guides

FLORENCE

DANA FACAROS & MICHAEL PAULS

About the authors

Dana Facaros and **Michael Pauls** have written over 30 books for Cadogan Guides, including all of the Italy series. They lived for three years in Umbria but have now moved to a farmhouse surrounded by vineyards in the Lot Valley.

About the contributor

Trained as a professional musician, **Nicky Swallow** has lived in Florence for 20 years. During that time, her enthusiasm for all things Tuscan has led to an in-depth knowledge of the region and an ongoing search for its less obvious attractions.

Cadogan Guides
Network House, 1 Ariel Way, London W12 7SL
cadoganguides@morrispub.co.uk
www.cadoganguides.com

The Globe Pequot Press
246 Goose Lane, PO Box 480, Guilford, Connecticut
06437–0480

Series design: Andrew Barker
Series cover design: Sheridan Wall
Art direction: Jodi Louw
Designer: Sarah Lyon
Photography: © Kicca Tommasi
Maps: © Cadogan, drawn by Map Creation Ltd
Additional map work: Angie Watts

Editorial Director: Vicki Ingle
Series Editor: Claudia Martin
Editor: Dominique Shead
Proofreading: Susannah Wight
Indexing: Isobel McLean
Production: Book Production Services
Printed in Italy by Legoprint
A catalogue record for this book is available from the British Library
ISBN 1860118305

Please help us to keep this guide up to date. We have done our best to ensure that the information in this guide is correct at the time of going to press. But places and facilities are constantly changing, and standards and prices in hotels and restaurants fluctuate. We would be delighted to receive any comments concerning existing entries or omissions. Authors of the best letters will receive a copy of the Cadogan Guide of their choice.

Nightlife and Entertainment p.235
Where to Stay p.211
LUNGARNOHOTEL
Sports and Green Spaces p.249
Walks p.153
The Guide p.41
Outside the Centre p.143
Shopping p.243
Eating Out p.223
Festivals p.256

Contents

Introducing

Introduction 1
The Neighbourhoods 2
Days Out in Florence 9
Roots of the City 19
Art and Architecture 35

The Guide

01
Travel 41

Getting There 42
Specialist Tour Operators 44
Entry Formalities 46
Arrival 47
Getting Around 48

02
Practical A–Z 53

Climate 54
Crime and the Police 54
Disabled Travellers 54
Electricity, Weights and Measures 55
Embassies and Consulates 55
Health, Emergencies and Insurance 56
Internet 56
Lost Property 56
Media 57
Money, Banks and Taxes 57
Opening Hours and Public Holidays 58
Packing 59
Photography 59
Post and Fax 59
Smoking 60
Students 60
Telephones 60
Time 61
Tipping 61
Toilets 61
Tourist Offices 61
Women Travellers 62
Working and Long Stays 62

03
The Medieval Core 63

Piazza del Duomo 66
The Duomo 66
The Baptistry 70
Museo dell'Opera del Duomo 71
Loggia del Bigallo 73
Via de' Calzaiuoli 73
Orsanmichele 73
Piazza della Signoria 75
Palazzo Vecchio 78
The Uffizi 81
Museo di Storia della Scienza 87
Ponte Vecchio 88
The Bargello 88
Badia Fiorentina 91
Piazza San Firenze 91
Palazzo Borghese 91
Casa di Dante 91
Santa Margherita de' Cerchi 92
Museo Nazionale di Antropologia ed Etnologia 92
Borgo degli Albizi 92

04
West Florence 93

San Lorenzo 96
Cappelle Medicee 97
San Lorenzo Market 98
Cenacolo di Foligno 98
Palazzo Medici-Riccardi 98
Santa Maria Novella 101
Stazione Centrale 105
The Croce del Trebbio 105
Palazzo Rucellai 106
Museo Marino Marini 106
Palazzo Strozzi 106
Piazza della Repubblica 107
Mercato Nuovo 107
Museo della Casa Fiorentina Antica 108
Santa Trínita 109
Ponte Santa Trínita 110
Piazza Goldoni 111
Galleria Corsini 111
Ognissanti 111

05
North and East Florence 113

San Marco 116
The Università and its Museums 117
Chiostro dello Scalzo 118
Sant'Apollonia 118
Along Via San Gallo 119
The Galleria dell'Accademia 119
Rotonda di Santa Maria degli Angeli 120
Santissima Annunziata 121
Spedale degli Innocenti 122
Museo Archeologico 122
Santa Maria Nuova 123
Museo di Firenze Com'Era 123
Collezione A. della Ragione 124
Teatro della Pergola 124
Santa Maria Maddalena dei Pazzi 124
Piazzale Donatello and the English Cemetery 125
Piazza d'Azeglio 125
Synagogue 125
Sant'Ambrogio 125
Piazza dei Ciompi 126

Casa Buonarroti 126
Santa Croce 126
Museo Horne 131

06
The Oltrarno 133
Palazzo Pitti 136
Giardino di Boboli 139
Santa Felicità 139
Casa Guidi 140
La Specola 140
Santo Spirito 140
Santa Maria del Carmine 141
Museo Bardini/Galleria Corsi 142

07
Outside the Centre 143
Forte di Belvedere and San Leonardo in Arcetri 145
San Miniato 145
Bellosguardo 147
The Cascine 147
Fortezzza da Basso 147
Russian Church 147
The Stibbert Museum 148
Museo delle Porcellane di Doccia 148
Ponte a Mensola and Settignano 148
The Certosa del Galluzzo 149
Carmignano 149
Comeana 149
Medici Villas 149

08
Walks 153
Dante's Florence 154
The Oltrarno 157
Fiesole 159

09
Siena 163
The Campo 172
Piazza del Duomo 175
South of the Centre 183
North of the Centre 184

10
Pisa 187
The Campo dei Miracoli 192
North of the Arno 196
South of the Arno 198

11
Lucca 201
Around the Town 206

Listings
Where to Stay 211
Eating Out 223
Nightlife 235
Entertainment 240
Shopping 243
Sports and Green Spaces 249
Children and Teenagers' Florence 252
Gay and Lesbian Florence 254
Festivals 256

Reference
Artists' Directory 258
Language 264
Index 269

Maps
Unmissable Florence *inside front cover*
The Neighbourhoods 2–3
The Medieval Core 65
West Florence 95
North and East Florence 115
The Oltrarno 135
Outside the Centre 144
Dante's Florence Walk 155
The Oltrarno Walk 158
Fiesole Walk 160
Siena 164–5
Pisa 188–9
Lucca 202–3
Hotels 214–5
Restaurants North of the Arno 226–7
Oltrarno Restaurants 232
Colour Street Maps *end of guide*
Off the Beaten Track *inside back cover*

Introduction

This city of Florence is well populated, its good air a healthy tonic; its citizens are well dressed, and its women lovely and fashionable, its buildings are very beautiful, and every sort of useful craft is carried on in them, more so than any other Italian city. For this many come from distant lands to see her, not out of necessity, but for the quality of its manufactures and arts, and for the beauty and ornament of the city.

Dino Compagni in his *Chronicle* of 1312

The precocious capital of Tuscany began to slip into legend back in the 14th century, during the lifetime of Dante; it was noted as different even before the Renaissance, before Boccaccio, Masaccio, Brunelleschi, Donatello, Leonardo da Vinci, Botticelli, Michelangelo, Machiavelli, the Medici... According to the tourist office, by the end of the 20th century, 688 years after Dino, a grand total of over 2,500,000 Americans, Germans, French and Britons (the top four groups), as well as Spanish, Brazilians, Egyptians and some 800,000 Italians, spent at least one night in a Florentine hotel. Some, perhaps, had orthodontist appointments. A large percentage of the others came to inhale the rarefied air of the cradle of Western civilization, to gaze at some of the loveliest things made by mortal hands and minds, to walk the streets of new Athens, the great humanist 'city built to the measure of man'. Calling Florence's visitors 'tourists', however, doesn't seem quite right. 'Tourism' implies pleasure, a principle alien to this dour, intellectual, measured town; 'pilgrims' is perhaps the better word, cultural pilgrims who throng the Uffizi, the Accademia, the Bargello to gaze upon the holy mysteries of our secular society, to buy postcards and replicas, the holy cards of our day.

Someone wrote a warning on a wall near Brunelleschi's Santo Spirito, in the Oltrarno: '*Turista con mappa/alla caccia del tesoro/per finire davanti a un piatto/di spaghetti al pomodoro*' (Tourist with a map, on a treasure hunt, only to end up in front of a plate of spaghetti with tomato sauce). Unless you pack the right attitude, Florence can be as disenchanting as cold spaghetti. It only blossoms if you apply mind as well as vision, if you go slowly and do not let the art bedazzle until your eyes glaze over in dizzy excess (a common complaint, known in medical circles as the Stendhal syndrome). Realize that loving and hating Florence at the same time may be the only rational response. It is the capital of contradiction; you begin to like it because it goes out of its way to annoy.

The Neighbourhoods

In this guide, the city is divided into the five neighbourhoods outlined on the map below, each with its own sightseeing chapter. This map also shows our suggestions for the Top Ten activities and places to visit in Florence. The following colour pages introduce the neighbourhoods in more detail, explaining the distinctive character and highlights of each.

Outside the Centre

West Florence

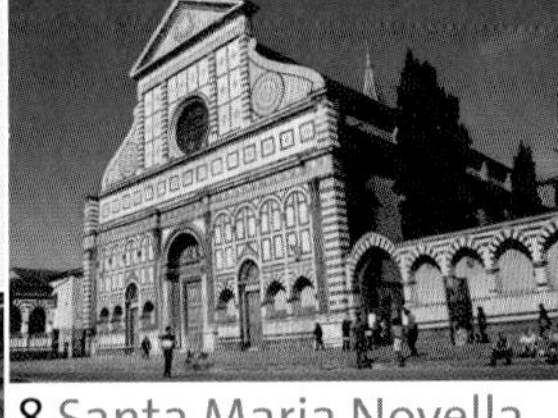

8 Santa Maria Novella, p.101

10 Designer boutiques and medieval palazzi around Via de' Tornabuoni, p.105

The Oltrarno

7 The Medici at home: the Pitti Palace and Boboli Gardens, p.136

9 The view over Florence from San Miniato, p.145

2 The Baptistry doors, p.71

1 Brunelleschi's dome, p.66

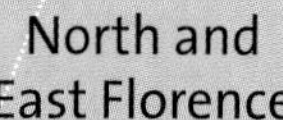

The Medieval Core

6 Dante's Florence and the Bargello, p.88

4 Piazza della Signoria, p.75

5 Santa Croce, Florence's pantheon, p.126

3 Renaissance art in the Uffizi, p.81

The Medieval Core

Few cities in the world can equal the dense concentration of art and monuments in the heart of Florence, in a tight web of streets under the Duomo dome, Brunelleschi's stunning tour de force. In only 10 minutes (if the streets aren't too crowded) you can walk from the Baptistry, the seed of the Florence miracle, to the Uffizi, where Botticelli and Leonardo da Vinci's paintings bring the Renaissance into full flower. Much of it would have been familiar to Dante, who was born in the shadow of the Badia and the medieval Bargello, now transformed into an Uffizi of sculpture, where Michelangelo and Donatello hold pride of place. The Piazza della Signoria and the Palazzo Vecchio, the seat of Florence's government, were the centre stage for its tumultuous history. Its powerful guilds lavished sculptures on their church, Orsanmichele; its gold merchants still deal along the picturesque Ponte Vecchio.

Clockwise from top: Detail on the Duomo façade, Duomo and Baptistry, Ponte Vecchio, the view from the Campanile.

The Medieval Core
The Medieval Core chapter p.63
Hotels p.212 Restaurants p.225 Bars p.236
Dante's Florence walk p.154

From top: Designer shopping, Mercato Nuovo, Santa Maria Novella (twice).

West Florence

In the early 15th century, the city's west end became the favourite address of its merchants and bankers; the Medici built the first Renaissance palace here, and the others quickly followed suit, each grander than the next. The Medici took over the parish church, San Lorenzo, and paid the greatest artists of the day to decorate it – Brunelleschi, Donatello and Michelangelo, who contributed the Medici tombs and library. Santa Maria Novella, close by, is another high shrine of Renaissance art, with landmark frescoes by Masaccio and Uccello; then there's Santa Trìnita, with its charming works by Ghirlandaio; and the Galleria Corsini, one of the city's most important private collections of art. The richness in the churches here is matched by the wares displayed in sleek windows along Florence's fanciest shopping street, Via de' Tornabuoni, but you'll find plenty of other places around here to spend money too, from the old Straw Market to the lively Mercato Centrale.

West Florence
West Florence chapter p.93
Hotels p.213 Restaurants p.225 Bars p.236

From top: Santa Croce, Spedale degli Innocenti, Piazza SS. Annunziata.

North and East Florence

The great space north of Florence's first medieval walls was in the old days the location of religious houses, schools and hospitals. Among the most important were San Marco, now the world's greatest collection of works by the Blessed Fra Angelico, and SS. Annunziata, another church/art gallery. In the vicinity, you'll find such Florentine essentials as the Accademia, home of Michelangelo's Goliath-sized *David*, and Brunelleschi's Spedale degli Innocenti, as well as the city's excellent archaeology museum, full of Etruscan curiosities. On the east side, central Florence's original working-class neighbourhood, the Franciscan church of Santa Croce, with its chapels by Giotto and its pantheon of great Florentines, is a must-see. Michelangelo has another shrine in the Casa Buonarroti. For fun, take in the city's flea market, at Sant'Ambrogio.

North and East Florence
North and East Florence chapter p.113
Hotels p.217 Restaurants p.229 Bars p.236

From top: Borgo San Frediano, Santa Maria del Carmine, Boboli Gardens.

The Oltrarno

'Over the Arno', Florence's left bank, is a pleasant place tucked under the pretty hills that close the south of the city. It offers no respite for the art pilgrim: the vast Pitti Palace, the last residence of the Medici Grand Dukes, has eight museums all by itself, although the lovely Boboli Gardens just behind wait to cure any symptoms of art glut. Much of the rest of the Oltrarno maintains a neighbourhood feel rare in Florence's *centro storico*. Its major churches each have a masterpiece: at Santa Maria del Carmine, Masaccio's precious frescoes in the Bracacci Chapel pointed the way to generations of painters; the elegant interior of Santo Spirito was Brunelleschi's last important work; while Santa Felicità has two masterpieces by the great Mannerist painter Pontormo.

The Oltrarno

The Oltrarno chapter p.133
Hotels p.218 Restaurants p.231 Bars p.237
Oltrarno walk p.157

Outside the Centre

Much of outer Florence has been engulfed in rather nondescript sprawl – much, but not all. Some of the hills overlooking the city, especially to the south, have changed little since Michelangelo planned Florence's defences, and offer splendid views over the city – from Bellosguardo you can see every church façade in the city. Another attraction are the many Medici villas and their lovely gardens – the one at the Villa di Castello is considered the very first *giardino all'italiano*. Fiesole, the 'mother of Florence' up on her hill, is featured in the 'Walks' chapter.

From top: San Miniato (twice), Forte di Belvedere.

Outside the Centre

Outside the Centre chapter p.143
Hotels p.219 Restaurants p.233
Fiesole walk p.159

Days Out in Florence

Couples' City p.10

Medici City p.16

Quirky City p.18

Medieval City p.12

Renaissance City p.14

COUPLES' CITY

The city of Dante and Beatrice, Florence brims over with art which just asks to be shared with a partner. Outside the galleries and churches, however, this merchants' city of stone can seem intimidating. When it gets to be too much, seek out its softer side – the views along the Arno or from the hills above, or the Boboli Gardens, are the most obvious, but also keep a lookout for the more out-of-the-way piazzas, peaceful cloisters, and lesser-known sights. As if to make up for its overall austerity, Florence has its share of romantic hotels, restaurants and cafés.

One

Start: Piazza San Marco.

Morning: It has to be done: join the crowds of couples and schoolgirls gawking at Michelangelo's mighty ***David*** in the Accademia. Then escape up to lofty **Fiesole**, Florence's highest balcony.

Lunch: **Pizzeria Etrusca**, where you can eat under the trees on Fiesole's main square.

Afternoon: Take in Fiesole's enchanting garden setting and lovely views, its Etruscan and Roman ruins and villas. If you're inspired, take the lovely walk down to Florence past Renaissance villas and medieval churches.

Dinner: A romantic setting and innovative food at **Alle Murate**.

Evening: Salsa the night away at **Maramao**.

Two

Start: Piazza Santa Maria Novella.

Morning: Visit one of Florence's great art churches, **Santa Maria Novella** (*photo right*), with its masterpieces by Giotto, Masaccio, Donatello, Filippino Lippi, Uccello and many more. Peruse the elegant shops of **Via de' Tornabuoni**, and buy each other a souvenir of Florence in the Straw Market (**Mercato Nuovo**).

Lunch: **Ristorante Ricchi**, a fish restaurant on magical Piazza Santo Spirito.

Afternoon: Visit Florence's quieter Left Bank, the **Oltrarno**, haunted by the gentle ghosts of Barrett and Browning. Then walk or take a taxi up to **Bellosguardo** for the magical view that takes in every church façade in Florence.

Dinner and evening: Dine and dance with the Florentines at the **Universale**, open till 2am.

Food and Drinks

Alle Murate, p.229
Pizzeria Etrusca, p.234
Ristorante Ricchi, p.232
Universale, p.239

Sights and Activities

Bellosguardo, p.147
David, p.119
Fiesole, p.159
Fiesole walk, p.159
Mercato Nuovo, p.107
Oltrarno, p.133
Santa Maria Novella, p.101
Via de' Tornabuoni, p.105

Nightlife

Maramao, p.238
Universale, p.239

MEDIEVAL CITY

Although we think of Florence as the cradle of the Renaissance, it didn't fall here from outer space but developed directly from the city's exceptionally lively artistic currents in the Middle Ages. Medieval Florence was one of the wealthiest cities in the world, but it was also one of the most violent, and self-defence was a prime consideration: old tower houses, walls and gates are everywhere in the city centre, while other corners of town, by Dante's house or Via delle Terme, remain resolutely medieval. Although frescoes and furnishings were lost or painted over as fashions changed, you can still get a good idea of what Florence was like when it was at the top of the world.

Three

Start: Piazza del Duomo.

Morning: Take time to study the detail and refinement that are the hallmarks of trecento Florentine art: the golden mosaics inside the **Baptistry**, Giotto's charming **campanile** (*photo bottom left*), the little **Museo del Bigallo**, and **Orsanmichele**, the chapel-shrine of the city's medieval guilds.

Lunch: **Buca Mario**, a traditional Florentine restaurant in the medieval district.

Afternoon: Take a bus up to the 11th-century church of **San Miniato** (*photos top right and middle left*), with its extraordinary geometrical façade, lavish interior and views over Florence, then make the pretty walk down by way of **San Leonardo in Arcetri**.

Dinner: **La Casalinga** in Piazza Santo Spirito, for hearty homecooking.

Evening: Stroll through the softly lit old streets in the centre – when the crowds have gone, medieval Florence is almost tangible.

Four

Start: Piazza Santa Croce.

Morning: **Santa Croce** (*photo above left*), where Michelangelo and dozens of other great men are buried, and where the walls are covered with superb trecento frescoes by Giotto, the Gaddis, Daddi and Maso di Bianco; don't miss the tremendous *Triumph of Death* by Orcagna in the church's Museo dell'Opera.

Lunch: A big salad or a full-blown meal at the excellent **Baldovino**.

Afternoon: Return to the time of **Dante**, visiting his 'house' and his old haunts around the **Badia** and **Bargello** (*photo above, far left*), where he grew up and first espied his Beatrice.

Dinner: **Cibreo**, the most classically Florentine of Florentine restaurants.

Evening: Listen to some live jazz at **Jazz Club**.

Food and Drinks

Baldovino, p.230
Buca Mario, p.228
La Casalinga, p.233
Cibreo, p.229

Sights and Activities

Badia, p.91
Bargello, p.88
Baptistry, p.70
Campanile of the Duomo, p.69
Dante's 'house', p.91
Museo del Bigallo, p.73
Orsanmichele, p.73
San Leonardo in Arcetri, p.145
San Miniato, p.145
Santa Croce, p.126

Nightlife

Jazz Club, p.241

RENAISSANCE CITY

Every so often in history, a city finds itself just bursting with talent, fresh ideas and the seismic energy to make a great leap forward and turn the past on its nose. Although the word 'Renaissance' came along later, 15th-century Florentines were already well aware that they were pioneers, rediscovering, imitating then competing to outdo the ancients in art and architecture. The new confidence made 'man the measure of all things', and gave birth to Humanism and a fresh interest in the sciences. The more you visit Florence and its Renaissance landmarks, the more astonishing it seems.

Five

Start: Piazza San Marco.

Morning: Start at the **convent of San Marco** (*photo far right*), designed by Michelozzo and filled with ethereally beautiful paintings by Fra Angelico. Head over to Brunelleschi's landmark **Spedale degli Innocenti**, admire his sublime **Duomo dome**, and linger over Ghiberti's 'Gates of Paradise' on the **Baptistry**.

Lunch: Indulge in a culinary masterpiece: the truffle tortellini at the **Taverna del Bronzino**.

Afternoon: Linger in the **Uffizi**, the garden of Renaissance art, where nearly all the brightest blooms are by Tuscans if not Florentines and (bad news for you) all worth a look.

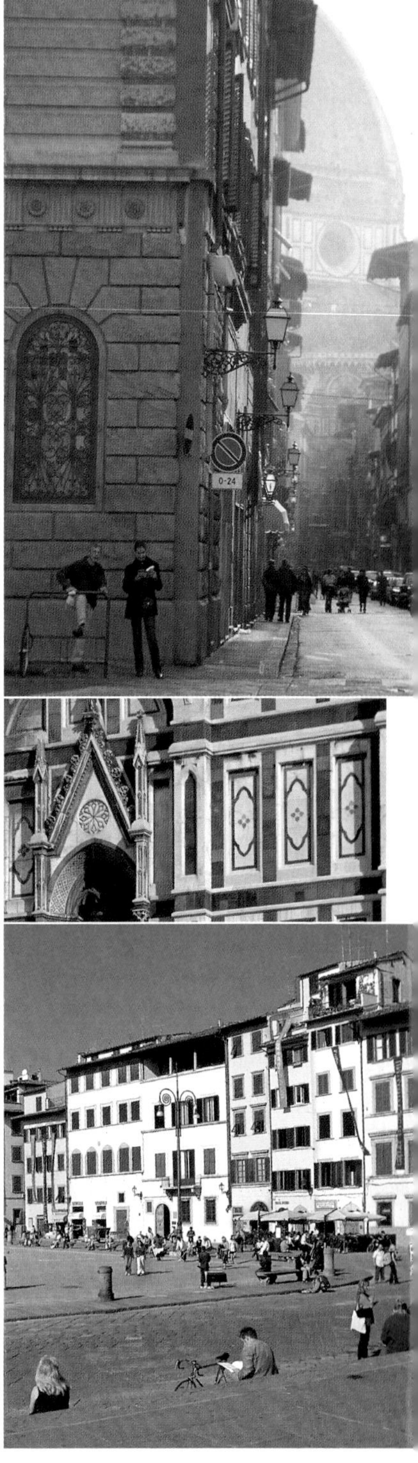

Dinner: Creative cooking in a lovely setting, at **Caffè Concerto**.

Six

Start: Piazza San Firenze.

Morning: Spend the morning with the greatest sculptors since the ancient Greeks: walk around the sublime outdoor sculpture gallery of **Orsanmichele** (*photo above*), then visit the **Bargello**, home to some of the finest works to come from the chisels of Donatello, Michelangelo, Cellini, Verrocchio, Giambologna and more.

Lunch: Recover from art overload at the **Trattoria del Carmine**.

Afternoon: Head for the **Brancacci Chapel**, with its fabled frescoes by Masaccio that inspired all that came after. Spend the rest of the day seeking out some of the after-shocks: Brunelleschi's **Santo Spirito**, with works by Lippi and Verrocchio; **Santa Trìnita**, with Ghirlandaio's masterpiece; the perfect **Palazzo Rucellai** and haywire **Palazzo Strozzi**; and Uccello's mesmerizing **Green Cloister in Santa Maria Novella** as dessert.

Dinner: **Osteria del Caffè Italiano**, set in a Renaissance palazzo.

Evening: Dance the night away with the modern Florentines at **Central Park**.

Food and Drinks

Caffè Concerto, p.229
Osteria del Caffè Italiano, p.230
Taverna del Bronzino, p.230
Trattoria del Carmine, p.233

Sights and Activities

Baptistry, p.70
Bargello, p.88
Brancacci Chapel, p.141
Convent of San Marco, p.116
Duomo dome, p.66
Green Cloister in Santa Maria Novella, p.104
Orsanmichele, p.73
Palazzo Rucellai, p.106
Palazzo Strozzi, p.106
Santa Trìnita, p.109
Santo Spirito, p.140
Spedale degli Innocenti, p.122
Uffizi, p.81

Nightlife

Central Park, p.237

MEDICI CITY

No major city anywhere has had its destiny so intertwined with a single family. Astute bankers, the Medici became the richest family in Europe by the early 1400s, and parlayed their fortune into influence over Florentine affairs for 350 years. Perhaps the greatest collectors in history, they commissioned sculptures and paintings, palaces, villas and gardens; they bought up libraries and supported scholars, poets and scientists, including Galileo. As Grand Dukes of Tuscany, they presided over and sometimes hastened Florence's decline, until the last Medici made up for many of their foibles by willing that all their accumulated treasures had to remain forever in Florence.

Seven

Start: Piazza della Signoria (*photo bottom left*).

Breakfast: A coffee and cornetto at the lovely **Rivoire**.

Morning: The **Palazzo Vecchio** (*photo top left*), the seat of Florentine government, full of Medici fluff and obsessions, followed by the nearby **Museo di Storia della Scienza** – the Medici, after all, were originally doctors, and in the 17th century founded the world's first scientific organization.

Lunch: A pizza outside on Piazza Santo Spirito at **Borgo Antico**.

Afternoon: The Medici Grand Dukes bought the enormous **Pitti Palace** and had no trouble filling it to the brim: visit their priceless painting collection (Raphaels, Rubens, etc.) in the Galleria Palatina. Then take a stroll in the **Boboli Gardens**, stage for the Grand Dukes' pageants.

Dinner: Try the seven-course *menu degustazione* at **Pane e Vino**.

Evening: The busy **bars around Piazza Santo Spirito**.

Eight

Start: Stazione Centrale.

Morning: Take the bus out to the best-preserved Medici villa, Lorenzo il Magnifico's charming **Poggio a Caiano**, where he wrote his finest poetry.

Lunch: Back in Florence for a *bistecca alla fiorentina* at **Sostanza**.

Afternoon: Start with Gozzoli's fairy-tale allegory of the Medici in their home base, the **Palazzo Medici-Riccardi**. Then head over to see the pomposity that followed at **San Lorenzo**: Michelangelo's tombs and the insanely opulent Princes' chapel, plus the masterpieces Cosimo il Vecchio commissioned from Donatello and Brunelleschi.

Dinner: Dine like a Medici Grand Duke at the **Enoteca Pinchiorri**.

Evening: Keep your brow high Medici style with an opera at the **Teatro del Maggio Musicale**.

Food and Drinks

Borgo Antico, p.233
Enoteca Pinchiorri, p.229
Pane e Vino, p.231
Rivoire, p.225
Sostanza, p.228

Sights and Activities

Boboli Gardens, p.139
Museo di Storia della Scienza, p.87
Palazzo Medici-Riccardi, p.98
Palazzo Vecchio, p.78
Pitti Palace, p.136
Poggio a Caiano, p.151
San Lorenzo, p.96

Nightlife

Bars around Piazza Santo Spirito, p.237
Teatro del Maggio Musicale, p.241

QUIRKY CITY

At times Florence can seem like a serious-minded schoolmistress whose slip never shows, so it can be fun to seek out its more playful, bizarre or embarrassing corners, or places where Medici good taste overflowed into the kitsch or grotesque, something that happened to the Grand Dukes themselves as they slid into dribbling decadence; see the Princes' Chapel or the seashell vases in the Museo degli Argenti.

Nine

Start: Via Romana.

Morning: Begin with the lifelike wax cadavers in **La Specola** museum, commissioned by one of the more morbid Grand Dukes; visit the hodge-podgey old **Casa Buonarotti**, Michelangelo's house that he never lived in; and seek out the detritus of Florence in the **Piazza dei Ciompi flea market**.

Lunch: Go native and order the cockscombs at **Trattoria Cibreo**.

Afternoon: See the amazing junk the Medici collected, in the **Museo degli Argenti** in the Pitti Palace. Follow Cosimo I's catwalk (the Vasari Corridor) to **Santa Felicità** to see the Pontormos, Mannerism at its most extreme. Cross the Arno to visit the little **English cemetery** in Piazzale Donatello, lost in a roaring traffic island – a strange experience at twilight.

Dinner: **Oliviero**, for its tasty if offbeat dishes and sleazy décor.

Evening: A drink at **La Rotonda** in an old Ferrari showroom.

Night: Dance the night away at **Soulciety**, a good alternative to the city's run-of-the-mill clubs, with its rococo décor.

Food and Drinks
Oliviero, p.228
Trattoria Cibreo, p.231

Sights and Activities
Casa Buonarotti, p.126
English cemetery, p.125
Museo degli Argenti, p.138
Piazza dei Ciompi flea market, p.126
Santa Felicità, p.139
La Specola, p.140

Nightlife
La Rotonda, p.236
Soulciety, p.238

Roots of the City

ETRUSCANS AND ROMANS 20

THE FLORENTINE REPUBLIC BATTLES WITH THE BARONS 21

GUELPHS AND GHIBELLINES 21

BUSINESS AS USUAL: RIOT, WAR, PLAGUES AND REVOLUTION 23

THE RISE OF THE MEDICI 24

LORENZO THE MAGNIFICENT 25

SAVONAROLA 27

THE END OF THE REPUBLIC 28

COSIMO I: THE MEDICI AS GRAND DUKES 31

KNICK-KNACKS AND TEDIUM: THE LATER MEDICI 32

POST-MEDICI FLORENCE 33

Etruscans and Romans

The identity of Florence's first inhabitants is a matter of dispute. There seems to have been some kind of settlement along the Arno long before the Roman era, perhaps as early as 1000 BC; the original founders may have been either native Italics or Etruscans. Throughout the period of Etruscan dominance, the village on the river lived in the shadow of *Faesulae* – Florence's present-day suburb of Fiesole was then an important city, the northernmost member of the Etruscan Dodecapolis. The Arno river cuts across central Italy like a wall. This narrow stretch of it, close to the mountain pass over to Emilia, was always the most logical place for a bridge.

Roman Florence can claim no less a figure than **Julius Caesar** for its founder. Like so many other Italian cities, the city began as a planned urban enterprise in an underdeveloped province; Caesar started it as a colony for his army veterans in 59 BC. The origin of the name – so suggestive of springtime and flowers – is another mystery. First it was *Florentia*, then *Fiorenza* in the Middle Ages, and finally *Firenze*. One guess is that its foundation took place in April, when the Romans were celebrating the games of the Floralia.

The original street plan of *Florentia* can be seen today in the neat rectangle of blocks between Via de' Tornabuoni and Via del Proconsolo, between the Duomo and Piazza della Signoria. Its forum occupied roughly the site of the modern Piazza della Repubblica, and the outline of its amphitheatre can be traced in the oval of streets just west of Piazza Santa Croce. Roman *Florentia* never really imposed itself on the historian. One writer mentions it as a *municipia splendidissima*, a major town and river crossing along the Via Cassia, connected to Rome and the thriving new cities of northern Italy, such as *Bononia* and *Mediolanum* (Bologna and Milan). At the height of Empire, the municipal boundaries had expanded out to Via de' Fossi, Via S. Egidio, and Via de' Benci. Nevertheless, *Florentia* did not play a significant role either in the Empire's heyday or in its decline.

After the fall of Rome, Florence weathered its troubles comparatively well. We hear of it withstanding sieges by the Goths around the year 400, when it was defended by the famous imperial general Stilicho, and again in 541, during the campaigns of Totila and Belisarius; all through the Greek–Gothic wars Florence seems to have taken the side of Constantinople. The Lombards arrived around 570; under their rule Florence was the seat of a duchy subject to the then Tuscan capital of Lucca. The next mention in the chronicles refers to Charlemagne spending Christmas with the Florentines in the year 786. Like the rest of Italy, Florence had undoubtedly declined; a new set of walls went up under Carolingian rule, about 800, enclosing an area scarcely larger than the original Roman settlement of 59 BC. In such times Florence was lucky to be around at all; most likely throughout the Dark Ages the city was gradually increasing its relative importance and strength at the expense of its neighbours. The famous Baptistry, erected some time between the 6th and 9th centuries, is the only important building from that troubled age in all Tuscany.

By the 1100s, Florence was the leading city of the County of Tuscany. **Countess Matilda**, ally of Pope Gregory VII against the emperors, oversaw the construction of a new set of walls in 1078, this time coinciding with the widest Roman-era boundaries. Already the city had recovered all the ground lost during the Dark Ages, and the momentum of growth did not abate. New walls were needed again in the 1170s, to enclose what was becoming one of the largest cities in

Before the 13th Century

Baptistry, built between the 6th and 9th centuries, p.70

Medieval lanes, home to the Palazzo di Parte Guelfa and the Palazzo dell'Arte della Seta, p.107

Museo Archeologico, for its Etruscan and Egyptian collections, p.122

Europe. In this period, Florence owed its growth and prosperity largely to the textile industry – weaving and 'finishing' cloth not only from Tuscany but wool shipped from as far afield as Spain and England. The capital gain from this trade, managed by the *Calimala* and the *Arte della Lana*, Florence's richest guilds, led naturally to an even more profitable business – banking and finance.

The Florentine Republic Battles with the Barons

In 1125, Florence once and for all conquered its ancient rival Fiesole. Wealth and influence brought with them increasing political responsibilities. Externally the city often found itself at war with one or other of its neighbours. Since Countess Matilda's death in 1115, Florence had become a self-governing *comune*, largely independent of the emperor and local barons. The new city republic's hardest problems, however, were closer to home. The nobles of the county, encouraged in their anachronistic feudal behaviour by representatives of the imperial government, proved irreconcilable enemies to the new merchant republic, and Florence spent most of the 12th century trying to keep them in line. Often the city actually declared war on a noble clan, as with the Alberti, or the Counts of Guidi, and razed their castles whenever they captured one. To complicate the situation, nobles attracted by the stimulation of urban life – not to mention the opportunities for making money – often moved their entire families into Florence itself. They brought their country habits with them, a boyish eagerness to brawl with their neighbours on the slightest pretext, and a complete disregard for the laws of the *comune*. Naturally, they couldn't feel secure without a little urban castle of their own, and before long Florence, like any prosperous Italian city of the Middle Ages, featured a remarkable skyline of hundreds of tower-fortresses, built as much for status as for defence. Many were over 60m in height. It wasn't uncommon for the honest citizen to come home from a hard day's work at the bank, hoping for a little peace and quiet, only to find siege engines parked in front of the house and a company of bowmen commandeering the children's bedroom.

But just as Florence was able to break the power of the rural nobles, those in the town also eventually had to succumb. The last tower-fortresses were chopped down to size in the early 1300s. But even without the nobles raising hell, the Florentines found new ways to keep the pot boiling. The rich merchants who dominated the government, familiarly known as the *popolo grosso*, resorted to every sort of murder and mayhem to beat down the demands of the lesser guilds, the *popolo minuto*, for a fair share of the wealth; the two only managed to settle their differences when confronted by murmurs of discontent from what was then one of Europe's largest urban proletariats. But even beyond simple class issues, the city born under the sign of Mars always found a way to make trouble for itself. Not only did Florentines pursue the Guelph–Ghibelline conflict with greater zest than almost any Tuscan city; according to the chronicles of the time, they actually started it. In 1215, men of the Amidei family murdered a prominent citizen named Buondelmonte de' Buondelmonti over a broken wedding engagement, the spark that touched off the factionalist struggles first in Florence, then quickly throughout Italy.

Guelphs and Ghibellines

In the 13th century, there was never a dull moment in Florence. Guelphs and Ghibellines, often more involved with some feud between powerful families than with real political issues, cast each other into exile and confiscated each other's property with every change of the wind. Religious strife occasionally pushed politics off the front page. In the 1240s, a curious foreshadowing of the Reformation saw Florence wrapped up in the **Patarene heresy**. This sect, closely related to the Albigensians of southern France, was as obsessed with the presence of Evil in the world as John Calvin – or Florence's own future fire-and-brimstone preacher, Savonarola. Exploiting a streak of religious eccentricity that has always seemed to be present in the Florentine psyche, the Patarenes thrived in the city, even electing their own bishop. The established Church was up to the challenge; St Peter Martyr, a bloodthirsty Dominican, led his armies of axe-wielding monks to the assault in 1244, exterminating almost the entire Patarene community.

In 1248, with help from Emperor Frederick II, Florence's Ghibellines booted out the Guelphs – once and for all, they thought, but two years later the Guelphs were back, and it was the Ghibellines' turn to pack their grips. The new Guelph regime, called the *primo popolo*, was for the first time completely in the control of the bankers and merchants. It passed the first measures to control the privileges of the turbulent, largely Ghibelline nobles, and forced them all to chop the tops off their tower-fortresses. The next decades witnessed a series of wars with the Ghibelline cities of Tuscany – Siena, Pisa and Pistoia – not just by coincidence Florence's habitual enemies. Usually the Florentines were the aggressors, and more often than not fortune favoured them. In 1260, however, the Sienese, reinforced by Ghibelline exiles from Florence and a few imperial cavalry, destroyed an invading Florentine army at the **Battle of Monteaperti**. Florence was at the Ghibellines' mercy. Only the refusal of Farinata degli Uberti, the leader of the exiles, to allow the city's destruction kept the Sienese from putting it to the torch – a famous episode recounted by Dante in the *Inferno*. (In a typical Florentine gesture of gratitude, Dante found a home for Uberti in one of the lower circles of hell.)

In Florence, a Ghibelline regime under Count Guido Novello made life rough for the wealthy Guelph bourgeoisie. As luck would have it, though, only a few years later the Guelphs were back in power, and Florence was winning on the battlefield again. The new Guelph government, the *secondo popolo*, earned a brief respite from factional strife. In 1289, Florence won a great victory over another old rival, Arezzo. This was the **Battle of Campaldino**, where the Florentine citizen army included young Dante Alighieri. In 1282, and again in 1293, Florence tried to clean up an increasingly corrupt government with a series of reforms. The 1293 *Ordinamenti della Giustizia* once and for all excluded the nobles from the important political offices. By now, however, the real threat to the Guelph merchants' rule did not come so much from the nobility, which had been steadily falling behind in wealth and power over a period of two centuries, but from the lesser guilds, which had been completely excluded from a share of the power, and also from the growing working class employed in the textile mills and the foundries.

Despite all the troubles, the city's wealth and population grew tremendously throughout the 1200s. Its trade contacts spread across Europe, and crowned heads from London to Constantinople found Florentine bankers ready to float them a loan. About 1253 Florence minted modern Europe's first gold coin, the *florin*, which soon became a standard currency across the continent. By 1300 Florence counted over 100,000 souls – a little cramped, even inside the vast new circuit of walls built by the *comune* in

13th Century

Bargello, which became the residence of the *podestà*, p.88

Duomo, begun in the 1290s, p.66

Palazzo dell'Arte della Lana, built for the powerful Wool Merchants Guild, p.75

Palazzo Vecchio, built by the Guelphs as the 'Palazzo del Popolo', p.78

Santa Croce, also part of the huge building programme of the 1290s, p.126

the 1280s. It was not only one of the largest cities in Europe, but certainly one of the richest. Besides banking, the wool trade was also booming: by 1300 the wool guild, the *Arte della Lana*, had over 200 large workshops in the city alone.

Naturally, this new opulence created new possibilities for culture and art. Florence's golden age began perhaps in the 1290s, when the *comune* started its tremendous programme of public buildings – including the Palazzo della Signoria and the cathedral; important religious structures, such as Santa Croce, were under way at the same time. Cimabue was the artist of the day; Giotto was just beginning, and his friend Dante was hard at work on the *Commedia*.

As in so many other Italian cities, Florence had been developing its republican institutions slowly and painfully. At the beginning of the *comune* in 1115, the leaders were a class called the *boni homines*, made up mostly of nobles. Only a few decades later, these were calling themselves *consules*, evoking a memory of the ancient Roman republic. When the Ghibellines took over, the leading official was a *podestà* appointed by the emperor. Later, under the Guelphs, the *podestà* and a new officer called the *capitano del popolo* were both elected by the citizens. With the reforms of the 1290s Florence's republican constitution was perfected – if that is the proper word for an arrangement that satisfied few citizens and guaranteed lots of trouble for the future. Under the new dispensation, power was invested in the council of the richer guilds, the *Signoria*; the new Palazzo della Signoria was designed expressly as a symbol of their authority, replacing the old Bargello, which had been the seat of the *podestà*. The most novel feature of the government, designed to overcome Florence's past incapacity to avoid violent factionalism, was the selection of officials by lot from among the guild members. In effect, politics was to be abolished.

Business as Usual: Riot, War, Plagues and Revolution

Despite the reforms of the *Ordinamenti*, Florence found little peace in the new century. As if following some strange and immutable law of city-state behaviour, no sooner had the Guelphs established total control than they themselves split into new factions. The radically anti-imperial **Blacks** and the more conciliatory **Whites** fought each other through the early 1300s with the same fervour they both had once exercised against the Ghibellines. The Whites, who included Dante among their partisans, came out losers when the Blacks conspired with the pope to bring Charles of Valois' French army into Florence; almost all the losing faction were forced into exile in 1302. Some of them must have sneaked back, for the chronicles of 1304 record the Blacks trying to burn them out of their houses with incendiary bombs, resulting in a fire that consumed a quarter of the city.

Beginning in 1313, Florence was involved in a constant series of inconclusive wars with Pisa, Lucca and Arezzo, among others. In 1325, the city was defeated and nearly destroyed by the great Lucchese general **Castruccio Castracani** (*see* Lucca, p.206). Castruccio died of a common cold while the siege was already under way, another instance of Florence's famous good luck, but unfortunately one of the last.

The factions may have been suppressed, but fate had found some more novel disasters for the city. One far-off monarch did more damage to Florence than its Italian enemies had ever managed – King Edward III of England, who in 1339 found it expedient to repudiate his foreign debts. Florence's two biggest banks, the Bardi and the Peruzzi, immediately went bust, and the city's standing as the centre of international finance was gravely damaged.

If anything was constant throughout the history of the republic, it was the oppression

14th Century

Campanile, designed by Giotto, p.69

Piazza dei Ciompi, where the wool-workers' revolt took place in 1378, p.126

Ponte Vecchio, rebuilt in 1345, replacing the old wooden bridge, p.88

of the poor. The ruling bankers and merchants exploited their labour and gave them only the bare minimum in return. In the 14th century, overcrowding, undernourishment and plenty of rats made Florence's poorer neighbourhoods a perfect breeding ground for epidemics. Famine, plagues and riots became common in the 1340s, causing a severe political crisis. At one point, in 1342, the Florentines gave over their government to a foreign dictator, Walter de Brienne, the French–Greek 'Duke of Athens'. He lasted only for a year before a popular revolt ended the experiment. The **Black Death** of 1348, which was the background for Boccaccio's *Decameron*, carried off perhaps one half of the population. Coming on the heels of a serious depression, it was a blow from which Florence would never really recover.

In the next two centuries, when the city was to be the great innovator in Western culture, it was already in relative decline, a politically decadent republic with a stagnant economy, barely holding its own among the turbulent changes in trade and diplomacy. For the time being, however, things didn't look too bad. Florence found enough ready cash to buy control of Prato, in 1350, and was successful in a defensive war against expansionist Milan in 1351. Warfare was almost continuous for the last half of the century, a strain on the exchequer but not usually a threat to the city's survival; this was the heyday of the mercenary companies, led by *condottieri* like **Sir John Hawkwood** (Giovanni Acuto), immortalized by the equestrian 'statue' in Florence's cathedral. Before the Florentines made him a better offer, Hawkwood was often in the employ of their enemies.

Throughout the century, the Guelph party had been steadily tightening its grip over the republic's affairs. Despite the selection of officials by lot, by the 1370s the party organization bore an uncanny resemblance to some of the big-city political machines common not so long ago in America. The merchants and the bankers who ran the party used it to turn the Florentine Republic into a profit-making business. With the increasingly limited opportunities for making money in trade and finance, the Guelph ruling class tried to make up the difference by soaking the poor. Wars and taxes stretched Florentine tolerance to breaking point and, finally, in 1378, came revolution. The **Ciompi Revolt** (*ciompi* – wage labourers in the textile industries) began in July, when a mob of workers seized the Bargello. Under the leadership of a wool-carder named Michele di Lando, they executed a few of the Guelph bosses and announced a new, reformed constitution. They were also foolish enough to believe the Guelph magnates when they promised to abide by the new arrangement if only the *ciompi* would go home. Before long di Lando was in exile, and the ruling class firmly back in the seat of power, more than ever determined to eliminate the last vestiges of democracy from the republic.

The Rise of the Medici

In 1393, Florentines celebrated the 100th anniversary of the great reform of the *Ordinamenti*, while watching their republic descend irresistibly into oligarchy. In that year **Maso degli Albizzi** became *gonfaloniere* (the head of the *Signoria*) and served as virtual dictator for many years afterwards. The ruling class of merchants, more than a bit paranoid after the Ciompi revolt, were generally relieved to see power concentrated in strong hands; the ascendancy of the Albizzi family was to set the pattern for the rest of the republic's existence. In a poisoned atmosphere of repression and conspiracy, the spies of the *Signoria*'s new secret police hunted down malcontents while whole legions of Florentine exiles plotted against the republic in foreign courts. Florence was almost constantly at war. In 1398 she defeated an attempt at conquest by Giangaleazzo Visconti of Milan. The imperialist policy of the Albizzi and their allies resulted in important territorial gains, including the conquest of Pisa in 1406, and the purchase of Livorno from the Genoese in 1421. Unsuccessful wars against Lucca finally disenchanted the Florentines with Albizzi rule. An emergency *parlamento* (the infrequent popular assembly usually called when a coming change of rulers was obvious) in 1434 decreed the recall from exile of the head of the popular opposition, **Cosimo de' Medici**.

Perhaps it was something that could only have happened in Florence – the darling of the plebeians, the great hope for reform, happened to be the head of Florence's biggest bank. The Medici family had their roots in the Mugello region north of Florence. Their name seems to suggest that they once were pharmacists (later enemies would jibe at the balls on the family arms as 'the pills'). For two centuries they had been active in Florentine politics, and many had acquired reputations as troublemakers; their names turned up often in the lists of exiles and records of lawsuits. None of the Medici had ever been particularly rich until **Giovanni di Bicci de' Medici** (1360–1429) parlayed his wife's dowry into the founding of a bank. Good fortune – and a temporary monopoly on the handling of the pope's finances – made the Medici Bank Florence's biggest.

Giovanni had been content to stay on the fringe of politics; his son, **Cosimo** (known in Florentine history as '**il Vecchio**', the 'old man') took good care of the bank's affairs but aimed his sights much higher. His strategy was as old as Julius Caesar – the patrician reformer, cultivating the best men, winning the favour of the poor with largesse and gradually, carefully, forming a party under a system specifically designed to prevent such things. In 1433 Rinaldo degli Albizzi had him exiled, but it was too late; continuing discontent forced his return only a year later, and for the next 35 years Cosimo would be the unchallenged ruler of Florence. Throughout this period, Cosimo occasionally held public office – this was done by lottery, with the electoral lists manipulated to ensure a majority of Medici supporters at all times. Nevertheless, he received ambassadors at the new family palace (built in 1444), entertained visiting popes and emperors, and made all the important decisions. A canny political godfather and usually a gentleman, Cosimo also proved a useful patron to the great figures of the early Renaissance – including Donatello and Brunelleschi. His father had served as one of the judges in the famous competition for the Baptistry doors, and Cosimo was a member of the commission that picked Brunelleschi to design the cathedral dome.

Cosimo did oversee some genuine reforms; under his leadership Florence began Europe's first progressive income tax, and a few years later the state invented the modern concept of the national debt – endlessly rolling over bonds to keep the republic afloat and the creditors happy. The poor, with fewer taxes to pay, were also happy, and the ruling classes, after some initial distaste, were positively delighted; never in Florence's history had any government so successfully muted class conflict and the desire for a genuine democracy. Wars were few, and the internal friction negligible. Cosimo died in August 1464; his tomb in San Lorenzo bears the inscription *Pater patriae*, and no dissent was registered when his 40-year-old son **Piero** took up the boss's role.

Lorenzo the Magnificent

Piero didn't quite have the touch of his masterful father, but he survived a stiff political crisis in 1466, outmanoeuvring a new faction led by wealthy banker Luca Pitti. In 1469 he succumbed to the Medici family disease, the gout, and his 20-year-old son **Lorenzo** succeeded him in an equally smooth transition. He was to last for 23 years. Not necessarily more 'magnificent' than other contemporary princes, or other Medici, Lorenzo's honorific reveals something of the myth that was to grow up around him in later centuries. His long reign corresponded to the height of the Florentine Renaissance. It was a relatively peaceful time, and in the light of the disasters that were to follow, Florentines could not help looking back on it as a golden age.

As a ruler, Lorenzo showed many virtues. Still keeping up the pretence of living as a private citizen, he lived relatively simply, always accessible to the voices and concerns of his fellow citizens, who would often see him walking the city streets. In the field of foreign policy he was indispensable to Florence and indeed all Italy; he did more than anyone to keep the precarious peninsular balance of power from disintegrating. The most dramatic affair of his reign was the **Pazzi conspiracy**, an attempt to assassinate Lorenzo plotted by Pope Sixtus IV and the wealthy Pazzi family, the pope's bankers and ancient rivals of the Medici. In 1478, two of the younger Pazzi attacked Lorenzo and his brother Giuliano during Mass at the cathedral. Giuliano was killed, but Lorenzo managed to escape into the sacristy. The botched murder aborted the planned revolt; Florentines showed little interest in the Pazzis' call to arms, and before nightfall most of the conspirators were dangling from the cornice of the Palazzo Vecchio.

Apparently, Lorenzo had angered the pope by starting a syndicate to mine for alum in Volterra, threatening the papal monopoly. Since Sixtus failed to murder Lorenzo, he had to settle for excommunicating him, and declaring war in alliance with King Ferrante of Naples. The war went badly for Florence and, in the most memorable act of his career, Lorenzo walked into the lion's cage, travelling to negotiate with the terrible Neapolitan, who had already murdered more than one important guest. As it turned out, Ferrante was only too happy to dump his papal entanglements; Florence found itself at peace once more, and Lorenzo returned home to a hero's welcome.

In other affairs, both foreign and domestic, Lorenzo was more a lucky ruler than a skilled one. Florence's economy was entering a long, slow decline, but for the moment the banks and mills were churning out just enough profit to keep up the accustomed level of opulence. The Medici Bank was on the ropes. Partly because of Lorenzo's neglect, it came close to collapsing on several occasions – and it seems that Lorenzo blithely made up the losses with public funds. Culturally, he was fortunate to be nabob of Florence at its most artistically creative period; future historians and Medici propagandists gave him a reputation as an art patron that is entirely undeserved. His own tastes tended towards bric-a-brac, jewellery, antique statues and vases; there is little evidence that he really understood or could appreciate the scores of great artists around him. Perhaps because he was too nearsighted to see anything very clearly, he did not ever commission an important canvas or fresco in Florence (except for Luca Signorelli's mysterious *Pan*, lost in Berlin during the last war). His favourite architect was the hack Giuliano da Sangallo.

The Medici had taken great care with Lorenzo's education; he was brought up with some of the leading humanist scholars of Tuscany for tutors and his real interests were literary. His well-formed lyrics and winsome pastorals have earned him a place among Italy's greatest 15th-century poets; they neatly reflect the private side of Lorenzo, the retiring, scholarly family man who enjoyed life better on one of the many rural Medici

15th Century

Loggia dei Lanzi, site of Florence's *parlamento*, p.76

Medici villas, rural retreats for the Medici in the 15th and 16th centuries, p.149

Orsanmichele, a showcase of 15th-century sculpture commissioned by the guilds, p.73

Palazzo Medici-Riccardi, the Medici's first family palace, p.98

Piazza della Signoria, site of the Bonfire of Vanities and the burning of Savonarola, p.75

villas than in the busy city. In this, he was perfectly in tune with his class and his age. Plenty of Florentine bankers were learning the joys of country life, reading Horace or Catullus in their geometrical gardens and pestering their tenant farmers with well-meant advice.

Back in town, they had thick new walls of rusticated sandstone between them and the bustle of the streets. The late 15th century was the great age of palace building in Florence. Following the example of Cosimo de' Medici, the bankers and merchants erected dozens of palaces (some of the best can be seen around Via de' Tornabuoni). Each one turns blank walls and iron-barred windows to the street. Historians always note one very pronounced phenomenon of this period – a turning inward, a 'privatization' of Florentine life. In a city that had become a republic only in name, civic interest and public life ceased to matter so much. The very rich began to assume the airs of an aristocracy, and did everything they could to distance themselves from their fellow citizens. Ironically, just at the time when Florence's artists were creating their greatest achievements, the republican ethos, the civic soul that had made Florence great, began to disintegrate.

Savonarola

Lorenzo's death, in 1492, was followed by another apparently smooth transition of power to his son **Piero**. But after 58 years of Medicean quiet and stability, the city was ready for a change. The opportunity for the malcontents came soon enough, when the timid and inept Piero allowed the invading King of France, **Charles VIII**, to occupy Pisa and the Tuscan coast. A spontaneous revolt chased Piero and the rest of the Medici into exile, while a mob sacked the family's palace. A new regime, hastily put together under **Piero Capponi**, dealt more sternly with the French (*see* p.76) and tried to pump some new life into the long-dormant republican constitution.

The Florence that threw out the Medici was a city in the mood for some radical reform. Already, the dominating figure on the political stage was an intense Dominican friar from Ferrara named **Girolamo Savonarola**. Perhaps not surprisingly, this oversophisticated and overstimulated city was also in the mood to be told how wicked and decadent it was, and Savonarola was happy to oblige. A spellbinding revival preacher with a touch of erudition, Savonarola packed as many as 10,000 into the Duomo to hear his weekly sermons, which were laced with political sarcasm and social criticism. Though an insufferable prig, he was also a sincere democrat. There is a story that the dying Lorenzo called Savonarola to his bedside for the last rites, and that the friar refused him absolution unless he 'restored the liberty of the Florentines', a proposal that only made the dying despot sneer with contempt.

Savonarola also talked Charles VIII into leaving Florence in peace. Pisa, however, took advantage of the confusion to revolt, and the restored republic's attempts to recapture it were in vain. Things were going badly. Piero Capponi's death in 1496 left Florence without a really able leader, and Savonarolan extremists became ever more influential. The French invasion and the incessant wars that followed cost the city dearly in trade, while the Medici, now in Rome, intrigued endlessly to destroy the republic. Worst of all, Savonarola's attacks on clerical corruption made him another bitter enemy in Rome – none other than **Pope Alexander VI** himself, the most corrupt cleric who ever lived. The Borgia pope scraped together a league of allies to make war on Florence in 1497.

This war proceeded without serious reverses for either side, but Savonarola was able to exploit it brilliantly, convincing the Florentines that they were on a moral crusade against the hated and dissolute Borgias, Medici, French, Venetians and Milanese. The year 1497 was undoubtedly the high point of Savonarola's career. The good friar's spies – mostly children – kept a close eye on any Florentines who were suspected of enjoying themselves, and collected books, fancy clothes and works of art for the famous **Bonfire of Vanities**. It was a climactic moment in the history of Florence's delicate psyche. Somehow the spell had been broken; like the deranged old Michelangelo, taking a hammer to his own work, the Florentines gathered the objects that had once been their greatest pride and put them to the torch. The bonfire was held in the centre of the Piazza della Signoria; a visiting Venetian offered to buy the whole lot, but the Florentines had someone hastily sketch his portrait and threw that on the flames, too.

One vanity the Florentines could not quite bring themselves to part with was their violent factionalism. On one side were the *Piagnoni* ('weepers') of Savonarola's party, on the other the party of the *Arrabbiati* ('the angry'), including the gangs of young delinquents who would demonstrate their opposition to piety and holiness by sneaking into the cathedral and filling Savonarola's pulpit with cow dung. A Medicean party was also gathering strength, a sort of fifth column sowing discontent within the city and undermining the war effort. Three times, unsuccessfully, the exiled Medici attempted to seize the city with bands of mercenaries. The Pisan revolt continued, and Pope Alexander had excommunicated Savonarola and was threatening to place all Florence under an interdict. In the long hangover after the Bonfire of Vanities, the Florentines were growing weary of their preacher. When the *Arrabbiati* won the elections of 1498, his doom was sealed. A kangaroo court found the new scapegoat guilty of heresy and treason. After some gratuitous torture and public mockery, the very spot where the Bonfire of Vanities had been held now witnessed a bonfire of Savonarola.

Pope Alexander still wasn't happy. He sent an army under his son, Cesare Borgia, to menace the city. Florence weathered this threat, and the relatively democratic 'Savonarolan' constitution of 1494 seemed to be working out well. Under an innovative idea, borrowed from Venice and designed to circumvent party strife, a public-spirited gentleman named **Piero Soderini** was elected *gonfaloniere* for life in 1502. With the help of his friend and adviser, **Niccolò Machiavelli**, Soderini kept the ship of state on an even keel. Pisa finally surrendered in 1509. Serious trouble returned in 1512, and once more the popes were behind it. As France's only ally in Italy, Florence ran foul of Julius II. Papal and Spanish armies invaded Florentine territory, and after their gruesome sack of Prato, designed specifically to overawe Florence, the frightened and politically apathetic city was ready to submit to the pope's conditions – the expulsion of Soderini, a change of alliance, and the return of the Medici.

The End of the Republic

At first, the understanding was that the Medici would live in Florence strictly as private citizens. But **Giuliano de' Medici**, son of Lorenzo and current leader, soon united the upper classes for a rolling back of Savonarolan democracy. With plenty of hired soldiers to intimidate the populace, a rigged *parlamento* in September 1512 restored Medici control. The democratic Grand Council was abolished; its new meeting hall in the Palazzo Vecchio (where Leonardo and Michelangelo were to have their 'Battle of the Frescoes') was broken up into apartments for soldiers. Soldiers were everywhere, and the Medicean restoration took on the aspect of a police state. Hundreds of political prisoners spent time undergoing torture in the Palazzo Vecchio's dungeons, among them Machiavelli.

Giuliano died in 1516, succeeded by his nephew **Lorenzo, Duke of Urbino**, a snotty young sport with a tyrant's bad manners. Nobody mourned much when syphilis carried him off in 1519, but the family paid Michelangelo to give both Lorenzo and Giuliano fancy tombs. Ever since Giuliano's death, however, the real Medici boss had been not Lorenzo, but his uncle Giovanni,

Know Your Medici

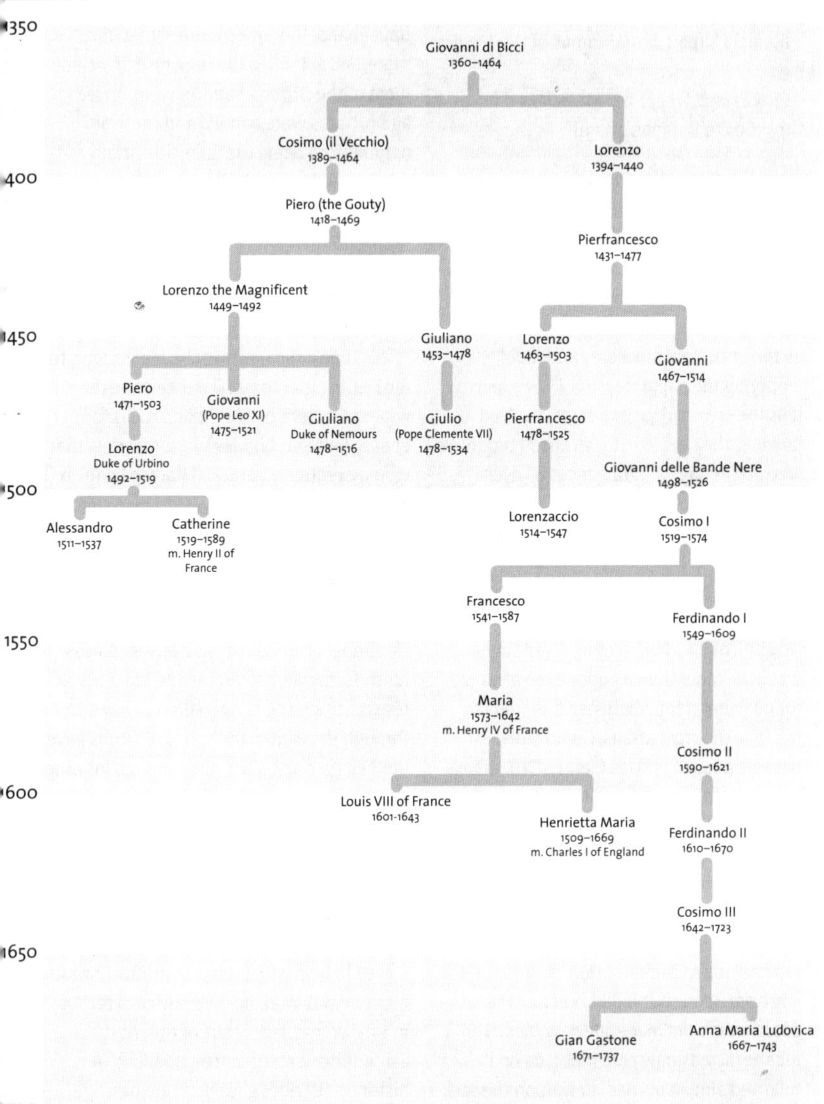

who in that year became **Pope Leo X**. The Medici, original masters of nepotism, had been planning this for years. Back in the 1470s, Lorenzo il Magnifico realized that the surest way of maintaining the family fortunes would be to get a Medici on the papal throne. He had little Giovanni ordained at the age of eight, purchased him a cardinal's hat at 13, and used bribery and diplomacy to help him accumulate dozens of benefices all over France and Italy.

For his easy-going civility (as exemplified in his famous quote: 'God has given us the papacy so let us enjoy it'), and his patronage of scholars and artists, Leo became one of the best-remembered Renaissance popes. On

16th Century

Fortezza da Basso, built by Charles V to prevent Florentine independence, p.147

Medici Chapels, burial tombs of the Medici, p.97

Pitti Palace, where the Medici lived from the 1500s to the 1700s, p.136

the other side of the coin was his criminal mismanagement of the Church; having learned the advantages of parasitism, the Medici were eager to pass it on to their friends. Upper-class Florentines descended on Rome like a plague of locusts, occupying all the important sinecures and rapidly emptying the papal treasury. Their rapacity, plus the tremendous expenses involved in building the new St Peter's, caused Leo to step up the sale of indulgences all over Europe – disgusting reformers like Luther and greatly hastening the onset of the Reformation.

Back in Florence, Lorenzo Duke of Urbino's successor Giulio, bastard son of Lorenzo il Magnifico's brother, the murdered Giuliano, was little more than a puppet; Leo always found enough time between banquets to manage the city's affairs. Giulio himself became pope in 1523, as **Clement VII**, thanks largely to the new financial interdependence between Florence and Rome, and now the Medici presence in their home city was reduced to two more unattractive young bastards, Ippolito and Alessandro, under the guardianship of Cardinal Silvio Passerini. As Leo had done, Clement attempted to run the city from Rome, but high taxes and the lack of a strong hand made the new Medici regime increasingly precarious; its end followed almost immediately upon the sack of Rome in 1527. With Clement a prisoner in the Vatican and unable to intervene, a delegation of Florentine notables discreetly informed Cardinal Passerini and the Medicis that it was time to go. They took the hint, and for the third time in less than a century Florence had succeeded in getting rid of the Medici.

The new republic, though initiated by the disillusioned wealthy classes, soon found radical Savonarolan democrats gaining the upper hand. The Grand Council met once more, and extended the franchise to include most of the citizens. Vanities were cursed again, books were banned and carnival parades forbidden; the Council officially pronounced Jesus Christ 'King of the Florentines', just as it had done in the heyday of the Savonarolan camp meetings. In an intense atmosphere of republican virtue and pious crusade, Florence rushed headlong into the apocalyptic climax of its history.

This time it did not take the Medici long to recover. In order to get Florence back, the witless Clement became allied to his former enemy, **Emperor Charles V**, a sordid deal that would eventually betray all Italy to Spanish control. Imperial troops were to help subdue Florence, and Clement's illegitimate son Alessandro was to wed Charles' illegitimate daughter. The bastards were closing in. Charles' troops put Florence under siege in December 1529. The city had few resources for the struggle, and no friends, but a heroic resistance kept the imperialists at bay all through the winter and spring. Citizens gave up their gold and silver to be minted into the republic's last coins. The councillors debated seizing little Catherine de' Medici, future Queen of France, but then a prisoner of the republic, and dangling her from the walls to give the enemy a good target. Few artists were left in Florence, but Michelangelo stayed to help with his city's fortifications (by night he was working on the Medici tombs in San Lorenzo, surely one of the most astounding feats of fence-straddling in history; both sides gave him safe passage when he wanted to leave Florence, and again when he decided to return).

In August of 1530, the Florentines' skilful commander, Francesco Ferruccio, was killed in a skirmish near Pistoia; at about the same time the republic realized that its mercenary captain within the walls, Malatesta Baglioni, had sold them out to the pope and emperor. When they tried to arrest him, Baglioni only laughed, and directed his men to turn their artillery on the city. The inevitable capitulation came on 12 August; after almost 400 years, the Florentine republic had breathed its last.

At first, this third Medici return seemed to be just another dreary round of history repeating itself. Again, a packed *parlamento* gutted the constitution and legitimized the Medici takeover. Again the family and its minions combed the city, confiscating back every penny's worth of property that had been confiscated from them. This time, however, was to be different. Florence had gone from being a large fish in a small Italian pond to a minuscule but hindersome nuisance in the pan-European world of papal and imperial politics. Charles V didn't much like republics, or disorderly politicking, or indeed anyone who might conceivably say no to him. The orders came down from the emperor in Brussels; it was to be Medici for ever.

Cosimo I: The Medici as Grand Dukes

At first little was changed; the shell of the republican constitution was maintained, but with the 20-year-old illegitimate **Alessandro** as 'Duke of the Florentine Republic'; the harsh reality was under construction on the height above the city's west end – the Fortezza da Basso, with its Spanish garrison, demanded by Charles V as insurance that Florence would never again be able to assert its independence. If any further symbolism was necessary, Alessandro ordered the great bell to be removed from the tower of the Palazzo Vecchio, the bell that had always summoned the citizens to political assemblies and the mustering of the army.

In 1537, Alessandro was treacherously murdered by his jealous cousin Lorenzaccio de' Medici. With no legitimate heirs in the direct line, Florence was in danger of falling under direct imperial rule, as had happened to Milan two years earlier, upon the extinction of the Sforza dukes. The assassination was kept secret while the Medici and the diplomats angled for a solution. The only reasonable choice turned out to be 18-year-old **Cosimo de' Medici**, heir of the family's cadet branch. This son of a famous mercenary commander, Giovanni of the Black Bands, had grown up on a farm and had never been involved with Florentine affairs; both the elder statesmen of the family and the imperial representatives thought they would easily be able to manipulate him.

It soon became clear that they had picked the wrong boy. Right from the start, young Cosimo had a surprisingly complete idea of how he meant to rule Florence, and also the will and strength of personality to see his commands carried out. No one ever admitted liking him; his puritanical court dismayed even the old partisans of Savonarola, and Florentines always enjoyed grumbling over his high taxes, going to support 'colonels, spies, Spaniards, and women to serve Madame' (his Spanish consort Eleanor of Toledo).

More surprising still, in this pathetic age when bowing and scraping Italians were everywhere else losing both their liberty and their dignity, Cosimo held his own against both pope and Spaniard. To back up his growing independence, Cosimo put his domains on an almost permanent war footing. New fortresses were built, a big fleet begun, and a paid standing army took the place of mercenaries and citizen levies. The skeleton of the old republic was revamped into a modern, bureaucratic state, governed as scientifically and rationally as any in Europe. The new regime, well prepared as it was, never had a severe test. Early in his reign Cosimo defeated the last-ditch effort of the republican exiles, unreconstructed oligarchs led by the banker Filippo Strozzi, at the **Battle of Montemurlo**, the last threat ever to Medici rule. Cosimo's masterstroke came in 1557, when with the help of an imperial army he was able to gobble up the entire Republic of Siena. Now the Medicis controlled roughly the boundaries of modern Tuscany; Cosimo was able to cap off his reign in 1569 by purchasing from the Pope the title of Grand Duke of Tuscany.

Knick-knacks and Tedium: The Later Medici

For all Cosimo's efforts, Florence was a city entering a very evident decline. Banking and trade did well throughout the late 16th century, a prosperous time for almost all of Italy, but there were very few opportunities for growth, and few Florentines interested in looking for it. More than ever, wealth was going into land, palaces and government bonds; the old tradition of mercantile venture among the Florentine élite was rapidly becoming a thing of the past. For culture and art, Cosimo's reign turned out to be a disaster. It wasn't what he intended; indeed the Duke brought to the field his accustomed energy and compulsion to improve and organize. Academies were founded, and research underwritten. Cosimo's big purse and his emphasis on art as political propaganda helped change the Florentine artist from a slightly eccentric guild artisan to a flouncing courtier, ready to roll over at his master's command.

Michelangelo, despite frequent entreaties, always refused to work for Cosimo. Most of the other talented Florentines eventually found one excuse or another to bolt for Rome or even further afield, leaving lapdogs like **Giorgio Vasari** to carry on the grand traditions of Florentine art. Vasari, with help from such artists as Ammannati and Bandinelli, transformed much of the city – especially the interiors of its churches and public buildings. Florence began to fill up with equestrian statues of Medici, pageants and plaster triumphal arches displaying the triumphs of the Medici, sculptural allegories (like Cellini's *Perseus*) reminding us of the inevitability of the Medici and, best of all, portraits of semi-divine Medici floating up in the clouds with little Cupids and Virtues.

It was all the same to Cosimo and his successors, whose personal tastes tended more to engraved jewels, exotic taxidermy and sculptures made of seashells. But it helped hasten the extinction of Florentine culture and the quiet transformation of the city into just another Mediterranean backwater. Cosimo himself grew ill in his later years, abdicating most responsibility to his son **Francesco** from 1564 to his death 10 years later. Francesco, the genuine oddball among the Medici, was a moody, melancholic sort who cared little for government, preferring to lock himself up in the family palaces to pursue his passion for alchemy, as well as occasional researches into such subjects as perpetual motion and poisons – his agents around the Mediterranean had to ship him crates of scorpions every now and then. Despite his lack of interest, Francesco was a capable ruler, best known for his founding of the port city of Livorno.

Later Medici followed the general course established by other great families, such as the Habsburgs and Bourbons – each one was worse than the last. Francesco's death in 1587 gave the throne to his brother, **Ferdinando I**, founder of the Medici Chapels at San Lorenzo and another indefatigable collector of bric-a-brac. Next came **Cosimo II** (1609–21), a sickly nonentity who eventually succumbed to tuberculosis, and **Ferdinando II** (1621–70), whose long and uneventful reign oversaw the impoverishment of Florence and most of Tuscany. For this the Medici do not deserve much blame. A long string of bad harvests, beginning in the 1590s, plagues that recurred with terrible frequency as late as the 1630s, and general trade patterns that redistributed wealth and power from the Mediterranean to northern Europe, all set the stage for the collapse of the Florentine economy. The fatal blow came in the 1630s, when the long-deteriorating wool trade collapsed with sudden finality. Banking was going too, partly a victim of the age's continuing inflation, partly of high taxes and lack of worthwhile investments. Florence, by mid-century, found itself with no prospects at all, a pensioner city drawing a barely respectable income from its glorious past.

With **Cosimo III** (1670–1723), the line of the Medici crossed over into the realm of the ridiculous. A religious crank and anti-Semite, this Cosimo temporarily wiped out free thought in the universities, allowed Tuscany to fill up with nuns and Jesuits, and decreed fantastical laws like the one that forbade any man to enter a house where an unmarried woman lived. To support his lavish court and pay the big tributes demanded by Spain and Austria (something earlier Medici would have scorned), Cosimo taxed what was left of the Florentine economy into an early grave. His heir was the incredible **Gian Gastone** (1723–37). This last Medici, an obese drunkard, senile and slobbering at the age of 50, has been immortalized by the equally incredible bust in the Pitti Palace. Gian Gastone had to be carried up and down stairs on the rare occasions when he ever got out of bed (mainly to disprove rumours that he was dead); on the one occasion he appeared in public, the chronicles report him vomiting repeatedly out of the carriage window.

As a footnote on the Medici there is Gian Gastone's perfectly sensible sister, **Anna Maria Ludovica**. As the very last surviving Medici, it fell to her to dispose of the family's vast wealth and hoards of art. When she died, in 1743, her will revealed that the whole bundle was to become the property of the future rulers of Tuscany – whoever they should be – with the provision that not one bit of it should ever, ever be moved outside Florence. Without her, the great collections of the Uffizi and the Bargello might long ago have been packed away to Vienna or to Paris.

Post-Medici Florence

When Gian Gastone died in 1737, Tuscany's fate had already been decided by the great powers of Europe. The Grand Duchy would fall to **Francis Stephen**, Duke of Lorraine and husband-to-be of the Austrian Empress Maria Theresa; the new duke's troops were already installed in the Fortezza da Basso a year before Gian Gastone died. For most of the next century, Florence slumbered peacefully under a benign Austrian rule. Already the first Grand Tourists were arriving on their way to Rome and Naples, sons of the Enlightenment like Goethe, who never imagined anything in Florence could possibly interest him and didn't stop, or relics like the Pretender Charles Edward Stuart, 'Bonnie Prince Charlie', Duke of Albany, who stayed two years. Napoleon's men occupied the city for most of two decades, without making much of an impression.

18th Century to the Present

Casa Guidi, where Robert and Elizabeth Barrett Browning set up house, p.140

Piazza della Repubblica, built in the late 19th century, p.107

Stazione Centrale, one of modern Italy's finest buildings, erected in 1935, p.105

After the Napoleonic Wars, the Habsburg restoration brought back the Lorraine dynasty. From 1824 to 1859, Florence and Tuscany were ruled by **Leopold II**, that most useful and likeable of all Grand Dukes. This was the age when Florence first became popular among the northern Europeans and the time when the Brownings, Dostoevsky, Leigh Hunt and dozens of other artists and writers took up residence, rediscovering the glories of the city and of the early Renaissance. Grand Duke Leopold was decent enough to let himself be overthrown in 1859, during the tumults of the Risorgimento. In 1865, when only the Papal State remained to be incorporated into the Kingdom of Italy, Florence briefly became the new nation's capital. King Vittorio Emanuele moved into the Pitti Palace, and the Italian Parliament met in the great hall of the Palazzo Vecchio.

It was really not meant to last. When the Italian troops entered Rome in 1870, Florence's brief hour as a major capital was at an end. Not, however, without giving the staid old city a memorable jolt towards the modern world. In an unusual flurry of exertion, Florence finally threw up a façade for its cathedral, and levelled the picturesque though squalid market area and Jewish ghetto to build the dolorous Piazza della Repubblica. Fortunately, the city regained its senses before too much damage was done. Throughout this century, Florence's role as a museum city has been confirmed with each passing year. The hiatus provided by the Second World War allowed the city to resume briefly its ancient delight in black-and-white political epic. In 1944–5, Florence offered some of the most outrageous spectacles of Fascist fanaticism, and also some of the most courageous stories of the Resistance – including that of the German consul Gerhard Wolf, who used his position to protect Florentines from the Nazi terror, often at great personal risk.

In August 1944, the Allied armies were poised to advance through northern Tuscany. For the Germans, the Arno made a convenient defensive line, requiring that all the bridges of Florence be demolished. All, except for the Ponte Vecchio, were saved in a last-minute deal, though the buildings on either side of it were destroyed to provide piles of rubble around the bridge approaches. After the war, all were repaired; the city had the Ponte Santa Trìnita rebuilt stone by stone exactly as it was. No sooner was the war damage redeemed, however, than an even greater disaster attacked Florence's patrimony. The flood of 1966, when water reached as high as 6.5m, did more damage than Nazis or Napoleons; an international effort was raised to preserve and restore the city's art and monuments. Since then the Arno's bed has been deepened under the Ponte Vecchio and 6m earthen walls have been erected around Ponte Amerigo Vespucci; video screens and computers monitor every fluctuation in the water level. If a flood happens again, Florence will have time to protect herself.

Far more insoluble is the problem of terrorism, which touched the city, in May 1993, when a bomb attack destroyed the Gregoriophilus library opposite the Uffizi and damaged the Vasari Corridor. Florence, shocked by this intrusion from the outside world into its holy of holies, repaired most of the damage in record time with funds which were raised by a national subscription.

Careful planning has saved the best of Florence's immediate countryside from a different sort of flood – post-war suburbanization – but much of the other territory around the city has been coated by an atrocity of suburban sprawl, some of the most degraded landscapes in all Italy. The building of a new airport extension, which the Florentines hope will help make up some of the economic ground they've lost to Milan, may also include the building of a whole new business city, a new Florence, nothing less than 'the greatest urban planning operation of the century' they say, with some of the old audacity of Brunelleschi. There are plans for an underground train system, and perhaps even a new high-speed train between Milan and Rome that would pass under Florence in a tunnel. Ideas there are, but getting them past the city's innate factionalism and its own mania for perfectionism has proved to be a mountain of a stumbling block.

Meanwhile Florence works hard to preserve what it already has. Although new measures to control the city's bugbear – the traffic problems of a city of 400,000 that receives 7 million visitors a year – have been enacted to protect the historic centre, pollution from nearby industry continues to eat away at monuments – Donatello's statue *St Mark* at Orsanmichele, perfectly intact 50 years ago, is now a mutilated leper. Private companies, banks and even individuals finance 90 per cent of the art restoration in Florence, with techniques invented by the city's innovative Institute of Restoration. Increasingly copies are made to replace original works. Naturally, half the city is for them, and the other half, against.

Art and Architecture

ETRUSCANS, ROMANS AND THE DARK AGES 36

THE MIDDLE AGES 37

THE RENAISSANCE 38

MANNERISM 40

THE REST COMPRESSED 40

For details on all the artists featured in this book, and their major works, *see also* the **Artists' Directory** on p.258.

Etruscans, Romans and the Dark Ages

Almost all Etruscan art derives from the Greek; the Etruscans built classical temples (unfortunately of wood, with terracotta embellishments, so little survives), carved themselves sarcophagi decorated with scenes from Homer, and painted their pottery in red and black after the latest styles from Athens or Corinth. Their talent for portraiture, among much else, was carried on by the Romans, and they bequeathed their love of fresco painting to the artists of the Middle Ages and Renaissance, who of course weren't even aware of the debt.

After destroying the Etruscan nation, the Romans also began the extinction of its

Florentine Schizophrenia

Dante's *Vita Nuova*, the autobiography of his young soul, was only the beginning of Florentine analysis; Petrarch, who was the introspective 'first modern man', was a Florentine born in exile; Ghiberti was the first artist to write an autobiography, Cellini wrote one of the most readable; Alberti invented art criticism; Vasari invented art history; Michelangelo's personality, in his letters and sonnets, looms as large as his art. In many ways Florence broke away from the medieval idea of community and invented the modern concept of the individual, most famously expressed by Lorenzo de' Medici's friend, Pico della Mirandola, whose *Oration on the Dignity of Man* tells us what the God on the Sistine Chapel ceiling was saying when he created Adam: '...And I have created you neither celestial nor terrestrial, neither mortal nor immortal, so that, like a free and able sculptor and painter of yourself, you may mould yourself entirely in the form of your choice.'

To attempt to understand Florence, remember one historical constant: no matter what the issue, the city always takes both sides, vehemently and often violently, especially in the Punch and Judy days of Guelphs and Ghibellines. In the 1300s this was explained by the fact that the city was founded under the sign of Mars, the war god; but in medieval astronomy Mars is also connected with Aries, another Florentine symbol and the time of spring blossoms. Whatever dispute rocked the streets, Great Aunt Florence often expressed her schizophrenia in art, floral Florence versus stone Florence, epitomized by the irreconcilable differences between the two most famous works of art in the city: Botticelli's graceful, enigmatic *Primavera* and Michelangelo's cold, perfect *David*. The 'city of flowers' seems a joke; it has nary a real flower, nor even a tree, in its stone streets; indeed, all effort has gone into keeping nature at bay, surpassing it with geometry and art. And yet the Florentines were perhaps the first since the Romans to discover the joys of the countryside. The rough, rusticated stone palaces, like fortresses or prisons, hide charms as delightful as Gozzoli's frescoes in the Palazzo Medici; Luca della Robbia's dancing children and floral wreaths are contemporary with the naked, violent warriors of the Pollaiuolo brothers; the writhing, quarrelsome statuary in the Piazza della Signoria is sheltered by a most delicate and beautiful loggia.

After 1500, all of the good, bad and ugly symptoms of the Renaissance peaked in the mass fever of Mannerism. Then, drifting into a debilitating twilight of *pietra dura* tables, gold gimcracks, and interior decoration, Florence gave birth to the artistic phenomenon known as kitsch. Since then, worn out perhaps, or embarrassed, this city built by merchants has kept its own counsel, expressing its argumentative soul in overblown controversies about traffic and art restoration. We who find her fascinating hope she some day remembers her proper role as the bearer of the torch of culture.

artistic tradition; by the Empire, there was almost nothing left that could be called distinctively Etruscan. What Tuscan painting survived followed styles current in Byzantium, a stylization that lingered into the 13th century in Tuscan panel painting.

The Middle Ages

In both architecture and sculpture, the first influence came from the north. Lombard masons filled Tuscany with simple Romanesque churches, although it wasn't long before two distinctive Tuscan forms emerged: the Pisan style, characterized by blind rows of colonnades, black and white zebra stripes, and lozenge-shaped designs; and the 'Tuscan Romanesque' which developed around Florence, notable for its use of dark and light marble patterns and simple geometric patterns, often with intricate mosaic floors to match (the Baptistry and San Miniato in Florence are the chief examples). In the cities in between, such as Lucca, there are interesting variations on the two different styles. Siena was perhaps the most receptive to Gothic styles from the north, but adapted to an Italian sensibility that produced not only churches but unique public buildings such as the Palazzo Comunale, all of good siena-coloured brick.

From the large pool of talent working on Pisa's great cathedral complex in the 13th century emerged Italy's first great sculptor, **Nicola Pisano**, whose Baptistry pulpit, with its naturalistic figures derived from ancient reliefs, finally broke away from the stiff hierarchic figures of Byzantium. His even more remarkable son, **Giovanni Pisano**, prefigures Donatello in the expressiveness of his statues and the vigour of his pulpits; his façade of Siena cathedral, though altered, is a unique work of art. **Arnolfo di Cambio**, a student of Nicola Pisano, became chief sculptor-architect of Florence during its building boom in the 1290s, designing its cathedral and Palazzo Vecchio with a hitherto unheard-of scale and grandeur.

Painting at first lagged behind the new realism and more complex composition of sculpture. The first to depart from Byzantine stylization, at least according to the account in Vasari's *Lives of the Artists* (*see* p.79), was **Cimabue**, in the late 1200s, who forsook Greek forms for a more 'Latin' or 'natural' way of painting. Cimabue found his greatest pupil, **Giotto**, as a young shepherd, chalk-sketching sheep on a piece of slate. Brought to Florence, Giotto soon eclipsed his master's fame (artistic celebrity being a recent Florentine invention) and achieved the greatest advances on the road to the new painting with a plain, rather severe approach that shunned Gothic prettiness while exploring new ideas in composition and expressing psychological depth in his subjects. Even more importantly, Giotto through his intuitive grasp of perspective was able to go further than any previous artist in representing his subjects as actual figures in space. In a sense Giotto actually invented space; it was this, despite his often awkward and graceless draughtsmanship, that so astounded his contemporaries. His followers, **Taddeo** and **Agnolo Gaddi** (father and son), **Giovanni da Milano**, and **Maso di Banco** filled Florence's churches with their own interpretations of the master's style. In the latter half of the 1300s, however, there also appeared the key figure of **Andrea Orcagna**, the most important Florentine sculptor, painter and architect of his day. Inspired by the more elegant style of **Andrea Pisano**'s Baptistry doors, Orcagna broke away from the simple Giottesque forms for a more elaborate, detailed style in his sculpture, while the fragments of his frescoes that survive have a vivid dramatic power which undoubtedly owes something to the time of the Black Death and social upheavals in which they were painted.

Siena never produced a Vasari to chronicle its accomplishments, though they were considerable; in the 13th and 14th centuries, Siena's Golden Age, the city's artists, like its soldiers, rivalled and often surpassed those of Florence. For whatever reason, it seemed purposefully to seek inspiration in different directions from Florence; at first from central Italian styles around Spoleto, then, with prosperity and the advent of **Guido da Siena** in the early 1200s, to the more elegant line and colour of Byzantium. Guido's work paved the way for the pivotal figure of **Duccio di Buoninsegna**, the catalyst who founded the essentials of Sienese art by uniting the beauty of Byzantine line and colour with the sweet finesse and new human warmth of western Gothic art. With Duccio's great followers **Pietro** and **Ambrogio Lorenzetti** and **Simone Martini**, the Sienese produced an increasingly elegant and rarefied art. They were less innovative than the Florentines, though they brought the 'International Gothic' style – flowery and ornate, with all the bright tones of May – to its highest form in Italy. Simone Martini introduced the Sienese manner to Florence in the early 1400s, where it influenced most notably the work of **Lorenzo Monaco**, **Masolino**, and the young goldsmith and sculptor, **Ghiberti**.

The Renaissance

Under the assaults of historians and critics over the last two centuries, the term 'Renaissance' has become a vague and controversial word. Nevertheless, however you choose to interpret this rebirth of the arts, and whatever dates you assign to it, Florence inescapably takes the credit for it. This is no small claim. Combining art, science and humanist scholarship into a visual revolution that often seemed pure sorcery to their contemporaries, a handful of Florentine geniuses taught the Western eye a new way of seeing. Perspective seems a simple trick to us now, but its discovery determined everything that followed, not only in art, but in science and philosophy as well.

Leading what scholars used self-assuredly to call the 'Early Renaissance' is a triumvirate of three geniuses: **Brunelleschi**, **Donatello** and **Masaccio**. Brunelleschi, neglecting his considerable talents in sculpture for architecture and science, not only built the majestic dome of Florence cathedral, but threw the Pandora's box of perspective wide open by mathematically codifying the principles of foreshortening. His good friend Donatello, the greatest sculptor since the ancient Greeks, inspired a new generation of both sculptors and painters to explore new horizons in portraiture and three-dimensional representation. The first painter to incorporate Brunelleschi and Donatello's lessons of spatiality, perspective and expressiveness was the young prodigy Masaccio, who along with his master Masolino painted the famous Brancacci Chapel in the Carmine, studied by nearly every Florentine artist.

The new science of architecture, sculpture and painting introduced by this triumvirate ignited an explosion of talent unequalled before or since – a score of masters, most of them Tuscan, each following the dictates of his own genius to create a remarkable range of themes and styles. To mention only the most prominent: **Lorenzo Ghiberti**, who followed Donatello's advice on his second set of Baptistry doors to cause a Renaissance revolution; **Leon Battista Alberti**, who took Brunelleschi's ideas to their most classical extreme in architecture, creating new forms in the process; **Paolo Uccello**, one of the most provocative of artists, who according to Vasari drove himself bats with the study of perspective and the possibilities of illusionism; **Piero della Francesca**, who explored the limits of perspective and geometrical forms to create the most compelling, haunting images of the quattrocento; **Fra Angelico**, who combined Masaccio's innovations and International Gothic colours and his own deep faith to create the most purely spiritual art of his time; **Andrea del Castagno**, who made use of perspective to create monumental, if often restless, figures.

And still more: **Benozzo Gozzoli**, whose enchanting springtime colours and delight in detail are a throwback to the International Gothic; **Antonio** and **Piero Pollaiuolo**, sons of a poultryman, whose new, dramatic use of line and form, often violent and writhing, would be echoed in Florentine Mannerism;

Masters and Students: The Progress of the Renaissance

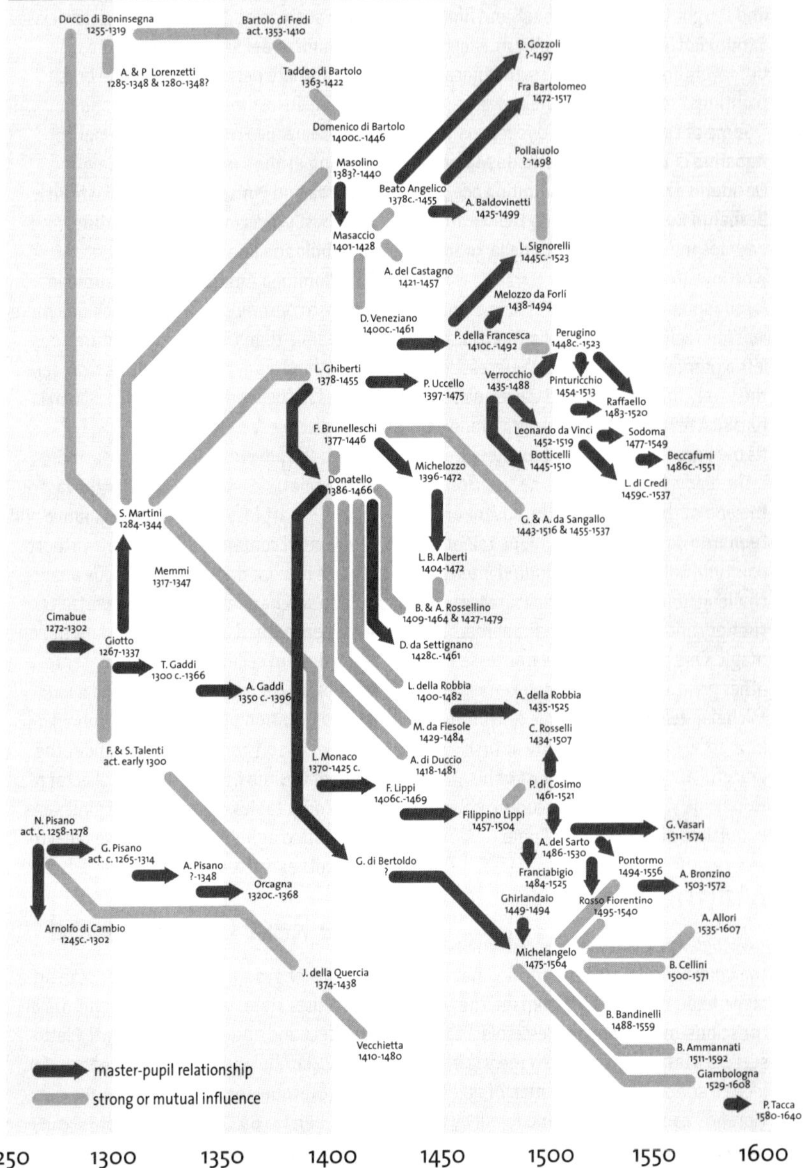

This chart shows who learned from whom – an insight into some 300 years of artistic continuity

Fra Filippo Lippi, a monk like Fra Angelico but far more earthly, the master of lovely Madonnas, teacher of his talented son **Filippino Lippi**; **Domenico Ghirlandaio**, whose gift of easy charm and flawless technique made him society's fresco painter; **Andrea del Verrocchio**, who could cast in bronze, paint, or carve with perfect detail; **Perugino** (Pietro

Vannucci) of Umbria, who painted the stillness of his native region into his landscapes and taught the young Raphael; and finally **Sandro Botticelli**, whose highly intellectual, but lovely and melancholy, mythological paintings are in a class of their own.

Some of Donatello's gifted followers were **Agostino di Duccio**, **Benedetto da Maiano**, **Desiderio da Settignano**, **Antonio** and **Bernardo Rossellino**, **Mino da Fiesole** and perhaps most famously **Luca della Robbia**, who invented the coloured terracottas his family spread throughout Tuscany. Siena's leading sculptor, **Jacopo della Quercia**, also left a number of works elsewhere, especially the lovely tomb of Ilaria del Carretto in Lucca (1408). A few decades later Lucca produced its own great sculptor, **Matteo Civitali**.

The 'Early Renaissance' came to a close near the end of the 1400s with the advent of **Leonardo da Vinci**, whose unique talent in painting, only one of his hundred interests, challenged the certainty of naturalism with a subtlety and chiaroscuro that approaches magic. One passion, however, obsessed the other great figure of the 'High Renaissance', **Michelangelo Buonarroti**: his consummate interest was the human body, at first graceful and serene as in most of his Florentine works, and later, contorted and anguished after he left for Rome.

Mannerism

Michelangelo left in Florence the seeds for the bold, neurotic avant-garde art that has come to be known as Mannerism. The first conscious 'movement' in Western art can be seen as a last fling amid the growing intellectual and spiritual exhaustion of 1530s Florence, conquered once and for all by the Medici. The Mannerists' calculated exoticism and exaggerated, tortured poses, together with the brooding self-absorption of Michelangelo, are a prelude to Florentine art's remarkably abrupt turn into decadence and prophesy its final extinction. Foremost among the Mannerist painters are two surpassingly strange characters, **Jacopo Pontormo** and **Rosso Fiorentino**, who were not in such great demand as the coldly classical **Andrea del Sarto** and **Bronzino**, consummate perfectionists of the brush, both much less intense and demanding. There were also charming reactionaries working at the same time, especially **Il Sodoma** and **Pinturicchio**, both of whom left their best works in Siena. In sculpture **Giambologna** and to a lesser extent **Bartolommeo Ammannati** specialized in virtuoso *contrapposto* figures, each one more impossible than the last. In sculpture, too, Siena shied away from Florentine exaggeration, as in the work of Jacopo della Quercia's chief disciple, **Vecchietta**.

With the advent of Giambologna and Ammannati's contemporary, **Giorgio Vasari**, Florentine art lost almost all imaginative and intellectual content, and became a virtuoso style of interior decoration perfectly adaptable to saccharine holy pictures, portraits of newly enthroned dukes, or absurd mythological ballroom ceilings. In the cinquecento, with plenty of money to spend and a long Medici tradition of patronage to uphold, this tendency soon got out of hand. Under the reign of Cosimo I, indefatigable collector of *pietra dura* tables, silver and gold gimcracks, and stuffed animals, Florence gave birth to yet another artistic phenomenon – kitsch.

The Rest Compressed

In the long, dark night of later Tuscan art a few artists stand out – the often whimsical architect and engineer **Buontalenti**; **Pietro Tacca**, Giambologna's pupil with a taste for the grotesque; the charming Baroque fresco master **Pietro da Cortona**. Most of Tuscany chose to sit out the Baroque, and we can race up to the 19th century for the delightful 'Tuscan Impressionists' or *Macchiaioli* ('Splatterers'; the best collection is in the Modern Art section of the Pitti Palace); and in the 20th century **Ottone Rosai**, the master of the quiet Florentine countryside.

Travel

GETTING THERE 42
By Air 42
By Train 43
By Coach 44

SPECIALIST TOUR OPERATORS 44

ENTRY FORMALITIES 46

ARRIVAL 47

GETTING AROUND 48
By Bus 48
By Train 49
By Car 50
By Taxi 51
By Carriage 51
By Motorbike or Bicycle 51

01

GETTING THERE

By Air

From the UK and Ireland

Scheduled Flights

From London Heathrow there are daily Alitalia and British Airways flights to the international airport at Pisa; from Gatwick there are daily flights to Florence with Alitalia and Meridiana. From Dublin, you can fly with either Alitalia or Aer Lingus to Milan, from where you can pick up a connecting flight to Florence; or else go through London for Tuscany. Keep your eye open for bargains and charters in the papers.

Aer Lingus, *Dublin*, **t** *(01) 886 8888; or Belfast*, **t** *0845 737747*, **w** *www.aerlingus.ie*.

Alitalia, *London*, **t** *08705 448259; Dublin*, **t** *(01) 677 5171*, **w** *www.alitalia.co.uk*.

British Airways, **t** *0845 77 333 77*, **w** *www.britishairways.com*.

Meridiana, **t** *(020) 7839 2222*, **w** *www.meridiana.it*.

Low-cost Airlines

Ryanair, **t** *08701 569569*, **w** *www.ryanair.com*. Fly to Pisa from Stansted (**t** 050 503770 in Pisa).

Go, **t** *0345 605 4321*, **w** *www.go-fly.com*. Fly to Bologna from Stansted (**t** 848 887766 in Italy).

Airlines Offices in Florence

Alitalia, **w** *www.alitalia.it: Lungarno Acciaioli 10/12r*, **t** *055 27881; Piazza dell'Oro 1*, **t** *1478 65643 (flight inquiries)*, **t** *1478 65642 (international reservations)*, **f** *050 278 8400*.

British Airways, **w** *www.britishairways.com: no longer have an office in Florence. For information and reservations they have a toll-free number:* **t** *478 12266, or use their office at Pisa airport*.

Meridiana, **w** *www.meridiana.it, Lungarno Vespucci 28r*, **t** *199 111333*.

TWA: *Via dei Vecchietti 4*, **t** *055 239 6856*, **f** *055 214634*.

Prices vary from £20 to £150 return, depending on booking periods, special offers, etc.

From the USA and Canada

Scheduled Flights

From the United States, the major carriers fly only to Rome or Milan, though British Airways has a New York–London–Pisa service. Your travel agent may find a much cheaper fare from your home airport to your Italian airport by way of London, Brussels, Paris, Frankfurt or Amsterdam. Alitalia flies direct to Italy from both the USA and Canada.

To be eligible for low cost or APEX fares, you'll have to have fixed arrival and departure dates and spend at least a week in Italy, but no more than 90 days. SuperAPEX, the cheapest normal fares available, must be purchased at least 14 days (or sometimes 21 days) in advance and there are penalties to pay if you change your flight dates. At the time of writing the lowest mid-week SuperAPEX between New York and Rome in the off-season is around $508, rising to the $900 zone in summer.

To sweeten the deal, Alitalia in particular often has promotional perks like rental cars (Jetdrive), or discounts on domestic flights within Italy, on hotels, or on tours. Ask your travel agent. Children under the age of two usually travel for free and both British Airways and Alitalia offer cheaper tickets on some flights for students and the under-25s.

Air Canada: **t** *1 888 247 2262*, **w** *www.aircanada.ca*.

Alitalia: *(USA)* **t** *800 223 5730*, **w** *www.alitaliausa.com*.

British Airways: **t** *800 AIRWAYS, TTY* **t** *1 877 993 9997*, **w** *www.britishairways.com*.

Continental, **t** *800 231 0856,or hearing impaired* **t** *800 343 9195, Canada* **t** *800 525 0280*, **w** *www.continental.com*.

Delta: **t** *800 241 4141*, **w** *www.delta.com*.

Northwest Airlines, **t** *800 225 2525*, **w** *www.nwa.com*.

TWA, **t** *800 892 4141*, **w** *www.twa.com*.

United Airlines, **t** *800 241 6522*, **w** *www.ual.com*.

Flights on the Internet

The best place to start looking for flights is the Web – just about everyone has a site where you can compare prices (*see* the airlines listed below), and booking online usually confers a 10–20% discount.

UK and Ireland

www.airtickets.co.uk
www.cheapflights.com
www.lastminute.com
www.skydeals.co.uk
www.sky-tours.co.uk
www.thomascook.co.uk
www.travelocity.com
www.travelselect.com

USA and Canada

www.xfares.com (carry on luggage only)
www.smarterliving.com
www.air-fare.com
www.expedia.com
www.flights.com
www.orbitz.com
www.priceline.com
www.travellersweb.ws
www.travelocity.com

Discounts, Students and Special Deals

Airhitch, *2790 Broadway, Suite 100, New York, NY 10025*, **t** *(212) 864 2000*, **w** *www.airhitch.org*.

Council Travel, *205 E 42nd Street, New York, NY 10017*, **t** *(800) 743 1823*. Major specialists in student and charter flights; branches all over the USA. Can also provide Eurail and Britrail passes.

Last Minute Travel Club, *132 Brookline Avenue, Boston, MA 02215*, **t** *800 527 8646*.

Now Voyager, *74 Varick St, Suite 307, New York, NY 10013*, **t** *(212) 431 1616*. For courier flights.

STA, *10 Downing Street, New York, NY 10014*, **t** *800 781 4040*, **t** *(212) 627 3111*, **w** *www.statravel.com; ASUC Building, 2nd Floor, University of California, Berkeley, CA 94720*, **t** *(510) 642 3000*. Also with branches at universities.

TFI, *34 West 32nd Street, New York, NY 10001*, **t** *(212) 736 1140, toll free* **t** *800 745 8000*.

Travel Cuts, *187 College St, Toronto, Ontario M5T 1P7*, **t** *(416) 979 2406*. Canada's largest student travel specialists; branches in most provinces.

By Train

From the UK and Ireland

Note that the train costs a lot more than the cheapest air fares, and it takes a lot longer. It's about 17 hours by Eurostar from London's Waterloo Station to Florence (changing in Paris), and will set you back around £225 for a standard return fare, including your couchette and reservations throughout. Travelling by train and ferry takes about 22 hours and costs around £176 for a second-class return. These trains are, if you take along a good book, a fairly painless way of getting there (contact Rail Europe, *see* below, for more details).

Discounts are available for senior citizens, families and for children, and anyone under 26. Get them from Rail Europe or Rail Choice (*see* below) and throughout Europe at student offices (CTS in Italy) in main railway stations. An Interail Pass (available to EU residents only) offers unlimited travel for all ages throughout Europe for up to a month. At the time of writing, a 22-day pass covering Zone G (Italy, Greece, Turkey, Slovenia) costs £129 for the under-26s and £185 if you're over 26; a month's pass covering Zone G and also Zone E (France, Belgium, Luxembourg and the Netherlands) costs £169 for under-26s and £239 for over-26s.

Various youth fares and inclusive rail passes are also available within Italy, and if you're planning on doing a lot of train travel solely in Italy you can organize these before leaving home at Rail Choice (*see* below). Rail Choice have further discounts for those students and under-26s using Eurostar.

Rail Europe Travel Centre, *179 Piccadilly, London W1V 0BA*, **t** *08705 848 848*, **w** *www.raileurope.co.uk*.

Eurostar, *EPS House, Waterloo Station, London SE1*, **t** *08705 186 186*, **w** *www.eurostar.com*.

Rail Choice, *15 Colman House, Empire Square, High Street, Penge, London SE20 7EX*, **t** *(020) 8659 7300*, **w** *www.railchoice.com and www.railchoice.co.uk*.

From USA and Canada

See above for notes on travelling to Italy by train from the UK. For information on Italian rail passes and special deals, contact:

CIT, *15 West 44th Street, 10th Floor, New York, NY 10036*, **t** *(212) 730 2121*, **w** *www.cittours.com or www.fs-on-line.com; (Canada) 80 Tiverton Court, Suite 401, Markham, Toronto L3R O94*, **t** *(905) 415 1060*.

Rail Choice, *15 Colman House, Empire Square, High Street, Penge, London SE20 7EX*, **t** *(020) 8659 7300*, **w** *www.railchoice.com*. They can send rail passes and Motorail tickets to the USA by Fedex.

Rail Europe, *226 Westchester Ave, White Plains, NY 10064*, **t** *(914) 682 2999*, **t** *800 438 7245*, **w** *www.raileurope.com*.

By Coach

Usually more expensive than a charter flight, the coach is the last refuge of airplane-phobic bargain-hunters. The journey time from London to Rome or Siena is around 32 hours, changing in Paris and/or Milan; the return fare is around £115. There are, again, discounts for under-26s, senior citizens and children.

Eurolines UK Ltd, *4 Cardiff Road, Luton LU1 1PP*, **t** *08705 143219*, **f** *(01582) 400694*, **w** *www.gobycoach.com*. **Open** *Mon–Fri 8am–8pm, Sun 10–2*.

SPECIALIST TOUR OPERATORS

In the UK

Abercrombie & Kent, *Sloane Square House, Holbein Place, London SW1W 8NS*, **t** *(020) 7559 8686*, **f** *(020) 7730 9376*, **e** *info@abercrombiekent.co.uk*. Exclusively tailored holidays in Tuscany.

Ace Study Tours, *Babraham, Cambridge CB2 4AP*, **t** *(01223) 835055*, **f** *(01223) 837394*, **w** *www.study-tours.org*. Cultural tours through Tuscany.

Alternative Travel (ATG), *69–71 Banbury Road, Oxford OX2 6PE*, **t** *(01865) 315678*, **f** *315697*, **w** *www.atg-oxford.co.uk*, **e** *info@atg-oxford.co.uk*. Offers walking, wild flower, art and cycling tours as well as truffle hunts and painting courses.

Andante Travels, *The Old Telephone Exchange, Winterborne Dauntsey, Salisbury SP4 6EH*, **t** *(01980) 610555*, **w** *www.andante-travels.co.uk*. Owned and run by archeologists, offers 'Romantic ruins in rural Italy': a 5-day tour of Tuscany's most important Etruscan archaeological sites, art and architecture.

Arblaster & Clarke Wine Tours, *Farnham Road, West Liss, Petersfield, Hants GU33 6JQ*, **t** *(01730) 893344*, **f** *(01730) 892888*, **w** *www.arblasterandclarke.com*. Wine tours, truffle hunts and gourmet cooking tours.

British Airways Holidays, *Astral Towers, Betts Way, Crawley, West Sussex RH10 2XA*, **t** *0870 242 4243/(01293) 723100*, **f** *(01293) 722702*, **w** *www.baholidays.co.uk*. Florentine city breaks.

Brompton Travel, *Brompton House, 64 Richmond Road, Kingston-upon-Thames, Surrey KT2 5EH*, **t** *(020) 8549 3334*, **w** *www.bromptontravel.co.uk*. Organizers of tailor-made trips, city breaks and opera tours.

The Caravan Club, *East Grinstead House, West Sussex RH19 1UA*, **t** *(01342) 326944*, **f** *(01342) 327989*, **w** *www.caravanclub.co.uk*. Arranges advance booking and pitch reservation.

Citalia, *Marco Polo House, 3–5 Lansdowne Road, Croydon CR9 1LL*, **t** *(020) 8686 5533, or* **t** *8681 0712*, **w** *www.citalia.co.uk*. Modest resort and self-catering holidays.

Erna Low, *9 Reece Mews, London SW7 3HE*, **t** *(020) 7584 2841*, **f** *(020) 7589 9531*, **w** *www.bodyandsoulholidays.com*. Pamper yourself at their spa resort in Grosseto.

Fine Art Travel, *15 Savile Row, London W1X 1AE*, **t** *(020) 7437 8553*, **f** *(020) 7437 1733*. Re-creates the spirit of the Grand Tour, staying in private villas and palazzi.

Inscape Fine Art Tours, *Austins Farm, High Street, Stonesfield, Witney, Oxfordshire OX8 8PU*, **t** *(01993) 891726*, **f** *(01993) 891718*. Escorted art tours with guest lecturers.

Italiatour, *9 Whyteleafe Business Village, Whyteleafe Hill, Whyteleafe, Surrey CR3 0AT*, **t** *(01883) 621900*, **f** *(01883) 625255*, **w** *www.italiatour.com*. Resort holidays, city breaks, cookery courses and horse-riding.

Kirker Holidays, *3 New Concordia Wharf, Mill Street, London SE1 2BB*, **t** *08700 270480*, **f** *(020) 7231 4771*, **w** *www.kirker.ping.co.uk*. City breaks and tailor-made tours; also arranges internal rail travel and any length of stay.

Magic of Italy, *227 Shepherd's Bush Road, London W6 7AS*, **t** *(020) 8748 7575*, **f** *(020) 8748 3731*, **w** *www.magictravelgroup.co.uk*. City breaks and villa or farmhouse holidays.

Magnum, *7 Westleigh Park, Blaby, Leicester*, **t** *(01162) 777123*. Organizes holidays for senior citizens in Florence.

Martin Randall Travel, *10 Barley Mow Passage, Chiswick, London W4 4PH*, **t** *(020) 8742 3355*, **f** *(020) 8742 7766*, **w** *www.martinrandall.com*. Imaginatively put together cultural tours with guest lecturers.

Prospect Music and Art Tours, *36 Manchester Street, London W1M 5PE*, **t** *(020) 7486 5704*, **f** *(020) 7486 5868*, **e** *sales@prospecttours.com*. Art tours in Florence; specialist holidays devoted to figures such as Dante and Piero della Francesca.

Ramblers Holidays, *Box 43, Welwyn Garden City, Hertfordshire AL8 6PQ*, **t** *(01707) 331133*, **f** *(01707) 333276*, **w** *www.ramblersholidays.co.uk*. Walking holidays.

Real Holidays, *66–68 Essex Road, London N1 8LR*, **t** *(020) 7359 3938*, **f** *(020) 7226 5800*, **w** *www.realhols.co.uk*. Designers of quirky holidays for demanding folk.

Rhodes School of Cuisine, **t** *(01428) 685140*, **f** *(01428) 683424*, **w** *www.rhodeschoolofcuisine.com*. Culinary holidays in a private villa in Vorno, near Lucca.

Sherpa Expeditions, *131a Heston Road, Hounslow, Middlesex TWR ORD*, **t** *(020) 8577 2717*, **f** *(020) 8572 9788*, **w** *www.sherpa-walking-holidays.co.uk*. Walking and cycling holidays.

Simply Tuscany and Umbria, *Kings House, Wood Street, Kingston-upon-Thames, Surrey KT1 1UG*, **t** *(020) 8541 2206*, **f** *(020) 8541 2280*, **w** *www.simply-travel.com*. Tailor-made itineraries, also art, architecture and vegetarian cookery courses, balloon flights, spa resorts and painting holidays.

Sovereign Tours, *2nd Floor, Astral Towers, Betts Way, Crawley, West Sussex*, **t** *(0161) 742 2255*, **w** *www.sovereign.com*. Wide range of 7–14-day package tours in the Florence and Chianti areas; 3- and 4-star accommodation.

Specialtours, *81 Elizabeth St, London SW1W 9PG*, **t** *(020) 7730 2297*, **f** *(020) 7823 5035*. Cultural tours of Tuscany.

Tasting Places, *Unit 40, Buspace Studios, Conlan Street, London W10 5AP*, **t** *(020) 7460 0077*, **f** *(020) 7460 0029*, **w** *www.tastingplaces.com*. Cookery courses.

Travelsphere, *Compass House, Rockingham Road, Market Harborough, Leicestershire LE16 7QD*, **t** *(01858) 464818*, **f** *(01858) 434323*, **w** *www.travelsphere.co.uk*. Singles holidays and coach tours.

Venice Simplon-Orient Express, *Suite 200, Hudson's Place, Victoria Station, London SW1V 1JL*, **t** *020 7928 6000*. London–Florence luxury rail tours.

Voyages Jules Verne, *21 Dorset Square, London NW1 6QG*, **t** *(020) 7616 1000*, **w** *www.vjv.co.uk*. Tours from May to November, staying in 4-star accommodation with escorted excursions.

Wallace Arnold, *Gelderd Road, Leeds LS12 6DH*, **t** *(01132) 310739*. Based in a hotel in Montecatini Terme, with excursions to Florence, Pisa and Lucca.

Waymark, *44 Windsor Road, Slough*, **t** *(01753) 516477*, **f** *(01753) 517016*. Walking tours.

In the USA and Canada

The Italian Tourist Office in New York can provide an extensive list of specialist tour operators. Here is a selection:

Abercrombie & Kent, *1520 Kensington Rd., Oak Brook, IL 60523 2141, **t** (630) 954 2944 or toll free **t** 800 323 7308, **w** www.abercrombiekent.com*. City breaks and walking holidays.

Archaeological Tours Inc., *Suite 904, 271 Madison Avenue, New York, NY 10016, **t** (212) 986 3054*. Etruscan sites.

Bike Riders' Tours, *PO Box 130254, Boston, MA 02113, **t** (617) 723 2354, **f** (617) 723 2355, **w** www.bikeriderstours.com*. Cycling tours, and a culinary 'Cucina Toscana' tour.

Butterfield & Robinson, *70 Bond Street, Suite 300, Toronto, Ontario M5B 1X3, **t** (416) 864 1354, **t** 800 678 1147, **f** (416) 864 0541, **w** www.butterfield.com*. Cycling and walking holidays in areas of Tuscany.

Certified Vacations, *300 Pinnacle Way, Norcross, GA 30093, **t** 800 241 1700.* Prepackaged or tailor-made FIT tours.

CIT Tours, *15 West 44th St, New York, NY 10173, **t** (212) CIT-TOUR, **w** www.cit-tours.com; also 9501 West Devon Ave, Rosemount, IL 60018, **t** 800 CIT-TOUR, and, in Canada, 80 Tiverton Court, Suite 401, Markham, Ontario L3R 0GA, **t** 800 387 0711.* Tailor-made tours for individuals and groups, plus cookery courses.

Esplanade Tours, *581 Boylston Street, Boston, MA 02116, **t** (617) 266 7465, toll free **t** 800 426 5492, **w** www.specialtytravel.com*. Art, architecture and FIT itineraries.

Europe Train Tours, *198 E. Boston Post Rd., Mamaroneck, NY 10543, **t** (914) 698 9426, toll free **t** 800 551 2085, **f** (914) 698 9516.* Escorted tours by train and car.

Italian Connection, *11 Fairway Drive, Suite 210, Edmonton, Alberta T6J 2W4, **t** 1 800 462 7911, **t** (780) 438 5712, **f** (780) 436 4085, **w** www.italian-connection.com*. Walking and culinary tours.

Italiatour, *666 5th Avenue, New York, NY 10103, **t** 800 845 3365 (US), **t** 888 515 5245 (Canada), **w** www.italiatour.com*. Fly-drive holidays and tours organized by Alitalia.

La Dolce Vita Wine Tours, *576 Fifth Street, Brooklyn, NY 11215, toll free **t** 888 746 0022, **t** (718) 788 6365, **f** (718) 499 2618, **w** www.dolcetours.com*. Wine tours with 'epicurean', walking or biking options.

Maupintour, *1421 Research Park Drive, Kansas 66049, **t** (785) 331 1000, toll free **t** 800 255 4266, **w** www.maupintour.com.* Sailing holidays along Tuscan waterways.

Rhodes School of Cuisine, ***t** 1 888 254 1070, **w** www.rhodeschoolofcuisine.com*. Culinary holidays in a private villa in Vorno, near Lucca.

Stay and Visit Italy, *5506 Connecticut Avenue NW, Suite 23, Washington, DC 20015, **t** (202) 237 5220, **t** 800 411 3728, **f** (202) 966 6972, **w** www.stayandvisit.com*. Tailor-made tours throughout Tuscany and Umbria.

Trafalgar Tours, *11 East 26th Street, New York, NY 10010, **t** (212) 689 8977, **w** www.trafalgartours.com*. Ask about their 10-day tour 'Rome and the Tuscan Highlights'.

Worldwide Classroom, *P.O. Box 1166, Milwaukee, WI 53201, **t** (414) 351 6311, toll free **t** (800) 276 8712, **f** (414) 224 3466, **w** www.worldwide.edu*. Database listing educational organizations around the world.

ENTRY FORMALITIES

Passports and Visas

To get into Italy you need a valid passport. EU citizens do not need visas; US, Canadian and Australian nationals do not need visas for stays of up to three months. If you mean to stay longer than three months in Italy you will have to get a *permesso di soggiorno*. For this you will need to state your reason for staying, be able to prove a source of income and have medical insurance. After a couple of thoroughly exasperating days filling out forms at some provincial *questura* office, you can then collect the *permesso*.

According to Italian law, you must register with the police within eight days of arriving, though few bother to do this. If you check into a hotel this is done automatically. If you come to grief in the mesh of rules and forms, you can at least get someone to explain it to you in English by calling the Rome Police Office for Visitors, **t** 06 4686 2928.

Customs

Since July 1999, duty-free goods have been unavailable on journeys within the European Union, but this does not necessarily mean that prices have gone up, as shops at ports, airports and the Channel Tunnel do not always choose to pass on the cost of the duty. It does mean that there is no limit on how much you can buy, as long as it is for your own use. Guidelines are issued (e.g., 10 litres of spirits, 800 cigarettes, 90 litres of wine, 110 litres of beer) and, if they are exceeded, you may be asked to prove that it is all for your own use.

Non-EU citizens flying from an EU country to a non-EU country (e.g., flying home from Italy) can still buy duty-free. Americans can take home 1 litre of alcohol, 200 cigarettes and 100 cigars, etc. Canadians can take home 200 cigarettes and 1.5 litres of wine or 1.14 litres of spirits or 8.5 litres of beer.

ARRIVAL

The Airports

If you are arriving in Tuscany by plane, you will fly into one of three airports.

Aeroporto Amerigo Vespucci, Florence

***t** 055 373498, 24hr flight info **t** 055 306 1702 (recorded message in Italian and English), **w** www.safnet.it.*

Florence's Peretola airport lies about 5km (3 miles) west of the city centre. It has grown from a dinky little place to a bustling airport taking as much, if not more, international traffic than Pisa. Due to the diminutive length of the runway, it only handles small planes, but through flights to Milan, Rome, Paris, London, Amsterdam, Frankfurt and Brussels, you can connect with flights to just about anywhere in the world.

A special airport bus (the Volainbus) connects with the city centre, stopping at the SITA bus station (near the main train station) and in Via S. Caterina da Siena (north of the train station). It runs every half-hour from 6am to 8.30 pm and then every hour until 11:30pm and takes about 30mins; tickets cost €4.13 and can be bought on the bus.

A taxi into central Florence will cost about €15.50 plus extra charges for luggage, night journeys and public holidays. Journey time about 20mins.

The fairly modest facilities at the airport include branches of the main car rental companies, a bank, a bar and a branch of the Tuscan tourist board. The latter is open daily from 7.30am to 11pm.

Aeroporto Galileo Galilei, Pisa

***t** 050 500707, **w** www.pisa-airport.com.*

Pisa airport lies just outside the city and some 80km (50 miles) west of Florence. It is connected to Florence by a dual carriageway (the 'Firenze–Pisa–Livorno') which runs into the airport. The airport handles flights from Italy and the rest of Europe, but there is more choice of destination from Florence. Through Milan, Rome, London, Paris, Brussels and Munich you can connect with international flights.

To get into Pisa city centre, either take the n5 bus from outside the arrivals building which runs every 15mins into Pisa Centrale train station (tickets from the info desk) or take a taxi which costs about €7.75.

Trains run from the airport to Florence and stations in between (Pisa Centrale, Pontederra and Empoli). For Siena, change at Empoli, for Livorno, Viareggio and Massa Carrara change at Pisa Centrale. For Arezzo change in Florence. There is also an infrequent service which runs to Lucca. Trains to Florence do not always coincide with flight arrivals and departures. They run roughly every hour from 10am to 5pm, but are much more infrequent before and after these times. Beware; the last train into Florence leaves Pisa airport at 7.14pm. You may find it better to take a bus or taxi into Pisa central station where connections are better. There is a full timetable at the info desk.

Airport facilities include a bar and restaurant, a bank, a post office, car hire offices, a tourist office (open 10.30–4.30 and 6pm–10pm), a small business centre, a children's play area and a few shops.

Aeroporto G. Marconi, Bologna

***t** 051 647 9615, **w** www.bologna-airport.it.*

Bologna Airport handles more flights than either Pisa or Florence and has two terminals. BA flights from London Gatwick to Bologna can be cheaper than those to Pisa, and Go fly here, so it is worth bearing in mind as an arrival point. Connections to other parts of Europe are also good.

The airport lies 6km north of central Bologna and is connected to the central station by a special bus service. This runs every 15mins, costs €3.60 and takes about 20mins. Tickets are available on board. Taxis into the station cost about €15.50. From Bologna Centrale station, trains into Florence can take from 50mins to over an hour depending on the type of train. The fastest are the Eurostars and these are also the most expensive as they require a supplement; travel on Fridays and Sundays requires a reservation. The cheaper and slower Intercities are less frequent but a good alternative.

If you hire a car, take the horrendous (because it is usually full of articulated lorries, there are many tunnels and it winds through the Appenines) A1 motorway south to Florence; journey time is about 1 hour 20mins.

Facilities include car hire offices, bank, bar and restaurant, VIP lounge, tourist info office (for Emilia Romagna only) and some shops.

GETTING AROUND

By Bus

In Florence, routes are labelled well; all buses charge flat fees for rides within the city limits and immediate suburbs, at the time of writing €1.03. Bus tickets must always be purchased before you get on, either at a tobacconist's, a newspaper kiosk, certain shops, in many bars, or from ticket machines near the main stops. Once you get on, you must 'obliterate' your ticket in the machines in the front or back of the bus; controllers stage random checks to make sure you've punched your ticket. Fines for cheaters are about €39, and the odds are about 12 to 1 against a check, so you may take your chances according to how lucky you feel. If you're good-hearted, you'll buy a ticket and help some overburdened municipal transit line meet its annual deficit.

From Florence SITA buses go to Siena, LAZZI to Lucca and Pisa and CLAP to Lucca; SITA buses run between Siena and Pisa; TRA-IN buses operate from Siena covering Siena province.

SITA *(near the station, Via S. Caterina da Siena 15, **t** 055 294955, **t** 800 373760, **w** www.sita-online.it)*: towns in the Val d'Elsa, Chianti, Val di Pesa, Mugello and Casentino; Anghiari, Arezzo, Bibbiena, Caprese, Castelfiorentino, Certaldo, Città di Castello, Consuma, Figline Valdarno, Firenzuola, Incisa Valdarno, Marina di Grosseto, Montevarchi, Poggibonsi (for San Gimignano and Volterra), Pontassieve, Poppi, Pratovecchio, Sansepolcro, Scarperia, Siena, Stia, Vallombrosa.

LAZZI *(Piazza Stazione 47r, **t** 055 351061 Mon–Fri, **t** 166 845010 24-hour recorded message, **w** www.lazzi.it)*: along the Arno to the coast, including Calenzano, Cerreto Guidi, Empoli, Forte dei Marmi, Livorno, Lucca, Marina di Carrara, Marina di Massa, Montecatini Terme, Montelupo, Montevarchi, Pescia, Pisa, Pistoia, Pontedera, Prato, Signa, Tirrenia, Torre del Lago and Viareggio. Also has information on RAMA buses to Grosseto.

Bus Tickets

There are various tickets available within Florence. All can be used over a certain timespan on as many buses as you wish.

60min ticket	€1.03
3hr ticket	€1.81
24hr ticket	€4.13
2-day pass	€5.68
3-day pass	€7.23
7-day pass	€12.14

CAP *(Via Nazionale 13, **t** 055 214637)*: Borgo S. Lorenzo, Impruneta, Pistoia, Prato. Also has info on COPIT buses.

CLAP: only runs buses within Lucca and its province.

COPIT *(Piazza S. Maria Novella, **t** 055 214637)*: Abetone, Cerreto Guidi, Pistoia, Poggio a Caiano, Vinci.

RAMA *(Lazzi Station, **t** 055 239 8840)*: Grosseto.

By Train

Train information from anywhere in Italy: ***t** 8488 88088 (open 7am–9pm), **w** www.fs-on-line.it, or **t** 055 2351, **w** www.trenitalia.com.*

Florence, Siena, Pisa and Lucca are linked by regular trains, so in theory it is possible to do a whistle-stop rail tour of all four cities in one day, but that would not leave a great deal of time for the sights! Florence is the central transport node for Tuscany and harder to avoid than to reach. The central station is Santa Maria Novella, **t** 055 235 2061, for reservations. Many long-distance trains arriving at night use Campo di Marte station (served by bus nos.12 and 70 at night).

There are trains roughly every hour between Florence and Siena (97km, 90mins) – the journey takes a little longer if you have to change at Empoli. (Note that it is actually quicker to get to Siena by bus; moreover the train station is a long way from the town centre.) Pisa, 81km from Florence, is on the main Florence–Livorno line with one or two trains every hour (55mins). Lucca can be reached from Florence hourly via the Florence–Pistoia–Viareggio line (78km, 80mins). The journey from Pisa to Lucca (24km) takes only 25 minutes. To travel from Siena to Lucca, you could go via either Florence or Pisa (125km, 2hrs).

Train fares have increased greatly over the last couple of years and only those without extra supplements can still be called cheap. Italy's national railway, the FS (Ferrovie dello Stato) is well run and often a pleasure to ride. Possible FS unpleasantnesses you may encounter, besides a strike, are delays and crowding (especially at weekends and in the summer). Tickets may be purchased not only in the stations, but at many travel agents. Reserve a seat in advance (*fare una prenotazione*). The fee is small and can save you hours standing. On Intercities you must pay a supplement but reservations are not obligatory. On the Eurostars, you pay a supplement and reservations are obligatory on Fridays and Sundays. Do check when you purchase your ticket in advance that the date is correct; tickets are only valid the day they're purchased unless you specify otherwise.

Be sure you ask which platform (*binario*) your train arrives at; the big permanent boards posted in the stations are not always correct. Always remember to stamp your ticket (*convalidare*) in the not-very-obvious machine at the head of the platform before boarding the train. Failure to do so will result in a fine. If you get on a train without a ticket you can buy one from the conductor, with an added 20 per cent penalty. You can also pay a conductor to move up to first class if there are places available.

There is a strict hierarchy of trains. A *Regionale* travels shortish distances, and tends to stop at all the stations. There are only a few *Espressi* trains left in service, but they are in poor condition, and mostly service the long runs from the south. No supplement is required. *Intercity* trains link Italian cities, with minimum stops. Some carry an obligatory seat-reservation requirement (free in this case), and all have a supplement. The true Kings of the Rails are the super-swish and super-fast (Florence–Rome in 90mins) *Eurostars*. These make very few stops, have both first- and second-class carriages, and carry a supplement. So, the faster the train, the more you pay.

The FS offers several **passes**. Two flexible option for visitors are the 'Flexi Card', which allows unlimited travel for either four days within a month (€144), 8 days within a month (€150), or 12 days within a month (€259) plus supplements and seat reservations on Eurostars; the other option is the Italy Rail Card (IRC), which allows 8, 15, 21 or 30 *consecutive* days of travel for about €182, €229, €275 and €320 respectively. Another ticket, the 'Kilometrico', gives you 3,000 kilometres of travel, made on a maximum of 20 journeys and is valid for two months (2nd class €177, 1st class €181 plus supplements); one advantage is that it can be used by up to five people at the same time. Other discounts, available only once you're in Italy, are 15 per cent on same-day return tickets and three-day returns (depending on the distance involved), and discounts for families of at least four travelling together. Senior citizens (men 65 and over, women 60) can also get a 'Carta d'Argento' ('silver card') for €25 entitling them to a 20 per cent reduction in fares. A 'Carta Verde' bestows a 20 per cent discount on people under 26 and costs €25.

Refreshments on routes of any great distance are provided by bar cars or trolleys; you can usually get sandwiches and coffee from vendors along the tracks at intermediary stops. Station bars often have a good variety of take-away travellers' fare; consider at least investing in a bottle of mineral water, since there's no drinking water on the trains. Besides trains and bars, Italy's stations offer other facilities. All have a *deposito bagaglio* (or computerized lockers) where you can leave your bags for 12 hours for €2.60. The larger ones have porters (who charge €2.60 per piece) and luggage trolleys; major stations have an *albergo diurno* ('day hotel', where you can have a shower, shave and haircut), information offices, currency exchanges open at weekends, hotel reservation services, kiosks with foreign papers. You can also arrange to have a rental car awaiting you at your destination – Avis, Hertz, and Maggiore provide this service.

By Car

You're probably better off not driving at all: parking is impossible (Florence and Siena both have traffic-free central zones), traffic impossible, deciphering one-way streets, signals and signs impossible. However, given these difficulties, a car does give you the freedom and possibility of making your way through Tuscany's lovely countryside.

Be prepared, however, to encounter some of the highest fuel costs in Europe and drivers who look at motoring as if it were a video game. The Italians, from 21-year-old madcaps to elderly nuns, turn into aggressive starfighters once behind the wheel, whose mission is to reach their destination in a certain allotted time (especially around lunch or dinner, if they think the pasta is already on the boil) regardless of minor nuisances such as other cars, road signs, traffic signals, solid no-passing lines, or blind curves on mountain roads. No matter how fast you trip along on the *autostrade* (Italy's toll motorways, official speed limit 130km/80miles per hour), someone will pass you going twice as fast.

If you aren't intimidated, buy a good road map of Italy or a more detailed one of Tuscany (the Italian Touring Club produces excellent ones). Many **petrol stations** close for lunch in the afternoon, and few stay open late at night, though you may find a 'self-service' where you feed a machine nice smooth notes. *Autostrada* tolls are high – for example, to drive on the A1 from Florence to Milan will cost you €20. The rest stops and petrol stations along the motorways are open 24 hours. Other roads – *superstrade* on down through the Italian grading system – are free of charge. The Italians are very good about signposting, and roads are almost all excellently maintained. Some highways seem to be built of sheer bravura, suspended on cliffs, crossing valleys on enormous piers – feats of engineering that will remind you, more than almost anything else, that this is the land of the ancient Romans. Beware that you may be fined on the spot for speeding, a burnt-out headlamp, etc; if you're especially unlucky you may be slapped with a *super multa*, a superfine, of €130–260. You may even be fined for not having a portable triangle danger signal (pick one up at the frontier or from an ACI office for €2.60).

The **Automobile Club of Italy** (ACI) is a good friend to the foreign motorist, and although they no longer offer free breakdown service, their prices are fair. They can be reached from anywhere by dialling **t** 116 – also use this number if you have an accident, need an ambulance, or simply have to find the nearest service station. If you need major repairs, the ACI can make sure the prices charged are according to their guidelines. Local ACI addresses are:

Florence: *Viale Amendola 36, **t** 055 24861, **w** www.aci.it; **bus** 8, 14, 31.*

Lucca: *Via Catalani 59, **t** (0583) 582626.*

Pisa: *Via Cisanello 168, **t** (050) 950111.*

Siena: *Viale Vittorio Veneto 47, **t** (0577) 49002.*

The best **maps** are Firenze Piantà (Touring Club Italiano, 1:12,500) and Firenze (Litografia Artistica, 1:9000); Siena City Plan (Freytag and Berndt, 1:5000); Pisa City Plan (Freytag and Berndt, 1:8000); Lucca Città Piantà (Studio F. M. B., 1:6000).

Hiring a car is fairly simple if not particularly cheap. Italian car rental firms are called *autonoleggi*. There are both large international firms through which you can reserve a car in advance, and local agencies, which often have lower prices. Air or train travellers should check out possible discount packages; nearly all require the driver to be at least 21, or 25 for powerful cars. Average car hire is from €55 a day for a Fiat Punto, but the cost goes down if you hire for longer. Rates become more advantageous if you take the car for a week with unlimited mileage. Some essential numbers:

Florence: Most firms are in easy walking distance of the station. Avis, Borgo Ognissanti 128r, **t** 199 100133; Europcar, Borgo Ognissanti 53r, **t** 800 014410; Hertz, Via M. Finiguerra 33, **t** 199 11 22 11; Maggiore-Budget, Via M. Finiguerra 31r, **t** 055 210238; Program, Borgo Ognissanti 135, **t** 055 282916; Italy by Car, Borgo Ognissanti 134r, **t** 055 287161.

Pisa Airport: Hertz, **t** 050 49187; Maggiore-Budget, **t** 050 42574; Avis, **t** 050 42028; Program (the most economical), **t** 050 500296.

By Taxi

Taxi metres will start at €2.21 plus extras, adding €0.74 per km. There is a minimum charge of €3.65. Each piece of baggage will cost extra, and there are surcharges for trips outside the official city limits (Fiesole, for example), trips between 10pm and 6am, and trips on Sundays and holidays.

By Carriage

The *carozze* of Florence are now used only by tourists, and there are very few of them. Negotiate times and dates before you begin: prices are about €25 for half an hour. They depart from Piazza della Signoria.

By Motorbike or Bicycle

The means of transport of choice for many Italians; motorbikes, mopeds and scooters or Vespas can be a delightful way to get between the cities and see the countryside. You should only consider it, however, if you've ridden them before – Italy's hills and aggravating traffic make it no place to learn. Helmets are compulsory. Hire costs for a *motorino* (moped) range from about €26.50 per day; Vespas (scooters) are somewhat more (from about €35). Try Florence by Bike (Scooters and Bikes), Via San Zanobi 120/120r, **t** 055 488992, **w** *www.florencebybike* (*open daily*), or Alinari, Via Guelfa 85r, **t** 055 280500 (*open daily*).

Italians are keen **cyclists** as well, racing drivers up the steepest hills; if you're not training for the Tour de France, consider the region's hills well before planning a bicycling tour – especially in the hot summer months. Bikes can be transported by train in Italy, either with you or within a couple of days – apply at the baggage office (*ufficio bagagli*). Hire prices range from about €10 per day, and to buy one costs upwards of €130, either in a bike shop or through the classified ad papers which are put out in nearly every city and region. Alternatively, if you bring your own bike, do check the airlines to see what their policies are on transporting them.

A new, fun way of getting around Florence is in one of the electric-powered **golf buggies**. Biancaneve hires them out for €15.50 for an hour, €103.50 for the day, **t** 055 713 4270. They can access pedestrian areas and take up to 4 people. Delivery and collection is included in the price.

Practical A–Z

02

Climate 54
Crime and the Police 54
Disabled Travellers 54
Electricity, Weights and Measures 55
Embassies and Consulates 55
Health, Emergencies and Insurance 56
Internet 56
Lost Property 56
Media 57
Money, Banks and Taxes 57
Opening Hours and Public Holidays 58
Packing 59
Photography 59
Post and Fax 59
Smoking 60
Students 60
Telephones 60
Time 61
Tipping 61
Toilets 61
Tourist Offices 61
Women Travellers 62
Working and Long Stays 62

Climate

Winter can be an agreeable time to visit the indoor attractions of the cities and avoid crowds, particularly in Florence, where it seldom snows but may rain for several days at a time.

Average Temperatures in °C (°F)

Jan	April	July	Oct
6 (42)	13 (55)	25 (77)	16 (60)

Crime and the Police

There is a fair amount of petty crime in the cities – purse snatchings, pickpocketing, minor thievery of the white-collar kind (always check your change) and car break-ins and theft – but violent crime is rare. Nearly all mishaps can be avoided with adequate precautions. Scooter-borne purse-snatchers can be foiled if you stay on the inside of the pavement and keep a firm hold on your property. Pickpockets most often strike in crowded buses and gatherings; don't carry too much cash or keep some of it in another place. Be extra careful in train stations, don't leave valuables in hotel rooms, and park your car in garages, guarded car parks, or on well-lit streets, with temptations like radios, cassettes, etc., out of sight. Purchasing small quantities of cannabis is legal although what a small quantity might be exactly is unspecified, so if the police don't like you to begin with, it will probably be enough to get you into big trouble.

Once the scourge of Italy, political terrorism has declined drastically in recent years, mainly thanks to special squads of the *carabinieri*, the black-uniformed national police, technically part of the Italian army. Local matters are usually in the hands of the *polizia urbana*; the nattily dressed *vigili urbani* concern themselves with directing traffic and handing out parking fines.

Florence: the Ufficio Stranieri, in the *questura*, Via Zara 2, **t** 055 49771 (*open Mon–Fri 8.30–12.30*), handles most foreigners' problems, and usually has someone around who speaks English. Good for residents' permits.

Siena: the Ufficio Stranieri is at Via del Castoro 6; call **t** 0577 201631 for an appointment Mon–Fri 8.30–10.30am.

Disabled Travellers

Recent access-for-all laws in Italy have improved the once dire situation: the number of ramps and stair lifts has increased a hundredfold in the past few years, and nearly every hotel has one or two rooms for the disabled – although most of the older ones don't have a lift, or one large enough for a chair. Curbs and streetcorners have now all been ramped, to help wheelchairs on and off pavements. Many museums and monuments are now accessible with ramps, lifts, toilets, etc.; ask at the tourist office for a list.

Most of the new types of buses have ramps and a designated space for a wheelchair. Accessible trains (including toilets and wheelchair areas in the carriages) have a disabled sign displayed on the outside. If you need assistance up the steep steps (there is no ramp), call **t** 055 235 2275. The disabled desk at Santa Maria Novella station is on platform 5. There are free disabled parking spaces throughout Florence, and if you display a sticker in your car you can also drive through pedestrian areas.

Specialist Organizations

In Italy

CO.IN (Consorzio Cooperative Integrate), *Via Enrico Giglioli 54a, 00169 Rome*, **t** *06 800 437631*, **f** *06 232 67505*. Their tourist information centre (*open Mon–Fri 9–5*) offers advice and information on accessibility.

In the UK and Ireland

Holiday Care Service, *2nd floor, Imperial Building, Victoria Road, Horley, Surrey RH6 7PZ*, **t** *(01293) 774535*. Provides information on accommodation, transportation, equipment hire, services, tour operators and contacts.

RADAR *(The Royal Association for Disability and Rehabilitation), 25 Mortimer Street, London W1*, **t** *(020) 7723 4004*.

Royal National Institute for the Blind, *224 Great Portland Street, London W15 5TB*, **t** *(020)*

7388 1266. Its mobility unit offers a 'Plane Easy' audio-cassette with advice for blind people travelling by plane. It will also advise on finding accommodation.

Tripscope, *Alexandra House, Albany Rd, Brentford, Middx TW8 0NE*, **t** *08457 585641*, **f** *(020) 8580 7022*, **w** *www.justmobility.co.uk/tripscope*. Practical advice and information on every aspect of travel and transport for elderly and disabled travellers. Information can be provided by letter or tape.

Irish Wheelchair Association, *Blackheath Drive, Clontarf, Dublin 3*, **t** *(01) 833 8241*, **w** *www.iwa.ie*. They publish guides with advice for disabled holiday-makers.

In the USA and Canada

American Foundation for the Blind, *15 West 16th Street, New York, NY 10011*, **t** *(212) 620 2000, toll free* **t** *800 2323 5463*. The best source of information in the USA for visually impaired travellers.

Federation of the Handicapped, *211 West 14th Street, New York, NY 10011*, **t** *(212) 747 4262*. Organizes summer tours for members; there is a nominal annual fee.

SATH (Society for the Advancement of Travel for the Handicapped), *Suite 610, 347 5th Av, New York, NY 10016*, **t** *(212) 447 7284*, **w** *www.sath.org*.

Electricity, Weights and Measures

The current is 220 volts, 50 hertz, and is compatible with all UK (but not US) appliances. You will need to bring with you a two-pin adaptor (hard to find in Italy).

Italy uses the metric system. Below is a conversion chart for quick reference.

1 kilogramme (1,000g) = 2.2lb
1 lb = 0.45kg
1 etto (100g) = 1/4lb (approx)
1 litre = 1.76 pints
1 pint = 0.568 litres
1 quart = 1.136 litres
1 imperial gallon = 4.546 litres
1 US gallon = 3.785 litres
1 mile = 1.61 kilometres

Useful Numbers

Police, Fire	**t** 113
Medical emergencies	**t** 118
Lost property	**t** 055 328 3942
Post office	**t** 055 27361
Train information	**t** 8488 88088
Tourist offices	**t** 055 234 0444
	t 055 212245

1 foot = 0.3048 metres
1 kilometre = 0.621 miles
1 metre = 39.37 inches

Embassies and Consulates

In Italy

Australia: *Via Alessandria 215, Rome*, **t** *06 852721*.

Canada: *Via G B de Rossi 27, Rome*, **t** *06 445981*.

Ireland: *Piazza Campitelli 3, Rome*, **t** *06 697 9121*.

New Zealand: *Via Zara 28, Rome*, **t** *06 440 2928*.

UK: *Lungarno Corsini 2, Florence*, **t** *055 284133*.

USA: *Lungarno Amerigo Vespucci 38, Florence*, **t** *055 239 8276*.

Abroad

Canada: *275 Slater St, Ottawa, Ontario K1P 5HG*, **t** *(613) 232 2401*, **f** *(613) 233 1484*, **e** *ambital@italyincanada.com*, **w** *www.italyincanada.com. Consulates in Toronto, Montreal and Vancouver.*

Ireland: *63–65 Northumberland Road, Dublin 4*, **t** *(01) 660 1744*, **f** *(01) 668 2759*, **e** *italianembassy@eircom.net*.

UK: *14 Three Kings Yard, London W1Y 4EH*, **t** *(020) 7312 2200*, **f** *(020) 7312 2230*, **e** *emblondon@embitaly.org.uk*, **w** *www.embitaly.org.uk. Consulates in Edinburgh, Manchester and Bedford.*

USA: *3000 Whitehaven St, NW Washington DC 20008*, **t** *(202) 612 4400*, **f** *(202) 518 2154*, **e** *stampa@itwash.org*, **w** *www.italyemb.org. Consulates in most major cities.*

Health, Emergencies and Insurance

You can insure yourself against almost any mishap – cancelled flight, stolen or lost baggage, and health – for a price. National health services in the UK and Australia have reciprocal health care agreements with Italy (pack an E-111 form). Citizens of other countries should check their current policies to see if they provide cover while abroad and under what circumstances, and judge whether a special traveller's insurance policy is required. Travel agencies sell policies, as well as insurance companies, but they are not cheap.

Minor illnesses and problems that crop up in Italy can usually be handled free of charge in a public hospital clinic or *ambulatorio*. If you need minor aid, Italian pharmacists are highly trained and can probably diagnose your problem; look for a *farmacia* (they all have a list in the window with details of which ones are open during the night and on holidays). Extreme cases should head for the *Pronto Soccorso* (A&E department/Casualty). Italian doctors are not always great linguists; contact your embassy or consulate for a list of English-speaking doctors.

Medical Emergencies

Florence: for an ambulance or first aid, Misericordia, Piazza del Duomo 20, **t** 055 212222. Doctor's night service, **t** 055 287788. The general hospital Santa Maria Nuova, in Piazza S. M. Nuova, **t** 055 27581, is the most convenient. Tourist Medical Service, 24 hours a day, is staffed by English- and French-speaking physicians at Via Lorenzo il Magnifico 59, ring first on **t** 055 475411. There is a pharmacy open 24 hours every day in S. Maria Novella Station, also Molteni, Via Calzaiuoli 7r and Taverna, Piazza S. Giovanni 20r, by the Baptistry.

Siena: ambulance, **t** 118; hospital **t** 585111; doctor's night service **t** 0577 586466/118; Farmacia Centrale, Via Banchi di Sotto 2.

Pisa: Hospital Santa Chiara, Via Roma 67, **t** 050 992111. Farmacia dell'Ospedale, Via Roma, **t** 050 992111.

Lucca: hospital: Campo di Marte, Via dell'Ospedale, **t** 0583 9701.

Internet

Florence is full of Internet points; you will have no difficulty finding one in the centre of town. Cyber cafés haven't caught on in Italy big-time, so you will most likely find a shop offering anything from basic computer and Internet services to those offering much more (proof reading and correction, CD burning, photocopying, international telephone lines, photo services etc.) plus, at most, a soft drinks machine.

Some of the main ones are:

Internet train, *Via Zannoni 1r (D2), **t** 055 211103, **w** www.internettrain.it. **Open** daily 9.30am–10.30pm*. Branches at Borgo San Jacopo 30r; Via dell'Oriuolo 40r; Via de' Benci 36r; Borgo la Croce 33r. Opening hours differ from branch to branch.

Intotheweb, *Via de' Conti 23r (D3), **t** 055 264 5628. **Open** daily 10am–midnight*. Uses Macs.

Nettyweb, *Via Santo Spirito 42r (C5), **t** 055 265 4549, **w** www.nettyweb.com. **Open** Mon–Fri 10am–8pm, Sat and Sun 12.30–10pm*. Meeting and business room available for rent.

The Netgate, *Via Sant'Egidio 10r (F4), **t** 055 234 7967, **w** www.thenetgate.it. **Open** daily 11–9.* Branches: Via Nazionale 156r; Via de' Cimatori 17r; Via dei Serragli 76r; Stazione Santa Maria Novella. Opening hours differ from branch to branch.

Lost Property

In Italian lost property is *oggetti smarriti* or *oggetti ritrovati*. The main office in Florence is at Via Circondaria 17b, **t** 055 328 3942 (bus 23, 33).

There is one **car pound** if your car gets towed away: in the Ponte a Greve car park, near the Ponte al Indiano in the west of the city, **t** 055 783882 (*open 24hrs; bus 44*).

Useful Websites

www.comune.it. Official Florence city council website. Info on the weather, what's on, visas, permits etc.

www.cultura.toscana.it. Official site of the region of Tuscany (regione toscana).

www.firenze.net. Info on Florence and Tuscany; entertainment, art, weather, traffic. Also provides a booking service for hotels and concerts.

www.firenzespettacolo.it. The website of Florence's excellent monthly listings magazine.

www.musei.provincia.siena.it. Museums in Siena and its province.

www.turismo.toscana.it. Everything for the tourist in Tuscany.

Media

Many of the main newsstands in Tuscan towns and cities sell English **newspapers**; in the summer months they arrive the same evening. The only American paper available is the *Herald Tribune* which has an *Italy Daily* insert. The same insert also comes with the Italian language *Corriere della Sera*. Even smaller newsstands stock *Time* and *Newsweek*.

For Italian speakers, a look at the local press always provides insights into the country you are visiting. Tuscany's most popular daily is *La Nazione*, a right-wing rag with lots of gossipy items. Each province has its own insert and it is useful for 'what's on' listings and flats-for-rent searches (in the Sunday edition). *La Repubblica* is a more reliable centre-left bet and has some excellent journalism. It is based in Rome, but has a Florence insert. The Milan-based *Corriere della Sera* is another decent paper with an English-language insert (*see* above). *Panorama* and *L'Espresso* are both good weekly current affairs magazines with some excellent journalism (in Italian).

There are several useful listings magazines in Florence. The best, *Firenze Spettacolo*, is published monthly (**w** *www.firenzespettacolo.it*) and costs €1.55. It is Florence-based, but has a certain amount of listings for the province of Florence and further afield. It is mainly in Italian but is easy to understand; it has a short listings section in English, too. It has good reviews, views and comment and a good 'going out' section (restaurants, bars, cafés, clubs, concerts etc.).

The new bi-monthly *Florence in your Pocket* (self-proclaimed 'Irreverent City Guide') also costs €1.55. It is entirely in English and has good tourist information (museums, monuments, practical info) as well as bi-monthly listings. *Florence Concierge Information* is a free English/Italian publication geared towards tourists and is available from hotels and tourist offices. *Vista* is a glossy quarterly which looks better than it reads: some Florence listings and the odd interesting article.

Italian **television** is pretty dire and even the more 'serious' state-owned RAI channels (1, 2 and 3) are dominated by game and quiz shows and by appalling 'variety' shows featuring an amazing amount of almost bare bums and cleavage. There are dozens of smaller TV stations; if you can manage to pick up Pistoia-based TVL, they show Sky News and CNN between about midnight and 8am.

There are endless **radio** stations available in Tuscany. The national networks RAI 1, 2 and 3 broadcast a mix of music and current affairs, while there are plenty of music stations.

Money, Banks and Taxes

It's a good idea to bring some euro notes with you; unforeseen delays and unexpected public holidays may foul up your plans to find a bank open when you arrive. Travellers' cheques remain the most secure way of financing your holiday in Italy; they are easy to change and an insurance against unpleasant surprises. Credit cards (American Express, Diner's Club, Mastercard, Access, Eurocard, Barclaycard, Visa) are accepted in most hotels, restaurants (though still not in some family-style trattorias), shops and most petrol stations. If you have a PIN number you can use the many cashpoint machines. Do not be surprised if you are asked to show identification when paying with a credit card.

Money can be sent to Italy through Thomas Cook travel agents, Western Union and American Express, or by having someone at home telexing the amount to an Italian bank for you to go and pick up. Technically, it shouldn't take more than a couple of days to arrive (but it always does). Make sure the telex includes the number of your passport, ID card, or driver's licence, or the Italians may not hand over the cash.

American Express: *Via Dante Alighieri 22r (E4)*, **t** *50981 (bus A)*.

Thomas Cook: *Lungarno Acciaiuoli 6/12 (D5)*, **t** *055 289781*.

Western Union *(freephone* **t** *800 464464), Agenzia STS, Via Zanetti 18 (D3)*, **t** *055 284183*.

The Euro

As from 1 January 2002, Italy has become one of 12 countries to adopt the euro as its currency. The official exchange rate is L1,936.27 = 1 euro.

ATMs in Italy will cough up €10, €20 and €50 notes; the authorities claim that they will be able to fill most of Italy's holes in the walls during the first week of circulation, so by the time this guide is published, all should be well. But how long it will take to convert all sorts of other money slots (take, for example, the light machines in churches) is anyone's guess.

Banking Hours

Banks are usually open 8.30am–1.20pm, and for one hour in the afternoon (3–4 or 4–5pm). They are closed on Saturdays, Sundays and national holidays. Some are worth visiting for their space-capsule doors alone.

Opening Hours and Public Holidays

Most of Tuscany closes down at 1pm until 3 or 4pm, to eat and properly digest the main meal of the day, although things are now beginning to change in the cities. Many more **shops** in the centre of town now stay open during lunch. Afternoon working hours are from 4 to 7, often from 5 to 8 in the hot summer months.

Food shops shut on Wednesday afternoons in the winter. They close on Saturday afternoons only from the end of June to the beginning of September. Sunday opening is becoming more usual, particularly for shops in the centre of town. Bars are often the only places open during the early afternoon and sometimes on a Sunday.

Churches have always been a prime target for art thieves and as a consequence are usually locked when there isn't a sacristan or caretaker to keep an eye on things. All churches, except for the really important cathedrals and basilicas, close in the afternoon at the same hours as the shops, and the little ones tend to stay closed. Always have a pocketful of coins to batten the light machines in churches, or what you came to see is bound to be hidden in ecclesiastical shadows. Don't do your visiting during services, and don't come to see paintings and statues in churches the week preceding Easter – you will probably find them covered with mourning shrouds.

Public Holidays

The Italians have cut down somewhat on their official national holidays, but note that every town has one or two holidays of its own – usually the feast day of its patron saint (*see* Festivals, p.256).

1 Jan	Capodanno (New Year's Day)
6 Jan	Epiphany
Mar/April	Easter Monday
25 April	Liberation Day
1 May	Labour Day
15 Aug	Ferragosto (Assumption)
1 Nov	Ognissanti (All Saints)
8 Dec	Immaculate Conception of the Virgin Mary
25 Dec	Christmas Day
26 Dec	Santo Stefano

The opening hours of **museums** vary considerably, particularly in Florence; some are now open until 10pm. Many museums are magnificent, many are run with shameful neglect, and many have been closed for years for 'restoration'. Expect to pay between €2 and €5 for museum entrance; more expensive ones run to €8 (Uffizi) and €6.50 (Accademia). The good news is that state-run museums and monuments are free if you're under 18 or over 60 (bring ID). If you're lucky, your visit will coincide with 'Settimana dei Beni Culturali' (free museum week). With an estimated one work of art per inhabitant, Italy has a hard time financing the preservation of its national heritage, and if there's something you really want to see, you would do well to enquire at the tourist office whether it's open or 'temporarily' closed before setting out.

Packing

You simply cannot overdress in Italy. Now, whether or not you want to try to keep up with the natives is your own affair and your own heavy suitcase – you may do well to compromise and just bring a couple of smart outfits for big nights out. It's not that the Italians are very formal; they simply like to dress up with a gorgeousness that adorns their cities just as much as those old Renaissance churches and palaces. The few places with dress codes are the major churches and basilicas (no shorts or sleeveless shirts), and the smarter restaurants.

Never take more than you can carry, but do bring the following: any prescription medicine you need, an extra pair of glasses or contact lenses, a pocket knife and corkscrew (for picnics), a torch (for dark frescoed churches and hotel corridors), a travel alarm (for those early trains) and a pocket Italian–English dictionary (for flirting and other emergencies). You may want to invest in earplugs. Your European electric appliances will work in Italy; just change your plug to the two-prong variety or buy a travel plug; American appliances need transformers as well.

Photography

Film and developing are much more expensive than they are in the USA or UK. You are not allowed to take pictures in most museums and in some churches. Most cities now offer one-hour processing if you need your pics in a hurry.

Post and Fax

The postal service in Italy used to have an extremely poor reputation, but has improved in the last couple of years. The new first-class mail, *posta prioritaria* (€0.62), is supposed to guarantee the arrival of a letter in Italy within 24 hours and to EU countries within 36. Or you can use registered delivery, *raccomandata*, for a €2.58 supplement. Stamps (*francobolli*) may also be purchased at tobacconists. Airmail letters to and from North America can quite often take up to two weeks. This can be a nightmare if you're making hotel reservations and are sending a deposit – emailing, faxing or telephoning ahead is far more secure if time is short.

Ask for mail to be sent to you in Italy either care of your hotel or addressed *Fermo Posta* (*poste restante*: general delivery) to a post office, or, if you're a card-holder, to an American Express office. When you pick up your mail at the *Fermo Posta* window, bring your passport for identification. Make sure that your mail is sent to the proper post office; the Posta Centrale is often the easiest option.

Main Post Offices

Florence: Via Pellicceria, near Piazza della Repubblica (D4), **t** 055 27361, open Mon–Fri 8.15–7, Sat 8.15–12.30; telegram office open Mon–Sat 8.15–7, or **t** 160.

Siena: Piazza Matteotti 37, **t** 0577 42178.

Pisa: Piazza Vittorio Emanuele II, **t** 050 5194.

Lucca: 2 Via Vallisneri, **t** 0583 46669.

The Italian post has made the process of sending packages a lot easier. You no longer have to wrap things in a certain way; the post offices have boxes if you want to use them. Whether they will be sent as a *lettera* or *pacco* depends on size, weight and contents. *Posta prioritaria* is good for parcels up to 2 kilos.

Smoking

Tobacconists (*tabacchi*) display a blue and white 'T' sign outside the shop; they and some bars sell cigarettes which are cheaper than in the UK.

Italy is still a great nation of smokers although recent legislation has banned smoking in public offices (post offices, banks etc.), on public transport (although trains have smoking compartments) and in any public places with inadequate air filtering. However these rules are frequently ignored, and you are unlikely to get much sympathy if you ask someone to stop blowing smoke in your face in a restaurant or in a non-smoking train carriage. No-smoking rooms in hotels are rare, as are non-smoking sections in bars and restaurants.

Students

Tuscany is full of students who come to study Italian, history of art, art, restoration and so on. Most are concentrated in Florence, but some choose the less touristy towns of Siena, Lucca and Pisa.

Università degli Studi di Firenze, *Piazza San Marco 4*, ***t*** *055 27571*, ***w*** *www.unifi.it*; ***bus*** *C, 1, 6*. Florence's university.

Istituto Universitario Europeo, *Via dei Roccettini 9, San Domenico di Fiesole*, ***t*** *055 46851*, ***w*** *www.iue.it*; ***bus*** *7*. A post-grad centre.

Università di Firenze Centro di Cultura per i Stranieri, *Via di Boldrone 2*, ***t*** *055 454016*, ***w*** *www.unifi.it/unifi/ccs*; ***bus*** *20, 28*. This cultural centre run by the University of Florence offers courses in Italian language at all levels and a whole range of other courses, all taught in Italian. You can study anything from the history of Italian literature, art or music to Italy today or contemporary art.

The British Institute of Florence, *Piazza degli Strozzi 2*, ***t*** *055 267781*, ***w*** *www.britishinstitute.it*; ***bus*** *A*. The British Institute offers language courses in English and Italian of various lengths, courses in history of art, Italian culture, drawing and even cooking.

Scuola Machiavelli, *Piazza Santo Spirito 4*, ***t*** *055 239 6966*, ***w*** *www.centromachiavelli.it*. A smaller school than the others listed here, the Machiavelli is run by a co-operative of teachers and offers a more personal approach. You can learn Italian in classes with a maximum of 12 students or through individual lessons, enrol in courses in commercial Italian, art history, art and artisan practical courses in professional workshops, food and beverage apprenticeships, cooking, and opera singing.

Istituto Lorenzo de' Medici, *Via Faenza 43*, ***t*** *055 287143*, ***w*** *www.lorenzodemedici.it*; ***bus*** *4, 17*. You can take language courses at various levels here or courses in many aspects of Italian culture including art history, cinema and cooking.

S.A.C.I., *Via Sant'Antonino 11*, ***t*** *055 289948*, ***w*** *www.saci-florence.org*. American school offering language courses but best known for its art courses: restoration, painting, drawing, sculpture and ceramics.

Telephones

To call Italy from abroad, dial **t** 00 39 followed by the area prefix – including the first 0. When telephoning within Italy, always include the 0, even when dialling a number in the same town, and always use the code.

Like many things in Italy, telephoning can be unduly complicated and usually costs over the odds to boot. Public phones will accept coins, as well as phone cards. These (the best option for phoning abroad) cost €2.58, €5.16 and €7.75 and are available in tobacconists, stationers (*cartolerie*), bars and newsstands. Hotels and bars sometimes have metered telephones. If you want to reverse charges (call collect), you can call from a phone box;

dial **t** 172 followed by the country code and you will be connected to an international operator.

Time

Italy is an hour ahead of the UK and clocks go forward and back in spring and autumn on the same day as in the UK.

Tipping

Refreshingly, there is not a lot of pressure in Italy to leave major tips. It was customary until the end of 2001 to round restaurant bills up a few thousand lire to the nearest 10,000 or 5,000; less in modest places. It remains to be seen how this will work out with the euro.

Most Florentines feel that taxis are so expensive that drivers deserve no tip, and they are right! Any tip should be minimal and drivers don't expect more. A few coins are sometimes expected in public loos for the caretaker (in motorway services or in stations). In hotels, the usual kinds of 'rules' apply: 10–15% , but it should reflect your general satisfaction with the service offered.

Toilets

Frequent travellers have noted an improvement over the years in the cleanliness of Italy's public conveniences; there are fewer holes in the ground, and loo paper is more generally on offer, although you will only find them in places like train and bus stations and bars. If you can't find a public loo, go into the nearest bar; they are legally obliged to let you use their *bagno*. In stations, motorway rest stops and the smarter cafés, there are washroom attendants who expect a few coins. Don't confuse the Italian plurals: *signori* (gents), *signore* (ladies).

Tourist Offices

Australia: *Level 26-44 Market Street, NSW 2000 Sydney,* **t** *(02) 92 621666,* **f** *(02) 92 621677,* **e** *lenitour@ihug.com.au.*

Canada: *175 Bloor Street East, Suite 907, South Tower, Toronto M4W 3R8 (ON),* **t** *(416) 925 4882,* **t** *925 3725,* **f** *(416) 925 4799,* **w** *www.italiantourism.com.*

New Zealand: *c/o Italian Embassy, 34 Grant Road, Thorndon, Wellington,* **t** *(04) 736065.*

UK: *Italian State Tourist Board, 1 Princes Street, London W1R 8AY,* **t** *(020) 7408 1254,* **f** *(020) 7493 6695,* **w** *www.enit.it,* **w** *www.italiantourism.com;* **Italian Embassy**, *14 Three Kings Yard, Davies St, London W1Y 2EH,* **t** *(020) 7312 2200,* **f** *(020) 7312 2230,* **w** *www.embitaly.org. uk.*

USA: *630 Fifth Avenue, Suite 1565, New York, NY 10111,* **t** *(212) 245 5095/4822,* **f** *(212) 586 9249; 500 N Michigan Avenue, Suite 2240, Chicago, IL 60611,* **t** *(312) 644 0996,* **f** *(312) 644 3019; 12400 Wilshire Boulevard, Suite 550, Los Angeles, CA 90025,* **t** *(310) 820 1898/9807,* **f** *(310) 820 6357,* **w** *www.italiantourism.com.*

In Florence

The tourist offices listed below all provide free maps, leaflets and guides in various languages. However, they only supply information concerning their own province.

Agenzia per il Turismo, *Via Alessandro Manzoni 16 (off maps),* **t** *055 23320,* **w** *www.firenze.turismo.toscana.it;* ***bus*** *6.* ***Open*** *Mon–Fri 8–6, Sat 8–2.* While this is the administrative headquarters of the provincial tourist board, it is rather out of the way and the main office in Via Camillo Cavour is much more central.

Agenzia per il Turismo, *Via Camillo Cavour 1r (E2),* **t** *055 290832,* **w** *www.provincia.firenze.it/istrcult/turismo/inform.htm;* ***bus*** *1, 6, 17.* ***Open*** *Mon–Sat 8.15–7.15, Sun 8.30–1.30.*

Ufficio Informazioni Turistiche, *Borgo Santa Croce 29r (F5),* **t** *055 234 0444,* **w** *www.comune.firenze.it;* ***bus*** *B, C.* ***Open*** *Mon–Sat 9–7, Sun and hols 9–2.*

Ufficio Informazioni Turistiche, *Piazza della Stazione 4 (C3),* **t** *055 212245,* **w** *www.comune.firenze.it;* ***bus*** *A, D, 17.* ***Open*** *Mon–Sat 8.30–7, Sun and hols 8.30–1.30.*

Consorzio Informazioni Turistiche Alberghiere, *inside the central train station (C2),* **t** *055 282893;* ***bus*** *A, 1, 17.* ***Open*** *daily*

8.45–8. A hotel booking agency which doesn't accept telephone bookings. Charges vary according to the level of hotel booked, and you must pay one night at the time of booking.

Florence Promhotels, *Viale Volta 72 (off maps)*, ***t*** *055 553941*, ***t*** *800 866022 (toll-free no. within Italy)*, ***w*** *www.promhotels.it*. A hotel booking service.

Women Travellers

Italy is a relatively safe country for women travelling alone, although you may find yourself hassled by men. This is rarely threatening, but it can be annoying and persistent; the best way to deal with such advances is to ignore them and walk away.

Most Tuscan towns and cities are safe at night but avoid badly lit streets after dark and the area around the train station in Florence at night. Taxis in Florence offer a 10% discount to women travelling alone after 9pm, but you may need to 'remind' the driver when it comes to paying.

For contact with women's organizations (mostly in Italian), the **Libreria delle Donne** in Borgo Pinti 2b, **t** 055 240384, is a useful address while Network is an American-run organization of professional women, mostly English-speaking, which holds monthly meetings. Call **t** 055 575299 for information.

Working and Long Stays

Tuscany is no longer an easy place to arrive in, find work and just 'hang out' for a while.

Rental prices (especially in Florence and Siena) are sky high, and jobs – both casual and otherwise – are hard to come by.

You must apply for a *carta di soggiorno* after three months in Italy. Members of the EU do not need special documents in order to find work, but some potential employers may ask for a *libretto di lavoro* which you can get from the *comune*. If your country is an EU member, it shouldn't be a problem, just a bureaucratic pain. Non EU members are given a *permesso di soggiorno*, but will encounter difficulties getting this if they don't have papers from their own countries. Americans must have a visa if they want to stay longer than three months. This must be done through the Italian consulate in the US.

One recent improvement is that if you are from the EU, officially resident in Italy and you have a valid *carta di soggiorno*, you are entitled to the same health service rights as an Italian citizen and can get your *libretto sanitaria* free. Apply to your local USL office for this. A bit like the UK, some medicines and treatments are free, while a contribution must be made to others. This is called paying *il ticket*.

Options for casual employment include English teaching, working on market stalls, picking up the odd piece of translation work (if you speak reasonable Italian), bar or restaurant work, house cleaning and babysitting.If you are after a 'proper' job, look in the local press (*La Pulce* is useful). For Italian speakers, jobs in the tourism industry are a good bet or you can try contacting conference organizers who employ hostesses and guides during big conferences. Buying offices and multinationals often look for English (or German and French) speakers for office jobs.

It can be useful to obtain residency in Italy and it is essential if you want to buy a car. This must be done at the 'Ufficio Circoscrizione' of your local town hall and requires yet more documents.

Finding somewhere to live is not easy and not cheap. Expect to pay €6,200–7,750 per month for a year's rental of a one-bedroomed flat in central Florence; more if you rent for a shorter period. The thrice-weekly *La Pulce* carries accommodation ads as does the Sunday edition of *La Nazione*. There are plenty of agencies dealing with short and long-term rentals ('Agenzia Immobiliare') although you will obviously have to pay an agency fee if you use one.

The Medieval Core

03

PIAZZA DEL DUOMO 66
The Duomo 66
The Baptistry 70
Museo dell'Opera del Duomo 71
Loggia del Bigallo 73

VIA DE' CALZAIUOLI 73
Orsanmichele 73

PIAZZA DELLA SIGNORIA AND AROUND 75
Loggia dei Lanzi 76
Palazzo Vecchio 78
The Uffizi 81
Museo di Storia della Scienza 87

PONTE VECCHIO 88

THE BARGELLO AND AROUND 88
The Bargello 88
Badia Fiorentina 91
Piazza San Firenze 91
Palazzo Borghese 91
San Martino del Vescovo 91
Casa di Dante 91
Santa Margherita de' Cerchi 92
Museo Nazionale di Antropologia ed Etnologia 92
Borgo degli Albizi 92

The Medieval Core

Between the Piazza del Duomo and Piazza della Signoria lies the medieval kernel from which the Florentine Renaissance emerged like a hot-house flower. On one end, the Piazza del Duomo has the Cathedral and Baptistry, not only the city's religious centre, but the prime focus of some of the city's greatest art and architecture. On the other end, the Piazza della Signoria, the seat of Florence's government and showcase of her civic virtue, also has the masterpieces of her greatest painters in the Uffizi. In between you'll find the medieval police station, the Bargello, home to superb sculptures by Donatello, Michelangelo and company; the unique church of Orsanmichele, a shrine built by the city's once all-powerful medieval guilds; and the narrow medieval lanes that Dante once called home.

To follow Dante's footsteps more closely, *see* the walk on 'Dante's Florence' on p.154.

1 Lunch

Antico Fattore, *Via Lambertesca 1/3r*, **t** *055 288975*; **bus** *B*. **Open** *Mon–Sat 12.15–2.45 and 7.15–10.30; closed two weeks in Aug*. ***Moderate***. A traditional, popular Florentine trattoria that serves excellent local dishes, reasonably priced.

2 Tea and Cakes

Caffè Italiano, *Via Condotta 56r*; **bus** *A*. ***Open*** *Mon–Sat 8am–8.30pm and 9.30pm–midnight; closed Aug*. Sit upstairs for delicious coffee, tea and cakes.

3 Drinks

Rivoire, *Piazza della Signoria 5r*; **bus** *A, B*. ***Open*** *Tues–Sun 8am–midnight*. A historic elegant bar/café with marble-detailed décor.

Highlights

Couples' City: Visit the Donatellos and other lovely sculptures in the Bargello, p.88

Medieval City: Orsanmichele, the church and shrine of Florence's guilds, p.73

Renaissance City: Brunelleschi's perfect dome and Ghiberti's Baptistry doors, pp.66 and 71

Medici City: The Uffizi – they built it, and chose most of the art, too, p.81

Quirky City: Galileo's finger, in the Museo di Storia della Scienza, p.87

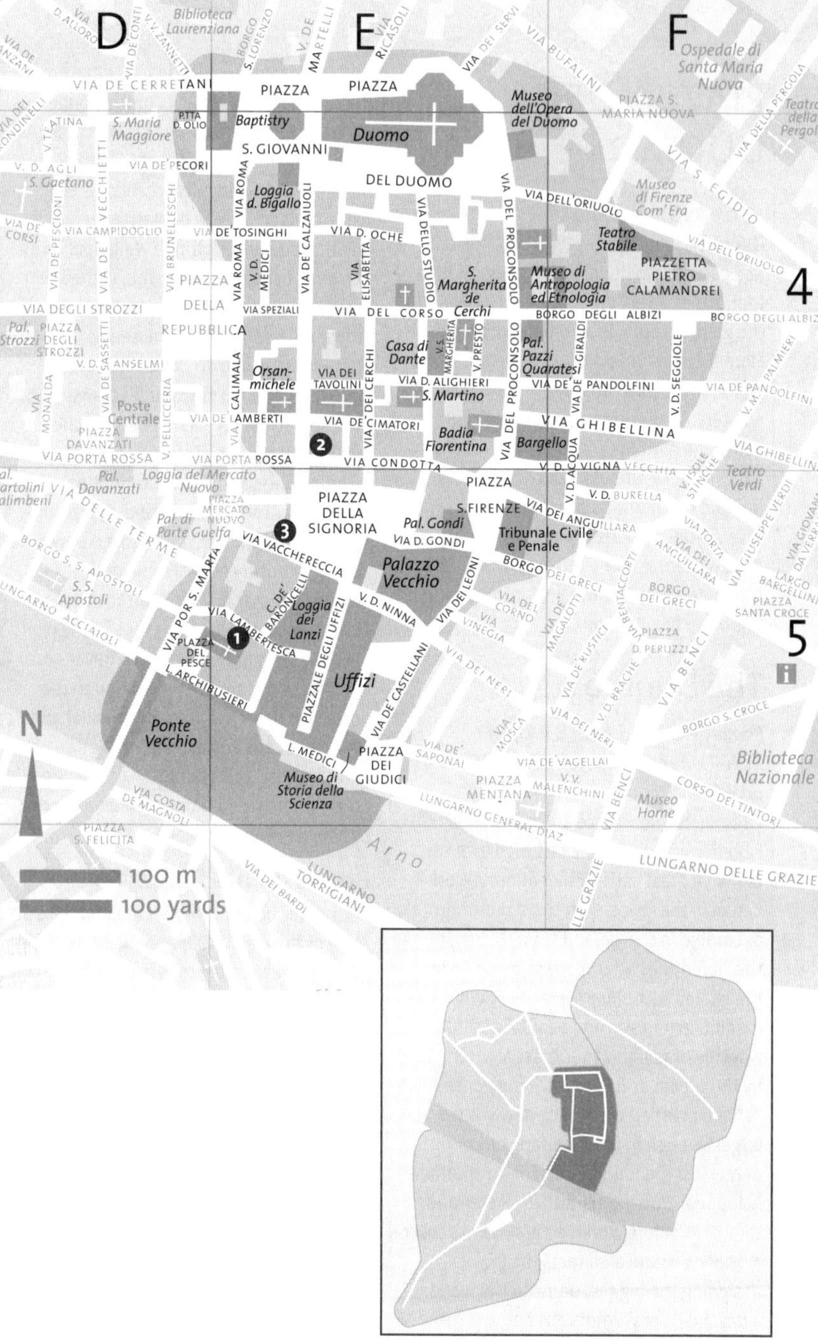

D
E
F
4
5
Biblioteca Laurenziana
Ospedale di Santa Maria Nuova
PIAZZA
PIAZZA
S. GIOVANNI
DEL DUOMO
Baptistry
Duomo
Museo dell'Opera del Duomo
S. Maria Maggiore
S. Gaetano
Loggia d. Bigallo
Teatro Stabile
PIAZZETTA PIETRO CALAMANDREI
S. Margherita de Cerchi
Museo di Antropologia ed Etnologia
PIAZZA DELLA REPUBBLICA
Pal. Strozzi
Casa di Dante
Pal. Pazzi Quaratesi
Orsanmichele
S. Martino
Poste Centrale
Badia Fiorentina
Bargello
Teatro Verdi
PIAZZA DELLA SIGNORIA
PIAZZA S. FIRENZE
Pal. Gondi
Tribunale Civile e Penale
Palazzo Vecchio
Loggia dei Lanzi
Uffizi
Ponte Vecchio
Museo di Storia della Scienza
PIAZZA DEI GIUDICI
Biblioteca Nazionale
Museo Horne
Arno
100 m
100 yards
N

PIAZZA DEL DUOMO

Florence's holy centre, the Piazza del Duomo, is in many way the key to the city, and essential to understanding everything that comes after. Tour groups circle around the great spiritual monuments of medieval Florence like sharks around their prey, preyed on in turn by postcard vendors and portrait painters. An occasional street musician serenades the human carnival from a hundred nations, while ambulances of a medieval first-aid brotherhood stand at the ready in case anyone swoons from ecstasy or art-glut. As bewildering as it often is, however, the Piazza del Duomo is the best introduction to this often bewildering city.

The Duomo E4

***Piazza del Duomo; bus** 1, 7, A. **Open** Mon–Thurs and Sat 9.30–5, Fri and Sun 1–5; **adm** free.*

For all its importance and prosperity, Florence was one of the last medieval cities to plan a great cathedral or duomo. Work began in the 1290s, with the sculptor Arnolfo di Cambio in charge, and from the beginning the Florentines attempted to make up for their delay with sheer audacity. 'It will be so magnificent in size and beauty', according to a decree of 1296, 'as to surpass anything built by the Greeks and Romans. In response Arnolfo planned what in its day was the largest church in Christendom; he confidently laid the foundations for an enormous octagonal crossing 146ft in diameter, and then died before working out a way to cover it, leaving future architects the job of designing the biggest dome in the world.

Beyond its presumptuous size, the cathedral of Santa Maria del Fiore shows little interest in contemporary innovations and styles; a visitor from France or England in the 1400s would certainly have found it somewhat drab and architecturally primitive. Visitors today often don't know what to make of it as they circle its grimy, ponderous bulk. Instead of the striped bravura of Siena or the elegant colonnades of Pisa, they behold an astonishingly eccentric green, white and red pattern of marble rectangles and flowers – like Victorian wallpaper or, as one critic better expressed it, 'a cathedral wearing pyjamas'. On a sunny day, the cathedral under its sublime dome seems to sport festively above the dun and ochre sea of Florence; in dismal weather it sprawls morosely across its piazza like a beached whale with a lace doily front.

The fondly foolish **façade** cannot be blamed on Arnolfo. His original design, only one-quarter completed, was taken down in a late 16th-century Medici rebuilding programme that never got off the ground. The Duomo turned a blank face to the world until the present neo-Gothic extravaganza was stuck on in 1888. Walk around to the north side to see what many consider a more fitting door, the **Porta della Mandorla** crowned with an Assumption of the Virgin in an almond-shaped frame, or *mandorla*, made by Nanni di Banco in 1420.

Brunelleschi's Dome

Yet if this behemoth of a cathedral, this St Mary of the Floral Wallpaper, was created for no other reason than to serve as a base for its dome, it would be more than enough. Brunelleschi's dome, more than any landmark, makes Florence Florence.

The dome repeats the rhythm of the surrounding hills, echoing them with its height and beauty; from those city streets fortunate enough to have a clear view, it rises among the clouds with all the confident mastery, proportions, and perfect form that characterize the highest aspirations of the Renaissance. But if it seems miraculous, it certainly isn't divine; unlike the dome of the Hagia Sophia, suspended from heaven by a golden chain, Florence's was made by man – one man, to be precise.

Not winning the competition for the baptistry doors was a bitter disappointment

Brunelleschi's Show of Perspective

Picking up where Euclid left off, medieval scholars such as Roger Bacon and Robert Grosseteste were keenly interested in the relationship between the viewer and the objects observed at any given moment, and how this relationship changed with every shift of distance or angle. Beginning with Giotto and Duccio, it became a problem of great interest to artists as well. Both scholars and painters sought to learn how to see the world, trusting their own eyes, and not old doctrines or pictures.

The man who made the great breakthrough in the discovery of the principles of visual perspective was Filippo Brunelleschi, and he did it in a way that was as empirical and untheoritical as a kitchen sink. He gave two public demonstrations in Florence of his discovery, once while standing in the central door of the Duomo. Using the doorway as his frame of vision of the Baptistry, and stretching strings across it to create a grid, he sketched and then painted the contents as he saw them, keeping a fixed distance at all times to accurately render geometry into two dimensions. It changed the history of painting and visual theory, which Alberti would later describe in his landmark *Della Pittura*. What didn't catch on was the way Brunelleschi showed viewers his completed picture of the Baptistry: he cut a peephole in the canvas at eye level and set up a mirror in front of it, to control the fixed distance of the spectator to the work and making it appear perfectly to scale.

to the hot tempered Filippo Brunelleschi. His reaction was typically Florentine; not content with being the second-best sculptor, he turned his talents to a field where he thought no one could beat him. He launched himself into an intense study of architecture and engineering, visiting Rome and probably Ravenna to snatch secrets from the ancients. When proposals were solicited for the cathedral's dome in 1418, he was ready with a brilliant *tour de force*. Not only would he build the biggest, most beautiful dome of the time, but he would do it without any need for expensive supports while work was in progress, making use of a cantilevered system of bricks that could support itself while it ascended – surpassing the technique of the ancients with a system far more simple than that of the dome builders of the Pantheon or Hagia Sophia. To the Florentines, a people who could have invented the slogan 'form follows function' for their own tastes in building, it must have come as a revelation; the most logical way of covering the space turned out to be a work of perfect beauty. Brunelleschi, in building this dome, put a crown on the achievements of Florence. The Pope himself came up to lead a vast procession of prelates and noblemen to celebrate its completion on Florentine New Year's day, 25 March 1436. After 565 years it is still the city's pride and symbol.

The best way to appreciate Brunelleschi's genius is by touring inside the two concentric shells of the dome (*see* p.68), but before entering, note the eight marble ribs that define its octagonal shape; hidden inside are the three huge stone chains that bind them together. Work on the balcony around the base of the dome, designed by Giuliano da Sangallo, was halted in 1515 after Michelangelo commented that it resembled a cricket's cage. As for the **lantern**, the Florentines were famous for their fondness for Doubting Thomas, and here they showed why. Even though they marvelled at the dome, they still doubted that Brunelleschi could construct a proper lantern, and forced him to submit to yet another competition. He died soon after, and it was completed to his design by Michelozzo.

The Interior

After the façade, the austerity of the Duomo interior is almost startling. There is plenty of room; contemporary writers mention 10,000 souls packed inside to hear the hellfire and brimstone sermons of

Savonarola. Even with that in mind, the Duomo hardly seems a religious building – more a Florentine building, with simple arches and counterpoint of grey stone and white plaster, full of old familiar Florentine things. Near the entrance, on the right-hand side, are busts of Brunelleschi and Giotto. On the left wall, posed inconspicuously, are the two most conspicuous monuments to private individuals ever erected by the Florentine Republic. The older one, on the right, is to **Sir John Hawkwood**, the famous English *condottiere* whose name the Italians mangled to Giovanni Acuto, a legendary commander who served Florence for many years and is perhaps best known to English speakers as the hero of *The White Company* by Arthur Conan Doyle. All along, Hawkwood had the promise of the Florentines to build him an equestrian statue after his death; it was a typical Florentine trick to pinch pennies and cheat a dead man – but they hired the greatest master of perspective, Paolo Uccello, to make a fresco that looked like a statue (1436). Twenty years later, they pulled the same trick again, commissioning another great illusionist, Andrea del Castagno, to paint the non-existent equestrian statue of another *condottiere*, Niccolò da Tolentino, victor of the battle of San Romano and friend of Cosimo il Vecchio, who was buried in the cathedral. A little further down, Florence commemorates its own secular scripture with Michelino's well-known fresco of Dante, a vision of the poet and his *Paradiso* outside the walls of Florence. Two singular icons of Florence's fascination with science stand at opposite ends of the building: behind the west front, a bizarre clock painted by Uccello, and in the pavement of the left apse, a gnomon fixed by the astronomer Toscanelli in 1475. A beam of sunlight strikes it every year on the day of the summer solstice.

For building the great dome, Brunelleschi was accorded a special honour – he is one of the few Florentines to be buried in the cathedral. His tomb may be seen in the **Excavations of Santa Reparata** (*the stairway descending on the right of the nave; open 10–5, closed Sun; adm €1.55*). Arnolfo di Cambio's cathedral was constructed on the ruins of the ancient church of Santa Reparata, which lay forgotten until 1965. Excavations have revealed not only the palaeo-Christian church and its several reconstructions, but also the remains of its Roman predecessor – a rather confusing muddle of walls that have been tidied up in an ambience that resembles an archaeological shopping centre. A coloured model helps explain what is what, and glass cases display items found in the dig, including the spurs of Giovanni de' Medici, who was buried here in 1351. In the ancient crypt of Santa Reparata are 13th-century tomb slabs, and in another section there's a fine pre-Romanesque mosaic pavement.

There is surprisingly little religious art – the Florentines for reasons of their own have carted most of it off into the Museo dell' Opera del Duomo. The only really conventional religious decorations are the hack but scarcely visible frescoes high in the dome (some 295ft up), mostly the work of Vasari. As you stand there squinting at them, try not to think that the cupola weighs an estimated 25,000 tons. In the central apse, a beautiful bronze urn by Ghiberti contains relics of the 4th-century Florentine bishop, St Zenobius. Under the dome are the doors to the two sacristies, under terracotta lunettes by Luca della Robbia; *The Resurrection* over the north sacristy is one of his earliest and best works. He also did the bronze doors, with tiny portraits on the handles of Lorenzo il Magnifico and his brother Giuliano de' Medici, targets of the Pazzi conspiracy in 1478 (*see* box opposite).

A door on the left aisle near the Dante fresco leads up into the **dome** (*open Mon–Fri 8.30–7, Sat 8.30–5.40, closed Sun; adm €5.16*). The complicated network of stairs and walks between the inner and outer domes (not too difficult, if occasionally claustrophobic and vertiginous) was designed by Brunelleschi for the builders, and offers an insight on how thoroughly the architect thought out the

Murder in the Cathedral

On 28 April 1478, at the moment of the elevation of the Host, Francesco Pazzi, Florentine banker to the Pope, and his bravo Bandini, and two priests jumped the Medici brothers, leading an attack conceived with the support of Pope Sixtus IV and the King of Naples. Pazzi plunged his dagger 21 times into the handsome 25-year-old Giuliano, while Lorenzo, cape wrapped around one arm as a shield, sword unsheathed, fought off his aggressors, leaping over the then-extant choir screen and taking refuge with his supporters behind the bronze door. He had only a scratch on his neck; his friend Ridolfi sucked it, in case of poison. At the very same moment, another intriguer, the archbishop of Pisa, Francesco Salviati, who hated Lorenzo for not making him archbishop of Florence, failed in his attempt to capture and seize power in the Palazzo Vecchio. His body was soon seen dangling from the window, joined shortly after by that of Francesco Pazzi and all their co-conspirators, hanged or defenestrated without trial, to the cheers of the pro-Medici mob. The mutilations and executions without trial of over a hundred people suspected to have been involved in the plot continued for days, for months; those who fled abroad were relentlessly tracked down by Medici agents.

The cultivated, refined Lorenzo then displayed the vindictiveness that was an integral part of the Medici character. The Pazzi, one of the oldest families in Florence, were annihilated, their goods were confiscated, their palazzi renamed, their dolphin symbol struck down everywhere. After he was tortured, stripped naked and hanged, the body of Jacopo, the chief of the clan, was exhumed from Santa Croce (where his spirit had been causing torrential downpours), dragged mockingly through the streets, the head used as a knocker against his own palace; he was then thrown into the Arno, then fished out again, and cudgelled until the bones were broken into tiny bits, before being tossed back into the river. Sandro Botticelli was paid 40 florins each for painting their likenesses on the Palazzo Vecchio's walls, with epitaphs composed by Lorenzo, so all Florence could witness their infamy. And Lorenzo, conveniently relieved of his popular brother, was undisputed master of Florence.

problems of the dome's construction, inserting hooks to hold up scaffolding for future cleaning or repairs; he even installed restaurants to save workers the trouble of descending for meals. There is also no better place to get an idea of the dome's scale; the walls of the inner dome are 12ft thick, and those of the outer dome six feet. These provide enough strength and support to preclude the need for further buttressing.

From the gallery of the dome you can get a good look at the lovely **stained glass** by Uccello, Donatello, Ghiberti and Castagno, in the seven circular windows, or *occhi*, made during the construction of the dome. Further up, the views through the small windows offer tantalizing hints of the breathtaking panorama of the city from the marble lantern. The bronze ball at the very top was added by Verrocchio, and can hold almost a dozen people when it's open.

Giotto's Campanile E4

***Open** summer daily 9–6.50, winter daily 9–4.20; **adm** €5.16.*

There's no doubt about it; the dome steals the show on Piazza del Duomo, putting one of Italy's most beautiful bell towers in the shade both figuratively and literally. The dome's great size – 364ft to the bronze ball – makes Giotto's Campanile look small, though 278ft is not exactly tiny.

Giotto was made director of the cathedral works in 1334, and his basic design was completed after his death (1337) by Andrea Pisano and Francesco Talenti. It is difficult to say whether they were entirely faithful to the plan. Giotto was an artist, not an engineer. After he died, his successors realized that the thing, then only 38ft high, was about to tumble over, a problem they overcame by doubling the thickness of the walls.

Besides its lovely form, the green, pink and white campanile's major fame rests with Pisano and Talenti's **sculptural reliefs** – a veritable encyclopaedia of the medieval world view with prophets, saints and sibyls, allegories of the planets, virtues and sacraments, the liberal arts and industries (the artist's craft is fittingly symbolized by a winged figure of Daedalus). All of these are copies of the originals now in the Cathedral Museum. If you can take another 400 steps or so, the terrace on top offers a slightly different view of Florence and of the cathedral itself.

The Baptistry E4

***Piazza di San Giovanni, at the west end of Piazza del Duomo; bus** 1, 7, A. **Open** Mon–Sat noon–7, Sun 8.30–2; **adm** €2.58.*

In order to begin to understand what magic made the Renaissance first bloom by the Arno, look here; this ancient and mysterious building is the egg from which Florence's golden age was hatched. By the quattrocento Florentines firmly believed their baptistry was originally a Roman temple to Mars, a touchstone linking them to a legendary past. Scholarship sets its date of construction between the 6th and 9th centuries, in the darkest Dark Ages, which makes it even more remarkable; it may as well have dropped from heaven. Its distinctive dark green and white marble facing, the tidily classical pattern of arches and rectangles that deceived Brunelleschi and Alberti, was probably added around the 11th century. The masters who built it remain unknown, but their strikingly original exercise in geometry provided the model for all of Florence's great church façades. When it was new, there was nothing remotely like it in Europe; to visitors from outside the city it must have seemed almost miraculous.

Every 25 March, New Year's Day on the old Florentine calendar, all the children born over the last 12 months would be brought here for a great communal baptism, a habit that helped make the baptistry not merely a religious monument but a civic symbol, in fact the oldest and dearest symbol of the republic. As such the Florentines never tired of embellishing it. Under the octagonal cupola, the glittering 13th- and 14th-century gold-ground mosaics show a strong Byzantine influence, perhaps laid by mosaicists from Venice. The decoration is divided into concentric strips: over the apse, dominated by a 26ft figure of Christ, is a *Last Judgement*, while the other bands, from the inside out, portray the *Hierarchy of Heaven*, *Story of Genesis*, *Life of Joseph*, *Life of Christ* and the *Life of St John the Baptist*, the last band believed to be the work of Cimabue. The equally beautiful mosaics over the altar and in the vault are the earliest, signed by a monk named Iacopo in the first decades of the 1200s. New lighting has been installed, making them much easier to view.

To match the mosaics, there is an intricate tessellated marble floor, decorated with signs of the Zodiac; the blank, octagonal space in the centre was formerly occupied by the huge font. The green and white patterned walls of the interior, even more than the exterior, are remarkable, combining influences from the ancient world and modern inspiration for something entirely new, the perfect source that architects of the Middle Ages and Renaissance would ever strive to match. Much of the best design work is up in the **galleries**, not accessible, but partially visible from the floor.

The baptistry is hardly cluttered; besides a 13th-century Pisan-style baptismal font, only the **Tomb of Anti-Pope John XXIII** by Donatello and Michelozzo stands out. This funerary monument, with scenographic marble draperies softening its classical lines, is one of the great prototypes of the early Renaissance. But how did this Anti-Pope John (a former Neapolitan pirate named Baldassare Cossa) deposed by the Council of Constance in 1415, earn the unique privilege of a fancy tomb in the baptistry? Why, it was thanks to him that Giovanni di Bicci de' Medici made the family fortune as head banker to the Curia.

The Gates of Paradise

Historians used to pinpoint the beginning of the 'Renaissance' as the year 1401, when the merchants' guild, the Arte di Calimala, sponsored a competition for the baptistry's north doors. The **South Doors** (the main entrance into the baptistry) had already been completed by Andrea Pisano in 1330, and they give an excellent lesson on the style of the day. The doors are divided into 28 panels in quatrefoil frames with scenes from the life of St John the Baptist and the eight Cardinal and Theological Virtues – formal and elegant works in the best Gothic manner.

The celebrated competition of 1401 – perhaps the first ever held in the annals of art – pitted the seven greatest sculptors of the day against one another. Judgement was based on trial panels on the subject of the Sacrifice of Isaac, and in a dead heat at the end of the day were the two by Brunelleschi and Lorenzo Ghiberti, now displayed in the Bargello. The judges asked them to collaborate; Brunelleschi lost his temper, refused and Ghiberti was left to complete the task on his own. It was a serendipitous outcome; he devoted nearly the rest of his life to creating the most beautiful bronze doors in the world while Brunelleschi went on to build the most perfect dome. Ghiberti's first efforts, the **North Doors** (1403–24), are contained, like Pisano's, in 28 quatrefoil frames. In their scenes on the Life of Christ, the Evangelists, and the Doctors of the Church, you can trace Ghiberti's progress over the 20 years he worked in the increased depth of his compositions, not only visually but dramatically; classical backgrounds begin to fill up the frames, ready to break out of their Gothic confines. Ghiberti also designed the lovely floral frame of the doors; the three statues, of John the Baptist, the Levite and the Pharisee, by Francesco Rustici, were based on a design by Leonardo da Vinci and added in 1511.

The doors were hardly up when Ghiberti was set loose on the **East Doors** (1425–52), which were to become one of the most sublime achievements of the age. A perfectionist, the artist drove his assistants crazy by recasting and recasting the panels to make each little detail more lifelike, until old age finally made him give up. Here Ghiberti (perhaps under the guidance of Donatello) dispensed with the small Gothic frames and instead cast ten large panels that depict the Old Testament in Renaissance high gear, re-interpreting the forms of antiquity with a depth and drama that have never been surpassed. Michelangelo declared them 'worthy to be the Gates of Paradise', and indeed, it's hard to believe that these are people, buildings and trees of bronze and not creatures frozen in time by some celestial alchemy. The doors (they're actually copies – some of the original panels, restored after flood damage, are on display in the Museo dell'Opera del Duomo) have been cleaned recently, and stand in gleaming contrast to the others which still carry the grime of centuries. In 1996 copies of Andrea Sansovino's marble statues of Christ and John the Baptist (1502) and an 18th-century angel were installed over the doors. The originals had begun to fall to bits in 1974; they too are now in the Museo dell'Opera.

Ghiberti wasn't exactly slow to toot his own horn; according to him, he personally planned and designed the Renaissance on his own. His unabashedly conceited *Commentarii* were the first attempt at art history and autobiography by an artist, and a work as revolutionary as his doors in its presentation of the creative God-like powers of the artist. It is also a typical exhibition of Florentine pride that he should put busts of his friends among the prophets and sibyls that adorn the frames of the East Doors. Near the centre, the balding figure with arched eyebrows and a little smile is Ghiberti himself.

Museo dell'Opera del Duomo E4

Piazza del Duomo 9, t 055 230 2885, w www.operaduomo.firenze, it; bus 1, 17. Open Mon–Sat 9–7.30, Sun 9–1.40; adm €5.16.

This museum is one of Florence's finest, and houses both relics from the actual construction of the cathedral and the masterpieces that once adorned it. The first room is devoted to the cathedral's sculptor-architect Arnolfo di Cambio and contains a drawing of his ornate, sculpture-filled façade that was but a quarter completed when the Medici had it removed in 1587. Here, too, are the statues he made for it: the unusual Madonna with the glass eyes, Florence's original patron saints, Reparata and Zenobius, and nasty old Boniface VIII, who sits stiffly on his throne like an Egyptian god. There are the four Evangelists, including a St John by Donatello, and a small collection of ancient works – Roman sarcophagi and an Etruscan cippus carved with dancers. Note the 16th-century 'Libretto', a fold-out display case of saintly odds and ends, all neatly labelled. The Florentines were never enthusiastic about the worship of relics, and long ago they shipped San Girolamo's jawbone, John the Baptist's index finger and St Philip's arm across the street to this museum.

A nearby room contains a collection of altarpieces, triptyches and paintings of saints including Giovanni del Biondo's *Saint Sebastian*. Also here are a series of marble relief panels by Baccio Bandinelli from the altarpiece of the cathedral. A small room adjacent to this contains a section (several fragments pieced together) of the door known as the 'Porta della Mandorla' on the north side of the Duomo. This is an intricately carved marble relief including a small figure of *Hercules* with his stick, significant in that it was the first representation of the adult male nude and a taste of things to come, more of a statue than a relief. Also in this room are two statues known as *The Profetini*, which once stood over the door and are attributed to the young Donatello.

On the landing of the stairs stands the *Pietà* that Michelangelo intended for his own tomb. The artist, increasingly cantankerous and full of *terribilità* in his old age, became exasperated with it and took a hammer to the arm of the Christ – the first known instance of an artist vandalizing his own creation. His assistant repaired the damage and finished part of the figures of Mary Magdalene and Christ. According to Vasari, the hooded figure of Nicodemus is Michelangelo's self-portrait.

Upstairs, the first room is dominated by the two **Cantorie**, two marble choir balconies with exquisite bas-reliefs, made in the 1430s by Luca della Robbia and Donatello and removed from the Duomo in 1688 to make room for a bigger choir for the wedding of Prince Ferdinando. Both *cantorie* rank among the Renaissance's greatest productions. Della Robbia's delightful horde of laughing children dancing, singing and playing instruments is a truly angelic choir, Apollonian in its calm and beauty, perhaps the most charming work ever to have been inspired by the forms of antiquity. Donatello's *putti*, by contrast, dance, or rather race, through their quattrocento decorative motifs with Dionysian frenzy. Grey and weathered prophets by Donatello and others stand along the white walls, taken from the façade of Giotto's campanile. According to Vasari, while carving the most famous one, the bald *Habbakuk* (nicknamed *lo Zuccone*, 'baldy'), Donatello would mutter 'Speak, damn you. Speak!' The next room contains other original works from the campanile: the panels on the *Spiritual Progress of Man* by Andrea Pisano.

The first thing you see as you enter the last room is Donatello's statue, *Mary Magdalene*, surely one of the most jarring figures ever sculpted, ravaged by her own piety and penance, her sunken eyes fixed on a point beyond this vale of tears. This room is dedicated to works removed from the baptistry, especially the lavish silver altar (14th–15th century), made by Florentine goldsmiths, portraying scenes from the life of the Baptist. Antonio Pollaiuolo used the same subject to design the 27 needlework panels that once were part of the priest's vestments. There are two 12th-century Byzantine mosaic miniatures, masterpieces of the intricate, and a *St Sebastian* triptych by Giovanni del Biondo that may well be the record for arrows; the poor saint looks like a hedgehog.

A ramp now leads into the new part of the museum from the room containing the panels from the campanile. Cases either side of this now display the collection of pulleys and other instruments used in the construction of the cathedral. At the bottom of the ramp on the left is Brunelleschi's death mask, facing a model of the lantern, which he was never to see. A window behind this model cleverly gives a close-up view of the cupola itself topped by that self-same lantern.

A series of rooms off a long corridor contain bits and pieces brought out of storage, including the four carved façades, artists' models for the design of the cricket's-cage pattern round the base of the cupola. The corridor leads into a room whose walls are filled with drawings of the Duomo from the 1875 competition to design the façade.

From here, a staircase leads down into the courtyard where eight of Ghiberti's panels from *The Gates of Paradise* are on display. The plan is to reconstruct the doors in their entirety, including the surrounds, and display them on the huge marble wall which has been constructed in the courtyard. However, the restoration of the final panels is not yet finished; meanwhile the blank marble wall sits there, rather bare but for the three statues at its foot.

Loggia del Bigallo E4

South of the Baptistry, near the beginning of Via de' Calzaiuoli.

This 14th-century porch, the most striking secular building on the Piazza del Duomo, was built for one of Florence's great charitable confraternities, the Misericordia, whose members in the 13th and 14th centuries courageously nursed and buried victims of the plague; their headquarters are still across the street, behind the parked ambulances. The Loggia itself originally served as a lost and found office, although instead of umbrellas it dealt in children; if unclaimed after three days they were sent to foster homes. In the 15th century the Misericordia merged with a similar confraternity called the Bigallo, and works of art donated to both charities over centuries are displayed in the diminutive but choice **Museo del Bigallo**, located next to the loggia at Piazza San Giovanni 1 (*open Mon 8.30–noon, Thurs 4–6pm; adm €2.60*). The most famous picture here is the fresco *Madonna della Misericordia*, featuring the earliest known view of Florence (1342); other 14th-century works (by Bernardo Daddi, Niccolò di Pietro Gerini, and sculptor Alberto Arnoldi) portray the activities of the brotherhood, members of which may still be seen wearing the traditional black hoods that preserve their anonymity.

East of the Loggia del Bigallo, between Via dello Studio and Via del Proconsolo, is a stone bench labelled '**Sasso di Dante**' – Dante's Stone' – where the poet would sit and take the air, observing his fellow citizens and watching the construction of the cathedral.

VIA DE' CALZAIUOLI

Of all the streets that radiate from the Piazza del Duomo, the straight, pedestrian-only Via de' Calzaiuoli is the one most people almost intuitively turn down, the Roman street that became the main thoroughfare of medieval Florence, linking the city's religious centre with the Piazza della Signoria. Widening of this 'Street of the Shoemakers' in the 1840s has destroyed much of its medieval character, and the only shoe shops to be seen are designer-label.

Orsanmichele E4

Via Arte della Lana; ***bus*** *A.* ***Open*** *daily 9–12 and 4–6; closed first and last Mon of month;* ***adm*** *free.*

This wonderfully eccentric church looks like no other church in the world: it rises up in a tall, neat, three-storey rectangle. It was built on the site of ancient San Michele ad Hortum (popularly reduced to

Guilds: The Original Ruling Class

After the Guelph triumph in the 13th century and the exile of the *Grandi* (or nobles) from politics, Florence was governed by an oligarchy of guilds, or *arti*. There were 21 *arti*, but political power lay in the hands of members of the seven elite guilds: the lawyers, the Arte dei Giudici e Notai; the great merchants, the Arte della Lana (wool), the Arte di Por Santa Maria (silk) and the Arte de Calimala (cloth); the bankers, the Arte del Cambio, the doctors, apothecaries, and spice sellers, the Arte dei Medici, Speziali e Merciai, and the leather and fur dealers, the Arte dei Vaccai e Pellicciai. The vast majority of Florence's population of humble workmen need not apply, nor did much of Florence's great wealth as a world capital in the 14th century seep down their way. By 1378 they were starving, leading to the soon-squelched revolt of the *ciompi* (*see* p.126).

Medieval Florence made her first fortune by taking in wool and silk from around Europe, refining, finishing and dyeing it. The wool guild was rich enough to build the Duomo; the bankers' guild, in 1252, made great fortunes easier to get when they minted a little gold coin known as the florin, that was soon used throughout Europe.

The oligarchy kept up a sheen of disinterest in the way it governed the republic. All guild members over the age of 30 had their names put in leather bags in Santa Croce, and every two months, nine names would be drawn, six from the seven major guilds, two from the 14 minor guilds, and one who was elected to be the Gonfaloniere, the city's standard bearer. For two months these lottery-chosen officials were the *priori*, or priors, who made up the government of the Signoria that ruled Florence. Upon election, they had to go and live in the Palazzo della Signoria. The food was good, however, and there was a jester on hand to keep them happy. If there was a serious crisis the *priori* couldn't deal with, the tower bell would summon all male Florentines over the age of fourteen to the Piazza della Signoria for a *parlamento*. When two-thirds had gathered, they would be asked to vote to give full powers to a *balìa*, or emergency committee.

The Florentines often patted their own backs for inventing this system as proof against tyrants but, in practice, it was as easily manipulated and rotten as any. Whichever family was richest and had the most supporters decided which names were put in the bag, and if somehow *priori* not favourable to their interests were chosen, they would call a rigged *parlamento* and vote for a *balìa* to dismiss them. It was as easy as that.

'Orsanmichele'), a 9th-century church located near a vegetable garden, which the *comune* destroyed in 1240 in order to erect a grain market; after a fire in 1337 the current market building (by Francesco Talenti and others) was erected, with a loggia on the ground floor and emergency storehouses on top where grain was kept against a siege.

The original market had a pilaster with a painting of the Virgin that became increasingly celebrated for performing miracles. The area around the Virgin became known as the Oratory, and when Talenti reconstructed the market, his intention was to combine its secular and religious functions; each pilaster of the loggia was assigned to a guild to adorn with an image of its patron saint (*see* box). In 1380, when the market was relocated, the entire ground floor was given over to the church, and Francesco Talenti's talented son Simone was given the task of closing in the arcades with lovely Gothic windows, which were later bricked in.

Orsanmichele grew into a magnificent showcase of 15th-century Florentine sculpture, a stylebook of the innovations that succeeded one another throughout the decades. Each guild sought to outshine the others by commissioning the greatest artists to sculpt their patron saints and the elaborate canopied niches that hold them. From Via de' Calzaiuoli turn left on Via de' Lamberti to see the work that got the ball rolling: Donatello's *St Mark*, patron of the linen dealers, finished in 1411, and the first free-standing marble statue of the Renaissance; note the subtle *contrapposto* position that makes the figure 'escape' from the confinement of the niche.

The niches continue around Via dell'Arte della Lana, named after the Wool Merchants' Guild, the richest after that of the bankers. Their headquarters, the **Palazzo dell'Arte della Lana** (linked by an overhead arch with Orsanmichele) was built in 1308 and restored in 1905 in a delightful William Morris style of medieval picturesque. The first statue on this façade of Orsanmichele is *St Eligio*, patron of smiths, by Nanni di Banco (1415), set in a niche embellished with the guild's emblem (black pincers) and a bas-relief below showing one of this rather obscure saint's miracles – apparently he shod a horse the hard way, by cutting off its hoof, shoeing it, then sticking it back on the leg. The other two statues on this street are bronzes by Ghiberti, the Wool Guild's *St Stephen* (1426) and the Exchange Guild's *St Matthew* (1422), the latter an especially fine work in a classical niche. On the Via Orsanmichele façade stands a copy of Donatello's famous *St George* (the original is in the Bargello) done in 1417 for the Armourers' Guild; the dramatic predella of the saint slaying the dragon is one of the first-known works making use of perspective. Next are the Stonecutters' and Carpenters' Guild's *Four Crowned Martyrs* (1415, by Nanni di Banco), inspired by Roman statues; by making them appear in an intimate conversation, Nanni managed to wedge them all in their niche. He also contributed the Shoemakers' *St Philip* (1415), while the next figure, *St Peter*, is commonly attributed to Donatello (1413). Around the corner on Via dei Calzaiuoli stands the bronze *St Luke*, patron of the Judges and Notaries, by Giambologna, a work of 1602. Facing Via dei Calzaiuoli, in a 15th-century niche, that originally held Donatello's *St Ludovico*, is the picturesque *Doubting of St Thomas* by Andrea del Verrocchio (1484), made not for a guild but the Tribunal of Merchandise, who like St Thomas always wanted to be certain before making a judgement. In the tabernacle of the cloth merchants, or Arte di Calamala, is Ghiberti's *St John the Baptist*, the first life-size bronze cast since antiquity. In the rondels above some of the niches are terracottas of the guilds' symbols by Luca della Robbia.

Orsanmichele's dark **interior** is ornate and cosy, with more of the air of a guildhall than a church. It makes a picturebook medieval setting for one of the masterpieces of the trecento: Andrea Orcagna's beautiful Gothic **Tabernacle**, a large, exquisite work in marble, bronze and coloured glass framing a contemporary painting of the Madonna (either by Bernardo Daddi or Orcagna himself), replacing the miraculous one, lost in a fire. The Tabernacle was commissioned by survivors of the 1348 Black Death. On the walls and pilasters are faded 14th-century frescoes of saints, placed as if they were members of the congregation; if you look at the pilasters on the left as you enter and along the right wall you can see the old chutes used to transfer grain from the storeroom above.

PIAZZA DELLA SIGNORIA AND AROUND

Italian city builders are renowned for effortlessly creating beautiful squares, but it's an art where the Florentines are generally all thumbs. Only here, in the city's civic stage, did they achieve a grand, meaningful space, although not by design – in the 13th century the victorious Guelphs knocked down the hated Ghibelline quarter that stood here, and no one wanted to rebuild on land polluted by their memory. Still, the piazza is an antidote to the stone gullies of the centre, a showcase for the sombre fortress of the Palazzo Vecchio and a lively gathering of some of the best and worst of Florentine sculpture, which form a fine backdrop to open-air concerts in the summer. Banks and insurance companies share the rest.

Although the Piazza della Signoria currently serves as Great Aunt Florence's drawing-room-cum-tourist-overflow-tank, in the old days it saw the public assemblies of the republic, which in Florence meant that the square often degenerated into a battle-ground for its impossibly inscrutable internecine intermural quarrels. These could be stirred up to mythic levels of violence; in the 14th century a man was eaten by a crowd maddened by a political speech. Such speeches were given from the *arringhiera*, or oration terrace in front of the Palazzo Vecchio, a word which gave us 'harangue'. It was in the Piazza della Signoria that Savonarola ignited his notorious Bonfire of Vanities in 1497, and here, too, the following year, the disillusioned Florentines ignited Savonarola himself. A small plaque in the pavement marks the exact spot, not far from Ammannati's fountain.

If, on the other hand, trouble came from without, the Florentines would toll the famous bell in the tower of the Palazzo Vecchio (it was nicknamed the *Vacca*, or cow, for its low mooing sound) and the square would rapidly fill with the gonfalons of the citizens' militia and the guilds. 'We will sound our trumpets!' threatened the French King Charles VIII, when the Florentines refused to shell out enough florins to make him and his army go away. 'And we will ring our bell!' countered the courageous republican Piero Capponi – a threat that worked; Charles had to settle for a smaller sum. When Alessandro de' Medici was restored as duke of Tuscany three years later, one of his first acts was to smash the bell as too potent a symbol of Florence's liberty.

Since the 1970s and 80s a different kind of battle has been waged here, spiced with good old-fashioned Florentine factionalism. At stake is the future of the Piazza della Signoria itself. In 1974, while searching for signs of the original paving stones, the Soprintendenza ai Beni Archeologici found, much to their surprise, an underground medieval kasbah of narrow lanes, houses and wells – the ruins of Ghibelline Florence, built over the baths and other portions of Roman and Etruscan *Florentia*. During the excavations, the remains of Roman dyeing vats were also found, an indication that Florence was associated with textiles even back then. The *comune* ordered the excavations filled in; from the city's point of view, the piazza, essential to the essential tourist trade, was untouchable. In the '80s, the communal government fell, and the excavations were reopened on the portion of the piazza near the Loggia. There are proposals to excavate the rest of the square, much to the horror of the *comune*, and to create eventually an underground museum. For the moment, at any rate, the digging party is in retreat and the pavement of Piazza Signoria is complete – no gaping holes.

Loggia dei Lanzi E5

Generally of a lower key than a political harangue was the *parlamento*, a meeting of eligible male citizens to vote on an important issue (perhaps because the outcome was usually decided in advance by the bosses). On these occasions, the Florentines heard speeches from the platform of this graceful three-arched loggia, also known as the Loggia della Signoria or the Loggia dell'Orcagna, after Andrea Orcagna, the probable architect.

Completed in 1382, when pointed Gothic was still the rage, the loggia with its lofty round arches looks back to classical antiquity and looks forward to the Renaissance; it is the germ of Brunelleschi's revolutionary architecture. If the impenetrable, stone Palazzo Vecchio is a symbol of the republic's muscle and authority, the Loggia dei Lanzi is a symbol of its capacity for beauty. Unfortunately there are plans to put in a railing of some kind around it 'to protect the statues'; one hopes that the traditionalists squawk loud enough to keep it open. At the time of writing, the statues are being restored one by one, so expect some scaffolding for the next year or two.

The loggia received its name 'of the lances' after the Swiss lancers, the private bodyguard of Grand Duke Cosimo I. It was Cosimo who, in 1545, was responsible for the most famous sculpture sheltered in the arcade, Cellini's newly restored *Perseus*: not by commissioning it from the volatile Cellini, but by scoffing, saying a life-sized bronze statue was impossible, infuriating Cellini, who proved him wrong, although it took him 10 years, and cost him his health and the roof of his house , which caught fire as he stoked the furnace to melt the bronze. The result, his masterpiece, is a Mannerist *tour de force* with its attention to detail and expressive composition, the figure of Perseus graceful and poised atop the gruesome bleeding trunk of Medusa, eyes averted from the horrible head with its petrifying gaze. The subject was a subtle hint to the Florentines, to inspire their gratitude for Grand Ducal rule which spared them from the monstrosity of their own unworkable republic. Another wager was behind the creation of Giambologna's *Rape of the Sabines* (1583): he took a rough block of marble all the other sculptors in Florence had rejected as impossible, on the bet that he could do something with it. Its curious shape 'liberated', as Michelangelo would say, became an old man, a young man and a woman spiralling upwards in a fluid *contrapposto* convulsion, one of the first sculptures designed to be seen from all sides: the title was stuck on after its completion. The loggia also shelters Giambologna's less successful *Hercules and Nessus*, a chorus line of six Roman vestal wallflowers, and several other works that contribute to the rather curious effect, especially at night, of people at a wild party frozen into stone by Medusa's magical gaze.

Statues in the Piazza della Signoria E5

The first two statues placed in the square (now copies) were carried there by republican enthusiasm. Donatello's *Judith and Holofernes* was hauled from the Medici palace and placed here in 1494 as a symbol of the defeat of tyranny. Michelangelo's *David* was equally seen as the embodiment of republican triumph (when it was finished in 1504, the Medici were in exile), although it is doubtful whether Michelangelo himself had such symbolism in mind: the statue was originally intended to stand next to the cathedral, only to be shanghaied to the Piazza della Signoria as a message for any would-be Goliath. In 1873, it was replaced by the copy you see today, when the original was relocated (with much pomp, on a specially built train) for safekeeping at the Accademia. Later Florentine sculptors attempted to rival the *David*, especially the awful Baccio Bandinelli, who managed to get the commission to create a pendant to the statue and boasted that he could surpass Il Divino himself. The pathetic result, *Hercules and Cacus*, was completed in 1534; as a reward, Bandinelli had to listen to his archrival Cellini insult the statue in front of their patron, Cosimo I. An 'old sack full of melons' he called it, bestowing the sculpture's alternative title.

Another overgrown victim of the chisel stands at the corner of the Palazzo Vecchio. Ammannati's **Neptune's Fountain** (1575) was dubbed *Il Biancone* ('Big Whitey') almost as soon as it was unveiled; Michelangelo pitied the huge block of marble Ammannati 'ruined' to produce Neptune, a lumpy, bloated symbol of Cosimo I's naval victories, wearing a silly crown of anti-pigeon spikes as he stands arrogantly over a low basin and a few half-hearted spurts of water, pulled along by four struggling sea steeds, mere hobbyhorses compared with Big Whitey himself.

The last colossus in Piazza della Signoria is the *Monument to Cosimo*, by Giambologna (1595), the only large-scale equestrian bronze of the Late Renaissance. The scheme on the panels below Cosimo depicts scenes of his brutal conquest of Siena, and of the 'Florentine Senate' and the Pope conferring the Grand Dukedom on Cosimo.

Directly behind Cosimo stands the **Tribunale di Mercanzia**, built in the 14th century as a commercial court for merchants of the guilds and adorned with heraldic arms. To the left of this (no. 7) is a fine, 16th-century contribution, the **Palazzo Uguccioni**, very much in the spirit of High Renaissance in Rome, and sometimes attributed to a design by Raphael.

Palazzo Vecchio E5

***Piazza della Signoria, t** 055 276 8465, **w** www.nuovopalazzovecchio.org; **bus** A, B. **Open** mid-June–mid-Sept Tues, Wed and Sat 9–7, Mon, Fri 9–11pm, Thurs and Sun 9–2; mid-Sept–mid-June Fri–Wed 9–7, Thurs 9–2; **adm** €5.68.*

When Goethe made his blitz-tour of Florence, the Palazzo Vecchio (also called the Palazzo della Signoria) helped pull the wool over his eyes. 'Obviously', wrote the great poet, 'the people ... enjoyed a lucky succession of good governments' – a remark which, as Mary McCarthy wrote, could make the angels in heaven weep.

But none of Florence's chronic factionalism mars Arnolfo di Cambio's temple of civic aspirations, part council hall and part fortress. In many ways, the Palazzo Vecchio is the ideal of stone Florence: rugged and imposing, with a rusticated façade that was to inspire so many of the city's private palaces, yet designed according to the proportions of the Golden Section of the ancient Greeks. Its dominant feature, the 308ft tower, is a typical piece of Florentine bravado, for long the highest point in the city.

The Palazzo Vecchio occupies the site of the old Roman theatre and the medieval Palazzo dei Priori. In the 13th century this earlier palace was flattened along with the rest of the Ghibelline quarter, and in 1299, the now ascendant Guelphs called upon Arnolfo di Cambio, master builder of the cathedral, to design the most impressive 'Palazzo del Popolo' (as the building was originally called) possible, with an eye to upstaging rival cities. The palace's unusual trapezoidal shape is often, but rather dubiously, explained as Guelph care not to have any of the building touch land once owned by Ghibellines. One doubts that even in the 13th century real estate realities allowed such delicacy of sentiments; nor does the theory explain why the tower has swallowtail Ghibelline crenellations, as opposed to the square Guelph ones on the palace itself. Later additions to the rear of the palace have obscured its shape even more, although the façade is essentially as Arnolfo built it, except for the bet-hedging monogram over the door hailing Christ the King of Florence, put up in the nervous days of 1529, when the imperial army of Charles V was on its way to destroy the last Florentine republic (the inscription replaces an earlier one left by Savonarola). The room at the top of the tower was used as prison for celebrities and dubbed the Alberghettino; inmates of the 'little hotel' included Cosimo il Vecchio before his brief exile, and Savonarola, who spent his last months, between torture sessions, enjoying a superb view of the city before his execution in the piazza below.

Today, the palazzo serves as Florence's city hall. Recently, it was used as the setting for some gruesome scenes in the film *Hannibal* (2000): Giancarlo Giannini's detective ends up hanging from the balcony under the tower, entrails dangling...

The Interior

With few exceptions, the interior decorations date from the time of Cosimo I, when he relocated his Grand Ducal self here from the Medici palace in 1540. To politically 'correct' its acres of walls and ceilings in the shortest amount of time, he turned to his court artist Giorgio Vasari, famed more for the speed at which he could execute a commission than for its quality. On the ground floor of the palazzo, before you buy your ticket, you can take a gander at some of Vasari's more elaborate handiwork in the **Courtyard**, redone for the occasion of Francesco I's unhappy marriage in 1565 to the plain and stupid Habsburg Joanna of Austria.

The First Professional Philistine

Many who have seen Vasari's work in Florence will be wondering how such a mediocre painter should rate so much attention. Ingratiating companion of the rich and famous, workmanlike over-achiever and tireless self-promoter, Vasari was the perfect man for his time. Born in Arezzo, in 1511, a fortunate introduction to Cardinal Silvio Passerini gave him the chance of an education in Florence with the young Medici heirs, Ippolito and Alessandro. In his early years, he became a fast and reliable frescoist gaining a reputation for customer satisfaction – a real innovation in an age when artists were increasingly becoming eccentric prima donnas. In the 1530s, after travelling around Italy on various commissions, he returned to Florence just when Cosimo I was beginning his plans to remake the city in the image of the Medici. It was a marriage made in heaven. Vasari became Cosimo's court painter and architect, with a limitless budget and a large group of assistants, the most prolific fresco machine ever seen in Italy – painting over countless good frescoes of the 1300s along the way.

But more than for his paintings, Vasari lives on through his book, the *Lives of the Artists*, a series of exhaustive biographies of artists. Beginning with Cimabue, Vasari traces the rise of art out of Byzantine and Gothic barbarism, through Giotto and his followers, towards an ever-improving naturalism, finally culminating in the great age of Leonardo, Raphael, and the divine Michelangelo, who not only mastered nature but outdid her. Leon Battista Alberti gets the credit for drafting the first principles of artistic criticism, but it was Vasari who first applied such ideas on a grand scale. His book, being the first of its kind, and containing a mine of valuable information on dozens of Renaissance artists, naturally has had a tremendous influence on all subsequent criticism. Art critics have never really been able to break out of the Vasarian straitjacket.

Much of Vasari's world seems quaint to us now: the idea of the artist as a kind of knight of the brush, striving for Virtue and Glory, the slavish worship of anything that survived from ancient Rome, artistic 'progress' and the conviction that art's purpose was to imitate nature. But many of Vasari's opinions have had a long and mischievous career in the world of ideas. His blind disparagement of everything medieval – really the prejudice of his entire generation – lived on until the 1800s. His dismissal of Sienese, Umbrian and northern artists – of anyone who was not a Florentine – has not been entirely corrected even today. Vasari was the sort who founded academies, a cheerful conformist who believed in a nice, tidy art that went by the book. With his interior decorator's concept of Beauty, he created a style of criticism in which virtuosity, not imagination, became the standard by which art was to be judged; history offers few more instructive examples of the stamina and resilience of dubious ideas.

Vasari's suitably grand staircase ascends to the largest room in the palace, the vast **Salone dei Cinquecento**. The *salone* was added at the insistence of Savonarola for meetings of the 500-strong Consiglio Maggiore, the reformed republic's democratic assembly. In 1503, art's two reigning divinities, Leonardo da Vinci and Michelangelo, were commissioned to paint the two long walls of the *salone* in a kind of Battle of the Brushes to which the city eagerly looked forward. Sadly, neither came anywhere near to completing the project; Leonardo managed to fresco a section of the wall, using the experimental techniques that were to prove the undoing of his *Last Supper* in Milan, while Michelangelo only completed the cartoons before being summoned to Rome by Julius II, who required the sculptor of the *David* to pander to his own personal megalomania.

In the 1560s Vasari removed what remained of Leonardo's efforts and refrescoed the entire room as a celebration of Cosimo's triumphs over Pisa and Siena – inane, big and busy scenes, crowded with men and horses who appear to have all the substance of overcooked past – topped by an apotheosis of the Grand Duke on the ceiling. The sculptural groups lining the walls of this almost uncomfortably large room (the Italian parliament sat here from 1865 to 1870 when Florence was the capital) are only slightly more stimulating. Even Michelangelo's *Victory*, on the wall opposite the entrance, is more virtuosity than vision, yet bitter and poignant: a vacuous young idiot poses with one knee atop a defeated old man half-submerged in stone, said to be Michelangelo's self-portrait. The neighbouring, muscle-bound duet, *Hercules and Diomedes* by Vicenzo de' Rossi, was probably inevitable in this city obsessed by the possibilities of the male nude.

Beyond the *salone*, behind a modern glass door, is a much more intriguing room, although it's not much bigger than a closet. This is the **Studiolo of Francesco I**, designed by Vasari in 1572 for Cosimo's melancholic and reclusive son, where he would escape to brood over his real interests in curiosities, chemistry, crystal and gem cutting and alchemy – so much so that at the end of his life he had his ministers meet him here so he could always keep an eye on his experiments (one of which led to an ingenious method for making porcelain as fine as that imported from China – thanks to its Grand Duke, Florence became the first place in Europe to manufacture it). The little study, windowless and more than a little claustrophobic, has been restored to its original appearance, lined with allegorical paintings by Vasari, Bronzino and Allori, and bronze statuettes by Giambologna and Ammannati; their refined, polished, and erotic mythological subjects are part of a carefully thought-out 16th-century programme on Man and Nature. The lower row of paintings conceals Francesco's secret cupboards where he kept his most precious pearls and crystals and gold.

After the *salone* a certain fuzziness begins to take over, in room after room of Medicean puffery provided by Cosimo I's propaganda machine and Vasari's fresco factory. The first rooms, known as the **Quartiere di Leone X**, carry ancestor worship to extremes, each one dedicated to a different Medici. In the first Cosimo il Vecchio returns from exile amid tumultuous acclaim; in the second Lorenzo il Magnifico receives ambassadors in the company of a dignified giraffe; the third and fourth are dedicated to the Medici popes; while the fifth, naturally, is for Cosimo I, who gets the most elaborate treatment of all.

Upstairs the next series of rooms is known as the **Quartiere degli Elementi**, with more by Vasari and co, depicting allegories of the elements. Beyond these are several rooms used to display works pilfered by the Nazis during the war and since recovered (*closed at the time of writing*). Many of the paintings were personally selected by Goering and Hitler, who were especially fond of *Leda and the Swan* and other mild mythological erotica. In a small room is the original of Verrocchio's *Boy with the Dolphin*, from the courtyard fountain.

A balcony across the Salone dei Cinquecento leads to the **Quartiere di Eleonora di Toledo**, Mrs Cosimo I's private apartments. Of special note here is her chapel, one of the masterpieces of Bronzino, who seemed to relish the opportunity to paint something besides Medici portraits. The next room, the **Sala dell'Udienza**, has a quattrocento coffered ceiling by Benedetto and Giuliano da Maiano, and walls painted with a rather fine romp by Mannerist Francesco Salviati (1550–60).

The last room, the **Sala dei Gigli** ('of the lilies') boasts another fine ceiling by the da Maiano brothers; it hovers over Donatello's bronze *Judith and Holofernes*, a late work of 1455; the warning to tyrants inscribed on its base was added when the statue was abducted from the Medici palace. Shown right before Judith strikes, with none of the gore popular at the time, it is one of Donatello's most naturalistic sculptures; the fact that it was done in eleven different pieces makes some critics wonder if sections, such as Holofernes' leg, weren't cast from real models. Off the Sala dei Gigli are two small rooms of interest: the **Guardaroba**, a unique 'wardrobe' adorned with 57 maps painted by Fra Egnazio Danti in 1563, depicting all the world known at the time. A bust and portrait of Machiavelli are in the **Cancelleria**, his office from 1498 to 1512, when he served the republic as secretary and diplomat. Poor Machiavelli died bitter and unaware of the notoriety that his works would one day bring him, and he would be amazed and probably appalled to learn that his name had become synonymous with cunning, amoral intrigue. After losing his job upon the return of the Medici, then tortured and imprisoned on a false suspicion of conspiracy, Machiavelli lived in enforced idleness in the country, where he wrote his political works and two fine plays, feverishly trying to return to favour, even dedicating his most famous book, *The Prince*, to Lorenzo, Duke of Urbino (a nonentity further glorified by Michelangelo's Medici tombs). Machiavelli's main concern throughout *The Prince* was to advise realistically, without mincing words, the fractious and increasingly weak Italians on how to create a strong state; his dark reputation came from openly stating what rulers do, rather than what they would like other people to think they do.

On the mezzanine before you exit the museum is the **Collezione Loeser**, a fine assortment of Renaissance art left to the city in 1928 by Charles Loeser, the Macy's department store heir.

The Uffizi E5

Entrance just south of the Palazzo Vecchio, w www.musa.uffizi.firenze.it; bus A, B. Open Tues–Sun 8.15–6.50; adm €8. Enormous queues in the summer are very common; try to arrive early, or book a ticket in advance on t 055 294883; you pay an extra €1.55 booking fee, and pick up the tickets and pay at the gallery at the time of your visit. Note that rooms in the Uffizi are often temporarily closed owing to either restoration work or staff shortages; a list of these is posted daily at the ticket counter.

Florence has the most fabulous art museum in Italy, and as usual we have the Medici to thank; for the building that holds these treasures, however, credit goes to Grand Duke Cosimo's much maligned court painter. Poor Giorgio Vasari! His roosterish boastfulness and the conviction that his was the best of all possible artistic worlds, set next to his very modest talents, have made him a comic figure in most art criticism. Even the Florentines don't like him. On one of the rare occasions when he tried his hand as an architect, though, he gave Florence something to be proud of. The Uffizi ('offices') were built as Cosimo's secretariat, incorporating the old mint (producer of the first gold florins in 1252), the archives, and the large church of San Pier Scheraggio, with plenty of room for the bureaucrats needed to run Cosimo's efficient, modern state. The matched pair of arcaded buildings have cold elegant façades that conceal Vasari's surprising innovation: iron reinforcements that make the huge amount of window area possible and keep the building stable on the soft, sandy ground. It was a trick that would be almost forgotten until the Crystal Palace and the first American skyscrapers.

Almost from the start the Medici began to store some of their huge art collection in parts of the building. There are galleries in the world with more works of art – the Uffizi counts a mere 1,800 – but the Uffizi overwhelms by the fact that every one is worth looking at.

The Uffizi has undergone major reorganization in the last few years. Some of this involved the restoration of remaining damage after the bomb (all but a very few paintings are now back on display), but improvements have also been made on a practical level. The most significant changes involve the ground floor which housed the state archive. Major restoration of the vaulted rooms has resulted in a vastly improved space; there are now three entrances (for individuals, for groups and for pre-paid tickets), bookshops, cloakrooms, video and computer facilities and information desks.

From the ticket counter you can take the lift or sweeping grand stair up to the second floor, where the Medici once had a huge theatre, a space now used as the **Cabinet of Drawings and Prints**. Although the bulk of this extensive and renowned collection is only open to scholars with special permission, a roomful of tempting samples gives a hint at what they have a chance to see.

Nowadays one thinks of the Uffizi as primarily a gallery of paintings, but for some hundred years after its opening, visitors came almost exclusively for the fine Hellenistic and Roman marbles. Most of these were collected in Rome by Medici cardinals, and not a few were sources of Renaissance inspiration. The **Vestibule** at the top of the stair contains some of the best, together with Flemish and Tuscan tapestries made for Cosimo I and his successors. **Room 1**, usually shut, contains excellent early Roman sculpture.

Rooms 2–6: 13th and 14th Centuries

The Uffizi's paintings are arranged chronologically. The roots of the Early Renaissance are strikingly revealed in **Room 2**, dedicated to the three great **Maestà** altarpieces by the masters of the 13th century. All portray the same subject of the Madonna and Child enthroned with angels. The one on the right, by Cimabue, was painted around the year 1285 and represents a breaking away from the flat, stylized Byzantine tradition. To the left is the so-called *Rucellai Madonna*, painted in the same period by the Sienese Duccio di Buoninsegna for Santa Maria Novella. It resembles Cimabue's in many ways, but has a more advanced technique for creating depth, and the bright colouring that characterizes the Sienese school. Giotto's altarpiece, painted some 25 years later, takes a great leap forward, not only in his use of 'false' perspective, but in the arrangement of the angels, standing naturally, and in the portrayal of the Virgin, gently smiling, with real fingers and breasts.

To the left, **Room 3** contains representative Sienese works of the 14th century, with a beautiful Gothic *Annunciation* (1333) by Simone Martini and the brothers Pietro and Ambrogio Lorenzetti. **Room 4** is dedicated to 14th-century Florentines: Bernardo Daddi, Nardo di Cione, and the delicately coloured *San Remigio Pietà* by Giottino. **Rooms 5 and 6** house Italian contributions to the International Gothic school, most dazzlingly Gentile da Fabriano's *Adoration of the Magi* (1423), painted for the banker Palla di Nonfri Strozzi, and a landmark: it was the first painting where the artist tried to capture light and shadow realistically, and it was the first in Florence that shows the client and his son – just behind the youngest king – as splendid full-sized figures directly involved in the action of the story, instead of being shunted off to one side, in miniature. The Strozzi's even prouder rivals, the Medici, would take the concept even further in their scene of the Magi in the Palazzo Medici (*see* p.98). The rooms also contain two good works by Lorenzo Monaco, and the *Thebaid* of Gherardo Starnina, depicting the rather unusual activities of the 4th-century monks of St Pancratius of Thebes, in Egypt – a composition strikingly like Chinese scroll scenes of hermits.

Rooms 7–9: Early Renaissance

In the Uffizi, at least, it's but a few short steps from the superbly decorative International Gothic to the masters of the Early Renaissance. **Room 7** contains minor works by Fra Angelico, Masaccio and Masolino, and three masterpieces. Domenico Veneziano's pastel *Madonna and Child with Saints* (1448) is one of the rare pictures by this Venetian master who died a pauper in Florence. It is a new departure not only for its soft colours and warm spring light, the hallmark of the new *pittura della luce* as advocated by Alberti but for the subject matter, unifying the enthroned Virgin and saints in one panel, in what is known as a *Sacra Conversazione*. Piero della Francesca's famous *Double Portrait of the Duke Federigo da Montefeltro and his Duchess Battista*

Sforza of Urbino (1465) depicts one of Italy's noblest Renaissance princes – and surely the one with the most distinctive nose. Piero's ability to create perfectly still, timeless worlds is even more evident in the allegorical 'Triumphs' of the Duke and Duchess painted on the back of their portraits. A similar stillness and fascination floats over into the surreal in Uccello's *Rout of San Romano* (1456), or at least the third of it still present (the other two panels are in the Louvre and London's National Gallery; all three once decorated the bedroom of Lorenzo il Magnifico in the Medici palace). Both Piero and Uccello were deep students of perspective, but Uccello went half-crazy; applying his principles to a violent battle scene has left us one of the most provocative works of all time – a vision of warfare in suspended animation, with pink, white and blue toy horses, robot-like knights, and rabbits bouncing in the background.

Room 8 is devoted to the works of the rascally romantic Fra Filippo Lippi, whose ethereally lovely Madonnas were modelled after the brown-eyed nun he loved. In his *Coronation of the Virgin* (1447) she kneels in the foreground with two children, while the artist, dressed in a brown habit, looks dreamily towards her; in his celebrated *Madonna and Child with Two Angels* (1445) she plays the lead before the kind of mysterious landscape Leonardo would later perfect. Lippi taught the art of enchanting Madonnas to his student Botticelli, who has some lovely works in this room and the next; Alesso Baldovinetti, a pupil of the far more holy Fra Angelico, painted the room's beautiful *Annunciation* (1447). **Room 9** has two small scenes from the *Labours of Hercules* (1470) by Antonio Pollaiuolo, whose interest in anatomy, muscular expressiveness and violence presages a strain in Florentine art that would culminate in the great Mannerists. He worked with his younger brother Piero on the refined, elegant *SS. Vincent, James and Eustace*, transferred here from San Miniato. This room also contains the Uffizi's best-known forgery. *The Young Man in a Red Hat*, or self-portrait of Filippino Lippi, is believed to have been the work of a clever 18th-century English art dealer who palmed it off on the Grand Dukes.

Botticelli: Rooms 10–14

To accommodate the bewitching art of 'Little Barrels' and his throngs of admirers, the Uffizi converted four small rooms into one great Botticellian shrine. Although his masterpieces displayed here have become almost synonymous with the Florentine Renaissance at its most spring-like and charming, they were not publicly displayed until the beginning of the 19th century, nor given much consideration outside Florence for another hundred years.

Botticelli's best works date from the days when he was a darling of the Medici – family members crop up most noticeably in *The Adoration of the Magi* (1476), where you can pick out Cosimo il Vecchio, Lorenzo il Magnifico and Botticelli himself (in the right foreground, in a yellow robe, gazing at the spectator). His *Annunciation* is a graceful, cosmic dance between the Virgin and the Angel Gabriel. In the *Tondo of the Virgin of the Pomegranate* the wistfully lovely goddess who was to become his Venus makes her first appearance.

Botticelli is best known for his sublime mythological allegories painted for the Medici and inspired by the Neoplatonic, humanistic and hermetic currents that pervaded the Florentine intelligentsia of the late 15th century. Perhaps no painting has been debated so fervently as *La Primavera* (1478). Commissioned by Lorenzo di Pierfrancesco, this hung for years in the Medici Villa at Castello. The subject of the Allegory of Spring may have been suggested by Marsilio Ficino, translator of Plato and natural magician; the figures and colour scheme supposedly represent the 'beneficial' planets able to dispel sadness. *Pallas and the Centaur* seems to be another subtle allegory of Medici triumph – the rings of Athene's gown were a family device. Other interpretations see the taming of the sorrowful centaur as a melancholy comment on reason and civilization. Botticelli's last great mythology, *The Birth of Venus*, was also commissioned by Lorenzo di Pierfrancesco and inspired by a poem by Poliziano, Lorenzo il Magnifico's Latin and Greek scholar, who described how Zephyr and Chloris blew the newborn goddess to shore on a scallop shell, while Hora hastened to robe her, a scene Botticelli portrays once again with dance-like rhythm and delicacy of line. Yet the goddess of love floats towards the spectator with a melancholy expression – perhaps reflecting the artist's own feelings of regret; artistically, the poetic, decorative style he perfected in this painting would be disdained and forgotten in his own lifetime. Spiritually, too, Botticelli turned a corner after creating this haunting, uncanny beauty – it would be his, and Florence's, farewell to a road not taken.

Although Vasari's biography portrays Botticelli as a prankster rather than a sensitive soul, the painter absorbed more than any other artist the *fin-de-siècle* neuroticism that beset Florence with the rise of Savonarola. So thoroughly did he reject his former Neoplatonism that he would only accept commissions of sacred subjects or supposedly edifying allegories like his *Calumny*, a small but disturbing work, and a fitting introduction to the dark side of the quattrocento psyche.

This large room also contains works by Botticelli's contemporaries. Two paintings of the Adoration of the Magi, one by Ghirlandaio and one by Filippino Lippi, show the influence of Leonardo's unfinished but radical work in pyramidal composition (in the next room); Leonardo himself got the idea from the large *Portinari Altarpiece* (1471) by Hugo van der Goes at the end of the room, a work brought back from Bruges by Medici agent Tommaso Portinari.

Rooms 15–24: More Renaissance

Room 15 is dedicated to Leonardo da Vinci's early career in Florence. His master Andrea del Verrocchio began *The Baptism of Christ* (1470), when called away, leaving the young Leonardo to paint the angel on the left, and the distant landscape, in oils; the story goes that Verrocchio took one look at it and was so awed that he put his brushes away for good, and concentrated on sculpture. Most critics concur that Leonardo's next work was the large *Annunciation* (1475) – the soft faces and blurring contours, the botanical details, the misty, watery background that would become the trademarks of his magical brush are there, although some bits, such as the Virgin's table, were completed by others (Leonardo often left paintings unfinished, his interest drawn by something else). His least finished, but most influential work that he left in Florence before moving off to Milan, was his wash drawing for *The Adoration of the Magi* (1481). Difficult to make out at first, the longer you stare, the better you'll see the strikingly unconventional composition, of a serene Madonna and Child surrounded by turmoil of anxious, troubled humanity, with an exotic background of ruins, trees and horsemen, all charged with expressive energy. Other artists in Room 15 include Leonardo's peers: Lorenzo di Credi, whose religious works have eerie garden-like backgrounds, and the wonderfully nutty Piero di Cosimo, whose dreamy *Perseus Liberating Andromeda* includes an endearing mongrel of a dragon that gives even the most reserved Japanese tourist fits of giggles. Tuscan maps adorn **Room 16**, as well as paintings by Hans Memling.

The octagonal **Tribuna** (Room 18) with its mother-of-pearl dome and *pietra dura* floor and table was built by Buontalenti in 1584 for Francesco I, and like the Studiolo in the Palazzo Vecchio, it was designed to hold Medici treasures. For centuries the best-known of these was the *Venus de' Medici*, a 2nd-century BC Greek sculpture, farcically claimed as a copy of Praxiteles' celebrated Aphrodite of Cnidos, the most erotic statue in antiquity. In the 18th century, amazingly, this rather ordinary girl was considered the greatest sculpture in Florence; today most visitors walk right past, snubbing her without a second glance (*see* box). Other

Trends in Taste

I took a quick walk through the city to see the Duomo and the Battistero. Once more, a completely new world opened up before me, but I did not wish to stay long. The location of the Boboli Gardens is marvellous. I hurried out of the city as quickly as I entered it.

Goethe, on Florence in *Italian Journey*

Goethe, the father of the Italian Grand Tour, on his way from Venice to Rome, did not have much time for the city that likes to call itself 'The Capital of Culture'. Like nearly every traveller in the 18th and early 19th centuries, he knew nothing of Giotto, Masaccio, Botticelli, or Piero della Francesca; it was Roman statues that wowed him, the very same ones that the modern visitor passes in the corridors of the Uffizi without a second glance. Shelley managed to write pages on his visits to the museum without mentioning a single painting.

Some Tuscan attractions never change – the Leaning Tower, Michelangelo's *David*, the villas, the gardens and the cheap wine. Others have gone through an amazing rise or fall in popularity, thanks in part to John Ruskin, whose *Mornings in Florence* introduced the charms of the Romanesque architecture, Giotto, and the masters of the trecento; for him Orcagna was the master of them all (but in the 18th century, the Giottos in Santa Croce were whitewashed over, while many works of Orcagna had been destroyed earlier, by Vasari). Botticelli went from total obscurity in the 18th century to become the darling of the Victorians.

But the story of the *Venus de' Medici* is perhaps the most instructive. The statue is a pleasant, if unremarkable Greek work of the 2nd century BC, but for two centuries it was Florence's chief attraction; the minute visitors arrived in Florence they would rush off to gaze upon her; those prone to write gushed rapturously of her perfect beauty. Napoleon kidnapped her for France, asking the great neoclassical sculptor Canova to sculpt a replacement; afterwards the Venus was one of the things Florence managed to get back, though her reign was soon to be undermined – Ruskin called her an 'uninteresting little person'. Since then she has stood forlornly in the Tribuna of the Uffizi, unnoticed and unloved.

Some things don't change. Over a hundred years after Goethe's blitz tour of Florence, Aldous Huxley had no time for the city, either: 'We came back through Florence and the spectacle of that second-rate provincial town with its repulsive Gothic architecture and its acres of Christmas card primitives made me almost sick. The only points about Florence are the country outside it, the Michelangelo tombs, Brunelleschi's dome, and a few rare pictures. The rest is simply dung when compared to Rome.'

antique works include *The Wrestlers* and *The Knife Grinder*, both copies of Pergamese originals, *The Dancing Faun*, *The Young Apollo*, and *The Sleeping Hermaphrodite* in the adjacent room, which sounds fascinating but is usually curtained off.

The real stars of the Tribuna are the Medici court portraits, many by Bronzino, who could not only catch the likeness of Cosimo I, Eleanor of Toledo and their children, but aptly portrayed the spirit of the day – these are people who took themselves very seriously indeed. They have for company Vasari's posthumous portrait of *Lorenzo il Magnifico* and Pontormo's *Cosimo il Vecchio*, Andrea del Sarto's *Girl with a Book by Petrarch*, and Rosso Fiorentino's *Angel Musician*, an enchanting work entirely out of place in this stodgy temple.

Two followers of Piero della Francesca, Perugino and Luca Signorelli, hold pride of place in **Room 19**; Perugino's *Portrait of a Young Man* is believed to be of his most famous pupil Raphael. Signorelli's *Tondo of the Holy Family* was to become the inspiration for Michelangelo's (*see* p.86). The Germans appear in **Room 20**, led by Dürer and his earliest known work, the *Portrait of* *my Father* (1490), done at age 19, and *The Adoration of the Magi* (1504), painted after his first trip to Italy. Also here are Lucas Cranach's Teutonic *Adam and Eve* and *Portrait of Martin Luther* (1543), not someone you'd expect to see in Florence. **Room 21** is dedicated to the great Venetians, most famously Bellini and his uncanny *Sacred Allegory* (1490s), the meaning of which has never been satisfactorily explained. There are two minor works by the elusive Giorgione, and a typically weird *St Dominic* by Cosmè Tura. Later Flemish and German artists appear in **Room 22**, works by Gerard David and proto-Romantic Albrecht Altdorfer, and a portrait attributed to Hans Holbein, *Sir Thomas More*. **Room 23** is dedicated to Correggio of Parma and Mantegna of the Veneto, as well as to Boltraffio's strange *Narcissus* with an eerie Leonardo-esque background.

Rooms 25–27: Mannerism

The window-filled **South Corridor**, with its views over the city and fine display of antique sculpture, marks only the halfway point in the Uffizi but nearly the end of Florence's contribution. In the first three rooms, however, local talent rallies to produce a brilliantly coloured twilight in Florentine Mannerism. By most accounts, Michelangelo's only completed oil painting, the *Tondo Doni* (1506), was the spark that ignited Mannerism's flaming orange and turquoise hues. Michelangelo was 30 when he painted this, in a medium he disliked (sculpture and fresco being the only fit occupations for a man, or so he believed). It is a typical Michelangelo story that when the purchaser complained that the artist was asking too much for it, Michelangelo promptly doubled the price. As shocking as the colours are the spiralling poses of the Holy Family, sharply delineated against a background of five nude, slightly out-of-focus young men of uncertain purpose (are they pagans? angels? boyfriends? or just filler?) – an ambiguity that was to become a hallmark of Mannerism and in particular of the Sistine Chapel ceiling. In itself, the *Tondo Doni* is more provocative than immediately appealing; the violent canvas in **Room 27**, Rosso Fiorentino's *Moses Defending the Children of Jethro*, was painted some 20 years later and in its intention to shock the viewer puts a cap on what Michelangelo began.

Room 26 is dedicated mainly to Raphael, who was in and out of Florence in 1504–8. Never temperamental or eccentric like his contemporaries, the good-natured Raphael was the sweetheart of the High Renaissance. His Madonnas, like *The Madonna of the Goldfinch*, a luminous work painted in Florence, have a tenderness that was soon to be over-popularized by others and turned into holy cards, a cloying sentimentality added like layers of varnish over the centuries. It's easier, perhaps, to see Raphael's genius in non-sacred subjects, like *Leo X with Two Cardinals*, a perceptive portrait study of the first Medici pope with his nephew Giulio de' Medici, the future Clement VII. The same room contains Andrea del Sarto's most original work, the fluorescent *Madonna of the Harpies* (1517), named after the figures on the Virgin's pedestal. Of the works by Pontormo, the best is in **Room 27**, *Supper at Emmaus* (1525), a strange canvas with peasant-faced monks emerging out of the darkness, brightly clad diners with dirty feet, and the Masonic symbol of the Eye of God hovering over Christ's head.

Rooms 28–45

Although we now bid a fond farewell to the Florentines, the Uffizi fairly bristles with masterpieces from the rest of Italy and abroad. Titian's delicious nudes, especially the incomparably voluptuous *Venus of Urbino*, raise the temperature in **Room 28**; Parmigianino's hyper-elegant *Madonna with the Long Neck* (1536) in **Room 30** is a fascinating Mannerist evolutionary dead-end, possessing all the weird beauty of a foot-long dragonfly. Sebastiano del Piombo's *Death of Adonis*, in **Room 32**, is notable for its melancholy, lagoony, autumn atmosphere and the annoyed look on Venus' face. **Room 34** holds Paolo Veronese's *Holy Family with St Barbara*, a late work bathed in a golden

Venetian light, with a gorgeously opulent Barbara gazing on. In **Room 35** his contemporary Tintoretto is represented by a shadowy *Leda* languidly pretending to restrain the lusty swan; the Uffizi's El Greco is here as well, reminding us that this most Mannerist of Mannerists learned how to do it in Venice.

Room 41 is Flemish domain, with brand-name art by Rubens and Van Dyck; the former's *Baccanale* may be the most grotesque canvas in Florence. **Room 42**, the *Sala della Niobe*, was reopened in December 1998 after the bomb damage was repaired. A series of statues, *Niobe and her Sons* (18th-century copies of Hellenic works), are housed in the high, arched-ceilinged room which is covered in pristine plaster and gold leaf. Struggle on gamely to **Room 43** to see three striking Caravaggios. His *Bacchus* and *The Head of Medusa* are believed to be self-portraits; in its day the fleshy and heavy-eyed Bacchus, half portrait and half still life, but lacking the usual mythological appurtenances, was considered highly iconoclastic. Here, too, is one of the best *Judith and Holofernes* by Artemisia Gentileschi; after she was allegedly raped by a fellow artist (who was acquitted in court), the subject of a woman slicing off a man's head became her favourite theme. There are three portraits by Rembrandt in **Room 44**, including two of himself, young and old, and landscapes by Ruysdael. **Room 45** is given over to some fine 18th-century works, including two charming portraits of children by Chardin, and others by Goya and Longhi, and Venetian landscapes by Guardi and Canaletto. Even more welcome by this time is the newly renovated bar at the end of the corridor, with a lovely summer terrace.

Corridoio Vasariano

***Open** for limited periods during the year and within limited hours, to individuals as well as groups; **t** 055 265 4321 for information and obligatory booking; **adm** €9.30.*

In 1565, when Francesco I married Joanna of Austria, the Medici commissioned Vasari to link their new digs in the Pitti Palace with the Uffizi and the Palazzo Vecchio in such a manner that the archdukes could make their daily rounds without having to rub elbows with their subjects. With a patina of 400 years, Florence wouldn't look quite right without this covered catwalk, leapfrogging on rounded arches from the back of the Uffizi, over the Ponte Vecchio, daintily skirting a medieval tower, and darting past the façade of Santa Felicità to the Pitti Palace. The Corridoio was reopened in September 1997 after bomb damage repairs, and it's worth visiting for the views of Florence and a celebrated collection of artists' self-portraits, beginning with Vasari himself before continuing in chronological order, past the Gaddis and Raphael to Rembrandt, Van Dyck, Velázquez, Hogarth, Reynolds, Delacroix, Corot and scores in between.

The **Contini Bonacossi Collection** that used to be housed in the Pitti is now in a room adjacent to the Uffizi (*entrance on Via Lambertesca; by appointment only, call Firenze Musei on **t** 055 265 4321*). This recent bequest includes works of Cimabue, Duccio and Giovanni Bellini, some sculpture and china, and also paintings by El Greco, Goya and Velázquez – the last represented by an exceptional work, *The Water Carrier of Seville*.

Museo di Storia della Scienza E5

***Piazza dei Giudici, behind the Uffizi, w www.imss.fi.it; bus** 23, B. **Open** June–Sept Mon and Wed–Fri 9.30–5, Tues and Sat 9.30–1, Oct–May Mon and Wed–Sat 9.30–5, Tues 9.30–1, second Sun of the month 9.30–5; **adm** €6.50.*

For all that Florence and Tuscany contributed to the birth of science, it is only fitting that this museum should be in the centre of the city. Much of the ground floor is devoted to instruments measuring time and distance that are often works of art in themselves: Arabian astrolabes and pocket sundials, Tuscan sundials in the shape of Platonic solids, enormous elaborate armillary spheres and a small reliquary holding the bone of Galileo's finger, erect, like a final gesture to the city that until 1737 denied him a Christian burial. Here, too, are two of his original telescopes and the lens with which he discovered the first four moons of Jupiter in 1610, and made known in a book called Medicea Sidera in honour of his benefactors. Other instruments come from the Accademia del Cimento (the 'test'), founded in 1657 by Galileo's disciples the Grand Duke Ferdinando and Cardinal Leopoldo de' Medici, the world's first scientific organization, dedicated to Galileo's principle of inquiry and proof by experimentation: 'Try and try again' was its motto. Members met and argued in the Pitti palace, and published important work for 10 years before breaking up in discord. One, Evangelista Torricelli, invented the barometer.

Upstairs, there's a large room filled with machines used to demonstrate principles of physics, which the ladies who run the museum will operate if you ask. Two unusual ones are the 18th-century automatic writer and the instrument of perpetual motion. The rooms devoted to medicine contain a collection of 18th-century wax anatomical models, designed to teach budding obstetricians about unfortunate foetal positions, as well as a fine display of antique surgical instruments.

PONTE VECCHIO D5

Bent bridges seeming to strain like bows
And tremble with arrowy undertide ...
Casa Guidi Windows,
Elizabeth Barrett Browning

Often at sunset the Arno becomes a stream of molten gold, confined in its walls of stone and laced into its bed with the curving arches of its spans. That is, during those months when it has a respectable flow of water. But even in the torrid days of August, when the Arno shrivels into muck and spittle, its two famous bridges retain their distinctive beauty. The most famous of these, the Ponte Vecchio, the 'Old Bridge', crosses the Arno at its narrowest point; the present bridge, with its three stone arches, was built in 1345, and replaces a wooden construction from the 970s, the successor to a span that may well have dated back to the Romans. The old wooden bridge had as its protector the Marzocco, or statue of Mars; at its foot in 1215, Buondelmonte dei Buondelmonti was murdered, setting off the wars of the Guelphs and Ghibellines. The original Marzocco was washed down the Arno in a 14th-century flood, and Donatello's leonine version that replaced it has been carted off to the Bargello.

Like old London Bridge, the Ponte Vecchio is covered with shops and houses. By the 1500s, for hygienic reasons, it had become the street of hog butchers, although after Vasari built Cosimo's secret passage on top, the Grand Duke, for olfactory reasons, evicted the butchers and replaced them with goldsmiths. They have been there ever since, and shoppers from around the world descend on it each year to scrutinize the traditional Florentine talent for jewellery – many of the city's great artists began their careers as goldsmiths, from Ghiberti and Donatello to Cellini, who never gave up the craft, and whose bust adorns the middle of the bridge. In the 1966 flood the shops did not prove as resilient as the Ponte Vecchio itself, and a fortune in gold was washed down the Arno.

THE BARGELLO AND AROUND

The Bargello E4

Via del Proconsolo,* t *055 238 8606,* w *www.sbas.firenze.it/bargello/index;* bus *A, 14.* Open *daily 8.15–1.50; closed the first, third and fifth Sun and the second and fourth Mon of each month;* adm *€4.

This battlemented urban fortress, well proportioned yet of forbidding grace, for centuries saw duty as Florence's police station and prison. Today its only inmates are men of marble, gathered together to form

Italy's finest collection of sculpture, a fitting complement to the paintings in the Uffizi. Note the iron lion scaling the flag pole.

The Bargello is 'stone Florence' squared to the sixth degree, rugged *pietra forte*, the model for the even grander Palazzo Vecchio. Even the treasures it houses are hard, definite – and almost unremittingly masculine. The Bargello offers the best insight available into Florence's golden age, and it was a man's world indeed.

Completed in 1255, the Bargello was intended as Florence's Palazzo del Popolo, though by 1271 it had become the residence of the foreign *podestà*, or chief magistrate, installed by Guelph leader Charles of Anjou. The Medici made it the headquarters of the captain of police (the *Bargello*), torture chamber and city jail, a function it served until 1859.

In the Renaissance it was the peculiar custom to paint portraits of the condemned on the exterior walls of the fortress; Andrea del Castagno was so good at it that he was nicknamed Andrea of the Hanged Men. All of these ghoulish souvenirs have long since disappeared, as have the torture instruments – burned in 1786, when Grand Duke Peter Leopold abolished torture and the death sentence in Tuscany, only a few months behind the Venetians, who were the first in the world to do so. After an imaginative restoration in the 1860s, the Bargello's **Gothic courtyard**, once site of the gallows and chopping block, is one of Florence's most romantic corners, its shadowy arcades and stately stairs encrusted with centuries of *podestà* armorial devices and plaques in a wild vocabulary of symbols, watched over benignly by big cowardly lions of Oz with rusting crowns.

The Ground-floor Gallery

The main gallery is dedicated to **Michelangelo** and his century, although it's an oddly decaffeinated Michelangelo on display here, low on his trademark angst and ecstasy.

His *Bacchus* (1496), a youthful work inspired by bad Roman sculpture, has all the personality of a cocktail-party bore. Better to invite his noble *Brutus* (1540), even if he's just a bust – the only one the sculptor ever made, in a fit of republican fervour after the assassination of Duke Alessandro de' Medici. Also by Michelangelo is the lovely *Pitti Tondo* and the unfinished *Apollo/David*. From Michelangelo's followers there's a tippling *Bacchus* by Sansovino, and Ammannati's *Leda and the Swan* (a work inspired by a famous but lost erotic drawing by Michelangelo).

The real star of the room is Benvenuto Cellini, who was, besides the many other things one can read about in his romp of an autobiography, an exquisite craftsman and daring innovator. His large bust *Cosimo I* (1548), with its fabulously detailed armour, was his first work cast in bronze, although the unidealized features did not curry favour with the boss that poor Cellini worked so avidly to please. Here, too, is a preliminary model of the *Perseus*, as well as four small statuettes and the relief panel from the original in the Loggia dei Lanzi.

The last great work in the room is by Medici court sculptor Giambologna, now again enjoying a measure of the appreciation he enjoyed during his lifetime; art historians consider him the key Mannerist figure between Michelangelo and Bernini. Giambologna's most famous work, the bronze *Mercury* (1564), has certainly seeped into popular consciousness as the representation of the way the god should look. The stairway from the courtyard leads up to the shady **Loggia**, now converted into an aviary for Giambologna's charming bronze birds, made for the animal grotto at the Medici's Villa di Castello.

Salone del Consiglio Generale

Upstairs the magnificent Salone del Consiglio Generale, formerly the courtroom of the *podestà*, contains Early Renaissance sculpture, most especially the masterpieces of **Donatello**. When Michelangelo's maudlin self-absorption and the Mannerists' empty virtuosity begin to seem tiresome, a visit to this room, to the profound clarity of the greatest of Renaissance sculptors, will prove a welcome antidote. Donatello's originality and vision are strikingly modern – and mysterious. Unlike Michelangelo, who went so far as to commission his own biography when Vasari's didn't please him, Donatello left few traces, not only of his long life, but of what may have been the sources of inspiration behind his three most celebrated works displayed here. The chivalric young *St George* (1416) is from the façade of Orsanmichele; his alert watchfulness, or *prontezza*, created new possibilities in expressing movement, emotion and depth of character in stone. Note the accompanying bas-relief of the gallant saint slaying the dragon, a masterful and very early work in perspective.

Donatello's fascinatingly androgynous bronze *David*, obviously not from the same planet as Michelangelo's *David*, is young, cool and suave, and conquers his Goliath more by his charming enigmatic smile than by his muscles. Cast for Cosimo il Vecchio in 1430, this was the first free-standing nude figure since antiquity, and one of the most erotic, exploring depths of the Florentine psyche that the Florentines probably didn't know they had.

The same erotic energy and mystery surrounds the laughing, dangerous-looking, precocious boy Cupid, or *Atys Amor*; with its poppies, serpents and winged sandals, it could easily be the ancient idol people mistook it for in the 1700s. Like Botticelli's mythological paintings, Cupid is part of the artistic and intellectual undercurrents of the period, full of pagan philosophy, a possibility rooted out in the terror of the Counter-Reformation and quite forgotten soon after.

Other Donatellos in the *salone* further display the sculptor's amazing versatility. The small, rather haughty marble *David* (1408) is his earliest known work – he was about 20 at the time. In the centre of the hall, his *Marzocco*, the symbol of Florence, long stood on the Ponte Vecchio. Although the two versions of Florence's patron saint, *John the Baptist*, are no longer attributed to Donatello, they show his influence in their desire to express the saint's spiritual character physically rather than by merely adding his usual holy accessories. The *Dancing Putto* and two busts are Donatello's; his workshop produced the gilded bas-relief of the Crucifixion.

On the wall hang the two famous trial reliefs for the second set of Baptistry doors, by Ghiberti and Brunelleschi, both depicting the *Sacrifice of Isaac*. Between the panels, the vigorous relief of a tumultuous *Battle Scene* is by the little-known Bertoldo di Giovanni, Donatello's pupil and Michelangelo's teacher. There are a number of other excellent reliefs and busts along the walls, by Agostino di Duccio and Desiderio da Settignano, and Luca della Robbia's sweet Madonnas.

First Floor

The remainder of the first floor houses fascinating collections of **decorative arts** donated to the Bargello. The **Sala della Torre** is devoted to Islamic art. The **Sala Carrand**, named after the French donator, contains splendiferous Byzantine and Renaissance jewellery, watches and clocks, and a Venetian astrolabe. Off this room is the **Cappella del Podestà** where the condemned were given their last rites, while their eyes were filled with a fresco of the Last Judgement by the school of Giotto, discovered under the plaster in the 1840s; note the scene of Paradise, which includes the earliest known portrait of Dante, with his piercing gaze and eagle's beak nose.

Some of the most interesting items are in the next rooms, especially the works in the **ivory collection** – Carolingian and Byzantine diptychs, an 8th-century whalebone coffer from Northumbria adorned with runes, medieval French miniatures chronicling 'The Assault on the Castle of Love', 11th-century chess pieces, and more.

Second Floor

A stairway from the ivory collection leads up to the second floor, where you'll find a colourful array of enamelled terracottas from the della Robbia family workshop, a room of portrait busts, beautiful works by Antonio Pollaiuolo and Verrocchio, including his *David* and a bust of the lovely *Young Lady with a Nosegay*, with her hint of a smile and long, sensitive fingers. There is also a collection of armour, and the most important collection of small Renaissance bronzes in Italy.

Badia Fiorentina E4

Piazza San Firenze, entrance in Via Dante Alighieri; bus A. Open Mon 3–6; voluntary donation.

The beautiful Romanesque campanile of this ancient Benedictine abbey, or Badia, was cited by Dante in the Paradiso. The Badia was founded at the end of the 10th century by the widow of Umberto, the Margrave of Tuscany, and further endowed by their son Ugo, 'the Good Margrave'. Dante would come here to gaze upon Beatrice, and some 50 years after the poet's death, Dante's first biographer, Boccaccio, used the Badia as his forum for innovative public lectures on the text of *The Divine Comedy*. It's surprising today to read that Boccaccio's (and later, the Renaissance's) principal criticism of the work is that Dante chose to write about lofty, sacred things in the vulgar tongue of Tuscany.

Under the celebrated campanile, the Badia is a hotchpotch from too many remodellings. Inside, however, are two beautiful things from the Renaissance: the *Tomb of Count Ugo* (1481) by Mino da Fiesole and the *Madonna Appearing to St Bernard* (1485), a large painting by Filippino Lippi. Through an unmarked door to the right of the choir, you can reach the upper loggia of the **Chiostro degli Aranci**, where the monks grew oranges. Built in the 1430s, it is embellished with a fine series of frescoes on the life of St Benedict, generally thought to be by Rossellino.

Piazza San Firenze E5

Piazza San Firenze, the strangely shaped square that both the Bargello and Badia call home, is named after the large church of **San Firenze**, an imposing ensemble, now partially used as Florence's law courts. Opposite, the **Palazzo Gondi** is a fine Renaissance merchants' palace built by Giuliano da Sangallo in 1489 but completed only in 1884; it's not easy to pick out the discreet 19th-century additions. In 1994, during roadworks, a section of Roman *Florentia*'s walls and a tower were discovered under the Piazza's pavement.

Palazzo Borghese E4

Via Ghibellina 110.

Up from the Bargello, this is one of the finest neoclassical buildings in the city. It was erected in 1822 – for a party in honour of Habsburg Grand Duke Ferdinand III. The host of this famous affair was one of the wealthiest men of his day, the Roman prince Camillo Borghese, husband of Pauline Bonaparte and the man responsible for shipping so many of Italy's artistic treasures off to the Louvre at her brother's behest. Note the Borghese dragons balancing precariously on the cornice.

San Martino del Vescovo E4

Piazza San Martino; bus A. Open Mon–Sat 10–12 and 3–5.

Founded in 986, Dante's parish church of San Martino was rebuilt in 1479 when it became the headquarters of the charitable Compagnia dei Buonuomini. The Compagnia commissioned a follower of Ghirlandaio to paint a series of colourful frescoes on the Life of St Martin and the Works of Charity, scenes which are acted out by quattrocento Florentines, in their own fashions on their own streets. The church also has a fine Byzantine Madonna, and one by Perugino, the latter by a rare surviving *finestra a tromba*, a window used to distribute bread during the plague.

Casa di Dante E4

North up an alley off Via S. Margherita; bus A. Open Mon, Tues and Thurs–Sat 9.30–12.30 and 3.30–6.30, Wed and Sun 9.30am–12.30pm.

Although the house was actually built in 1911 over the ruins of an amputated tower house of the Giuochi family, scholars all agree that the Alighieri lived somewhere close by. Since 1960, this museum dedicated to Dante has made a game attempt to evoke Dante's life and times, in spite of neglect and stingy Florentine low-watt light bulbs. There is a model of Florence as it was in the 13th century, and mock-ups of the battle of Campaldino, where Dante as a soldier fought Arezzo. Near the entrance is an edition of *The Divine Comedy*, all printed in tiny letters on a poster by a mad Milanese. Of the manuscript reproductions, the most interesting is an illumination of the infamous murder of Buondelmonte dei Buondelmonti, with the Ponte Vecchio and a statue of Mars, the original *Marzocco*, in place. Upstairs there are copies of Botticelli's beautiful line illustrations for the *Commedia*.

Santa Margherita de' Cerchi E4

*Via S. Margherita; **bus** A. **Open** daily 10–12 and 3–5.*

This church, built in 1032, is where Dante as a boy first espied the young Beatrice in 1273 and where he would later wed his second choice, Gemma Donati, whose family arms still emblazon the 13th-century porch. Both Beatrice and Gemma were buried here in their family tombs; no trace remains today although you can still see the tombstone of Monna Tessa, Beatrice's nurse.

Museo Nazionale di Antropologia ed Etnologia E4

*Palazzo Nonfinito, Via Proconsolo 12; **bus** A, 14. **Open** Wed–Mon 9am–1pm; **adm** €1.54.*

The Palazzo Nonfinito, begun in 1593 and never completed, holds the first ethnological museum in Italy, founded in 1869. It contains Peruvian mummies, musical instruments collected by Galileo Chini (who decorated the Liberty-style extravaganzas at Viareggio), plus lovely and unusual items made by Japan's mysterious Caucassian people, the Ainu, and Pakistan's Kafiri, and skulls from all over the world.

Next door at No.10 is the elegant **Palazzo Pazzi-Quaratesi**, built in 1472 by Giuliano da Maiano for Jacopo de' Pazzi; it was the headquarters of the banking family that organized the murder conspiracy against Lorenzo and Giuliano de' Medici.

Borgo degli Albizi F4

This fine old street was the ancient Via Cassia, linking Rome with Bologna; it deserves a leisurely stroll for its palaces and perhaps even its boutiques. At No.26, the **Palazzo Ramirez di Montalvo** built by Ammannati in 1568 for Cosimo I's favourite, Antonio Moltalvo, is decorated with elaborate graffito and a de luxe model of Cosimo's coat of arms, although the whole is rather worse for wear, sheltering auctioneers and Florence's Jehovah's Witnesses. You can't miss No.18, the cinquecento **Palazzo Valori**, nicknamed 'Palazzo dei Visacci' or 'Funny Face Palace' for its owner's desire to immortalize Florence's great men (Dante, Boccaccio, Vespucci, Alberti, etc.) with surreal, semi-relief herm-busts in blue draperies on three floors of the façade. Borgo degli Albizi ends up in one of Florence's most picturesque little squares, **Piazza San Pier Maggiore**; only the arched portico remains of the church that once stood here and had to be destroyed in 1784 because of its decided lean; the rooms on top of the portico look like one of the cosiest addresses in the city.

West Florence

AROUND SAN LORENZO 96
San Lorenzo 96
Cappelle Medicee 97
San Lorenzo Market 98
Cenacolo di Foligno 98
Palazzo Medici-Riccardi 98

AROUND SANTA MARIA NOVELLA 101
Santa Maria Novella 101
Stazione Centrale 105
The Croce del Trebbio 105

AROUND VIA DE' TORNABUONI 105
Palazzo Rucellai 106
San Pancrazio/Museo Marino Marini 106
Palazzo Strozzi 106

PIAZZA DELLA REPUBBLICA 107
Mercato Nuovo 107
Museo della Casa Fiorentina Antica 108

AROUND SANTA TRÍNITA 109
Santa Trínita 109
Ponte Santa Trínita 110
Piazza Goldoni 111
Galleria Corsini 111
Ognissanti 111

04

West Florence

West ends are so often the fashionable parts of a city (the prevailing winds and the smells they carried is one reason) and medieval Florence was no exception to the rule. The area around San Lorenzo was the stomping ground of the banking family whose members through luck, pluck and bucks hit the jackpot and became Grand Dukes: the Medici palace, chapel and tombs are all in a very small area. Their peers built their huge stone palazzi nearby, off Via de' Tornabuoni, which is now the most prestigious shopping street in Florence. On either side of it are Santa Maria Novella, one of the city's greatest art churches, and Santa Trínita, which has its share of lovely art.

Highlights

Couples' City: Window shop along Via de' Tornabuoni, p.105

Medieval City: Gothic Santa Maria Novella, on the cusp of the Renaissance, p.101

Renaissance City: Michelangelo's tombs and Donatello's pulpits in San Lorenzo, p.96

Medici City: The Palazzo Medici-Riccardi and Gozzoli's charming fresco, p.98

Quirky City: The two heavyweights: Palazzo Strozzi and the Princes' Chapel, pp.106 and 97

1 Lunch

Il Latini, *Via dei Palchetti 6r*, **t** *055 210916*, **w** *www.illatini.com*; **bus** *A, B.* **Open** *Tues–Sun 12.30–2.30 and 7.30–10.30; closed Aug.* ***Moderate***. A Florentine institution, noisy and fun. Their meat dishes are particularly good.

2 Tea and Cakes

Gilli, *Piazza della Repubblica 13–14r*; **bus** *A.* **Open** *Wed–Mon 8am–midnight*. Large historic café that has been going since 1733, with a stunning *belle époque* interior.

3 Drinks

Capocaccia, *Lungarno Corsini 12/14r*, **t** *055 210751*; **bus** *A, B.* **Open** *Tues–Sun noon–2am*. This is an elegant and popular bar that in summer spills out onto the Lungarno.

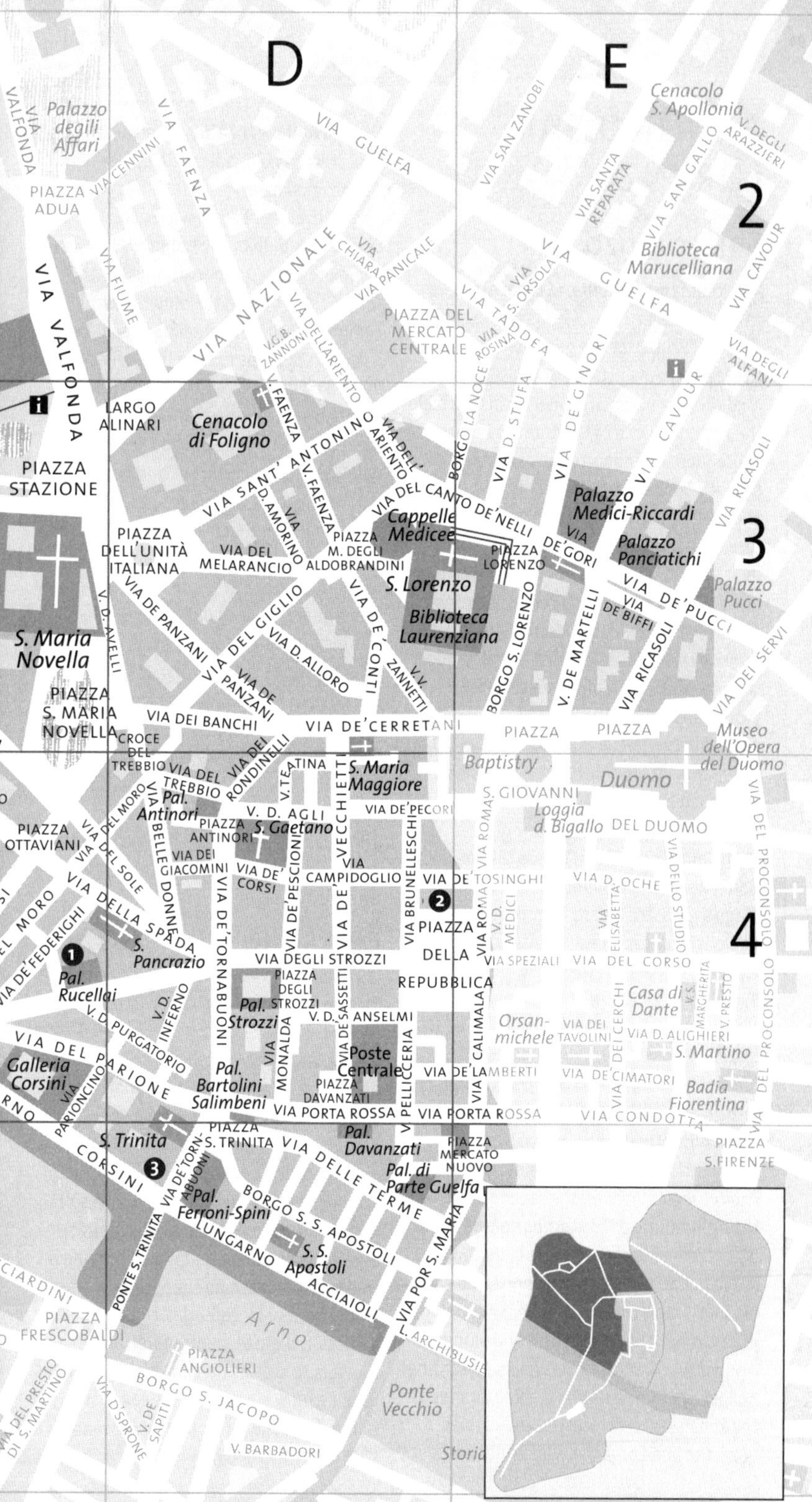

D
E
2
3
4
Cenacolo S. Apollonia
Palazzo degli Affari
Biblioteca Marucelliana
Piazza Adua
Piazza del Mercato Centrale
Largo Alinari
Cenacolo di Foligno
Piazza Stazione
Cappelle Medicee
Palazzo Medici-Riccardi
Palazzo Panciatichi
Palazzo Pucci
Piazza dell'Unità Italiana
Piazza M. degli Aldobrandini
Piazza S. Lorenzo
S. Lorenzo
Biblioteca Laurenziana
S. Maria Novella
Piazza S. Maria Novella
Croce del Trebbio
S. Maria Maggiore
Baptistry
Duomo
Museo dell'Opera del Duomo
Piazza S. Giovanni
Piazza del Duomo
Loggia d. Bigallo
Pal. Antinori
Piazza Antinori
S. Gaetano
Piazza Ottaviani
Piazza della Repubblica
S. Pancrazio
Pal. Rucellai
Piazza degli Strozzi
Pal. Strozzi
Casa di Dante
Orsanmichele
S. Martino
Galleria Corsini
Poste Centrale
Pal. Bartolini Salimbeni
Piazza Davanzati
Badia Fiorentina
Piazza S. Trinita
S. Trinita
Pal. Davanzati
Piazza Mercato Nuovo
Pal. di Parte Guelfa
Piazza S. Firenze
Pal. Ferroni-Spini
S. S. Apostoli
Piazza Frescobaldi
Piazza Angiolieri
Arno
Ponte Vecchio
Via Valfonda
Via Nazionale
Via Guelfa
Via Faenza
Via Cavour
Via Ricasoli
Via de' Ginori
Via de' Cerretani
Via de' Tornabuoni
Via degli Strozzi
Via Porta Rossa
Via Calzaiuoli
Via del Corso
Via Condotta
Via del Proconsolo
Via dei Servi
Via de' Pucci
Via dei Banchi
Via della Spada
Via del Parione
Lungarno Corsini
Lungarno Acciaioli
Borgo S. S. Apostoli
Via delle Terme
Via Por S. Maria
Ponte S. Trinita
Borgo S. Jacopo
V. Barbadori
Via Roma
Via de' Pecori
Via Speziali
Via de' Lamberti
Via de' Cimatori
Via D. Alighieri

AROUND SAN LORENZO

San Lorenzo D3

Piazza San Lorenzo; ***bus*** *1, 17.* ***Open*** *Mon–Sat 10–5;* ***adm*** *€2.50.*

The lively quarter has been associated with the Medici ever since Giovanni di Bicci de' Medici commissioned Brunelleschi to rebuild the ancient church of San Lorenzo in 1420; subsequent members of the dynasty lavished bushels of florins on its decoration and Medici pantheon, and on several projects commissioned from Michelangelo. The mixed result of all their efforts could be held up as an archetype of the Renaissance, and one which Walter Pater described as 'great rather by what it designed or aspired to do, than by what it actually achieved'.

One can begin with San Lorenzo's façade of corrugated brick, the most *nonfinito* of all of Michelangelo's unfinished projects; commmissioned by Medici Pope Leo X in 1516, the project never got further than Michelangelo's scale model, on display in the Casa Buonarroti. To complete the church's dingy aspect, the piazza in front contains a universally detested 19th-century statue of Cosimo I's dashing father, Giovanni delle Bande Nere, who died at the age of 28 of wounds received fighting against Emperor Charles V.

The **interior**, although completed after Brunelleschi's death, is true to his design, classically calm in good grey *pietra serena*. The artistic treasures it contains are few but choice, beginning with the second chapel on the right housing *The Marriage of the Virgin* (1523) by the Mannerist Rosso Fiorentino. Rosso makes Joseph, usually portrayed as an old man, into a Greek god with golden curls in a flowing scene of hot reds and oranges – a powerful contrast to the chapel's haunting, hollow-eyed tomb slab of the Ray Charles of the Renaissance, Francesco Landini (died 1397), the blind organist whose madrigals were immensely popular and influential. At the end of the right aisle, there's a lovely delicately worked tabernacle by Desiderio da Settignano.

Most riveting of all, however, are **Donatello's pulpits**, the sculptor's last works, completed by his pupils after his death in 1466. Cast in bronze, the pulpits were commissioned by Donatello's friend Cosimo il Vecchio, perhaps to keep the sculptor busy in his old age. Little in Donatello's previous work, however, prepares the viewer for these scenes of Christ's Passion and Resurrection with their rough, distorted, and impressionistic details, their unbalanced, highly emotional and overcrowded compositions, more reminiscent of Rodin than anything Florentine; one critic wrote that they represent 'the first style of old age in the history of art'. Unfortunately they were set up on columns in the 17th century, just above eye level, like so many things in Florence, a fault somewhat redeemed by a new lighting system. Nearby, directly beneath the dome, lies buried Donatello's patron and Florence's original godfather, Cosimo il Vecchio; the grille over his grave bears the Medici arms and the simple inscription, *Pater Patriae*, 'the Father of his Country'.

Old Sacristy

It was the godfather's father, Giovanni di Bicci de' Medici, who in 1420 commissioned Brunelleschi to build the Old Sacristy off the left transept. Often cited as one of the first and finest works of the early Renaissance, Brunelleschi designed this cube of a sacristy according to carefully calculated mathematical proportions, emphasized with a colour scheme of white walls, articulated in soft grey *pietra serena* pilasters and cornices; a dignified decoration that would become his trademark, something Florentine architects would borrow for centuries. Donatello contributed the terracotta tondi and lunettes, as well as the bronze doors, embellished with lively Apostles. The Sacristy was built to hold the sarcophagi of Giovanni di Bicci de' Medici and his wife; in 1472 Lorenzo il

Magnifico and his brother Giuliano had Verrocchio design the beautiful bronze and red porphyry wall tomb for their father Piero the Gouty and their uncle Giovanni. Unfortunately Verrocchio saw fit to place this in front of Brunelleschi's original door, upsetting the careful balance.

The **chapel** across the transept from the entrance to the Old Sacristy houses a 19th-century monument to Donatello, who was buried here at his request near Cosimo il Vecchio. The lovely *Annunciation* is by Filippo Lippi; the large, colourful fresco of the *Martyrdom of St Lawrence* around the corner in the aisle is by Bronzino and has just been restored. Just beyond the Bronzino a door leads into the 15th-century **cloister**.

Biblioteca Laurenziana

***Access from the cloister. Open** Mon–Sat 8.30–1.30; **adm** free.*

If Brunelleschi's Old Sacristy heralded the Renaissance, Michelangelo's library is Mannerism's prototype, or Brunelleschi gone haywire, no longer serene and mathematically perfect, but complicated and restless, the architectural elements stuck on with an eye for effect rather than for any structural purpose. The vestibule barely contains the remarkable stair, flowing down from the library like a stone cascade, built by Ammannati after a drawing by Michelangelo. This grand entrance leads into a fabulous collection of books begun by Cosimo de' Medici and includes a very rare 5th-century Virgil and other Greek and Latin codices, beautifully illuminated manuscripts, and the original manuscript of Cellini's autobiography; ask for a look around.

Cappelle Medicee D3

***Piazza Madonna degli Aldobrandini (behind San Lorenzo church); bus** 1, 17. **Open** daily 8.15–5; closed the second and fourth Sun and the first, third and fifth Mon of the month; **adm** €6.*

The entrance to the Medici chapels leads through the crypt, a dark and austere place where many of the Medici are actually buried, the Archdukes with their jewelled crowns on their heads and their sceptres at their side. Their main monument to themselves, the family obsession, is just up the steps: the **Chapel of the Princes**, a stupefying, fabulously costly octagon of death that, as much as the Grand Dukes fussed over it, lends their memory an unpleasant aftertaste of cancerous bric-a-brac that grew and grew. Perhaps only a genuine Medici could love its insane, trashy opulence; all of Grand Duke Cosimo's descendants, down to the last, Anna Maria Ludovica, worked like beavers to finish it according to the plans left by Cosimo's illegitimate son, dilettante architect Giovanni de' Medici. Yet even today it is only partially completed, the *pietre dure* extending only part of the way up the walls. The 19th-century frescoes in the cupola are a poor substitute for the originally planned *Apotheosis of the Medici* in lapis lazuli, and the two statues in gilded bronze in the niches over the sarcophagi (each niche large enough to hold a hippopotamus) are nothing like the intended figures to be carved in semi-precious stone. Inlaid *pietra dura* arms of Tuscan towns subjected by the Medici provide the best of the interior decoration, topped by the family arms, with their familiar six red boluses blown up as big as beachballs. These balls probably derive from the family's origins as pharmacists (*medici*), and opponents sneeringly called them 'the pills'. Medici supporters, however, made them their battle cry in street fights: 'Balls! Balls! Balls!'

New Sacristy

A passageway leads to Michelangelo's New Sacristy, commissioned by Leo X to occupy an unfinished room built to balance Brunelleschi's Old Sacristy. Michelangelo's first idea was to turn it into a new version of his unfinished, lamented overly ambitious Pope Julius tomb in Rome, a hope quickly quashed by his Medici patrons, who requested instead four wall tombs. Michelangelo managed to finish two, as well as the New Sacristy itself, creating a silent and gloomy mausoleum, closed in and grey, a chilly introspective cocoon that can depress even the chattiest tour groups.

Nor are the famous tombs guaranteed to cheer. Both honour nonentities: that of *Night and Day* belongs to Lorenzo il Magnifico's son, Giuliano, the Duke of Nemours, and symbolizes the Active Life, while the *Dawn and Dusk* is of Guiliano's nephew, Lorenzo, Duke of Urbino (and dedicatee of *The Prince*), who symbolizes the Contemplative Life (true to life in one respect – Lorenzo was a disappointment to Machiavelli and everyone else, passively obeying the dictates of his uncle Pope Leo X). Idealized statues of the two men, in Roman patrician gear, represent these states of mind, while draped on their sarcophagi are Michelangelo's four allegorical figures, *The Times of Day*, so heavy with weariness and grief they seem ready to slide off onto the floor. The most finished figure, *Night*, has always impressed the critics; she is almost a personification of despair, the mouthpiece of Michelangelo's most bitter verse:

Sweet to me is sleep, and even more to be like stone
While wrong and shame endure;
Not to see, nor to feel, is my good fortune.
Therefore, do not wake me; speak softly here.

Both statues of the dukes look towards the back wall, where a large double tomb for Lorenzo il Magnifico and his brother Giuliano was originally planned, to be decorated with river gods. The only part of this tomb ever completed is the statue of the *Madonna and Child* now in place, accompanied by the Medici family patrons, the doctor saints *Cosmas and Damian*.

In 1975, charcoal drawings were discovered on the walls of the little room off the altar. They were attributed to Michelangelo, who may have hidden here in 1530, when the Medici had regained Florence and would only forgive the artist for aiding the republicans if he finished their tombs. But Michelangelo had had enough of their ducal pretences and went to Rome, never to return to Florence. Ask at the cash desk for a permit to see the drawings, as only 12 people can enter at one time.

San Lorenzo Market D3

Via dell'Ariento and around. Food market Mon–Sat 7–2 and Sat pm; clothes market Mon–Sat 8.30–7.

What makes the neighbourhood around San Lorenzo so lively is its street market, which the Florentines run with an almost Neapolitan flamboyance. Stalls selling clothes and leather extend from the square up Via dell'Ariento and vicinity (nicknamed 'Shanghai') towards the **Mercato Centrale**, Florence's main food market, a cast-iron and glass confection of the 1870s, brimful of fresh fruit and vegetables upstairs, and leering boars' heads and mounds of tripe on the ground floor.

Cenacolo di Foligno D3

Via Faenza 42; ***bus*** *1, 17, 22, 29.* ***Open*** ***by appointment, t*** *055 286982, Mon–Sat 9–12; ring bell.*

In the 1490s, the great Umbrian painter Perugino painted a Last Supper in the refectory of the Florentine convent of the Tertiary Franciscans of Foligno. It was rediscovered only in the 1850s, and has recently been restored.

Palazzo Medici-Riccardi E3

Via Cavour 3; ***bus*** *1, 17.* ***Open*** *Thurs–Tues 9–7;* ***adm*** *€4.*

The early Medici, in sharp contrast to their archducal descendants, were fairly publicity shy. Cosimo il Vecchio, the richest man in Europe, walked about the streets in simple attire, and never with a bodyguard. But in the 1440s, when his business became too big for his father's house in Piazza del Duomo, he decided it was time for a new palace, bought a site on the widest street in Florence and asked Brunelleschi to design it. His wooden model was so splendid that Cosimo was embarrassed, and asked Michelozzo to come up with something more discreet. Brunelleschi in rage broke his model into bits.

Michelozzo's palace was a landmark in Florentine architecture. Until then, the mansions of the elite resembled little fortresses (see the Palazzo Spini, in Piazza Santa Trínita); Michelozzo did away with the towers and battlements, and instead created a far more classical structure. One of his innovations was the rusticated ground floor 'to unite an appearance of solidity and strength, with the light and shadow so essential to beauty under the glare of the Italian sun'. This was the Medici bank headquarters, where Cosimo stowed his florins, and it originally had no windows. The two upper floors, where the family lived, are considerably lighter with their arched bays of windows; the top floor was originally an open loggia (the 'kneeling windows' that glassed it in were designed by Michelangelo) and the huge overhanging cornice was inspired by Roman temples. Others, like the Rucellai, Strozzi and Pitti, would be far grander, but stylistically all begin here with Michelozzo.

This would be the principal address of the Medici for a hundred years, home to Florence's unofficial court, where ambassadors would call, kings would lodge, and important decisions would be made, until Cosimo I abandoned it in favour of larger quarters in the Palazzo Vecchio and the Pitti Palace. In 1659 the Riccardi purchased the palace, enlarged it and did everything to keep it glittering until Napoleon and his debts drove them to bankruptcy in 1809. The palace is now used as the prefecture.

In their day, the Medici lived with the likes of Donatello's delightful *David*, and his *Judith and Holofernes*, Uccello's *Battle of San Romano* and other masterpieces now in the Uffizi and Bargello. Frescoes are much harder to move, however, and the Palazzo Medici has one of the most charming ones in Italy, Benozzo Gozzoli's 1459 *Procession of the Magi*, located in the **Cappella dei Magi** upstairs (*open daily exc Wed 9–7; adm €4; you can reserve a time,* ***t*** *055 276 0340*).

Painting in a delightful, decorative manner more reminiscent of International Gothic than the awakening Renaissance style of his contemporaries, Gozzoli created a merry, brilliantly coloured pageant of beautifully dressed kings, knights and pages, accompanied by greyhounds and a giraffe, who travel through a springtime landscape of jewel-like trees and castles; wrapped around three walls of the small chapel to create a glowing fairytale world. The 'Three Kings' lead the annual pageant of the *Compagnia dei Magi*, Florence's richest confraternity. Most of the identifiable figures are of the Medici family, or celebrities who came to Florence in the Council of 1439 (*see* box overleaf): on the wall in front of the altar, surrounded by pages, is the melancholy Byzantine Emperor John VII Palaeologos in his unique head dress, while behind him ride three teenage daughters of Piero the Gouty. Their 10-year-old brother Lorenzo il Magnifico is the idealized young king in front, dressed in gold (note the Medici balls on the horse's trappings) followed by Cosimo il Vecchio on the white horse bearing the motto '*semper*'; his brother Lorenzo rides next to him on a mule. The Magnificent Lorenzo's younger brother Giuliano rides the pale horse with the star, and next to him, their hatless father, Piero the Gouty. Gozzoli, who would never again paint anything as splendid, certainly had no qualms about identifying himself among the crowd of figures in the back ground, between two Greek scholars, with 'opus Benotii' written on his red cap. In the foreground, note the black man carrying a bow. Blacks, as well as Turks, Circassians, Tartars and others, were common enough in Renaissance Florence, who could legally be bought as slaves after a plague in 1336 left an acute shortage of servants. By the 1400s, however, contemporary writers mention them as artisans, fencing masters, soldiers and one famous archery instructor, who may be the man pictured here.

The Council of Florence

That this council, a last ditch attempt to heal the old schism between the Western and Eastern churches in 1438–39, happened in Florence had much to do with Europe's richest man, Cosimo de' Medici, offering to foot the bill. Cosimo wanted Florence to have the prestige of hosting the long awaited reconciliation of Christendom, but he wasn't immune, either, to the possibilities the council would give him of arranging new business deals in the east.

The Greek party of 700 officials, scholars, theologians and interpreters was led by the Patriarch of Constantinople and the Emperor John VII Palaeologos, who was anxious to sort out the irritating doctrinal differences so the west would send him aid against the Ottoman Turks. The Western delegation was led by Pope Eugenius IV, a friend of Cosimo's. But his first city of choice was Ferrara – before the huge expense of hosting so many guests and an outbreak of plague drove the pope to accept Cosimo's offer.

The Florentines marvelled at their exotic, sumptuously costumed guests, their Mongol servants and rare animals, many of whom found their way into paintings – as in Gozzoli's fresco in the Medici palace. Much of the serious business, however, took place in Santa Maria Novella, where the Pope's party lodged and council committee meetings were held. Here, after very subtle negotiations between the advisors of the Pope and Patriarch, a compromise on the main sticking point between the two churches – the nature of the Holy Ghost – was reached, and on 6 July 1439 there was a moving announcement in the cathedral that 'the wall which divided the Western and Eastern Churches has fallen. Peace and concord have returned.' Florence celebrated, but when the Emperor returned to Constantinople, the Council's compromises were blasted and had to be retracted. Nor did any of the vaguely promised aid against the Turks ever arrive from Italy, and in 1453 Contantinople fell.

The visiting Greeks, however, inspired more than colourful costumes in Florentine art. Among the dignitaries who accompanied the emperor were Gemistos Plethon and his student Johannes Bessarion, both leading scholars of Plato at a time when the philosopher was merely known as the name of Aristotle's teacher in the west. Plethon, although a friend of the emperor, was regarded with deep suspicion by the Orthodox establishment who thought he took Plato and classicism too far by advocating a return to the glory (and pagan) days of Greek civilization. As Machiavelli later would, he advised the emperors on how to run a proper city-state, while his increasingly esoteric philosophy combined Christianity with symbols of classical polytheism – Christ infused with the spirit of Apollo.

During the Council, Plethon and Bessarion often gave talks about Plato in the evenings. Cosimo and his humanist friends ate it up, and when Cosimo asked the two scholars to stay on in Florence after the Council, they did (Bessarion settled in Italy for good, and became a cardinal). Before Plethon left for Greece, he wrote a treatise for the Florentines, comparing the philosphies of Plato and Aristotle.

Fired with enthusiasm, Cosimo sponsored a Latin translation of Plato from his pet scholar Marsilio Ficino; he opened up his fabulous library so his friends could study freely, and he founded the Platonic Academy in Villa Careggi (*see* p.150). Plethon's more esoteric musings, nursed along by Ficino, would also have descendants in Renaissance philosophy, literature and art, including much that seems strange and enigmatic to us because we've lost the key – as in Botticelli's mythologies (*see* p.83).

The altarpiece, a copy of a *Madonna* by Filippo Lippi, has just been restored and is now housed in the room dedicated to Sidney Sonnino. This forms the antechamber to the other room of the palace opened to visitors, the **Gallery**, located up the second flight of stairs on the right from the courtyard. It's hard to imagine a more striking contrast than that between Gozzoli and the Neapolitan Luca Giordano (nicknamed *Luca fa presto* or 'Quick-draw Luke'), who painted this hilarious ceiling for the Riccardi in 1683, as a left-handed compliment to the Medici for selling them the palace. No longer mere players in a religious pageant, the Medici, or at least the over-stuffed Grand Duke Cosimo III and his unspeakable heir Gian Gastone, take the leading roles, defying the laws of gravity and good taste in an apotheosis of marshmallow clouds.

AROUND SANTA MARIA NOVELLA

Santa Maria Novella C3

Piazza S. Maria Novella; bus A, 1, 17. Open Mon–Thurs and Sat 9.30–5, Fri and Sun 1–5; adm €2.58.

As in Venice and so many other Italian cities, the two churches of the great medieval preaching orders – the Dominicans' Santa Maria Novella and the Franciscans' Santa Croce – became the largest and most prestigious in the city, where wealthy families vied to create the most beautiful chapels and tombs.

Santa Maria Novella has the prettier face – the stupendous black and white marble **façade** is the finest in Florence. The lower section, with its looping arcades, is Romanesque work in the typical Tuscan mode, finished before 1360. In 1456 Giovanni Rucellai commissioned Alberti to complete it, a remarkably fortunate choice. Alberti's upper half not only perfectly harmonizes with the original, but perfects it with geometrical harmonies to create a kind of Renaissance sun temple. To Alberti it seemed a logical progression: the original builders had oriented Santa Maria to the south instead of the usual west, so that at noon the sun streams through the 14th-century rose window. The only symbol Alberti put on the façade is a blazing sun; the unusual sundials, over the arches on the extreme right and left, were added by Cosimo I's court astronomer Egnazio Danti. Note how the base of the façade is also the base of an equilateral triangle, with Alberti's sun at the apex.

The beautiful frieze depicts the Rucellai emblem (a billowing sail), as on the Palazzo Rucellai. The wall of Gothic recesses to the right, enclosing the old cemetery, are *avelli*, or family tombs.

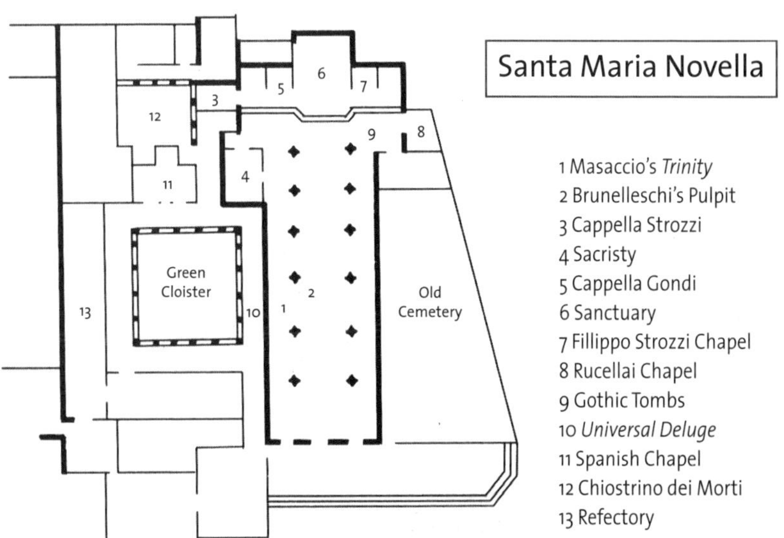

The Disenchantment of the World

Death was on everyone's mind when the Great Plague rolled through Italy in 1348. In art, the most striking memories of those harrowing days are the powerful frescoes by the Master of the Triumph of Death in Pisa's Campo Santo; in literature, no account surpasses Boccaccio's introduction to his masterpiece, *The Decameron*, the 'Human Comedy' that complements *The Divine Comedy* of his fellow Florentine.

Boccaccio, the son of a prosperous banker, was the first great writer from the urban middle class. Born either in Florence or in the Florentine town of Certaldo in 1313, he spent much of his youth in the literate, art-loving court of Robert of Anjou in Naples. He returned to Florence shortly before 1348, when the sight of the bodies of plague victims piled in the street sent deep cracks into his belief about the divinely ordered medieval cosmos that he had been reared on and loved in *The Divine Comedy*. Boccaccio's great feat would be to disenchant Dante's world in the most entertaining way possible.

He takes a detached view of the great theatre of life from the very beginning of *The Decameron*. Despite the Church's claims that the plague was 'a punishment signifying God's righteous anger at our iniquitous way of life', Boccaccio notes that in fact it was a highly contagious disease that had come out of the East, and that fate and chance alone seemed to spare some Florentines while others were struck down whether they responded to the plague by praying for deliverance, hiding out, or living riotously as if there would be no tomorrow.

His ten young storytellers gather in Santa Maria Novella and escape the plague for a country villa, where they pass the days by telling tales. These stories sparkle with a secular, spunky vitality and sense of humour that is fresh and new; sex, for the first time in literature, becomes a pleasurable end in itself. Fate and chance, however, decide most of the plots and outcomes of the hundred tales they tell; with few exceptions, the belief in the just outcome of human endeavour is an illusion.

In his old age Boccaccio wrote exclusively in Latin and earned himself a reputation as one of the great humanists of the 14th century, regretting the frivolity of *The Decameron* in his old age. As Giuliano Procacci wrote, 'He put himself in the position of a calmly objective recorder of life's dramas and chances; it was a difficult and exhausting mental standpoint, and a new one, demanding nervous energy and courage. Is it any wonder that Boccaccio too, in his premature old age, should have sought comfort and refuge in study and piety?'

For a century after Boccaccio Florence led the world in humanistic thought. The horrors of the plague were forgotten as victories in diplomacy and the battlefield, a hitherto unknown prosperity, and tremendous strides in architecture, art and science made the city radiate confidence. The fatalism of *The Decameron* seemed unduly pessimistic by the end of the 15th century. The humanists were keenly aware of Florence's special destiny, as described by Leonardo Bruni in his proud, patriotic *Laudatio Florentinae Urbis* or in Coloccio Salutati's 'What city, not merely in Italy but in the whole world, is stronger within the circle of its walls, prouder in palaces, richer in temples, more lovely in buildings... Where is trade richer in its variety, abler in subtle understandings? Where are there more famous men?' – brave new words before the mass neurotic religious revival orchestrated by Savonarola and the return of the wrath of God as the prime mover. Even Pico della Mirandola, the most optimistic of humanists, himself fell under the fanatic's spell.

Florence was never the same, and the repercussions were dire: for a city that practically invented humanism to toss its books and art in the proto-Ayatollah's bonfire of the vanities cast long shadows onto everyone's future. Don't forget that only in the 20th century has *The Decameron* been translated complete with all the naughty bits.

The Interior

The interior is vast, lofty and more Gothic in feel than any other church in Florence. No thanks to Vasari, though, who was set loose to remodel the church to 16th-century taste, painting over the original frescoes, removing the rood screen and Dominicans' choir from the nave, and remodelling the altars. Then in the 1800s restorers did their best to de-Vasari Santa Maria with neo-Gothic details. Neither party, however, could touch two of the interior's most distinctive features – the striking stone vaulting of the nave and the perspective created by the columns marching down the aisles, each pair placed a little closer together as they approach the altar.

Over the portal is a fresco lunette by Botticelli that has recently been restored, as well as an anonymous 14th-century *Annunciation* in an elaborate 'Tuscan' frame. Santa Maria Novella's best-known fresco is over the third altar on the left (although the altar itself has now been removed): Masaccio's recently restored *Trinity*, painted around 1425, a key work of the Renaissance. This is the first known fresco that makes use of perspective as demonstrated by Brunelleschi: even today you can make out the spot just under the cross where Masaccio stuck a nail into the wall to mark the vanishing point, and the strings he pressed into the plaster to use as guides. Combined with his pioneering use of architectural elements, derived from Brunelleschi's Spedale degli Innocenti, the perpective lends his composition a novel physical and intellectual depth. The flat wall becomes a deeply recessed chapel, calm and classical, enclosed in a coffered barrel vault, dominated by a commanding figure of God the Father; at the foot of the fresco a bleak skeleton decays in its tomb, bearing a favourite Tuscan reminder: 'I was that which you are, you will be that which I am.' Above this morbid suggestion of physical death kneel the two donors; within the celestially rational inner sanctum the Virgin and St John stand at the foot of the Cross, providing humanity's link with the mystery of the Trinity.

Brunelleschi designed the pulpit nearby, where Galileo was first denounced by the Inquisition (and whispered his perhaps apocryphal *eppur si muove* (*see* p.199). There is little else to detain you in the aisles, but don't miss the elevated chapel in the left transept, the **Cappella Strozzi**. This is one of the most evocative corners of 14th-century Florence, frescoed entirely by Nardo di Cione and his brother, Andrea Orcagna. On the vault pictures of *St Thomas Aquinas and the Virtues* are echoed in Andrea's lovely altarpiece *The Redeemer Donating the Keys to St Peter and the Book of Wisdom to St Thomas Aquinas*; on the left wall there's a crowded scene of Paradise, with the righteous lined up in a medieval school class photograph. On the right wall, Nardo painted a striking view of Dante's *Inferno*, with all of a Tuscan's special attention to precise map-like detail.

Giotto's recently restored *Crucifix* (*c*.1300), one of the artist's first works, hangs very dramatically in the middle of the nave, suspended from the ceiling. You can compare it, in the **Gondi Chapel**, to another famous *Crucifix*, carved in wood by Brunelleschi, which, according to Vasari, so astonished his friend Donatello that when he first set eyes upon it, he dropped all the eggs he was carrying in his apron for their lunch.

The charming fresco cycle in the **Sanctuary** (1485–90), painted by Domenico Ghirlandaio, portrays the *Lives of the Virgin, St John the Baptist and the Dominican Saints* in magnificent architectural settings; little Michelangelo was among the students who helped him complete it. Nearly all of the bystanders are portraits of Florentine quattrocento VIPs, including the artist himself (in the red hat, in the *Expulsion of St Joachim from the Temple*), but most prominent are the ladies and gents of the Tornabuoni house. More excellent frescoes adorn the **Filippo Strozzi Chapel**, the finest work ever to come from the brush of Filippino Lippi, painted in 1502 near the end of his life; the exaggerated, dark and violent scenes portray the lives of *St Philip* (his crucifixion and his subduing of the dragon before the Temple of Mars, which creates such a stench it kills the heathen prince) and of *St John the Evangelist* (raising Drusiana from the dead and being martyred in boiling oil). The chapel's beautifully carved tomb of Filippo Strozzi is by Benedetto da Maiano.

The **Rucellai Chapel** contains a marble statue of the Madonna by Nino Pisano and a fine bronze tomb by Ghiberti. Of the three Gothic tombs nearby in the right transept, one contains the remains of the Patriarch of Constantinople, who died in the city in 1439 during the Council of Florence (*see* p.100).

The Cloisters

Entrance just to the left of the church. Open Mon–Thurs 9–2, Sat and Sun 8–1; adm €2.58.

More great frescoes await in Santa Maria Novella's cloisters, all recently restored and open as a city museum. The first cloister, the **Green Cloister** (*c.* 1440) is one of the masterpieces of Paolo Uccello, deriving its name from the *terraverde* or green earth pigment used by the artist, which lends the scenes from Genesis their eerie, ghostly quality. Much damaged by time and neglect, they are nevertheless striking for their two Uccellian obsessions – perspective and animals, the latter stealing the scene of the *Creation*. His well-preserved *Universal Deluge* verges on the surreal, a picture framed by not one but two arks (symbolizing the Eastern and Western churches, which were briefly united at the Council of Florence), whose steep walls have the uncanny effect of making the scene race out of its own vanishing point, a vanishing point touched by divine wrath in a searing bolt of lightning. In between the claustrophobic arks the flood rises, tossing up a desperate ensemble of humanity, waterlogged bodies, naked men bearing clubs, crowded in a jam of flotsam and jetsam and islets rapidly receding in the dark waters. In the right foreground, amidst the panic and under a dove of peace, stands a tall robed man, recently identified as Cosimo il Vecchio (Florence's Noah, saving all on the ship of state) while a flood victim seizes him by the ankles. Some of Uccello's favourite perspective studies were of headgear, especially the wooden hoops called *mazzocchi* which he puts around the necks and on the heads of his figures like life savers.

The **Spanish Chapel**, where the Inquisition had its headquarters in Florence, opens up at the far end of the cloisters and takes its name from the Spanish court followers of Eleonora di Toledo who worshipped here. This chapel, too, is famous for its frescoes, the masterpiece of a 14th-century artist named Andrea di Buonaiuto, whose subject was the Dominican cosmology, perhaps not something we have much empathy for these days, but here beautifully portrayed so that even the *Hounds of the Lord* (a pun on the Order's name, the 'Domini canes') on the right wall seem more like pets than militant bloodhounds sniffing out heresy. The church behind the scene with the hounds is a fairy pink confection of what Buonaiuto imagined the Duomo would look like when finished; it may well be Arnolfo di Cambio's original conception. Famous Florentines, including Giotto, Dante, Boccaccio and Petrarch, stand to the right of the dais supporting the pope, emperor and various sour-faced hierophants. Off to the right the artist has portrayed four rather urbane looking Vices with dancing girls, while the Dominicans lead stray sheep back to the fold. On the left wall, *St Thomas Aquinas* dominates the portrayal of the Contemplative Life, surrounded by Virtues and Doctors of the Church.

The oldest part of the monastery, the **Chiostrino dei Morti** (1270s), contains some 14th-century frescoes, while the **Great Cloister** beyond is now off limits, the property of the Carabinieri, the new men in black charged with keeping the Italians orthodox. Off the Green Cloister, the **Refectory** is a striking hall with cross vaulting and frescoes by Alessandro Allori, now serving as a museum of fresco fragments and bits and pieces from the church.

Piazza Santa Maria Novella C3

By some twitch of city planning, both of the city's sacred art galleries of Santa Maria Novella and Santa Croce dominate broad, stale squares that do not invite lingering. In the irregular Piazza Santa Maria Novella you may even find yourself looking over your shoulder for the ghosts of the carriages that once raced madly around the two stout obelisks set on turtles, just as in a Roman circus, in the fashionable carriage races of the 1700s. The arcade on the south side, the **Loggia di San Paolo**, was modelled after Brunelleschi's Spedale degli Innocenti; the lunette over the door, by Andrea della Robbia, is *The Meeting of SS. Francis and Dominic*.

Stazione Centrale C2

*Piazza Stazione; **bus** 1, 7, 2, and many others.*

Just behind, but a world apart from Santa Maria Novella, another large, amorphous square detracts from one of modern Italy's finest buildings – Florence's Stazione Centrale, designed by the Tuscan Giovanni Michelucci in 1935. Adorned by only a glass block canopy at the entrance (and an early model of that great Italian invention, the digital clock), the station is nevertheless remarkable for its clean lines and impeccable practicality; form following function in a way that even Brunelleschi would have appreciated.

The Croce del Trebbio D4

*Via delle Belle Donne; **bus** A.*

Via delle Belle Donne, one of the medieval lanes leading south from Piazza Santa Maria Novella, was once famed for its brothels. Today it has one of the few crossroads in Italy marked by a cross, a Celtic custom that never caught on here – an Italian would much prefer a corner shrine to the Madonna. The origins of the Croce del Trebbio (from trivium, 'three roads') are a bit sinister: it marks the spot of a massacre of Patarene heretics in the 1240s, after a sermon delivered by the fire-eating Inquistor St Peter Martyr from the pulpit of Santa Maria Novella.

AROUND VIA DE' TORNABUONI

The streets between Santa Maria Novella and Piazza Santa Trínita have always been the choicest district of Florence, and Via de' Tornabuoni the city's smartest shopping street. Milan's current status as headquarters of Italy's fashion industry is a sore point with Florence, which used to be top dog and lost its position in the 1970s for lack of a large international airport. Florence, in a few words, wants its business back. Pitti Uomo, the biannual men's ready-to-wear trade fair, is now the most important event of its kind in Italy, and the increase in traffic at the local airport has made the city considerably more accessible. Via de' Tornabuoni and the surrounding streets sport window displays that could hold their own anywhere.

In the bright and ambitious 1400s, when Florence was the centre of European high finance, Via de' Tornabuoni and its environs was the area the new merchant élite chose for their palaces. Today's bankers build great skyscrapers for the firm and settle for modest mansions for themselves; in Florence's heyday, things were reversed. Bankers and wool tycoons really owned their businesses. Their homes were imposing city palaces, often with their offices on the ground floor, all built in the same conservative style and competing with each other in size like some Millionaires' Row in 19th-century America.

At the north end of Via de' Tornabuoni stands the beautiful golden **Palazzo Antinori** (1465, architect unknown), home to one of Tuscany's most prolific wine-producing families; it has the city's grandest Baroque church **San Gaetano** (1648, by Gherardo Silvani) as its equally golden companion, its façade decorated with statues that would fit alright in Rome but look like bad actors in Florence. Further along is the Gucci boutique, where George Eliot lived in 1860.

Palazzo Rucellai C4

Via della Vigna Nuova 18; bus A.

Just off Via de' Tornabuoni, the Palazzo Rucellai is the most celebrated example of domestic architecture in Florence. Its builder, Giovanni Rucellai, was a quattrocento tycoon (he made his fortune, and derived his name, from *oricello*, the celebrated Florentine red dye) and an intellectual, whose *Zibaldone* or commonplace book is one of the best sources available on the life and tastes of the educated Renaissance merchant. In 1446 Rucellai chose his favourite architect, Leon Battista Alberti, to design his palace. Actually built by Bernardo Rossellino, it follows Alberti's precepts and theories in its use of the three classical orders; instead of the usual rusticated stone, the façade has a far more delicate decoration of incised irregular blocks and a frieze, elements that would influence subsequent Italian architecture – though far more noticeably in Rome than Florence itself. Originally the palace was only five bays wide, and when another two bays were added later the edge was left ragged, unfinished: a nice touch, as if the builders could return at any moment and pick up where they left off. The façade's frieze, like that commissioned on Santa Maria Novella by Rucellai, portrays the devices of the Medici and Rucellai families (Giovanni's son married a daughter of Piero the Gouty), a wedding feted in the **Loggia dei Rucellai** across the street, which was also designed by Alberti.

San Pancrazio/Museo Marino Marini D4

Piazza San Pancrazio; bus A. Open Mon and Wed–Sat 10–5, Sun 10–1, plus Thurs 10–11pm in summer; adm €4.

Behind the Rucellai palace stands the ancient church of **San Pancrazio**, with an antique-style porch by Alberti, guarded by two lions so mossy and mouldering that one resembles a St Bernard and the other a muffin. At one point in its up-and-down career the church served as a tobacco factory. Now it's been given a new life as the Museo Marino Marini containing 180 works by Marini (1901–80), one of the greatest Italian sculptors of the 20th century. Marini also worked as a painter and lithographer, and his portraits and favourite subjects (especially the *Horse and Rider*) are known for their sensuous surfaces and uncanny psychological intensity.

If you come on a Saturday at 5.30 (but not in July, August, or September), the **Rucellai Chapel** (*open Mon–Sat 10–12*) behind San Pancrazio at 18 Via della Spada should be open for Mass. It's your only chance to see a perfect Renaissance gem designed in 1467 by Alberti: the Tempietto del Santo Sepolcro, an idealized reconstruction to scale of the Holy Sepulchre in Jerusalem that is Giovanni Rucellai's funerary monument.

Palazzo Strozzi D4

Palazzo Strozzi was the champion of Florence's millionaire palaces, a rusticated stone cube of such fearful dimensions that it squats in its own piazza just up from Via de' Tornabuoni like the inscrutable monolith in *2001: A Space Odyssey*, radiating waves of megalomania. It was begun by Benedetto da Maiano in 1489 for the extraordinarily wealthy Filippo Strozzi, head of one of Florence's greatest banking clans and adviser to Lorenzo il Magnifico. When he died in 1491, the façade facing Piazza Strozzi was almost complete, but future generations had neither the money nor the interest to finish the massive cornice. And one wonders whether his son, also called Filippo, ever took much pleasure in it; although at first a Medici ally like his father and wed to Piero de' Medici's daughter, Filippo later led a band of anti-Medici exiles against Florence. Captured and imprisoned in the Fortezza da Basso, he stabbed himself, while many other Strozzi managed to escape to Paris to become bankers and advisers to the king of France.

There are few architectural innovations in the Palazzo Strozzi, but here the typical Florentine mansion is blown up to the level of the absurd: although it has three storeys like other palaces, each floor is as tall as three or four normal ones; even the rings for tying up horses are big enough for elephants. Like Michelangelo's *David*, Florence's other beautiful monster, it emits what Mary McCarthy called the 'giganticism of the human ego', the will to surpass not only antiquity but nature herself. But the Strozzi, it turns out, were only pikers in the ego stakes; in spite of its enormous dimensions, their Ponderosa could fit neatly into the courtyard of the Pitti Palace (*see* p.136). Nowadays, at least, the Strozzi palace is moderately useful as a space to hold temporary exhibitions.

PIAZZA DELLA REPUBBLICA D4

On the map, it's easy to pick out the small rectangle of narrow, straight streets around Piazza della Repubblica, just behind the Palazzo Strozzi; these remain unchanged from the little *castrum* of Roman days. At its centre, the old forum deteriorated through the Dark Ages into a shabby market square and the Jewish ghetto, a piquant, densely populated quarter known as the Mercato Vecchio, the epitome of the picturesque for 19th-century tourists but an eyesore for the movers and shakers of the new Italy, who tore down its alleys and miniature *piazze* to create a fit symbol of Florence's reawakening. They erected a triumphal arch to themselves and proudly blazoned it with the inscription: 'THE ANCIENT CITY CENTRE RESTORED TO NEW LIFE FROM THE SQUALOR OF CENTURIES'. The sad result of this well-intentioned urban renewal, the Piazza della Repubblica, is one of the most ghastly squares in Italy, a brash intrusion of ponderous 19th-century buildings and parked cars. Just the same it is popular with locals and tourists alike, full of outdoor cafés, and something of an oasis among the narrow, stern streets of medieval Florence.

Mercato Nuovo E5

Via Por S. Maria and Via Porta Rossa.

The Mercato Nuovo, the old Straw Market, bustles under a beautiful loggia built by Grand Duke Cosimo in the 1500s. Although you won't see more than a wisp of straw these days, there is no lack of leather bags and belts, scarves, toys, umbrellas, embroidered linens and knick-knacks. In medieval times this was the merchants' exchange, where any merchant who committed the crime of bankruptcy was publicly spanked before being carted off to prison; in times of peace it sheltered Florence's battle-stained *carroccio* – the ox cart every medieval city took with it to war, bearing an altar and banners, that served to rally the troops (*see* box, p.108). Florentines often call the market the '*Porcellino*' (piglet) after the large bronze boar erected in 1612, a copy made by Pietro Tacca of the ancient statue in the Uffizi (the *porcellino* here is a new copy of the copy). The drool spilling from its mouth reminds us that unlike Rome, Florence is no splashy city of fountains. Rub the piglet's shiny snout, and they say destiny will one day bring you back to Florence. The pungent aroma of the tripe sandwiches sold nearby may give you second thoughts.

Medieval Lanes D5

Just south of the Mercato Nuovo is a well-preserved pocket of the medieval city. The **Palazzo di Parte Guelfa** at Piazza di Parte Guelfa, off the south end of Via Pellicceria, was the 13th-century headquarters of the Guelph party, and often the real seat of power in the city, paid for by property confiscated from the Ghibellines. In the 15th century Brunelleschi added a hall on the top floor and an extension. Next door is the guildhall of the silk makers, the 14th-century

Tuscany on Wheels

Tuscans have always loved a parade, and to the casual reader of Renaissance history, it seems they're forever proceeding somewhere or another, even to their own detriment – during outbreaks of plague, holy companies marched through afflicted areas, invoking divine mercy, while in effect spreading the pestilence.

During the centuries of endless war each Tuscan city rolled out its war chariot or battle wagon, called the *carroccio*, invented by a Milanese bishop in the 11th century. A *carroccio*, drawn by six white oxen, was a kind of holy ship of state in a hay cart; a mast held up a crucifix while a battle standard flew from the yard-arm; there was an altar for priests to say Mass during the battle and a large bell to send signals over the din to the armies. The worst possible outcome of a battle was to lose one's *carroccio* to the enemy, as Fiesole did to Florence. One is still in operation, in Siena, rumbling out twice a year for the Palio.

Medieval clerical processions, by the time of Dante, became melded with the idea of the Roman 'triumph' (*trionfo*); in Purgatory, the poet finds Beatrice triumphing with a cast of characters from the Apocalypse. Savonarola wrote of a *Triumph of the Cross*; Petrarch and Boccaccio wrote allegorical triumphs of virtues, love and death. More fun, however, are the secular Roman-style triumphs which were staged by the Medici, especially at Carnival (the name of which, according to Burckhardt, comes from a cart, the pagan *carrus navalis*, the ship of Isis, launched every 5 March to symbolize the reopening of navigation). You can get a hint of their splendour from the frescoes at Poggio a Caiano (*see* p.151); the best artists of the day would be commissioned to design the decorations – two particularly famous *trionfi* in Florence celebrated the election of the Medici Pope Leo X.

Two lovely memories of Florence's processions remain. One is Gozzoli's fresco in the chapel of the Medici palace, showing the annual procession staged by the Compagnia de' Re Magi, the most splendid and aristocratic of pageants. The other comes from the Florentine Carnival, famous for its enormous floats, in which scenes from mythology were portrayed to songs and music. One year, for the masque of Bacchus and Ariadne, Lorenzo de' Medici composed the loveliest Italian poem to come out of the Renaissance, with the melancholy refrain:

Quanto è bella giovinezza,
Che si fugge tuttavia!
Chi vuol esser lieto, sia:
Di doman non c'è certezza.
(How fair is youth,
How fast it flies away!
Let him who will, be merry:
Of tomorrow nothing is certain.)

Palazzo dell'Arte della Seta, still bearing its bas-relief emblem, or 'stemma', of a closed door, the age-old guild symbol.

Just around the corner from the Guelph Palace, take Via Pellicceria to see a fine ensemble of medieval buildings on the tiny square near Via delle Terme, where Roman *Florentia* kept her baths.

Museo della Casa Fiorentina Antica D5

Palazzo Davanzati, Via Porta Rossa 13; bus B. Unfortunately closed probably until early 2004 for extensive restoration. There is an exhibition of what you would see were it open on the ground floor (open 8.30–1.50; closed alternative Sundays and Mondays).

This delightful museum offers an idea of what day-to-day life was like inside these sombre palaces some 600 years ago. Built in the mid-14th century for the Davizzi family, the house was purchased by merchant Bernardo Davanzati in 1578 and stayed in the family until the 1900s. Restored by an antique collector in 1904 who filled it with period furnishings, it is the best-preserved medieval–Renaissance house in Florence.

The façade is basically as it was, except for a 16th-century addition of a fifth-floor loggia, replacing the battlements – in the rough-and-tumble 14th century, a man's home literally had to be a castle. But it was also a showroom for his prosperity, and by the standards of the day, the dwellers of this huge palace were multi-millionaires. Below the grand loggia, used for sumptuous public entertainment, the palace is entered by way of a striking vertical **Courtyard**, which could be cut off from the street in times of danger. The ground floor was also used for storage; no family felt safe without a year's store of grain and oil – against famine, siege, plagues or inflation. One storeroom is now used for an audio-visual history of the house. The well in the corner served all the floors, and there is a medieval dumb waiter, waiting to transport the shopping up to the kitchen.

Until the rest of the museum reopens, you'll have to imagine the formal **Sala Grande**, the bright **Sala dei Pappagalli**, frescoed with parrots, a rare en-suite bedroom, and another, the **Sala dei Pavoni**, topped by a frieze of peacocks and other exotic birds flitting among the trees, the **Salone** with its 15th-century Flemish tapestries and a portrait of Giovanni di Bicci de' Medici, the **Sala Piccola** with its *cassoni*, or elaborately painted wedding chests, the **Camera della Castellana di Vergi**, decorated with a lovely fresco from a medieval French romance, and the **kitchen**, as usual on the top floor in the hope that in case of fire, only it would burn.

AROUND SANTA TRÍNITA

Piazza Santa Trínita D5

Three old Roman roads – Via Porta Rossa, Via delle Terme and Borgo SS. Apostoli – converge in the irregularly shaped Piazza Santa Trínita. This boasts an exceptional architectural ensemble, grouped around the 'Column of Justice' from the Roman Baths of Caracalla, given by Pius IV to Cosimo I, and topped with a red statue of Justice by Francesco del Tadda. Its pale granite is set off by the surrounding palaces: the High Renaissance–Roman **Palazzo Bartolini-Salimbeni** by Baccio d'Agnolo (1520) on the corner of Via Porta Rossa, once the fashionable Hôtel du Nord where Herman Melville stayed; the medieval **Palazzo Buondelmonti**, with a 1530 façade by Baccio d'Agnolo, home to a 19th-century reading room where Dumas, Browning, Manzoni and Stendhal once browsed; and the magnificent curving **Palazzo Spini-Feroni** to the right of Borgo SS. Apostoli, the largest private medieval palace in Florence, built in 1289 and still retaining its grim battlements. The Spini were ancient rivals of the Medici, who came close to pinching the highly profitable papal banking business from them in 1420, before going suddenly bankrupt; now it's part of the Salvatore Ferragamo empire, with a museum displaying 60 years of fashion designs (*open 9–1 and 2–6 Mon–Fri by appointment only, t 055 336 0456; closed Aug; adm free*). One of Florence's oldest churches, the 11th century **SS. Apostoli** is just up from here, in the sunken Piazzetta del Limbo, the old cemetery of unbaptized babies.

Around the corner on Lungarno Corsini, the British Consulate occupies the **Palazzo Masetti**. Ironically this was once home to the flamboyant Countess of Albany, wife of Bonnie Prince Charlie, who found happiness by leaving the Pretender for Italian dramatist Vittorio Alfieri, but insisted to the end that she was Britain's rightful Queen Louise.

Santa Trínita D5

Piazza Santa Trínita; ***bus*** *A, B.* ***Open*** *Mon–Sat 8–12 and 4–6, Sun 4–6;* ***adm*** *free.*

The church of Santa Trínita has stood on the west side of the piazza, in one form or another, since the 12th century; its unusual accent on the first syllable (from the Latin Trinitas) is considered to be proof of its ancient foundation.

Although the pedestrian façade added by Buontalenti in 1593 isn't very welcoming, step into its shadowy 14th-century interior for several reasons, beginning with the **Bartolini-Salimbeni Chapel** (fourth on the right), frescoed in 1422 by the Sienese Lorenzo Monaco, whose *Receiving of the Virgin* on the left takes place in a wonderful Tuscan fantasy backdrop of pink towers. He also painted the chapel's graceful, ethereally coloured altarpiece of the Annunciation.

The **Sassetti Chapel**, the second to the right of the high altar, is one of the masterpieces of Domenico Ghirlandaio, completed in 1495 for Francesco Sassetti, general (and generally incompetent) manager of the Medici bank. The chapel is dedicated to the *Life of St Francis*, but also to the life of Francesco Sassetti: the scene above the altar, of Francis receiving the Rule of the Order, is transferred to the Piazza della Signoria, where Sassetti (to the right, with the fat purse) and his boss, Lorenzo il Magnifico look on, while on the steps stands the great Latinist Poliziano with Lorenzo's three sons. The *Death of St Francis* pays homage to Giotto's similar composition in Santa Croce. The altarpiece, the *Adoration of the Shepherds* (1485), is one of Ghirlandaio's best-known works, in its way the archetypal Renaissance painting. It is a contrived but charming classical treatment of a biblical scene – the Magi arrive through a triumphal arch, the stable is a ruined temple, the manger a Roman sarcophagus, while sibyls pose in the vault; the one on the outer arch supposedly announced the birth of Christ to Augustus.

Santa Trínita is a Vallombrosan church and the first chapel to the right of the altar holds the Order's holy of holies, a **painted crucifix** formerly located up in San Miniato. The story goes that on a Good Friday, a young nobleman named Giovanni Gualberto was on his way to Mass when he happened upon the man who had recently murdered his brother. But rather than take his revenge, Gualberto pardoned the assassin in honour of the holy day. When he arrived at church to pray, this crucifix nodded in approval of his mercy. Giovanni was so impressed that he went on to found the Vallombrosan order in the Casentino.

The **Sanctuary** was frescoed by Alesso Baldovinetti, though only four Old Testament figures survive on the ceiling. In the second chapel to the left the marble *Tomb of Bishop Benozzo Federighi* (1454) is by Luca, the first and greatest of the della Robbias, and features his trademark enamelled terracotta in bouquets of flowers. On the north side of the nave, in the fourth chapel, a detached fresco by Neri di Bicci portrays San Giovanni Gualberto and his fellow Vallombrosan saints; over the arch you can see him forgiving the murderer of his brother, although it's not easy to make out. Lastly, in the third chapel on the left, there's a gold-ground altarpiece, the *Coronation of the Virgin*, by Bicci di Lorenzo (1430).

Ponte Santa Trínita D5

In the summer of 1944, the Arno briefly became a German defensive line during the slow, painful retreat across Italy. Before leaving Florence, the Nazis blew up every one of the city's bridges, saving only, on Hitler's special orders, the Ponte Vecchio, though they blasted a large number of ancient buildings on each side of the span to create piles of rubble to block its approaches. Florence's most beautiful span, the Ponte Santa Trínita, was the most tragic victim.

Immediately after the war the Florentines set about replacing the bridges exactly as they were: for Santa Trínita, old quarries had to be reopened to duplicate the stone, and old methods revived to cut it (modern power saws would have done the job too cleanly). The graceful curve of the three arches was a problem; they could not be constructed geometrically, and considerable speculation went on over how the architect (Ammannati, in 1567) did it. Finally, recalling that Michelangelo had advised Ammannati on the project, someone noticed that the same arch could be seen on Michelangelo's tombs in the Medici Chapel, constructed by pure artistic imagination. Fortune lent a hand in the rebuilding; almost all the pieces of the bridge's original statues of the Four Seasons were fished out of the Arno and put back together. Only Spring's head was missing, until divers found it by accident in 1961.

Piazza Goldoni C4

Further down the Arno is the only square in Florence named after a Venetian, the great comic playwright who made all Italy laugh in the 18th century. The most important building here is the **Palazzo Ricasoli**, built in the 15th century but bearing the name of one of unified Italy's first prime ministers, Bettino 'Iron Baron' Ricasoli, whose other claim to fame was developing the formula of grapes that go into Chianti.

The bridge here, the **Ponte alla Carraia**, is new and nondescript, but its 1304 version played a leading role in that year's most memorable disaster: a company staging a water pageant of the *Inferno*, complete with monsters, devils and tortured souls, attracted such a large crowd that the bridge collapsed under the weight, and all were drowned. Later it was drily commented that all the Florentines who went to see Hell that day found what they were looking for.

Galleria Corsini C4

Palazzo Corsini, Lungarno Corsini (enter from Via Parione); ***bus*** *A, B.* ***Open*** *by appointment only,* ***t*** *055 218994, Mon, Wed and Fri 9am–noon.*

The city's most flamboyant piece of Roman Baroque extravagance, Palazzo Corsini was begun in 1650 and crowned with a bevy of statues. The Corsini, the most prominent family of 17th- and 18th-century Florence, were reputedly so wealthy that they could ride from Florence to Rome entirely on their own property. Like all great patrician families they loved art; the Galleria Corsini has works by Giovanni Bellini, Signorelli, Filippino Lippi and Pontormo, and *Muses* from the ducal palace of Urbino, painted by Raphael's first master, Timoteo Viti. It also has the rarest of Florentine amenities: a garden, a 17th-century oasis of box hedges, Roman statues, lemon trees and tortoises, surrounded by large trees once used as *ragnaie*, strung with nets to trap small birds for the spit. Further east on Lungarno Corsini stood the Libreria Orioli, which published the first edition of *Lady Chatterley's Lover* in 1927.

While walking here, stop to enjoy the hugely varied Florence skyline from this vantage point. Lining the river, the palaces themselves are of all shapes and sizes, contrasting with the cluster of red rooftops near San Frediano. Add to these the various bell towers, the Ponte Vecchio, the near hills with San Miniato and Forte di Belvedere surrounded by lofty cypresses to the east, and the higher ground of the Valombrosa beyond that. Do this at midday, and a wild symphony of bells will assail you from all directions.

Ognissanti C4

All Saints, Borgo Ognissanti 42; ***bus*** *B.* ***Open*** *daily 8–12.30 and 5–7.30.*

To the west of Piazza Goldoni lies the old neighbourhood of the only Florentine to have a continent named after him. Amerigo Vespucci, or Americus Vespucius in Latin (1451–1512), was a Medici agent in Seville, and he made two voyages from there to the New World on the heels of Columbus. His parish church, Ognissanti, is set back from the river behind a dingy Baroque façade, on property donated in 1256 by the Umiliati, a religious order that specialized in wool-working.

The Vespucci family tomb is below the second altar to the right, and little Amerigo himself – although it may be another Florentine talltale – is said to be pictured next to the Madonna in the fresco of the Madonna della Misericordia. Also buried in Ognissanti was the Filipepi family, one of whom was Botticelli. Ghirlandaio's *St Jerome in his Study* and young Botticelli's *St Augustine in his Study* hang in the church.

Ognissanti's best art is kept in the **Convent** (*open Mon, Tues and Sat 9–12*), just to the left of the church at No.42, where the refectory was frescoed with a great *Cenacolo* by Domenico Ghirlandaio in 1480. It's hard to think of a more elegant Last Supper, here a garden party with fruit trees and exotic birds; a peacock sits in the window, cherries and peaches litter the lovely tablecloth.

As you leave, note the extraordinary Art Deco building at No.60r Borgo Ognissanti, an unexpected sight in this sober street. Piazza d'Ognissanti is dominated by two five-star hotels, but the most notable building is the **Palazzo Lenzi**, from the first half of the 15th century and lavishly covered with graffiti; it now houses the French Consulate.

North and East Florence

05

AROUND SAN MARCO 116
San Marco 116
The Università and its Museums 117
Chiostro dello Scalzo 118
Sant'Apollonia 118
Along Via San Gallo 119
The Galleria dell'Accademia 119
Opificio delle Pietre Dure 120
Rotonda di Santa Maria degli Angeli 120

AROUND SANTISSIMA ANNUNZIATA 121
Santissima Annunziata 121
Spedale degli Innocenti 122
Museo Archeologico 122
Santa Maria Nuova 123
Museo di Firenze Com'Era 123
Collezione A. della Ragione 124
Piazzale Donatello and the English Cemetery 125
Piazza d'Azeglio 125
Synagogue 125
Sant'Ambrogio 125
Casa Buonarroti 126

AROUND SANTA CROCE 126
Santa Croce 126
Museo Horne 131

North and East Florence

As the Florentines made their fortunes in the Middle Ages, they were often plagued by nagging visions of hell, where rich men, especially bankers, or usurers, were doomed. The Church offered charity as a way out, and the north end of Florence soon filled up with monasteries, convents and hospitals. With the Library of San Marco, the University and the Accademia, the neighbourhood also evolved into the city's centre of learning. It is home to the two mighty opposites of the Florentine Renaissance – the gentle spiritual masterpieces of the blessed Fra Angelico in San Marco and the overweening *David* of Michelangelo in the Accademia – who, as One of the Most Famous Sculptures in the World, gets all the crowds. But there are plenty of other beautiful things to see in the Accademia, as well as in Florence's often overlooked Archaeology Museum, and in the aristocratic church of SS. Annunziata.

Heading south and east, you run into Brunelleschi's serene foundlings' hospital, Florence's funky flea market, with forays into Tuscan Baroque in between, and Michelangelo's house. But there's more: down by the Arno waits the grand temple of Florentine contradiction, Santa Croce, both the city's pantheon and one of its prime galleries of 14th-century frescoes.

1 Lunch

Enoteca Pinchiorri, *Via Ghibellina 87*, ***t** 055 242777;* ***bus** A, 14.* ***Open** Mon and Wed 7.30pm–10, Tues and Thurs–Sat 12.30–2 and 7.30–10; closed Aug.* ***Expensive***. Splurge at the only restaurant in Florence with two Michelin rosettes.

2 Tea and Cakes

La Via del Tè, *Piazza Ghiberti 22r;* ***bus** A, C.* ***Open** Mon–Sat 9.30–2 and 4–7.30.* Choose from a wide selection of teas. Also serves sweet and savoury snacks.

3 Drinks

Caffè Cibreo, *Via del Verrocchio 5r,* ***t** 055 234 5853;* ***bus** A, C.* ***Open** Tues–Sun 8am–1am; closed Aug.* A chic, pretty café/bar next to the busy Sant' Ambrogio food market. Located opposite the famous sister restaurant.

Highlights

Couples' City: Join the crowds ogling *David* in the Accademia, p.119

Medieval City: Trecento frescoes in Santa Croce, p.126

Renaissance City: Brunelleschi's Spedale degli Innocenti, p.122

Medici City: One of the family's pet projects: San Marco and the beautiful works by Fra Angelico, p.116

Quirky City: The Sant'Ambrogio flea market, p.125

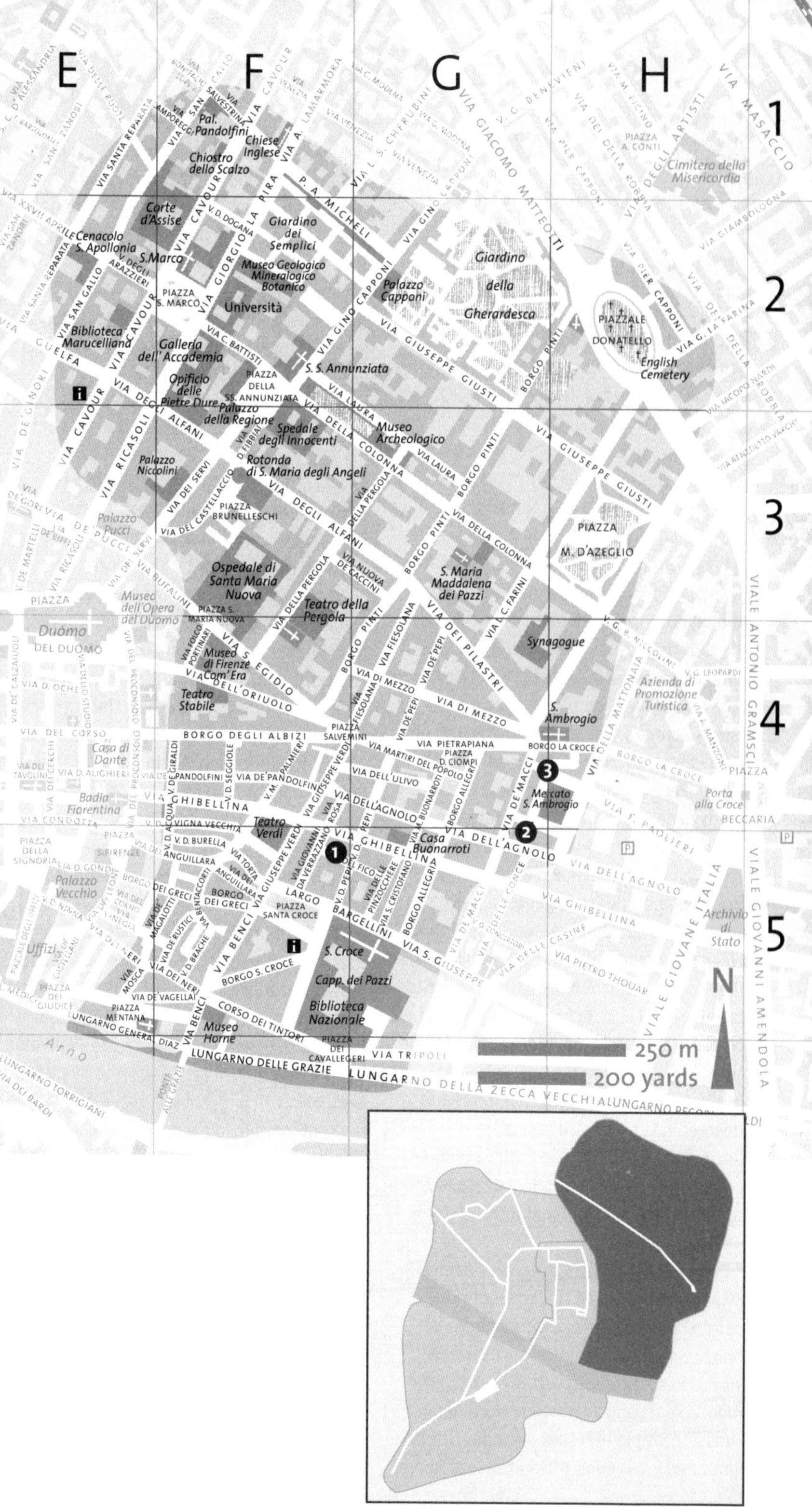

AROUND SAN MARCO

San Marco F2

***Piazza San Marco; bus** 1, 17. **Open** Sun–Fri 8.15–1.50, Sat 8.15–6.50; closed first, third, fifth Sun and second and fourth Mon in month; **adm** €4. **Church open** daily 7–12 and 4–7.*

On the north edge of the Renaissance city, the Dominican Convent of San Marco was Cosimo il Vecchio's favourite pious project; he became close friends with the prior Antonino Pierozzi (who was canonized in 1523) and in 1437 he commissioned Michelozzo to rebuild it, and add a library for all the religious books and manuscripts he donated to the monks (he kept the classics for himself). The Medici library was confiscated by the Signoria in 1494 and brought here, and it became, briefly, Europe's first lending library; the fines for neglectful borrowers were hundreds of florins. Pope Leo X, however, used Vatican funds to buy the library back for the Medici, and it's now in the Biblioteca Laurenziana.

San Marco is best known for the works of the other-worldly **Fra Angelico** (*c.* 1400–55). His spiritual qualities were endorsed in 1982 when he was beatified by John Paul II; in 1984 the Pope declared him the patron of artists, taking over St Luke's old job. In residence here between 1436 and 1447, Angelico was put in charge of decorating the new convent constructed by Cosimo. His paintings and frescoes in San Marco, in a setting unchanged from the 1400s, offer a unique opportunity to see his works in the peaceful, contemplative environment in which they were meant to be seen.

Every painter in the 15th century earned his living painting sacred subjects, but none painted them with Angelico's deep conviction and faith, communicating his biblical visions in soft angelic pastels, bright playroom colours and an ethereal blondness, so clear and limpid that they just had to be true. 'Immured in his quiet convent', wrote Henry James, 'he apparently never received an intelligible impression of evil; and his conception of human life was a perpetual sense of sacredly loving and being loved.' He knelt to pray each day before picking up his brushes, and often wept in pity for Christ's pains while painting Crucifixions. The gentle friar was entirely up to date in his art, and studied the works of Masaccio and artificial perspective in his technique.

The Pilgrims' Hospice

A visit to San Marco begins with Michelozzo's harmonious **Cloister of Sant' Antonino**, decorated with corner frescoes by Fra Angelico. Just off the cloister, the **Pilgrims' Hospice**, also by Michelozzo, has been arranged as a gallery of the master's paintings, which have been gathered here from all over Florence. Here you'll find his great *Last Judgement* altarpiece (1430), a serenely confident work, where the graves recede into the depths of a dark sky and dawning resurrection. All the saved are well-dressed Italians holding hands, led by an angel in a celestial dance. They are allowed to keep their beautiful clothes, while the bad (mostly princes and prelates) are stripped to receive their interesting tortures.

The charming *Thirty-five Scenes from the Life of Christ*, acted out before strikingly bare, brown Tuscan backgrounds, were painted as cupboard doors for Santissima Annunziata (three of the scenes are by Angelico's apprentice, Alesso Baldovinetti). Sadly, the *Madonna and Child with Angels and Eight Saints* (*c.* 1440) commissioned by Cosimo il Vecchio was washed with acid during a botched 19th-century cleaning and has lost its brilliant colours, although Fra Angelico's then novel creation of space still shines through – it is one of the very first panel paintings that makes use of perspective. The noble, gracefully lamenting figures in the magnificent *Deposition* altarpiece from Santa Trínita stand before an elegant townscape dominated by Angelico's ziggurat-style Temple in Jerusalem. The **Tabernacle of the Linaioli** (the flax-workers) has an exceptionally beautiful predella, as does the *Pala di San Marco*, which shows SS. Cosmas and Damian, patrons of medicine and the Medici, in the act of performing history's first leg transplant.

Other rooms off the cloister contain works by Fra Bartolommeo, another resident of the convent, whose portraits capture some of the more sincere spirituality of the late 15th century. The **Chapterhouse** contains Angelico's fresco *Crucifixion and Saints*, a painting over-restored and lacking his accustomed grace; in the refectory there's a more pleasing *Last Supper* by the down-to-earth Domenico Ghirlandaio.

The Convent

Stairs lead up to Michelozzo's beautiful convent, where at the top your eyes meet the Angelic Friar's masterpiece, a miraculous *Annunciation* that must have earned him his beatification. The subject was a favourite with Florentine artists, not only because it was a severe test – expressing a divine revelation in a composition of strict economy – but because the Annunciation, falling near the spring equinox, was New Year's Day for Florence until the Medici finally adopted the pope's calendar in the 1600s.

The Dominicans of San Marco each had a small white cell with a window and a fresco to serve as a focal point for their meditations. Angelico and his assistants painted 44 of these; those believed to have been done by the master are along the outer wall (cells 1–9, the *Noli me Tangere*, another *Annunciation*, a *Transfiguration*, a *Harrowing of Hell*, a *Coronation of the Virgin*, and others). He also painted the scene in the large cell used occasionally by Cosimo il Vecchio and other visiting celebrities. The cells in one corridor are all entirely painted with scenes of the Crucifixion, all the same but for some slight difference in the pose of the Dominican monk at the foot of the Cross; walking past and glancing in the cells successively gives the strange impression of watching an animated cartoon. The **Prior's cell** at the end, where Savonarola lived, has simple furniture of the period and a *Portrait of Savonarola* in the guise of St Peter Martyr (with an axe in his brain) by his friend Fra Bartolommeo. In a nearby corridor hangs a copy of the anonymous painting in the Corsini Gallery, of Savonarola and two of his followers being burned at the stake in the Piazza della Signoria.

The **Library**, entered off the corridor, is one of Michelozzo's greatest works, as light and airy as the cloisters below, radiating serenity in its vaulted nave and aisles; it contains a collection of beautiful choir books.

The Church of San Marco

San Marco was rebuilt, along with the convent, in the 15th century, although the interior was later rearranged by Giambologna and the Baroque façade added in 1780. It has several works of note: the right aisle has a large Ravenna-style mosaic (705) of the virgin praying originally in Pope John VII's Oratory in Rome, and an excellent painting by Fra Bartolommeo, the *Madonna and Six Saints*. To the left of the altar is the theatre-like chapel of Sant'Antonio by Giambologna; there's a *Resurrection* by Allori (1584), and in the left aisle, by the second altar and a statue of Savonarola, the tombstones of three great humanists from the circle of Lorenzo il Magnifico: Angelo Poliziano (d. 1494), Giovanni Pico della Mirandola (d. 1494) and Girolamo Benivieni (d. 1542). Also have a look at the famous fresco of the Annunciation on the back wall, by Jacopo di Cione (1371, but later repainted), and a large Crucifix by the school of Giotto.

The Università and its Museums F2

Piazza San Marco.

Piazza San Marco often overflows with students from Florence's university, which occupies the former buildings of the Grand Ducal stables. The university was founded in 1321 as the Studio Fiorentino, when the great university of Bologna was under a ban of excommunication. Although Pisa would always be considered the main university in

Tuscany (carefully fostered by the Medici, to soften opposition to their rule), Florence's university taught many future humanists, including Poggio Bracciolini, who ferreted out lost Latin classics from monastery cellars in France, Germany and Switzerland, and (when he couldn't buy them) copied them out in a clean, easily legible hand based on Carolingian script, that became the origin of the Roman type and handwriting we use today.

In the 15th century, Florence was known as the only place in Europe where Greek was properly taught. After the Council of Florence (*see* p.100), a number of scholars had moved here from Constantinople, and in 1488 they oversaw the first printed text of Homer. Some of their students were English, such as Thomas Linacre (who would help found the Royal College of Physicians), William Latimer and William Grocyn, who all collaborated on a translation of Aristotle into Latin.

The university runs several small museums just north at Via G. La Pira 4; nearly all the collections were begun by the indefatigable Medici. The **Geology and Palaeontology Museum** (*open Tues–Sat and second Sun of the month 9–1; adm €3.10*) has one of Italy's best collections of fossils, many of which were uncovered in Tuscany, including antiquated elephants from the Valdarno. The **Mineralogy and Lithology Museum** (*same opening hours and adm as Geology and Palaeontology Museum, above, except closed Sat*) houses strange and beautiful rocks, especially from Elba, a treasure island of minerals; there's a topaz weighing in at 151kg, meteorites, and a bright collection of Medici trinkets, worked from stones in rainbow hues. The **Botanical Museum** (*open by request only,* **t** *055 275 7462; adm free*) houses one of the most extensive herbariums in the world and exquisite wax models of plants made in the early 1800s. On Via P. Micheli 3 is the entrance to the University's **Giardino dei Semplici**, the botanical garden created by Cosimo I (*open Mon–Fri 9–1*). The garden maintains its original layout, with medicinal herbs, Tuscan plants, flowers and tropical plants in its greenhouses .

Chiostro dello Scalzo F1

***Off Piazza S. Marco at Via Cavour 69; bus** 1, 6, 17. **Open** Mon, Thurs and Sat 9–1.*

Of the Confraternity of San Giovanni Battista, all that has survived is this cloister, frescoed (1514–24) with scenes of the *Life of St John the Baptist* by Andrea del Sarto and his pupil Franciabigio. Del Sarto, Browning's 'perfect painter', did these in monochrome grisaille, and while the scene of the *Baptism of Christ* is beautiful, some of the other panels are the most unintentionally funny things in Florence – the scene of Herod's banquet is reduced to a meagre breakfast where the king and queen look up indignantly at the man bringing in the platter of the Baptist's head as if he were a waiter who had made a mistake with their order.

Almost opposite, at Via Cavour 57, the huge **Court of Appeals** building started off in 1574 as the Casino de San Marco, built in 1574 by Bernardo Buontalenti for Francesco I, who kept his alchemy and other labratories here. Before then, a much smaller casino served as Lorenzo de' Medici's informal school of sculpture, where he kept many of the family masterpieces and paid young artists, most famously Michelangelo, to attend.

Sant'Apollonia E2

***The entrance to the museum and** cenacolo **is on Via XXVII Aprile 1; bus** 1, 6. **Open** daily 8.30–1.30; closed the second and fourth Mon and the first, third and fifth Sun of the month. The entrance to the cloister (now part of the university) is on Via San Gallo.*

Cenacoli, or frescoes of the Last Supper, were *de rigueur* in monastic refectories; in several cases the Last Supper fresco is all that remains of an entire complex. Until 1860, the Renaissance convent of Sant'Apollonia was the abode of cloistered nuns. When the convent was suppressed, and the fresco discovered under coats of whitewash, the critics believed it to be the work of Paolo Uccello, but have since unanimously attributed it to Andrea del Castagno, painted sometime between 1445 and 1450. The other walls have Castagno's *sinopie* of the Crucifixion, Entombment and Resurrection; in the vestibule there are good works by Neri di Bicci and Paolo Schiavo.

Along Via San Gallo E2

Just up Via San Gallo you'll find the handsome **Palazzo Marucelli** at No.10, built by Gherado Silvani in 1634, and remarkable for its bizarre satyrs squirming around the door; note too the locomotive in the medallion, added in the 19th century. The palazzo is now the History and Geography faculty of the University. A little further up on the left is the old **convent of S. Apollonia**, which became a military depot in 1808, and now belongs to the University; the door on Via San Gallo may have been designed by Michelangelo and leads into a charming cloister. Further up on the right, the 14th-century church of **San Giovannino dei Cavalieri** was the oratory of the Knights of Malta, and in its restored interior has a striking Crucifix by Lorenzo Monaco. A bit further up at No.74, the elegant and monumental **Palazzo Pandolfini** was built *c.* 1520 to a design by Raphael, while further up on the left at No.83, under a loggia, was the **Ospedale di Bonifazio**, founded in 1377 by Bonifazio Lupi; in the 18th century, under Vincente Chiarugi, it became the first psychiatric hospital in the world. It's now the Questura (police headquarters).

The Galleria dell'Accademia F2

Via Ricasoli 60, t 055 238 8609, w www.sbas.firenze.it/accademia; bus 1, 6, 7. Open Tues–Sun 8.15–6.50; summer Sat 8.15–10pm; to book call t 055 294883; adm €6.50. Note that from autumn 2002 until spring 2003 Michelangel's* David *will be cleaned bit by bit, but the statue will always be visible.

Although Lorenzo il Magnifico ran an informal art school, the idea died with him until 1562, when Cosimo I and sculptor Baccio Bandinelli founded the Accademia, the first formal academy of art and architecture in the world, which did away with the old artist-pupil relationship in favour of the more impersonal (and state controlled) approach. In 1935 its building was graced with the loggia from the former hospital of San Matteo, a work inspired by the Spedale degli Innocenti, complete down to the della Robbia lunettes.

The Accademia's street, Via Ricasoli, makes a beeline for the Duomo, but on most days the view is obstructed by crowds milling here. In the summer the queues are as long as those at the Uffizi, everyone anxious to get a look at Michelangelo's *David*. This precocious symbol of republican liberty originally stood in the rain in the Piazza della Signoria, but in 1873 it was installed, with much pomp, in a specially built classical exedra in this gallery.

Michelangelo completed the *David* for the city of Florence in 1504, when he was 29, and it was the work that established the overwhelming reputation he had in his own time. The monstrous block of marble – 16ft high but unusually shallow – had been quarried 40 years earlier by the Cathedral Works and spoiled by other hands. The block was offered to other artists, including Leonardo da Vinci, before young Michelangelo decided to take up the challenge of carving the largest statue since Roman times. And it is the dimensions of the *David* that remain the biggest surprise in these days of endless reproductions. Certainly as a political symbol of the Republic, he is excessive – the irony of a David the size of a Goliath is disconcerting – but as a symbol of the artistic and intellectual aspirations of the Renaissance he is unsurpassed.

And it's hard to deny, after gazing at this enormous beefcake *alla fiorentina*, that these same Renaissance aspirations by the 1500s began snuggling uncomfortably close to the frontiers of kitsch. Disproportionate size is one symptom; the calculated intention to excite a strong emotional response is another. In the *David* (whose hair was originally gilded, until the rain washed it away) virtuosity eclipses vision, and commits the even deadlier kitsch sin of seeking the sterile empyrean of perfect beauty – most would argue that Michelangelo here achieves it, perhaps capturing his own feelings about the work in the *David*'s chillingly vain, self-satisfied expression. This is also one of the few statues to have actually injured someone. During a political disturbance in the Piazza della Signoria, its arm broke off and fell on a farmer's toe. In 1991 it was *David*'s toe which fell victim when a madman chopped it off. Since then, the rest of his anatomy has been shielded by glass.

In the Galleria next to the *David* are four of Michelangelo's famous *nonfiniti*, the *Prisoners* or Slaves, worked on between 1519 and 1536, sculpted for Pope Julius' tomb and left in various stages of completion, although it is endlessly argued whether this is by design or through lack of time. Whatever the case, no works better illustrate Michelangelo's view of sculpture as a prisoner in stone just as the soul is a prisoner of the body.

The Accademia's Gallery was founded by Grand Duke Pietro Leopold in 1784 to provide students with examples of art from every period. The big busy Mannerist paintings around the *David* are by Michelangelo's contemporaries, among them Pontormo's *Venus and Cupid*, with a Michelangelesque Venus among theatre masks. Other rooms contain a good selection of quattrocento painting, including the *Madonna del Mare* by Botticelli, a damaged Baldovinetti, the *Thebaid* by a follower of Uccello, and Perugino's *Deposition*. The painted frontal of the **Adimari chest** shows a delightful wedding scene of the 1450s with the Baptistry in the background, a work that has been reproduced in half the books ever written about the Renaissance.

The hall off to the left of the *David* was formerly the women's ward of a hospital, depicted in a greenish painting by Pontormo. Now it is used as a gallery of plaster models by 19th-century members of the Accademia, a surreal, bright white neoclassical crowd.

The excellent **collection of old musical instruments**, once housed in the Palazzo Vecchio, has now moved to the Accademia. Some 150 exhibits, including several violins and cellos by Cremona greats like Stradivarius and Guarneri, are on display.

Opificio delle Pietre Dure F2

***Via degli Alfani 78; bus** 1, 17. **Open** Mon–Wed, Fri and Sat 8.15–2, Thurs 8.15–7; **adm** €2.*

Cosimo I was the first to promote actively what was to become Florence's special craft, and it was Ferdinando I who founded the Opificio in 1588 as a centre for craftsmen, whose main task was to supply *pietre dure* (inlaid 'hard stones' or semi-precious stones) by the square yard for the Medici chapels. In the late 18th century, the Lorraine dukes made this plain convent of San Nicoló into their workshop and museum, and they've been here ever since, creating 'paintings in stones'; some, like the *Veduta del Pantheon* by Ferdinando Partini, are extraordinarily detailed, catching light and shadow in their cold, meticulous perfection.

Rotonda di Santa Maria degli Angeli F3

***Via degli Alfani, across Via dei Servi; bus** 1, 17.*

This octagonal church was one of Brunelleschi's last works, begun in 1434, and one of the first centralized buildings of the Renaissance. It was designed as a chapel for the convent of Santa Maria degli Angeli (now entirely incorporated in the Hospital of Santa Maria Nuova), where in the 14th and 15th centuries, the sons of rich Florentine merchants, including Cosimo il Vecchio, learned their Latin, French and German, and had their early grounding in the classics.

AROUND SANTISSIMA ANNUNZIATA

Piazza Santissima Annunziata F2

This lovely square was the beginning of a revolution in urban design: the first Renaissance attempt at such a unified architectural ensemble became the direct ancestor of the royal squares of 17th-century Paris and the residential squares of 18th-century London. The piazza is surrounded on three sides by arcades. In its centre, gazing down the splendid vista of Via dei Servi towards the Duomo, stands the equestrian **statue of Ferdinand I** (1607) by Giambologna and his pupil Pietro Tacca, made of bronze from Turkish cannons captured during the Battle of Lepanto. But more intriguing than Ferdinand are Tacca's bizarre **Baroque fountains** that share the square. Recently restored and possessed of a nominally marine theme, they resemble overflowing tureens of *bouillabaisse* that any ogre would be proud to serve.

Santissima Annunziata F2

Piazza Santissima Annunziata; bus C, 1, 6. Open daily 7–12.30 and 4–6.30; adm free.

Florence's high society church, Santissima Annunziata, was founded n 1250 to house a miraculous picture of the Virgin. It attracted so many pilgrims that in 1444 the Medici paid for Michelozzo, their favourite architect, to enlarge and rebuild it. To shelter the crowds, Michelozzo designed the **Chiostrino dei Voti** in front of the church, a glass-roofed atrium that was originally packed with ex-votos that the Florentines have since lost and tidied away – among them, a famously life-like wax effigy of the Magnificent Lorenzo by Verrocchio, placed here in thanksgiving for his close call in the Pazzi Conspiracy. Most of the Chiostrino's frescoes are by Andrea del Sarto and his students, but the most enchanting work is Alesso Baldovinetti's *Nativity* (1462), although it's sadly faded, with the ghost of a transcendent landscape. Also present are two youthful works: Pontormo's *Visitation* and Rosso Fiorentino's Mannerist *Assumption*.

The interior, the only one the Florentines ever spent much money on during the Counter-Reformation, is the most sumptuous and lush Baroque work in the city. Michelozzo's design features an unusual polygonal **Tribune** around the sanctuary, a concept derived from antique buildings and entered by way of a triumphal arch designed by Leon Battista Alberti. Directly to the left as you enter is Michelozzo's **Tempietto**, hung with lamps and candles, built to house the miraculous *Annunciation*, painted by a monk with the help of an angel who painted the Virgin's face. Its construction was funded by Piero the Gouty de' Medici, who couldn't resist adding the inscription on the floor that 'The marble alone cost 4000 florins'. The ornate canopy over the *tempietto* was added in the 17th century.

The next two chapels on the left side contain frescoes by Andrea del Castagno, painted in the 1450s but whitewashed over by the Church when it read Vasari's phoney story that Castagno murdered his fellow painter Domenico Veneziano – a difficult feat, since Veneziano outlived his supposed murderer by several years. Rediscovered in 1864, Castagno's fresco *St Julian and the Saviour* in the first chapel has some strange Baroque bedfellows by Giambattista Foggini. The next chapel contains Castagno's daring *Vision of St Jerome*, showing the saint torn by his privations in the wilderness looking up to a vision of the Holy Trinity. This demanded such extreme foreshortening that Castagno in frustration ended up painting red cherubs *a secco* over the lower part of Christ's body, although these have partly peeled off over time. The right aisle's fifth chapel contains a fine early Renaissance tomb, that of the obscure Orlando de' Medici by Bernardo Rossellino. The neighbouring chapel in the transept has a painted crucifix by Baldovinetti, while in the next one the *Pietà* is the funerary monument of Cosimo I's court sculptor and Cellini's archrival Baccio Bandinelli; in this *Pietà* he put his own features on Nicodemus, as Michelangelo did in the *Pietà* in the Museo del Duomo. Bandinelli's most lasting contribution (or piece of mischief) was his collusion with Cosimo in creating the Accademia (*see* p.119).

Nine semicircular chapels radiate from the Tribune. The one at the rear contains the tomb of Giambologna, a far more talented follower of Michelangelo; his pupil Pietro Tacca is buried with him, in this chapel designed by Giambologna before his death. The next chapel to the left contains a *Resurrection* by Bronzino, one of his finest religious paintings. To the left of Alberti's triumphal arch, under a statue of St Peter, is the grave of Andrea del Sarto; next to it is one of Florence's loudest Counter-Reformation blasts, the tomb of bishop Angelo Marzi Medici (1546).

The **Chiostro dei Morti**, off the left transept, is most notable for Andrea del Sarto's fresco, the *Madonna del Sacco* (1525), an unusual work named after the sacks of grain on which St Joseph leans. The **Cappella di San Luca** off the cloister belongs to the Accademia and contains the graves of Cellini, Pontormo, Franciabigio and other artists (*open on request 7–12.30 and 4–6.30*).

Spedale degli Innocenti F3

Piazza della SS. Annunziata; bus C, 1, 6. Open Thurs–Tues 8.30–2; adm €3.

In the 1420s, the hot-tempered genius Filippo Brunelleschi struck the first blow for classical calm in this piazza when he built the Spedale degli Innocenti and its famous portico – an architectural landmark, but also a monument to Renaissance Italy's long, hard and ultimately unsuccessful struggle towards some kind of social consciousness.

Even in the best of times, Florence's poor were treated like dirt, although babies, at least, were treated a little better. No one really knew how many there were (births were registered by putting beans in a box, a black one for a boy, a white one for a girl). No one wanted to know about the unwanted ones or their fate, until the foundation of the Spedale degli Innocenti, the first hospital for foundlings in the world; at the left end of the loggia you can still see the original window-wheel, where babies were left anonymously, until 1875. The place still serves as an orphanage, as well as a nursery school.

The Spedale was Brunelleschi's first completed work as an architect and demonstrates his use of geometrical proportions adapted to traditional Tuscan Romanesque architecture. His lovely portico is adorned with the famous blue and white tondi of infants in swaddling clothes by Andrea della Robbia, added as an appeal to charity in the 1480s after several children died of malnutrition. Brunelleschi also designed the two beautiful cloisters of the convent; the **Chiostro delle Donne**, reserved for the hospital's wet nurses, is especially fine. Upstairs, the **Museo dello Spedale** contains a number of detached frescoes from Ognissanti and other churches, among them an unusual series of red and orange prophets by Alessandro Allori; other works include a *Madonna and Saints* by Piero di Cosimo, a *Madonna and Child* by Luca della Robbia, and the brilliant *Adoration of the Magi* (1488) painted by Domenico Ghirlandaio for the hospital's church, a crowded, colourful composition featuring portraits of members of the Arte della Lana, or Wool Guild, who funded the Spedale.

Museo Archeologico G3

Via della Colonna 38, t 055 23575; bus C. Open Mon 2–7, Tues and Thurs 8.30–7, Wed, Fri and Sun 8.30–2; in summer Sat 8.30–2 and 8–11pm; adm €4.

Florence's excellent archaeology museum occupies the 17th-century Palazzo della

Crocetta, built for Grand Duchess Maria Maddalena of Austria. Just like nearly every other museum in Florence, this impressive collection was begun by the Medici, beginning with Cosimo il Vecchio and accelerating with the insatiable Cosimo I and his heirs. The Medici were especially fond of Etruscan things, while the impressive Egyptian collection was begun by Leopold II in the 1830s.

The **Etruscan collection** is on the first floor, including the famous bronze *Chimera*, a remarkable beast with the three heads of a lion, goat and snake. This 5th-century BC work, dug up near Arezzo in 1555 and immediately snatched by Cosimo I, had a great influence on Mannerist artists. There is no Mannerist fancy about its origins, though; like all such composite monsters, it is a religious icon, a calendar beast symbolizing the three seasons of the ancient Mediterranean agricultural year. In the same corridor stands the *Arringatore*, or Orator, a monumental bronze of the Hellenistic period, a civic-minded and civilized-looking gentleman, dedicated to Aulus Metellus, and the statue of *Minerva*. Also in this section are other Etruscan bronzes, big and small. The cases here are full of wonderful objects, anything from tiny animals to jewellery, carved mirrors and household objects such as plates – there's even a strainer. All these show just how skilled the Etruscans were in casting bronze.

The beautifully lit **Egyptian collection**, also on the first floor, has recently been expanded and modernized. It includes some interesting small statuettes, mummies, canopic vases, and a unique wood-and-bone chariot, nearly completely preserved, found in a 14th-century BC tomb in Thebes.

On the second floor there is plenty of Greek art; Etruscan noble families were wont to buy up all they could afford. The beautiful Hellenistic horse's head once adorned the Palazzo Medici-Riccardi. The *Idolino*, a bronze of a young athlete, is believed to be a Roman copy of a 5th-century BC Greek original. There is an excellent *Kouros*, a young man in the archaic style from 6th-century BC Sicily. An unusual, recent find, the silver *Baratti Amphora*, was made in the 4th century BC in Antioch and covered with scores of small medallions showing mythological figures. Scholars believe that the images and their arrangement may encode an entire system of belief, the secret teaching of one of the mystic-philosophical cults common in Hellenistic times, and they hope some day to decipher it. There's a vast collection of Greek pottery (including the massive *François vase* in Room 2), and large Greek, Roman and Renaissance bronzes, recently brought out of storage. There are also several fabulous Greek marble sculptures dating from *c.* 500 BC.

There is virtually nothing displayed on the ground floor now, although temporary exhibitions are held there. Out in the garden are several reconstructed Etruscan tombs.

The fabulous collection of precious stones, coins and, most notably, cameos (amassed by the Medici) is now permanently on display in the corridor which runs between the museum and the church of Santissima Annunziata.

Santa Maria Nuova F3

Piazza di Santa Maria Nuova.

Florence's oldest and busiest hospital, Santa Maria Nuova was founded in 1286 by the father of Dante's Beatrice, Folco Portinari. Readers of Iris Origo's *The Merchant of Prato* will recognize it as the work-place of the good notary, Ser Lapo Mazzei. The portico of the hospital, by Buontalenti, was finished in 1612.

Museo di Firenze Com'Era F4

***Via dell'Oriuolo 24; bus** A. **Open** Fri–Wed 9–2; **adm** €2.58.*

The Museum of Florence As It Was is not large; it contains a number of plans and maps, as well as a collection of amateurish watercolours of Florence's sights from the 18th century, and paintings of Florence's surroundings by Ottone Rosai, a local favourite who died in 1957. Its jewel is right out in front: the nearly room-sized *Pianta della Catena*, most beautiful of the early views of Florence. It is a copy, as the original made in 1490 by an unknown artist – that handsome fellow pictured in the lower right-hand corner – was lost in a Berlin museum during the last war. This fascinating painting captures Florence at the height of the Renaissance, a city of buildings in bright white, pink and tan; the great churches are without their façades, the Uffizi and Medici chapels have not yet appeared, and the Medici and Pitti palaces are without their later extensions.

Today's Florentines seem much less interested in the Renaissance than in the city of their grandparents. For some further evidence, look around the corner of Via S. Egidio, where some recent remodelling has uncovered posters over the street from 1925, announcing plans for paying the war debt and a coming visit of the Folies Bergère. The Florentines have restored them and put them under glass.

Collezione A. della Ragione F4

Complesso delle Oblate, Via Sant' Egidio 21; bus A. Reopening summer 2002 for visits by appointment only (call tourist office for details). Once the museum is fully functional it will open as normal, Wed–Mon 9–2; adm €2.

Florence's only gallery of modern art, Italian style, has been relocated from the Piazza Signoria to the newly renovated Complesso delle Oblate, and at the time of writing is not yet open to the public.

There are typical still lifes by De Pisis; equally still landscapes by Carlo Carra; mysterious baths by De Chirico, all three of them members of Ferrara's Metaphysical school; Tuscan landscapes by Mario Mafai, Antonio Donghi and Ottone Rosai; a speedy Futurist horse by Fortunato Depero and a window with doves by Gino Severini; a number of richly coloured canvases by Renato Guttuso and paintings after Tintoretto by Emilio Vedova, and many others, surprises, perhaps, if you're unfamiliar with more recent Italian art.

Teatro della Pergola F3–4

Via della Pergola 12/32. Visits by appointment only, generally in the mornings (t 055 263 1807 for information).

When it was built in wood in 1656 by Ferdinando Tacco (son of the sculptor) the Pergola was one of the first theatres with seats arranged in tiers. Cardinal Gian Carlo de' Medici and his friends, the Accademia degli Immobili, built it and supplied the actors. It opened to the general public in 1718. Rebuilt in the early 19th century, it is one of Italy's beautiful theatres, where prose, chamber music concerts and opera are regularly staged.

Benvenuto Cellini lived on this street, at No.59, where that he set set the roof alight while casting his *Perseus*, and where he died in 1571.

Santa Maria Maddalena dei Pazzi G3

Borgo Pinti 58; bus C, 6. Open 9–12 and 5–7; voluntary donation.

One of the city's least known churches, Santa Maria Maddalena was founded in the 13th century, then rebuilt in classical Renaissance style by Giuliano da Sangallo, then given the full Baroque whack when it was rededicated to the Counter-Reformation saint of the Pazzi family. Inside it's all high theatre, with a gaudy *trompe-l'oeil* ceiling, paintings by Luca Giordano, florid chapels, and a wild marble chancel. From the Sacristy a door leads down into a labyrinth-crypt to the **Chapter House** (*token adm*) which contains a fresco of the Crucifixion (1496), one of Perugino's masterpieces. Arranged in three arches that lend a vague *trompe l'oeil* feel to the room, the symmetry and quiet, contemplative grief of the five figures at the foot of the Cross and the magic stillness of the luminous Tuscan–Umbrian landscape have a powerful impact, as if existing just on the other side of the looking glass. The fresco has never been restored; in the 1966 flood, the water came within four inches of the scenes, and stopped. There's also Perugino's sinopia of Christ coming down from the Cross to comfort St Francis.

Piazzale Donatello and the English Cemetery H2

***Bus** 8, 33.*

Donatello's name has suffered terrible indignities of late (many young people know him only as a Teenage Mutant Ninja Turtle) but the Florentines, at least, could spare their greatest sculptor something more dignified than Piazzale Donatello, a swollen artery in the city's frenetic system of *viali* that take traffic around the centre. Pity, too, Elizabeth Barrett Browning (1809–61) and the other expatriates buried in the piazza's English Cemetery – now a traffic island choked in eternal fumes.

Piazza d'Azeglio H3

***Bus** 6, 31, 32.*

In contrast to Piazzale Donatello, this shady and elegant piazza is Florence's one experiment with a London square. No.35 bears a plaque in memory of Pellegrino Artusi (d. 1911), renowned chef and author of *La Scienza in Cucina e L'Arte de Mangiar Bene*, the Tuscan culinary bible.

Synagogue G4

*Via L. C. Farini 4; **bus** A, 6. Security is tight, but the synagogue may be **open** April, May, Sept, Oct, Sun–Thurs 10–5, Fri 10–2; June–Aug, Sun–Thurs 10–6, Fri 10–1; Nov–Feb, Sun–Thurs 10–2; **adm** €3.09. **Museum open** same hours, **t** 055 234 6654 for information.*

Florence's Jewish community, although today only 1,200 strong, was one of the most important in Italy. Jews were invited to Florence by the Republic in 1430, but repeatedly exiled and readmitted until Cosimo I founded Florence's Ghetto in 1551. When the Ghetto was opened up in 1848 and demolished, this new Synagogue (1874–82) was built, a tall Mozarabic Pre-Raphaelite hybrid inspired by the Hagia Sophia and the Transito Synagogue of Toledo. Although seriously damaged by the Nazis in August 1944 – and later by the Arno in 1966 – it has been lovingly restored. There's a small **Jewish Museum** upstairs, with a documentary history of Florentine Jews as well as ritual and ceremonial items from the synagogue's treasure.

Sant'Ambrogio H4

*Piazza Sant'Ambrogio; **bus** A, C. **Open** daily 8–12.30 and 4–7.30.*

The streets of Sant'Ambrogio, south of the synagogue, are among the most dusty and piquant in the city centre, a neighbourhood where tourists seldom venture. Life revolves around Sant'Ambrogio, one of the oldest churches in Florence and its adjacent market made of cast iron in 1873.

Rebuilt in the 13th century, and given a simple façade in 1888, it has no lack of treasures. The second chapel on the right has a lovely fresco, *Madonna Enthroned with Saints* by Orcagna (or Agnolo Gaddi), and the **Cappella del Miracolo**, just left of the high altar, where a priest in 1230 found drops of blood in the chalice rather than wine, contains Mino da Fiesole's celebrated marble *Tabernacle* (1481) and his own tomb. The chapel has a beautiful fresco of the Procession of the Chalice by Cosimo Rosselli, with 15th-century Florentine celebrities including Pico della Mirandola and Rosselli himself (in a black hat, in the group on the left), and a view of Sant'Ambrogio's old façade. Andrea Verrocchio is buried in the fourth chapel on the left; on the wall by the second altar, there's a beautiful painting of the *Nativity with Angels and Saints* by Alesso Baldovinetti. The deteriorated fresco of an atypical St Sebastian on the entrance wall is by Agnolo Gaddi, along with a *Deposition* by Niccoló di Piero Gerini.

Piazza dei Ciompi G4

***Bus** A, C.*

From Sant'Ambrogio, Via Pietrapiana leads to bustling Piazza dei Ciompi, named after the wool-workers' revolt of 1378. In the morning, Florence's flea market or **Mercatino** takes place here, the best place in town to buy that 1940s radio or outdated ball gown you've always wanted. One side of the square is graced with the **Loggia del Pesce**, decorated with terracotta seafood, built by Vasari in 1568 for the fishmongers of the Mercato Vecchio, and moved here when the Mercato Vecchio was demolished to make way for Piazza della Repubblica.

Casa Buonarroti G5

*Via Ghibellina 70, **w** www.casabuonarotti.it; **bus** A, 14. **Open** Wed–Mon 9.30–4; **adm** €6.20.*

Michelangelo never lived in this house, although he purchased it in 1508. Making himself at home wasn't the point, not to an artist who had no thought for his own personal comfort, or anyone else's – he never washed, and never took off his boots, even in bed. Real estate, however, was an obsession of his, as he struggled to restore the status of the semi-noble but impoverished Buonarroti. His nephew Leonardo inherited the house and several works of art in 1564; later he bought the two houses next door to create a memorial to his uncle, hiring artists to paint scenes from Michelangelo's life. In the mid-19th century, the house was opened to the public as a museum.

The ground floor is dedicated to mostly imaginary portraits of the artist, and works of art collected by his nephew's descendants, including an eclectic Etruscan and Roman collection and a lovely predella of the *Life of St Nicolas of Bari* by Giovanni di Francesco. The main attractions, however, are upstairs, beginning with Michelangelo's earliest known piece, the beautiful bas-relief *The Madonna of the Steps* (1490–1), the precocious work of a 16-year-old influenced by Donatello and studying in the household art school of Lorenzo il Magnifico; the relief *Battle Scene*, inspired by classical models, dates from the same period. Small models and drawings of potential projects that never came off line the walls; there's the wooden model for the façade of San Lorenzo, and designs for some of the statues Michelangelo intended to fill in its austere blank spaces – as usual, his ideas were far too grand for his patron's purse and patience, even when the patrons were the Medici.

The next four rooms were painted in the 17th century to illustrate the master's life, virtues and apotheosis, depicting a polite, deferential and pleasant Michelangelo hobnobbing with popes. Those who know the artist from *The Agony and the Ecstasy* may think they painted the wrong man by mistake. One of the best sections is a frieze of famous Florentines in the library.

AROUND SANTA CROCE

Santa Croce G5

*Piazza S. Croce; **bus** B. **Open** summer Mon–Sat 9.30–5.30, Sun 3–5.30; winter Mon–Sat 9.30–12.30 and 3–5.30, Sun 3–5.30; **adm** free.*

No place in Florence so feeds the urge to dispute as the church of Santa Croce, Tuscany's 'Westminster Abbey', the largest Franciscan basilica in Italy. It was here that Stendhal had his revelation: 'I had attained to that supreme degree of sensibility where the divine intimations of art merge with the impassioned sensuality of emotion. As I emerged from the port of Santa Croce, I was seized with a fierce palpitation of the heart; I walked in constant fear of falling to the ground.' But don't be put off; most people manage to emerge from a visit without tripping over themselves.

The contradictions begin in the **Piazza Santa Croce**, which has its fine points – the row of medieval houses with projecting upper storeys, supported by stone brackets; the faded bloom of dancing nymphs on the **Palazzo dell'Antella**; and the curious 14th-century **Palazzo Serristori-Cocchi**, opposite the church. Surveying the scene is a grim 19th-century statue of Dante (if Dante really looked like that, no wonder his Bice married someone else); perhaps the Florentines felt obliged to make him glower at them as punishment for his exile. Because this piazza is the lowest-lying in the city, it suffered the worst in the 1966 flood, when 18ft of oily water poured in: note the small plaque high up on the corner of the Piazza and Via Verdi. It's hard to visualize – but it was nearly as bad once before; just under it another plaque records that the water also rose in 1557. The watermark is most evident on the palazzo on the opposite side of Via Verdi.

Piazza Santa Croce was once the scene of splendid tournaments and jousts, most famously the ones in honour of Lorenzo and Giuliano de' Medici, who naturally won the prizes; the point was to put on a good show, so no one was hurt or got their magnificent silks and golden brocades dirty. It was also, more seriously, a training ground. Having a citizens' militia, as opposed to relying on foreign mercenaries, answered one of Machiavelli's requirements for a well-governed state, and to build up their endurance, the republic's citizens played a ball game similar to rugby, which is still played here each June, when the usually immaculate Florentines in their Renaissance duds mix it up (*see* box). Fighting is more than permitted, as long as it's one to one (and they get dirty).

As a backdrop to all this sweat and dirt rises Santa Croce's neo-Gothic **façade**, built in 1857–63 and financed by Sir Francis Sloane, whose Sloane Square in London has more admirers than this white with green and pink striped design, derived from Orcagna's Tabernacle in Orsanmichele. Yet of all the façades grafted on to Italy's churches in order to atone for the chronic Renaissance inability to finish any project, this is one of the least offensive.

Santa Croce was reputedly founded by St Francis himself, and it's probably true; during repairs after the flood, vestiges of a small early 13th-century church were discovered under the present structure. It went by the board in the colossal building programme that changed the face of Florence in the 1290s. The great size of the new church

Calcio in Costume

The eternal argument of Santa Croce heats up with rib-crunching violence every year, when the various neighbourhoods of Florence compete in a Renaissance football match. Its origins go back to 17 February 1530, when the friendless republic of Florence had been besieged by the army of Charles V for three months. People were cold, hungry and miserable, but they were grimly determined to repel the emperor's troops, who could look down on Piazza Santa Croce from the surrounding hills. It was then decided to give them something worth looking at, to show them exactly what the Florentines thought of their siege: they played a rowdy, noisy game of football.

To commemorate this last great thumbing-of-the-communal-nose at the forces of reaction that would smother Florence for centuries, every year around the summer solstice, young bloods from the four quarters of the city don hose, baggy doublets and brightly plumed hats . After a good deal of pageantry, banner waving, gonfalon tossing, and a magnificent display of caparisoned horses, the 27 players on each side take the field – an immense rectangle of sand laid in the centre of the piazza. A cannon is fired, and the two sides charge at each other, butting heads, swinging fists, kicking, and grappling in a mix of no-holds-barred rugby, football, and Roman wrestling, anything to get the ball into the adversaries' goal. The prize: a pure white calf.

speaks for the immense popularity of Franciscan preaching. Arnolfo di Cambio planned it, and it was largely completed by the 1450s. Unfortunately, just as in Santa Maria Novella, Giorgio Vasari and the blinding forces of High Renaissance mediocrity were unleashed upon the **interior** a century later. Vasari never had much use for the art of Andrea Orcagna – he not only left him out of his influential *Lives of the Artists* but in Santa Croce he destroyed Orcagna's great fresco cycle that once covered the nave, replacing it with uninspired side altars.

Like many Franciscan churches, Santa Croce's large size, its architectural austerity and open timber roof resemble a barn, but at the end there's a lovely polygonal sanctuary, which shimmers with light and colour streaming through the 14th-century stained glass.

For centuries it was the custom to install monuments to illustrious men here but, perversely, the greater the person, the uglier their memorial. A member of the Pazzi conspiracy, Francesco Nori, is buried by the first pillar in the right aisle, and is graced by one of the loveliest works of art, the *Madonna del Latte* (1478), a bas-relief by Antonio Rossellino, while the **Tomb of Michelangelo** (1570, the first in the right aisle) by Vasari is one of the least attractive. Michelangelo died in Rome in 1564, refusing for 35 years to return to Florence while alive, but agreeing to give the city his corpse. Dante has fared even worse, with an 1829 neoclassical monument that's as disappointing as the fact (to the Florentines) that Dante is buried in Ravenna, where he died in 1321.

Facing the nave, Benedetto da Maiano's **marble pulpit** (1476) is one of the most beautiful that the Renaissance ever produced. Behind it, the neoclassical **Vittorio Alfieri Monument** (1809) was sculpted by Antonio Canova and paid for by Alfieri's lover, the Countess of Albany. Next is the nondescript 18th-century **Monument of Niccolò Machiavelli**, and then Donatello's pristine *Annunciation* (*c.* 1435), a tabernacle in gilded limestone, the angel wearing a remarkably sweet expression as he gently breaks the news to a grave Madonna.

Bernardo Rossellino's **Tomb of Leonardo Bruni** (1447), another masterpiece of the Renaissance, is perhaps the one monument that best fits its man. Bruni, a good friend of Cosimo il Vecchio, was a Greek scholar, an eloquent humanist who urged the Florentines to be worthy successors of the ancient Athenians, and the author of the first major historical work of the period, *The History of Florence*, a copy of which his tranquil effigy holds. The tomb, with its Brunelleschian architectural setting, inspired other artists, most obviously Desiderio da Settignano and his equally beautiful tomb of **Carlo Marsuppini** (1453), another humanist, directly across the nave as well as the more imitative monument to composer **Giocchino Rossini** crowded in to the left. The last tomb in the aisle belongs to Greek–Italian poet and patriot Ugo Foscolo.

Santa Croce is especially rich in trecento frescoes, which provide a unique opportunity to compare the work of Giotto with his followers. The south transept's **Castellani Chapel** has later, more decorative compositions by Agnolo Gaddi (*Scenes from the Lives of Saints*, 1380s). The beautiful **Baroncelli Chapel** was painted with *Scenes from the Life of the Virgin* by Agnolo's father Taddeo, Giotto's assistant in the 1330s, and includes a bright gilded altarpiece, the *Coronation of the Virgin* by Giotto and his workshop.

The next door gives on to a **Corridor** and the **Medici Chapel** (*open for Mass at 6pm daily*), both designed by Michelozzo; inside are one of Andrea della Robbia's finest altarpieces and a 19th-century fake Donatello, a relief *Madonna and Child* that fooled the experts for decades. From the corridor a door leads to the **Sacristy**, its walls frescoed by Taddeo Gaddi (*The Crucifixion*), Spinello Aretino and Niccolò di Pietro Gerini. Behind the 14th-century grille, the **Rinuccini Chapel** was frescoed by one of Giotto's most talented followers, the Lombard Giovanni da Milano, in the 1360s.

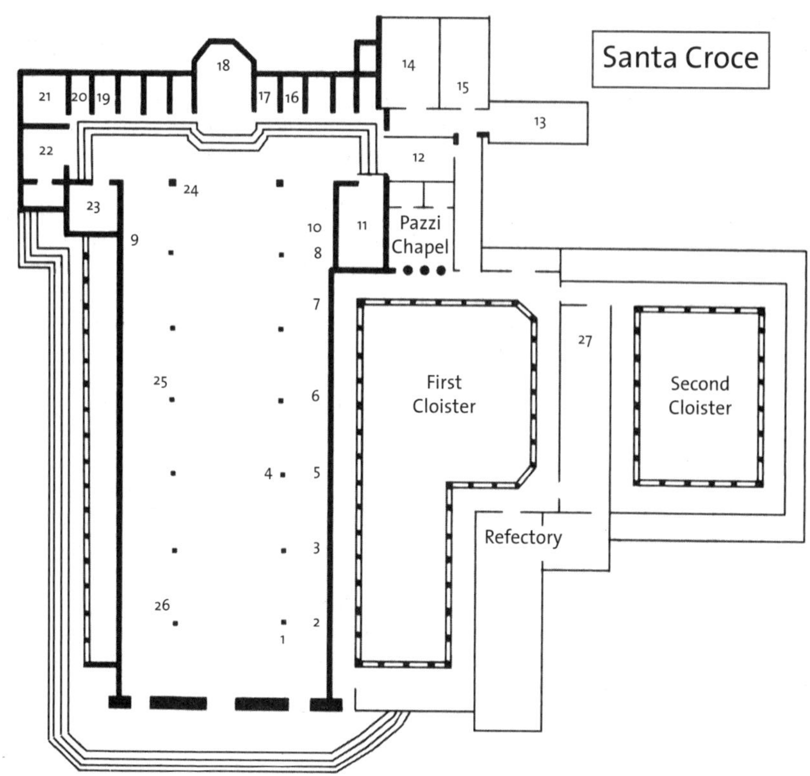

1 *Madonna del Latte*
2 Tomb of Michaelangelo
3 Monument to Dante
4 Benedetto da Maiano's Pulpit
5 Vittorio Alfieri's Tomb
6 Tomb of Machiavelli
7 Donatello's *Annuniciation*
8 Tomb of Leonardo Bruni
9 Tomb of Carlo Malaspini
10 Tomb of Rossini
11 Castellani Chapel
12 Baroncelli Chapel
13 Medici Chapel
14 Sacristy
15 Rinuccini Chapel
16 Peruzzi Chapel
17 Bardi Chapel
18 Sanctuary
19 Bardi di Libertà Chapel
20 Bardi di Vernio Chapel
21 Niccolini Chapel
22 Bardi Chapel
23 Salviati Chapel
24 Monument to Alberti
25 Tomb of Lorenzo Ghiberti
26 Galileo's Tomb
27 Museo dell'Opera di S. Croce

Giotto: The Peruzzi and Bardi Chapels

The two chapels to the right of the sanctuary, the Peruzzi Chapel and the Bardi Chapel, belonged to the two richest families in Florence until England's Edward III ruined them by repudiating his debts to their banks in 1339. Just before then, however, they hired Giotto, Italy's most famous and prestigious artist, to supply the frescoes. Giotto at the time was at the height of his powers, having just returned from Padua after completing his masterpiece, the Arena chapel.

The frescoes have not fared well during the subsequent 660 years. Firstly Giotto painted large sections *a secco* (on dry plaster) instead of *affresco* (on wet plaster), presenting the same kind of preservation problems that bedevil Leonardo's *Last Supper*; secondly, the 18th century thought so little of the frescoes that they were whitewashed over as eyesores. Rediscovered some 150 years later and finally restored in 1959, the frescoes now, even though fragmentary, look more or less as Giotto painted them. The Peruzzi Chapel contains scenes from the *Lives of St John the Evangelist and the Baptist*. In the Bardi Chapel the subject is the *Life of St Francis*. The contrast between Giotto's frescoes and the chapel's 13th-century altarpiece, also on the *Life of St Francis*, is a fair yardstick for measuring the breadth of the Giottesque revolution. Ruskin fixed his attention on St Louis, and spent breathless page upon page in his *Mornings in Florence*, praising it as the perfect example of Giotto's style, never suspecting that the entire figure had been added only a few years previously by the frescoes' restorer.

Agnolo Gaddi designed the stained glass around the **Sanctuary**, as well as the fascinating series of frescoes on the *Legend of the True Cross* (*see* box). To the left are more chapels frescoed by followers of Giotto: the fourth, the **Bardi di Libertà Chapel**, by Bernardo Daddi and the last, the **Bardi di Vernio Chapel**, by Maso di Banco, one of the most innovative and mysterious artists of the trecento. The frescoes illustrate the *Life of the Pope St Sylvester* – his baptism of Emperor Constantine, the resurrection of the bull, the closing of the dragon's mouth and resurrection of two sorcerers; on the other wall of the chapel are a *Dream of Constantine* and *Vision of SS. Peter and Paul*. In the corner of the transept, the richly marbled **Niccolini Chapel** (1584) built by Antonio Dossi in 1584 and decorated with paintings by Allori offers a Mannerist change of pace. Next, the second **Bardi Chapel** houses the famous *Crucifix* by Donatello that Brunelleschi called 'a peasant on the Cross'. The last of the funeral monuments, near the door, belong to Lorenzo Ghiberti and Galileo; for falling foul of the Inquisition, Galileo was not permitted a Christian burial until 1737.

Pazzi Chapel

***Open** winter Thurs–Tues 10–5, summer Thurs–Tues 10–6; **adm** €4.10.*

The Pazzi Chapel carries an entrance fee, but it's well worth it. Brunelleschi, who could excel on the monumental scale of the cathedral dome, saved some of his best work for small places. Unless you know something of the architect and the austere religious tendencies of the Florentines, the Pazzi Chapel is inexplicable, a Protestant reformation in architecture unlike anything ever built before. The 'vocabulary' is essential Brunelleschi, the geometric forms emphasized by the simplicity of the decoration: *pietra serena* pilasters and rosettes on white walls, arches, twelve terracotta tondi of the Apostles by Luca della Robbia, coloured rondels of the Evangelists in the pendentives by Donatello, and a small stained-glass window by Baldovinetti. Even so, that is enough. The contemplative repetition of elements makes for an aesthetic that posed a direct challenge to the International Gothic of the time.

Leaving the Pazzi Chapel (notice Luca della Robbia's terracotta decorations on the portico), a doorway on the left of the cloister leads to another work of Brunelleschi, the **Second Cloister**, designed with the same subtlety and one of the quietest spots in Florence.

Museo dell'Opera di Santa Croce G5

*In the old monastic buildings off the first cloister; **bus** B. **Open** winter Thurs–Tues 10–5, summer Thurs–Tues 10–6; **adm** €4.13.*

Here you can see Cimabue's celebrated *Crucifix*, devastated by the 1966 flood, and partly restored after one of Florence's perennial restoration controversies. The refectory wall has another fine fresco by Taddeo Gaddi, the *Tree of the Cross* and the *Last Supper*, while fragments of Orcagna's frescoes salvaged from Vasari and company offer

The Legend of the True Cross

This popular medieval story was part of the Golden Legend by the 13th-century bishop of Genoa, the Blessed Jacopo de Voragine, and remained an inspiration to artists until the Counter-Reformation suppressed it for its historical inaccuracies. It begins with Noah's son, Seth, as an old man, asking for the essence of mercy. The Angel Gabriel replies by giving Seth a branch, saying that 5,000 years must pass before mankind may know true redemption. Seth plants the branch over Adam's grave on Mount Sinai, and it grows into a magnificent tree. King Solomon orders the tree cut, but as it is too large to move, the trunk stays where it is and is used as the main beam of a bridge. The Queen of Sheba is about to cross the bridge when she has a vision that the saviour of the world will be suspended from its wood, and that his death will mark the end of the Kingdom of the Jews. She refuses to cross the bridge, and writes of her dream to Solomon, who has the beam buried deep underground. Nevertheless, it is dug up and used to make the cross of Christ.

The cross next appears in the Emperor Constantine's dream before the Battle of Milvian Bridge, when he hears a voice saying that under this sign he will conquer. When it proves true, he sends his mother Helen to find the cross in Jerusalem. There she meets Judas Cyriacus, a pious Jew who knows where Golgotha is, but won't tell until Helen has him thrown in a well and nearly starved to death. When at last he agrees to dig, a sweet scent fills the air, and Judas Cyriacus is immediately converted. To discover which of the three crosses they find is Christ's, each is held over the coffin of a youth; the True Cross brings him back to life. After all this trouble in finding it, Helen leaves the cross in Jerusalem, where it is stolen by the Persians. Their King Chosroes thinks its power will bring him victory, but instead he loses the battle, and Persia, to Emperor Heraclius, who decides to return the holy relic to Jerusalem. But the gate is blocked by the Angel Gabriel, who reminds the proud Heraclius that Jesus entered the city humbly, on the back of an ass. And so, in a similar manner, the emperor returns the cross to Jerusalem.

powerful, nightmarish vignettes in *The Triumph of Death and Hell*. Donatello's huge gilded bronze statue *St Louis of Toulouse* (1423) – a flawed work representing a flawed character, according to Donatello – was made for the façade of Orsanmichele. The museum also contains works by Andrea della Robbia, and a painting of Florence's Mayor Bargellini with a melancholy Santa Croce submerged in the 1966 flood for a backdrop. Under the colonnade there's the statue *Florence Nightingale*, born in and named after the city in 1820.

Museo Horne F5

Via de' Benci 6; bus A, B. Open Tues–Sat 9–1, Mon 9–1 and 8.30–11.30; adm €5.

Florence owes this delightful museum to Herbert Percy Horne (1844–1916), English art historian, biographer of Botticelli, and Florentinophile, who bequeathed his collection to the nation. There are some excellent works: on the first floor, a large *Deposition*, the last work of Gozzoli, sadly darkened with age, a painting by the great Sienese Pietro Lorenzetti, and a tondo by Piero di Cosimo. In the next room hangs Horne's prize, Giotto's golden painting of young St Stephen; other works include Signorelli's *Redeemer* (a beardless, girlish youth), Beccafumi's *Decalione e Pirra*, and a saccharine *St Sebastian* by Carlo Dolci. Room Three has a rousing quattrocento battle scene, taken from a marriage chest, good 15th-century wood inlays, and a relief of the head of St John the Baptist by Desiderio da Settignano. Upstairs a diptych attributed to Barna da Siena holds pride of place, together with an impressive array of Renaissance furniture and household objects.

Florence's East End

The east end of Florence, which is a rambling district packed with artisans and small manufacturers, was the artists' quarter in Renaissance times. Still one of the livelier neighbourhoods, with a few lingering artists lodged in the upper storeys, hoping to breathe inspiration from the very stones where Michelangelo walked, it is a good place to observe the workaday Florence behind the glossy façade. Just west of Piazza Santa Croce is a series of streets – **Via Bentaccordi** (where a plaque marks Michelangelo's boyhood home), **Via Torta** and **Piazza dei Peruzzi** – which makes an almost complete ellipse. These mark the course of the inner arcade of the Roman amphitheatre, some stones of which can still be seen among the foundations of the palaces.

The Oltrarno

06

AROUND THE PITTI PALACE 136
Palazzo Pitti 136
Giardino di Boboli 139
Santa Felicità 139
Casa Guidi 140
La Specola 140

AROUND SANTO SPIRITO 140
Santo Spirito 140
Santa Maria del Carmine 141

EAST OF THE PONTE VECCHIO 142
Museo Bardini/Galleria Corsi 142

The Oltrarno

The Oltrarno – the 'beyond' the Arno – is both Florence's populist left bank and the stage for the biggest chunk of Medici megalomania of them all, the Pitti Palace. It isn't large – a chain of hills squeezes it against the river, and their summits afford some of the best views over the city.

***See also* the Oltrarno walk on p.157.**

Highlights

Couples' City: A stroll around the delightful Giardino di Boboli, p.139

Medieval City: Orcagna's striking Crucifixion fresco in the Refectory by Santo Spirito, p.141

Renaissance City: Masaccio's Cappella Brancacci, one of the seminal works of the Renaissance, p.141

Medici City: Their Pitti Palace, chock-a-block with treasures, p.136

Quirky City: La Specola's museum of waxes, p.140

1 Lunch

Trattoria del Carmine, *Piazza del Carmine 18r*, ***t*** *055 218601*; ***bus*** *D, 6.* ***Open*** *Mon–Sat noon–2.30 and 7–10.30; closed 3 weeks in Aug.* ***Inexpensive***. A friendly neighbourhood trattoria with a long, reasonably priced menu. Outdoor seating, too.

2 Tea and Cakes

Hemingway, *Piazza Piattellina 9r*, ***t*** *055 284781*; ***bus*** *D, 6.* ***Open*** *Tues–Thurs 4.30pm–1am, Fri and Sat 4.30pm–2am, Sun 11am–8pm.* Teas, coffees and handmade chocolates are the specialities at this elegant café/bar done out in pale blues with rattan furniture.

3 Drinks

Cabiria Café, *Piazza Santo Spirito 4r*; ***bus*** *D.* ***Open*** *Mon, Wed and Thurs 8am–1.30am, Fri–Sun 8am–2.30am.* Noisy, laid-back, trendy bar. One of Florence's most *recherché* terraces for a Campari.

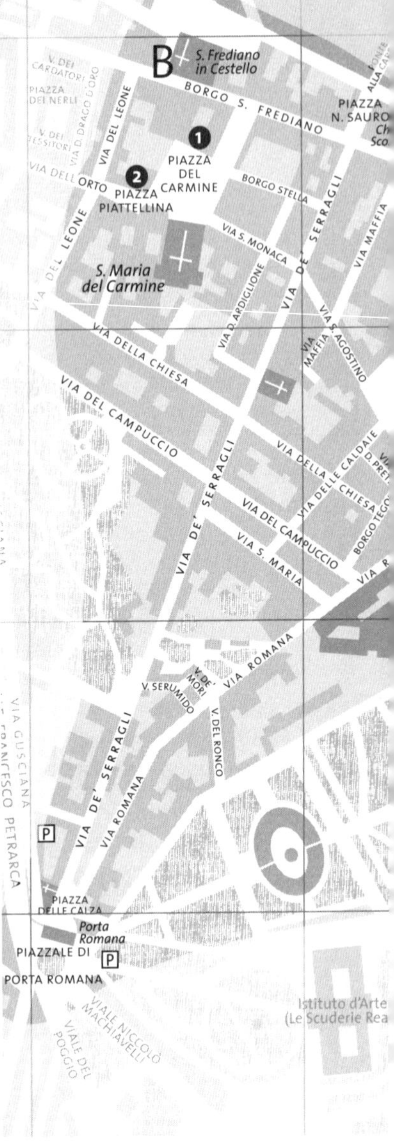

C
D
E
F
5
6
7
8
Arno
LUNGARNO GUICCIARDINI
VIA DI S. SPIRITO
Pal. Guicciardini
S. Trinita
PIAZZA S. TRINITA
Pal. Davanzati
PIAZZA MERCATO NUOVO
PIAZZA DELLA SIGNORIA
PIAZZA S.FIRENZE
Pal. Gondi
Tribunale Civile e Penale
Palazzo Vecchio
Loggia dei Lanzi
Pal. di Parte Guelfa
Pal. Ferroni-Spini
S.S. Apostoli
BORGO S.S. APOSTOLI
VIA DELLE TERME
LUNGARNO ACCIAIOLI
PIAZZA FRESCOBALDI
BORGO S. JACOPO
Uffizi
Ponte Vecchio
Museo di Storia della Scienza
PIAZZA DEI GIUDICI
PIAZZA MENTANA
Museo Horne
S. Spirito
PIAZZA S. SPIRITO
V. BARBADORI
VIA DEI VELLUTI
VIA MAGGIO
V. DE GUICCIARDINI
PIAZZA S. FELICITA
Santa Felicità
VIA COSTA DE MAGNOLI
COSTA DI S. GIORGIO
Palazzo Guadagni
PIAZZA DE' PITTI
Casa Guidi
PIAZZA S. FELICE
Palazzo Pitti
La Specola Museo Zoologico
LUNGARNO TORRIGIANI
VIA DEI BARDI
COSTA SCARPUCCIA
Pal. Torrigiani
PIAZZA DE MOZZI
Museo Bardini
VIA DE' RENAI
VIA DI S. NICCOLÒ
LUNGARNO SERRISTORI
PONTE ALLE GRAZIE
LUNGARNO GRAZIE
Porta San Giorgio
VIA DI BELVEDERE
Forte di Belvedere
Giardino di Boboli
Museo delle Porcellane
Villa S. Leonardo
VIA DI S. LEONARDO
V. MADONNA DELLA PACE
N
250 m
200 yards

AROUND THE PITTI PALACE

Palazzo Pitti C–D6

*Piazza dei Pitti; **bus** D.*

As the Medici consolidated their power in Florence, they made a point of confiscating or buying up the most important properties of their former rivals, especially their family palaces. The most spectacular example of this was the Grand Duchess Eleanor's acquisition in 1549 of the Pitti Palace, built in 1457 by a banker named Luca Pitti, an influential part of the Medici machine who occasionally had vague ambitions of toppling the Medici and becoming the big boss himself.

With its extensive grounds, now the Boboli Gardens, the palace was much more pleasant than the medieval Palazzo Vecchio, and at Eleanor's insistance she and Cosimo I moved in there for good. The palace remained the residence of the Medici, and later the House of Lorraine, until 1868. The original building, probably designed by Brunelleschi, was only as wide as the seven central windows of the façade. Succeeding generations found it too small for their burgeoning hoards of bric-a-brac, and added several stages of symmetrical additions, resulting in a long bulky profile, resembling a rusticated Stalinist ministry. The very smart new forecourt sloping from Via de' Guicciardini to Piazza Pitti was completed for the European Summit in June 1996. Would the Medici have approved? In the 17th century, the gate of the Pitti was hung with wine bottles like many other Florentine palazzi, advertizing wine for sale in the cellars.

There are eight separate museums in the Pitti, including collections dedicated to clothes, ceramics and carriages – a tribute to Medici acquisitiveness in their centuries of decadence, a period from which, in the words of Mary McCarthy, 'flowed a torrent of bad taste that has not yet dried up . . . if there had been Toby jugs and Swiss weather clocks available, the Grand Dukes would certainly have collected them'. For the diligent visitor who wants to see it all, the Pitti is pitiless, and impossible to take in in a single day.

Galleria Palatina

t** 055 238 8614. **Open** daily 8.30–6.50, until 10pm on Sat in summer; **adm** €6.50. **The ceiling frescoes are gradually being restored in all the main rooms over 2002–4, resulting in some rooms being partially closed; in this case the paintings will be moved.

The Pitti museum that most people see is the Galleria Palatina, containing the Grand Dukes' famous collection of 16th–18th-century paintings, stacked on the walls in enormous gilt frames under the berserk opulence of frescoed ceilings celebrating planets, mythology and, of course, the Medici. The gallery occupies the first floor of the right half of the palace; the ticket office is on the ground floor, off Ammannati's exaggerated rustic courtyard, a Mannerist masterpiece of colossal proportions. The size of it was determined by the Pitti, who, out of spite for the Strozzi family, made it large enough to swallow the entire Palazzo Strozzi (*see* p.106).

After the entrance to the Galleria is the neoclassical **Sala Castagnoli**, with the *Tavola delle Muse* in its centre, itself an excellent introduction to the Florentine 'decorative arts'; the table, a paragon of the intricate art of *pietra dura*, was made in the 1870s. The Galleria's best paintings are in the five former reception rooms off to the left, with colourful Baroque ceilings painted in the 1640s by Pietro da Cortona.

However, the set route takes you through the other part of the palace first, starting with the **Sala di Prometeo** containing Filippo Lippi's lovely *Tondo of the Madonna and Child* and Baldassare Peruzzi's unusual *Dance of Apollo*. Next you can peek into the **Sala di Bagni**, the Empire bathroom of Elisa Baciocchi, Napoleon's sister, who ruled the Département de l'Arno between 1809 and 1814, and seemingly spent much of those years redecorating the Pitti. Caravaggio's

Sleeping Cupid is in the **Sala dell'Educazione di Giove**. The next room to this is the pretty **Salla della Stufa**, frescoed with the *Four Ages of the World* by Pietro da Cortona.

The first of the reception rooms, the **Sala dell'Iliade** (frescoed in the 19th century), has fine portraits by the Medici court painter and Rubens' friend, Justus Sustermans. Two *Assumptions of the Virgin* by Andrea del Sarto, *Philip II* by Titian, *La Maddalena* by Artemisia Gentileschi and a Velázquez equestrian *Portrait of Philip IV* share the room with one of the most unexpected residents of the gallery, *Queen Elizabeth*, who looks a bit uncomfortable in their company.

In the **Sala di Saturno** Raphael dominates, with several paintings done in his early Florence days: the portraits of *Maddalena and Agnolo Doni* (1506) and the *Madonna 'del Granduca'*, influenced by the paintings of Leonardo. Ten years later, Raphael had found his own style, evident in his famous *Madonna della Seggiola* ('of the chair'), one of the most popular works he ever painted, and one that is far more complex and subtle than it first appears. The rounded, intertwining figures of the Madonna and Child are seen as if through a slightly convex mirror, bulging out – one of the first examples of conscious illusionism in the Renaissance.

The **Sala di Giove**, used as the Medici throne room, contains one of Raphael's best-known portraits, the lovely and serene *Donna Velata* (1516). The small painting *The Three Ages of Man* is usually attributed to Giorgione. Salviati, Perugino, Fra Bartolommeo and Andrea del Sarto are also represented here.

The **Sala di Marte** has two works by Rubens, *The Four Philosophers* and the *Consequences of War*, as well as some excellent portraits by Tintoretto and Van Dyck (*Cardinal Bentivoglio*), and Titian's rather dashing *Cardinal Ippolito de' Medici* in Hungarian costume. Although destined for the Church, Ippolito was one of the more high-spirited Medici, and helped to defend Vienna from the Turks before being poisoned at the age of 24.

In the **Sala di Apollo** there's more Titian – his *Portrait of a Grey-eyed Noble Man* who resembles the perfect 16th-century English gentleman, a romantic character with an intense gaze, and his more sensuous than penitent *Mary Magdalene* – as well as more by Andrea del Sarto and Van Dyck.

The last reception room is the **Sala di Venere**, with works by Titian, including the famous *Concert*, a work perhaps partly painted by Giorgione and a powerful *Portrait of Pietro Aretino*, Titian's close and caustic friend, who complained to the artist that it was all too accurate and gave it to Cosimo I. There are two beautiful, optimistic landscapes by Rubens, painted at the end of his life, and an uncanny self-portrait, entitled *La Menzogna* (the Falsehood), by Neapolitan Salvator Rosa. The centrepiece statue, the *Venus Italica*, was commissioned by Napoleon from neoclassical master Antonio Canova in 1812 to replace the *Venus de' Medici* which he 'centralized' off to Paris – a rare case of the itchy-fingered emperor trying to pay for something he took.

Paintings to ferret out include Filippino Lippi's *Death of Lucrezia* and Raphael's *Madonna dell'Impannata*, both in the adjacent **Sala di Ulisse**.

Beyond the Sala delle Nicchie are the **State Apartments**, situated in the right half of the Pitti. These were last redone in the 19th century by the Dukes of Lorraine, with touches by the Kings of Savoy, who occupied them during Florence's interlude as national capital. Among the heavy, garish but expensive furnishings, there is a fine series of Gobelin tapestries ordered from Paris by Elisa Baciocchi.

Galleria d'Arte Moderna

***t** 055 238 8616. **Open** daily 8.15–1.50; closed second and fourth Sun and first, third and fifth Mon of each month; **adm** €5 (inc. costume museum). Tickets on the ground floor.*

Florence keeps its works from the late 18th and 19th centuries on the second floor above the Galleria Palatina. Though the monumental stair may leave you breathless (the latter Medici negotiated it with sedan chairs and strong-shouldered servants), the sunny paintings of the Italy of your great-great grandparents have a sweet charm all their own. The 'Splatterers' or *Macchiaioli* (Tuscan Impressionists) illuminate **Room 16** and the rest of the museum, offering an excellent introduction to the works by Silvestro Lega, Giovanni Fattori, Nicolo Cannicci, Francesco Gioli, Federigo Zandomeneghi and Telemaco Signorini, punctuated here and there by enormous Risorgimento battle scenes. What comes as a surprise, especially if you've been touring around Florence for a while, is that the marriage between painting and sculpture that characterizes most of its art history resulted in a nasty divorce in the late 1800s: while the canvases radiate light, the statues becomes disturbingly kitsch, morbidly, stupefyingly obsessed with death and beauty, culminating with the *Pregnant Nun* and the *Suicide*, by Antonio Ciseri in **Room 19**.

The gallery was reorganized and extended in 1999 and there are now over 30 rooms, the last of which contain the most recent paintings covering 1900–23. There are plans to open more rooms for the years 1923–45.

Museo degli Argenti

Same opening hours as Arte Moderna; adm €2.

The ground floor on the left flank of the Pitti was used as the Medici summer apartments and now contains a museum showing off the family's incredible hoard of jewellery, vases, trinkets and pricey curiosities.

The Grand Duke's guests would be received in four of the most delightfully frescoed rooms in Florence, beginning with the **Sala di Giovanni di San Giovanni**, named after the artist who frescoed much of it in the 1630s. The theme is the usual Medici tooting their own horns – but here playing nostalgic golden oldies. Here Apollo and the Muses, chased from Parnassus, find refuge with Lorenzo il Magnifico; a fresco by Francesco Furini shows him in the Platonic Academy at Careggi, and in a fresco by Ottavio Vannini Lorenzo smiles as he studies a bust of a Faun presented by a young Michelangelo.

His real passion, a collection of antique vases carved of semi-precious stones or crystal, is displayed in a room off to the left; the vases were dispersed with the rise of Savonarola, but Lorenzo's nephew Cardinal Giulio had no trouble in relocating them, as Lorenzo had LAUR.MED. deeply incised into each. The three **Reception rooms** were painted in shadowy blue *trompe l'oeil* by two masterly Bolognese illusionists, Agostino Michele and Angelo Colonna.

The Grand Dukes' treasure is up on the mezzanine. These golden toys are only a small fraction of what the generations of Medici had accumulated; despite the terms of Anna Maria's will, leaving everything to Florence, the Lorraines sold off the most valuable pieces and jewels to finance Austria's wars. Among the leftovers here, however, is an apoplexy of fantastical bric-a-brac: jewelled bugs, cameos, sea monster pendants, interlaced ivory cubes, carved cherry pits, gilt nautilus shells, chalices made of ostrich eggs, enough ceramic plates to serve an army, a Mexican bishop's mitre made of feathers, intricate paper cut-outs, buffalo horn cups, and 17th-century busts and seashell figurines that would not shame the souvenir stand of any seaside resort.

Other Museums

The recently reopened **Museum of Costumes** (*same hours as Argenti and Arte Moderna; adm €5, inc Arte Moderna*) is housed in the Meridiana pavilion, the south extension of the Pitti, a dull addition added by the Lorraines; its prize exhibit is the reconstructed dress that Eleanor of Toledo was buried in – the same one that she wears in Bronzino's famous portrait. The **Porcelain Museum**, with even more plates (*open 9–1.30, closed the second and fourth Sun and the first, third and fifth Mon of each month; adm €2.06, inc the Boboli Gardens*) is housed in the airy casino of Cosimo III, in the Giardino del Cavaliere in the Boboli Gardens (follow the signs). The **Museo delle Carrozze**, with Medici and Lorraine carriages and sedan chairs, has been closed for years.

Giardino di Boboli C–D7

***Bus** D. **Open** daily 9am until one hour before sunset; closed first and last Sun of the month; **adm** €2.06. Entrances at the Pitti Palace, Via Romana and at Porta Romana.*

Stretching back invitingly from the Pitti, the shady green of the Boboli Gardens, Florence's largest (and only) central garden of any size, is an irresistible oasis in the middle of a stone-hard city. Some of its acres once belonged to the Bogoli family, and a corruption of their name stuck to the place.

Laid out by Buontalenti, the Boboli reigns as queen of all formal Tuscan gardens, the most elaborate and theatrical, a Mannerist–Baroque co-production of Nature and Artifice laid out over a steep hill, full of shady nooks and pretty walks and beautifully kept. The park is populated by a platoon of statuary, many of them copies of Roman works, while others are fond Mannerist pieces like Cosimo I's court dwarf Morgante posing as a chubby Bacchus astride a turtle (near Vasari's Corridor).

Just beyond this lies the remarkable **Grotta di Buontalenti**. One of the architect's most imaginative works, it seems to anticipate Gaudì with his dripping, stalactite-like stone, from which fantastic limestone animals struggle to emerge. Casts of Michelangelo's *nonfiniti* slaves stand in the corners, replacing the originals put there by the Medici, while in the shadowy depths stands a luscious Venus coming from her bath by Giambologna.

The **Amphitheatre**, ascending in regular tiers from the palace, was designed like a small Roman circus to hold Medici court spectacles, most famously in 1661 a performance of Il Mondo Festeggiante, a play that included a lavish display of balleton horseback, tableaux vivants, and phantasmagoria all in the most splendid costumes, attended by 20,000 people in honour of the marriage of the lugubrious Grand Duke Cosimo III to the frisky Marguerite-Louise, niece of Louis XIV. It has a genuine obelisk, of Rameses II from Heliopolis, snatched by the ancient Romans and shipped here by the Medici branch in Rome. The granite basin, large enough to submerge an elephant, came from the Roman Baths of Caracalla. Straight up the terrace is the **Neptune Fountain**; a path leads from there to the pretty **Kaffeehaus**, a boat-like pavilion with a prow and deck offering a fine view of Florence and drinks in the summer. Other signs from the Neptune Fountain point the way up to the secluded **Giardino del Cavaliere**, located on a bastion on Michelangelo's fortifications (*open same hours as the Porcelain Museum*). Cosimo III built the casino here to escape the summer heat in the Pitti Palace; the view over the ancient villas, vineyards and olives is pure Tuscan enchantment.

Santa Felicità D6

*Piazza Santa Felicità; **bus** D. **Open** daily 9–12 and 3–6.*

Although rebuilt in 1736, Santa Felicità is one of Florence's most ancient churches, founded (or so they say) by the Syrian Greek traders who introduced Christianity to the city, and who established the first Christian cemetery in the small square in front of the church. The dome was destroyed in the mid-16th century to make way for Cosimo I's catwalk, the Vasari Corridor, which is awkwardly part of the upper façade. There is one compelling reason to enter, and it's in the first chapel on the right, the *ne plus ultra* of Mannerism: Pontormo's weirdly luminous *Deposition* (1528), painted in shimmering chromatic pinks, oranges and blues that cut through the darkness of the little chapel. Michelangelo wrote that 'One paints with the head, not with the hand': and here naturalism gives way to idea, Pontormo's weightless figures, almost seeming to dance in a circle with the dead Christ. Flaunting all convention, a blue rag holds centre stage in the composition; there is no sign of a cross, the only background is a single cloud. Sharing the chapel is Pontormo's *Annunciation* fresco, a less idiosyncratic work, as well as four tondi of the Evangelists in the cupola, partly the work of Pontormo's pupil and adopted son, Bronzino.

Casa Guidi C6

***Piazza San Felice 8; bus D. Open** April–Nov Mon, Wed and Fri 3–6; **adm** free, voluntary donation.*

In the 17th century the neighbourhood around the Pitti was a fashionable address, but in the 19th century rents for a furnished palace were incredibly low. Shortly after their secret marriage, Robert and Elizabeth Barrett Browning found one of these, the Casa Guidi, the perfect place to settle (Elizabeth, an invalid, had been ordered to Italy by her doctor). During their 13 years here Elizabeth became obsessed with Italian politics, and wrote the *Casa Guidi Windows* (1851) in an attempt to gain sympathy for Florence. Robert wrote little during his Florence years, outside of the poetry in *Men and Women*, but after his beloved Elizabeth died in 1861 after taking a chill, he took their young son and left for London, although Italian subjects would always remain an inspiration. The house is now owned by the Browning Institute and contains some original furnishings, personal belongings and a library with an extensive collection of books by and about the Brownings.

Dostoevsky wrote *The Idiot* while living nearby, at No.21 Piazza Pitti. Note the doorbells at No.13, 10 little wrought-iron gargoyles waiting to have their heads pulled.

La Specola C6–7

*Via Romana 17; **bus** D. **Open** Thurs–Tues 9–1; **adm** €3.10.*

The former Palazzo Torrigiani was nicknamed La Specola after Grand Duke Pietro Leopold made it an astronomical observatory in the 1770s and founded the **Museo Zoologico**, a charmingly old-fashioned collection of nearly everything that walks, flies or swims, from the humble sea worm to the rare Madagascar aye-aye or the swordfish, with an accessory case of different blades. Some trophies bagged by the hunt-crazy House of Savoy are displayed, while near the end come small wax models of human and animal anatomy, wax eggs, a wax peeled chicken and wax skinned cat.

The real horror show stuff, however, is kept hidden away in the **Museum of Waxes**. Dotty, prudish old Cosimo III was a hypochondriac and morbidly obsessed with diseases, which his favourite artist, a Sicilian priest named Gaetano Zumbo, was able to portray in wax with revolting realism for his patron to fret over – macabre anatomical models that were a popular sight for 18th-century Grand Tourists.

AROUND SANTO SPIRITO

Piazza Santo Spirito C6

***Bus** D.*

Piazza Santo Spirito is the centre of Oltrarno life. Sleepy in the morning, except for a few market stalls under the plane trees and a quiet café or two, in the evening the bars fill until the early hours with people who meet and chat in the piazza and on the steps of Santo Spirito.

Santo Spirito C5

*Piazza S. Spirito. **Open** Mon–Fri 8.30–12 and 4–6, Sat and Sun 4–6; **adm** free.*

A plain 18th-century façade (currently under restoration until late summer 2002) hides Brunelleschi's last and perhaps greatest church. He designed Santo Spirito in 1440 and lived to see only one column erected, but subsequent architects were faithful to his elegant plan for the interior. This is done in Brunelleschi's favourite pale grey *pietra serena* articulation, a rhythmic forest of columns with semicircular chapels gracefully recessed into the transepts and the three arms of the crossing. The effect is somewhat spoiled by the ornate

17th-century *baldacchino*, which sits in this enchanted garden of pure architecture like a 19th-century bandstand.

Most of the good paintings in Santo Spirito were sold off over the years. The best that remain are Filippino Lippi's beautiful *Madonna and Saints* in the right transept and Verrocchio's jewel-like *St Monica and Nuns*, an unusual composition and certainly one of the blackest paintings of the Renaissance, pervaded with a dusky, mysterious quality; Verrocchio, who taught both Leonardo and Botticelli, was a Hermetic alchemist on the side. The fine marble altarpiece and decoration in the next chapel is by Sansovino; the elaborate barrel-vaulted **Vestibule** and octagonal **Sacristy**, entered from the left aisle, are by Giuliano da Sangallo, inspired by Brunelleschi.

Also hanging in Santo Spirito is a painted wooden ***Crucifix***, discovered in the church in 1963 and believed by most scholars to be a documented one by Michelangelo. The *contrapposto* position of the slender body, and the fact that only Michelangelo would carve a nude Christ weigh in favour of the attribution.

To the left of the church, in the **refectory** (*open 10.30–1.30, until 12.30 Sun, closed Mon; adm €2.06*) of the long gone 14th-century convent, are the scanty remains of a *Last Supper* and a well-preserved, highly dramatic *Crucifixion* by Andrea Orcagna, in which Christ is seen alone against an enormous dark sky, with humanity ranged below and angels like white swallows swirling around in a cosmic whirlwind. The refectory also contains an interesting collection of Romanesque odds and ends, including 13th-century stone sea lions from Naples.

Santa Maria del Carmine B5

*Piazza del Carmine; **bus** D. **Cappella Brancacci open** Mon and Wed–Sat 10–5 (last adm 4.45), Sun and hols 1–5; **adm** €3.10. Only 30 people admitted at a time for 15 minutes; you can usually avoid waiting if you go at lunch time.*

There is little to say about the rough stone façade or the interior of Santa Maria del Carmine, which burned in 1771 and was reconstructed shortly after. Miraculously, the **Cappella Brancacci**, one of the seminal works of Florentine Renaissance painting, survived both the flames and attempts by the authorities to replace it with something more fashionable. Three artists worked on the Brancacci's frescoes: Masolino, who began them in 1425, and who designed the cycle, his pupil Masaccio, who worked on them alone for a year before following his master to Rome, where he died at the age of 27, and Filippino Lippi, who finished them 50 years later, when the Brancacci, who were silk merchants exiled by the Medici in 1436, were permitted to return. By then Masaccio's work was legendary and had been closely studied by all the painters in Florence, and Filippino took care to imitate him as closely as possible, giving the frescoes the appearance of stylistic unity. Between 1981 and 1988 the chapel was subject to one of Italy's most publicized restorations, cleansed of 550 years of dirt and overpainting and, controversially, Adam and Eve's fig leaves, enabling us to see what so thrilled the painters of the Renaissance.

Masaccio in his day was a revolution and a revelation in his solid, convincing naturalism; his powerful figures, inspired by Donatello's sculptures, are real men and women's bodies, without any fussy ornamentation or Gothic grace, feeling real emotions. One only has to compare the elegant *Temptation of Adam* by Masolino, where the beautiful figures gracefully gesture under the gaze of the woman-headed serpent, with Masaccio's *Expulsion of Adam and Eve*, opposite; the despair of the first two humans, weeping and howling as they leave the exceedingly narrow gate of paradise, is one of the most memorable and harrowing images created in the Renaissance. Next to it, in the *Rendering of the Tribute Money*, the young artist displays his mastery of Brunelleschian artificial perspective and light effects. The three episodes in the fresco show an official demanding tribute from the city (in the centre), St Peter fetching it on Christ's direction from the mouth of a fish (on the left) and, lastly, his handing over of the money to the official on the right. It is an unusual subject in art, and it seems that Felice Brancacci especially chose it as a comment to show his support for the introduction of a property register in Florence, even though it would make it easier to tax rich men like himself. Other works by 'Shabby Tom' include *St Peter Baptizing the Neophytes* (note the realistic shivver and wetness) and *St Peter Healing with his Shadow* both on the upper register, and *St Peter Enthroned and Resurrecting the Son of the King of Antioch* from a shroud filled with bones, the right half of which was finished by Filippino Lippi. The elegant and graceful Masolino's *Healing of the Cripple and the Raising of Tabitha* (*c.* 1425) was also revolutionary for its time, with the action taking place in a typical Italian piazza, complete with clothes on the line and a pet monkey. He was responsible for the rest, except for the lower register's *Release of St Peter from Prison*, *St Peter Crucified* and *St Paul Visiting St Peter in Prison*, all by Filippino Lippi, based on Masaccio's sketches.

Among the detached frescoes displayed in the cloister and refectory is a good one by Filippino's dad, Fra Filippo Lippi, who was born nearby in Via dell'Ardiglione.

For more information on this area, the **walk** on p.157 covers the western Oltrarno.

EAST OF THE PONTE VECCHIO

Many great medieval bankers erected their palaces in the Oltrarno. Several may still be seen along Via de' Bardi, east of the Ponte Vecchio, a street once entirely owned by the Bardi. John Pope Henessy lived in No.28 until his death in 1994. Palazzo Capponi (No.36) has a ghoulish gargoyle incorporated into its stone crest above the door. On the right, now a garden, a little plaque commemorates a stay by St Francis in 1211. The church of Santa Lucia dei Magnoli on the left has a della Robbia-like relief above the door, and on the next right-hand corner is the 'Smallest Art Gallery in the World'.

Museo Bardini/ Galleria Corsi F6

Piazza dei Mozzi. Currently closed for restoration for an indefinite time.

This eclectic collection of art and architectural fragments was left to the city in 1922 by the great antique dealer and Risorgimento veteran Stefano Bardini. Bardini built his rather lugubrious palace, re-using bits of the church of San Gregorio della Pace that once stood here, along with doorways, ceilings and stairs that he salvaged from the demolition of the Mercato Vecchio and other buildings in central Florence. San Gregorio's crypt came in handy to install his collection of tombs and altarpieces (there's an especially fine one by Andrea della Robbia). Also outstanding are Tino di Camaino's trecento *Charity*, a *Madonna* attributed to Donatello, a panel painting of *St Michael* by Antonio Pollaiuolo, and a magnificent set of Persian carpets, old musical instruments, a cardinal's hat that may have belonged to Silvio Piccolomini, the future Pius II, 15th-century papier-mâché dummies, a wooden model of Pisa Baptistry, furniture and armour. More of the Bardini collection, recently left to the city by Stefano's son, will soon be open in the elegant 13th–14th-century **Palazzo dei Mozzi**, also in the piazza.

The bridge here, the nondescript postwar **Ponte alle Grazie,** replaced a famous medieval bridge with seven chapels on it, home to seven nuns, who one imagines spent much of their time praying that the Arno wouldn't flood.

Outside the Centre

FORTE DI BELVEDERE AND SAN LEONARDO IN ARCETRI 145
SAN MINIATO 145
BELLOSGUARDO 147
THE CASCINE 147
FORTEZZA DA BASSO 147
RUSSIAN CHURCH 147
THE STIBBERT MUSEUM 148
MUSEO DELLE PORCELLANE DI DOCCIA 148
PONTE A MENSOLA AND SETTIGNANO 148
THE CERTOSA DEL GALLUZZO 149
CARMIGNANO 149
COMEANA 149
MEDICI VILLAS 149

07

Outside the Centre
N
5 km
2.5 miles
Prato
Prato Calenzano
Settimello
Sesto Fiorentino
Museo delle Porcellane di Doccia
Firenze Nord
Quinto
Cercina
Pratolino
R. Mugnone
Caldine
Villa di Castello
Villa la Petraia
Trespiano
Pian di Mugnone
Villa Careggi
Fiesole
Castello
Firenze Nova
VIA BOLOGNESE
S. Domenico
Stibbert Museum
Maiano
Florence
Rifredi
Novoli
Peretola
Peretola Airport
Campi Bisenzio
Poggio a Caiano
Carmignano
R. Ombrone
A11
AUTOSTRADA FIRENZE MARE
SS66
S325
Arno
Le Cascine
Russian Church
Fortezza da Basso
Settignano
Ponte a Mensola
Ippodromo
Stazione Centrale
Campo di Marte
L'Isolotto
Ponte della Vittoria
Duomo
SS67
Signa
Lastra a Signa
Villa Artimino
Firenze Signa
Ponte a Greve
Bellosguardo
Boboli Gardens
Forte di Belvedere
Rovezzano
Porta Romana
Gavinana
Badia a Ripoli
Soffiano
San Leonardo in Arcetri
San Miniato
Bagno a Ripoli
Scandicci
Villa il Gioiello
Greve
Villa di Poggio Imperiale
Ponte a Ema
Ema
Firenze Sud
A1
AUTOSTRADA DEL SOLE
Certosa del Galluzzo
Montelupo Fiorentino
TUSCANY
S. Donato in Collina
Grassina
Firenze Certosa
Tavarnuzze
To Pisa
Chiesanuova
To Siena

Great Aunt Florence, with her dour complexion and severe, lined face, never was much of a looker from street level, but improves with a bit of distance, from one of her hilltop balconies: the Forte di Belvedere, San Miniato, Piazzale Michelangelo, Bellosguardo, Fiesole or Settignano. Few cities, in fact, are so well endowed with stunning vistas; and when you look down on Florence's palaces and towers, her loping bridges and red tile roofs and famous churches, Brunelleschi's incomparable dome seems even more remarkable, hovering like a benediction over the city.

Down below, the newer sections of the city are irredeemably dull. Much of Florence's traffic problem is channelled through its ring of avenues, or *viali*, laid out in the 1860s by Giuseppe Poggi to replace the demolished walls. On and along them are scattered points of interest, including the old city gates; the distances involved and danger of carbon monoxide poisoning on the *viali* make the idea of walking insane.

A bit further afield, the outskirts of the city have long lured the Florentines out of their streets of history into some of Tuscany's loveliest countryside. Lofty Fiesole, Florence's grandmother, and a set of Medici villas are all easily reached by public transport; and as Fiesole is such a popular outing we've made it into a walk (*see* p.159).

Forte di Belvedere D7 and San Leonardo in Arcetri E8

***Bus** 13, then walk.*

One of Florence's best and closest balconies is the **Belvedere Fort**, a graceful six-point star designed by Buontalenti and built in 1590–5, not so much for the sake of defence but to remind any remaining Florentine republicans who was boss. Since 1958, it has been used for special exhibitions, but you can always enjoy the unforgettable views of Florence and the countryside from its ramparts (*currently under restoration until probably 2003*). It is a lovely place for a break when sightseeing gets to be too much, with a big lawn on one side to stretch out on.

There are two ways to get there: from the Boboli Gardens, or by ascending one of Florence's prettiest streets, **Costa San Giorgio**, which begins in Piazza Santa Felicità, just beyond the Ponte Vecchio, and winds up the hill, past old villas and walled gardens. The villa at No.19 was the home of Galileo, from 1610 to 1631, when he was invited to Florence by Cosimo II. The top of the street is closed by the arch of the **Porta San Giorgio**, bearing a 13th-century relief of St George and dragon.

Above Porta San Giorgio, yet only 10 minutes' walk from the Ponte Vecchio, you're in the middle of the country, a rolling landscape of olives and cypresses, villas and gardens: rural Tuscany begins right at the city wall. A 10-minute walk along winding Via San Leonardo will take you to the 11th-century **San Leonardo in Arcetri** (*usually open Sunday mornings*). There is a wonderful 13th-century pulpit, originally in San Pier Scheraggio, and a small rose window, made according to legend from a wheel of Fiesole's *carroccio*, captured by Florence in 1125. A half-kilometre further on, past the Viale Galileo crossroads, Via San Leonardo changes its name to Via Viviani, where it passes the **Astrophysical Observatory** (which you can visit, day or night) and the **Torre del Gallo**, a reconstruction of a 14th-century tower by art dealer Stefano Bardini. Another kilometre further on Via Viviani reaches the settlement of Pian de' Giullari, where Galileo spent the last years of his life, in the 16th-century **Villa il Gioiello**, virtually under house arrest after his encounter with the Inquisition in 1631, and where Milton probably visited him.

San Miniato G8

*Up the stepped Via di San Salvatore al Monte from Porta San Miniato, or **bus** 13 up the scenic Viale dei Colli from the station or Piazza del Duomo. **Open** summer daily 8–7.30, winter daily 8–12.30 and 2.30–7.30; **adm** free. Come*

at 4.30pm (winter) or 5.30pm (summer) to hear the Gregorian chant.

High atop its monumental steps, San Miniato's distinctive and beautiful façade can be seen from almost anywhere in Florence, although relatively few visitors take the time to visit one of the finest Romanesque churches in Italy.

San Miniato was built in 1015, over an earlier church that marked the spot where the head of St Minias, a 3rd-century Roman soldier, bounced when the Romans axed it off. The church has always been one of the dearest to the Florentines' hearts. The remarkable geometric pattern of green, black and white marble that adorns its façade was begun in 1090, though funds only permitted the embellishment of the lower, simpler half of the front; the upper half, full of curious astrological symbolism (someone has just written a whole book about it), was added in the 12th century, paid for by the Arte di Calimala, the guild that made a fortune buying bolts of fine wool, dyeing them a deep red that no one else in Europe could imitate, then selling them back for twice the price; their proud gold eagle stands at the top of the roof. The glittering mosaic of Christ, the Virgin and St Minias came slightly later.

The Calimala was also responsible for decorating the interior; as in many Romanesque churches with an important martyr's tomb, the crypt gets centre stage, and the presbytery is raised above it. As the Calimala became richer, so did the fittings; the delicate intarsia **marble floor** of animals and zodiac symbols dates from 1207. The lower walls were frescoed in the 14th and 15th centuries, and include an enormous St Christopher. At the end of the nave stands Michelozzo's unique, free-standing **Cappella del Crocifisso** (1448) magnificently carved and adorned with terracottas by Luca della Robbia, built to hold the crucifix that spoke to St John Gualberto (now in Santa Trínita).

Off the left nave is one of Florence's Renaissance showcases, the **Chapel of the Cardinal of Portugal** (1461–6). The 25-year-old cardinal, a member of the Portuguese royal family, happened to die in Florence at an auspicious moment, when the Medici couldn't spend enough on publicly prominent art, and when some of the greatest artists of the quattrocento were at the height of their careers. The chapel was designed by Manetti, Brunelleschi's pupil; the ceiling was exquisitely decorated with enamelled terracotta and medallions by Luca della Robbia; the tomb of the Cardinal was beautifully carved by Antonio Rossellino; the fresco of the Annunciation was charmingly painted by Alesso Baldovinetti; the altarpiece *Three Saints* is a copy of the original by Piero Pollaiuolo.

Up the steps of the choir more treasures await. The marble transenna and pulpit were carved in 1207, with art and a touch of medieval humour. Playful geometric patterns frame the mosaic in the apse, *Christ between the Virgin and St Minias*, made in 1297 by artists imported from Ravenna, and later restored by Baldovinetti. The colourful **Sacristy** on the right was frescoed by Spinello Aretino in 1387, but made rather flat by subsequent restoration. In the **Crypt** an 11th-century altar holds the relics of St Minias; the columns are topped by ancient capitals. The **cloister** has frescoes of the Holy Fathers by Paolo Uccello, remarkable works in painstaking and fantastical perspective, rediscovered in 1925.

The panorama of Florence from San Miniato is lovely to behold, but such thoughts were hardly foremost in Michelangelo's mind during the Siege of Florence. The hill was vulnerable, and to defend it he hastily erected the fortress (now surrounding the cemetery to the left), placed cannons in the unfinished 16th-century campanile (built to replace an original which fell over), and shielded the tower from artillery with mattresses. He grew fond of the small church below San Miniato, **San Salvatore al Monte**, built by Cronaca in the late 1400s, which he called his 'pretty country lass'.

With these associations in mind, the city named the vast, square car park below

Piazzale Michelangelo. This is the most popular viewpoint only because it is the only one capable of accommodating an unlimited number of tour buses. On Sunday afternoons, crowds of Florentines habitually make a stop here as well during their after-lunch *passeggiata*. Besides another copy of the *David* and a fun, tacky carnival atmosphere, the Piazzale offers views that can reach as far as Pistoia on a clear day.

Bellosguardo Off maps

***Bus** 11, 36, 37, then 20min walk.*

Many would argue that the finest of all views over Florence is to be had from Bellosguardo, located almost straight up from Porta Romana at the end of the Boboli Gardens or Piazza Torquato Tasso. Non-mountaineers may want to take a taxi; the famous viewpoint, from where you can see every church façade in the city, is just before Piazza Bellosguardo. The area is a peaceful little residential oasis of superb villas and houses gathered round a square. The grandest villa, Villa Bellosguardo, was built in 1780 for Marquis Orazio Pucci, ancestor of the late Florentine fashion designer Emilio Pucci. The great tenor Enrico Caruso bought it for his retirement, although he lived there for only three years before he died, in 1921.

The Cascine Off maps

***Bus** 17 from the station or Duomo.*

The Cascine is the long (3.5km), narrow public park lining the north bank of the Arno. It was originally the Medici's dairy farm, or *cascina*, and later a Grand Ducal hunting park and theatre for public spectacles.

A windy autumn day in the Cascine in 1819 inspired Shelley to compose the 'Ode to the West Wind'. Three years later Shelley's drowned body was burnt on a pyre in Viareggio, by his friend Trelawny; curiously, a similar incineration took place in the Cascine in 1870 when the Maharaja of Kohlapur died in Florence. According to Hindu ritual his body had to be burned near the confluence of two rivers, in this case, the Arno and Mugnone at the far end of the park, on a spot now marked by the **Ponte all'Indiano** (the Indian's Bridge), a modern, bright rust-coloured road bridge which can be seen for miles around.

Florentines come to the Cascine to play; it has a riding school, race tracks, rides and zoo for children, tennis courts, and a swimming-pool; the Grand Ducal railway terminus, Stazione Leopolda, is situated at the city end of the park and is a large performance space. At night, the *viale* which runs parallel to the river and the Cascine is the favourite hang-out for transvestites and the car drivers who ogle them.

Fortezza da Basso C1

*Near the train station; **bus** 23.*

Cars and buses hurtle around the Fortezza da Basso, an enormous bulk built by Antonio da Sangallo on orders from the extravagant authoritative Duke Alessandro de' Medici in 1534. The rest of the city hated the citadel, 'built with the blood of her unhappy people as a prison and slaughter-house for the unhappy citizens'. The talk inspired Alessandro's fame-seeking cousin and bosom companion, Lorenzo de Pierfrancesco (or Lorenzaccio) de' Medici, to lure the duke to his house with the promise of a sexual adventure and stab him as he slept. As a fortress, the place never saw any action as thrilling or vicious as the annual Pitti fashion shows that take place here.

Russian Church Off maps

***Bus** 14. Services Sat 6pm and Sun 10.30am. Call **t** 055 490148 to arrange a visit.*

Just east of the Fortezza, at the corner of Via Leone X and Viale Milton, an unexpected sight rises above the sleepy residential neighbourhood – the five graceful and lofty colour-tiled onion domes of the Russian Church, made even more exotic by the palm tree tickling its side. In the 19th century, Florence was a popular winter retreat for

Russians who could afford it, among them Dostoievsky and Maxim Gorky. Completed by Russian architects in 1904, it is a pretty jewel box of brick and majolica decoration, open on the third Sunday of the month at 10.30am when the priest from Nice comes to hold services in Russian.

The Stibbert Museum Off maps

***Via Stibbert 26; bus** 4 from the station, or 1km walk from Piazza della Libertà up Via Vittorio Emanuele. **Open** Mon–Wed 10–2, Fri–Sun 10–6; **adm** €5.*

Frederick Stibbert (1838–1906) fought with Garibaldi and hobnobbed with Queen Victoria, and you can savour his lifetime's accumulations in Florence's most bizarre museum, and its nicest small park, laid out by Stibbert, complete with a mouldering Egyptian temple sinking in a pond.

Stibbert's Italian mother left him a 14th-century house, which he enlarged, joining it to another house to create a sumptuous Victorian version of what a medieval Florentine house should have looked like – 64 rooms to contain a pack-rat's hoard of all things brilliant and useless, from an attributed Botticelli to snuff boxes, to what a local guide intriguingly describes as 'brass and silver basins, used daily by Stibbert'. Stibbert's serious passion, however, was armour, and he amassed a magnificent collection from all times and places. The best pieces are not arranged in dusty cases, but, with a touch of Hollywood, on grim knightly mannequins ranked ready for battle.

Museo delle Porcellane di Doccia Off maps

*Via Pratese 31, Sesto Fiorentino. **Train** to Sesto Fiorentino (10min journey), or **bus** 28A from the station (40min journey). **Open** Tues, Thurs and Sat 9.30–1 and 3.30–6.30; **adm** €5.17.*

You can change gears again by heading out a little further in the sprawl to Sesto Fiorentino, a suburb that since 1954 has been home to the famous Richard-Ginori china and porcelain firm. Founded in 1735, the firm has opened this mueum to display a neat chronology of its production of Doccia ware, including many Medici commissions (a ceramic Venus de' Medici), fine painted porcelain, and some pretty Art Nouveau works.

Ponte a Mensola and Settignano Off maps

***Bus** 10 from the station or Piazza San Marco.*

The least touristy of all the balconies over Florence sits under the village of Settignano. The road up passes by way of Ponte a Ménsola, where Boccaccio spent his childhood in the Villa Poggio Gherardo, and where it is believed he set the first three days of *The Decameron*. In the 9th century, a Scottish Benedictine saint named Andrew founded the church of San Martino a Mensola, just beyond the villa on a little square. Rebuilt in the 1400s, the church has three good trecento works: Taddeo Gaddi's *Triptych of the Madonna with SS. Lucy and Margherita*, his son Agnolo's panel paintings *St Andrew's Casket*, and on the high altar another triptych by the school of Orcagna, dated 1391. From the quattrocento there's a *Madonna and Saints* by Neri di Bicci on the first altar on the left.

If you leave the church and keep left, you'll soon come to **Villa i Tatti**, on the enchanting road up to Fiesole (*see* walk, p.161). If you turn right instead of left at San Martino a Ménsola you'll come to **Settignano**, a delightful bourg surrounded by villas. During the Renaissance it was a cradle of sculptors, producing Desiderio da Settignano and the brothers Antonio and Bernardo Rossellino; Michelangelo spent his childhood here as well, in the Villa Buonarroti. Not one left anything behind to remember them by; the good art in the parish church of the Assunta is by Andrea della Robbia (an enamelled terracotta, the *Madonna and Child*) and Buontalenti (the pulpit). There are, however, splendid views of Florence from Piazza Desiderio, and plenty of places to quaff a glass of Chianti.

The Certosa del Galluzzo Off maps

South of Poggio Imperiale, on a hill off the Siena road; bus 37 from the station. Open Tues–Sun 9–12 and 3–6; adm free.

One of the landmarks near Florence, the fortress-like Certosa del Galluzzo (or Certosa di Firenze) sits high over the Siena road on a hill planted with olives and cypresses. It was founded for the Carthusians in 1341 by one of Andrea Castagno's 'Great Men' in the Uffizi, Niccolò Acciaiuoli, tycoon, *condottiere* and good friend of Petrarch and Boccaccio. Since 1958 it has been inhabited by Cistercians, one of whom takes visitors around. The Certosa has a fine 16th-century courtyard and church of San Lorenzo, with lots of 17th-century art and the pretty Cappella di Santa Maria of 1404, while the subterranean chapels contain impressive and perfectly preserved tombs of the Acciaiuoli family, including a handsome Gothic one of the founder, and a superb one to Cardinal Agnolo II Acciaiuoli, once attributed to Donatello. A door leads into the Coro dei Padri (where the Carthusians worshipped), with its beautifully carved stalls of 1570 and a sumptuous late 16th-century altar.

The visit continues into the equally lavish monastery, first to the Colloquio with its 16th-century stained glass, then the Chiostro Medio and the frescoed Sala del Capitolo, and then the **Chiostro Grande**, a pure Renaissance work (1498–1516) surrounded by the monks' cells, and decorated with 66 majolica tondi of prophets and saints by Giovanni della Robbia and assistants; one cell is opened for visits, and is almost cosy. The Gothic stone **Palazzo degli Studi** was intended by the founder as a school of liberal arts, and is now part of the Certosa's Pinacoteca containing five superb lunettes by Pontormo, painted while he and his pupil Bronzino hid out here from the plague in 1522.

Carmignano Off maps

A local bus continues 5km southwest of Poggio a Caiano (see p.151) to Carmignano. Guided tours of San Michele by appointment only, t 055 871 2046.

There is one compelling reason to visit Carmignano and its church San Michele: Pontormo's uncanny painting *The Visitation* (1530s), one of the masterpieces of Florentine Mannerism. There are no concessions to naturalism here – the four soulful, ethereal women, draped in Pontormo's startling luminous colours, barely touch the ground, standing before a scene as substantial as a stage backdrop. The result is one of the most unforgettable images from the 16th century.

Comeana: Etruscan Tombs Off maps

3km south of Poggio a Caiano (see p.151), at Comeana Montefortini, t 0574 24112. Tomba di Montefortini open Tues–Sun 9–2; adm free. Tomba dei Boschetti temporarily closed; call above number for information.

The well-preserved Etruscan **Tomba di Montefortini** is a 7th-century BC burial mound, 36ft high and 262ft in diameter, covering two burial chambers. A long hall leads down to the vestibule and rectangular tomb chamber, both carefully covered with false vaulting; the wide shelf in the chamber was probably used for the gifts an Etruscan needed for the afterlife.

An equally impressive tomb nearby, the **Tomba dei Boschetti**, was seriously damaged over the centuries by local farmers.

Medici Villas Off maps

Like their Bourbon cousins in France, the Medici liked to pass the time acquiring new palaces for themselves. In their case, however, the reason was less self-exaltation than simple property speculation; one secret of the Medici's success was that they always thought several generations ahead. As a result the countryside is littered with their villas, most of them privately owned, although some are partly open to the public.

Villa Careggi

Viale Pieraccini 17, t 055 427 9755; bus 14C from the station. You can visit all rooms on Sat, and some rooms Mon–Fri. Open Mon–Fri 9–1, Sat 9–6. You can stroll through its gardens and woods.

Perhaps the best-known Medici villa is Careggi, a fortified farmhouse that was enlarged for Cosimo il Vecchio by Michelozzo in 1434. It became synonymous with the birth of Humanism when Cosimo founded his Platonic Academy here, which was eagerly continued by his grandson, the Magnificent Lorenzo. The greatest Latin and Greek scholars of the day, Ficino, Poliziano, Pico della Mirandola and Argyropoulos, would meet here and hold philosophical discussions in imitation of a Platonic symposium; every 7 November they would hold a splendid banquet in honour of Plato's birthday. As Cosimo il Vecchio and Piero had both died at Careggi, when Lorenzo felt the end was near at age 43, he had himself carried out to the villa, with Poliziano and Pico della Mirandola to bear him company, and Savonarola to confess him. After his death, the villa was burned by Florentine republicans, although Cosimo I later had it rebuilt, and Francis Sloane had it restored. It is now used as health authority offices.

Villa La Petraia

Via della Petraia 40. Frustrating to reach if you're on your own; take a taxi or, if you are adventurous, bus 28 from the station, and get off after the wastelands, by Via Reginaldo Giuliano. Open daily 9–4.30; closed the second and fourth Mon of the month; in spring and summer, the hours extend in the evening; adm €2.06 (includes Villa di Castello).

Further east, amid the almost continuous conurbation of power lines and industrial landscapes that blight the Prato road, the Villa la Petraia manages to remain Arcadian on its steeply sloping hill. La Petraia was purchased by Grand Duke Ferdinando I in 1557 and rebuilt as a splendid villa by Buontalenti, who kept the tower of the original country castle intact. Unfortunately Vittorio Emanuele II liked it as much as the Medici, and when Florence was the capital of Italy, he had it redesigned to suit his relentlessly bad taste. Still, the interior has its charms. The ornate Baroque court is frescoed with a pastel history of the Medici by 17th-century masters Volterrano and Giovanni di San Giovanni; Vittorio Emanuele II added the glass roof so that he could use the space as a ballroom. Of the remainder of the palace, you're likely to remember best the Chinese painting of Canton and the games room, with billiard tables as large as football fields and perhaps the world's first pinball machine, made of wood. A small room contains Giambologna's endearing *Venus Wringing Water from Her Hair*. La Petraia's beautiful hanging garden on the right side of the villa, with its elegant marble fountain, was designed for the pre-Medici owners by sculptor Niccolò Pericoli Tribolo and the park, shaded by ancient cypresses, is open throughout the afternoon.

If you walk up Via della Petraia, on the left is the grandiose Villa Corsini, a rare example of an intact Baroque villa, with a theatrical façade from the early 18th century.

Villa di Castello

Via di Castello 40; bus 28 from station. From La Petraia, turn right at Via di Castello for 450m. Gardens open daily 9–4.30; closed the second and third Monday of the month; in spring and summer, extended hours in the evening. See Villa La Petraia for adm.

One of Tuscany's most famous gardens is just down the hill from La Petraia, at Villa di Castello. The villa was bought in 1477 by Lorenzo di Pierfrancesco and Giovanni de' Medici, cousins of Lorenzo il Magnifico who were Botticelli's patrons, and they hung the walls of this villa with his mythological paintings that are now the big stars of the

Uffizi. The villa was sacked in the 1530 siege, then restored by Cosimo I, and today is the headquarters of the Accademia della Crusca, founded by Grand Duke Francesco in 1583 and dedicated to maintaining the purity of the Tuscan (now Italian) language; originally it was so strict and pro-Florentine that it exiled a playwright, Girolamo Gigli, for daring to suggest that St Catherine of Siena wrote better than Boccaccio. Less stuffy and pedantic than the more recent Académie Française, members are currently compiling a historical dictionary, and look at their task as linguistic 'baking'; one room has all their names carefully preserved, not on the usual coats of arms, but on bakers' shovels (*no adm*).

The **Garden**, one of the prototypes for the classic *giardino all'italiana*, was laid out for Cosimo I by Tribolo in the 1540s. Tribolo also designed the fountain in the centre, with a bronze Hercules and Antenaeus by Ammannati. Directly behind the fountain, a fantastical artificial stalactite cave, the **Grotto degli Animali**, is lined with pebble and seashell mosaics and filled by Ammannati and Giambologna with a fountain and marvellous, true-to-life statues of every animal, fish and bird known to man (some are copies of Giambologna's originals in the Bargello). The shady terrace above offers the best view over the geometric garden below; Ammannati's large statue of January, or *Gennaio*, emerges shivering from a pool of water among the trees.

A 20-minute walk north from Villa di Castello to Quinto takes you to two unusual 7th-century BC **Etruscan tombs**: La Montagnola, Via Filli Rosselli 95, and La Mula, Via della Mula 2. Neither has any art, but the chambers under their 26ft artificial hills resemble others elsewhere in the Mediterranean – the domed tholos tombs of Mycenaean Greece, corbelled passages like the navetas of Majorca, and entrances that look like the sacred wells of Sardinia. Unfortunately both are closed for several years due to work on a new high-speed rail line.

Villa Demidoff

Pratolino, 12km north of Florence along Via Bolognese; bus 25A or a SITA bus from Piazza Stazione. Open Mar and Oct Sun 10–6, April–Sept Thurs–Sun 10–8.

In 1568, the infatuated Duke Francesco I built this charming villa as a gift to his mistress, the beautiful Venetian Bianca Capello, whom the rest of Florence hated as much as he loved. Francesco commissioned Buontalenti – artist, architect, and hydraulics engineer, nicknamed 'delle Girandole' (of the Catherine wheel) for the fantastic fireworks he made – to design the enormous gardens, and he made Pratolino the marvel of its day, full of water tricks, ingenious automata, grottoes with changeable scenery, musical waterfalls and organs and a famous menagerie, all of which greatly impressed Montaigne during a visit in 1581. Sadly, none of Buontalenti's wonders have survived, except for the largest-ever example of this play between art and environment – Giambologna's massive *Appennino*, a giant rising from stone, part stalactite, part fountain himself. The Medici liked to trace their descent back to one Averardo, a knight who fought with Charlemagne and killed a giant who had been terrorizing the Mugello just north of here. In the battle, the giant bashed deep dents in Averardo's shield, which Charlemagne made his coat of arms, the famous Medici *palle* or balls.

When the Lorraines inherited the place, they made the rest of the park into an English garden and demolished the house. Prince Paolo Demidoff bought the estate in 1872 and restored the servants' quarters as his villa; today it is an invitingly cool refuge from a sweltering Florentine summer afternoon .

Poggio a Caiano

COPIT buses go past every half-hour, departing from the McDonald's on the north side of the station. Villa, t 055 877012, open daily Nov–Feb 8.15–3.30; April, May, Sept 8.15–5.30; Mar and Oct 8.15–4.30; June–Aug

***8.15–6.30; adm €2.07. Grounds open** Mon–Sat 9–6.30, winter till 4.30, Sun 9–12.30.*

Of all the Medici villas, Poggio a Caiano is the most evocative of the country idylls described in Lorenzo il Magnifico's beautiful poems on the Tuscan countryside; this was not only his favourite retreat, but is generally considered the very first Italian Renaissance villa. Lorenzo purchased a farmhouse here in 1480, and commissioned Giuliano da Sangallo to rebuild it in a classical style. It was Lorenzo's sole architectural commission (not by choice: his mishandling of the family bank drove it to bankruptcy) and its classicism matched the mythological nature of the poems he composed here, most famously *L'Ambra*, which was inspired by the stream Ombrone that flows nearby. Sangallo designed the villa according to Alberti's description of the perfect country house, anticipating Palladio, and added a classical frieze (now a copy) on the façade, sculpted with the assistance of Andrea Sansovino. Some of the other features – the clock, the curved stair and central loggia – were later additions. **Inside**, Sangallo designed an airy, two-storey *Salone*, for which the two Medici popes commissioned frescoes from Pontormo, Andrea del Sarto, Franciabigio and Allori on their favourite subject: the Medici, here dressed as Romans in historical scenes that parallel events in their lives. In the right lunette, around a large circular window, Pontormo painted the lovely *Vertumnus and Pomona* (1521), a languid and beautifully coloured summer scene under a willow tree. In another room, Francesco I and Bianca Cappello his wife died in 1587, only 11 hours apart; Francesco was always messing about with poisons but malaria seems to have been the killer.

Fine old trees and a 19th-century statue of Lorenzo's *L'Ambra* dot the grounds; in Lorenzo's day there was also a menagerie, with a famous sweet-natured giraffe, a present from the Sultan of Babylon.

Villa Artimino

*There is a very infrequent CAP **bus** from Poggio a Caiano to Artimino. **Villa open** summer Tues 9–12.30 and 3–6, winter Tues 8.30–12 and 2–4. **Guided tours** only by appointment, **t** 055 875 1427. **Museum open** Mon–Sat 9.30–1, Sun 9.30–12.30; **adm** €4.13.*

The Etruscan city of Artimino, 4km west, was destroyed by the Romans and is now occupied by a small town and yet another Medici property, the Villa Artimino ('La Ferdinanda'), built as a hunting lodge for Ferdinando I by Buontalenti. Buontalenti gave it a semi-fortified air with buttresses, but the total effect is simple and charming, the long roofline punctuated by innumerable chimneys; the graceful stair was added in the last century from a drawing by the architect in the Uffizi. In the basement, an **Etruscan Archaeological Museum** contains items found in the tombs, among them a unique censer with two basins and a boat, bronze vases, and a red figured krater painted with initiation scenes, found in a 3rd-century tomb . There's a convenient place for lunch in the grounds. Also in Artimino is an attractive Romanesque church, **San Leonardo**, built of stones salvaged from earlier buildings.

Poggio Imperiale

*Viale del Poggio Imperiale, 1km south of Porta Romana; **bus** 11. **Open** Wed 10–12 by request, **t** 055 220151.*

One last Medici villa, the Villa di Poggio Imperiale, stands majestically at the summit of Viale del Poggio Imperiale, a street lined with a stately escort of cypress sentinels. Cosimo I grabbed this huge villa from the Salviati family in 1565, and it remained a ducal property until there were no longer any dukes to duke. Its neoclassical façade was added in 1808, and the audience chamber was decorated in the 17th century by the under-rated Rutilio Manetti and others. Much of the villa is now used as a girls' school.

Walks

DANTE'S FLORENCE WALK 154
OLTRARNO WALK 157
FIESOLE WALK 159

08

DANTE'S FLORENCE WALK

In 1265 Dante Alighieri was born under the sign of Gemini in the San Piero quarter of Florence. Much of what we know about him is supplied by his own writings: although he disregards his immediate family, we know that he was nine, attending Candlemas, 'when first the glorious Lady of my mind was made manifest to mine eyes; even she who was called Beatrice by many who know not wherefore'. Beatrice, however, went on to wed another, and died suddenly in 1290; Dante tried to forget his disappointment and grief in battle, fighting in the wars against Arezzo and Pisa, then in writing his revolutionary 'autopsychology' *La Vita Nuova*. Like the other great poets of Florence's literary awakening, Guido Calvacanti and Foreses Donati, Dante was a keen student of Bruneto Latini, who urged his followers to strive for excellence and fame and, with Aristotle and Cicero as their models, to use their talents to serve their city state, Florence.

In 1302, as a White Guelph, he was exiled from his beloved city; a friend just managed to rescue the manuscript of the *Inferno* from the crowds who came to sack and pillage his home. His exile, although mostly in the palazzi of rich patrons, was hard to bear, 'Bitter is the taste of another man's bread...' as he wrote in the *Paradiso*. In *The Divine Comedy*, Dante interwove his personal trials and solutions with the trials then facing Italy, all set against the poem's great allegory of the fall of man, as his protagonist (generally understood to be himself) is exiled from God in the *Inferno*, spiritually awakened in *Purgatorio* (where he put most of Florence's great poets and painters) and finally fulfilled by union in the city of heaven, beyond the nightmare of history and beyond his very self.

Dante was never allowed to return home, and died in Ravenna just after the completion of his masterpiece in 1321, where the city boss Guido Novello da Polenta, nephew of the famous Francesca da Rimini, had taken him in.

To the end, Florence was never far from his mind, and he refers to the city, its monuments and events from his life there all through the *Commedia*. The best place to summon the shade of Italy's greatest poet is in these narrow medieval lanes. This walk will not only follow sites associated with the poet, but hopefully evoke a little of what his Florence was like along the way. It starts, like so much in Florence, at the Ponte Vecchio.

Start: Ponte Vecchio.
Finish: Piazza Santa Croce.
Walking time: 40 minutes, not including museum visits.
Lunch and drinks stops: Ottorino, *see* p.125; Antico Fattore, *see* p.125; Coquinarius, p.125; Vini e Vecchi Sapori, *see* p.125; Caffè Italiano, *see* p.125; Rivoire, *see* p.125.

In the *Paradiso* (*canto 16, 145–7*) Dante recalls the murder of Buondelmonte dei Buondelmonti in 1215 (*see* p.21), the event that touched off the eternal wars of Guelph and Ghibelline: 'How fitting for this battered stone that guards the bridge, that Florence should make its peace a victim here...' The stone was of course the *Marzocco*, the ancient statue of the war god Mars. In 1333, only 12 years after Dante's death, an Arno flood washed away stone, bridge and all; the replacements would be the bridge you see today, and a new *Marzocco* sculpted by Donatello.

Once over the bridge on the northern side, you would be facing the old walls along the Arno, and the main gate, Porta Santa Maria. The walls are long gone, but the gate's name lives on in the street that carries the bridge traffic into the city. **Via Por Santa Maria** was the business centre of medieval Florence, lined with the green tables of money-changers in front of the buildings, where many of the city's first big bankers and merchants had their headquarters – including, most likely, those upstarts the Medici; Giovanni Bicci di Medici's banking

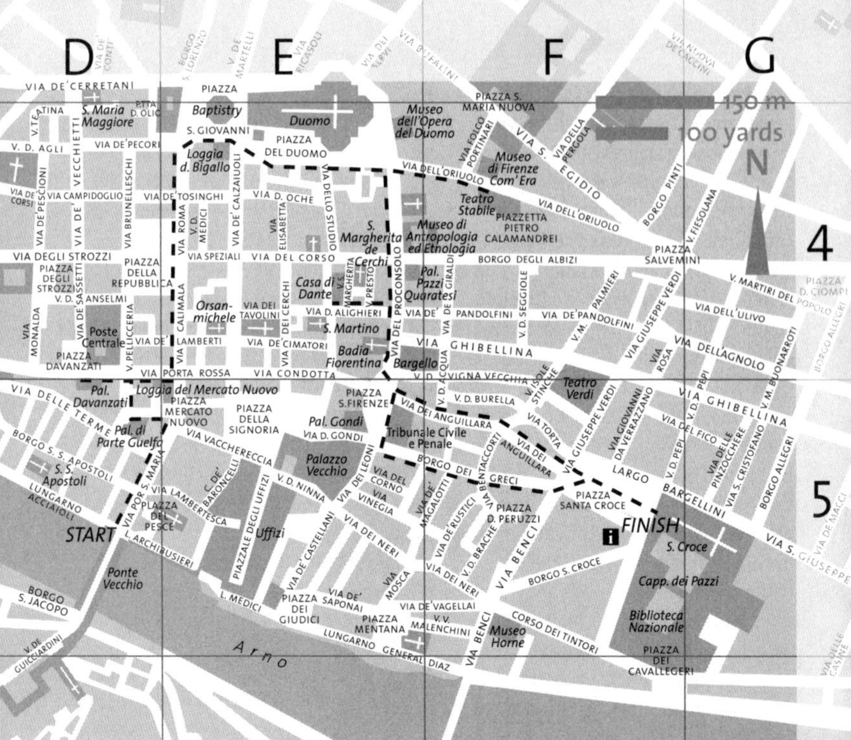

house, a few decades after Dante's death, would be just around the corner on Via Porta Rossa, off the Mercato Nuovo.

To see the best surviving example of these office-palace complexes, turn left at the end of Via Por Santa Maria, through the market-place and into Via Porta Rossa for the **Palazzo Davanzati**, begun just after Dante's death and now home of the Museo della Casa Fiorentina Antica (*currently closed indefinitely for restoration*).

Now retrace your steps on Via Porta Rossa, and turn left on Via Calimala. Here you'll see two more famous relics of Dante's time, the **Palazzo dell'Arte della Lana** (1308) on the right, and home of the powerful textile guild, and behind it the singular combination church/communal granary, **Orsanmichele** (*see* p.73), built in 1337. (Before Dante was exiled, he would have known the original, with a loggia by Arnolfo da Cambio; it burned while he was in exile in 1304, when the current building was begun.)

Continuing on Via Calimala/Via Roma will take you up to Piazza del Duomo. Dante may or may not have watched the building of the Duomo from an old stone bench which stood on a spot now occupied by the Sasso di Dante restaurant in Piazza delle Pallottole just off Piazza del Duomo towards Via del Proconsolo. A plaque on the piazza itself (between Nos.54r and 44r) commemorates the '**Sasso di Dante**'.

Just across stands that 'most Florentine of buildings', already the ancient repository of the city's soul: the **Baptistry** (*see* p.70). While Santa Maria in Fiore was under construction, this was used as Florence's cathedral. Dante, like every other Florentine, would of course have been baptized '*nel mio bel San Giovanni*', following the tradition by which every Florentine child got its baptism communally on the Annunciation – also the start of the new year in the Florentine calendar. In the *Inferno* (*canto 19, 13–21*), he describes the fate of the simoniacs in hell, stuffed head-down into pits; it reminded him of an incident from his younger days, when he tipped over one of the deep baptismal urns here to save a child who had crawled in and was drowning. In the Duomo itself, there is the famous fresco *Domenico di Michelino* (1465), showing Dante with all his poetic cosmology in the background.

From behind the Duomo, take Via dell' Oriuolo east to the **Museo di Firenze Com'Era** (*see* p.123). Here, '*com'era*' largely means the Florence of the Renaissance or the 19th century, but stop in anyhow for a look at the enlargement of the famous Pianta della Catena. Dante's Florence, for all its confusion and factional fights, was just growing into opulence in his day. The two great projects that would dominate the city of the future, the Duomo and the Palazzo della Signoria, were already underway. Look at the finely detailed Pianta and imagine the town without them – little towers and red tile roofs, with the Ponte Vecchio and the new Bargello (begun 1255, finished 1346) the major landmarks of the town, along with a few more of the noble tower-fortresses that the republic was still gradually demolishing. Florence was just beginning.

Retrace your steps a bit, and a left on Via del Proconsolo will take you into the poet's old neighbourhood. Three streets down on the right is **Via Dante Alighieri**, where the entrance to the **Badia Fiorentina** (*see* p.91), another medieval landmark, is on your left a little way along the street. Dante's nostalgia for Florence appears in little things all through his great work; in the *Paradiso* (*canto 15, 97–9*) he recalls how the Badia's bells marked the hours of the day in his old haunts. Most scholars believe Dante was born here in Via Dante Alighieri. The poet only mentions the neighbourhood: San Piero, the sixth of Florence's six *sestrieri*. If this was indeed the street, young Dante would have had a good seat for festivals; medieval Florence had a Palio, like Siena's, and this street was part of the course. In 1911, one of its houses was declared the **Casa di Dante** and fancifully restored (*see* p.91).

A modern bas-relief on one of the buildings on Via Dante Alighieri, opposite Via Santa Margherita, shows the sights that would have been familiar to Dante – the Bargello, the Badia campanile, and the sturdy well-preserved **Torre della Castagna**, which stands just ahead on the left, on the corner of Via Dante Alighieri and Via dei Magazzini, one of scores of similar tower houses that once made Florence's skyline resemble Manhattan's. This was the residence of the *priori*, the governors of the city, before the construction of the Palazzo Vecchio. Dante himself was a *priore* once (elected by lot from the list of citizens, as in many medieval Italian city-republics) and he would have spent his two-month term of office living here, as the law required.

Retrace your steps to Via Proconsolo and take a right; this will take you south past the façade of the Badia and, opposite, the **Bargello** (*see* p.88) – and if you haven't been, you could stop here to see the fragment of a fresco in the chapel, attributed to Giotto and long believed by the Florentines to be a portrait of Dante himself, among the fortunate in heaven.

Beyond these two buildings is Piazza San Firenze, and a left here on Via dell'Anguillara or Via Borgo dei Greci will end this walk among the Dantean memorials of **Santa Croce** (*see* p.126). Inside, in this church that has become a kind of Pantheon of Tuscan worthies, is the poet's empty neoclassical tomb, with its portentous inscriptions and mourning pensive deities. Florence never gave up hope of getting the body back one day.

And out in the piazza, where medieval Franciscans preached to the masses, is the famous grim-faced **Dante statue**. No mistake, this is one very large piece of Risorgimento propaganda. The sculptor's name was Enrico Pazzi, and the celebrated *disdegno* (disdain) he put in Dante's face is only meant to underscore the line below from the *Divina Commedia*: 'O Italy enslaved, in sorrow.'

Pazzi originally planned the thing for the poet's tomb in Ravenna, but that city politely declined it. After that, the Florentines proposed to pay for it and give it to Turin, then capital of what was becoming a united Italy. A year later, when Tuscany joined the kingdom and the capital was moved to Florence, the Florentines decided to keep it after all. This scowling mug might not make Dante very happy, if he could see it, but this is Florence, and a statue is a statue.

OLTRARNO WALK

Florence's left bank, the Oltrarno, is relatively small, squeezed in between the Arno and the hills, but it manages to seem more green and serene than the dense stone canyons that characterize the right bank. Its streets were fashionable in the 12th and 13th centuries, when the feisty nobility lived in tower houses during the violent scrums between the Guelphs and Ghibellines. Afterwards, wealthy merchants and bankers developed the neighbourhood – the Bardi clan, most notably, who bought up a whole street of a slum known as Borgo Pigiglioso ('flea pit') and lined it in almost its entirety with family palazzi. Once in fashion, the Oltrarno never really fell out, especially once the Grand Dukes took up residence in the Pitti Palace. Today the Oltrarno is central Florence's last real residential neighbourhood, the streets lined with bakeries and barber shops instead of boutiques and restaurants. It is also now a really sought-after area to live in (property prices in Santo Spirito are among the highest in Florence) and has become increasingly trendy in the past 10 years, so there are also lots of bars, restaurants and nightspots here too.

Start: Ponte Vecchio.
Finish: Porta San Frediano.
Walking time: 45 minutes.
Lunch and drinks stops: Antico Ristoro di Cambi, *see* p.231; Angiolino, *see* p.231; Momoyama, *see* p.231; La Vecchia Bettola, *see* p.233; Ashoka, *see* p.233; Sabatino, *see* p.233; Trattoria del Carmine, *see* p.233; Hemingway, *see* p.233.

Although at first glance even these streets seem severe, there are plenty of details to pick up – don't keep your eyes at street level. If you look up, the buildings reveal intricate stone carvings, wrought-iron work and frescoes. The Italians tend not to draw their curtains, so after dark you'll often see amazing ceilings and chandeliers through the tall windows of the *piano nobile*. Rooftop terraces and gardens are always a delight, especially in spring and summer when they are a riot of flowers. If you find doorways to grand buildings open, step inside if you dare; there's often a spectacular courtyard or hidden garden waiting to be discovered. Even when they are closed, these doors, often immensely thick with all sorts of decorations or great studs in them, are worth a glance. Don't forget the doorbells – there are some wonderful little wrought-iron gargoyles about. The names on the buzzers of the flats, or on the shop signs of the butcher's or furniture restorer's, are often the very same that shine in Florence's chronicles. Also keep an eye peeled for the plaques marking the high water-mark of the flood of 1966; some old façades still bear a faded mark as well.

Start by strolling over the Ponte Vecchio. **Vasari's corridor** runs along the top of the bridge on the left-hand side. This was built in 1564 for Cosimo I when he moved from the Palazzo Vecchio into the Pitti Palace, at the insistance of his wife, Eleanor of Toledo, whose health was failing; they had hoped the gardens and more airy and spacious halls of the Pitti would make her better (it didn't – she died within two years). The Corridor, linking the new Medici residence to Cosimo's new office building, the Uffizi, was built post-haste – four builders were killed on the site – because Cosimo had already survived more than one assassination attempt, including an ingenious one discovered by his spies before it was too late – a *cheval-de-frise*, bristling with swords and spikes, sunk under the Arno just where the Grand Duke liked to dive in to cool off in the summer.

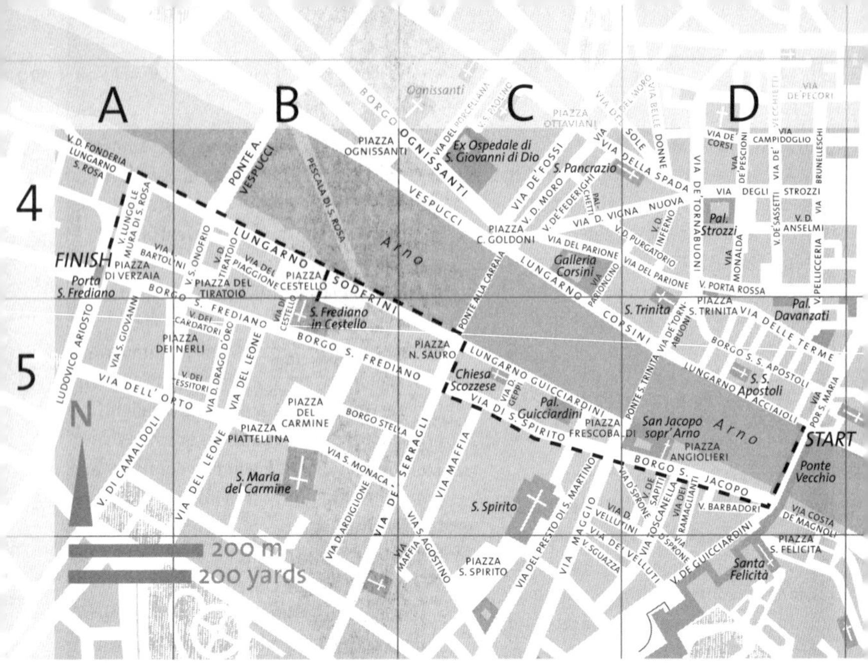

The buildings opposite the end of the Ponte Vecchio were rebuilt after the war, after the fleeing Germans blew them to smithereens to block access to the bridge. To the left, at the end of the bridge, the Corridor was forced to snake on brackets around the medieval Torre dei Mannelli when the owner adamantly refused to let Vasari ram it through the interior of the building. Opposite, towards Borgo San Jacopo, the the bottom floor of the **Casa dei Templari**, once headquarters of the Knights Templar in Florence, survived the Nazi dynamite, while the rest was carefully rebuilt '*dové era, com'era*' (where it was, as it was).

Turning right into Borgo San Jacopo at the end of the Ponte Vecchio, opposite you will see the **Torre dei Rossi Cerchi**, a typical tower house from the 1200s, with a fountain at its foot made of a Roman sarcophagus (or rather a copy of one, blown up in the war) topped by a handsome if anonymous bronze 16th-century *Bacchus*. Continuing along Borgo San Jacopo, you'll find two other 13th-century tower houses (the Torre di Belfredeli on the right and the Torre dei Barbadori opposite) that have been restored on either side at the corner of Via Ramaglianti, and another further on at No.17, the **Torre dei Marsili**, marked by a beautiful Della Robbia *Annunciation* in a lavish frame, with two kneeling angels on the sides.

Next comes the pretty façade of the 11th-century church of **San Jacopo sopr'Arno**, sporting a series of delightful little gargoyles above the three arches of its portico, supported by ancient columns and others from the 12th century. In preparation for his great dome on the cathedral, Brunelleschi practised building a dome here without supports, over the Cappella Ridolfi, although it was destroyed when the interior was remodelled in the 18th century.

Borgo San Jacopo ends in the **Piazza Frescobaldi** and the fountain with its Medici crest under the triangular room on the corner of Borgo San Jacopo and Via dello Sprone.

Via di Santo Spirito is lined with fine palaces and medieval towers pruned by the Republic, belonging to some of the oldest noble families in Florence, embellished with coats of arms above doorways, and some marvellous internal gardens if you are lucky enough to find doors open. Note the little carved arches at waist level, built into the buildings. Some have been blocked up, are used as postboxes or simply as decoration, but they were originally used to dispense wine to thirsty passers-by. Note too the terracotta Madonna on the left-hand corner just past Via Maggio; at No.27 the R painted on the wall is the kind of relic still common in many Italian cities: it stands for *rifugio* – a bomb shelter from the war.

The westernmost quarter within the medieval walls, **Borgo San Frediano** is known for its workshops and unpretentious antique dealers. Via S. Spirito ends in Piazza Sauro (leading to the Ponte alla Carraia). From here, take the Lungarno Soderini and follow the river along to the parish church, **San Frediano in Cestello**, its blank unfinished poker face a landmark along this stretch of the Arno. This was an early church, rebuilt in 1698, with an elegant cylindrical drum and a funny puny Baroque campanile. The interior is grandly Baroque, and contains among the 18th-century frescoes, a famous 13th-century smiling polychrome statue of the Virgin, the *Madonna del Sorriso* (third chapel on the left). The massive low building at the end of the piazza was a granary built by Cosimo III in 1695. At the end of the Lungarno Soderini, the **Torrino di Santa Rosa**, often remodelled after it was built in 1324 has a tabernacle protecting an early 18th-century *Pietà*, attributed to Ghirlandaio.

Going left from here, you can make out a last stretch of Florence's medieval walls, leading towards the massive **Porta San Frediano** (1334), a tall tower gate built by Andrea Pisano guarding the Pisa road, with its old wooden door, mighty nails and locks still in place.

FIESOLE WALK

Florence liked to look at itself as the daughter of Rome, and in its fractious heyday explained its quarrelsome nature by the fact that its population from the beginning was of mixed race, of Romans and 'that ungrateful and malignant people who of old came down from Fiesole', according to Dante (of course, Dante's family claimed to be descended from a Roman soldier).

Start: Piazza Mino, Fiesole (a 20min trip up on bus 7 from Florence station or Piazza San Marco).

Finish: Either Fiesole or walk/take bus 7 back down to Florence.

Walking time: 2 hours (Fiesole sights only).

Tourist information: Fiesole tourist office, Via Portigiani 3 (near the entrance to the Teatro Romano), **t** 055 598720, **f** 055 598822, **w** *www.comune.fiesole.fi.it/infoturismo*. Open Mon–Sat 8.30–7.30, Sun 10–7, hols 10–4. One ticket costing €6.20 covers entrance to all Fiesole's museums.

Lunch and drinks stops: 45 Piazza Mino, *see* p.233; Pizzeria Etrusca, *see* p.234; Piazzeria San Domenico, *see* p.234; Blue Bar, *see* p.234.

First settled in the 2nd millennium BC, Fiesole grew to become the most important Etruscan city in the region. Yet from the start Etruscan *Faesulae*'s relationship with Rome was rocky, especially after sheltering Catiline and his conspirators in 65 BC. Because of its lofty position, Fiesole was too difficult to capture, so the Romans built a camp below on the Arno to cut off its supplies. Eventually Fiesole was taken, and it dwindled as the Roman camp below grew into *Florentia*, growth the Romans encouraged to spite the feisty old Etruscans on their hill. This easily defended summit, however, ensured Fiesole's survival in the Dark Ages. When times became safer, families began to move back down to the Arno to rebuild Florence. They returned to smash up most of Fiesole after defeating it in 1125; since then the little town has remained aloof, an independent *comune*, letting Florence dominate and choke in its own juices far, far below.

But ever since the days of the *Decameron*, whose storytellers retreated to its garden villas to escape the plague, Fiesole has played the role of Florence's aristocratic suburb; its cool breezes, beautiful landscapes and belvedere views make it the perfect refuge from the torrid Florentine summers. There's no escaping the tourists, however; we foreigners have been tramping up and down Fiesole's hill since the days of Shelley.

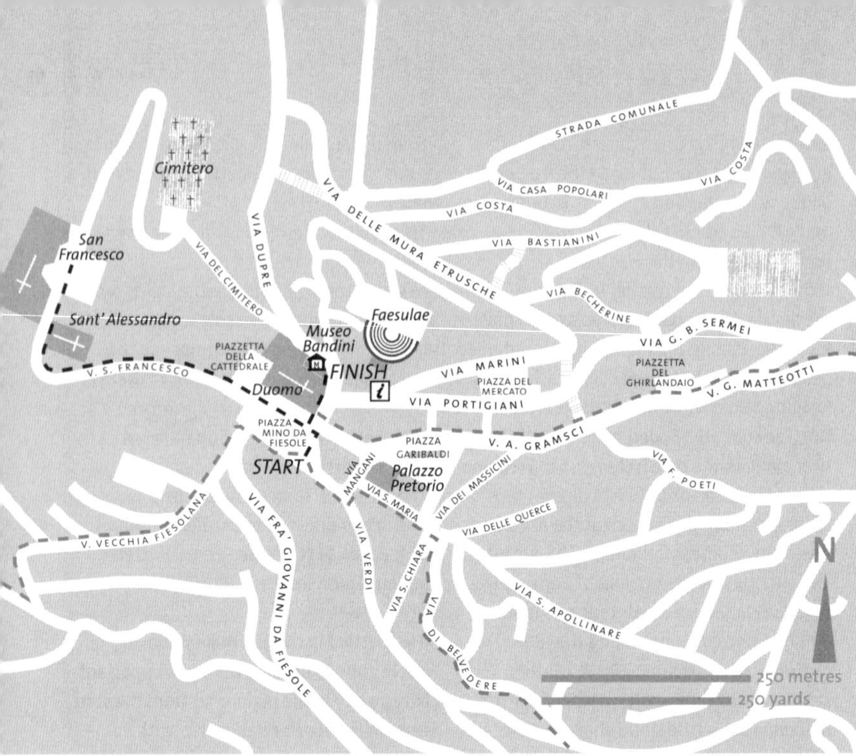

The bus will leave you on the long sloping stage of **Piazza Mino**, the ancient forum and still Fiesole's centre, with its cafés, restaurants, and the **Palazzo Pretorio** (14th–15th century) at the far end, its loggia and façade encrusted with coats of arms of the *podestàs* who governed here. A market is held in front of the Palazzo Pretorio on Saturday mornings. The square is named after a favourite son, the quattrocento sculptor Mino da Fiesole, whom Ruskin preferred to all others. An example of his work may be seen in the **Duomo**, the side of which dominates the north side of the piazza. Built in 1028, it was the only building spared by the vindictive Florentines in 1125. It was subsequently enlarged and given a scouring 19th-century restoration, leaving the tall, crenellated campanile as its sole distinguishing feature. Still, the interior has an austere charm, with a raised choir over the crypt similar to San Miniato. Up the steps to the right are two beautiful works by Mino da Fiesole: the *Tomb of Bishop Leonardo Salutati* and an altar front. The main altarpiece in the choir, of the Madonna and saints, is by Lorenzo di Bicci, from 1440. Note the two saints frescoed on the columns; it was a north Italian custom to paint holy people as if they were members of the congregation. The crypt, holding the remains of Fiesole's patron, St Romulus, is supported by ancient columns bearing doves, spirals and other early Christian symbols.

By the Cathedral, take rather steep Via S. Francesco up to the hill that served as the Etruscan and Roman acropolis. Halfway up is a little garden with extraordinary views of Florence and the Arno sprawl, with a monument to the three gallant *carabinieri* who gave themselves up to be shot by the Nazis in 1944 to prevent them from taking civilian reprisals. Above this is another panoramic terrace and, opposite, the **Basilica di Sant'Alessandro** was constructed over an Etruscan/Roman temple in the 6th century, reusing its lovely cipollino marble columns and Ionic capitals, one still inscribed with an invocation to Venus. At the top of the hill, square on the ancient acropolis, stands the **monastery of San Francesco** (founded in 1399), its church containing a famous early cinquecento *Annunciation* by Raffaellino del Garbo, an *Immaculate Conception* by

Piero di Cosimo and a triptych by Bicci di Lorenzo. A grab-bag of odds and ends collected from the four corners of the world, especially from Egypt and China, is displayed in the quaint Franciscan Missionary Museum in the cloister; it also has an Etruscan collection (*open Tues–Fri 10–12 and 3–5, Sat and Sun 3–5*).

Return to Piazza Mino, walk past the cathedral and turn left into Via Dupré. The **Museo Bandini** (*open Wed–Sun winter 9.30–5, summer 9–7*) is tiny (only three rooms) but contains more sacred works, including numerous della Robbia terracottas (*currently being restored*), and some good trecento paintings by Lorenzo Monaco, Neri di Bicci and Taddeo Gaddi.

Diagonally across the road is the entrance to what remains of ***Faesulae*** (*open Wed–Sun winter 9.30–5, summer 9–7*). Because Fiesole stayed out of trouble in the Dark Ages, its Roman monuments have survived in much better shape than those of Florence; although hardly spectacular, the ruins are charmingly set amid olive groves and cypresses. The small Roman Theatre has survived well enough to host plays and concerts in the summer; Fiesole would like to gently remind you that in ancient times it had the theatre and plays while Florence had the amphitheatre and wild beast shows. Within the Roman complex are the rather confusing remains of two superimposed temples, the baths, and a stretch of Etruscan walls (best seen from Via delle Mure Etrusche, below) that proved their worth against Hannibal's siege. The **Archaeology Museum** (*within the same complex; open Wed–Sun winter 9.30–5, summer 9–7*) is housed in a small 20th-century Ionic temple, displaying some very early small bronze figurines with flapper wing arms, Etruscan funerary urns and stelae, including the 'stele Fiesolana' with a banquet scene. It also contains the Costantini Collection of pottery from Greece, Magna Grecia and Etruria.

These are the main sights of Fiesole, but there are several lovely options for more walking if you have the time and energy. One is a walk from Piazza Mino into Borgunto, the east end of town, starting by the Palazzo Pretorio. Take Via S. Maria, eventually becoming panoramic Via Belvedere, which leads to another enchanting view over Florence. Continue left on Via Adriano Mari, along a long stretch of Etruscan walls. In a couple of kilometres you'll come to the bucolic **Monte Ceceri**, a wooded park where Leonardo da Vinci performed his flight experiments, and where the Florentine architects found their dark *pietra serena* in quarries which are now abandoned but open for exploration.

The other two walks will take you down towards Florence. For scenery, the most enchanting (but quite lengthy) route is to take Via G. Matteotti, Via Francesco Ferrucci and Via di Vincigliata and pass by Fiesole's castles, the **Castel di Poggio** and the **Castel di Vincigliata** (site of summer concerts), built on the site of a ruin dating back to 1031, while further down is American critic Bernard Berenson's famous **Villa I Tatti**, which he left in 1959, along with a distinguished collection of Florentine art and his rich library, to Harvard University as the Centre of Italian Renaissance Studies (*write ahead if you want to visit*). From here the road descends towards Ponte a Mensola and Settignano, with buses back to Florence (*see* p.148).

The second road down, the steep and narrow Via Vecchia Fiesolana, passes, on the left, the Tavernacolo del Proposto, with a fresco attributed to Perugino. When you reach Yiuzzo degli Angeli, look right to the remains of an Etruscan gate, and look left to see the **Villa Medici** (or Belcanto) built by Michelozzo for Cosimo il Vecchio; in its lovely garden on the hillside, Lorenzo and his friends of the Platonic Academy would come to get away from the world; it was also the lucky Iris Origo's childhood home (*adm free*). The terrace just below was Queen Victoria's favourite spot in Florence.

At the bottom on the lane, in Piazzale San Domenico, the convent of San Domenico di Fiesole is where Giovanni da Fiesole first entered his monkish world as Fra Angelico.

The 15th-century church of **San Domenico** contains his lovely *Madonna with Angels and Saints*, in the first chapel on the left, as well as a photograph of his *Coronation of the Virgin*, which Napoleon snapped up in 1809 and sent to the Louvre. Across the nave there's a *Crucifixion* by the school of Botticelli, an unusual composition of verticals highlighted by the cypresses in the background. In the chapterhouse (*ring the bell at No.4*) Beato Angelico left a fine fresco of the Crucifixion before moving down to Florence and San Marco.

It's a five-minute walk down the Via Badia to the **Badia Fiesolana**, built in the 9th century by Fiesole's bishop, an Irishman named Donatus and, until 1026, the cathedral of Fiesole, with a fine view over the rolling countryside and Florence in the background. Although later enlarged, perhaps by Brunelleschi, it has preserved the Tuscan Romanesque façade of the older church, a charming example of the geometric green and white marble inlay decoration. The interior (*open only on Sunday mornings,* ***t*** *055 46851*) is highlighted with *pietra serena* in the style of Brunelleschi. The convent buildings next door are now the home of the European University Institute.

You can take a No.7 bus back to Florence from Piazza San Domenico or continue down Via San Domenica, Via della Piazzuola and Via delle Forbici, passing by **Villa Il Reppiedi**, where the words on the wall read: *A Matre et filia aeque disto* (I am have halfway between the Mother, Fiesole, and the Daugher, Florence). Further down on the right is the **Villa Bondi**, also known as Il Garofano, which once belonged to the Alighieri family, before passing onto the Portinari in 1322. On the left, is the grand Villa Ventaglio, wih its magnificent park. Further down, the road runs into Viale Volta (where buses 3 and 7 will take you back to the centre).

Siena

HISTORY 164
GETTING THERE 167
TOURIST INFORMATION 167
WHERE TO STAY 167
EATING OUT 168
THE CAMPO 172
PIAZZA DEL DUOMO 175
SOUTH OF THE CENTRE 183
NORTH OF THE CENTRE 184

09

Draped on its three hills, Siena (pop. 61,400) is the most beautiful city in Tuscany, a flamboyant medieval ensemble of palaces and towers cast in warm, brown, Siena-coloured brick. Its soaring skyline is its pride, dominated by the blazing black and white banner of the cathedral and the taut needle of the Torre del Mangia; and yet the Campo, the very centre of Siena, is only four streets away from olive groves and orchards. The contrast is part of the city's charm: densely built-up brick urbanity, and round the corner a fine stretch of long Tuscan farmland that fills the valleys within the city's walls.

Here art went hand in hand with a fierce civic pride to make Siena a world of its own, and historians go so far as to speak of 'Sienese civilization' in summing up the achievements of this unique little city.

History

Everywhere in Siena you'll see the familiar Roman symbol of the she-wolf suckling the twins. This is Siena's symbol as well; according to legend, the city was founded by the sons of Remus, Senius and Ascius. One rode a black horse, the other a white, and the simple comunal shield of black and white halves (the *balzana*) has been the other most enduring symbol of Siena over the centuries. It is most likely that somebody was living on these three hills long before this mythological pair. Excavations have found traces of Etruscan and even Celtic habitation. The almost impregnable site, dominating most of southern Tuscany, would always have been of great interest. Roman-era *Sena Julia* which was refounded by Augustus as a colony for his veterans, never achieved much importance, and we know little about the place until the early 12th century, when the emerging *comune* began keeping written records. In 1125, an increasingly independent Siena elected its first consuls. By 1169, the *comune* wrested political control away from the bishop, and some 10 years later Siena developed its own written constitution.

The political development is complex, and with good reason. Twelfth-century Siena was

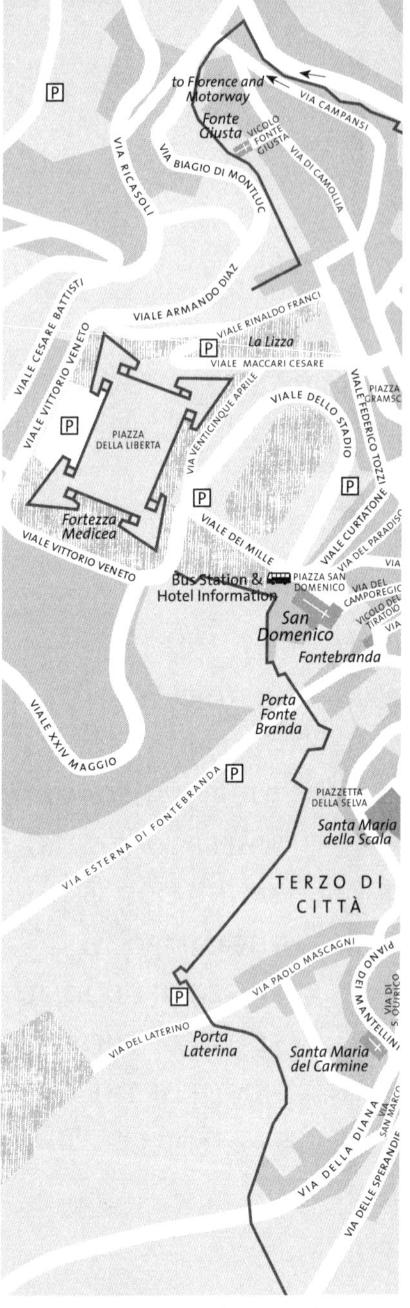

a booming new city; control over its rich countryside, supplying some of the best wool in Italy, helped start an important cloth industry, and a small silver mine, acquired from Volterra in the 1160s, provided seed capital for what was to become one of the leading banking towns of Europe. Like so many other Italian cities, Siena was able early

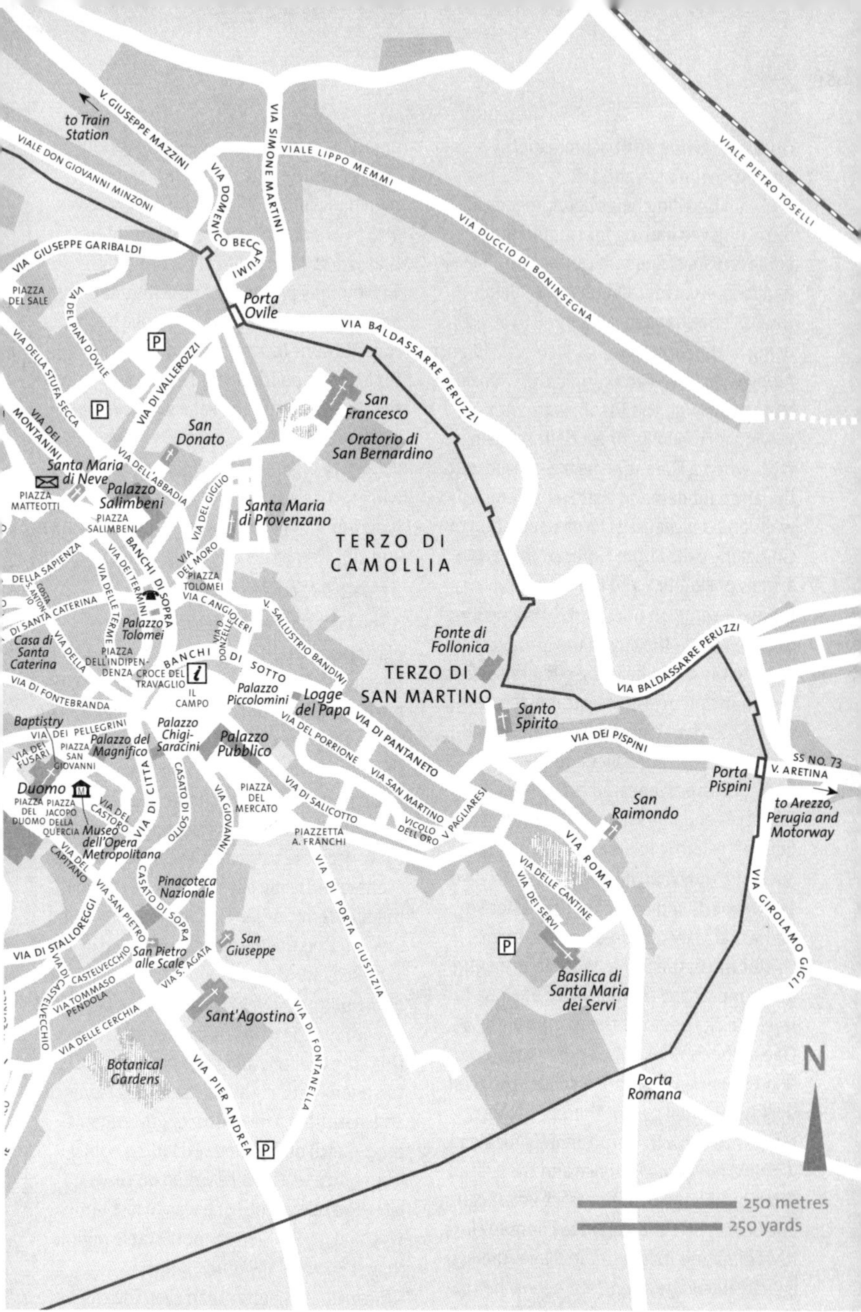

on to force its troublesome rural nobles to live within its walls, where they built scores of tall defence towers, fought pitched battles in the streets and usually kept the city divided into armed camps; in the narrowest part of the city, the *comune* once had to lay out new streets parallel to Via Camollia because of one particularly boisterous nobleman whose palace most Sienese were afraid to pass. Yet Siena was never completely able to bring its titled hoodlums under control. The businessmen made the money, and gradually formed their city into a sophisticated self-governing republic, but the nobles held on to many of their privileges for centuries, giving an anachronistically feudal tinge to Siena's life and art.

Like its brawling neighbours, medieval Siena enjoyed looking for trouble; in the endless wars of the 13th century they never had to look very far. Originally a Guelph town, Siena changed sides early to avoid being in the same camp as archrival Florence. Along with Pisa, Siena carried the Ghibelline banner through the Tuscan wars with varying fortunes. Its finest hour came in 1260, when a Florentine herald arrived with the arrogant demand that Siena demolish its walls and deliver up its large population of Ghibelline exiles from Florence. If not, the armies of Florence and the entire Guelph League – some 40,000 men – were waiting outside to raze the city to the ground. Despite the overwhelming odds, the Sienese determined to resist. They threw the keys of the city on the altar of the yet unfinished cathedral, dedicating Siena to the Virgin Mary (a custom repeated ever since when the city is endangered, most recently just before the battle for liberation in 1944). In the morning, they marched out to the **Battle of Monteaperti** and beat the Florentines so badly that they captured their *carroccio*.

After the battle Siena had Florence entirely at her mercy and naturally was anxious to level the city and sow the ground with salt. One of the famous episodes in the *Inferno* relates how the Florentine exiles, who made up a substantial part of the Sienese forces, refused to allow it. Unfortunately for Siena, within a few years Florence and the Tuscan Guelphs had the situation back under control and Siena was never again to come so close to dominating Tuscan affairs. Nevertheless the city would be a constant headache to Florence for the next three centuries. When things were quiet at the front, the Sienese had to settle for bashing each other. The constant stream of anti-Siena propaganda in Dante isn't just Florentine bile; medieval Siena had a thoroughly earned reputation for violence and contentiousness. The impressive forms and rituals of the Sienese Republic were merely a façade concealing endless, pointless struggles between the various factions of the élite. Early on, Siena's merchants and nobles divided themselves into five *monti*, syndicates of self-interest that worked like political parties only without any pretence of principle. At one point, this Tuscan banana republic had 10 constitutions in 27 years, and more often than not its political affairs were settled in the streets. Before the Palio was invented, Siena's favourite civic sport was the *Gioco del Pugno*, a general fist-fight in the Campo with 300 on a side. Sometimes tempers flared, and the boys would bring out the axes and crossbows.

Siena's Golden Age

The historical record leaves us with a glaring paradox. For all its troubles and bad intentions, Siena often managed to run city business with disinterest and intelligence. An intangible factor of civic pride always made the Sienese do the right thing when something important was at hand, like battling with the Florentines or selecting a new artist to work on the cathedral. The Battle of Monteaperti may have proved a disappointment in terms of territorial ambitions, but it inaugurated the most brilliant period of Sienese culture, and saw the transformation of the hilltop fortress town into the beautiful city we see today. In 1287, under pressure from the Guelphs and their Angevin protectors, Siena actually allied itself with Florence and instituted a new form of government: the '**Council of the Nine**'. Excluding nobles from office, as Florence would do six years later, the rule of the Nine was to last until 1355, and it gave Siena a more stable regime than it knew at any other period.

Business was better than ever. The city's bankers came to rival Florence's, with offices in all the trading centres and capitals of Europe. A sustained peace, and increasing cultural contacts with France and Naples, brought new ideas and influences into Siena's art and architecture, just in time to embellish massive new building programmes like the **Cathedral** (begun 1186, but not substantially completed until the

Getting There

The fastest route by **car** from Florence to Siena (68km) is the unnumbered toll-free Superstrada del Palio (1hr); the most scenic is the Chiantigiana SS222 through the heart of Chianti and the Via Cassia (SS2), which weave amongst the hills the Superstrada avoids (2hrs). Cars are forbidden to enter the centre, but there are clearly defined parking areas along all entrances to the city.

Siena's **train** station is located below the city, 1.5km from the centre down Viale G. Mazzini and is linked to the centre by frequent buses. Siena's main line runs from Empoli (on the Florence–Pisa line) to Chiusi (Florence–Rome). There are trains roughly every hour, with frequent connections to Florence from Empoli (97km, 1hr), and less frequently to Pisa from Empoli (125km, 2hrs). To save a trip to the station, all rail information/tickets are available at Agency Il Caroccio, Via Montanini 73/75, **t** 0577 226964.

Almost every town in southern Tuscany can be reached by **bus** from Piazza San Domenico, the big transport node on the western edge of Siena, with hotel information booths. A board lists departure times and the location of stops; the ticket office (with a fancy, computer-operated information dispenser) is in the little building next to San Domenico church. The name of the company serving the whole of Siena province is TRA-IN, Piazza Gramsci (in the underpass), **t** 0577 204246, **e** *train@comune.siena.it*, **w** *www.comune.siena.it/train*. Other companies depart for other cities like Florence (SITA, about once every hour, Rome, Perugia, Pisa, etc.), but all leave from San Domenico.

Tourist Information

Piazza del Campo 56, **t** 0577 280551, **f** 0577 270676, **e** *aptsiena@siena.turismo.toscana.it*, **w** *www.siena-turismo.toscana.it*. Open Mon–Sat 8.30–7.30, Sun 9–3.

Post Office: Piazza Matteotti 37.

Hotel Reservations: Piazza San Domenico, **t** 0577 288084, **f** 0577 280290, **e** *info@hotelsiena.com*, **w** *www.hotelsiena.com*.

Festivals

For the **Palio**, Siena's great horse race, *see* p.173. A week of **concerts** is held in July, associated with the Chigiana music school. **Incontri in Terra di Siena** consists of 10 days of international chamber music concerts in late July based at La Foce, writer Iris Origo's estate near Montepulciano, **t** 0578 69101, **w** *www.lafoce.com*. **Santa Cecilia festival** celebrates the patroness of music, with concerts on 22 November.

Shopping

Siena, with its population of only 60,000, is blissfully short of designer boutiques and so on. Most shops in Siena close at lunch time.

Where to Stay

Many of Siena's finest and most interesting hotels are in the lovely countryside, or near the city gates. What's left, in the centre, is simple but comfortable enough. Book ahead in summer, as rooms are in short supply.

Luxury

*****La Certosa di Maggiano**, *Via Certosa 82, near the Porta Romana*, ***t** 0577 288180*, ***f** 0577 288189*, ***e** info@certosadimaggiano.it*, ***w** www.certosadimaggiano.it*. About 1km southeast of the city, this is one of the most remarkable establishments in Italy, a restored 14th-century Carthusian monastery. There are only 14 rooms, and the luxuries include a heated pool, a quiet chapel and cloister, an excellent restaurant, and a library that would be an antiquarian's dream. €350.

*****Continentale**, *Via Banchi di Sopra 85*, ***t** 0577 56011/44204*, ***f** 0577 560 1555*, ***e** info@grandhotelcontinentalesiena.it*, ***w** www.grandhotelcontinentalesiena.it*. Siena's only luxury hotel in the city centre, with 51 rooms furnished with fine fabrics and antiques. Some rooms have panoramic views. €484.

***Park Hotel**, *Via Marciano 18*, ***t** 0577 44803*, ***f** 0577 49020*, ***e** info@parkhotelsiena.it*, ***w** www.parkhotelsiena.it*. A 16th-century building designed by Peruzzi, situated on the hill that dominates Siena, with stunning views of the Tuscan landscape. €400.

Expensive

***__Palazzo Ravizza__, *Pian dei Mantellini 34, near the Porta Laterina, just inside the walls,* **t** *0577 280462,* **f** *0577 221597,* **e** *bureau@ palazzoravizza,* **w** *www.palazzoravizza.it*. An elegant 19th-century palazzo with upmarket rooms furnished with antiques. There is a lovely garden at the back and a restaurant too. €227 half board (obligatory in season).

***__Villa Liberty__, *Viale V. Veneto 11,* **t** *0577 44966,* **f** *0577 44770,* **e** *info@villaliberty.it,* **w** *www.villaliberty.it*. A pleasant and elegant 'Liberty style' villa situated near San Domenico and set in a garden. Rooms are well furnished; two have private terraces. €250.

****__Villa Patrizia__, *Via Fiorentina 58,* **t** *0577 50431,* **f** *0577 50442,* **e** *info@villapatrizia.it,* **w** *www.villapatrizia.it*. A large old villa north of the town with tennis and a pool. €248.

****__Villa Scacciapensieri__, *Strada Scacciapensieri 10, 3km north of the city,* **t** *0577 41441,* **f** *0577 270854,* **e** *villassa@tin.it,* **w** *www.tin.it/villascacciapensieri*. There are sunset views over Siena from this quiet country house; also a pool and a good restaurant with an outdoor terrace. €230.

Moderate

***__Duomo__, *Via Stalloreggi 34, south of the Duomo,* **t** *0577 289088,* **f** *0577 43043,* **e** *hduomo@comune.siena.it,* **w** *www. hotelduomo.it*. A friendly, comfortably old-fashioned choice close to the centre. Rooms are a bit stark, but clean. €135.

***__Santa Caterina__, *Via Enea Silvio Piccolomini 7,* **t** *0577 221105,* **f** *0577 271087,* **e** *hsc@sienanet. it,* **w** *www.sienanet.it/hsc*. An 18th-century house not far from Porta Romana, with 19 attractive rooms. €144.

Inexpensive

***__Antica Torre__, *Via di Fieravecchia 7,* **t/f** *0577 222255*. Siena's most popular small (only 8 rooms) hotel: a restored 16th-century tower, with marble floors, antiques and beamed ceilings. €105.

__Canon d'Oro__, *Via Montanini 28, near the bus station,* **t *0577 44321,* **f** *0577 280868*. Pleasant, friendly and good value. Rooms have all been renovated within the last couple of years. €85.

***__Chiusarelli__, *Viale Curtatone 15,* **t** *0577 280562,* **f** *0577 271177,* **e** *info@chiusarelli.com,* **w** *www.chiusareli.com*. An attractive villa in a pretty garden, with the bonus of a car park. Plain rooms but a frescoed reception. €109.

__Il Giardino__, *Via Baldassare Peruzzi 35,* **t *0577 285290,* **f** *0577 221197*. Highly recommended in readers' letters, situated near the Porta Pispini, with views and a pool. €110.

__Lea__, *Viale XXIV Maggio 10,* **t/f *0577 283207*. Friendly hotel, centrally located at the end of the pedestrian zone. €85.

***__Minerva__, *Via Garibaldi 72,* **t** *0577 284474,* **f** *0577 43343,* **e** *minerva@sienanet.it,* **w** *www. sienanet.it/minerva*. Situated on a busy road but all the rooms are ranged round an inner courtyard; some have been upgraded and cost a little more. €96.

***__Moderno__, *Via B. Peruzzi 19,* **t** *0577 288453,* **f** *0577 270596,* **e** *moderno@sienanet.it,* **w** *www.sienanet.it/moderno*. A large hotel in a central location; garden and parking. €98.

__Piccolo Hotel Etruria__, *3 Via delle Donzelle off Via Banchi di Sotto near the Campo,* **t *0577 283685,* **f** *0577 288461,* **e** *hetruria@tin.it*. Friendly, clean and a good bargain. Four rooms in annexe opposite. Cheap restaurant next door also owned by the hotel. €96.

Cheap

__Centrale__, *Via Angiolieri 26,* **t *0577 280379,* **f** *0577 42152*. Very near the Campo. The 7 rooms are spacious and comfortable. €67.

__La Perla__, *Via delle Terme,* **t *0577 47144. Cash only*. Basic, but fairly central. €65.

__Piccolo Hotel Il Palio__, *Piazza del Sale 19,* **t *0577 281131,* **f** *0577 281142*. A little way from the centre, but it has the advantages of a quiet location and a friendly, English-speaking proprietress.

*__Tre Donzelle__, *Via delle Donzelle,* **t** *0577 280358*. Basic but clean. €57.

Eating Out

Siena being a university town, snacks and fast food of all kinds are common; a *cioccina* is Siena's special variation on pizza; *pici* (thick south Tuscan spaghetti) with a sauce prepared from ground fresh pork, *pancetta*, sausages and chicken breasts, added to tomatoes cooked with Brunello wine, is the city's favourite pasta dish.

Certosa di Maggiano, *Via di Certosa 82 (1km southeast of Porta Romana),* **t** *0577 288180.* ***Open*** *daily 7.30–10.30pm. Booking advised.* In an exquisite setting: part of a luxury hotel housed in a former Carthusian monastery, with 14th-century cloisters. Modern, *haute cuisine* dishes served with some pomp. €75.

Antica Trattoria Botteganova, *Via Chiantigiana 29,* **t** *0577 284230.* ***Open*** *Tues–Sun 12.30–2 and 8–10. Booking advised.* A few kms northeast of Siena on the SS408 to Montevarchi. Meats such as the stuffed rabbit are earthy, or try the more delicate fish choices such as the tomato flan with basil-flavoured sturgeon fillets. €46.50.

Da Enzo, *Via Camollia 49,* **t** *0577 281277.* ***Open*** *Mon–Sat 12.30–2 and 7.30–9.30; closed mid–end July*. The menu in this traditional restaurant is long and varied with plenty of choice between fish and meat. The classic garlicky spaghetti with clams (*vongole*) is good, and there is a roast fish of the day. €34.

Osteria Le Logge, *Via del Porrione 33,* **t** *0577 48013.* ***Open*** *Mon–Sat noon–3 and 7.30–11. Booking advised.* The high-ceilinged and airy main room of this restaurant must be one of the most pleasant places to eat in Siena. A tempting choice of antipasti precedes such dishes as wild boar with juniper berries and polenta, or rabbit ravioli with pecorino cheese and mint. €33.50.

Ai Marsili, *Via del' Castoro 3,* **t** *0577 47154.* ***Open*** *Tues–Sun 12.30–2 and 7.30–10.* An elegant setting for a large choice of excellent Sienese dishes. Among the meat courses is Catherine de' Medici's famous dish *faraona alla Medici*, guinea fowl roasted with pine nuts, almonds and plums. €32.

Guido, *Vicolo Pier Pettinato 7,* **t** *0577 280 042.* ***Open*** *daily 12.30–2.30 and 7.30–10*. A central, traditional Sienese restaurant with a somewhat medieval feel. The grilled lamb, veal and *bistecca* are excellent. €25.

Osteria di Ficomezzo, *Via dei Termini 71,* **t** *0577 222384.* ***Open*** *Mon–Sat 12.30–3 and 7.30–10.30*. Lunch is a simple affair here. In the evening more inventive dishes such as guinea fowl cooked with tarragon appear alongside the more traditional *pici*, hearty soups, and stews. €23.

Tullio ai Tre Cristi, *Vicolo Provenzano,* **t** *0577 280608.* ***Open*** *Wed–Mon 10.30–2.30 and 7.30–10*. On this site since about 1830, this is perhaps the most authentic of Sienese restaurants, and it is the traditional restaurant of the giraffe *contrada*. Its menu includes things like *ribollita* and roast boar from the Maremma. Tables outside. €22.

Osteria di Castelvecchio, *Via Castelvecchio 65,* **t** *0577 49586.* ***Open*** *Wed–Mon 12.30–2.30 and 7.30–9.30*. The decor here is original and modern, but this building was once the stable block of one of Siena's oldest palazzi. Traditional recipes (penne with *salsiccia* and peppers, risotto with fresh herbs) with an emphasis on vegetarian dishes. The *menu degustazione* (€23) is good value. €21.

Osteria La Chiacchiera, *Via Costa Sant' Antonio 4,* **t** *0577 280631.* ***Open*** *daily noon–3 and 7–midnight*. This friendly, highly recommended little trattoria serves excellent *pici*, *ribollita*, kidneys, cockscombs (*cibreo*), stews or a simple *bistecca*. Outdoor tables. €15.

La Torre, *Via Salicotto 7,* **t** *0577 287548.* ***Open*** *Fri–Wed noon–3 and 7–10.* A fun, family-run trattoria. Home-made pasta, and there is a wide choice of roast meats and poultry. €15.

Il Grattacielo, *Via dei Pontani 8,* **t** *0577 289326.* ***Open*** *Mon–Sat 8–2 and 5–8.* A popular student hangout; avoid the lunch-time rush. The roast pork and other simple dishes are good, and the wine flows freely. €12.

Pizzeria Carlo e Franca, *Via Pantaneto 138,* **t** *0577 284385.* ***Open*** *Thurs–Tues 11–3 and 5–12.* Antipasti and pizzas at reasonable prices not far from the centre. €10.

Gelaterie

For luscious home-made flavours try:

Gelateria Caribia, *Via Rinaldini, behind the Piazza del Campo.* ***Open*** *Feb–Nov*. The best!

Gelateria Costarella, *Via di Città 33. Closed Tues.*

Fonte Gaia, *Piazza del Campo 21.* ***Open*** *daily.*

1380s) and the **Palazzo Pubblico** (1295–1310). Beginning with Duccio di Buoninsegna (1260–1319) Sienese artists took the lead in exploring new concepts in painting and sculpture and throughout the 1300s they contributed as much as or more than the Florentines in laying the foundations for the Renaissance. Contemporary records betray an obsessive concern on the part of bankers and merchants for decorating Siena and impressing outsiders. At the height of its fortunes, in the early 14th century, Siena ruled most of southern Tuscany. Its bankers were known in London, in the Baltic and in Constantinople, and its reputation for beauty and culture was matched by few cities in Europe.

The very pinnacle of civic pride and ambition came in 1339, with the fantastical plan to expand the as yet unfinished cathedral into the largest in all Christendom. The walls of that great effort, a nave that would have been longer than St Peter's in Rome, stand today as a monument to the dramatic event that snapped off Siena's career in full bloom. The **Black Death** of 1348 carried off three-fifths of the population – a mortality not greater than some other Italian cities, perhaps, but the plague hit Siena at a moment when its economy was particularly vulnerable, and started a slow but irreversible decline that was to continue for centuries. Economic troubles led to political instability, and in 1355 a revolt of the nobles, egged on by Emperor Charles IV, who was then in Tuscany, overthrew the Council of the Nine. Then in 1371, seven years before the Ciompi revolt in Florence, the wool-workers staged a genuine revolution. Organized in a sort of trade union, the **Compagnìa del Bruco**, they seized the Palazzo Pubblico and instituted a new government with greater popular representation.

The decades that followed saw Siena devote more and more of its diminishing resources to buying off the marauding mercenary companies that infested much of Italy at this time. By 1399 the city was in such straits that it surrendered its independence to **Giangaleazzo Visconti**, the tyrant of Milan, who was then attempting to surround and conquer Florence. After his death Siena reclaimed its freedom. Political confusion continued throughout the century, with only two periods of relative stability. One came with the pontificate (1458–63) of Pius II, the great Sienese scholar **Aeneas Silvius Piccolomini**, who exerted a dominating influence over his native city while he ruled at Rome. In 1487, a nobleman named **Pandolfo Petrucci** took over the government; as an honest broker, regulating the often murderous ambitions of the *monti*, he and his sons kept control of the republic until 1524.

The Fall of the Republic

Florence was always waiting in the wings to swallow up Siena, and finally had its chance in the 1500s. The real villain of the piece, however, was not Florence but that most imperious emperor, **Charles V**. After the fall of the Petrucci, the factional struggles resumed immediately, with frequent assassinations and riots, and constitutions changing with the spring fashions. Charles, who had bigger prey in his sights, cared little for the fate of the perverse little republic; he feared, though, that its disorders, religious toleration, and wretched financial condition were a disease that might spread beyond its borders. In 1530, he took advantage of riots in the city to install an imperial garrison. Yet even the emperor's representatives, usually Spaniards, could not keep Siena from sliding further into anarchy and bankruptcy on several occasions, largely thanks to Charles's war taxes. Cultural life was stifled as the Spaniards introduced the Inquisition and the Index. Scholars and artists fled, while poverty and political disruptions made Siena's once proud university cease to function.

In 1550, Charles announced that he was going to build a fortress within the city's walls, and that the Sienese were going to pay for it. Realizing that even the trifling liberty still left to them would soon be extinguished, the Sienese ruling class began intrigues with Charles' great enemy, France. A French army which was led by a Piccolomini, arrived in July 1552. Inside the walls the people revolted and locked the Spanish garrison up in its own new fortress. The empire was slow to react, but inevitably, in late 1554, a huge force of imperial troops, along with those of Florence, entered Sienese territory. The siege was prosecuted with remarkable brutality by Charles's commander, the **Marquis of Marignano**, who laid waste much of the Sienese countryside (which did not entirely recover until this century), tortured prisoners and even hired agents to start fires inside the walls. After a brave resistance, led by a republican Florentine exile named **Piero Strozzi** and assisted by France, Siena was starved into surrendering in April 1555. Two years later, Charles's son Philip II sold Siena to Duke Cosimo of Florence, and the ancient republic disappeared into the new Grand Duchy of Tuscany.

If nothing else, Siena went out with a flourish. After the capture of the city, some 2,000 republican bitter-enders escaped to make a last stand at Montalcino. Declaring 'Where the *Comune* is, there is the City', they established what must be the world's first republican government-in-exile. With control over much of the old Sienese territory, the '**Republic of Siena at Montalcino**' held out against the Medici for another four years.

With its independence lost and its economy irrevocably ruined, Siena withdrew into itself. For centuries there was to be no recovery, little art or scholarship, and no movements towards reform. The Sienese aristocracy, already decayed into a parasitic *rentier* class, made its peace with the Medici dukes early on; in return for their support, the Medici allowed them to keep much of

The Terzi and the Contrade

From Il Campo, Siena's central square, the city unfolds like a three-petalled flower along three ridges. it has been a natural division since medieval times, with the oldest quarter, the **Terzo di Città**, including the cathedral, so the southwest; the **Terzo di San Martino** to the southeast; and the **Terzo di Camollia** to the north.

The Sienese have taken the ***contrade*** for granted so long that their history is almost impossible to trace. Basically, the word denotes the 17 neighbourhoods into which Siena is divided. Like the *rioni* of Rome, they were once the original wards of the ancient city – not merely geographical boundaries, but self-governing entities; the ancients often referred to them as the city's 'tribes'. In Siena, the *contrade* survived and prospered all through classical times and the Middle Ages. More than anything else, they maintained the city's traditions and sense of identity through the dark years after 1552. Incredibly enough, they're still there now, unique in Italy and perhaps all Europe. Once Siena counted over 60 *contrade*. Now there are 17, each with a sort of totem animal for its symbol:

Aquila (eagle), *Onda* (dolphin), *Tartuca* (turtle), *Pantera* (panther), *Selva* (rhinoceros) and *Chiocciola* (snail); all southwest of the Campo in Terzo di Città.

Leocorno (unicorn), *Torre* (elephant), *Nicchio* (mussel shell), *Civetta* (owl) and *Valdimontone* (ram); in Terzo di San Martino southeast of the Campo.

Oca (goose), *Drago* (dragon), *Giraffa* (giraffe), *Lupa* (wolf), *Bruco* (caterpillar) and *Istrice* (porcupine); all in the north in the Terzo di Camollia.

Sienese and Italian law recognize each of these as being legally chartered communities; today a *contrada* functions as a combination social and dining club, neighbourhood improvement organization, religious confraternity and mutual assistance fund. Each elects its own officials annually in May. Each has its own chapel, museum and fountain, its own flag and colours, and its own patron saint who pulls all the strings he can in Heaven to help his beloved district win the Palio.

their power and privileges. The once great capital of trade and finance shrank rapidly into an overbuilt farmers' market, its population dropping from a 14th-century high of 60–80,000 to around a mere 15,000 by the year 1700. This does much to explain why medieval and Renaissance Siena is so well preserved today – for better or worse, nothing at all has happened to change it.

By the 'Age of Enlightenment', with its disparaging of everything medieval, the Sienese seem to have quite forgotten their own history and art, and it is no surprise that the rest of Europe forgot them too. During the first years of the Grand Tour, no self-respecting northern European would think of visiting Siena. Few had probably ever heard of it, and the ones who stopped overnight on the way to Rome were usually dismayed at the 'inelegance' of its medieval buildings and art. It was not until the 1830s that Siena was rediscovered, with the help of literati like the Brownings, who spent several summers here, and that truly Gothic American, Henry James. The Sienese were not far behind in rediscovering it themselves. The old civic pride that had lain dormant for centuries yawned and stretched like Sleeping Beauty and went diligently back to work. Before the century was out, everything that could still be salvaged of the city's ancient glory was refurbished and restored. More than ever fascinated by its own image and eccentricities, and more than ever without any kind of an economic base, Siena was ready for its present career as a cultural attraction, a tourist town.

THE CAMPO

There is no lovelier square in Tuscany than the Campo, and none more beloved by its city. The Forum of ancient *Sena Julia* was on this spot, and in the Middle Ages it evolved into its present fan shape, rather like a scallop shell or a classical theatre. The Campo was paved in brick as early as 1340; the nine sections into which the fan is divided are in honour of the Council of the Nine, rulers of the city at the time. Thousands crowd over the bricks here every year to see the Palio, run on the periphery.

The Fonte Gaia

For a worthy embellishment to their Campo, the Sienese commissioned for its curved north end the Fonte Gaia from Jacopo della Quercia who was their greatest sculptor, though what you see now is an uninspired copy of 1868.

Della Quercia worked on it from 1408 to 1419, creating the broad rectangle of marble with reliefs of Adam and Eve and allegorical virtues. It was to be the opening salvo of Siena's Renaissance, an answer to the Baptistry doors of Ghiberti in Florence (for which della Quercia himself had been one of the contestants). Perhaps it was a poor choice of stone, but the years have been incredibly unkind to this fountain; the badly eroded remains of the original can be seen up on the loggia of the Palazzo Pubblico.

No one can spend much time in Siena without noticing its fountains. The Republic always made sure each part of the city had access to good water; medieval Siena created the most elaborate engineering works since ancient Rome to bring the water in. Fonte Gaia, and others such as the Fontebranda on Via Santa Caterina, are fed by underground aqueducts that stretch for miles across the Tuscan countryside. The original Fonte Gaia was completed in the early 1300s; there's a story that, soon after, some citizens dug up a beautiful Greek statue of Venus, signed by Praxiteles himself. The delighted Sienese carried it in procession through the city and installed it on top of their new fountain. With the devastation of the Black Death, however, the preachers were quick to blame God's wrath on the indecent pagan on the Fonte Gaia. Throughout history, the Sienese have always been ready to be shocked by their own sins; in this case, with their neighbours dropping like flies around them, they proved only too eager to make poor Venus the scapegoat. They chopped her into little bits,

The Palio

The thousands of tourists who come twice a year to see the Palio, Siena's famous horse race around the Campo, probably think the Sienese are doing it all just for them. Yet like the *contrade* which contest it, the Palio is an essential part of Sienese culture, something that means as much to the city as it did centuries ago. The oldest recorded Palio was run in 1283, though no one can say how far the custom goes back. The course is three times around the periphery of the Campo, though earlier it was run on various routes through the city's main streets.

The *palio* (Latin *pallium*) is an embroidered banner, the prize offered for winning the race. Two races are held each year, on 2 July and 16 August, and the *palio* of each is decorated with an image of the Virgin Mary. The course has room for only 10 horses in each race. Some of the 17 *contrade* are chosen by lot for each race to ensure that everyone has a fair chance. The horses are also selected by lot, but the *contrade* are free to select their own jockeys. Although the race itself only lasts a minute and a half, there's a good hour or two of pageantry preceding the event; the famous flag-throwers or *alfieri* of each participating *contrada* put on a dazzling show, while the medieval *carroccio*, drawn by a yoke of white oxen, is pressed into service to circle the Campo, bearing the prized *palio* itself.

The Palio is no joke; baskets of money ride on each race, not to mention the sacred honour of the district. To obtain divine favour, each *contrada* brings its horse into its chapel on race morning for a special blessing (and if a little horse manure drops during the ceremony, it's a sign of good luck). The only rule stipulates that you can't seize the reins of an opponent. There are no rules against bribing opposing jockeys, making alliances with other *contrade*, or ambushing jockeys before the race. The course around the Campo has two right angles. Anything can happen; recent Palii have featured not only jockeys but *horses* flying through the air. The Sienese say no one has ever been killed at a Palio. There's no reason to believe them. They wouldn't believe it themselves; it is an article of faith among the Sienese that fatalities are prevented by special intervention of the Virgin Mary. The post-Palio carousing, while not up to medieval standards, is still impressive; in the winning *contrada* the party might go on for days.

No event in Italy is as infectiously exhilarating as the Palio. There are two ways to see it, either from the centre of the Campo, which is packed tight and always very hot, or from an expensive (€130–260) seat in a viewing stand, which you must book well in advance. Several travel agencies offer special Palio tours; otherwise book by April (ask at the tourist office). Tickets can be bought from shops around the Campo too, but they are difficult to find because the event is primarily for the Sienese (the *contrade* buy most of the tickets) and not for tourists.

and a party of Sienese disguised as peasants smuggled the pieces over the border and buried them in Florentine territory to pass the bad luck on to their enemies.

Palazzo Pubblico

The Campo. Torre del Mangia* open *Nov–mid-Mar 10–4, mid-Mar–June and Sept–Oct 10–7, July and Aug 10am–11pm;* adm *€5.16.

If the Campo is like a Roman theatre, the main attraction on stage since 1310 has been this brick and stone palace, the enduring symbol of the Sienese Republic and still the town hall today. Its façade is the face of Siena's history, with the she-wolf of Senius and Ascanius, Medici balls, the IHS of San Bernardino, and squared Guelph crenellations, all in the shadow of the tremendous **Torre del Mangia**, the graceful, needle-like tower that Henry James called 'Siena's Declaration of Independence'. At 335ft, the tower was the second tallest ever raised in medieval Italy (only the campanile in Cremona beats it). At the time, the cathedral tower up on its hill completely dominated

Siena's skyline; the Council of the Nine wouldn't accept that the symbol of religious authority or any of the nobility's fortress-skyscrapers should be taller than the symbol of the republic, so its Perugian architects, Muccio and Francesco di Rinaldo, made sure its height would be hard to surpass.

There was a practical side to it, too. At the top hung the *comune*'s great bell, which had to be heard in every corner of the city tolling the hours and announcing the curfew, or calling the citizens to assemble in case of war or emergency. One of the first men to hold the job of bell-ringer gave the tower its name, a fat, sleepy fellow named *Mangiaguadagni* ('eat the profits') or just Mangia for short; there is a statue of him in one of the courtyards.

Climb the tower's endless staircase for the definitive view of Siena – on the clearest days you will also be able to see about half of the medieval republic's territory, a view that is absolutely, positively worth the slight risk of cardiac arrest (*open daily 9–5.30; winter until 2.15pm; adm*). At the foot of the tower, the marble **Cappella della Piazza**, with its graceful rounded arches, stands out clearly from the Gothic earnestness of the rest of the building. It was begun in 1352, in thanks for deliverance from the Black Death, but not finally completed until the mid-15th century.

Museo Civico

w www.comune.siena.it/museocivico. Open Nov–mid-Mar daily 10–6.30, mid-Mar–June and Sept–Oct daily 10–7, July and Aug daily 10am–11pm; adm €6.19.

Most of the Palazzo Pubblico's ground floor is still used for city offices, but the upper floors have been made into the city's museum.

Here the main attraction is the series of state rooms done in frescoes, a sampling of the best of Sienese art throughout the centuries. The first, the historical frescoes in the **Sala del Risorgimento**, were done by an artist named A. G. Cassioli only in 1886: the meeting of Vittorio Emanuele II with Garibaldi, his coronation, portraits and epigrams of past patriots, and an 'allegory of Italian Liberty', all in a colourful and photographically precise style. If anything, it is a tribute to Sienese artistic conservatism; finally liberated after 300 years of Florentine rule, they immediately went back to their good old medieval habits.

Next on the same floor is the **Sala di Badia** with frescoes depicting the story of Alessandro VII and some vigorous battle scenes by the Sienese Spinello Aretino (1300s) and the *Sixteen Virtues* by Martino di Bartolomeo. The adjoining **anticamera del Concistoro** has a lovely *Madonna and Child* by Matteo di Giovanni. In the **Sala del Concistoro**, Gobelin tapestries adorn the walls while the great Sienese Mannerist Beccafumi contributed a ceiling of frescoes in the 1530s celebrating the political virtues of antiquity; that theme is continued in the vestibule to the **Chapel**, with portraits of ancient heroes from Cicero to Judas Maccabeus, all by Taddeo di Bartolo. These portrayals, along with more portraits of the classical gods and goddesses and an interesting view of ancient Rome, show clearly just how widespread was the fascination with antiquity even in the 1300s. Intruding among the classical crew, there's also a king-sized St Christopher covering an entire wall. Before setting out on a journey it was good luck to catch a glimpse of this saint, and in Italy and Spain he is often painted extra large so you won't miss him. In a display case in the hall, some of the oldest treasures of the Sienese Republic are kept: the war helmet of the Captain of the People, and a delicate **golden rose**, a gift to the city from the Sienese pope, Pius II.

The **Chapel** (*Cappella del Consiglio*) is surrounded by a lovely wrought-iron grille designed by Jacopo della Quercia; when it is open you can see more frescoes by Taddeo di Bartolo, an altarpiece by Il Sodoma, and some exceptional carved wood seats, by Domenico di Nicolò (*c.* 1415–28). In the adjacent chamber (the **Sala del Mappamondo**), only the outline is left of Lorenzetti's cosmological fresco, a diagram of the universe including all the celestial and angelic spheres, much like the one in the Campo Santo at Pisa. Above it, there is a very famous fresco by Simone Martini (*c.* 1330), showing the redoubtable *condottiere* **Guidoriccio da Fogliano** on his way to attack the castle of Montemassi, during a revolt against Siena. Also by Martini is an enthroned Virgin, or *Maestà*, that is believed to be his earliest work (1315).

When you enter the **Sala dei Nove** (or Sala della Pace), meeting room of the Council of the Nine, you'll understand at a glance why they ruled Siena so well. Whenever one of the councillors had the temptation to skim some cream off the top, or pass a fat contract over to his brother-in-law the paving contractor, or tighten the screws on the poor by raising the salt tax, he had only to look up at Ambrogio Lorenzetti's great frescoes to really feel like a worm. There are two complementary sets, with scenes of Siena under good government and bad, and allegorical councils of virtues or vices for each. Enthroned Justice rules the good Siena, with such counsellors as Peace, Prudence and Magnanimity; bad Siena groans under the thumb of one nasty piece of work, sneering, fanged Tyranny and his cronies: Pride, Vainglory, Avarice and Wrath among others. The good Siena is a happy place, with buildings in good repair, well-dressed folk who are dancing in the streets, and well-stocked shops where the merchants appear to be making a nice profit. Bad Siena is almost a mirror image, only the effects of the Tyrant's rule are plain to see: urban blight, crime in broad daylight, buildings crumbling and abandoned, and business bad for everybody – a landscape which for many of us modern city dwellers will seem all too familiar.

In the next room is Guido da Siena's large *Madonna and Child* (mid-1200s), the earliest masterpiece of the Sienese school. If you're not up to climbing the tower, at least take the long, unmarked stairway by the Sala del Risorgimento that leads up to the **loggia**, with the second-best view over Siena and the disassembled bits and pieces of della Quercia's reliefs from the Fonte Gaia, not particularly impressive in their worn and damaged state, although *The Expulsion from Paradise* retains something of its power.

Croce del Travaglio

Two of Siena's three main streets form a graceful curve around the back of the Campo; where they meet the third, behind the Fonte Gaia, is the corner the Sienese call the Croce del Travaglio (a mysterious nickname: the 'cross of affliction').

Here, the three-arched **Loggia della Mercanzia**, in a sense Siena's Royal Exchange, was the place where the Republic's merchants made their deals and settled their differences before the city's famed commercial tribunal. The Loggia marks the transition from Sienese Gothic to the early Renaissance style – begun in 1417, it was probably influenced by Florence's Loggia dei Lanzi. The five statues of saints around the columns are the work of Antonio Federighi and Vecchietta, the leading Sienese sculptor after della Quercia.

The three streets that meet here lead directly into the **three *terzi*** of Siena. All three are among the city's most beautiful streets.

PIAZZA DEL DUOMO

The Duomo

***Piazza del Duomo. Open** Nov–mid-Mar Mon–Sat 7.30–1 and 2–5, Sun and hols 2.30–5, mid-Mar–Oct Mon–Sat 7.30–7.30, Sun and hols 2.30–7.30.*

Siena's Cathedral may not be a transcendent expression of faith, nor an important landmark in architecture, but it is certainly one of the most delightful, decorative ornaments in Christendom. Begun around 1200, it was one of the first Gothic cathedrals in central Italy. It started in good Gothic tradition as a communal effort and was not really a project of the Church. There doesn't seem

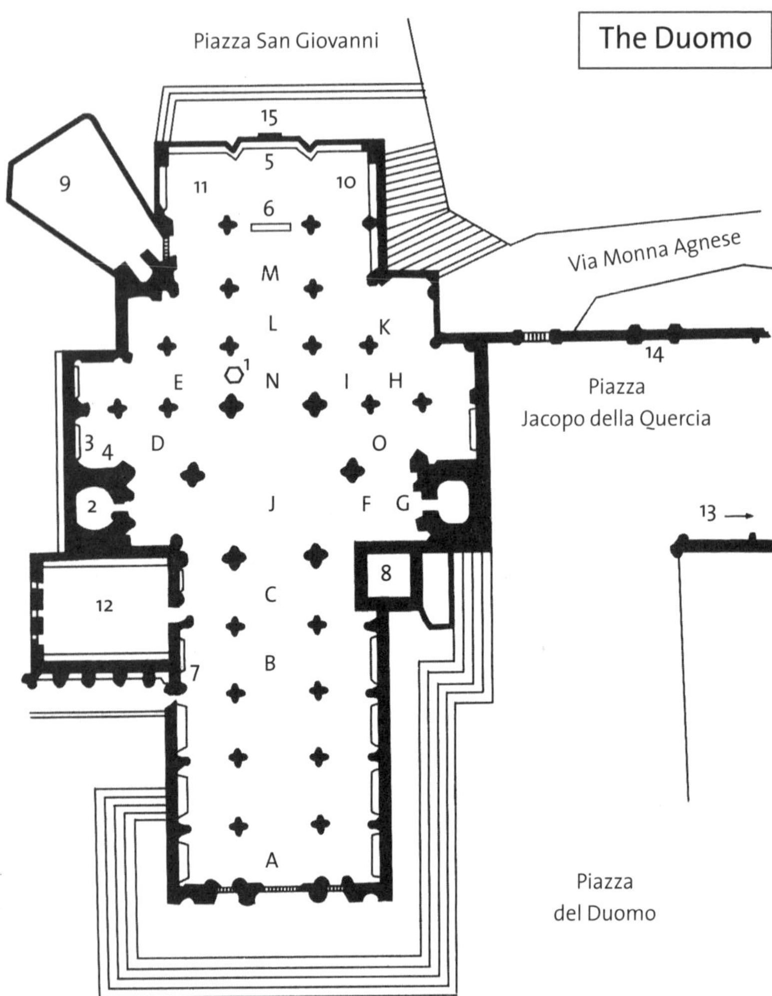

1 Pisano's Pulpit
2 Chapel of San Giovanni Battista
3 Tomb of Cardinal Pecci (Donatello)
4 Tomb of Cardinal Petroni (Tino da Camaino)
5 Stained Glass of Duccio
6 High Altar
7 Piccolomini Altar (della Quercia, Michelangelo)
8 Campanile
9 Sacristy
10 Cantorie
11 Choir
12 Piccolomini Library
13 To Cathedral Museum
14 Cathedral Extension
15 Bapistry (lower level)

A *Hermes Trismegistus*
B *Allegory of Virtue*
C *Wheel of Fortune*
D *Massacre of the Innocents*
E *Judith Liberating Bethulia*
F *Seven Ages of Man*
G *Allegories of Faith, Hope and Charity*
H *Story of Absalom*
I *Emperor Sigismund on his Throne*
J *Sacrifice of Elias, Execution of the False Prophets*
K *Samson and the Philistines*
L *David the Psalmist*
M *Sacrifice of Abraham*
N *Moses Receives the Commandments*
O *Story of Jephta*

to have been very much voluntary labour. Even in the Middle Ages Italians were a little too blasé for that – but every citizen with a cart was expected to bring two loads of marble from the quarries each year, earning him a special indulgence from the bishop. One load must have been white and the other black, for under the influence of Pisa, the Sienese built themselves one thoroughly striped cathedral – stripes darker and bolder than Pisa's or Lucca's. The campanile, with its distinctive fenestration, narrowing in size down six levels, rises over the city like a giant ice-cream parfait. Most of the body of the church was finished by 1270, and 14 years later Giovanni Pisano was called in to create the sculpture for the lavish **façade**, with statues of biblical prophets and pagan philosophers. The upper half was not begun until the 1390s, and the glittering mosaics in the gables are, like Orvieto's, the work of Venetian artists of the late 19th century.

The Interior

The interior is a treasure-box. Upon entering the main portal, the ferociously striped pilasters and the Gothic vaulting, a blue firmament painted with golden stars, inevitably draw the eye upwards. However, the most spectacular feature is at your very feet – the **marble pavement**, where the peculiar figure smiling up at you is *Hermes Trismegistus*, the legendary Egyptian father of alchemy (*see* box), depicted in elegant *sgraffito* work of white and coloured marble.

In fact, the entire floor of the cathedral is covered with almost 12,000 square metres of virtuoso *sgraffito* in 56 scenes which include portraits, mystical allegories and events from the Old Testament. Like the Biccherna covers in the Palazzo Piccolomini, they are a tradition carried on over centuries. Many of Siena's best artists worked on them, beginning in 1369 and continuing into the 1600s; Giorgio Vasari claimed that Duccio di

Hermes Trismegistus

As you pass through the main portal of Siena cathedral, the figure before you on the famous marble pavement comes as a surprise – Hermes Trismegistus, someone rarely seen in art, though a mysterious protagonist in a great undercurrent of Renaissance thought. 'Thrice-great Hermes', mythical author of a series of mystic philosophical dialogues from the 2nd century AD, had a profound influence on Greek and Arabic thought, gradually becoming associated (correctly or not) with the Egyptian god Thoth, inventor of writing and father of a deep mystical tradition that continues to this day. In the 1400s, the Hermetic writings were introduced in the West, largely the work of Greek scholars fleeing the Ottoman conquest of Constantinople and Trebizond. They made quite a splash. Marsilio Ficino, the Florentine humanist and friend of Cosimo de' Medici, completed the first Latin translation of the Hermetic books in 1471.

To the men of the Renaissance, Hermes was a real person, an Egyptian prophet, who lived in the time of Moses and was perhaps his teacher. They saw, revealed in the Hermetic books, an ancient, natural religion, prefiguring Christianity and complementary to it – and in fact much more fun than Christianity, for the magical elements in it were entirely to the taste of neo-Platonists like Ficino. From a contemporary point of view, the recovery of Hermes Trismegistus was one of the main intellectual events of the century, a century that witnessed a tremendous revival of natural magic, alchemy and astrology.

The memorable Hermes in Siena is surrounded by a bevy of 10 sibyls: those of Cumae and Tivoli (the Italians), Delphi, Libya, the Hellespont, Phrygia and the rest. These ladies, part of a pan-Mediterranean religious tradition even older than Hermes Trismegistus, are far more common in Tuscan religious iconography (as in the Baptistry and Santa Trínita in Florence, or most famously on Michelangelo's Sistine Chapel ceiling), for the belief that they all foretold the birth of Christ.

Buoninsegna himself first worked in this medium, though none of the pictures here is his.

Even in a building with so many marvels – the Piccolomini Library, Nicola Pisano's pulpit, Duccio's stained glass, works by Donatello, della Quercia, Pinturicchio, Michelangelo, Bernini and many others – this pavement perhaps takes pride of place. The greatest limitation of Sienese art was always the conservatism of its patrons, accustomed to demanding the same old images in the same old styles. Commissions from the Office of Cathedral Works, controlled by the state, were usually more liberal, allowing the artists to create such unique, and in some cases startling images, one of the greatest achievements of Renaissance Siena.

The *Hermes* on the cathedral pavement, by Giovanni di Stefano, was completed in the 1480s, a decade after Ficino's translation; it shows him together with Moses, holding a book with the inscription 'Take up thy letters and laws, O Egyptians'. Hermes is covered over, along with many of the other stonework figures, for much of the time. On either side, all 10 prophetic *Sibyls* done by various artists at the same time decorate the aisles of the church. Nor are Hermes and the sibyls the only peculiar thing on this floor. Directly behind him begins a series of large scenes, including a *Wheel of Fortune*, with men hanging on to it for dear life, another wheel of uncertain symbolism, and emblems of Siena and other Tuscan and Latin cities. Oddest of all is a work by Pinturicchio, variously titled the *Allegory of Virtue* or the *Allegory of Fortune*; on a rocky island full of serpents, a party of well-dressed people has just disembarked, climbing to the summit where a figure of 'Socrates' accepts a pen from a seated female figure, and another, 'Crates', empties a basket of gold and jewels into the sea. Below, a naked woman with a gonfalon stands with one foot in a boat, and another on land.

Unfortunately, many of the best scenes, under the crossing and transepts, are covered most of the year to save them from wear. You'll need to come between 15 August and 15 September to see the visionary works of Alessandro Franchi – *The Triumph of Elias* and other events in that prophet's life – and Domenico Beccafumi's *Sacrifice of Elias* and the *Execution of the False Prophets of Baal*. (Hasn't anyone in Siena ever heard of plexiglass?) Other works uncovered all year include *The Seven Ages of Man* by Antonio Federighi, *Scenes From the Life of Moses* by Beccafumi, Matteo di Giovanni's *Massacre of the Innocents* (always a favourite subject in Sienese art), and best of all the beautifully drawn *Judith Liberating the City of Bethulia* which was a collaboration of Federighi, Matteo di Giovanni and Urbano da Cortona.

Perhaps the greatest attraction above floor level is the great Carrara marble **pulpit** done by Nicola Pisano in the 1280s. Pisano started on it directly after finishing the one in Pisa; one of the assistants he brought here to help with the work was the young Arnolfo di Cambio. The typical Pisano conception is held up by allegorical figures of the seven liberal arts – more sibyls, prophets, Christian virtues and saints tucked away in the odd corners, and vigorous, crowded relief panels from the Passion as good as the ones in Pisa. Nearby, in the left transept, the **chapel of San Giovanni Battista** has frescoes by Pinturicchio and a bronze statue of St John the Baptist by Donatello, who also contributed the **Tomb of Giovanni Pecci**, a 1400s Sienese bishop. Another tomb worth a look is that of Cardinal Petroni, an influential early Renaissance design from 1310 by Tino di Camaino.

Some of the stained glass in the cathedral is excellent, especially the earliest windows, in the apse, designed by Duccio, and the rose window with its cornucopia. Over the high altar is a bronze baldachin by Vecchietta, with bronze angels (the two lower ones by Francesco di Giorgio Martini,1499) and in the north aisle, the Piccolomini altar includes four early statues of saints which are by Michelangelo, and one by Torrigiani, the fellow who broke Michelangelo's nose and ended up in exile, working in Westminster Abbey. There is also a *Madonna* by Jacopo della Quercia. Throughout the cathedral, as everywhere else in Siena, be sure to keep an eye out for details – little things like the tiny, exquisite heads of the popes that decorate the clerestory wall. The Office of Works never settled for anything less than the best, and even such trifles as the holy water fonts, the choir stalls, the iron grilles and the candlesticks are works of genuine artistic merit.

The Piccolomini Library

***Open** Nov–mid-Mar Mon–Sat 10–1 and 2.30–5, Sun and hols 2.30–5, mid-Mar–Oct Mon–Sat 9–7.30, Sun and hols 2.30–7.30; **adm** €1.54.*

The Piccolomini Library contains the famous frescoes by Pinturicchio maintained as part of the cathedral complex. It was built to hold the library of Aeneas Silvius, the greatest member of Siena's greatest noble family. The entrance is off the left aisle, near the Piccolomini Altar.

In 1495, 31 years after his death, Cardinal Francesco Piccolomini, a man who would

Siena's Renaissance Man

Aeneas Silvius Piccolomini (1405–64), eventually to become Pope Pius II, was the very definition of a Renaissance man. One of 18 children who were born into a branch of the mighty Piccolomini family, little Aeneas's quick intelligence soon attracted a great deal of attention, and he received the finest humanist education Siena could offer. To this he added natural charm, good looks, excellent Latin and an innate sense of diplomacy that soon earned him posts of responsibility with the leading ecclesiastics of the day.

Aeneas Silvius' interests ranged wide, and his keen observations and objective point of view on all aspects of life were invaluable to the scholarship of the day, especially in geography and topography. His *On Europe*, *On Asia* and *An Account of Bohemia* were among the most important works since ancient times; *On Asia* was closely studied by Columbus. Aeneas had enough time left over to write weighty tomes on history, on the lives of great men, on education and on antiquities; he was gifted enough in literature (he wrote poetry, a comedy and an erotic novella) to be crowned Poet Laureate. In politics, he worked fitfully to reform the Church of Rome and the constitution of Siena. He was the first to detail and describe the beauties of the Italian landscape, in which he found the greatest delight, as well as the little scenes of daily life that struck him. These, along with his thoughts and ambitions, even the unseemly, unflattering ones, went into his *Commentaries*, the most vivid and personal autobiography until Benvenuto Cellini's, and the only one ever published by a pope.

Aeneas Silvius took holy orders in 1446, marking a new serious turn in his life. Thanks to his service to popes Eugenius IV, Nicholas V and Calixtus III he became a bishop and cardinal, and was elected pope in 1458, in a corrupt conclave that he described in frank detail. His election hardly put an end to his womanizing, although his peers, who thought they had elected a worldly humanist, were astonished at Pius II's dedicated efforts to promote the papacy and defend the faith by preaching a Crusade against the Turks who had just captured Constantinople. His chief memorial is the little Renaissance city of Pienza, southeast of Siena, which Bernardo Rossellino created out of the humble village of his birth, Corsignano. But because of the honesty of his autobiography, Pius II has never been considered a very good pope, although 15th-century historians praised his truthfulness, courage and consistency. The irony is that other Renaissance popes were surely just as conniving and ambitious if not worse (for one thing, Pius II was one of the first who didn't believe in magic or astrology); the difference is they never wrote down their thoughts.

become Pope Pius III, decided his celebrated uncle's life would make a fine subject for a series of frescoes. He gave the job to Pinturicchio, his last major commission; among his assistants was the young, still impressionable Raphael – anyone who knows his *Betrothal of the Virgin* will find these paintings eerily familiar. The 10 scenes include Aeneas Silvius' attendance at the court of James I in Scotland – a Scotland with a Tuscan landscape – where he served with an embassy. Later he is shown accepting a poet laureate's crown from his friend Emperor Frederick III, and presiding over the meeting of Frederick and his bride-to-be, Eleanor of Aragon. Another fresco depicts him canonizing St Catherine of Siena. The last, poignant one portrays a view of Ancona, and its cathedral on Monte Guasco, where Pius II went in 1464, planning a crusade against the Turks. While waiting for the help promised by the European powers, help that never came, he fell ill and died.

Art historians and critics, following the sniping biography of the artist by Vasari, are not always kind to Pinturicchio. As with Gozzoli's frescoes for the Medici Palace in Florence, the consensus seems to be that this is a less challenging sort of art, or perhaps just a very elevated approach to interior decoration. Certainly Pinturicchio seems extremely concerned with the latest styles in court dress and coiffure. However, the incandescent colour, fairy-tale backgrounds and beautifully drawn figures prove irresistible. These are among the brightest and best-preserved of all quattrocento frescoes; the total effect is that of a serenely confident art, concerned above all with beauty for beauty's sake, even when chronicling the life of a pope. Aeneas Silvius' books have all been carted away somewhere but one of his favourite things remains, the *Three Graces* marble statue, a copy of the work by Praxiteles that was much studied by the artists of the 1400s.

Around the side of the cathedral, off the right transept, Piazza Jacopo della Quercia is the name the Sienese have given to the doomed nave of their 1330s **cathedral extension**. All around the square, the heroic pilasters and arches rise, some incorporated into the walls of later buildings.

Museo Metropolitana

***w** www.operaduomo.it. **Open** Nov–mid-Mar daily 9–1.30, mid-Mar–Sept daily 9–7.30, Oct daily 9–6; **adm** €5.16.*

Beyond the big, blank façade of the cathedral extension, a little door on the right gives entrance to the Museo Metropolitana, built into what would have been one of the cathedral transepts.

This is the place to go to inspect the cathedral façade at close range. Most of the statues now on the façade are modern copies, replacing the works of great sculptors like Nicola Pisano, Urbano da Cortona and Jacopo della Quercia. The originals have been moved to the museum for preservation, and you can look the cathedral's marble saints right in the eye (many of these remarkable statues, fairly alive with early Renaissance *prontezza* (alertness), seem ready to hop off their pedestals and start declaiming if they suspect for a minute you've been skipping Sunday Mass).

Besides these, there are some architectural fragments and leftover pinnacles, as well as some bits of the marble pavement that had to be replaced. On the first floor, a collection of Sienese paintings includes Duccio di Buoninsegna's masterpiece, the *Maestà* that hung behind the cathedral's high altar from 1311 until 1505. Painted on both sides, the main composition is a familiar Sienese favourite, the enthroned Virgin flanked by neat rows of adoring saints – expressive faces and fancy clothes with a glittering gold background. Among the other paintings and sculptures are works by Pietro and Ambrogio Lorenzetti, Simone Martini, Beccafumi and Vecchietta.

Among the works on the top floor is the *Madonna dagli Occhi Grossi* ('of the Big Eyes') by an anonymous artist of the 1210s, a landmark in the development of Sienese painting and the original cathedral altarpiece. There's a hoard of golden croziers, reliquaries, and crucifixes from the Cathedral Treasure, including another lovely golden rose from the Vatican; this was probably a gift from Aeneas Silvius. A stairway leads up to the top of the **Facciatone**, the 'big façade' of the unfinished nave, where you can enjoy a view over the city.

Cathedral Baptistry

***Piazza San Giovanni. Open** winter daily 10–1 and 2.30–5, summer daily 9–7.30; **adm** €2.06.*

In this unusual but prominent setting the Office of Works architects squeezed in perhaps the only baptistry in Italy situated directly under a cathedral apse. Behind its unfinished 1390s Gothic façade, this baptistry contains some of the finest art in Siena. It's hard to see anything in this gloomy cellar, though; bring plenty of coins for the lighting machines.

Frescoes by Vecchietta, restored to death in the 19th century, decorate much of the interior. The crown jewel, however, is the **baptismal font**, a king-sized work embellished with some of the finest sculpture of the quattrocento. Of the gilded reliefs around the sides, *Herod's Feast* is by Donatello, and the *Baptism of Christ* and *St John in Prison* by Ghiberti. The first relief, with the *Annunciation of the Baptist's Birth*, is the work of Jacopo della Quercia, who also added the five statues of prophets above. Two of the statues at the corners of the font, the ones representing the virtues Hope and Charity, are also by Donatello.

Pinacoteca Nazionale

***Via San Pietro 29. Open** Tues–Sat 8.15–7.15, Mon 8.30–1.30, Sun and hols 8.15–1.15; **adm** €4.13.*

This is the temple of Sienese art, a representative sampling of this inimitable city's style; many of the works have been recently restored. The collection, housed in the 14th-century Palazzo Buonsignori, is arranged roughly chronologically, beginning on the ground floor with Guido da Siena and his school in the mid-13th century (**Room 2**), continuing through an entire room of delicate, melancholy Virgins by Duccio and his followers, reaching a climax with Duccio's luminous though damaged *Madonna dei Francescani* in **Room 4**. More Madonnas and saints fill room after room, including important works by Siena's greatest 14th-century artists. One of the most famous is Simone Martini's *Madonna and Child*; the story goes that this Madonna was a great Palio fan. When everyone had gathered in the Campo for the event, she would wander out in the empty streets and tiptoe over for a look. One day, she lingered too long in the Campo and had to run back home, losing her veil in her haste. She has yet to find it and, according to the Sienese, she weeps sweetly during the Palio, probably because she can't get through the Pinacoteca's security system. Other Madonnas that stand out are those of Pietro and Ambrogio Lorenzetti (*Madonna Enthroned* and the *Annunciation*, both in **Room 7**) and Taddeo di Bartolo (*Triptych*, in **Room 9**), with their rosy blooming faces and brilliant colour, a remarkable counterpoint to the relative austerity of contemporary painting in Florence.

Sienese Renaissance painters are well represented, often betraying the essential conservatism of their art and resisting the new approaches of Florence: Domenico di Bartolo's 1433 *Madonna* in **Room 9**; Nerocchio and Matteo di Giovanni of the 1470s (**Room 14**); Sano di Pietro, the leading painter of the 1440s (**Rooms 16–18**). The first floor displays some of Il Sodoma's most important works, especially the great *Scourging of Christ* which is in **Room 31** (1514); in **Room 37** the *Descent into Hell* is one of the finest works by Siena's great Mannerist, Beccafumi.

Ospedale di Santa Maria della Scala

***Piazza del Duomo, e** infoscala@comune.siena.it, **w** www.santamaria/comune.siena.it. **Open** winter daily 10.30–4.30, summer daily 10–6; **adm** €5.16.*

Opposite the old cathedral façade, one entire side of the piazza is occupied by the great Ospedale di Santa Maria della Scala, believed to have been founded in the 9th century. For centuries one of the largest and finest hospitals in the world, this is now Italy's biggest and most exciting museum project.

According to legend, the hospital had its beginnings with a pious cobbler named Sorore, who opened a hostel and infirmary for pilgrims who were on their way to Rome. (Siena was an important stop on medieval Europe's busiest pilgrimage route, the Via Francigiana.) Sorore's mother, it is said, later had a vision here – of babies ascending a ladder into heaven, and being received into the arms of the Virgin Mary – and consequently a foundling hospital was soon added. A meticulous attention to the health of its citizens was always one of the most praiseworthy features of Siena; in the 14th century it insisted on such revolutionary practices as the washing of hands by doctors and nurses, meals adapted to each patient's illness, and the use of iron beds (to prevent the spread of bedbugs). To encourage donations, laws were passed allowing wealthy Sienese to deduct gifts from their taxes (remember, this is the 14th century) and not a few left huge sums in their wills; after the plague of 1348, the hospital was up to its ears in gold. Even in the decadence of the 1700s advances in such things as inoculations were being made here.

In recent years, the hospital functions have been gradually moved out to more accessible locations (one of the last to die here was novelist and folktale compiler, Italo Calvino). As the place closed up, there was talk of converting it into a museum. Now they're doing it, and in a big way. The Sienese say that their new museum, dedicated to all the arts of the city's history, will be one of the largest in the world, with three times the exhibition space of the Pompidou Centre. Don't ask when it will be finished; the point of this innovative exercise is that it will *never* be finished. An international competition was held to plan the new complex; the winner, Professor Guido Canali of Parma, came up with the idea of a *cantiere didattico*, an 'educational construction site' so to speak, where the process of museum-building itself is part of the attraction. Nevertheless, they should have much of the permanent exhibits in place in 10 years or so, along with shops, temporary exhibits and restoration workshops. In a typical gesture of Sienese civic pride, the *comune* declined to ask for state help in getting this project done; they mean to keep control of it by paying the whole bill themselves.

For now, it's definitely worth the price of admission just to see the big frescoes in the **Sala dei Pellegrini**, the hospital's main reception hall. Another pioneering fresco cycle devoted to a secular subject, like those in the Palazzo Pubblico, this is a tribute to old Siena's advanced, humanistic outlook; all the scenes are devoted to the history of the hospital, including the vision of Sorore's mother, and everyday views of the hospital's activities. In the best of them, Domenico di Bartolo shows how Sienese art was still keeping up with the Florentines in 1441 with his *Reception, Education and Marriage of a Daughter of the Hospital*; care of abandoned children, the *getatelli* (literally, 'little ones thrown away'), was one of the hospital's important functions. Other frescoes, by different Sienese artists, portray in loving detail the care of the sick, the distribution of alms to the poor, and the paying of the wetnurses of the *getatelli*.

Already, there is plenty more to see, including a collection of precious golden reliquaries and other church paraphernalia, some of it from medieval Constantinople, in refurbished chambers cheerfully marked *isolamento dei contagiosi*. Some other original features of the hospital include the **Capella del Sacro Chiodo**, with damaged frescoes by Vecchietta, the elaborate **Capella SS. Annunziata**, and the thoroughly spooky **Capella di Santa Caterina**, which begins with a leering skull and ends with an altarpiece by Taddeo di Bartolo. Old views and relics of the hospital are displayed in many of the long hallways of the complex; in some of the oldest, you can see how the façade was originally covered with frescoes, a colourful counterpoint to the cathedral façade across the way.

Museo Archeologico

***Under the Oratorio of Santa Caterina della Notte. Open** winter daily 10.30–4.30, summer daily 10–6; second and fourth Sun of month 10.30–1; **adm** with above museum.*

The Museo Archeologico was reopened here in its new home in early 2001. It contains a small collection of mainly Etruscan artefacts from sites around Siena.

SOUTH OF THE CENTRE

Palazzo Piccolomini

*Via Banchi di Sotto 52. **Open** Mon and Fri 8–2, Tues–Thurs 8–5.30, Sat 8–1.45; **adm** free. Closed for restoration at the time of writing.*

Siena's most imposing *palazzo privato*, it was built in the Florentine style by Rossellino in the 1460s. The palace now houses the old Sienese state archive – not a place you might consider visiting but for the presence of the famous *Tavolette della Biccherna* (the account books of the *Biccherna*, or state treasury). Beginning in the 1200s, the Republic's custom was to commission the best local artists to decorate the covers of the *tavolette*; the most interesting show such prosaic subjects as medieval citizens coming in to pay their taxes, city employees counting their pay and earnest monks trying to make the figures square – all are Cistercians from San Galgano, the only people medieval Siena trusted to do the job. Among the other manuscripts and documents you'll find Boccaccio's will.

Nearby, the **Loggia del Papa** was designed by Federighi and decorated by Francesco di Giorgio Martini. It was given to Siena by Aeneas Silvius Piccolomini in 1462.

Santa Maria dei Servi

*Via dei Servi. **Open** summer daily 7–12 and 3–7, winter daily 3–6.*

Its massive campanile looming over Piazza Alessandro Manzoni, Santa Maria dei Servi is situated in the heart of the *contrada* of the *Valdimontone* (ram). Here, in the north transept, is one of the earliest and best Sienese nativities, the altarpiece in the second north chapel by Taddeo di Bartolo. Among the many other good paintings in this church is a *Madonna* by Coppo di Marcovaldo and the *Madonna del Popolo* by Lippo Memmi. An interesting comparison can be made between two versions of that favourite Sienese subject, the *Massacre of the Innocents*: one from the early trecento by Pietro Lorenzetti, and another from 1491 by Matteo di Giovanni.

Sant'Agostino

*Piazza Sant'Agostino. **Open** summer daily 7–12 and 3–7, winter daily 3–6.*

This gloomy bulk conceals a happy rococo interior of 1749 by Vanvitelli, a Dutchman born Van Wittel who was the chief architect of the kings of Naples. Most of the building dates back to the 13th century, however, and there are surviving bits of trecento frescoes and altarpieces all around. On the right, seek out Perugino's *Crucifixion*, a rare non-Sienese painting. After the war, the other works of art were gathered together in the nearby Piccolomini chapel: the fine painting *Epiphany* by Il Sodoma, with a background reminiscent of Leonardo da Vinci, a horrific *Massacre of the Innocents* by Matteo di Giovanni, one of his favourite subjects, and a lovely *Madonna and Saints*, frescoed in the lunette by Ambrogio Lorenzetti. In the

Cappella Bichi, frescoes were uncovered in 1978, believed to be by Francesco di Giorgio Martini, an artist who went on to become more famous for his military engineering.

NORTH OF THE CENTRE

Santa Maria di Provenzano

***Via Provenzano Salvani. Open** summer daily 7–12 and 3–7, winter daily 3–6.*

This 1594 proto-Baroque parish church of the *contrada* of the Giraffe is one of the last important churches erected in Siena, built by Flaminio del Turco, with the most imposing interior after the Cathedral itself; lofty pillars support a daring dome. This particular Virgin Mary, a terracotta image said to be left by St Catherine (*see* p.185), has had one of the most popular devotional cults in Siena since the 1590s; the Palio of 2 July is in her honour, and the banner is usually kept here along with a vast array of ex-votos.

San Francesco

***Piazza S. Francesco. Open** summer daily 7–12 and 3–7, winter daily 3–6.*

One of the city's largest churches, San Francesco was begun in 1326. It's a sad tale; after a big fire in the 17th century, this great Franciscan barn was used for centuries as a warehouse and barracks. Restorations were begun in the 1880s, and the 'medieval' brick façade was completed only in 1913. The striped interior is still one of the most impressive in Siena, a monolithic rectangle with vivid stained glass (especially so in the late afternoon) and good transept chapels in the Florentine manner. A few bits of art have survived, including damaged frescoes by both Lorenzettis in the north transept, a *Crucifixion* by Pietro, and two fine works by Ambrogio – the strangely coloured *Martyrdom of the Franciscans at Ceuta* and *St Louis d'Anjou at the Feet of Boniface VIII*.

Oratorio di San Bernardino

***Open** mid-Mar–end Oct. Upper chapel not usually open, but ring for the doorkeeper.*

Next to San Francesco is the equally simple oratorio di San Bernardino, begun in the late 1400s to hold the heart of Siena's famous Franciscan (1380–1444), considered the foremost and most persuasive Italian preacher of the 15th century. If Bernardino wasn't entirely successful in taming the worldly pride of Siena's nobles, his motto 'Make it clear, make it short, and keep it to the point' has earned him a difficult posthumous job as the patron saint of advertising.

The upper chapel of the oratory is one of the monuments of the Sienese Renaissance, containing fine frescoes by Beccafumi, Il Sodoma, and the almost forgotten High Renaissance master Girolamo del Pacchia, few of whose works survive.

Biblioteca Comunale degli Intronati

***Via Sapienza 5, w** www.biblioteca.comune.siena.it. **Open** Mon–Fri 9–7, Sat–Sun 9–2; closed Sun Sept–June; **adm** free.*

The Biblioteca has a precious collection of manuscripts – among them, some of St Catherine's 400 letters and a copy of the *Divine Comedy* with illustrations by Botticelli.

Santuario e Casa di Santa Caterina

***Costa Sant'Antonio. Open** daily 9–12.30 and 2.30–6; **adm** free.*

The sanctuary, behind a grand portico donated in the 1940s by the cities of Italy, occupies the whole of the Benincasa home and the dyer's workshop, each room converted into a chapel, many with ceiling

St Catherine

St Catherine was the last but one of the 25 children born into the family of a wool dyer. At an early age, the visions started. By her teens she had turned her room at home into a cell and, while she never became a nun, she lived like a hermit, a solitary ascetic in her own house, sleeping with a stone for a pillow. After she received the stigmata, like St Francis, her reputation as a holy woman spread across Tuscany. But Catherine was quite a different kettle of fish. Unlike the charming, other-worldly Francis, she was tremendously political and involved in the temporal affairs of her day. The records say she never smiled. Completely illiterate, she corresponded through a secretary with popes, emperors and towns that asked her to settle disputes, and her letters are powerful masterpieces of direct, simple, righteous prose, although it has been noted that her favourite words were 'fire' and 'blood'. So complete was the moral authority conferred by her saintliness and humility that she could say: 'What I want, I order.' She wasn't always obeyed: her letter to the *condottiere* Sir John Hawkwood (of the equestrian fresco in Florence cathedral) asking him to lead a Crusade, met with a polite 'No, thank you'.

In 1378, Florence was under a papal interdict, and the city asked Catherine to plead its case at the papal court in Avignon. She went, but with an agenda of her own – convincing Pope Gregory XI (whom in her 'holy insolence' she addressed as *Babbo mio* or 'Daddy') to move the papacy back to Rome where it belonged. As a woman, and a holy woman to boot, she was able to tell the pope to his face what a corrupt and worldly Church he was running, without ending up dangling from the palace wall.

Talking the pope (a French pope, mind you) into leaving the civilized life in Provence for turbulent, barbaric 14th-century Rome is only one of the miracles with which Catherine was credited. Political expediency probably helped more than divine intervention – much of Italy, including anathemized Florence, was in revolt against the absentee popes. She followed them back, and died in Rome in 1380, at the age of only 33, her heart broken when she heard that an anti-pope had been enthroned in Avignon, beginning the Great Schism. Canonization came in 1460 and in the 20th century she was declared co-patron of Italy (along with St Francis) and one of the Doctors of the Church. She and St Teresa of Avila are the only women to hold this honour, both of them for their inspired devotional writings and practical, incisive letters enouraging church reform.

frescoes by 15th- and 16th-century Sienese artists, although oddly none was inspired to paint his best. There are four oratories in the house, and relics such as St Catherine's rock-pillow. The old kitchen, now the upper oratory, has a beautiful 17th-century tile floor; another oratory now serves as the *Oca*'s *contrada* chapel (note the goose in the detail of the façade).

San Domenico

Piazza San Domenico. Open winter daily 9–1 and 3–6, summer daily 7–1 and 3–7.

The bold Gothic lines of the apse and transepts of San Domenico give a great insight into the straightforward, strangely modern character of much of Sienese religious architecture.

Inside, the church is as big and empty as San Francesco; among the relatively few works of art is the only portrait from the life of St Catherine, on the west wall, done by her friend, the artist Andrea Vanni. This church was the scene of many incidents in the saint's life – she was known to go into ecstasy in the Cappella della Volte, where many Sienese watched the Host go flying from the hand of the priest directly into her mouth. Her head is ensconced in a golden reliquary (the Romans, suspecting she would be canonized one day, cut her body into bits when she died – the Venetians made off with a foot). The real attraction, though, is the wonderfully hysterical set of frescoes by Il Sodoma in the **Cappella Santa Caterina**, representing the girl in various states of serious exaltation. The lateral fresco on the left depicts one of the more disturbing scenes from her letters: a Sienese, Niccolo di Tuldo, was condemned to death for some misdemeanour and in rage filled his prison cell with curses. Catherine arrived to calm him down and succeeded so well in convincing him to submit to his own sacrifice that the two of them went off to the site of execution as if going to a party; Catherine undid his collar for him, and let his head drop on her own lap after the chop. The saint wrote: 'When the cadaver was taken away, my soul rested in such delicious peace and I rejoiced so in the perfume of that blood that I did not wish them to take away that thing that lay upon my clothes.'

Fortezza Medicea

*Piazza della Libertà, **t** 0577 288497, **e** enoteca@enoteca-italiana.it, **w** www.enoteca-italiana.it. **Open** Tues–Sat noon–1am, Mon noon–8.*

Though the site is the same, this is not the hated fortress Charles V compelled the Sienese to build in 1552; as soon as the Sienese chased the imperial troops out, they razed it to the ground. Cosimo I forced its rebuilding after annexing Siena, but to make the bitter pill easier to swallow he employed a Sienese architect, Baldassare Lanci, and let him create what must be the most elegant and civilized, least threatening fortress in Italy. The Fortezza, a long, low rectangle of Siena brick profusely decorated with Medici balls, seems more like a setting for garden parties or summer opera than anything designed to intimidate a sullen populace. The Sienese weren't completely won over; right after Italian reunification they renamed the central space of the fortress **Piazza della Libertà**. The grounds are now a city park, and the vaults of the munition cellars have become the **Enoteca Nazionale**, the 'Permanent Exhibition of Italian Wines'. Almost every variety of wine Italy produces can be bought here – by the glass or by the bottle.

Pisa

HISTORY 188
GETTING THERE 190
TOURIST INFORMATION 190
WHERE TO STAY 190
EATING OUT 191
THE CAMPO DEI MIRACOLI 192
NORTH OF THE ARNO 196
SOUTH OF THE ARNO 198

10

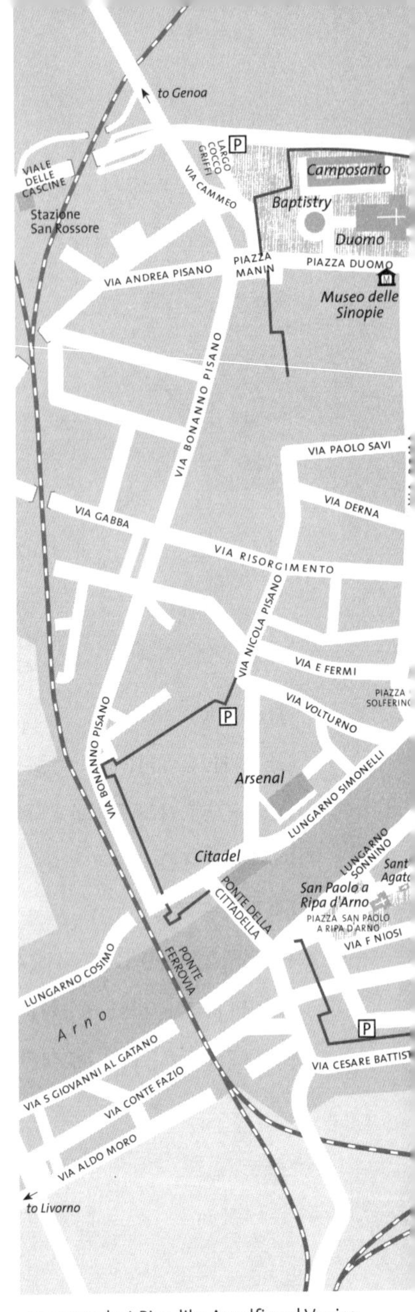

Pisa (pop. 104,000) is at once the best-known and the most mysterious of Tuscan cities. Its most celebrated attraction has become, along with the Colosseum, gondolas and spaghetti, a symbol for the entire Italian republic. Tour buses disgorge thousands every day into the Field of Miracles; visitors spend a couple of hours, buy a plastic tower, and leave again for places more tangible. At night even the Pisani make a mass exodus into the suburbs, as if they sense that the city is too big for them, not physically, but in terms of unfulfilled ambitions, of past greatness nipped in the bud.

Yet go back to about 1100, when according to the chroniclers, precocious Pisa was 'the city of marvels', the 'city of ten thousand towers', with a population of 300,000 – or so it seemed to the awed writers of that century, who, at least outside Venice, had never seen such an enormous, cosmopolitan and exotic city in Christian Europe since the fall of Rome. Pisan merchants made themselves at home all over the Mediterranean, bringing back new ideas and new styles in art in addition to their fat bags of profit. Pisan Romanesque, with its stripes and blind arcades, which had such a wide influence in Tuscany, was inspired by the great Moorish architecture of Andalucía; Nicola Pisano, first of a long line of great sculptors, is as important to the renaissance of sculpture as Giotto is to painting.

Like a Middle Eastern city, Pisa has put all its efforts into one fabulous spiritual monument, while the rest of the city wears a decidedly undemonstrative, almost anonymous, face, a little run down. It is a subtle place, a little sad perhaps, but strangely seductive if you give it a chance. After all, one can't create a Field of Miracles in a void.

History

In the Middle Ages, Pisa liked to claim that it began as a Greek city, founded by colonists from Elis. Most historians, however, won't give them credit for anything earlier than 100 BC or so, when a Roman veterans' colony was settled there. Records of what followed are scarce, but Pisa, like Amalfi and Venice, must have had an early start in building a navy and establishing trade connections. By the 11th century, the effort had blossomed into opulence; Pisa built itself a small empire, including Corsica, Sardinia, and for a while the Balearics. Around 1060, work was begun on the great cathedral complex, inaugurating the Pisan Romanesque. The city was a

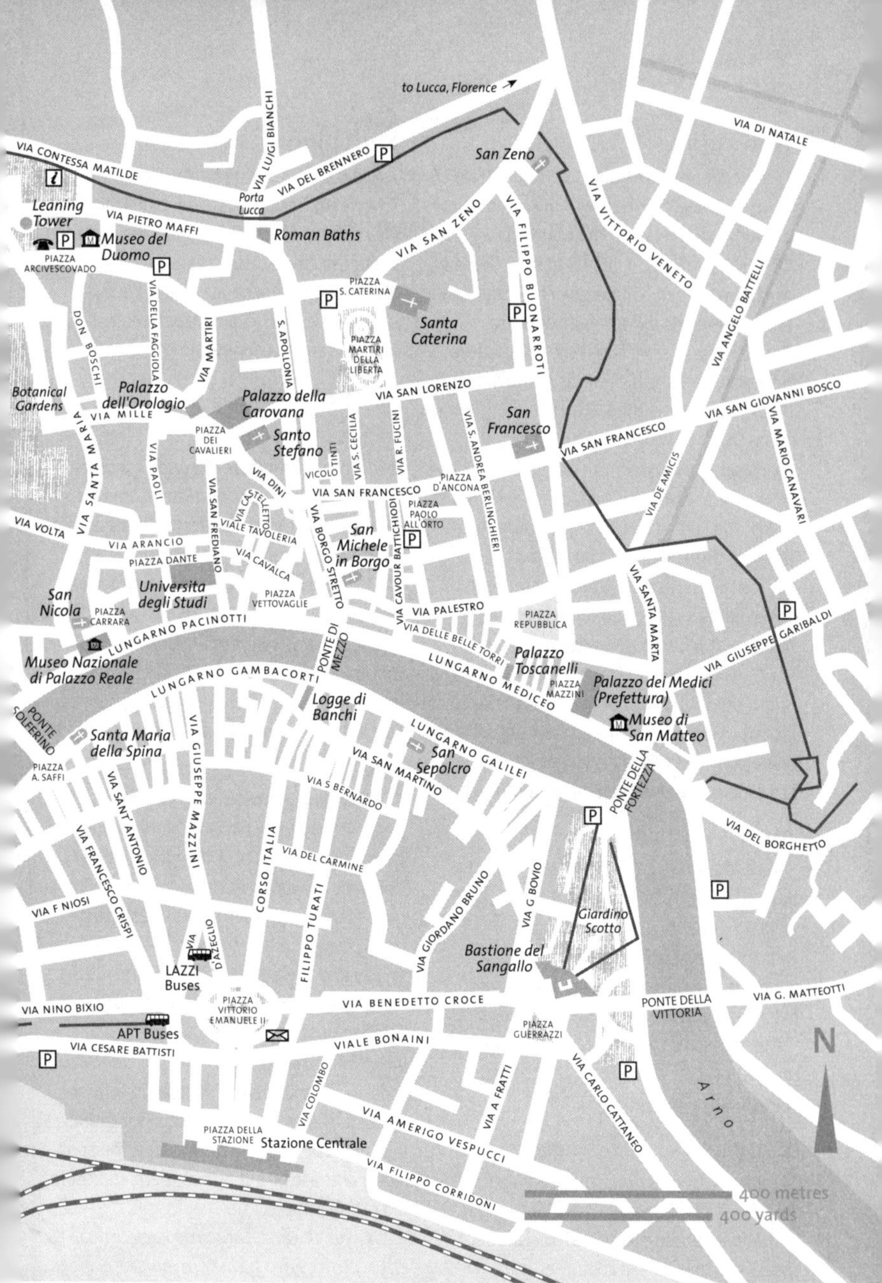

wonder to all who saw it: the great traveller Benjamin Tudela wrote that it had 10,000 towers. No wonder they made one or two lean, just to stand out.

The First Crusade (1090s), when Pisa's battling archbishop led the entire fleet in support of the Christian knights, turned out to be an economic windfall for the city. Unlike its greatest rival in the Western Mediterranean, Amalfi, Pisa from the start had adopted a course of combat with the states of the Muslim world, less from religious bigotry than a clear eye on the main chance; the same attitude led the city to capture and sack Amalfi itself in 1135.

When the Pisans weren't battling with the Muslims of Spain and Africa, they were learning from them. A steady exchange of

Getting There

There are regular **trains** to Pisa Centrale from Florence; the journey time is just over an hour. Pisa is also on the main Rome–Genova train line. To get there from Siena or Arezzo, you need to change in Florence. Many trains also stop at Pisa's Stazione San Rossore; if you're making Pisa a day trip you may want to get off there, as it's only a few blocks from the cathedral and Leaning Tower.

The LAZZI **bus** company runs a regular coach service between Lucca and Pisa, **t** 0583 584876. You can catch a coach from Florence to Pisa via Lucca (**t** LAZZI 055 351061). All intercity buses depart from in front of the station, near Piazza Vittorio Emanuele II.

Pisa lends itself well to **bicycles**; you can hire one at A Ruota Libera (also a pizzeria), Via Galli Tassi 6, near the Leaning Tower.

Tour operators who organize **day trips** to Pisa from Florence include: CAF, **t** 055 283200, **w** *www.caftours.com*; Amici del Turismo, **t** 055 218413, **w** *www.mercurio_italy.org*.

Tourist Information

Via C. Cammeo 2, **t** 050 560464, near the baptistry.

Piazza della Stazione, **t** 050 42291.

Pisa Airport, **t** 050 503700.

Internet for all: **e** *aptpisa@pisa.turismo.toscana.it*, **w** *www.pisa.turismo.toscana.it*.

There is also a free **hotel booking** service at the first office, **t** 050 830253, **f** 050 830243, **w** *www.traveleurope.it/pisa.htm*.

Festivals

Epiphany, or *La Befana*, on 6 Jan is a children's festival in Italy, and a public holiday. The *Befana* is an old lady and in Pisa she appears in the form of costumed parachutists who land in the piazzas bringing presents to the children. The **Festa di San Ranieri** on 16–17 June is a lights festival and historic regatta. **Gioco del Ponte** on 25 June consists of a traditional bridge tug-of-war game with a cart in the middle (on the Ponte di Mezzo). And the **San Sisto festival** on the first weekend of August is a traditional thanksgiving festival.

Shopping

Apart places selling light-up Leaning Towers in the Campo dei Miracoli, most of Pisa's shops are to be found in the main shopping street, pedestrian-only Corso Italia, leading down from the station. Piazza Vettovaglie is Pisa's arcaded market square, with a market every morning except Sunday.

Where to Stay

Moderate

******D'Azeglio**, *Piazza Vittorio Emanuele II 18/B*, ***t** 050 500310*, ***f** 050 28017*. Convenient for the station with comfortable, modern air-conditioned rooms and a restaurant. €134.

******Grand Hotel Duomo,** *Via Santa Maria 94*, ***t** 050 561894*, ***f** 050 560418*, ***e** hotelduomo@csinfo.it*, ***w** www.grandhotelduomo.it*. This may be the best Pisa has to offer, but don't expect too much from this rather dreary four-star hotel near the Campo dei Miracoli. €173.

Inexpensive

*****Giardino**, *Piazza Manin 1*, ***t** 050 562101*, ***f** 050 831 0392*, ***e** giardino@csinfo.it*, ***w** www.csinfo.it/giardino*. This little hotel just outside the walls off Piazza dei Miracoli has just been upgraded to a smart three-star establishment. Rooms and baths are modern and stylish and there is a pleasant terrace. €103.

*****Hotel Francesco**, *Via Santa Maria 129*, ***t** 050 554109*, ***f** 050 556145*, ***e** info@hotelfrancesco.com*, ***w** www.hotelfrancesco.com*. Small and friendly with an excellent restaurant next door, this hotel is located just south of the Field of Miracles. The spotless rooms are bright and modern and there is a pretty terrace. €118.

*****Royal Victoria**, *Lungarno Pacinotti 12*, ***t** 050 940111*, ***f** 050 940180*, ***e** mail@royalvictoria.it*, ***w** www.royalvictoria.it*. A hotel since 1839 the Royal Victoria overlooks the Arno and has bags of atmosphere. The spacious rooms (still very much in '30s style) are sparsely furnished with heavy antiques. Dickens and Ruskin stayed here. €102.

*****Di Stefano**, *Via S. Apollonia 35–37*, ***t** 050 553559*, ***f** 050 556038*, ***e** hds@csinfo.it*, ***w** www.hoteldistefano.pisa.it*. Behind Piazza dei Cavallieri, this friendly little hotel was upgraded 3 stars in 2002. Not all of the modern rooms have private bathrooms. €85.

***Villa di Corliano**, *Loc. Rigoli, 56010 Pisa,* ***t** 050 818193, **f** 050 818897, **e** villadicorliano@villadicorliano.com, **w** www.villadicorliano.com*. A villa since the 16th century but now rather faded. Simple accommodation in a glorious setting; Baroque frescoes, antique furniture and lovely grounds. €113.

Cheap

***Galileo**, *Via Santa Maria 12, **t/f** 050 40621.* Not all of the nine rooms in this simple hotel have private baths, but several of them have frescoes. €55.

***Gronchi**, *Piazza Arcivescovado 1, **t** 050 561823*. Tucked away in a quiet corner near the Campo dei Miracoli, the charming Gronchi is the nicest hotel in this category. None of the rooms have private baths. €32.

***Helvetia**, *Via Don Boschi 31, **t** 050 553084*. Clean and cheap and near the Campo dei Mracoli. Some rooms have private baths. €57.

Eating Out

Pisan restaurants tend to feature the wilder side of Tuscan cuisine: eels and squid, *baccalà*, tripe, wild mushrooms, 'twice-boiled soup' and dishes that waiters cannot satisfactorily explain.

Beny, *Piazza Gambacorti 22, **t** 050 25067. **Open** Mon–Sat 1–2.30 and 8–10.30. Booking essential.* A delightful little fish restaurant in a quiet piazza just off Corso Italia. The owner, Damiano, is knowledgeable and enthusiastic about food and wine. €45.

Al Ristoro dei Vecchi Macelli, *Via Volturno 49, **t** 050 20424. **Open** 12.30–2.30 and 8–10.30, closed Sun lunch and Wed*. A 15th-century slaughter house provides the setting for this sophisticated and popular restaurant. A must for pasta lovers particularly. €42.

Cagliostro, *Via del Castelletto 26/30, **t** 050 575413. **Open** 1–2.30 and 8–midnight, closed Tues*. The decor here is extraordinary. Try tagliolini with truffles, filet of ostrich with orange sauce, or one of the ever-present vegetable *sformati* (a kind of flan without pastry). People come from miles around to taste the steamed chocolate soufflé. €30.

Osteria dei Cavalieri, *Via San Frediano 16, **t** 050 580858. **Open** 12.30–2 and 7.45–10, closed Sat lunch and Sun*. A modern, airy *osteria* near Piazza dei Cavalieri. Food is basically Tuscan, but prepared with some degree of innovation; there is a good wine list. €25.

Il Nuraghe, *Via Mazzini 58, **t** 050 44368. **Open** Tues–Sun 12.30–2.30 and 8–10.30*. A traditional trattoria where the chef is Sardinian, so Tuscan and Sard specialities rub shoulders. *Maialino sardo* – roast suckling piglet – is one such dish. €25.

La Mescita, *Via D. Cavalca 2, **t** 050 544294. **Open** Tues–Sun for dinner, and Fri–Sun for lunch 12.30–2.30 and 8–11*. At the heart of the busy Vettovaglie market area, the Mescita is an attractive trattoria with a huge wine list. Dishes include *gnocchi* with courgette flowers and goats' cheese, and boned rabbit stuffed with green olives and pine nuts. €22.

Trattoria S. Omobono, *Piazza S. Omobono 6, **t** 050 540847. **Open** Mon–Sat 12.30–2 and 7.30–10*. A simple, rustic trattoria in a little square just off the main market place. Risotto with porcini, spaghetti *alla marinara*, *stoccafisso* (stockfish) with potatoes, and a wonderful fish *fritto misto*. €18.

San Lorenzo, *Piazza Chiara Gambacorti 17a, **t** 050 26360. **Open** Mon 12.30–2, Tues–Fri 12.30–2 and 8–10.30, Sat & Sun evenings only*. In a small piazza just off Via del Corso, this cheerful trattoria serves pizzas, pastas, meat and fish dishes. €15.

Vineria di Piazza, *Piazza delle Vettovaglie 13 (no phone). **Open** Mon–Sat 12.15–2.45 and 7.30–10*. The food here is simple, cheap and very tasty; bean soup with 'pioppini' mushrooms, fish soup, risotto with radicchio and gorgonzola. Tables right in the market. €10.

Cafés and Gelaterie

Bar Moderno Gelateria, *Via del Mille 10*. For stylish post-modern ice cream in summer.

Bottega del Gelato, *Piazza Garibaldi 11*. A wide choice, and heavenly frozen yoghurts.

Pasticceria Federico Salza, *Borgo Stretto 46*. The best cakes in Pisa and a lovely big terrace.

ideas brought much of medieval Arab science, philosophy and architecture into Europe through Pisa's port. Pisa's architecture, the highest development of the Romanesque in Italy, saw its influence spread from Sardinia to Apulia in southern Italy; when Gothic arrived in Italy Pisa was one of the few cities to take it seriously, and the city's accomplishments in that style rank with Siena's. In science, Pisa contributed a great though shadowy figure, that most excellent mathematician Leonardo Fibonacci, who either rediscovered the principle of the Golden Section or learned it from the Arabs, and also introduced Arabic numerals to Europe. Pisa's scholarly traditions over the centuries would be crowned in the 1600s by its most famous son, Galileo Galilei.

Pisa was always a Ghibelline city, the greatest ally of the emperors in Tuscany if only for expediency's sake. When a real threat came, however, it was not from Florence or any of the other Tuscan cities, but from the rising mercantile port of Genoa. After years of constant warfare, the Genoese devastated the Pisan navy at the Battle of Meloria (an islet off Livorno) in 1284. It signalled the end of Pisan supremacy, but all chance of recovery was quashed by an even more implacable enemy: the Arno. Pisa's port was gradually silting up, and when the cost of dredging became greater than the traffic could bear, the city's fate was sealed.

The Visconti of Milan seized the economically enfeebled city in 1396, and nine years later Florence snatched it from them. Excepting the period 1494–1505, when the city rebelled and kept the Florentines out despite an almost constant siege, Pisa's history was ended. The Medici dukes did the city one big favour, supporting the university and even removing Florence's own university to Pisa. In the last 500 years of Pisa's long, pleasant twilight, this institution has helped the city stay alive and vital, and in touch with the modern world; one of its students was the nuclear physicist Enrico Fermi.

THE CAMPO DEI MIRACOLI

For the museums and monuments on the Field of Miracles, you can save by getting the joint ticket for €10 (but it doesn't include the Leaning Tower).

Almost from the time of its conception, the Field of Miracles was the nickname given to medieval Italy's most ambitious building programme. As with Florence's cathedral, too many changes were made over two centuries of work to tell exactly what the original intentions were. But of all the unique things about this complex, the location strikes one first – a broad expanse of green lawn at the northern edge of town, just inside the walls. The cathedral was begun in 1063, the famous Leaning Tower and the baptistry in the middle 1100s, at the height of Pisa's fortunes, and the Campo Santo in 1278.

The Leaning Tower

***Open** summer daily 8–7.40, winter daily 9–4.40; **adm** €15. A maximum of 30 people are allowed up at once, accompanied by a guide. You cannot book ahead at present; there are 10–12 tours per day. Each visit lasts 30mins and there are 300 steps to climb to the top. Children under 8 not permitted, 8–12-yr-olds must be hand-held by an adult, 12–18-yr-olds must be accompanied by an adult.*

The stories claiming the tilt of the Leaning Tower was accidental were most likely pure fabrications, desperate tales woven to account for what, before mass tourism, must have seemed a great civic embarrassment. The argument isn't very convincing. It seems hard to believe that the tower would start to lean when only 33ft tall; half the weight would still be in the foundations. The argument then insists that the Pisans doggedly kept building it after the lean commenced. The architects who measured the stones in the last century to get to the bottom of the mystery concluded that the tower's odd state was absolutely intentional from the day it was begun in 1173.

The leaning campanile is hardly the only strange thing in the Field of Miracles. The more time you spend here, the more you will notice: little monster-griffins, dragons and such, peeking out of every corner of the oldest sculptural work, skilfully hidden where you have to look twice to see them, or the big bronze griffin sitting on a column atop the cathedral apse (a copy) and a rhinoceros by the door, Muslim arabesques in the Campo Santo, perfectly classical Corinthian capitals in the cathedral nave and pagan images on the pulpit. The elliptical cathedral dome, in its time the only one in Europe, shows that the Pisans had not only the audacity but the mathematical skills to back it up. You may have noticed that the baptistry too is leaning – about 4ft, in the opposite direction. And the cathedral façade leans outwards about a foot, disconcerting from the right angle. This could hardly be accidental. So much in the Field of Miracles gives evidence of a sophisticated, strangely modern taste for the outlandish. Perhaps the medieval master masons simply thought that perpendicular buildings were becoming a little trite.

Whatever, the campanile is beautiful and something unique in the world – also an expensive bit of whimsy, with its 190 marble and granite columns. It has also proved expensive to the local and national governments as they tried to decide how best to shore up the tower. The first phase was completed a few years back, when counterweights (800 tonnes of lead ingots) were stacked at the base of the tower's leaning side, stopping the tilt. The next stage was rather trickier: replacing the lead ingots with an underground support, laying a ring of cement around the foundations, and anchoring it to 10 steel cables attached to the bedrock 164ft underground. In 1998 the tower was given a rather unsightly girdle of plastic-coated steel braces, attached by a pair of 72ft steel cables to a counterweight system hidden among the buildings on the north end of the Campo dei Miracoli. The last project involved removing soil from under the north, east and west sides of the tower from a depth of about six metres below ground level, thereby decreasing the difference in depth between the north and south side. This seems to have worked; the tower is not only stable but has actually righted itself about 40cm. It was finally reopened to the public in December 2001.

The Duomo

***Open** summer Mon–Sat 10–7.40, Sun 1–7.40, winter Mon–Sat 10–12.45 and 3–4.45, Sun 3–4.45; **adm** €2.*

One of the first and finest works of the Pisan Romanesque, the cathedral façade, with four levels of colonnades, turned out to be a little more ornate than Buscheto, the architect, had planned back in 1063. These columns, with similar colonnades around the apse and the Gothic frills later added around the unique elliptical dome, are the only showy features on the calm, restrained exterior. On the south transept, the late 12th-century **Porte San Ranieri** has a fine pair of bronze doors by Bonanno, one of the architects of the Leaning Tower. The Biblical scenes are enacted among real palms and acacia trees; the well-travelled Pisans would have known what such things looked like.

Of the interior, little of the original art survived a fire in 1595. The roof went, as well as the Cosmati pavement, of which only a few patches still remain. A coffered Baroque ceiling and lots of bad painting were contributed during the reconstruction, but some fine work survives. The triumphal arch still has its fresco of the Madonna and Child by the Maestro di San Torpè (St Tropez) and the great mosaic of Christ Pantocrator in the apse by Cimabue, and there are portraits of the saints by Andrea del Sarto framed on the entrance pier (the charming *St Agnes*), in the choir and his *Madonna della Grazia* in the right nave. Giambologna's bronze angels stand at the entrance to the choir, and in the right transept note the sarcophagus carved by Tino di Camaino for Emperor Henry VII, who enjoyed his election for less than a year before he died near Siena in 1313.

The **pulpit** (*c.* 1300), by Giovanni Pisano, is the acknowledged masterpiece. The men of 1595 used the fire as an opportunity to get rid of this nasty old medieval relic, and the greatest achievement of Pisan sculpture sat disassembled in crates, quite forgotten until the late 20th century. Works of genuine inspiration often prove profoundly disturbing to ages of certainty and good taste. Pisano's pulpit is startling, mixing classical and Christian elements with a fluency never seen before his time. St Michael, as a telamon, shares the honour of supporting the pulpit with Hercules and the Fates, while prophets, saints and sibyls look on from their appointed places. The relief panels, jammed with expressive faces, diffuse an electric immediacy equal to the best work of the Renaissance. Notice particularly the *Nativity*, the *Massacre of the Innocents*, the *Flight into Egypt*, and the *Last Judgement*.

Next to the pulpit is a 16th-century bronze lamp known as the **Lamp of Galileo**, which Galileo observed when it was newly hung on its long rope. It swung for a long time, and Galileo noticed that although the swings shortened, they didn't seem to go any slower or faster; it formed the basis for his calculations on oscillations and his discovery of the principle of the pendulum.

The Baptistry

***Open** summer daily 8–7.40, winter daily 9–4.40; **adm** €5.*

The Pisan Baptistry is the biggest of its kind in Italy; those of many other cities would fit neatly inside. The original architect, Master Diotisalvi ('God save you'), saw the lower half of the building done in the typical stripes-and-arcades Pisan style. A second colonnade was intended to go over the first, but as the Genoese gradually muscled Pisa out of trade routes, funds ran short. In the 1260s, Nicola and Giovanni Pisano, members of that remarkable family of artists who did so much to re-establish sculpture in Italy, redesigned and completed the upper half in a harmonious Gothic crown of gables and pinnacles. The Pisanos also added the dome over Diotisalvi's original prismatic dome, still visible from the inside. Both domes were impressive achievements, among the largest attempted in the Middle Ages.

Inside, the austerity of the simple, striped walls and heavy columns of grey Elban granite is broken by two superb works of art. The great **baptismal font** is the work of Guido Bigarelli, the 13th-century Como sculptor who decorated it with 16 exquisite marble panels. These are finely carved in floral and geometrical patterns of inlaid stones, a northern, almost monochrome variant on the Cosmati work of medieval Rome and Campania. Nicola Pisano's **pulpit** (1260) was one of the first of that family's masterpieces, and established the form for their later pulpits, the columns resting on fierce lions, the relief panels crowded with intricately carved figures in impassioned New Testament episodes, a style that seems to owe much to the reliefs on old Roman triumphal arches and columns. The baptistry is famous for its uncanny acoustics; try singing a few notes from as near to centre as they will allow you.

The Campo Santo

***Open** summer daily 8–7.40, winter daily 9–4.40; **adm** €5.*

If one more marvel in the Campo dei Miracoli is not excessive, there is the Campo Santo, a remarkable cloister and graveyard as unique in its way as the Leaning Tower. Basically, the cemetery is a rectangle of gleaming white marble, unadorned save for the blind arcading around the façade and the beautiful Gothic tabernacle of the enthroned Virgin Mary over the entrance. With its uncluttered, simple lines, the Campo Santo seems more like a work of our own century than the 1300s.

The cemetery began, according to legend, when Archbishop Lanfranchi, who led the Pisan fleet into the first Crusade, came back with boatloads of soil from the Holy Land for extra-blessed burials. Over the centuries, thousands of dead Pisans and an exceptional hoard of frescoes and sculpture accumulated here. Much of it went up in flames on a terrible night in July 1944, when an Allied incendiary bomb hit the roof and set it on fire. Many priceless works of art were destroyed and others, including most of the frescoes, damaged beyond hope of ever being perfectly restored. The biggest loss was the set of frescoes by Benozzo Gozzoli – the *Tower of Babylon, Solomon and Sheba, Life of Moses* and the *Grape Harvest* and others; in their original state they must have been as fresh and colourful as his famous frescoes in Florence's Medici Palace. Even better known, and better preserved, are two 14th-century frescoes, the *Triumph of Death* and the *Last Judgement* by an unknown artist (perhaps Andrea Orcagna of Florence), whose failure to sign his work has passed him down to posterity with an unfortunate Halloween name, the 'Master of the Triumph of Death'. In this memento of the century of plagues and trouble, Death (in Italian, feminine: *La Morte*) swoops down on frolicking nobles, while in the *Last Judgement* (which has very little heaven) the damned are variously cooked, wrapped up in snakes, poked, disembowelled, banged up and chewed on; still, they are some of the best paintings of the trecento, and somehow seem less gruesome and paranoid than similar works of centuries to come (though good enough to have inspired that pop classic, Lizst's *Totentanz*).

For another curiosity, there's the *Theological Cosmography* of Piero di Puccio, a vertiginous diagram of 22 spheres of the planets and stars, angels, archangels, thrones and dominations, cherubim and seraphim, etc.; in the centre, the small circle trisected by a 'T' was a common medieval map pattern for the known earth. The three sides represent Asia, Europe and Africa, and the three lines the Mediterranean, the Black Sea and the Nile. Among the sculpture in the Campo Santo, there are sarcophagi and Roman bath tubs, and in the gallery of prewar photographs of the lost frescoes, a famous Hellenistic marble vase with bas-reliefs.

Museo delle Sinopie

***Piazza del Duomo. Open** summer daily 8–7.40, winter daily 9–4.40; **adm** €5.*

Housed in the 13th-century Ospedale Nuovo di Misericordia, this museum contains the pre-painted sketches on plaster of the frescoes lost in the Campo Santo fire. The name *sinopia* comes from Sinope, a Turkish port on the Black Sea, from where the reddish pigment originally derived; once the *sinopia* was drawn, the artist would cover the area he meant to paint in one day with wet plaster (*grasello*). When a fresco is detached from the wall, it is often possible to save the sinopia. During the restoration of the Campo Santo, these works of art in their own right were brought here – the *Triumph of Death* and the *Last Judgement* and others that were lost in the bombing.

Museo dell'Opera del Duomo

***Piazza Arcivescovado. Open** summer daily 8–7.40, winter daily 9–4.40; **adm** €5.*

The collection is arranged in the old Chapterhouse. The first rooms contain the oldest works – beautiful fragments from the cathedral façade and altar and two Islamic works, the very strange, original **Griffin** from the top of the cathedral, believed to have come from Egypt in the 11th century, and a 12th-century bronze basin with an intricate decoration. Statues by the Pisanos from the baptistry were brought in from the elements too late; worn and bleached, they resemble a convention of mummies. Other sculptures in the next room survived better: Giovanni Pisano's grotesque faces, his gaunt but noble *St John the Baptist* and the lovely *Madonna del Colloquio*, so named because she speaks to her child with her eyes; in the next room are fine works by Tino di Camaino, including the tomb of San Ranieri and his sculptures from the tomb of Emperor Henry VII, sitting among his court like some exotic oriental potentate. In **Room 9** are works by Nino Pisano and in **Rooms 10–11**, containing the Cathedral Treasure, Giovanni Pisano's lovely ivory *Madonna and Child* steals the show, curving to the shape of the elephant's tusk; there's an ivory coffer and the cross that led the Pisans on the First Crusade. Upstairs are some extremely big angels used as candlesticks, intarsia and two rare illuminated 12th- and 13th-century scrolls (called exultet rolls); the deacon would unroll them from the pulpit as he read so the congregation could follow the story with the pictures. The remaining rooms have some Etruscan and Roman odds and ends (including a good bust of Caesar) and prints and engravings of the original Campo Santo frescoes made in the 19th century. The courtyard has a unique view of the Leaning Tower, which seems to be bending over to spy inside.

NORTH OF THE ARNO

Via Santa Maria

For centuries the main artery between the Campo dei Miracoli and the Arno has been the gracefully curving Via Santa Maria, one of Pisa's finest streets, lined with elegant palaces and old tower houses. Be sure to look at the curiosities of the façades, and poke your head in the doors for a look at the secret gardens and courtyards.

Piazza dei Cavalieri

Encircled by beautiful palaces, this piazza in the old days was Piazza delle Sette, where the medieval Pisans clobbered each other in the *Gioco del Mazzascudo*, 'Club and Shield Game', the precursor of today's somewhat more civilized Gioco del Ponte (*see* p.190). Duke Cosimo I started what was probably the last crusading order of knights, the Cavalieri di Santo Stefano, in 1562. The crusading urge had ended long before, but the duke found the order a useful tool for placating the anachronistic fantasies of the Tuscan nobility – most of them newly titled bankers – and for licensing out freebooting expeditions against the Turks. Cosimo had Vasari build the **Palazzo della Carovana** for the order, conveniently demolishing the old Palazzo del Popolo, the symbol of Pisa's lost independence. Vasari gave the palace an outlandishly ornate *sgrafitto* façade; the building now holds the prestigious Scuola Normale Superiore, founded by Napoleon in 1810. In front of it stands a statue of Cosimo I by Francavilla.

Next to the palace is the order's church, **Santo Stefano**, built by Vasari in 1565, though the façade was designed by a young Medici dilettante (*open Mon–Fri 10.30–4.30, Sat until 6pm, Sun 1–6; adm €1.50*). The history of the order is told on the lavish coffered ceiling, and its pirate trophies are on display – eight gilded leather lanterns and long, fantastical pennants snatched by the order's pirates from defeated Turkish and North African galleys; one is claimed to have been captured from the flagship of Ali Pasha in the Battle of Lepanto. On the left hangs a *Nativity* by Bronzino and a *Holy Family* by Gentileschi.

Also on the Piazza, the Palazzo dell'Orologio was built around the '**Hunger Tower**' (right of the big clock – see plaque), famous in Dante's story of Count Ugolino della Gherardesca, the Pisan *podestà* who was walled in here with his sons and grandsons after the fickle city began to suspect him of intrigues with the Genoese after Pisa's defeat at Meloria in 1284. If the intent was to kill off the family and its progeny, the cruel punishment failed: the Gherardeschi ruled as *signori* from 1316 to 1341, and in 1330 founded Pisa's university.

Santa Caterina

Piazza Santa Caterina. Open Mon–Sat 8.30–12.30 and 4–6, Sun mornings only.

Pisa's Dominican headquarters, Santa Caterina has a beautiful, typically Pisan marble façade of 1330 in two tiers, with a lovely spoked rose window. The equally attractive interior, with one enormous assymetrical nave, is decorated with liquorice candystripes; there's a sculptural group of the *Annunciation* on its high altar and the *Tomb of Archbishop Saltarelli* on the left, all the work of Nino Pisano. On the left there's a *Madonna and Saints* by Fra Bartolommeo, a pietà by Santi ti Tito and a large painting from the 1340s attributed to Francesco Traini and Francesco Memmi, of the *Apotheosis of Saint Thomas Aquinas*, with Plato and Aristotle in attendance and the defeated infidel philospher Averroes below.

San Francesco

***Via San Francesco. Open** daily 7.30–noon and 3.30–6.15.*

Built in three stages between the 13th and 17th centuries, San Francesco is essentially Gothic behind a plain marble façade that Ferdinand DUX de' Medici financed in order to write his name in big letters on top. The vast interior (as always a testimony to the extraordinary religious revival inspired by the preaching orders) was 'restored to its primitive splendour in year XI' according to the Fascist-era plaque at the back. It contains some fine art: a marble 15th-century high altarpiece by Tomaso Pisano and frescoes from 1342 in the vault by Taddeo Gaddi. The altar is incongruously illuminated with an almost fluorescent light, clashing with the otherwise dim and restful interior. Flanking the altar, the second chapel on the right is shared by a beautiful 14th-century Florentine polyptych and the tomb of the unfortunate Count Ugolino, his sons and grandsons. A case of reliquaries in the transept contains a cassock of St Francis. In the last chapel on the left, look up to see the *sinopie*, also by Taddeo Gaddi. The sacristy was frescoed with *Scenes from the Life of the Virgin* by Taddeo di Bartolo in 1397; in the Chapterhouse are more frescoes, this time by Niccolò di Pietro Gerini. After seeing the church, take a minute to look into the cloisters.

Museo Nazionale di San Matteo

***Lungarno Mediceo, t** 050 541865. **Open** Tues–Sat 9–7, Sun 9–2; **adm** €4.15.*

The old convent attached to the church of San Matteo served as prison for many years; now it immures much of the best of Pisan art from the Middle Ages and Renaissance.

The ground floor contains a fine collection of medieval ceramic plates from the Middle East, brought home by old Pisan sea dogs; a large cache of jugs were found right under the Hunger Tower. Upstairs, is a well-arranged collection of 12th- and 13th-century works gathered from the city's churches, including Byzantine-style *Crucifixions* by Giunta di Capitinio (or Pisano), possibly of Greek origin, and believed to be the first artist ever to sign his work (early 1200s), and another signed by Berlighiero (d. 1236): they mark the beginning of more 'humanized' representations of Christ in response to the preaching of St Francis. Other works are by the conservative Maestro di San Martino, one of the leading Pisan painters of the day, and by Ranieri di Ugolino, who was inspired by the then avant-garde Cimabue in the Duomo.

From the 14th century – not a good time for Pisa, after its defeat at Meloria – there's a superb golden polyptych by Simone Martini (1319), and paintings from the brush of the excellent Francesco di Traini, Taddeo di Bartolo, Agnolo Gaddi, Antonio Veneziano and Turino Vanni. Pisa found its best expression in sculpture; the marble polychrome *Madonna del Latte* by Andrea and Nino Pisano (father and son) is often pointed out as a key work in the translation of Giotto's revolution into three dimensions. Note the fine bas-relief of the *Nativity* by Tino di Camaino (d. 1337), the star pupil of Giovanni Pisano who worked directly with Giotto.

After all the trecento works, the Early Renaissance comes as a startling revelation: here is Neri di Bicci's wonderfully festive *Coronation of the Virgin*, bright with ribbons, a *Madonna* from the decorative Gentile da

Fabriano, a recently restored *Madonna and Saints* by Ghirlandaio, a sorrowful *St Paul* by Masaccio, whose features and draperies are softly moulded, an anonymous *Madonna with Angel Musicians*, and a beautifully coloured *Crucifixion* by Gozzoli that looks more like a party than an execution. The last great work is Donatello's gilded bronze reliquary bust *San Lussorio*.

Museo Nazionale di Palazzo Reale

Entrance Lunargno Pacinotti 46. ***Open*** *Mon–Fri 9–2.30, Sat 9–1.30;* ***adm*** *€3.*

This royal palace was begun in 1559 by Cosimo I and has recently found a new life as a museum. It now functions as an annexe to the Museo Nazionale di San Matteo, housing a fine collection of old armour dusted off every June for the annual Gioco del Ponte as well as some 900 other pieces from the 15th to the 17th centuries. Another section soon to be installed will concentrate on paintings, sculptures and collectables (mostly from the 15th–18th centuries) from the Medici and Lorraine archducal hordes.

Domus Galilaeana

Via Santa Maria 26, ***w*** *www.domus-galilaeana.it.* ***Open*** *by appointment Mon–Fri 9.30–12.30,* ***t*** *050 23726.*

Although experts can't agree where Galileo's actually lived, this is an institute dedicated to his life and work, founded in 1939. The library has some 40,000 volumes on the history of science, plus some Galileo first editions and one of his letters.

San Nicola

Via Santa Maria 2. ***Open*** *Mon–Sat 7.45–noon and 5–7, Sun 8.30–noon and 5–7.*

Twelfth-century San Nicola conserves part of its original façade; the rest looks as if it had been scoured off. Take a good look at the bell tower, cylindrical at the bottom, octagonal in the middle, and hexagonal on top. Designed by Nicola Pisano, it has exactly the same kind of tilt as the Leaning Tower itself, built to lean forward before curving back again towards perpendicular. Ask the sacristan to show you the famous spiral stair inside, which Vasari claimed inspired Bramante's Belvedere stair in the Vatican. The church itself, patched together here and there over the centuries, shelters a fine painting of the Madonna by Traini, a wooden sculpture of the same by Nino Pisano in the fourth chapel on the left, a quattrocento painting of St Nicholas of Tolentino shielding Pisa from the plague (fourth chapel on the right), and just to the left of the presbytery, a *Crucifixion* attributed to Giovanni Pisano.

Roman Ships

Arsenale Mediceo, Lungarno Simonelli, ***t*** *050 21441,* ***w*** *www.navipisa.it.* ***Open*** *summer Tues–Fri 10–7, Sat–Sun 11–1 and 2–10;* ***adm*** *€7. Guided visits only; booking required.*

In 1998, builders were working on a new administrative building for the state railways when they unearthed the first evidence of the remains of Pisa's Roman/Etruscan harbour. Excavations soon came up with the remains of a number of 2,000-year-old ships. To date, 16 have been discovered; some of them are in excellent condition, their wooden structure intact. The remains of a wharf, a pier and lots of bits and pieces have also been found.

SOUTH OF THE ARNO

Santa Maria della Spina

Lungarno Gambacorti. ***Open*** *summer Mon–Fri 11–1.30 and 2.30–6, Sat and Sun until 8pm but shorter hours otherwise.*

A reliquary for one of the thorns from Christ's crown of thorns brought back from the Crusades, Santa Maria della Spina is one of the few outstanding achievements of

The Heresy of Science

Born in 1564, the young Galileo was nurtured in the lofty intellectual environment of Late Renaissance Tuscany. His father introduced him early to the Medici academies, where he was drawn irresistibly to mathematics from an early age.

Before Galileo was appointed professor of mathematics at Pisa (1589) and Padua (1592), all scientific learning came from books arguing for or against Aristotle's writings. Galileo taught that you could learn much more by studying nature, and in the process became the founding father of experimental physics – he showed that air had weight by weighing a pig's bladder full of air, then puncturing it to show the difference; he defied the Aristotelian concept of opposites in nature by inventing the principle of the thermometer, demonstrating that hot and cold were merely relative aspects of the same phenonemon, which he called temperature; he debunked Aristotle's precept that heavy bodies had a tendency to fall and light ones to rise with his famous Leaning Tower experiment, when he dropped variously sized balls and bullets and weights simultaneously and they all hit the ground at once.

In 1609, news reached Galileo of a Dutch spectacle-maker who had made a pipe with lenses that enabled one to see ships far out to sea. Galileo quickly put together one of his own with a convex lens in front, and a concave lens behind, that he soon improved to make the first telescope – with a magnification power of 30. Even so, when Galileo pointed his instrument at the heavens, it was an incredible revelation: he was the first man ever to see the surface of the moon, the moons of Jupiter, what appeared to be ears on Saturn (his telescope was too weak to discern the rings), the phases of Venus, the the Milky Way, and sunspots, although the last discovery permanently affected his eyesight. In 1610 he published all his discoveries in a little book called *Sidereus Nuncius*, 'The Starry Messenger'. An instant celebrity, Cosimo de' Medici made him Grand Ducal mathematician and philosopher.

Galileo (along with many Jesuits) had long believed in Copernicus's *De Revolutionibus Orbium Coelestium* (1543) and its theory that the earth revolved around the sun. However, by 1615, so many theologians thought that the theory was inconsistent with biblical teachings that, in spite all of Galileo's energetic efforts in Rome, *De Revolutionibus* was placed on the Index of prohibited books until it could be amended with a statement that it was an unproved hypothesis. The Holy Office then forbade Galileo from teaching it.

In 1624, the 60-year-old scientist went to Rome and asked Pope Urban VIII to discuss Copernicanism in a new book, emphasizing to the Pope that it was to the glory of the Catholic Church to promote learning. He spent the next five years writing (in Italian, instead of the usual Latin) the first-ever book of popular science, a witty and lively masterpiece called the *Dialogue on the Two Chief Systems of the World*, in which three characters (a Copernican, an Aristotelian and an amateur) discuss the two systems, with the Copernican clearly winning the argument. Although at first greeted with enthusiasm, the *Dialogue* was soon withdrawn by the Pope, who believed he had been duped. A special commission he set up agreed with him: that Galileo was advocating an unproved hypothesis as the truth and disobeying the order from the Holy Office of 17 years ago not to teach Copernicanism. In the famous Inquisition trial he was accused of relapsing – a much worse crime than heresy – and made to recant his belief that the earth moved, although, legend has it, with the famous aside:'*eppur si muove!*', 'But it does move!'

The Inquisition was lenient with the old man, first placing him under house arrest in Siena, and then in his villa at Arcetri, just outside Florence. There he wrote his even more influential *The Two New Sciences* (1638), on the mathematical study of motion and the strength of materials, a work that became the basis for the study of physics as a science. He died in 1642, if not a martyr, at least a hero to science.

The Original Romantic Revolutionary

Giuseppe Mazzini was born in Genoa in 1805. His career as an active revolutionary began in 1827 when he joined the Carbonari, a strict, hierarchical secret society which plotted armed revolution in Italy. He was, however, not one to obey orders blindly , and in 1830 he was betrayed to the police by his own local leader and sent to prison. During that time, Mazzini developed a political philosophy that never wavered: a belief in the unity and perfect equality of humanity (including women and workers) and in humanity's ability to progress thanks to education. He believed in God, but a God incarnate in the will of the people: his religion was democracy.

To make all this possible, Mazzini thought that the first goal of revolution should be an independent, unified Italy. From exile in Switzerland, he founded his own semi-secret society called *La Giovine Italia*, 'Young Italy', with the goal of instilling a sense of national identity in the Italian people and helping them to lead the revolution that would make Italy a democratic republic. One of the first recruits was a sailor named Garibaldi.

Mazzini's sense of mission meant he spent most of his life writing and plotting in exile, under the threat of the death penalty back home in Genoa. His first insurrection in 1834 was a fiasco after his commander, entrusted with Young Italy's funds, lost all the money gambling in Paris. It led, however, to over a decade of exile for Mazzini in London, where he kept the flame of revolt alive by making contacts and writing.

Mazzini next returned to Italy in 1849 when the Roman Republic was declared. Thanks to his reputation and integrity, he was acclaimed its natural leader, and gave the city the most tolerant, enlightened government it ever had in its entire history – while working for no pay and dining every day in a workers' canteen. The experiment, however, lasted only three months before the French troops summoned by Pius IX arrived and squashed the heroic defence of the Republic by the people of Rome, led by the dashing Garibaldi.

Hopelessly romantic republican insurrections supported by Mazzini in 1853 and 1857 went down to tragic defeat in Milan and Naples. Ironically, it was an equally hopeless insurrection in 1860, in which Mazzini had no direct part, that finally succeeded when Garibaldi and his Thousand volunteers took Sicily. But Mazzini declared that what actually resulted from all of Garibaldi's noble efforts was not the real Italy either, not the tolerant democracy of his dreams, and he refused to live in it.

Although Mazzini helped in the organization of the First International in London, his beliefs in private property and his insistence on a social as well as political revolution saw his influence quickly lose out to Marx. In 1872, he returned clandestinely to Italy under the alias of John Brown, the fiery American abolitionist, only to die on this spot in Pisa.

Italian Gothic. Originally it wasn't Gothic at all, but when partially rebuilt in 1323, the new architect – perhaps one of the Pisanos – turned it into an extravaganza of pointed gables and blooming pinnacles. All the sculptural works are first class, especially the figures of Christ and the Apostles in the 13 niches facing the streets. Although its placement on the Lungarno Gambacorti is perfect, it was not originally here at all, but located at the mouth of the Arno, where it suffered so many floods that it was at the point of vanishing in 1871, when the city decided to dismantle and rebuild it on this new site. Inside the luminous zebra interior, the statues of the Madonna and Child, SS. Peter and John are by Andrea and Nino Pisano.

Domus Mazziniana

Via Mazzini 71. Open Mon, Wed, Fri 8.30–1.30, plus Tues and Thurs 3–5.30; Sat 8.30–noon.

Here you can pay your respects to the revolutionary activist Giuseppe Mazzini (*see* box).

Lucca

11

HISTORY 202
GETTING THERE 204
TOURIST INFORMATION 204
WHERE TO STAY 204
EATING OUT 205
AROUND THE TOWN 206

Of all Tuscany's great cities, Lucca (pop. 92,500) is the most cosy, sane and domestic, a tidy gem of a town encased within its famous walls. Yet even these hardly seem formidable, more like garden walls than something that would keep the Florentines at bay. The old ramparts and surrounding areas, once the outworks of the fortifications, are now full of lawns and trees, forming a miniature green belt; on the walls, where the little city's soldiers once patrolled, now the citizens ride their bicycles and walk their dogs, and stop to admire the view.

Like paradise, Lucca is entered by way of St Peter's Gate. Once inside you'll find tidy, well-preserved Romanesque churches and medieval towers that destroyed Ruskin's romantic notion that a medieval building had to be half-ruined to be beautiful, a revelation that initiated his study of architecture. Nor do Lucca's numerous Liberty-style shop signs show any sign of rust; even the mandatory, peeling ochre paint and green shutters of the houses seem part of some great municipal housekeeping plan.

Bicycles have largely replaced cars within the walls. At first glance it seems too bijou, a good burgher's daydream. But after its long and brave history it has certainly earned the right to a little quiet. The annual hordes of Tuscan tourists leave Lucca alone for the most part, though there seems to be a small number of discreet visitors, many of them German and Swedish, who come back every year. They don't spread the word, apparently trying to keep one of Italy's most beautiful cities to themselves.

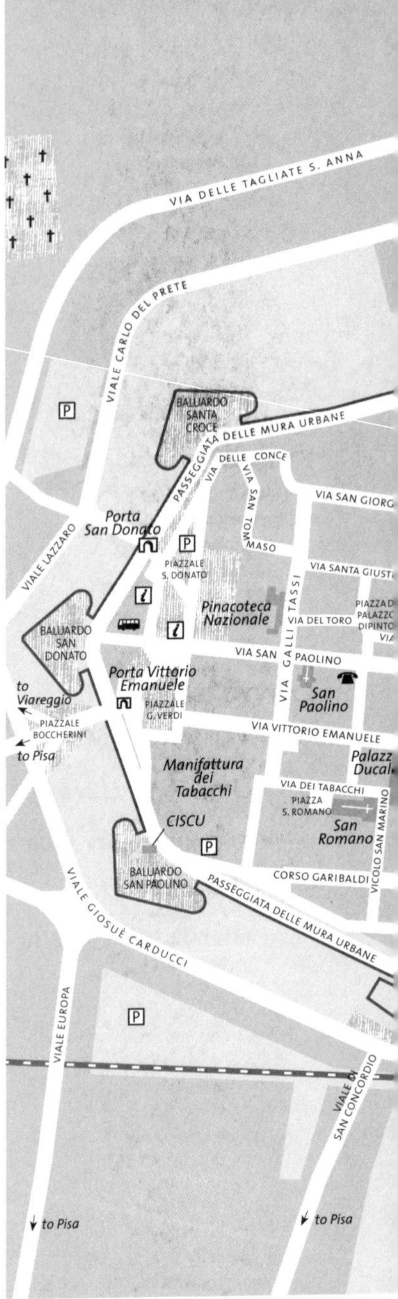

History

Lucca's rigid grid of streets betrays its Roman origins; it was founded as a colony in 180 BC as *Luca*, and in 56 BC entered the annals of history when Caesar, Pompey and Crassus met here to form the ill-fated First Triumvirate. It was converted to Christianity early on by St Peter's disciple Paulinus, who became first bishop of Lucca. The city did especially well in the Dark Ages; in late Roman times it was the administrative capital of Tuscany, and under the Goths managed to repulse the murderous Lombards. Its extensive archives were begun in the 8th century, and many of its churches were founded shortly after. By the 11th and 12th centuries Lucca emerged as one of the leading trading towns of Tuscany, special-

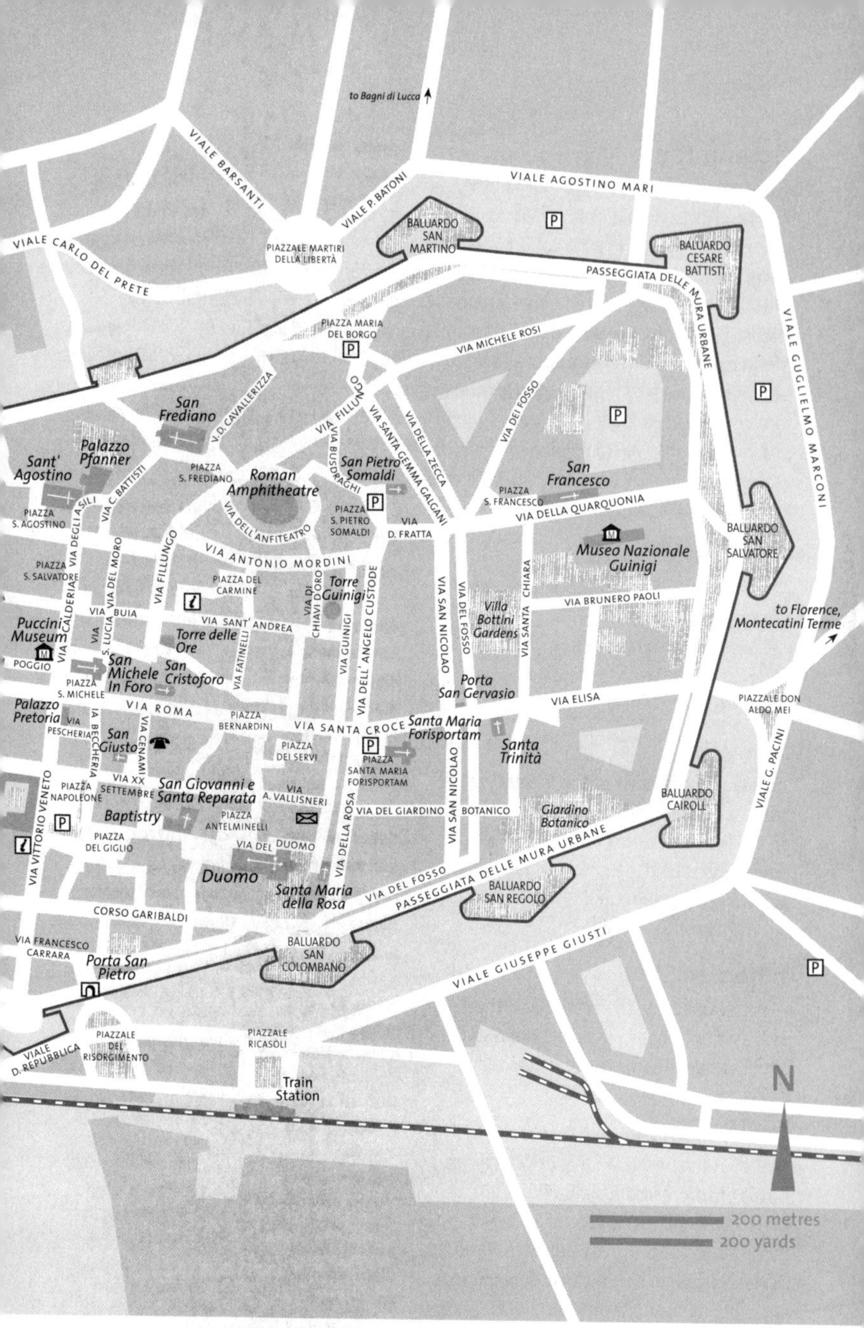

izing in the production of silk, sold by colonies of merchants in the East and West, who earned enough to make sizeable loans to Mediterranean potentates. A Lucchese school of painting developed, such as it is, and beautiful Romanesque churches were erected, influenced by nearby Pisa.

Ghibellines and Guelphs, and then Black and White Guelphs, made nuisances of themselves as they did everywhere else, and Lucca often found itself pressed to maintain its independence from Pisa and Florence.

In 1314, at the height of the city's wealth and power, the Pisans and Ghibellines finally

Getting There

The **railway station** is just south of the walls on Piazza Ricasoli, on the Viareggio–Lucca–Florence line, **t** 1478 88088. LAZZI **buses** leave from Piazzale Verdi, just inside the walls on the western end, for Florence, Pistoia, Pisa, Prato, Abetone, Bagni di Lucca, Montecatini and Viareggio, **t** 0583 584876. Get around Lucca by hiring a **bicycle** from the tourist office in Piazzale Verdi (*open spring and summer only*) or from Poli (**t** 0583 493787) or Bizzatti (**t** 0583 496031), both in Piazza Santa Maria (*open year-round*).

Tourist Information

. Vecchia Porta San Donato, Piazzale Verdi, **t** 0583 583150.

Piazza Santa Maria, **t** 0583 919931, **f** 0583 469964, **e** *info@luccaturismo.it*, **w** *www.luccaturismo.it*.

Festivals

On 12 July, the **Feast of San Paolino**, there are parades and games. On 13–14 September, on the **Feast of Santa Croce**, a candlelit procession is held in honour of the *Volto Santo* (11th-century crucifix), followed by a fair the next day in Piazza San Michele.

Where to Stay

Lucca can be less than charm city if you arrive without booking ahead; there simply aren't enough rooms to meet demand.

Luxury

*****__Locanda L'Elisa__, *outside the city, at Massa Pisana on Via SS 12bis*, **t** *0583 379737*, **f** *0583 379019*, **e** *locanda.elisa@lunet.it*. *Closed Nov*. Castruccio Castracani's own palace, built for the great Lucchese warlord in 1321. Surrounded by 18th-century gardens and a pool. Thoroughly modern inside. €275.

Expensive

****__Ilaria__, *Via del Fosso 20*, **t** *0583 47558*, **e** *info@hotelilaria.com*, **w** *www.hotelilaria.com*. Recently upgraded to a four-star hotel, the Ilaria has parking, and smart comfortable rooms in a contemporary decor. €210.

Moderate–inexpensive

***__La Luna__, *Corte Compagni 12*, **t** *0583 493634*, **f** *0583 490021*, **e** *laluna@onenet.it*, **w** *www.hotellaluna.com*. In a quiet part of the centre, this is a cosy place, with a private garage; recently renovated. €99.

***__Piccolo Hotel Puccini__, *Via di Poggio 9*, **t** *0583 55421*, **f** *0583 53487*, **e** *info@hotelpuccini.com*, **w** *www.hotelpuccini.com*. A small, busy, comfortable hotel right in the heart of things, with 14 rooms. Book ahead. €83.50.

***__Rex__, *Piazza Ricasoli 19*, **t** *0583 955443*, **f** *0583 954348*, **e** *iinfo@hotelrexlucca.com*, **w** *www.hotelrexlucca.com*. A good hotel with 25 rooms, all but one with a bathroom. €110.

***__Universo__, *Piazza del Giglio 1*, **t** *0583 493678*, **f** *0583 954854*, **e** *hoteluniverso@lunet.it*, **w** *www.hoteluniverso.it*. Inside the walls: a slightly frayed, thoroughly delightful place, although some rooms are nicer than others. Ruskin slept here. €140.

Cheap

__Diana__, *Via del Molinetto 11, near the cathedral*, **t *0583 592202*, **f** *0583 467795*, **e** *info@albergodiana.com*, **w** *www.albergodiana.com*. Friendly and well run with some of the nicest inexpensive rooms in Tuscany, some with bath. €62. Now has a more upmarket annexe nearby (€93).

__Moderno__, *Via V. Civitalli 38*, **t *0583 55840*, **f** *0583 53830*, **e** *info@albergomoderno.com*, **w** *www.albergomoderno.com*. A central location. Modern, comfortable and rarely crowded. €65.

__Villa Casanova__, *Via Casanova, Balbano, just outside the city (city bus 5 and then a 2.5km uphill walk, or take a taxi)*, **t *0583 548429*, **f** *0583 368955*. Simple rooms but a pleasant garden, tennis and a swimming pool to lounge by. €67.

San Frediano Youth Hostel, *Via della Cavallerizza 12*, **t** *0583 469957*, **f** *0583 461009*. *Open year-round*.

Affitacamere

Affittacamere are guesthouses only doing B&B that are too small (six rooms or less) to qualify as a real hotel. Many are economical; ask at the tourist office for a full list.

Affittacamere San Frediano, *Via degli Angeli 19, tel 0583 469630, **e** sanfredianolu@onenet.it, **w** www.sanfrediano.com*. Offers comfortable and well-furnished rooms; half of them have private bathrooms. €120.

****Alla Corte degli Angeli**, *Via degli Angeli 23, **t** 0583 469204, **f** 0583 991989, **e** info@cortedegliangeli.com, **w** www.cortedegliangeli. com*. Only two years old. The attractive rooms, in Anglo-Italian style, are cosy and comfortable; bathrooms have jacuzzis. €144.

****Palazzo Alexander**, *Via S. Giustina 48, **t** 0583 583571, **f** 0583 583610, **e** info@palazzo-alexander.it, **w** www.palazzo-alexander.it*. The lavish, ornate style of this new guest house, located in a 13th-century palazzo, will not be to everybody's taste, but it is a luxurious place to stay. Marble bathrooms. €153.

Eating Out

As usual, prices given are for a three-course meal excluding wine.

Puccini, *Corte S. Lorenzo 1/3, **t** 0583 316116. **Open** 12.30–2.30 and 8–10.30, closed Tues (in winter)*. Just opposite Casa Puccini, this modern and elegant restaurant is one of the best in Lucca. Fish predominates. €44.

Giglio, *Piazza del Giglio, **t** 0583 494058. **Open** Thurs–Mon 12.15–2.45 and 7.15–10, Tues 12.15–2.45*. A big open fireplace heats the elegant and sober dining room in winter, and in summer tables are set outside on the piazza. Fish is the speciality here. €30.

Antica Locanda dell' Angelo, *Via Pescheria 21, **t** 0583 467711. **Open** Tues–Sat 12.15–3 and 7.30–10.15, Sun 12.15–3*. A rustically elegant place with unusual dishes such as risotto with shrimps and green apples flavoured with curry. Home-made desserts. €30.

La Buca di Sant' Antonio, *Via della Cervia 3, **t** 0583 55881. **Open** 12.30–2.30 and 7.30–11, Sun 11–3, closed Sun dinner, Mon*. A justly popular restaurant – booking is advisable. Try the artichoke omelette, pappardelle with hare sauce or the traditional Zuppa di Farro. €30.

Buatino, *Via del Borgo Giannotti 508, **t** 0583 343207. **Open** Mon–Sat noon–2 and 7.30–10, closed Sun*. Classic Lucchese dishes: tasty, succulent roast pork (*Arista di Maiale*) or, of course, Zuppa di Farro. A couple of evenings a week there's live jazz or cabaret. €21.

Da Leo, *Via Tegrini 1, **t** 0583 492236. Open Mon–Sat noon–2.30 and 7.30–10.30*. Pretty chaotic, and full of locals and tourists alike. Rabbit stewed with olives, and veal with green peppers; fish only on Fridays. €18.

Da Giulio in Pelleria, *Via della Conce 45, **t** 0583 55948. **Open** Tues–Sat noon–3 and 7–10.30*. Traditional dishes at rock-bottom prices. Popular enough to warrant reservations, with top-quality 'peasant' fare. €16.

Gli Orti di Via Elisa, *Via Elisa 17, **t** 0583 491241. **Open** Fri–Mon 12.30–2.30 and 7.30–10.30, Thurs 7.30–10.30, closed Wed, Thurs*. Run by the son of the owner of La Buca (*see* above), this cheerful trattoria is great for a cheap and cheerful meal. Pizzas, salads, plus good pastas etc. €14.

Da Guido, *Via Cesare Battisti 28, **t** 0583 467219. **Open** Mon–Sat noon–2.30 and 7.30–10*. This basic but popular trattoria usually has the TV on. However, it's full of character and the food is wholesome and portions generous. €11.

Cafés, Bars, Gelaterie

Li per Li, *Via Fillungo 150*. Order a *frullato* (milk shake) made with fresh fruit, a crêpe (both sweet and savoury), a *centrifuga* (such as carrot, apple, ginger and parsley juice) or a *piadina*, a kind of hot sandwich.

Anfiteatro Caffè, *Piazza del Anfiteatro 51*. Drinks and snacks from dawn till late in a great spot for watching the piazza at play.

Pasticceria Taddeucci, *Piazza San Michele 34*. A long, narrow, old-fashioned *caffè*, Taddeucci makes traditional Lucchese cakes and biscuits such as *buccellato*, a simple cake made with raisins and fennel seed.

Antico Caffè delle Mura, *Piazzale Vittorio Emanuele 2*. A smart *caffè* and restaurant perched on the ramparts. Great views.

Caffè di Simo, *Via Fillungo 58*. Brimming with 'belle-époque' atmosphere, this is Luca's most historic *caffè*.

Gelateria Veneta, *Via Vittorio Veneto 74. Closed Jan and Feb*. Lucca's most revered *gelateria*.

managed to seize Lucca. But Lucca had a trump card up a secret sleeve: a remarkable adventurer named Castruccio Castracani. Castracani, an ambitious noble who for years had lived in exile – part of it in England – heard the bad news and at once set forth to rescue his home town. Within a year he had chased the Pisans out and seized power for himself, leading Lucca into its most heroic age, capturing most of Western Tuscany to form a little Luccan empire, subjugating even big fish like Pisa and Pistoia. After routing the Florentines at Altopascio in 1325, Castracani was planning to snatch Florence too, but died of malaria just before the siege was to begin – another example of Florence's famous good luck. Internal bickering between the powerful families soon put an end to Lucca's glory days, though in 1369 the city managed to convince Emperor Charles IV to grant it independence as a republic, albeit a republic ruled by oligarchs like Paolo Guinigi, the sole big boss between 1400 and 1430.

But Lucca continued somehow to escape being gobbled up by its voracious neighbours, functioning with enough tact and tenacity to survive even after the arrival of the Spaniards – a fact one can attribute not so much to its great walls as to its relative insignificance. Amazingly enough, after the Treaty of Château-Cambrésis, Lucca found itself standing together with Venice as the only truly independent states in Italy. And like Venice, the city was an island of relative tolerance and enlightenment during the Counter-Reformation, its garden walls in this case proving stout enough to deflect the viperous Inquisition. In 1805 Lucca's independence ended when Napoleon gave the republic to his sister Elisa Baciocchi, who ruled as its princess; it was given later to Marie Louise, Napoleon's widow, who governed well enough to become Lucca's favourite ruler and earn a statue in the main Piazza Napoleone. Her son sold it to Leopold II of Tuscany in 1847, just in time for it to join the Kingdom of Italy.

AROUND THE TOWN

San Martino Cathedral

Piazza San Martino. ***Open*** *winter Mon–Sat 7–5, summer Mon–Sat 7–7, Sun 9–9.50, 11.30–11.50 and 1–5.*

Begun by Pope Alexander II in 1070 and completed in the 15th century, this is perhaps the outstanding work of the Pisan style outside Pisa. Above the singular **porch**, with three different sized arches, are stacked three levels of colonnades, with pillars arranged like candy sticks, while behind and on the arches are exquisite 12th- and 13th-century reliefs and sculpture – the best work Lucca has to offer. See especially the *Adoration of the Magi* by Nicola Pisano over the left doorway, the two highly elaborated organ cases facing each other across the aisle, the column carved with the Tree of Life, with Adam and Eve crouched at the bottom and Christ on top, and a host of fantastical animals and hunting scenes, the months and their occupations, mermaids and dragons, a man embracing a bear, even *Roland at Roncevalles*, all by unknown masters. On the right side of the portico, there's also a medieval maze, which you can trace with your finger. Walk round the back, where the splendidly ornate apse and transepts are set off by the green lawn. The **Campanile**, crenellated like a battle tower, dates from 1060 to 1261.

The Interior

The dark interior offers a good introduction to the works of Lucca's only great artist, Matteo Civitali (1435–1501), who worked as a barber until his mid-30s, when he decided he'd rather be a sculptor. He deserves to be better known, but may never be since everything he made is still in Lucca.

His most famous work is the octagonal **Tempietto** (1484), a marble tabernacle in the middle of the left aisle, containing Lucca's most precious holy relic, the world-weary

Volto Santo ('Holy Image'), a cedar-wood crucifix said to be a true portrait of Jesus, sculpted by Nicodemus, an eyewitness to the crucifixion. Saved from the iconoclasts, it was set adrift in an empty boat and floated to Luni, where the bishop was instructed by an angel to place it in a cart drawn by two white oxen; where the oxen should halt, there too should the image remain. They made a lumbering beeline for Lucca, where the *Volto Santo* has remained ever since. Its likeness appeared on the republic's coins, and there was a devoted cult of the image in medieval England; Lucca's merchant colony in London cared for a replica of the *Volto Santo* in old St Thomas's, and according to William of Malmesbury, King William Rufus always swore by it, '*per sanctum vultum de Lucca*'. Long an object of pilgrimage, the image goes out for a night on the town in a candlelight procession each 13 September.

Further up the left aisle a chapel contains Fra Bartolommeo's *Virgin and Child Enthroned*. Here, too, is an altar by Giambologna, of *Christ with Saints Peter and Paul*. Civitali carved the cathedral's high altar, and also two expressive tombs in the south transept. A door from the right aisle leads to the sacristy (€1.60), where you can see Lucca's real icon, the remarkable **Tomb of Ilaria del Carretto** (1408), perhaps Jacopo della Quercia's most beautiful work, a tender, tranquil effigy of the young bride of boss Paolo Guinigi, complete with the family dog at her feet, waiting for his mistress to awaken. In fact the city has always had a strange love–hate relationship with this lovely statue. Right after her husband was overthrown they hustled the state out of the cathedral, and she didn't come back for centuries. Near the statue is the *Madonna Enthroned with Saints* by Domenico Ghirlandaio. A side altar near the sacristy has a typically strange composition from the Venetian Tintoretto, a *Last Supper* with a nursing mother in the foreground and cherubs floating around Christ. In the centre, unfortunately often covered up, is a particularly fine section of the inlaid marble floor; on the entrance wall, a 13th-century sculpture of St Martin has been brought in from the façade.

Museo della Cattedrale

***Open** summer daily 10–6, winter Mon–Fri shorter hours; **adm** €3.50.*

This newly opened museum next to the cathedral displays more of the cathedral's treasures, including the ornaments (the crown and garments) of the *Volto Santo*, della Quercia's *St John the Baptist* and tapestries and paintings from San Giovanni.

Santa Maria Forisportam

*Piazza S. Maria Forisportam. **Open** Mon–Sat 9–12 and 3–5, Sun 3–5.*

In the early 12th century, when the first church was built outside the gates, it took the name Santa Maria Forisportam ('outside the gates'). It is set in a charming square with a column, once used as a turning post in Lucca's medieval *Palio*. Its marble façade is topped off by brick and, inside, there is yet another carved organ case.

A pretty church with blind arcades in the Pisan style, it was Santa Maria Forisportam that converted Ruskin (and through Ruskin, millions of others) to medieval architecture: 'Here in Lucca I found myself suddenly in the presence of twelfth-century buildings, originally set in such balance of masonry that they could all stand without mortar; and in material so incorruptible, that after six hundred years of sunshine and rain, a lancet could not now be put between their joins. Absolutely for the first time I now saw what medieval builders were and what they meant. I took the simplest of façades for analysis, that of Santa Maria Foris-Portam, and thereon literally *began* the study of architecture.' Inside, it not only looks but smells terribly old. The font is made from a Palaeo-Christian sarcophagus and there are two paintings by Guercino, by the fourth altar on the right and in the left transept;

near the latter is a remarkable 14th-century painting on wood, the *Dormition and Assumption of the Virgin*.

Museo Nazionale Guinigi

Villa Guinigi, Via della Quarquonia, t 0583 496033. Open Tues–Sat 8.30–7, Sun 8.30–1; adm €6.50.

The palatial brick Villa Guinigi was built in 1418 by the big boss Paolo Guinigi in his glory days. Its ground floor houses an interesting collection of Romanesque reliefs, capitals and transennas, some of which are charmingly primitive – St Michael slaying the dragon, Samson killing the lion, a 9th-century transenna with birds and beasts, spirals and daggers. **Room IV** has a lovely *Annunciation* by Civitali, and beyond, a set of neoclassical reliefs from the Palazzo Ducale of the *Triumphs of Duchess Maria Luisa*. The painting gallery upstairs contains intarsia panels from the cathedral, each with scenes of Lucca as seen from town windows, some trecento works by the Lucca school and a charming quattrocento *Madonna and Child* by the 'Maestro della Vita di Maria'. Other rooms contain a miasma of oversize 16th-century canvases, some by Vasari.

Torre Guinigi

Via Sant' Andrea, t 0583 491243. Open daily Mar–Sept 9–7.30, Oct 10–6, Nov–Feb 9–5.30; adm €3.10.

In a neighbourhood of Lucca that has scarcely changed in the past 500 years the medieval ancestors of the Guinigi had their stronghold in a block of 14th-century houses and the Torre Guinigi.

This is one of Lucca's landmarks, with a tree sprouting out of the top – the best example of this quaint Italian fancy that you'll see here and there throughout the country. One of the most elaborate of medieval family fortresses, the tower has recently been restored, and it's worth the slight risk of cardiac arrest to climb the 230 steps for the view over the city and the marbly Apuan Alps.

Piazza dell'Anfiteatro

The **Roman amphitheatre** is the most remarkable relic of Roman Lucca. Like a fossil, only outlines of its arches are still traceable in the outer walls, while within the inner ring only the form remains – the marble was probably carted off to build San Michele and the cathedral – but Lucca is a city that changes so gradually and organically that the outline has been perfectly preserved. The foundations of the grandstands now support a perfect ellipse of medieval houses. Duchess Marie Louise cleared out the old buildings in the former arena, and now, where gladiators once slugged it out, there is a wonderfully atmospheric piazza, where the boys play football and the less active sit musing in sleepy cafés. The amphitheatre is also home to some great shops.

San Frediano

Piazza S. Frediano. Open Mon–Sat 8.30–noon and 3–5, Sun 9–11.30 and 3–6.

San Frediano, with its tall church and even taller campanile, was built in the early 1100s and shimmers with the colours of the large 13th-century mosaic on its upper façade, showing Christ and the Apostles in an elegant flowing style, often attributed to Berlinghiero Berlinghieri. The 11th-century bronze Arabian falcon at the top is a copy – the original is so valuable that it's locked away. The palatial **interior** houses Tuscany's most remarkable baptismal font, the 12th-century *Fontana lustrale*, covered with reliefs; behind is an equally beautiful terracotta lunette of the Annunciation by Andrea della Robbia. The chapels are richly decorated – the fourth on the left has an altarpiece in the form of a Gothic polyptych by Jacopo della Quercia, who also sculpted the two tombstones. The second on the left has frescoes painted by Amico Aspertini in 1508 (*currently under restoration*).

The bedecked mummy is St Zita, patroness of domestic servants; born in 1218, she entered the service of a family in Lucca at the age of 12 and remained with them until her death. She would not only give her clothes and food to the poor, but that of her masters, which at first caused her to be maltreated. Ever since her canonization in 1696 she has been greatly venerated, not only in Italy, but in England, where maids belonged to the Guild of St Zita. The Lucchesi are very fond of her, and on 26 April they bring her uncorrupted body out to caress.

Palazzo Pfanner

***Via degli Asili 33, t 0583 491243. Garden open** summer daily 9–7, winter daily 10–4; by appointment only.*

An 18th-century palace with a delicious, statue-filled garden (for a look into it and at San Frediano's handsome apse, climb up the city wall beyond), it has a famous grand stairway of white marble, and is used to display a collection of silks made in Lucca.

Via Fillungo

Medieval Via Fillungo is Lucca's main street, making up, with its surrounding lanes, the busy shopping district, packed on Saturday and Sunday afternoons when the Lucchesi are out for their afternoon *passeggiata*. It is a tidy nest of straight and narrow alleys where the contented cheerfulness that distinguishes Lucca from many of its neighbours seems somehow magnified. In this area, don't just keep your eyes at eye-level; the streets are narrow, and if you don't look up, you will miss some wonderful stone carving above doors and windows.

A number of shopfronts have remained unchanged for over a century – one of the most charming is the jeweller's at No.20, and there is another at No.95 with frescoed ceilings. Even older are the loggias of the 14th-century palaces, now bricked in, and the ancient **Torre dell' Ore**, which since 1471 has striven to keep the Lucchesi on time, and perhaps now suggests that it's time for a coffee in Lucca's historic **Caffè di Simo** at No.58. There's of course a church to be seen, 13th-century **San Cristoforo**, now used for exhibitions. It is also Lucca's war memorial.

San Michele in Foro

*Piazza San Michele. **Open** daily 7.30–12.30 and 3–6.*

Situated in Piazza San Michele, Lucca's Roman forum, San Michele in Foro is a masterpiece of Pisan Gothic and a church so grand that many people mistake it for the cathedral. The ambitious **façade** rises high above the level of the roof, to make the building look even grander (the Italians call the style 'wind-breaker'). Every column in the five levels of Pisan arcading is different: some doubled, some twisted like corkscrews, inlaid with mosaic Cosmati work or carved with monsters, while in between are friezes richly carved with animals. The whole is crowned by a giant statue of the Archangel, and on the corner of the façade is a *Madonna* by Civitali, paid for by the city in gratitude for deliverance from a plague in 1480; the graceful, rectangular campanile is Lucca's tallest and loveliest.

The **interior** is more austere, but there's a glazed terracotta *Madonna and Child* attributed to Luca della Robbia, a striking 13th-century *Crucifixion* hanging over the high altar, and a painting of plague saints by Filippino Lippi. Giacomo Puccini began his musical career here as a choirboy (his father and grandfather had been organists in the cathedral).

Museo Puccini

***Entrance in Corte San Lorenzo 9. Open** June–Sept daily 10–6, Oct–Dec Tues–Sun 10–1 and 3–6, mid-Mar–May Tues–Sun 10–1 and 3–6; **adm** €3.*

Puccini lived in narrow Via di Poggio 30, just opposite San Michele's façade. His house is now a little Puccini Museum. It has a few odds and ends left by Puccini (1858–1924), including manuscripts, letters, mementoes, his overcoat and other bits and pieces, as well as his piano. Once his operas had made him famous, he bought a villa at Torre del Lago, just south of Viareggio, where he said, 'I can practise my second favourite instrument, my rifle' on the coots and ducks in Lake Massaciuccoli; he was famous for terrorizing the local peasants by tearing around like a demon in his motorcar. His villa is also a museum, rather more extensive than the one here, and the maestro is buried in the adjacent chapel – he died just after having run through his last opera, *Turandot*, with Toscanini. In July and August, Torre del Lago hosts an opera festival in Puccini's honour.

Pinacoteca Nazionale

Palazzo Mansi, Via Galli Tassi 43. Open Tues–Sat 8.30–7, Sun 8.30–1; adm €6.50.
Most of the art in the Pinacoteca Nazionale, as well as the rich furnishings in several of the rooms, dates from the 17th century; the few paintings which might be interesting, portraits by Pontormo and Bronzino, are all indefinitely at the restorer's. In the study hangs a dark and damaged Veronese, and Tintoretto's *Miracle of St Mark Freeing the Slave*, showing, with typical Tintorettian flamboyance, Venice's patron saint dive-bombing from heaven to save the day. The 1600s frescoes are more fun than the paintings, especially the *Judgement of Paris*, which Venus wins by showing a little leg. And one can't help but wonder what rococo dreams tickled the fancy of the sleeping occupants of the amazing bedroom.

Piazza Napoleone

The shady twin squares of Piazza Napoleone and Piazza Giglio are Lucca's civic centre and the focus of its evening *passeggiata*. The yellow hodgepodge of a palace in Piazza Napoleone, formerly the seat of the lords of Lucca and the republican council, has been known as the **Palazzo Ducale** ever since it was used by Lucca's queens for a day, Elisa Bonaparte and Duchess Marie Louise; now it contains local government offices. The most important architect to have a crack at it was Ammannati in the 16th century, and signs of his Mannerist handiwork survive in the courtyard.

The Walls

Lucca's lovely bastions evoke images of the walled rose gardens of chivalric romance, enclosing a smaller, perfect cosmos. They owe their charm to Renaissance advances in military technology. Prompted by the beginning of the Wars of Italy, Lucca began to construct the walls in 1500.

The councillors wanted up-to-date fortifications to counter new advances in artillery, and their (unknown) architects gave them the state of the art, a model for the new style of fortification that would soon be transforming the cities of Europe. Being Renaissance Tuscans, the architects also gave them a little more elegance than was strictly necessary. The walls were never severely tested. Today, with the outer ravelins, fosses and salients cleared away (such earthworks usually took up more space than the city itself), Lucca's walls are just for decoration; under the peace-loving Duchess Marie Louise they were planted with a double row of plane trees to create a splendid elevated garden boulevard that extends around the city for nearly 4km, offering a continuous bird's-eye view over Lucca. They are among the best preserved in Italy. Of the gates, the most elaborate and flowery is the Porta San Pietro (1566) near the station, its portcullis still intact, with Lucca's proud motto of independence, LIBERTAS, inscribed over the top.

One of the best ways to explore the walls is by bike. Hire one in Piazza Santa Maria (*see* p.204) and do a circular tour.

Where to Stay

The Medieval Core 212
West Florence 213
North and East Florence 217
The Oltrarno 218
Fiesole 219
Villa Hotels in the Hills 220
Rooms to Let 221
Youth Hostels 221
Camping 222
Villa Rentals 222

Florence has some exceptionally lovely hotels, and not all of them at Grand Ducal prices, although base rates here are the highest in Tuscany and, indeed, among the highest in Italy. In this town historic old palace-hotels are the rule rather than the exception; those listed below are some of the more atmospheric and charming. Some hotels with a restaurant will require half board, and many will lay down a heavy breakfast charge as well that is supposed to be optional.

If you have a certain place in mind, it is essential to book in advance as soon as possible (considering the slowpoke Italian post, preferably by fax or phone, or increasingly through the Internet). If your Italian is non-existent, the National Tourist Office's Travellers' Handbook has a sample letter and list of useful terms.

There are almost 400 hotels in Florence, but not enough for anyone who arrives at Easter, June or September (and, to a lesser extent, July and August) without a reservation. Don't despair: there are several hotel consortia that can help you find a room in nearly any price range for a small commission. If you're arriving by car or train, the most useful will be ITA.

ITA: in Santa Maria Novella station, **t** 055 282893, open 9–9; in the AGIP service station at Peretola, to the west of Florence on A11, **t** 055 421 1800. No bookings can be made over the telephone and a booking fee of between €2.32 and €7.75 is charged, according to the category of hotel.

Price Categories

Price categories are based on the price of a double room in high season, including a private bath.

luxury	€250 and up
expensive	€180–250
moderate	€130–180
inexpensive	€75–130
cheap	up to €75

For rooms without bath, subtract 20–30 per cent. For a single room, count on paying two-thirds of a double; to add an extra bed in a double will add 35 per cent to the bill. (A *camera matrimoniale* is a room with a double bed, a *camera doppia* has twin beds, a *camera singola* is a single.) Taxes and service charges are included in the given rate. Also note that if rooms are listed without bath, it simply means the shower and lavatory are in the corridor. Costs are often a third less if you travel in the low season.

The Medieval Core

Luxury

Brunelleschi**** E4

Via dei Calzaiuoli/Piazza Santa Elizabetta, ***t*** *055 27370,* ***f*** *055 219653,* ***e*** *info@hotelbrunelleschi.it,* ***w*** *www.hotelbrunelleschi.it;* ***bus*** *A.*

The comfortable Brunelleschi is centrally situated in a quiet piazzetta. Built around a Byzantine tower, it offers everything you would expect from a 4-star hotel, if not a lot of character in the bedrooms. Restaurant, TV, air conditioning, babysitting service, cots, and parking nearby.

Savoy***** E4

Piazza della Repubblica 7, ***t*** *055 283313,* ***f*** *055 284840,* ***e*** *reservations@hotelsavoy.it,* ***w*** *www.rfhotels.com; wheelchair accessible;* ***bus*** *A.*

The Rocco Forte Hotels group rescued the crumbling old Savoy from ruin and reopened it in spring 2000. It is now a sleek, slick hotel which appeals to both business and leisure clients for its central location, smooth contemporary interiors and creature comforts. TV, air conditioning, babysitting service, and cots available. Parking nearby (extra cost). Restaurant.

Expensive

Calzaiuoli*** E4

Via Calzaiuoli 6, ***t*** *055 212456,* ***f*** *055 268310,* ***w*** *www.calzaiuoli.it;* ***bus*** *A.*

Just a few steps from Piazza Signoria and on a traffic-free street, this is a comfortable hotel with modern, nicely decorated rooms and wonderful views from the top floor. Air conditioning, TV, cots, babysitting service, parking nearby.

Hermitage*** D5

Vicolo Marzio 1, ***t*** *055 287216,* ***f*** *055 212208,* ***w*** *www.hermitagehotel.com;* ***bus*** *B.*

You have to look hard to find this little hotel tucked away behind the Ponte Vecchio on the north side of the river. It is built upside down; the lift takes you to the fifth floor with its ravishing roof garden, reception and elegant blue and yellow sitting room. From here you go down to the bedrooms which are on the small side, but charmingly furnished with antiques and tasteful fabrics. Some have river views. Air conditioning, TV, babysitting service, cots, parking.

Relais Uffizi E5

Chiasso de' Baroncelli/Chiasso del Buco 16, ***t*** *055 267 6239,* ***f*** *055 265 7909,* ***e*** *info@relaisuffizi.it,* ***w*** *www.relaisuffizi.it; wheelchair accessible;* ***bus*** *B.*

The only hotel which overlooks historic Piazza della Signoria, the Relais Uffizi is hidden down a series of narrow lanes. The 13 rooms of varying shapes and sizes are decorated and furnished with style while the atmosphere is informal. You can relax in the sitting room and watch the ever-changing piazza below. TV, air conditioning, cots available.

Inexpensive

Firenze* E4

Piazza dei Donati 4, ***t*** *055 214203,* ***f*** *055 212370; wheelchair accessible;* ***bus*** *A.*

The location of this newly renovated *pensione*, between Piazza Signoria and the Duomo, is excellent. The rather unimaginative rooms all now have bathrooms. Air conditioning, TV, parking nearby.

Maxim* E4
Via dei Medici 4, **t** *055 217474,* **f** *055 283729,* **e** *hotmaxim@tin.it,* **w** *www.firenzealbergo.it/home/hotelmaxim; wheelchair accessible;* **bus** *A.*
This centrally located budget hotel has had a recent facelift. The reception area is bright and elegant, and the bedrooms (which sleep two or three) are well furnished and modern. All are en suite and one even has a jacuzzi. Air conditioning, and parking nearby.

West Florence

Luxury

Astoria**** D3
Via del Giglio 9, **t** *055 239 8095,* **f** *055 214632,* **e** *manager@astoria.boscolo.com,* **w** *www.boscolo.com;* **bus** *1, 7, 17.*
This comfortable hotel has more character than many of those located near the station. Recently refurbished, it is in a grand 16th-century palazzo near San Lorenzo market. Public rooms are suitably impressive and some of the bedrooms likewise. Avoid those on the lower floors on the street. Frequently used by upmarket tour groups.

Excelsior***** C4
Piazza Ognissanti 3, **t** *055 2715,* **f** *055 210278,* **e** *marco_milocco@westin.com,* **w** *www.westin.com/excelsiorflorence; wheelchair accessible;* **bus** *B.*
Napoleon's sister Caroline once lived in the building which is now one of Florence's top hotels. Recently renovated, the huge dimensions and neoclassical lines feature tons of marble, lots of dark mahogany and stained glass to create an old-fashioned and luxurious atmosphere. Bedrooms are all that you would expect for the prices with antiques, heavy drapes and marble bathrooms. Some have a view of the Arno. TV and air conditioning in rooms; babysitting services, and parking nearby.

Grand***** B4
Piazza Ognissanti 1, **t** *055 2716,* **f** *055 217400,* **e** *marco_milocco@westin.com,* **w** *www.luxurycollection.com/grandflorence; wheelchair accessible;* **bus** *B.*
You can't really mention one without the other; sister hotel to the Excelsior, and facing it over the piazza, the Grand is equally plush. It was fully renovated some four years ago and no expense was spared. An immense hall with stained-glass ceiling, columns, marble floors, and lofty potted plants combines lounge, cocktail bar and restaurant. The more expensive bedrooms (regularly inhabited by the rich and famous) are decorated in early Florentine style with hand-crafted wood and paintwork. Carpets are thick and fabrics rich. TV, air conditioning, babysitting service, and parking nearby.

Helvetia & Bristol***** D4
Via dei Pescioni 2, **t** *055 287814,* **f** *055 288353,* **e** *information_hbf@charminghotels.it,* **w** *www.charminghotels.it;* **bus** *A.*
If you prefer luxury on a smaller scale, this hotel is the obvious choice. There are only 52 bedrooms and each one is different, all exquisitely furnished with rich fabrics adorning windows, walls and beds; service is discreet and the atmosphere understated. Many illustrious names have appeared in the hotel's register, including Stravinsky, D'Annunzio, Bertrand Russell and Pirandello. There are many superb antiques in both public rooms and bedrooms, and an excellent restaurant. TV, air conditioning, cots, babysitting service, and parking nearby.

Kraft**** Off maps
Via Solferino 2, **t** *055 284273,* **f** *055 239 8267,* **e** *info@krafthotel.it,* **w** *www.krafthotel.it;* **bus** *B, D.*
In a useful location if you are in Florence for the opera season (it is 2 minutes' walk from the Teatro Comunale), the Kraft has the added advantage of a small rooftop pool. Bedrooms are light and sunny, comfortably furbished with cheerful fabrics. The suites on the top floor have great views. There is a restaurant; also TV, air conditioning, and parking nearby.

Principe**** Off maps
Lungarno Vespucci 34, **t** *055 284848,* **f** *055 283458,* **e** *hotelprincipe@hotelprincipe.com,* **w** *www.hotelprincipe.com; closed Aug;* **bus** *B.*
Among the many hotels along the Arno, this is one of the most pleasant – a small, comfortable hotel, centrally air-conditioned and sound-proofed, with a little garden at the back; the nicer rooms have terraces over the Arno. TV, cots, parking nearby.

Expensive

Beacci Tornabuoni*** D4
Via Tornabuoni 3, **t** *055 212645,* **f** *055 283594,* **e** *info@bthotel.it,* **w** *www.bthotel.it;* **bus** *A, B, 6.*
An excellent small hotel, which puts you in the centre of fashionable Florence, on the top three floors of an elegant Renaissance palace. The rooms are comfortable, air-conditioned and equipped with mini-bars, though it's more fun to sit over your drink on the panoramic roof terrace. TV, cots, babysitting service, parking nearby.

Moderate

Alessandra** D5
Borgo SS. Apostoli 17, **t** *055 283438,* **f** *055 210619,* **e** *info@hotelalessandra.com,* **w** *www.hotelalessandra.com;* **bus** *A, B, 6.*
This modest hotel on a central, but quiet, back street has 25 rooms of varying standards, and not all have private baths. The best have waxed parquet floors and antique furniture, and prices are reasonable. TV, air conditioning in some rooms, babysitting service, parking nearby.

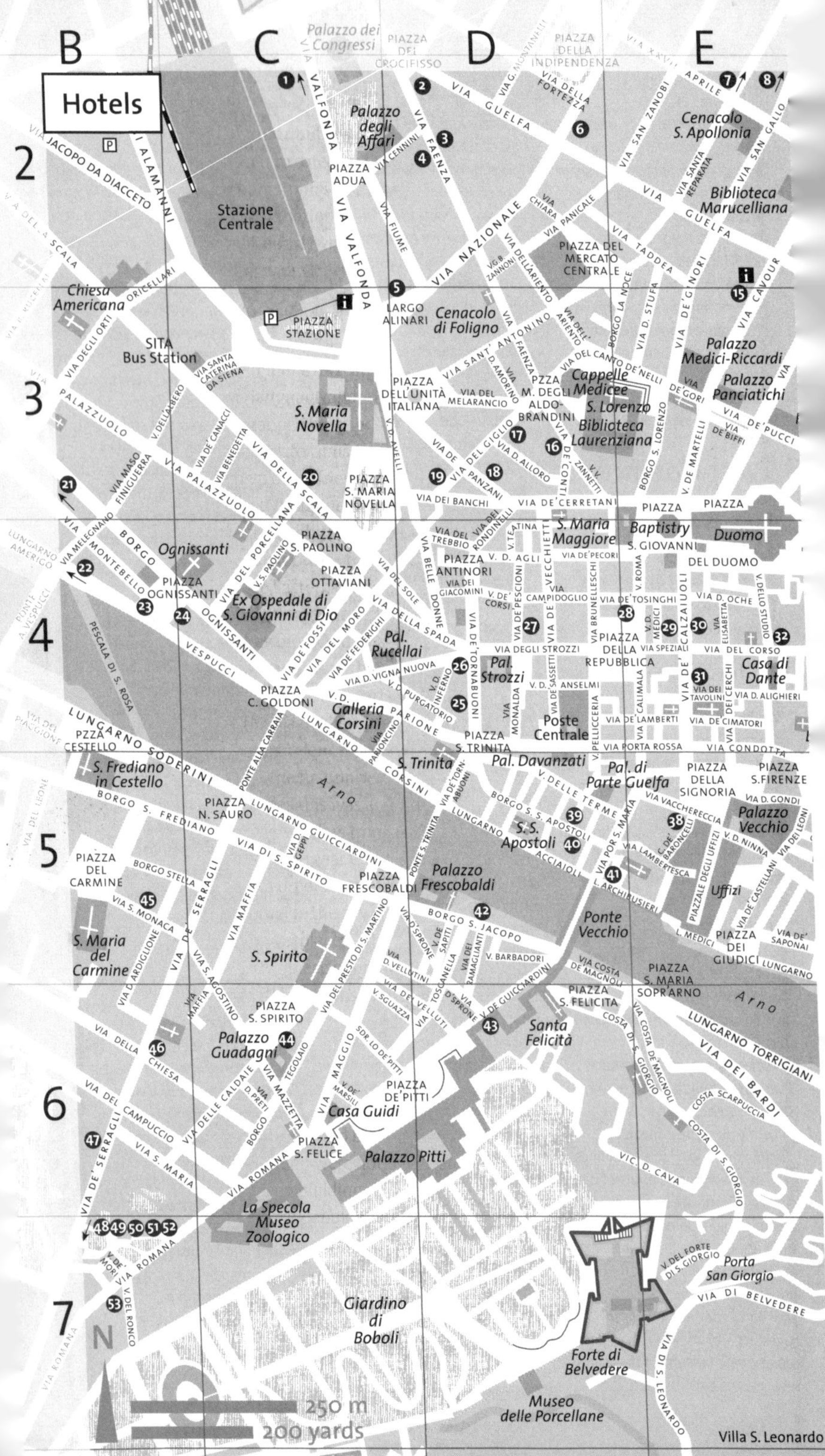

Hotels
B
C
D
E
2
3
4
5
6
7
Palazzo dei Congressi
PIAZZA DEL CROCIFISSO
PIAZZA DELLA INDIPENDENZA
VIA XXVII APRILE
VIA VALFONDA
VIA GUELFA
VIA DELLA FORTEZZA
VIA G. MONTANELLI
Palazzo degli Affari
VIA FAENZA
VIA CENNINI
PIAZZA ADUA
VIA SAN ZANOBI
Cenacolo S. Apollonia
VIA SAN GALLO
VIA SANTA REPARATA
Biblioteca Marucelliana
VIA JACOPO DA DIACCETO
VIA ALAMANNI
VIA DELLA SCALA
Stazione Centrale
VIA FIUME
VIA NAZIONALE
VIA CHIARA
VIA PANICALE
PIAZZA DEL MERCATO CENTRALE
VIA TADDEA
VIA DE' GINORI
VIA CAVOUR
VIA DELL'ARIENTO
V.G.B. ZANNONI
Chiesa Americana
VIA ORICELLARI
PIAZZA STAZIONE
LARGO ALINARI
Cenacolo di Foligno
BORGO LA NOCE
VIA D. STUFA
VIA DEGLI ORTI
SITA Bus Station
VIA SANTA CATERINA DA SIENA
VIA SANT' ANTONINO
VIA D. AMORINO
VIA DEL CANTO DE' NELLI
Palazzo Medici-Riccardi
Palazzo Panciatichi
VIA PALAZZUOLO
VIA DELL'ALBERO
S. Maria Novella
PIAZZA DELL'UNITÀ ITALIANA
VIA DEL MELARANCIO
PZZA M. DEGLI ALDO-BRANDINI
Cappelle Medicee
S. Lorenzo
Biblioteca Laurenziana
VIA DE' GORI
VIA DE' PUCCI
VIA DE' BIFFI
VIA DE' CANACCI
VIA BENEDETTA
VIA MASO FINIGUERRA
VIA DE' AVELLI
VIA DE' PANZANI
VIA DEL GIGLIO
VIA D. ALLORO
VIA DE' CONTI
V.V. ZANNETTI
BORGO S. LORENZO
VIA DE' MARTELLI
PIAZZA S. MARIA NOVELLA
VIA DEI BANCHI
VIA DE' CERRETANI
PIAZZA
Duomo
Baptistry
S. Maria Maggiore
VIA MELEGNANO
BORGO OGNISSANTI
Ognissanti
VIA DEL PORCELLANA
V. S. PAOLINO
PIAZZA S. PAOLINO
VIA DEL TREBBIO
VIA DEI RONDINELLI
V. TEATINA
PIAZZA S. GIOVANNI
DEL DUOMO
LUNGARNO AMERIGO
VIA MONTEBELLO
PIAZZA OGNISSANTI
PIAZZA OTTAVIANI
VIA DEL SOLE
PIAZZA ANTINORI
V. D. AGLI
VIA DE' PECORI
VIA DEI GIACOMINI
V. DE' CORSI
VIA BELLE DONNE
VIA CAMPIDOGLIO
VIA DE' TOSINGHI
VIA D. OCHE
VIA DELLO STUDIO
PONTE A. VESPUCCI
Ex Ospedale di S. Giovanni di Dio
VIA DELLA SPADA
VIA DEL MORO
VIA DE' FOSSI
VIA DE' FEDERIGHI
Pal. Rucellai
VIA DE' TORNABUONI
VIA DE' PESCIONI
VIA DE' VECCHIETTI
VIA BRUNELLESCHI
PIAZZA DELLA REPUBBLICA
V. D. MEDICI
VIA ELISABETTA
VIA DEGLI STROZZI
VIA SPEZIALI
VIA DEL CORSO
PESCAIA DI S. ROSA
VESPUCCI
VIA D. VIGNA NUOVA
V. D. INFERNO
V. D. PURGATORIO
Pal. Strozzi
VIA MONALDA
V. D. ANSELMI
V. DE' SASSETTI
Casa di Dante
VIA DEI TAVOLINI
VIA DE' CERCHI
VIA D. ALIGHIERI
PIAZZA C. GOLDONI
V. D. PARIONE
Galleria Corsini
VIA PARIONCINO
Poste Centrale
VIA DE' LAMBERTI
VIA CALIMALA
VIA DE' CALZAIUOLI
VIA DE' CIMATORI
VIA DEL PIAGGIONE
PZZA CESTELLO
LUNGARNO SODERINI
PONTE ALLA CARRAIA
LUNGARNO CORSINI
PIAZZA S. TRINITA
V. PELLICCERIA
VIA PORTA ROSSA
VIA CONDOTTA
S. Frediano in Cestello
S. Trinita
VIA DE' TORNABUONI
Pal. Davanzati
Pal. di Parte Guelfa
PIAZZA DELLA SIGNORIA
PIAZZA S. FIRENZE
VIA DEL LEONE
BORGO S. FREDIANO
Arno
PIAZZA N. SAURO
LUNGARNO GUICCIARDINI
V. DELLE TERME
BORGO S. S. APOSTOLI
VIA VACCHERECCIA
VIA D. GONDI
Palazzo Vecchio
VIA DEI LEONI
VIA D. CEPPI
PONTE S. TRINITA
LUNGARNO
S.S. Apostoli
C. DE' BARONCELLI
V. D. NINNA
PIAZZA DEL CARMINE
BORGO STELLA
VIA DI S. SPIRITO
PIAZZA FRESCOBALDI
Palazzo Frescobaldi
ACCIAIOLI
VIA POR S. MARIA
VIA LAMBERTESCA
PIAZZALE DEGLI UFFIZI
L. ARCHIBUSIERI
Uffizi
VIA DE' CASTELLANI
VIA S. MONACA
VIA DE' SERRAGLI
VIA MAFFIA
BORGO S. JACOPO
Ponte Vecchio
L. MEDICI
PIAZZA DEI GIUDICI
VIA DE' SAPONAI
S. Maria del Carmine
VIA D'ARDIGLIONE
VIA S. AGOSTINO
S. Spirito
VIA DEL PRESTO DI S. MARTINO
VIA D. VELLUTINI
V. D'SPRONE
V. DE' SAPITI
VIA TOSCANELLA
VIA DE' RAMAGLIANTI
V. BARBADORI
VIA COSTA DE' MAGNOLI
PIAZZA S. MARIA SOPR'ARNO
LUNGARNO
VIA MAFFIA
PIAZZA S. SPIRITO
V. SGUAZZA
VIA DEI VELLUTI
V. D'SPRONE
V. DE' GUICCIARDINI
PIAZZA S. FELICITA
Santa Felicità
COSTA DI S. GIORGIO
VIA COSTA DE' MAGNOLI
LUNGARNO TORRIGIANI
VIA DEI BARDI
VIA DELLA CHIESA
Palazzo Guadagni
TEGOLAIO
VIA MAGGIO
SDR. LO DE' PITTI
V. DE' MARSILI
PIAZZA DE' PITTI
COSTA SCARPUCCIA
VIA DEL CAMPUCCIO
VIA DELLE CALDAIE
VIA D. PRETI
VIA MAZZETTA
BORGO
Casa Guidi
COSTA DI S. GIORGIO
VIA DE' SERRAGLI
VIA S. MARIA
PIAZZA S. FELICE
Palazzo Pitti
VIA ROMANA
VIC. D. CAVA
La Specola Museo Zoologico
V. DE' MORI
VIA ROMANA
V. DEL FORTE DI S. GIORGIO
Porta San Giorgio
VIA DI BELVEDERE
V. DEL RONCO
Giardino di Boboli
N
Forte di Belvedere
VIA DI S. LEONARDO
VIA ROMANA
250 m
200 yards
Museo delle Porcellane
Villa S. Leonardo

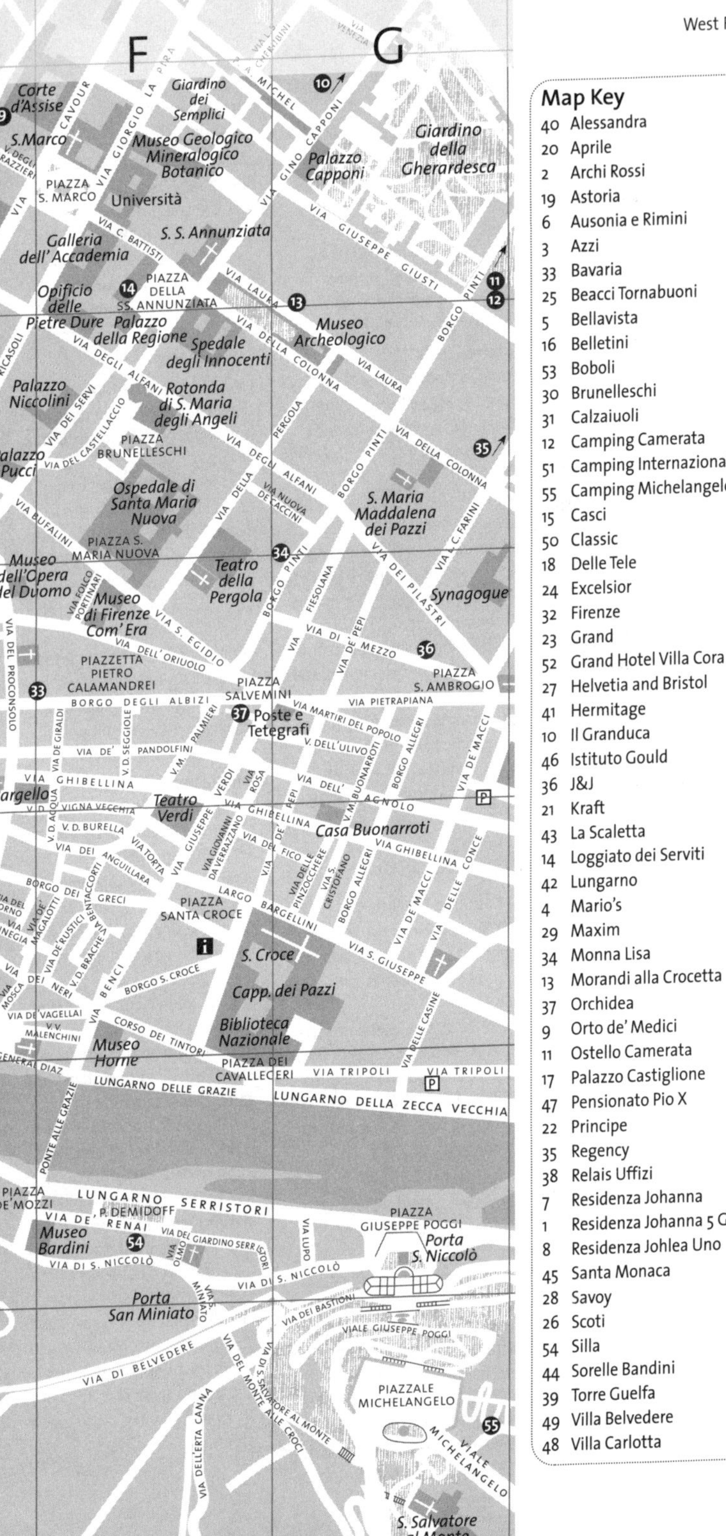

Map Key

- 40 Alessandra
- 20 Aprile
- 2 Archi Rossi
- 19 Astoria
- 6 Ausonia e Rimini
- 3 Azzi
- 33 Bavaria
- 25 Beacci Tornabuoni
- 5 Bellavista
- 16 Belletini
- 53 Boboli
- 30 Brunelleschi
- 31 Calzaiuoli
- 12 Camping Camerata
- 51 Camping Internazionale
- 55 Camping Michelangelo
- 15 Casci
- 50 Classic
- 18 Delle Tele
- 24 Excelsior
- 32 Firenze
- 23 Grand
- 52 Grand Hotel Villa Cora
- 27 Helvetia and Bristol
- 41 Hermitage
- 10 Il Granduca
- 46 Istituto Gould
- 36 J&J
- 21 Kraft
- 43 La Scaletta
- 14 Loggiato dei Serviti
- 42 Lungarno
- 4 Mario's
- 29 Maxim
- 34 Monna Lisa
- 13 Morandi alla Crocetta
- 37 Orchidea
- 9 Orto de' Medici
- 11 Ostello Camerata
- 17 Palazzo Castiglione
- 47 Pensionato Pio X
- 22 Principe
- 35 Regency
- 38 Relais Uffizi
- 7 Residenza Johanna
- 1 Residenza Johanna 5 Giornate
- 8 Residenza Johlea Uno
- 45 Santa Monaca
- 28 Savoy
- 26 Scoti
- 54 Silla
- 44 Sorelle Bandini
- 39 Torre Guelfa
- 49 Villa Belvedere
- 48 Villa Carlotta

Aprile*** C3
Via della Scala 6, **t** *055 216237*, **f** *055 280947*, **e** *info@hotelaprile.it*, **w** *www.hotelaprile.it*; **bus** *A, 12*.
Convenient for the station, and appropriately there is a bust of Cosimo I above the door of what was once a Medici palace. Vaulted ceilings and frescoes remain intact, and the bedrooms all have period furniture although some are on the gloomy side. The breakfast room, however, is very pleasant, and there is the added advantage of a shady courtyard. The hotel has recently expanded into an adjacent palazzo, where the rooms are more uniform and modern. TV, air conditioning, cots, and parking nearby.

Mario's*** D2
Via Faenza 89, **t** *055 216801*, **f** *055 212039*, **e** *hotelmarios@hotelmarios.com*, **w** *www.hotelmarios.com*; **bus** *1, 7, 17*.
In a street with more than its fair share of hotels, many of them of dubious quality, Mario's is a haven. Convenient for the station and a block ar two from the central market, the atmosphere is friendly and the decor rustic Florentine. A generous breakfast is served in a pretty room at long tables and guests are pampered with fresh flowers and fruit on arrival. If you don't want to sleep with your windows closed, ask for a room at the back; the street can be noisy.

Palazzo Castiglione D3
Via del Giglio 8, **t** *055 214886*, **f** *055 274 0521*, **e** *pal.cast@flashnet.it*, **w** *www.venere.it/firenze/palazzocastiglione*; **bus** *1, 7, 17*.
A new B&B located in an elegant palazzo near the central market, the six-roomed Castiglione is under the same ownership as the Torre Guelfa (*see* below). It has been immaculately restored and elegantly furnished. The two superior rooms are huge while others are beautifully frescoed. TV, air conditioning, babysitting service, cots, and parking.

Delle Tele** D3
Via Panzani 10, **t** *055 290797*, **f** *055 238 2419*; **bus** *1, 7, 17*.
On the busy street which runs from the station to the Duomo, bedrooms at the front of this hotel are well double-glazed. Recently renovated. *trompe l'oeil* decorations add character. TV, air conditioning, and parking nearby.

Torre Guelfa*** D5
Borgo SS. Apostoli 8, **t** *055 239 6338*, **f** *055 239 8577*, **e** *torre.guelfa@flashnet.it*, **w** *www.torreguelfa.3000.it*; *closed 3 days at Christmas*; **bus** *A, B, 6*.
Boasting the tallest privately owned tower in Florence from whence you can sip an aperitivo and marvel at the 360° view, this small hotel is bang in the middle of the *centro storico*. The grand double salon, a sunny breakfast room, stylish bedrooms in pastel shades with wrought-iron and hand-painted furniture plus, of course, the tower, make this a very pleasant place to stay. TV, air conditioning, cots, babysitting service, parking nearby.

Inexpensive

Ausonia e Rimini* D2
Via Nazionale 24, **t** *055 496547*, **f** *055 462 6615*, **e** *info@kursonia.com*, **w** *www.kursonia.com*; **bus** *31, 32*.
Near the station, these are actually two hotels on adjacent floors of a crumbling building. Both basic but clean. TV, air conditioning in some rooms, and parking nearby.

Azzi* D2
Via Faenza 56, **t/f** *055 213806*, **e** *hotelazzi@hotmail.com*; **bus** *1, 7, 17*.
Aimed at students and budget travellers, the Azzi is a simple *pensione* in a street full of cheap options near the station. But this one has been given something of a facelift recently and is a friendly and homely place to be based. Only three rooms have en-suite facilities, but the big terrace is a bonus.

Bellavista* D3
Largo Alinari 15, **t** *055 284528*, **f** *055 284874*, **e** *bellavistahotel@iol.it*; **bus** *1, 7, 17*.
A simple and clean choice which is convenient for both train and bus stations. A couple of the rooms have views of the Duomo; a few have private bathrooms. TV and air conditioning.

Belletini** D3
Via de' Conti 7, **t** *055 213561*, **f** *055 28355*, **e** *hotelbellettini@dada.it*, **w** *www.firenze.net/hotelbelletini*; **bus** *1, 7, 17*.
The rooms in this friendly hotel near to the Medici chapels are decorated in traditional Florentine style; a couple have stunning views of the nearby domes. Breakfasts are generous and good. A newly opened annexe just around the corner houses an additional six stylishly furnished rooms, which are slightly more expensive. TV, air conditioning, cots, and parking nearby.

Residenza Johanna Cinque Giornate** Off maps
Via Cinque Gionate 12, **t/f** *055 473377*, **e** *cinquegiornate@johanna.it*, **w** *www.johanna.it*; **bus** *4, 28*.
Like the Residenza Johanna (*see* below), this new home-from-home offers good value for money in a city where bargains are few and far between. Some way from the centre (near the Fortezza da Basso), the villa stands in its own garden, which also offers car parking (reserve ahead). The six bedrooms are prettily and comfortably furnished, a breakfast tray and electric kettle is provided in each room, and there is a sitting room with plenty of reading material. This is not really a hotel (hence the lack of official star rating) in that there is no night porter, and guests are very much left to themselves, but other facilities are of a three-star standard. TV, air conditioning in three rooms, cots.

Cheap

The obvious place to look is the seedy, crowded, tourist-student inferno that surrounds the station, especially in Via Nazionale, Via Fiume, Via Guelfa and Via Faenza down to Piazza Indipendenza. Many of the cheapest places post minions in the station to snatch up weary backpackers. Although convenient if you arrive by train, few of these hotels will brighten your stay in Florence; grouchy owners who lock the door at midnight seem to be the rule.

Scoti* D4
*Via de' Tornabuoni 7, **t** 055 292128, **e** hotelscoti@hotmail.com; **bus** A, B, 6.*
A surprisingly upmarket address for this simple and cheap *pensione* which could be ideal if you would rather splurge on the wonderful clothes in the surrounding shops than on your hotel. Facilities are basic – large rooms of up to four beds (there are a couple of more intimate singles), no private bathrooms, simple furniture, but there is bags of atmosphere starting with the floor-to-ceiling frescoes in the sitting room. The friendly owners (Doreen is Australian) are constantly making improvements.

North and East Florence

Luxury

J&J****** G4
*Via di Mezzo 20, **t** 055 234 5005, **f** 055 240282, **e** jandj@dada.it, **w** www.jandjhotel.com; **bus** A. C.*
The J&J occupies an unassuming building, an ex-convent in a quiet residential street near Sant' Ambrogio. In spite of its 16th-century origins, the interiors are fresh and new, combining original features and antique furniture with chic contemporary design. Each room is totally different. The suites are enormous with sitting areas and luxurious bathrooms; one even has a bathtub in the room. TV, air conditioning, babysitting, cots, and parking nearby.

Monna Lisa****** G3
*Borgo Pinti 27, **t** 055 247 9751, **f** 055 247 9755, **e** hotel@monnalisa.it, **w** www.monnalisa.it; **bus** 14, 23.*
A Renaissance palace now owned by the descendants of sculptor Giovanni Dupre, this is one of the most charming small hotels in Florence, hiding behind its stern façade. The palazzo is well preserved, the furnishings are family heirlooms, as are the many works of art. Try to reserve one of the tranquil rooms that overlook the garden; all are air-conditioned and have frigo-bars. TV, babysitting, cots, and private parking.

Regency******* H3
*Piazza d'Azeglio 3, **t** 055 245247, **f** 055 234 6735, **e** info@regency_hotel.com, **w** www.regency_hotel.com; **bus** C, 6.*
In Florence's plane-tree shaded 'London Square', there's the small Regency, charming and intimate with only 33 air-conditioned rooms; between the two wings there's an elegant town garden. The public rooms are beautifully panelled, and the fare in the dining room superb; there's a private garage for your car. TV, air conditioning, babysitting service, cots.

Expensive

Loggiato dei Serviti**** F2
*Piazza SS. Annunziata 3, **t** 055 289592, **f** 055 289595, **e** info@loggiatodeiservitihotel.it, **w** www.loggiatodeiserviti.it; **bus** C, 6.*
Located on Florence's most beautiful square (now traffic-free), the front rooms of this delightful hotel overlook Brunelleschi's famous portico. The 16th-century building was originally a convent, and many of the architectural features remain. Rooms are furnished with lovely antiques and tasteful fabrics; each is very different from the next. Highly recommended. TV, air conditioning, cots available, and parking nearby

Moderate

Casci**** E3
*Via Cavour 13, **t** 055 211686, **f** 055 239 6461, **e** casci@italyhotel.com, **w** www.hotelcasci.com; **bus** 1, 7, 17.*
The Lombardis, who run the Casci in this 15th-century palazzo (once home to Rossini), emphasize that it is very much a family hotel. The atmosphere is relaxed and cheerful, the reception area is full of helpful information, the breakfast room sports a frescoed ceiling while the recently refurbished bedrooms are bright and modern. The choice few look onto a garden at the back. Good value. TV, air conditioning, babysitting, cots, and parking nearby.

Morandi alla Crocetta**** G2
*Via Laura 50, **t** 055 234 4747, **f** 055 248 0954, **w** www.welcomehotelmorandi.it; wheelchair accessible; **bus** C, 6.*
This small, popular hotel (it has only 10 rooms) is situated in the university area northeast of Piazza San Marco. Run by an Irish–Italian family, the building was a convent in the 16th century, and some of the comfortable and pleasant rooms still have the odd fresco. Two have private terraces. Babysitting service, cots, and parking nearby.

Orto de' Medici**** E2
*Via San Gallo 30, **t** 055 483427, **f** 055 461276, **e** hotel@ortodeimedici.it, **w** www.ortodeimedici.it; wheelchair accessible; **bus** 7, 10.*
This new hotel was opened in August 2001 having undergone extensive renovation. Just north of the central market, it is located in an elegant little palazzo. Public rooms have wonderful old parquet floors and delightful frescoes while bedrooms have been fully modernized; a few have terraces and most have splendid marble bathrooms. There is a big terrace off the breakfast room for chilling out in the evenings. TV, air conditioning, cots available.

Inexpensive

Bavaria* F4
*Borgo degli Albizi 26, **t/f** 055 234 0313, **w** www.eidnet.com/hotelbavaria; **bus** A.*
The 16th-century palazzo in which this *pensione* is housed is most impressive – the façade is said to be frescoed by Vasari – but don't get your hopes up. The accommodation is decidedly spartan with minimal formica furniture, but the rooms (some of them vast) are clean and cheap; only three are en suite. Some have splendid views of the city.

Il Granduca** Off maps
*Via Pier Capponi 13, **t** 055 572803, **f** 055 579252; **bus** 33.*
One of the nicest hotels in this category, with a garden and garage, although a bit out of the centre, between Piazzale Donatello and Piazza della Libertà. All rooms but one are en suite. Parking nearby.

Residenza Johlea Uno Off maps
*Via San Gallo 80, **t** 055 463 3292, **f** 055 463 4552, **e** johlea@johanna.it, **w** www.johanna.it; **bus** 1, 7, 17.*
A remarkable bargain in terms of what it offers for the price, the Johlea is under the same ownership as the Johannas above and below. Situated 10 minutes' walk north of the central market, the rooms are comfortable and well furnished with taste and style and all have excellent bathrooms. Breakfast is supplied on trays in the rooms. On the top floor is a small sitting room and a roof terrace affording 360° views of the city. If all the rooms here are full, there is a sister 'residenza' (the Johlea Due) a few doors down. TV, air conditioning, cots available.

Cheap

Residenza Johanna Off maps
*Via Bonifacio Lupi 14, **t** 055 481896, **f** 055 482721; **bus** 1, 17.*
Only a tiny brass plaque over the bell gives away the location of this 'non-hotel'. There are no TVs or phones in the room and no doorman (guests are given their own keys), but furnishings are comfortable, bedrooms prettily decorated with floral papers and there's lots of reading material supplied. All rooms but two are en suite. Breakfast is not served, so there is a do-it-yourself tray in each room, and kettles in the corridor. Great value if you are prepared to be a little way from the centre of town, north of Piazza San Marco. Cots available; parking nearby.

Orchidea* F4
*Borgo degli Albizi 11, **t/f** 055 248 0346, **e** hotelorchidea@yahoo.it; **bus** A.*
Dante's in-laws once lived in the 12th-century building where the Anglo-Italian family who run the Orchidea offer seven cheerful rooms. Only one (a triple) has a private shower, and the best look onto a garden at the back. It is cosier than many similar establishments.

The Oltrarno

Luxury

Grand Hotel Villa Cora**** Off maps
*Viale Machiavelli 18–20, **t** 055 229 8451, **f** 055 229086, **e** reservations@villacora.it, **w** www.villacora.com; **bus** 12, 13.*
A luxurious choice near Piazzale Michelangelo, this opulent 19th-century mansion is set in a beautiful formal garden overlooking the Oltrarno. Built by the Baron Oppenheim, it later served as the residence of the wife of Napoleon III, Empress Eugénie. Its conversion to a hotel has dimmed little of its splendour; some of the bedrooms have frescoed ceilings and lavish 19th-century furnishings – all are air-conditioned and have frigo-bars, and there's a pretty pool. In the summer meals are served in the garden, and there's a fine view of Florence from the roof terrace. TV, babysitting service, cots, and free parking.

Lungarno**** D5
*Borgo San Jacopo 14, **t** 055 27261, **f** 055 268437, **e** lungarnohotels@lungarnohotels.com, **w** www.lungarnohotels.com; wheelchair accessible; **bus** D.*
This discreet hotel enjoys a marvellous location on the river, only 2 minutes' walk from the Ponte Vecchio. The ground-floor sitting/breakfast room and bar take full advantage of this with picture windows looking onto the water. The building is fairly modern, but incorporates a medieval tower. The whole hotel has just been refurbished; the smallish bedrooms are decorated in smart blue and cream and the best have balconies with 'The View'. You need to book way ahead if you want one of these. There is now a restaurant specializing in fish dishes. TV, air conditioning, babysitting service, cots, parking nearby.

Expensive

Villa Carlotta**** Off maps
*Via Michele di Lando 3, **t** 055 233 6134, **f** 055 233 6147, **e** villacarlotta@slashnet.it, **w** www.venere.it/firenze/villacarlotta; wheelchair accessible; **bus** 12, 13.*
This Tuscan–Edwardian hotel is in a quiet residential district in the upper Oltrarno, close to the Porta Romana. The 26 sophisticated rooms have recently been tastefully refurnished and have every mod con. There's a garden and glassed-in veranda, where the large breakfasts are served; a private garage offers safe parking. TV, air conditioning, babysitting service, cots.

Moderate

Classic Hotel*** Off maps
*Viale Machiavelli 25, **t** 055 229351, **f** 055 229353, **e** info@classichotel.it, **w** www.classichotel.it; closed 9 days in Aug; **bus** 12, 13.*
If you are travelling by car, staying in the centre of town is more

trouble (and expense) than it's worth. Even if you are not, the Classic offers excellent value for money, and a very pleasant location just above Porta Romana on the way to Piazzale Michelangelo. A 5-minute walk will take you to a bus stop for downtown. The pink-washed villa stands in a shady garden (a welcome respite from the heat of the city), and breakfast is served in the conservatory in summer. Rooms are furnished with a mixture of old and new, walls are white, parquet floors are polished and plaster work has been recently restored. There is even the odd fresco. TV, air conditioning, babysitting service, cots, and free parking.

Silla*** F6
*Via dei Renai 5, **t** 055 234 2888, **f** 055 234 1437, **e** hotelsilla@tin.it, **w** www.hotelsilla.it; **bus** D.*
Ten minutes' walk east of the Ponte Vecchio on the south bank of the river, the Silla's location is central, yet in a quiet and relatively green neighbourhood. The old-fashioned *pensione* is on the first floor of a 16th-century palazzo (there is no lift up the two flights of external steps), and the spacious breakfast terrace has great views over the Arno and beyond. The interior decor may be a little over the top, but rooms are spotless and spacious. TV, air conditioning, babysitting service, cots and parking on site.

Villa Belvedere**** Off maps
*Via Benedetto Castelli 3, **t** 055 222501, **f** 055 223163, **e** reception@villabelvedere.com, **w** www.villa-belvedere.com; closed several days at end Dec; **bus** 11.*
Not one of the more interesting buildings to be found in this part of peripheral Florence (a kilometre above Porta Romana), but the Belvedere offers a very pleasant alternative to central accommodation with a beautiful garden, tennis court, a nice little pool and good views (as befit its name). Rooms are modern and comfortable with lots of wood and plenty of space; those with terraces cost more. For trips into town, you can leave your car and catch a nearby bus. Light meals are served in the restaurant. TV, air conditioning, babysitting service, cots, private parking.

Inexpensive

Boboli** B7
*Via Romana 63, **t** 055 229 8645, **f** 055 233 7169, **e** hotelboboli@hotelboboli.com; **bus** 11, 36, 37.*
As the name suggests, this modest hotel is located near the back entrance of the Boboli gardens. The brightest rooms are right at the top of the four-storey building, but there is no lift. Or if you want quiet (Via Romana is quite noisy), go for a room on the inner courtyard. Breakfast is served on a little terrace in summer. Parking nearby.

La Scaletta** D6
*Via Guicciardini 13, **t** 055 283028, **f** 055 289562, **w** www.lascaletta.com; **bus** D.*
Between the Ponte Vecchio and the Pitti Palace, this friendly *pensione* also has the advantage of a roof garden and great views into Boboli. The 12 bedrooms (not all with bathrooms and some of which sleep up to four) are decently furnished, the nicest with some antique pieces. Public rooms maintain a feel of the 15th-century origins of the building, and a very moderately priced dinner is served in a vaulted dining room.

Sorelle Bandini* C6
*Piazza Santo Spirito 9, **t** 055 215308, **f** 055 282761; **bus** D, 11.*
In spite of its state of disrepair and relatively high prices, the Sorelle Bandini remains popular. This is partly due to the romantic loggia which runs along one side of the fourth-storey hotel, but also to its location on fascinating Piazza Santo Spirito, bustling by day and lively (and noisy) at night. Expect uncomfortable beds, cavernous rooms, heavy Florentine furniture and a certain shabby charm.

Cheap

Istituto Gould B6
*Via dei Serragli 49, **t** 055 212576, **f** 055 280274, **e** gould.reception@dada.it; wheelchair accessible; **bus** 11, 36, 37.*
An excellent budget choice near Santo Spirito, the Isitituto Gould is run by the Valdese church. Rooms vary in size from singles (a couple) to quads and not all have their own bathrooms; book early to secure singles or doubles. The best rooms have access to a terrace and the noisiest are on Via dei Serragli. No smoking is allowed in the building and you have to check in during office hours.

Pensionato Pio X B6
*Via dei Serragli 106, **t** 055 225044. €15 per person per night; **bus** 11, 36, 37.*
Another religious institution offering cheap accommodation, the Pio X is run by a couple of formidable (but kind) ladies. Most rooms are multi-bedded (and single-sex) although there are two singles and most share common bathrooms. The place is simply and sparsely furnished but spotless. There is a dining room where you can eat picnic food. House rules include no smoking and a midnight curfew.

Fiesole

Many frequent visitors to Florence wouldn't stay anywhere else: it's cooler, quieter, and at night the city far below twinkles as if made of fairy lights. If money is no object, the superb choice is:

Villa San Michele*****
*Via Doccia 4, **t** 055 567 8200, **f** 055 567 8250, **e** reservation@villasanmichele.net, **w** www.villasanmichele_orient_express.com; **bus** 7. **Luxury**.*
In a breathtaking location just below Fiesole with a façade and loggia reputedly designed by Michelangelo himself. Originally a monastery in the 14th century, it

was carefully reconstructed after bomb damage in the Second World War to create one of the most beautiful hotels in Italy, set in a lovely Tuscan garden, complete with a pool. Each of its 29 rooms is richly and elegantly furnished and air-conditioned; the more plush suites have jacuzzis. The food is delicious, and the reasons to go down to Florence begin to seem insignificant; a stay here is complete in itself. Paradise, however, comes at a stratospheric price. One of the better suites will cost around €1,800. A lot of VIPs stay here. TV, babysitting service, cots, free parking.

Villa Fiesole***
Via Beato Angelico 35, Fiesole, ***t*** *055 597252,* ***f*** *055 599133,* ***e*** *info@villafiesole.it,* ***w*** *www.villafiesole.it; wheelchair accessible;* ***bus*** *7.* ***Luxury****.*
This new hotel was once part of the San Michele convent, indeed it shares part of its driveway with the hotel of the same name. It's a lot cheaper, however. The smart, neoclassical-style interiors are variations on a fresh blue and yellow colour scheme. Bedrooms are extremely comfortable with thick carpeting, rich fabrics and gleaming new paintwork. Light meals are served in a sunny dining room or on the adjacent terrace, and there is a pool. Don't be misled by the three-star rating. The facilities (and prices) here are of a four-star standard. TV, air conditioning, babysitting service, cots, and free parking.

Villa Aurora****
Piazza Mino 38, Fiesole, ***t*** *055 59100,* ***f*** *055 59587,* ***e*** *h.aurora@fi.flashnet.it,* ***w*** *www.logicaa.net/aurora;* ***bus*** *7.* ***Expensive****.*
This agreeable 19th-century villa is located right on Fiesole's famous piazza from where the No.7 bus will whisk you down to central Florence in 20 minutes. There are 25 bedrooms – the best have rustic antiques and splendid views over the city. Some of the bathrooms are pokey. There is a restaurant on a terrace overlooking Florence in the summer, and the bar next door (noisy at times) is under the same ownership. TV, air conditioning, babysitting service, cots, and free parking.

Le Cannelle
Via Gramsci 52–56, ***t*** *055 597 8336,* ***f*** *055 597 8292,* ***e*** *info@lecannelle.com,* ***w*** *www.lecannelle.com;* ***bus*** *7.* ***Moderate–inexpensive****.*
Two enthusiastic sisters run this reasonably priced and immaculate little B&B on Fiesole's main street. In spite of double glazing, the quieter rooms are at the back and the top rooms have great views. TV and air conditioning.

Pensione Bencistà***
Via Benedetto di Maiano 4, ***t/f*** *055 59163,* ***e*** *pensionebencista@iol.it; closed 10 Dec–1 Feb;* ***bus*** *7.* ***Inexpensive****.*
The views offered from the Bencistà's fragrant, flower-decked terrace are every bit as good as those at Villa San Michele (*above*), and the welcome will be more friendly. This former monastery has been added to over the years, and a complicated series of stairs and passageways lead to the bedrooms, each one different from the next, but all comfortably furnished with solid antique pieces. Obviously, those with a view of the city are most sought after, and two even have terraces. The three little sitting rooms are particularly inviting in cooler weather when fires are lit. Half board – breakfast and either lunch or dinner – is obligatory here, but prices are reasonable. Free parking.

Villa Baccano*
Via Bosconi 4, ***t/f*** *055 59341,* ***e*** *villabaccano@fiesolehotels.com,* ***w*** *www.villabaccano.it;* ***bus*** *7.* ***Cheap****.*
In the hills, 2km out of the centre of Fiesole. Simple rooms in a lovely garden setting, half of which have private bath. TV, air conditioning, and free parking.

Villa Sorriso*
Via Gramsci 21, ***t*** *055 59027,* ***f*** *055 597 8075,* ***e*** *s.benigni@inwind.it,* ***w*** *www.paginegialle.it/albergosorriso-01;* ***bus*** *7.* ***Cheap****.*
In the centre, an unpretentious, comfortable hotel with a terrace overlooking Florence. All but two rooms have baths. Air conditioning, and parking nearby.

Villa Hotels in the Hills

If you're driving, you may consider lodging outside the city where parking is hassle free and the summer heat is less intense. Some places are within very few kms of the city.

Luxury

Torre di Bellosguardo****
Via Roti Michelozzi 2, ***t*** *055 229 8145,* ***f*** *055 229008,* ***e*** *torredibellosguardo@dada.it,* ***w*** *www.torrebellosguardo.com.*
In the 12th century a tower was built at Bellosguardo, enjoying one of the most breathtaking views over the city. It was later purchased by the Cavalcanti, friends of Dante, and a villa was added below the tower; Cosimo I confiscated it; the Michelozzi purchased it from the Medici; Elizabeth Barrett Browning wrote about it. In 1988 it opened its doors as a small hotel. Frescoes by Baroque master Poccetti adorn the entrance hall, fine antiques adorn the rooms, each unique and fitted out with a modern bath. The large and beautiful terraced garden has a pool. For a splurge, reserve the two-level tower suite, with fabulous views in four directions. The superb formal gardens look down to the city below, and light lunches are served around the pool in summer. TV, air conditioning, babysitting service, cots, and free parking.

Villa La Massa***

*Via La Massa 6, **t** 055 62611, **f** 055 633102, **e** villalamassa@galactica.it, **w** www.villamassa.com.*

A lovely choice, located up the Arno some 6km from Florence at Candeli. The former 15th-century villa of Count Giraldi, the hotel retains the old dungeon (now one of two excellent restaurants), the family chapel (now a bar), and other early Renaissance amenities, combined with 20th-century features like tennis courts, a pool and air conditioning. The furnishings are fit for a Renaissance princeling, there's dining and dancing by the Arno in the summer, a shady garden, and a hotel bus to whizz you into the city. The hotel has recently undergone a much publicized and costly re-vamp and is now under the same ownership as the famous Villa d'Este hotel on Lake Como. David Bowie and Imman got married here. TV, babysitting service, cots, and free parking.

Expensive

Paggeria Medicea**

*Viale Papa Giovanni XXIII 3, Artimino, near Carmignano, **t** 055 871 8081, **f** 055 875 1470, **e** hotel@artimino.com, **w** www.artimino.com; closed 21 Dec–3 Jan; wheelchair accessible.*

You can play the Medici in the refurbished outbuildings of Grand Duke Ferdinand's villa. It has some unusual amenities – a hunting reserve and a lake stocked with fish, also a pool and tennis court, and pleasant modern rooms, many with balconies, all air-conditioned. TV, free parking and cots available.

Villa Poggio San Felice

*Via San Matteo in Arcetri 24, **t** 055 220016, **f** 055 233 5388, **e** ilpoggio@tin.it, **w** www.wel.it/Sanfelice; closed Dec–Feb.*

This lovely 15th-century villa opened as a discreet B&B only recently. It is set in beautiful grounds on a hill just south of Porta Romana and is run by a charming young couple. The five bedrooms are furnished with family antiques; one has a huge private terrace. Free minibus to the city centre.

Villa le Rondini***

*Via Vecchia Bolognese 224, **t** 055 400081, **f** 055 268212, **e** mailbox@villalerondini.it, **w** www.villalerondini.it.*

In a pleasant setting about 7km north of Florence, this hotel has several separate buildings and is surrounded by olive and cyprus trees. The most interesting rooms are in the original 16th-century villa. There is a very pleasant pool. TV, air conditioning, babysitting service, cots, and free parking.

Villa Villoresi***

*Via Campi 2, Colonnata di Sesto Fiorentino, **t** 055 443692, **f** 055 442063, **e** cvillor@tin.it, **w** www.ila-chateau.com/villores.*

A lovely oasis in the middle of one of Florence's more unlovely suburbs. One of its charms is that it hasn't been too pristinely restored, and Contessa Cristina Villoresi's family home has retained much of its slightly faded appeal as well as its frescoed ceilings, antiques and chandeliers. The villa boasts the longest loggia in Tuscany, and five of the best, and grandest, bedrooms have direct access to this. Other rooms are much plainer – and cheaper. TV, air conditioning, swimming pool, cots, and free parking.

Moderate

Il Trebbiolo***

*Via del Trebbiolo 8, Molin del Piano, Fiesole, **t** 055 830 0098, **f** 055 830 0583, **e** iltrebbiolo@libero.it, **w** www.iltrebbiolo.it; wheelchair accessible.*

This small and elegant hotel is situated about 7km north of Fiesole in open countryside surrounded by olives and vines. The bedrooms are furnished with taste and flair, and the public rooms are equally inviting with antique furniture and modern art on the walls. The peaceful garden has wonderful hill views, and there is a restaurant serving dinner. Swimming pool, cots, and free parking.

Inexpensive

Casa Palmira

*Loc. Feriolo, Via Faentina, **t/f** 055 840 9749, **e** palmira@cosmos.it, **w** www.casapalmira.it; closed Jan–Mar.*

This delightful B&B is situated in the hills north of Florence (about 16km) on the way to the lovely Mugello area. A rustic barn has been converted by the owners into a welcoming and comfortable place to stay; there is a huge open fireplace, lots of squashy sofas, garden, mountain bikes and even a Smart car to hire. Cots and high chairs available.

Hermitage***

*Via Gineparia 112, Bonistallo, **t** 055 877040, **f** 055 879 7057, **e** hotelhermitageprato@tin.it, **w** www.hotelhermitageprato.it; wheelchair accessible.*

Further afield, near Poggio a Caiano, this is a fine affordable choice for families; there's a pool in the grounds, air-conditioned rooms, not to mention gallons of fresh air and quiet. TV, babysitting service, and free parking.

Rooms to Let

Besides hotels, a number of institutions and private homes let rooms – there's a complete list in the back of the annual provincial hotel book. Many take women only, and fill up with students in the spring when Italian schools make their annual field trips.

Youth Hostels

There are four youth hostels to choose from in Florence. The purpose-built, well-equipped and fully wheelchair-accessible **Archi Rossi** (D2), Via Faenza 94r, **t** 055 290804 (bus 1, 7, 17), is the nearest hostel to the station. Book a place after 6am; rooms can be occupied after 2.30. Phone bookings are accepted and there is a 12.30am curfew. **Ostello Europa Villa Camerata**, Viale A. Righe 2/4 (bus 17B from the station), **t** 055 601451, has 500 beds for people with IYHF cards. Located in an old palazzo with gardens, it is a popular place, and you'd be wise to show up at 2pm to get a spot in the summer; maximum stay three days. **Ostello Santa Monaca** (B5), Via Santa Monaca 6, **t** 055 268338 (bus D, 11, 36, 37), has 111 beds near the Carmine church; sign up for a place in the morning. **Istituto Gould** (B6), Via dei Serragli 44 in the Oltrarno (*see* p.219), is so popular that you must book well in advance, **t** 055 212576.

Camping

All of the following are off the area covered by our maps, unless stated:

Campeggio Panoramico
*Via Peramondo 1, Fiesole, **t** 055 599069. **Open** all year.*
The most picturesque site around Florence. Apart from space for tents and caravans, there are self-catering bungalows for rent which sleep 4.

Camping La Camerata
*Viale Righi 2/4, **t** 055 601451; **bus** 17; wheelchair accessible. **Open** all year.*
20mins by bus out of the centre of town, this campsite is in the spacious and pleasant grounds of the youth hostel.

Camping Internazionale
*Via S. Cristofano 2, south of the city in Bottai Tavarnuzze, **t** 055 237 4704. **Open** end Mar–mid-Oct.*
Near the A1 exit of the Autostrada Firenze–Certosa; convenient for motorists.

Camping Michelangelo G7
*Viale Michelangelo 80, **t** 055 681 1977, **f** 055 689348, **w** www.ecvacanze.it; **bus** 12, 13 from the station.*
Has fine views over the city and free hot showers; arrive early to get a spot. On the other hand, there's no shade and a disco until 1am.

Mugello Verde International Camping
*25km north of Florence on the road to Bologna, at Via Masso Rondinaio 2, in San Piero a Sieve, **t** 055 848511. **Open** April–Oct.*
Very pleasant setting among hills and forests, and frequent buses down to Florence.

Villa Rentals

See p.44 for UK-based holiday villa rental companies. Below is a list of local agencies:

Casaclub
*Via Termini 83, Siena, **t** 0577 44041, **f** 0577 247053, **e** casaclub@interbusiness.it, **w** www.casaclub.it.*
Villas throughout Tuscany, Umbria and Lazio.

Eurocasa
*Via XX Settembre 6, 52047 Marciano della Chiana, **t** 0575 845348, **f** 0575 845462, **e** info@eurocasa.com, **w** www.eurocasa.com.*
Apartments and villas in Tuscany and Umbria.

Toscanamare Villas
*Via W della Gheradesca 5, Castagneto Carducci (LI), **t** 0565 776333, **f** 0565 744339.*
Villas on the Versilia coast.

Tuscan Enterprises
*Casella Postale 34, Via delle Mura 22, Castellina in Chianti, 53011 Siena, **t** 0577 740623, **f** 0577 740950, **w** www.tuscanenterprise.it.*
Houses in Tuscany and Umbria.

Vela
*Via Colombo 16, Castiglione della Pescaia, **t** 0564 933495, **e** lavela@ouverture.it.*
Villas and flats at the seaside and in panoramic locations.

Eating Out

Florentine Specialities 224
Eating Out 224
The Medieval Core 225
West Florence 225
North and East Florence 229
The Oltrarno 231
Fiesole 233
Outside the Centre 234

Florentine Specialities

Florence in its loftier moods likes to call itself the 'birthplace of international haute cuisine', a claim that has very much to do with Catherine de' Medici, a renowned trencherwoman, who brought a brigade of Florentine chefs with her to Paris and taught the Frenchies how to eat artichokes, but has little to do with the city's contribution to the Italian kitchen.

Florentine food is on the whole extremely simple, with the emphasis on the individual flavours and fresh ingredients. A typical *primo* could be *pappardelle*, a type of wide tagliatelle egg-pasta, served usually with a meat sauce, or game such as wild boar, rabbit and duck. Soups are also popular: try the *minestrone toscano* with a base of *cavolo nero*, a kind of black cabbage with long, slim crinkly leaves and peculiar to Tuscany, *borlotti* beans and potatoes.

The most famous main course in Florence is the *bistecca alla fiorentina*, a large steak on the bone, 2 inches thick, cut from loin of beef and cooked on charcoal simply seasoned with salt and pepper. Offal lovers should go for *trippa alla fiorentina*, tripe stewed with tomatoes and sprinkled with parmesan. As for the vegetables, you could try *piselli alla fiorentina*, peas cooked with oil, parsley and diced bacon, or *tortino di carciofi*, a delicious omelette with fried artichokes, *fagioli all'uccelletto*, cannellini beans stewed with tomatoes, garlic and sage and *spinaci saltati*, fresh spinach sautéed with garlic and olive oil.

Florentine desserts tend to be sweet and fattening: *bomboloni alla crema* are vanilla-filled doughnuts and *le fritelle di San Giuseppe* are bits of deep-fried batter covered in sugar. If you prefer cheese, try the sturdy *pecorino toscano*.

For better or worse, the real Florentine specialities don't turn up on many restaurant menus, and you'll probably never learn what a Florentine cook can do with cockscombs or calves' feet.

Tuscan Wines

Quaffing glass after glass of Chianti inspired Elizabeth Barrett Browning to write her best poetry, and the wines of Tuscany may bring out the best in you as well.

Tuscany produces 39 DOC (Denominazione di Origine Controllata) and DOCG (the G stands for Garantita) wines, including some of Italy's noblest reds: the dry, ruby red Brunello di Montalcino and the garnet Vino Nobile di Montepulciano, deep red with the fragrance of violets. Chianti may be drunk young or as a Riserva (aged longer), especially the higher octane Chianti Classico. There are seven other DOC Chianti wines (Montalbano, Rufina, Colli Fiorentini, Colli Senesi, Colli Aretini, Colline Pisa and simple Chianti). Sangiovese is the chief grape of all Chianti as well as all the classified red wines of Tuscany.

Lesser known DOC reds include dry, bright red Rosso delle Colline Lucchesi, from the hills north of Lucca; hearty Pomino Rosso, from a small area east of Rufina in the Mugello; Carmignano, a consistently fine ruby red that can take considerable ageing, produced just west of Florence; and Morellino di Scansano, from the hills south of Grosseto, a dry red to be drunk young or old. The three other DOC reds from the coast are Parrina Rosso, from Parrina which is near Orbetello; Montescudaio Rosso; and Elba Rosso, a happy island wine, little of which makes it to the mainland. All three have good white versions as well.

Of the Tuscan whites, the most notable is Vernaccia di San Gimignano (also a Riserva), dry and golden in colour, the perfect complement to seafood; delicious, but more difficult to find, are dry, straw-coloured Montecarlo from the hills east of Lucca and Candia dei Colli Apuani, a light wine from the mountains of marble near Carrara. From the coast comes Bolgheri, white or rosé, both fairly dry. Cortona and its valley produce Bianco Vergine Valdichiana, a fresh and lively wine; from the hills around Montecatini comes the golden, dry Bianco della Valdinievole. Bianco di Pitigliano, of a yellow straw colour, is a celebrated accompaniment to lobster.

Eating Out

Like any sophisticated city with lots of visitors, Florence has plenty of fine restaurants; even in the cheaper places standards are high, and if you don't care for anything fancier, there will be lots of good red Chianti to wash down your meal.

In many places you'll often find restaurants offering a *menu turistico* – full, set meals usually of meagre inspiration for €12–15. Good, imaginative chefs often offer a *menu degustazione* – a set-price gourmet meal that allows you to taste their daily specialities and seasonal dishes. Both of these are cheaper than if you had ordered the same food à la carte. When you leave a restaurant you will be given a receipt (*ricevuto fiscale*) which according to Italian law you must take with you out of the door and carry for at least 300m.

When you eat out, mentally add to the bill (*conto*) the bread and cover charge (*pane e coperto*, €1.30–2.60) and a 10 per cent service charge. This is often included in the bill (*servizio compreso*); if not, it will say *servizio non compreso*, and you'll have to do your own arithmetic. Additional tipping is at your discretion; in family-owned and -run places just round up to the nearest couple of euros.

Note that many of the best places are likely to close for at least part of August; you would also be wise to call ahead and reserve, even a day or two in advance.

Price Categories

Prices quoted for meals in this book are for an average complete meal Italian-style, with wine, for one person.

expensive €42 and up
moderate €20–42
inexpensive below €20

The Medieval Core

Restaurants

There are not many good restaurants in this area.But central Florence, by popular demand, is full of *tavole calde*, pizzerias, cafeterias and snack bars, where you can grab a sandwich or a salad, if the restaurants below don't take your fancy.

Moderate

Antico Fattore E5
Via Lambertesca 1/3r, ***t*** *055 288975,* ***w*** *www.anticofattore.it;* ***bus*** *B; wheelchair accessible.* ***Open*** *Mon–Sat 12.15–2.45 and 7.15–10.30; closed 2 weeks in Aug.*
This traditional Florentine trattoria, popular with locals and tourists alike, suffered serious damage in the 1993 Uffizi bomb, but it is back in business now and serving excellent and reasonably priced local dishes. Try pasta with wild boar or deer sauce, 'Il Fritto' (deep-fried rabbit, chicken and brains) and *involtini* with artichoke hearts.

The Fusion Bar D5
Gallery Hotel Art, Vicolo dell'Oro 5, ***t*** *055 27263,* ***w*** *www.lungarno hotels.com;* ***bus*** *A, B; wheelchair accessible.* ***Open*** *Tues–Sun 7.30pm–10.30, Sat and Sun brunch 11.30–2.30.*
If you are fed up with rustic food and rustic decor, go for something completely different in the ultra-cool, East-meets-West atmosphere of the Gallery hotel's bar and restaurant. Their version of 'fusion food' (rather strange sushi combinations such as those involving foie gras or ratatouille and mayonnaise) is not completely convincing, but the setting makes up for it. They also serve light lunches, and brunch at the weekends.

Ottorino E4
Via delle Oche 12/16r, ***t*** *055 21515;* ***bus*** *A; wheelchair accessible.* ***Open*** *Mon–Sat 12.15–2.30 and 7.15–10.30; closed the second half of Aug.*
An elegant restaurant just south of the Duomo which serves typically Tuscan food, including a mixed platter of deep-fried brains, tiny lamb cutlets and vegetables.

Inexpensive

Coquinarius E4
Via della Oche 15r, ***t*** *055 230 2153;* ***bus*** *A; limited wheelchair accessibility.* ***Open*** *Sept–April daily 9am–11pm, May–Aug Mon–Sat 9am–11pm.*
You can eat or drink just about anything at this café/wine bar/restaurant. It is a useful stop-off for a light meal or snack in the centre of tourist land. Snacks include a series of hot *crostini* (toasted Tuscan bread with various toppings) and various salads, but you can also order a pasta dish, *carpaccio*, or a vegetarian dish. Wines by the bottle or the glass.

Vini e Vecchi Sapori E5
Via dei Magazzini 3r, ***t*** *055 293045;* ***bus*** *B.* ***Open*** *Tues–Sat noon–3 and 7–10, Sun noon–3. Cash only.*
A convenient stop-off near Piazza Signoria, this traditional wine bar serves plates of cheeses, salamis and mixed *crostini* as well as hot dishes such as *ribollita*, polenta with mushrooms and hot pecorino with honey.

Cafés

Caffè Italiano E4
Via Condotta 56r, ***t*** *055 291082. Cash only.*
On two levels; downstairs for standing at the bar, upstairs for a longer sit. Coffee, tea and cakes are great, and you can also enjoy a light lunch here.

Rivoire E5
Piazza della Signoria 5r.
Florence's most elegant and classy watering hole is, with a marble-detailed interior, as lovely as the piazza itself.

Gelaterie

Festa del Gelato E4
Via del Corso 75r.
Over 100 variations of ice cream.

Il Granduca E4
Via dei Calzaiuoli 57r. Closed Wed.
Creamy concoctions that challenge those of nearby rival Perché No.

L'Oasi E4
5 Via dell'Oriuolo, near the Duomo.
Sophisticated flavours and a good choice of cakes.

Perché No E4
Via Tavolini 194, near Via Calzaiuoli.
Another challenger for the *gelato* throne with wonderful ice cream in 1940s surroundings.

West Florence

Restaurants

Expensive

The Bristol D4
Via dei Pescioni 2, ***t*** *055 287814;* ***bus*** *A.* ***Open*** *daily 8–11pm.*
On the whole, hotel restaurants are not the best bet in Florence, but the Bristol (at the Helvetia & Bristol hotel) is a notable exception, featuring Tuscan or international dishes, all well prepared and impeccably served. Surroundings are intimate and elegant with lots of dark velvet and antique paintings.

Coco Lezzone D4
Via del Parioncino 26r, off Lungarno Corsini, ***t*** *055 287178;* ***bus*** *6, B.* ***Open*** *Mon–Sat 12.30–2 and 8–10.30.*
In old Florentine dialect, the name means big, smelly cook, but this shouldn't put you off. The food here – Tuscan classics using ingredients of the highest quality – is

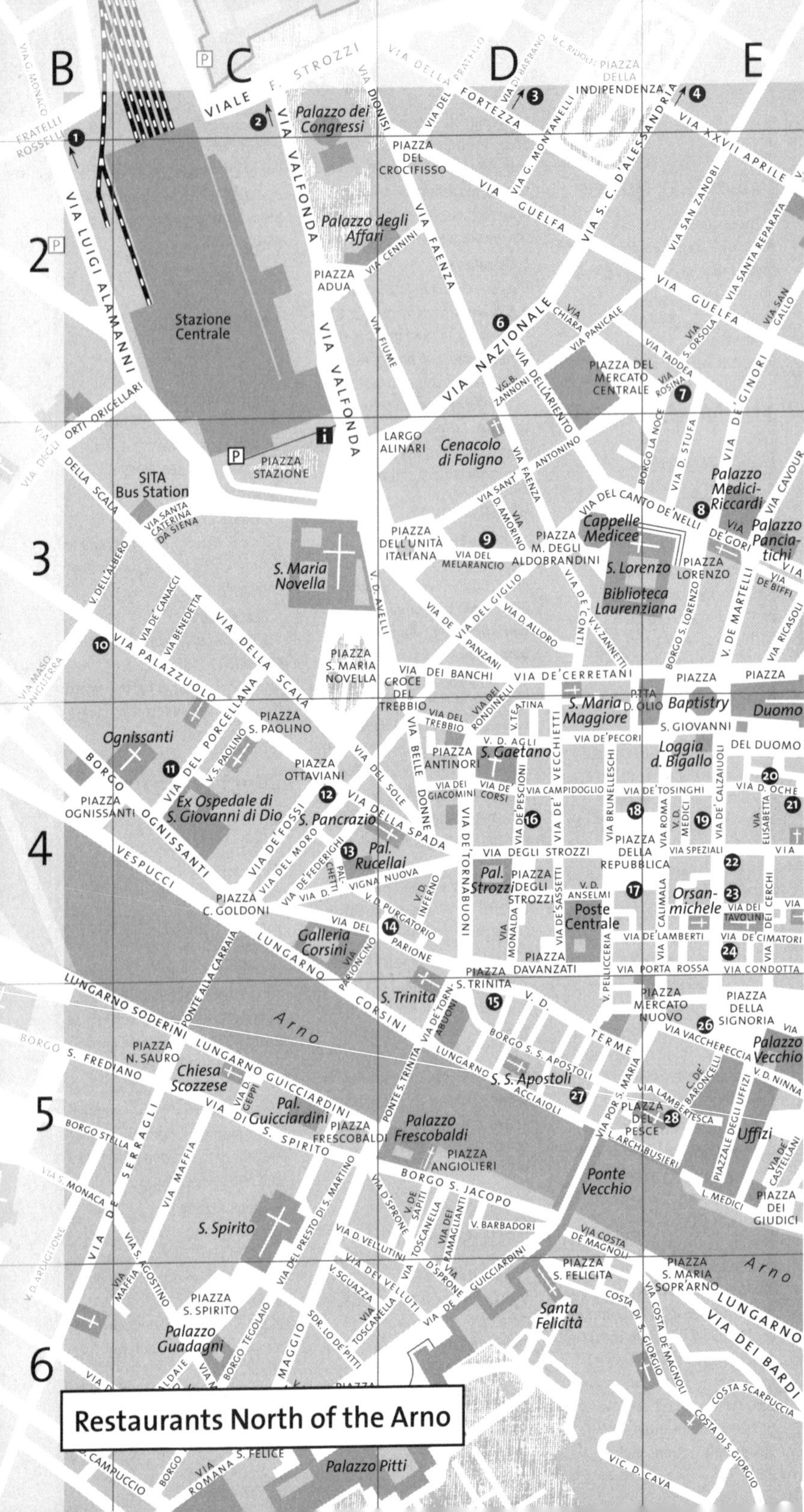

Restaurants North of the Arno
B
C
D
E
2
3
4
5
6
Stazione Centrale
Palazzo dei Congressi
Palazzo degli Affari
Cenacolo di Foligno
SITA Bus Station
S. Maria Novella
Cappelle Medicee
S. Lorenzo
Biblioteca Laurenziana
Palazzo Medici-Riccardi
Palazzo Panciatichi
Baptistry
Duomo
S. Maria Maggiore
Loggia d. Bigallo
S. Gaetano
Ognissanti
Ex Ospedale di S. Giovanni di Dio
S. Pancrazio
Pal. Rucellai
Pal. Strozzi
Poste Centrale
Orsanmichele
Galleria Corsini
S. Trinita
Palazzo Vecchio
S. S. Apostoli
Uffizi
Chiesa Scozzese
Pal. Guicciardini
Palazzo Frescobaldi
Ponte Vecchio
S. Spirito
Santa Felicità
Palazzo Guadagni
Palazzo Pitti
Arno

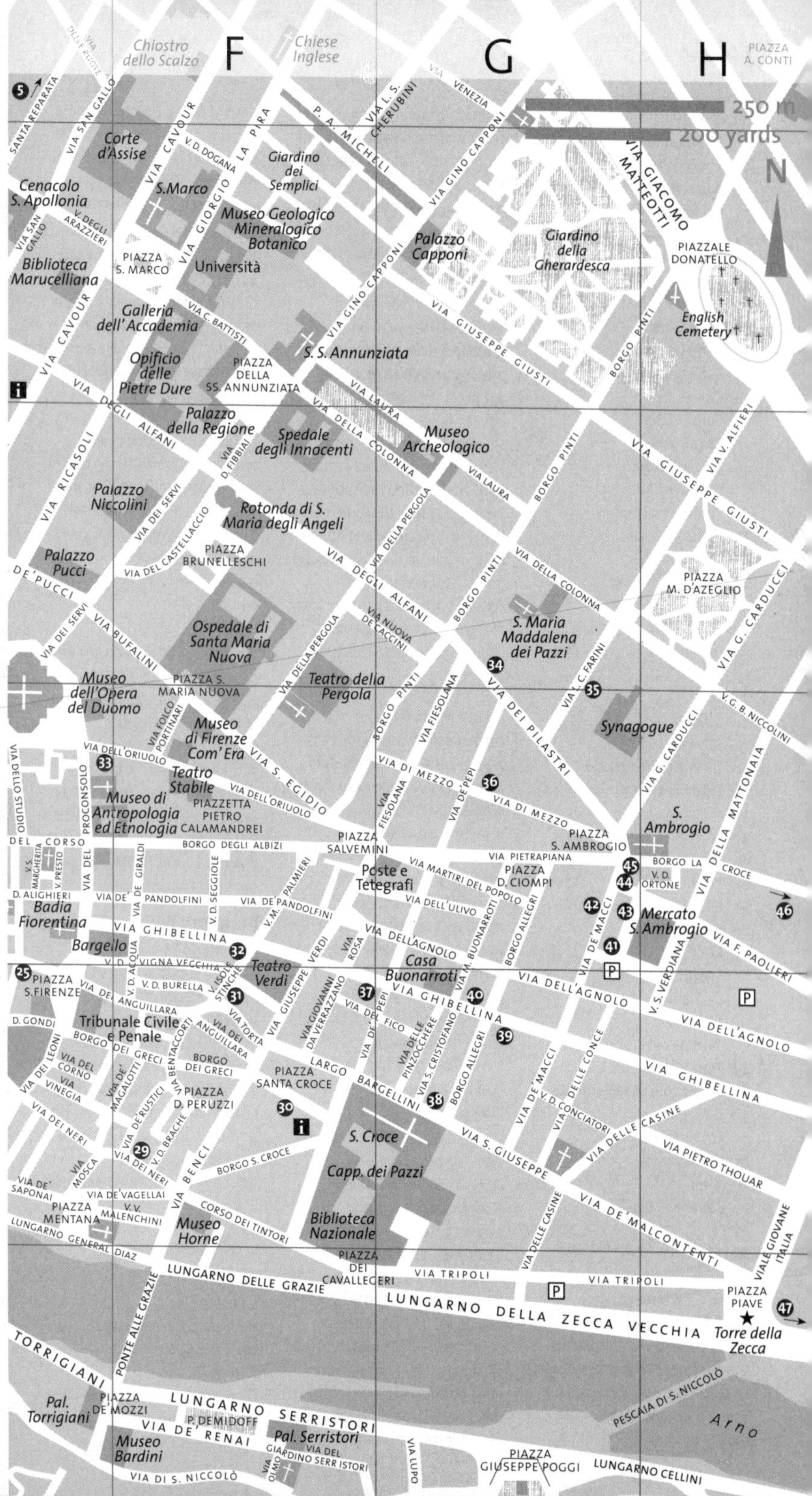

F
G
H
250 m
200 yards
N
Chiostro dello Scalzo
Chiese Inglese
Piazza A. Conti
Corte d'Assise
S.Marco
Giardino dei Semplici
Cenacolo S. Apollonia
Museo Geologico Mineralogico Botanico
Palazzo Capponi
Giardino della Gherardesca
Piazzale Donatello
English Cemetery
Biblioteca Marucelliana
Piazza S. Marco
Università
Galleria dell' Accademia
Opificio delle Pietre Dure
Piazza della SS. Annunziata
S.S. Annunziata
Palazzo della Regione
Spedale degli Innocenti
Museo Archeologico
Palazzo Niccolini
Rotonda di S. Maria degli Angeli
Palazzo Pucci
Piazza Brunelleschi
Piazza M. D'Azeglio
Ospedale di Santa Maria Nuova
S. Maria Maddalena dei Pazzi
Museo dell'Opera del Duomo
Piazza S. Maria Nuova
Teatro della Pergola
Synagogue
Museo di Firenze Com' Era
Teatro Stabile
Museo di Antropologia ed Etnologia
Piazzetta Pietro Calamandrei
Piazza Salvemini
S. Ambrogio
Piazza S. Ambrogio
Poste e Tetegrafi
Piazza D. Ciompi
Badia Fiorentina
Mercato S. Ambrogio
Bargello
Teatro Verdi
Casa Buonarroti
Piazza S.Firenze
Tribunale Civile e Penale
Piazza Santa Croce
Piazza D. Peruzzi
S. Croce
Capp. dei Pazzi
Piazza Mentana
Museo Horne
Biblioteca Nazionale
Piazza dei Cavalleggeri
Piazza Piave
Torre della Zecca
Pal. Torrigiani
Piazza de' Mozzi
P. Demidoff
Pal. Serristori
Museo Bardini
Piazza Giuseppe Poggi
Arno
Via delle Ruote
Via Santa Reparata
Via San Gallo
Via Cavour
V. D. Dogana
Via Giorgio La Pira
P. A. Micheli
Via L. S. Cherubini
Via Venezia
Via Gino Capponi
Via Giacomo Matteotti
Via San Gallo
V. degli Arazzieri
Via C. Battisti
Via Giuseppe Giusti
Borgo Pinti
Via Laura
Via della Colonna
Via degli Alfani
Via Ricasoli
Via D. Fibbiai
Via dei Servi
Via del Castellaccio
Via della Pergola
Via V. Alfieri
Via Nuova de' Caccini
Via Bufalini
De' Pucci
Via L. C. Farini
Via dei Pilastri
Via G. Carducci
V. G. B. Niccolini
Via Folco Portinari
Via dell'Oriuolo
Via S. Egidio
Via di Mezzo
Via de' Pepi
Via Fiesolana
Via della Mattonaia
Via dello Studio
Via del Proconsolo
Del Corso
Borgo degli Albizi
Via Pietrapiana
Borgo la Croce
V. D. Ortone
V. S. Margherita
V. Presto
Via de' Giraldi
V. D. Seggiole
Via M. Palmieri
Via Martiri del Popolo
D. Alighieri
Via de' Pandolfini
Via dell'Ulivo
Via de' Macci
Via Ghibellina
Via Rosa
Via dell'Agnolo
Via M. Buonarroti
Borgo Allegri
Via F. Paolieri
V. D. Vigna Vecchia
V. Isole Stinche
Via Giuseppe Verdi
V. S. Verdiana
V. D. Acqua
V. D. Burella
Via dei Anguillara
Via Giovanni da Verrazzano
Via del Fico
Via delle Pinzocchere
Via S. Cristofano
D. Gondi
Borgo dei Greci
Via Torta
Via Bentaccordi
Via de' Magalotti
Largo Bargellini
Via delle Conce
Via dei Leoni
Via del Corno
Via Vinegia
Via de' Rustici
V. D. Conciatori
Via delle Casine
Via dei Neri
V. D. Brache
Via Benci
Via S. Giuseppe
Via Pietro Thouar
Borgo S. Croce
Via Mosca
Via de' Saponai
Via de' Vagellai
V. V. Malenchini
Corso dei Tintori
Via de' Malcontenti
Lungarno General Diaz
Viale Giovane Italia
Lungarno delle Grazie
Via Tripoli
Lungarno della Zecca Vecchia
Ponte alle Grazie
Torrigiani
Lungarno Serristori
Pescaia di S. Niccolò
Via de' Renai
Via del Giardino Serristori
Via dell'Olmo
Via Lupo
Lungarno Cellini
Via di S. Niccolò
5
25
29
30
31
32
33
34
35
36
37
38
39
40
41
42
43
44
45
46
47
i
P

Map Key

40 Alle Murate
28 Antico Fattore
34 Aquacotta
38 Baldovino
39 La Baraonda
30 Boccadama
16 The Bristol
12 Buca Mario
43 Caffè Cibreo
47 Caffè Concerto
24 Caffè Italiano
44 Cibreo
14 Coco Lezzone
21 Coquinarius
46 Dolci e Dolcezze
3 Don Chisciotte
37 Enoteca Pinchiorri
22 Festa del Gelato
27 The Fusion Bar
29 Gelateria dei Neri
18 Gilli
17 Giubbe Rosse
19 Il Granduca
13 Il Latini
7 Da Mario
33 L'Oasi
15 Oliviero
32 Osteria Caffè Italiano
10 Osteria dei Cento Poveri
20 Ottorino
9 Peking
36 La Pentola dell'Oro
23 Perché No
42 Il Pizzaiuolo
26 Rivoire
35 Ruth's
1 Santa Lucia
8 Da Sergio
11 Sostanza
5 Taverna del Bronzino
45 Trattoria Cibreo
6 Il Triangolo delle Bermude
4 Il Vegetariano
41 La Via del Tè
25 Vini e Vecchi Sapori
31 Vivoli
2 Zibibbo

excellent, and the ambience is informal.

Don Chisciotte Off maps
Via C. Ridolfi 4r (between the Fortezza Basso and Piazza dell' Indipendenza), ***t*** *055 475430;* ***bus*** *4, 14.* ***Open*** *Tues–Sat 12.30–3 and 8–10.30, Sun and Mon 8–10.30; closed Aug. Booking essential.*
A small restaurant serving inventive Italian food with a particular emphasis on fish and vegetables. Let yourself be tempted by baked baby squid, delicate warm fish and vegetable salad or green tagliatelle with scampi and courgettes.

Oliviero D5
Via delle Terme 51r, 5 minutes from the Piazza della Signoria, ***t*** *055 212421;* ***bus*** *B.* ***Open*** *Mon–Sat 7.30pm–1am; closed Aug. Booking advised at weekends.*
Don't be put off by the rather sleazy decor (red velvet seating, pink candles), and the slightly bizarre clientele; the food is excellent. Feast on such curiosities as *gnudi di fiori di zucchina e ricotta* (ravioli stripped of its pasta coating with ricotta cheese and courgette flowers) and boned pigeon stuffed with chestnuts.

Moderate

Buca Mario C4
Piazza degli Ottaviani 16r, ***t*** *055 214179;* ***bus*** *A.* ***Open*** *Thurs–Tues 12.30–2.30 and 7.30–10.30. Booking advised.*
A steep flight of stairs will take you down into one of Florence's traditional 'cellar restaurants'; a place full of Florentine atmosphere with a menu to match. The soups here are superb – *pappa al pomodoro* and *ribollita* – or you could try the tagliatelle with *porcini. Ossobuco* is also excellent (cooked in tomato sauce, Florentine-style), and the *bistecca* is of the best quality.

Il Latini C4
Via dei Palchetti 6r (by Palazzo Rucellai), ***t*** *055 210916,* ***w*** *www.illatini.com;* ***bus*** *A, B.* ***Open*** *Tues–Sun 12.30–2.30 and 7.30–10.30; closed Aug.*
Il Latini is an institution in Florence, among both Italians and tourists. It is crowded (be prepared to queue – they don't accept bookings) and noisy but fun. You sit at long tables and are served huge portions of Florentine classics. The *primi* aren't great; this place is for serious carnivores in need of a fix, a *bistecca* or, more unusual, the *gran pezzo* – a vast rib roast of beef. The house wine (the family have a large estate) is good – try one of the riservas.

Osteria dei Cento Poveri B3
Via Palazzuolo 31r, ***t*** *055 218846;* ***bus*** *1, 17.* ***Open*** *May, June, Sept and Oct Thurs–Mon noon–2.30pm, rest of year Wed–Mon 7–11.30pm; closed last week Jan, first week Feb and two weeks in Aug. Booking recommended.*
A tiny restaurant near the train station which is often full of tourists and which serves refined versions of traditional Tuscan dishes. Fish plays an important part on the menu; try the gnocchi with lobster and sea bass roasted whole on a bed of sliced potatoes and black olives.

Sostanza C4
Via della Porcellana 25r (just west of Santa Maria Novella), ***t*** *055 212691;* ***bus*** *12, A.* ***Open*** *Mon–Fri 12.30–2 and 7.30–9.30.*
One of the few remaining authentic Florentine trattorias, this is a good place to eat *bistecca*. One of their most famous dishes is the simple, but delectable *petto di pollo al burro*, chicken breast sautéed in butter.

Inexpensive

Da Mario E2
Via delle Rosina 2r, ***t*** *055 218550;* ***bus*** *1, 7, 17.* ***Open*** *Mon–Sat noon–2pm. Cash only.*
Mario's trattoria, located at the back of the central market, is always buzzing, and there is usually a queue for the few rather cramped tables; don't expect a table to yourself. The food is pure Tuscan, excellent and cheap; *ribollita, spezzatino con patate* (beef stew with potatoes) and mixed boiled meats with a deliciously pungent *salsa verde*.

Peking D3
Via Melarancio 21r, ***t*** *055 282922;* ***bus*** *1, 7, 17.* ***Open*** *daily noon–3 and 6.30–11.*
There are now dozens of Chinese restaurants in Florence. Il Pechino

was among one of the first and it is still one of the more reliable ones, although don't expect more than fairly run-of-the-mill choices on the menu. Near the station.

Santa Lucia Off maps
*Via Ponte alle Mosse 102r (north of the Cascine), **t** 055 353255; **bus** 17. **Open** Thurs–Tues 7.30pm–1am; closed Aug. Cash only.*
There are three pizzerias in town where the pizza is genuinely Neapolitan, and this noisy, steamy, unromantic place, run by Neapolitans, is possibly the best (and the cheapest). They are topped with the sweetest tomatoes and the creamiest *mozzarella di buffala*. There are also some good seafood antipasti.

Da Sergio E3
*Piazza San Lorenzo 8r, **t** 055 281941; **bus** 1, 7, 17. **Open** Mon–Sat noon–2; closed hols.*
Hidden behind the market stalls, this family-run trattoria serves Florentine standards in two big rooms where you sit at communal tables; it bustles with locals and tourists 'in the know'. On Tuesdays and Fridays they also serve fish dishes: *baccalà* (salt cod) in tomato sauce and a deliciously sweet *inzimino* (squid and Swiss chard stew).

Cafés

Gilli D4
*Piazza della Repubblica 13–14r. **Open** Wed–Mon.*
Dates back to 1733, when the Mercato Vecchio still occupied this area; its two panelled back rooms are especially pleasant in the winter.

Giubbe Rosse D4
Piazza della Repubblica.
Another famous café, rendezvous of Florence's literati at the turn of the century; the chandelier-lit interior has changed little since.

Gelaterie

Il Triangulo delle Bermude D2
Via Nazionale 61r.
Has a superb choice.

North and East Florence

Restaurants

Expensive

Caffé Concerto Off maps
*Lungarno C. Colombo 7, **t** 055 677377; **bus** 31, 32. **Open** Mon–Sat noon–2.30 and 8–11; closed 3 weeks in Aug. Booking essential at weekends.*
The setting on the north bank of the Arno to the east of the centre is lovely, and the interior is warm wood and glass with good lighting and lots of greenery. The creative cooking features hearty portions of traditional ingredients, yet prepared with a different twist. Vegetarian options available. The wine list is exceptional.

Cibreo G4
*Via dei Macci 118r, **t** 055 234 1100; **bus** A, C. **Open** Tues–Sat 12.50–2.30 and 7.30–11.15; closed Aug. Booking essential.*
One of the most Florentine of Florentine restaurants, Cibreo is a stone's throw from the lively market of Sant'Ambrogio. The decor is simple – food is the main concern, and all of it is market-fresh. You can go native and order tripe antipasto, pumpkin soup, and cockscombs and kidneys, or play it safe with prosciutto from the Casentino, a fragrant soup (no pasta here) of tomatoes, mussels and bell-pepper, leg of lamb stuffed with artichokes or duck with sultanas and pine nuts. Top it off with a delicious lemon *crostata* or cheesecake; accompany it with an excellent choice of Italian or French wines, or a prized bottle of Armagnac. Their chocolate cake is the answer to every chocaholic's dreams.

Enoteca Pinchiorri F5
*Via Ghibellina 87, near the Casa Buonarroti, **t** 055 242777; **bus** A, 14. **Open** Mon and Wed 7.30–10pm, Tues and Thurs–Sat 12.30–2 and 7.30–10; closed Aug. Booking essential.*

Couples' City

Try one of these for a romantic meal: **Enoteca Pinchiorri**, *see* p.229; **Alle Murate**, *see* p.229; **Caffè Concerto**, *see* p.229; **Oliviero**, *see* p.228; **Osteria del Caffè Italiano**, *see* p.230; **The Bristol**, *see* p.225; **Rivoire**, *see* p.225; **Gilli**, *see* p.229; **Hemingway**, *see* p.233.

One of the finest gourmet restaurants in Italy; the owners inherited the building, a wine shop, some 10 years ago, and converted it into a beautifully appointed restaurant, with meals served in a garden court in the summer. They've also increased what was already in the cellars to an astonishing collection of some 80,000 bottles of the best Italy and France have to offer. The cooking, a mixture of nouvelle cuisine and traditional Tuscan recipes, wins prizes every year, and they have been awarded two Michelin rosettes. They also do a series of set menus; you can choose between Tuscan, fish or the day's menu based on market availability. Italians tend to complain about the minute portions. Prices are reckoned to be €130 excluding wine, but the sky's the limit if you go for a more interesting bottle.

Alle Murate G5
*Via Ghibellina 52r, **t** 055 240618, **w** www.florence-gourmet.it; **bus** A, 14. **Open** Tues–Sun 7.45pm–midnight. Booking advisable.*
This elegant, romantic, relaxed restaurant is very popular for its 'creative traditional' food. There are two set menus, one of Tuscan dishes and the other offering something a little different. Even when old friends such as lasagne and *bistecca* appear, they are given an innovative touch. There is plenty of fish – recommended dishes include spaghetti with sea bass, steamed octopus on a bed of mashed potato, and squid and mangetout. Meat lovers might try lamb's brain salad, pigeon stuffed with peppers and potatoes, or duck's livers with ceps and rosemary.

Vegetarian Restaurants

Florence has only two vegetarian restaurants, Ruth's and Il Vegetariano, but there are many restaurants offering vegetarian options. And of course there are always vegetarian pasta and pizza dishes to be had.

The following offer **vegetarian options**: Caffè Concerto, *see* p.229; Baldovino, *see* p.230; La Pentola dell'Oro, *see* p.231; Borgo Antico, *see* p.233; Boccadama, see p.230.

Ruth's G3
*Via Farini 2/A, **t** 055 248 0888; **bus** A, C. **Open** Sun–Thurs 12.30–2.30 and 8–10.30, Fri 12.30–2.30, Sat 8–10.30. **Inexpensive**.*
With a bright and modern interior, this new kosher vegetarian restaurant next to the synagogue also serves fish and Middle Eastern dishes. One of their specialities is the brick, which tastes better than it sounds: a kind of savoury pastry, filled with fish, potatoes or cheese, and fried. In the evenings there is a spicy fish couscous.

Il Vegetariano Off maps
*Via delle Ruote 30/r, **t** 055 47030; **bus** 10, 31, 32. **Open** Tues–Sat lunch and dinner, Sun dinner. **Inexpensive**.*
One-year membership (€1) is required for entrance to this vegetarian centre, which has excellent fresh food with a wide choice of soups, salads and more substantial dishes in pleasant surroundings.

Taverna del Bronzino Off maps
*Via delle Ruote 25–27r, **t** 055 495220; **bus** 1, 17. **Open** Mon–Sat 12.30–2.30 and 7.30–10.30, closed 3 weeks in Aug. Booking advisable.*
An elegant, traditional restaurant in a residential area north of the Duomo. The menu features plenty of traditional and less traditional Tuscan dishes – the *bistecca alla fiorentina* is succulent and tender, and the truffle-flavoured tortellini famous; there are also several fish choices for each course.

Moderate

Baldovino G5
*Via Giuseppe 22r (Piazza S. Croce), **t** 055 241773; **bus** C; wheelchair accessible. **Open** Tues–Sun 11.30–2.30 and 7–11.30.*
This excellent trattoria/pizzeria has been given a complete face-lift by a young Scotsman, who offers anything from a big salad, a filled foccaccia or a pizza (baked in a wood-burning oven) to a full menu of pastas, fish and meat (vegetarian options too). The steaks served in various ways, originate from the Val di Chiana (where all good steaks should come from). The wine list is interesting: the same owner runs a wine bar just across the road.

La Baraonda G5
*Via Ghibellina 67r, **t** 055 234 1171; **bus** A, 14; wheelchair accessible. **Open** Mon 7.30–10.30pm, Tues–Sat 12.30–2.30 and 7.30–10.30. Booking advised. Amex not accepted.*
A calm and civilized restaurant near Santa Croce which serves variations on traditional dishes: lettuce risotto, roast suckling pig with apple sauce (unusual in Tuscany), and stuffed baby squid.

Boccadama F5
*Piazza Santa Croce 25–26r, **t** 055 243640; **bus** B, C; wheelchair accessible. **Open** Tues–Sun 11.30–2.30 and 7.30–11 for meals, 8am–midnight for wine, cheese, and cold dishes.*
This café/wine bar/restaurant enjoys a stunning location on Piazza Santa Croce; the ambience is 'new' rustic and mellow with background jazz and a laid-back crowd in the evenings. Lunch times are a bit touristy and the menu is simpler. Try one of the *sformati* (vegetable flans), *farro* (spelt) soup with asparagus or lamb with artichokes; there are also good vegetarian options. The set *menu degustazione* is excellent value at about €25.

Osteria del Caffè Italiano F4
*Via Isola delle Stinche 11, **t** 055 289368, **w** www.florence-gourmet.it; **bus** A, 14; wheelchair accessible. **Open** Tues–Sat noon–1am. Booking advisable evenings and weekends.*
Located in beautiful and elegant rooms in a Renaissance palazzo, the food here is pure Tuscan, as is the superb wine list, and although prices are quite steep, the setting is gorgeous. Excellent salamis and cured hams, pasta with *sugo di cinghiale* (wild boar), grilled meats and home-made desserts. Wine and cold dishes are available all day; more substantial fare at meal times. Outdoor seating too.

Zibibbo Off maps
*Vai di Terzollina 3r, **t** 055 433383; **bus** 14; wheelchair accessible. **Open** Mon–Sat 1–3 and 8–11.*
Zibibbo is a wonderful restaurant serving what is essentially very traditional Tuscan fare but in a very stylish, un-Tuscan setting (pink-varnished floorboards, contemporary furniture, big windows looking over Florence). There is lots of choice between meat and fish dishes: *pasta e fagioli*, delicious *spaghetti alle vongole*, *inzimino* (squid stew with Swiss chard), tripe *alla fiorentina*, fricassée of rabbit and pigeon wrapped in *lardo* and cooked with prunes. Worth the trip up to the northernmost extremes of town.

Inexpensive

Aquacotta G3
*Via dei Pilastri 51r (north of Piazza S. Ambrogio), **t** 055 242907; **bus** A, C. **Open** Mon–Sat 7.30–10pm.*
The bread soup which lends this trattoria its name is a simple but delicious dish. You could follow that by deep-fried rabbit accompanied by crisply fried courgette flowers.

Il Pizzaiuolo G4
*Via dei Macci 113r, near Sant'Ambrogio, **t** 055 241171; **bus** C. **Open** Mon–Sat 12.30–3.30 and 7.30–1; closed Aug.*
One of the best pizzerias in town. The *pizzaiuolo* (pizza maker) is

Neapolitan, and his creations are puffy and light. There's lots more to choose from as well – especially seafood – if you can get past the queues.

La Pentola dell' Oro G4
*Via di Mezzo 24, north of Piazza Salvemini, **t** 055 241821; **bus** A. **Open** Mon–Sat 7.30–11.30pm. Booking advisable.*
Also known as Da Alessi after the mythical owner, this is one of the best value-for-money places in Florence. The menu is long and varied, and many of the superb dishes are based on ancient recipes. There are a number of vegetarian and salad choices. It is technically a club, so you may be asked to pay a small membership fee.

Trattoria Cibreo G4
*Via de' Macci 114, at the back of Cibreo, **t** 055 234 1100; **bus** C. **Open** Tues–Sat 12.50–2.30 and 7.30–11.15.*
This little annexe to smart Cibreo (*see* above) is a real find. The food is exactly the same (excluding the odd more extravagant dish), but it is served at rustic wooden tables on less expensive porcelain. So you can still eat the exquisite yellow pepper soup, cockscombs, stuffed rabbit and superb chocolate cake while gloating over the fact that your bill will be a third of that of your neighbours round the corner.

Cafés

Caffè Cibreo G4
Via del Verrocchio 5r.
Next to the Sant' Ambrogio food market; bustling at market times, more elegant in the evening.

Dolci e Dolcezze Off maps
*Piazza Cesare Beccaria 8r, at the top of Ponte San Niccolò, **t** 055 234 5438. **Open** Tues–Sun.*
The most delicious cakes, pastries and marmalades in the city – the *crostate, torte* and *bavarese* are expensive but worth every euro. It now has another shop in Via del Corso 41r.

La Via del Té G4
Piazza Ghiberti 22r.
Looking onto the Sant' Ambrogio food market, with a huge range of teas to choose from plus sweet and savoury snacks.

Gelaterie

Gelateria dei Neri F5
*Via dei Neri 20/22r, near Santa Croce. **Open** Thurs–Tues.*
Tasty cones, but no seats.

Vivoli F5
*Via Isola delle Stinche 7r (between the Bargello and S. Croce). **Open** Tues–Sun.*
Florence's claim to being the ice-cream capital of the world owes much to the decadently delicious confections and rich *semifreddi* served here.

The Oltrarno

Restaurants

Expensive

Pane e Vino E6
*Via San Niccolò 70r, just in from Ponte alla Grazie, **t** 055 247 6956; **bus** C, D. **Open** Mon–Sat 7.30pm–midnight. Booking advisable.*
This pleasant and informal restaurant started life as an *enoteca* and still has a superb wine list and very knowledgeable staff to go with it. If you are happy to trust the chef's choice, go for the *menu degustazione*; it changes daily, has seven small courses and is very good value. With any luck, the porcini mushroom flan will be available – it is superb.

Moderate

Angiolino C5
*Via Santo Spirito 57r, **t** 055 239 8976; **bus** 11, 36, 37. **Open** Tues–Sun 12.30–2.30 and 7.30–10.*
Although it has lost some of its genuinely 'characteristic' qualities after recent renovation, Angiolino is still a fairly reliable place to eat Tuscan standards. The vegetable antipasti are especially good, and the simple *pollastrina sulla griglia* (grilled spring chicken) is mouth-wateringly tasty.

Antico Ristoro di Cambi B4
*Via Sant'Onofrio 1r, **t** 055 217134; **bus** 6, D. **Open** Mon–Sat noon–2.30 and 7.30–10.30. Booking advisable.*
Some way to the west of the centre, this is a very popular place with the Florentine intelligentsia. The food is genuinely Florentine, the decor rustic. The soups – classic *ribollita* and *pappa al pomodoro* – are tasty and warming, and the *bistecca alla fiorentina* the real McCoy.

Cavolo Nero B5
*Via dell' Ardiglione 22, **t** 055 294744; **bus** D, 11, 36, 37. **Open** Mon–Sat noon–2.30 and 8–11; closed 2 weeks mid-Aug. Diners Club not accepted.*
This little restaurant, tucked away in a side street near Piazza del Carmine, has quite a following among Florentine trendies. The interior is white on yellow with tables crowded into the attractive room and there is a pretty garden at the back with outdoor seating. The food is mainly Mediterranean with a twist (curried monk fish, rabbit with wild fennel), but there are also plenty of local standards such as spaghetti with clams.

Il Guscio A5
*Via dell'Orto 49, **t** 055 224421; **bus** D; wheelchair accessible. **Open** Tues–Sat 8–11; closed Aug. Booking essential at weekends.*
This re-vamped trattoria which serves dishes from Tuscany and beyond is always busy. Try the *guanciali* (literally 'pillows') stuffed with ricotta and spinach with a pigeon sauce, fillet of beef topped with a slab of liver paté and laced with a rich sauce or roast suckling pig with potatoes. There are some fish dishes too. Desserts (including a tangy cheesecake) are excellent, and there is a long wine list. Outdoor seating too.

Momoyama C5
*Borgo San Frediano 10r, **t** 055 291840, **w** www.fionline.it/worldbusiness/yama.htm; **bus** D, 11;*

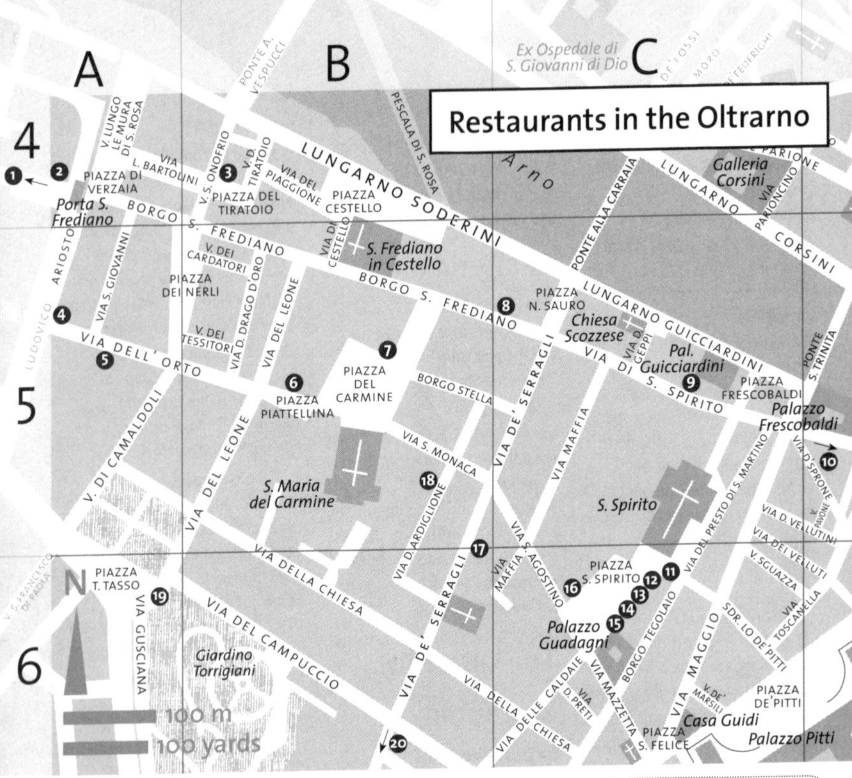

Map Key

9 Angiolino
3 Antico Ristoro di Cambi
1 Ashoka
13 Borgo Antico
12 Cabiria Café
11 La Casalinga
18 Cavolo Nero
17 Da Ginone
5 Il Guscio
6 Hemingway
8 Momoyama
16 Osteria Santo Spirito
10 Pane e Vino
15 Ricchi (*gelateria*)
14 Ristorante Ricchi
20 Da Ruggero
2 Sabatino
19 Al Tranvai
7 Trattoria del Carmine
4 La Vecchia Bettola

wheelchair accessible. ***Open*** *Tues–Sun 8pm–11.30, Sun brunch noon–3.30; closed Aug. Amex not accepted.*

The sushi (prepared in an open kitchen) in this restaurant is excellent. Minimalist designer decor, a series of intimate rooms, an art gallery in the basement and a menu featuring both Japanese (sushi, sashimi, tekkadon, tempura) and creative Italian dishes attracts a chic and sleek clientèle.

Osteria Santo Spirito C6
Piazza Santo Spirito 16r, ***t*** *055 238 2383;* ***bus*** *D.* ***Open*** *daily 12.30–2.30 and 7.30–11.30.*

Sit outside this osteria and enjoy a choice of cold dishes, pastas (try the gnocchi with melted cheese infused with truffle oil), vegetarian dishes and more. The decor inside is unusual for Florence – warm red paintwork with contemporary lighting.

Ristorante Ricchi C6
Piazza Santo Spirito 8r, ***t*** *055 215864,* ***w*** *www.caffericchi.it;* ***bus*** *D, 6; wheelchair accessible.* ***Open*** *Mon–Sat 8pm–10.30.*

This new fish restaurant has tables on magical Piazza Santo Spirito. Inside, the decor is contemporary and elegant, with tables lined up against the walls. The generous plate of antipasto is good and main courses include the catch of the day roasted on a bed of potatoes and tomatoes. There are a few meat dishes too.

Da Ruggero Off maps
Via Senese 89r, ***t*** *055 220542;* ***bus*** *11, 36, 37.* ***Open*** *Mon and Thurs–Sun noon–2.30 and 7.30–10.30; closed 3 weeks July/Aug. Booking essential.*

There are only two rather cramped rooms in Ruggero's family-run trattoria, so you must book in advance. The dark wood panelling and laden counter just inside the entrance are typical of old-style eateries in Florence, and so is the menu. Choose from the traditional soups (the *minestra di farro* – spelt soup – is wonderful), roast and grilled meats or Florentine braised beef with potatoes.

La Vecchia Bettola A5
Viale Ariosto 32–34r, west of the Carmine, ***t*** *055 224158;* ***bus*** *12, 13.* ***Open*** *Tues–Sat noon–2.30 and 7.30–10.*
Marble-topped tables, wooden stools and benches and tiled walls make up the interior of this noisy trattoria. The food is great; the menu changes daily, but you can nearly always find their classic *tagliolini con funghi porcini* (egg pasta with ceps). The grilled meats are tasty and succulent, and the ice cream comes from Vivoli.

Inexpensive

Ashoka Off maps
Via Pisana 86r, ***t*** *055 224446;* ***bus*** *6; wheelchair accessible.* ***Open*** *Mon–Sat 7pm–midnight.*
One of several Indian restaurants in Florence, the Ashoka is situated just outside Porta San Frediano. As long as you don't make comparisons to Indian food in the UK, you will be satisfied with the well-cooked if fairly standard fare on offer here, and it makes a welcome change from pasta and *bistecca*.

Borgo Antico C6
Piazza Santo Spirito 6, ***t*** *055 210437;* ***bus*** *D.* ***Open*** *daily 12.30–2.30 and 7.30–11.30.*
This pizzeria is popular with a young trendy crowd, and you may have to wait, especially in summer for a table in the square. Inside, the background music can be loud. But the pizza is good, and there are plenty of other choices – interesting pastas, big salads, vegetarian dishes, and more substantial meat and fish dishes.

La Casalinga C6
Via Michelozzi 9r, ***t*** *055 218624;* ***bus*** *D; wheelchair accessible.* ***Open*** *Mon–Sat noon–2.30 and 7–9.45.*
This family-run trattoria near Piazza Santo Spirito is always busy, and it's not surprising given the quality of the simple home cooking and the low prices. The *ribollita* (a hearty bread-based soup) is excellent.

Da Ginone B5–6
Via dei Serragli 33r, ***t/f*** *055 218758;* ***bus*** *11, 36, 37; wheelchair accessible.* ***Open*** *Mon–Sat noon–3.30 and 6.30–10.30; closed 3 weeks Aug.*
Ginone (Big Gino) serves up excellent home-cooked food in his friendly trattoria and prices range from a dirt cheap *menu turistico* (€10.50) to very reasonable. Go for *funghi porcini* in season or fish on Fridays. Special prices for guests of the nearby hostels. Outdoor seating too.

Sabatino A4
Via Pisana 2r, ***t*** *055 225955;* ***bus*** *6, D; wheelchair accessible.* ***Open*** *Mon–Fri noon–2.30 and 7.30–10.30; closed Aug.*
Now in new premises just outside the old city gate of San Frediano, this simple, family-run trattoria in the heart of the San Frediano district feels as if it has always been that way. Cooking methods, too, are of the old-fashioned variety, and prices are similarly retro. Hearty soups, tripe and kidneys are usually on the menu.

Al Tranvai A6
Piazza Torquato Tasso 14r (just south of the Carmine), ***t*** *055 225197;* ***bus*** *D.* ***Open*** *Mon–Fri 7.30–10.30pm. Booking essential in the evenings.*
The two rows of tables in this cheerful little trattoria – and the tables outside – are always full, and you may not get much elbow room. The varied menu changes daily, but the *crostini misti* (little rounds of toast with various toppings) are always on offer. Offal features strongly – tripe, *lampredotto* (intestines), chicken gizzards and other mysterious bits and pieces.

Trattoria del Carmine B5
Piazza del Carmine 18r, ***t*** *055 218601;* ***bus*** *D, 6; wheelchair accessible.* ***Open*** *Mon–Sat noon–2.30 and 7–10.30; closed 3 weeks in Aug. Booking advised on weekend evenings.*
Very much a neighbourhood trattoria, this place is friendly and has a long, reasonably priced menu. The *piatti del giorno* change daily and may include risotto with courgette flowers, Neapolitan octupus (with a spicy tomato sauce) or *pasta e fagioli* (hearty Tuscan bean soup). The Tuscan standards are always available. Outdoor seating too.

Cafés

Cabiria Café C6
Piazza Santo Spirito.
One of Florence's most recherché terraces for a Campari. Pleasant by day, noisy and trendy at night.

Hemingway B5
Piazza Piattellina 9r, ***t*** *055 284781;* ***bus*** *D, 6.* ***Open*** *Tues–Thurs 4.30pm–1am, Fri and Sat 4.30pm–2am, Sun 11am–8pm.*
Hemingway is a beautifully appointed bar done out in pale blues with rattan furniture. Although teas, coffees and, above all, chocolate are specialities, you can also enjoy cocktails, savoury snacks and light meals. Brunch is served on Sundays.

Gelaterie

Ricchi C6
Piazza Santo Spirito. Closed Sun and first half of Aug.
A huge choice and a scrumptious tiramisú.

Fiesole

45 Piazza Mino
Piazza Mino 45, ***t*** *055 599854,* ***w*** *www.contactgroup.it/45mino.htlm.* ***Open*** *Tues–Sun 12.30–3 and 7.30–midnight.* ***Moderate.***

This elegant restaurant with its pretty terrace specializes in fish dishes, but there is plenty of choice for meat-eaters too. There are two set menus or you can choose à la carte: spaghetti with mixed seafood, tagliatelle with lobster, chestnut tagliatelle with cheese and truffles, *bistecca* or the catch of the day. There is a simpler (and cheaper) lunch menu, and brunch is served at weekends from noon to 1.30pm.

Pizzeria Etrusca
*Piazza Mino 2, **t** 055 599484. **Open** Fri–Wed noon–3 and 7–1. **Moderate**.*

This bar and restaurant/pizzeria has a terrace with tables under the trees bordering Fiesole's central piazza. It is open for drinks and snacks outside meal times and serves full meals plus pizzas (which are less expensive) both at lunch and in the evenings. They are not the greatest, but it is a fun place for people watching.

Pizzeria San Domenico
*Piazza San Domenico, **t** 055 59182. **Open** Tues–Sun noon–3 and 7–1.30. **Inexpensive**.*

This bustling restaurant in the hamlet of San Domenico (on the way up to Fiesole and on the bus route) serves excellent pizzas at lunch and dinner, but lots more besides; the pasta dishes and main course salads are also good. There is a terrace and air conditioning.

Blue Bar
*Piazza Mino 39, **t** 055 597235. **Open** daily 8.30am–midnight; closed Tues in winter.*

This popular bar serves drinks and snacks (sandwiches, cakes and ice cream) throughout the day, but you can also eat a light meal at lunch time or in the evening when they serve salads, a choice of pastas and cold dishes. There is a wonderful big terrace which overlooks Florence and which makes an excellent cool-down spot after the sights of Fiesole.

Outside the Centre

Da Stefano
*Via Senese 271, Galuzzo, **t** 055 204 9105; **bus** 36, 37. **Open** Mon–Sat 7.30pm–11. Booking essential. **Expensive**.*
Now generally acknowledged to be the best fish restaurant in town, Stefano's message is *solo pesce, solo fresco a solo la sera* (only fish, only fresh and only in the evening). His fish is extraordinarily fresh; how else could he dare to serve it raw on an impressive platter of ice with tangy mayonnaise? Another visually impressive dish that doesn't fail to satisfy the palate is the *spaghetti alla Stefano* – a mountainous pile of steamy spaghetti brimful of shellfish. There is now a sushi chef, wielding a cleaver for more exotic dishes. After 10pm you can choose from a cheaper 'bistro' menu. Fun, lively, noisy place, and worth the 10-minute drive south out of town.

Bibé
*Via delle Bagnese 1r, **t** 055 204 9085; **bus** 36, 37, then taxi. **Open** Fri–Tues 12.30–2 and 7.30–9.45, Thurs 7.30–9.45pm. Booking advisable at weekends. **Moderate**.*
This old farmhouse is situated a couple of kms south of Porta Romana. It has a lovely garden (somewhat marred by its proximity to the road and mosquitos) with outdoor seating, although the inside is very pleasant, too. The food is basically Tuscan, but with the odd twist. The ceps soup with chickpeas is a good way to follow the classic *crostini* (toast topped with chicken livers), or try the *crespelle alla fiorentina* – light crepes filled with ricotta cheese and spinach. The roasts are good, as is the fried chicken and rabbit. Desserts here are creative and divine.

Da Delfina
*Via della Chiesa, Artimino, near Carmignano, **t** 055 871 8074. **Open** Tues–Sat 12.30–2.30 and 8–10.30, Sun 12.30–2.30pm. **Moderate**.*
Worth the drive out for its enchanting surroundings, lovely views, the charming atmosphere and sublime cooking – home-made tagliatelle with a sauce made from greens, risotto with garden vegetables, wild asparagus, succulent kid and lamb dishes. Outdoor seating too.

Osteria al Ponte Rotto
*Via Certaldese 8, San Casciano, **t** 055 828090; wheelchair accessible. **Open** Mon, Wed and Thurs 12.30–2pm, Fri and Sat 12.30–2 and 8–10, Sun 8–10pm. **Inexpensive**.*
Once a little trattoria at the back of the family-run grocery, things here have been smartened up, but the Osteria is still a simple place serving home-cooked food. The *zuppa lombarda* (a warming bean and bread soup) is excellent as are the grilled meats, or try the rabbit stewed with black olives. Outdoor seating too. From San Casciano (a few kms down the Siena *superstrada*) follow the signs to Montespertoli-Certaldo.

Nightlife

Bars 236
Clubs 237

Nightlife with Great Aunt Florence is still awaiting its Renaissance; according to the Florentines she's conservative, somewhat deaf and retires early – 1am is very, very late in this city. However, there are plenty of people who wish it weren't so, and slowly, slowly, Florence by night is beginning to mean more than the old *passeggiata* over the Ponte Vecchio and an ice cream, and perhaps a late trip up to Fiesole to contemplate the lights.

Meeting Places

The evening in Florence will usually begin by meeting up in a piazza. For typical crowds, head to Piazza Michelangelo (G7), where local lads and lasses perch on their scooters eating ice cream. Or stroll along to the central Piazza della Repubblica (D4) then down Via Calzaiuoli to the Ponte Vecchio and back again.

For the more alternative and trendy crowd, head for Piazza Santo Spirito (C6), especially in the summer months when the piazza and the church steps are packed with young people served by the surrounding pubs and bars. You could meet in Il Cabiria or on Piazza del Carmine in front of La Dolce Vita disco bar. Other summer meeting places include Parterre and Anfiteatro delle Cascine (*see* 'Outdoor Summer Venues', below).

Bars

The Medieval Core

Astor Caffè E4
Piazza Duomo 20r, ***t*** *055 239 9000;* ***bus*** *1, 7, 17.* ***Open*** *Mon–Sat 7am–1am; closed 2 weeks in Aug.*
A relatively new stop-off on the trendy night circuit, Astor is a huge space in the shadow of the Duomo done out in chrome and red overtones. Occasional live gigs pepper live DJ jazz-dance nights and you can also play at the Internet points.

JJ Cathedral Pub E3–4
Piazza San Giovanni 44r, ***t*** *055 280260;* ***bus*** *A, 1, 7.* ***Open*** *daily 11am–1am.*
The tiny balcony of this Irish pub looks straight onto the Baptistry and makes for prime people-watching territory on warm evenings; the bar is on two floors and a popular watering hole.

West Florence

Apollo D3
Via dell'Ariento 41r, ***t*** *055 215672;* ***bus*** *1, 17.* ***Open*** *Tues–Sat noon–3 and 6pm–3am, Sun noon–3 and 9pm–3am; closed 2 weeks in Aug.*
Full of sleek Italians, this energetic bar gets packed late at night when Djs take over from cocktails and nibbles.

Il Bovaro Off maps
Via Pisana 3r, ***t*** *055 220 7057;* ***bus*** *6.* ***Open*** *Mon–Fri and Sun 7pm–1am, Fri and Sat 7pm–2am.*
One of an increasing number of microbreweries in Tuscany, Il Bovaro brews pretty good beer on the premises; there is a choice of four types. You can also eat here and there are tables outside.

Caffè Megara D4
Via della Spada 15–17r, ***t*** *055 211837;* ***bus*** *A, 6.* ***Open*** *Mon–Sat 8am–2am.*
Just off chic Tornabuoni, this relaxed and friendly bar is a great place for daytime drinks and snacks, evening cocktails (happy hour 5–8pm) and night owls. It offers student discounts after 9pm and has loads of reading material if you want to chill out with a newspaper or magazine.

Capocaccia C4–D5
Lungarno Corsini 12/14r, ***t*** *055 210751;* ***bus*** *A, B.* ***Open*** *Tues–Sun noon–2am.*
This elegant bar has been flavour of the month among Florentine trendies for a while now. Its enviable location on the river attracts crowds all day long, but at *apperitivo* time (7pm and on), things liven up and there is a generous buffet of nibbles in the central room; punters spill out onto the Lungarno in warmer weather, and loud music accompanies the action.

The Fiddler's Elbow C3
Piazza Santa Maria Novella 7r, ***t*** *055 215056;* ***bus*** *A, 12.* ***Open*** *Mon–Thurs 3pm–1am, Friday 3pm–2am, Sat 2pm–2am, Sun 2pm–1am. Cash only.*
One of the original pubs, some live music and an expat atmosphere. A handy place to wait for a train, but a bit grim.

Rose's C–D4
Via del Parione 26r, ***t*** *055 287090;* ***bus*** *A, B.* ***Open*** *Mon–Sat 8am–1.30am, Sun 5pm–1.30am.*
Rose's has been up there among the Chosen Few of Florentine hip bars for years now. It is a sophisticated yet relaxed place where you can eat sushi from 7 to 11pm (excluding Mon) or sit on high stools at the bar or in one of the back rooms.

La Rotonda Off maps
Via Il Prato 10/16r, ***t*** *055 265 4644;* ***bus*** *D, 12.* ***Open*** *daily 7.30pm–1am.*
This circular building used to be a Ferrari showroom. Now it is a noisy, crowded, multilevelled pizzeria/pub modelled on an American saloon bar which hosts DJs and, from Thurs to Sun, live bands. Fun, if you like that kind of thing.

North and East Florence

Caffè Cibreo G4
Via del Verrocchio 5r, ***t*** *055 234 5853;* ***bus*** *A, C.* ***Open*** *Tues–Sun 8am–1am; closed Aug. Cash only.*
Next to the Sant' Ambrogio food market; bustling at market times, more elegant in the evening.

Enoteca Baldovino G5
Via San Giuseppe 18r, ***t*** *055 234 7220;* ***bus*** *C.* ***Open*** *daily noon–midnight; closed 4–6pm and on Mon in winter.*
One of only a handful of wine bars in Florence that stay open till late, Baldovino is located down the northern side of Santa Croce. There is a substantial menu

offering hot and cold dishes, but you can also while away the evening with a bottle of wine chosen from the comprehensive list. There are also plenty of wines by the glass.

H2O2 F4–G5
*Via Ghibellina 47r, **t** 055 243239; **bus** 14. **Open** Thurs–Tues 9am–midnight.*
A good pre-clubbing bar frequented by local posers getting into the mood with progressive house and drum'n'bass sounds. Minimum drinks charge on Fri and Sat.

The Lion's Fountain F4
*Borgo degli Albizi 34r, **t** 055 234 4412; **bus** A, 14. **Open** daily 6pm–2am; closed Aug. Cash only.*
A nice pub which also serves food.

Porfirio Rubirosa C–D1
*Viale Strozzi 18/20r, **t** 055 490965; **bus** 4, 12, 13, 14. **Open** Tues–Sun 7am–2am.*
A very slick, smart bar with a clientele to match just opposite the Fortezza da Basso. Drinks, snacks and light meals.

Rex Caffè G4
*Via Fiesolana 25r, **t** 055 248 0331; **bus** C, 6. **Open** Mon–Thurs and Sun 5pm–1.30am, Fri and Sat 5pm–2.30am; closed June–beginning Sept.*
Another super-cool music bar that has been around awhile. The decor is sensual modernist and DJs play the latest session sounds. Happy hour (5–9.30) is accompanied by tapas and the cocktails are great.

The William F5
*Via Magliabecchi 7–11r, **t** 055 263 8357; **bus** A, B. **Open** Mon–Thurs and Sun 1pm–1am, Fri and Sat 1pm–2am.*
Pastiche of an English pub.

The Oltrarno

Cafè Cabiria D6
*Piazza Santo Spirito 4r, **t** 055 215732; **bus** D. **Open** Mon, Wed and Thurs 8am–1am, Fri–Sun 8am–1.30am. Cash only.*
Small, quiet by day, trendy and heaving at night.

Il Rifrullo F–G6
*Via S. Niccolò 55r, **t** 055 234 2621; **bus** D. **Open** daily 8am–2am; closed 2 weeks in Aug.*
An older pub/wine bar, with a great spread of free nibbles during cocktail hour. There's no word for 'cosy' in Italian, but the Rifrullo does the best it can.

Le Volpi e l'Uva D5–6
*Piazza de' Rossi, **t** 055 239 8132; **bus** D. **Open** Mon–Sat 11am–8pm.*
A tiny, modern wine bar tucked away in a little piazza just south of the Ponte Vecchio, Le Volpi e L'Uva is a great place to sample lesser-known Italian wines either by the glass, perched on one of the high stools at the bar, or by the bottle to take away. The owners are knowledgeable and helpful and will help you choose. To sop up the wine, there is a selection of excellent cheeses, patés and other nibbles.

Clubs

Information on clubs is given in the monthly *Firenze Spettacolo* listings magazine. Check out each one's offerings as many places have themed evenings. Or head to one of the squares listed under 'Meeting Places' above and ask around to find out what's going on.

West Florence

Auditorium Flog Off maps
*Via Michele Mercati 24b, **t** 055 490437; **bus** 4, 14, 28. **Open** Tues–Sat, times vary; **adm** €5.20.*
Dance music and live concerts. Northwest of the city centre.

Central Park Off maps
*Parco delle Cascine; **bus** 1, 9, 26, 27. **Open** Tues–Sat 11pm–4am; **adm** €16 (includes one drink).*
Club with live music, three dance floors and shows. Thursdays are drum 'n' bass nights. In summer, the place trebles in size, becoming an ersatz desert island. Cocktails and dinner served from 9.30pm, dancing from 11pm.

Outdoor Summer Venues

There are lots of outdoor summer venues in Florence. All are free, and they offer live music on most nights, which can be anything from jazz and blues to world, folk or classical. They all have a bar, some have a restaurant or pizzeria, and some turn into dance spots later on.

Anfiteatro delle Cascine
*Parco delle Cascine; **bus** 17.*

Le Murate
*Via dell'Agnolo; **bus** A.*
An ex-prison, now a performance space. Cosy, with deliciously imaginative specialities and a garden.

Notti d'Estate
*Piazza Santo Spirito; **bus** D, 36, 37.*

Parterre
*Piazza della Libertà; **bus** 1, 17, 25.*

Rime Rampanti
*Piazza Poggia; **bus** D.*
On a lovely terrace above Piazza Poggia and overlooking the river.

Eskimo C3
*Via dei Canacci 12 (no phone); **bus** A, 12. **Open** daily 6pm–4am.*
This tiny club is very much a student dive, but a lively and fun one. Live music every evenings features a whole mix of sounds and standards. You need to pay the annual membership fee of €6.

Full-Up F4
*Via della Vigna Vecchia 25r; **bus** B, 23. **Open** Tues–Sat 11pm–4am.*
Mirrored walls and disco lighting. Dated music.

Girasol Off maps
*Via del Romito 1, **t** 055 474948; **bus** 14. **Open** Tues–Sun 8pm–2.30am.*
If it's Latin sounds you are into, head north to Girasol for live bands and DJs who supply a good mix of Cuban, flamenco, Brazilian, Caribbean and salsa rhythms. The space is small, so arrive early if you want a table.

Loonees D4
*Via Porta Rossa 15r, **t** 055 212249; **bus** A, B, 6. **Open** Tues–Sun 8pm–3am; closed Aug.*
A packed, studenty, live music venue popular with a foreign crowd. The free shots offered when you buy a beer make for a noisy atmosphere!

Maracanà D2
*Via Faenza 4; **bus** 17, 1, 7. **Open** Tues–Sun midnight–4am; closed June–Aug; **adm** €8–16.*
For live samba, mambo and bossanova. A bit sleazy.

Meccanó Off maps
*Viale degli Olmi 1, **t** 055 331371; **bus** 1, 9, 27. **Open** Tues–Sat 11pm–4am; closed Tues and Wed in winter; **adm** €13.50.*
A huge, popular club with restaurant and multiple dance floors. The garden opens in summer.

Space Electronic C3
*Via Palazzuolo 37, **t** 055 293082; **bus** 1, 17, A. **Open** daily 10pm–4am; closed most of Nov; **adm** €14.*
A high-tech noise box. Popular with foreigners who know no better.

Tenax Off maps
*Via Pratese 46, out near the airport, **t** 055 308160, **w** www.tenax.org; **bus** 29, 30, and special bus from Piazza Indipendenza. **Open** Thurs–Sat 10.30–4am; closed mid-May–Sept; **adm** €8 and up, depending on live act.*
Live bands range from international names to local groups. A DJ session always follows concerts; there are also pool tables, computers and several bars.

Yab D4
*Via Sassetti 5r, **t** 055 215160, **w** www.yab.it; **bus** A. **Open** Wed–Mon 9pm–4am; closed May–Sept. Minimum drinks charge at weekends.*
Yab has been around for a long time, and so have some of the punters who hang out there; it is favoured by a decidedly older crowd. It has recently been completely redesigned and has a vast dance space and a great sound system. Dance music varies throughout the week, but Thurs–Sat is commercial and disco with international DJs taking to the consoles on Tuesdays. Live '70s and '80s bands on Sundays.

North and East Florence

Ex-Mood F5
*Corso dei Tintori 4, **t** 328 817 9809 (mobile phone); **bus** B, C, 13. **Open** Wed–Sun 10pm–4am.*
The old Mood club has been revamped and given an appropriate new name. Still a cool venue, it is located below ground in a cavernous basement with bar and decent dance space. Sounds change every evening; Fridays is house and Saturdays drum'n'bass.

Jazz Club G3
*Via Nuova de' Caccini 3, **t** 055 247 9700; **bus** 6, C. **Open** Tues–Fri 9.30pm–2am, Sat 9.30pm–2.30am; **adm** €2.50. Cash only.*
A pleasant but smokey atmosphere with live jazz on Friday and Saturday nights, and a free jam session on Tuesdays.

Lido Off maps
*Lungarno Pecori Giraldi 1r; **bus** 12, 13, 14. **Open** Tues–Sat 12.30pm–2am, Sun 1pm–2am; closed Jan and Feb.*
A pretty setting on the Arno. Small, with mixed music and a mixed crowd. Comes into its own in summer. Small dance floor. Fridays are house nights.

Maramao G5
*Via dei Macci 79r; **bus** A, C, 14. **Open** Tues–Sat 11pm–3am; closed May–Sept; **adm** €11 (includes a drink).*
The music in this slick, cool venue is often Latin-American.

Soulciety E1–2
*Via San Zanobi 114b, **t** 055 830 3513; **bus** 1, 6, 17. **Open** Tues–Sun 11.30pm–4am; closed June–Sept; **adm** €6.*
Popular with Florence's Senegalese community but otherwise a relatively little-known dance venue, Soulciety is a good alternative to the city's run-of-the-mill clubs and, with its rococo decor, has an exotic, alternative feel to it. Funk, soul and hip-hop sounds dominate.

The Oltrarno

Caffè Notte C6
*Via delle Caldaie 28r, **t** 055 215864; **bus** D, 36, 37. **Open** Mon–Sat 7am–1am; closed 2 weeks in Jan.*
A true neighbourhood hangout with a regular clientele made up of lots of local colour. In summer, drinkers crowd around the few outside tables, while in winter the action moves indoors where there are board games and cards supplied.

Cafe La Torre Off maps
*Lungarno Cellini 65r, **t** 055 239 9863; **bus** D, 23. **Open** daily 10.30am–3am.*
Easily recognizable thanks to the neon tower over the door, La Torre (located on the river bank) is one of the few bars to cater for true night owls. It is also a good live music venue with sounds ranging from acid jazz to salsa through blues and roots. A mellow wind-down after a night's dancing.

Dolce Vita B5
*Piazza del Carmine, **t** 055 284595, **w** www.dolcevitafirenze.it; **bus** D, 6. **Open** summer Mon–Sat 10.30am–1.30am, Sun 6pm–1.30am, winter daily 6pm–1.30am.*
Although it is no longer the only game in town as far as cool bars go, Dolce Vita still attracts a sleek and sophisticated crowd who spill off the large terrace area into the piazza in summer months.

Fuori Porta F7
*Via Monte alle Croci 10r, **t** 055 234 2483, **w** www.fuoriporta.it; **bus** D, 23. **Open** Mon–Sat 12.30–3.30pm and 7pm–12.30am.*
This wine bar, one of the city's best, lies in the San Niccolò district, just under the old city gate. The wine list consists of about 600 different labels with some 40 on offer by the glass at any given time. There is an enticing menu of snacks and more substantial fare which

complements the wine perfectly. A pretty terrace provides fresh air in summer.

James Joyce Off maps
*Lungarno B Cellini 1r, **t** 055 658 0856, **w** www.florencepubs.com; **bus** D, 12, 23. **Open** Sun–Thurs 6pm–1.30am, Fri and Sat 6pm–2.30am.*
An Irish pub with literary pretensions, the James Joyce enjoys a pleasant location with a big garden near the river. Books and magazines are on hand for browsing.

Negroni F6
*Via dei Renai 17r, **t** 055 243647; **bus** D, 23. **Open** Mon–Sat 8am–2am.*
A new bar situated in a picturesque square near the river in the San Niccolò neighbourhood. Inside, the clean, contemporary look makes for a sophisticated ambience while outside there is a big terrace which is rather spoilt by traffic noise. At cocktail hour (7pm on), there is a great spread of nibbles to go with your favourite drink.

Sottosopra B6
*Via dei Serragli 48r, **t** 055 282 3400; **bus** 11, 36, 37. **Open** daily 6.30pm–1.30am; closed June–end Sept.*
A friendly, neighbourhood club on two levels. Sopra is the small bar area where you can hang out on high stools, sip a cocktail and graze at the nibbles, while in the basement Sotto, the more spacious dance floor, hosts a laid-back and un-intimidating crowd and a good mix of sounds.

Universale Off maps
*Via Pisana 77r, **t** 055 221122, **w** www.universalefirenze.it; **bus** 6. **Open** Tues–Sun 8.30pm–2am; closed June–Sept.*
The Universale is a vast, stunningly converted space in the shell of a '50s cinema; it was opened as a club in early 2001. There is something for everyone: civilized cocktail-bar, restaurant and pizzeria, dance floors, a giant video screen and the odd live music night.

Zoe F6
*Via dei Renai 13r, **t** 055 243111; **bus** D, 23. **Open** Mon–Thurs 8am–1pm, Fri and Sat 8am–2am, Sun 6pm–1am.*
Another bar in this increasingly trendy corner of the Oltrarno, Zoe is not cheap, but it's often packed. The cocktails are excellent.

Entertainment

Music 241

Cinema 242

Ballet and Dance 242

Theatre 242

Look for listings of concerts and events in Florence's daily, *La Nazione*; the tourist office's free *Florence Today* contains bilingual monthly information and a calendar, as does a booklet called *Florence Concierge Information*, available in hotels and tourist offices; the monthly *Firenze Spettacolo*, sold at newsstands, is written mainly in Italian but has a short English section and fills you in on ecology and trekking activities, film societies, bar music and the latest New Age mumbo jumbo to rock Florence. The annual guide *Guida Locali di Firenze* also gives listings.

Music

Rock and Jazz

Rock concerts are arranged by Toscana Music Pool, **t** 055 243280. Box Office, Via Faenza 139r, **t** 055 210804, is a useful ticket agency.

Rock

Auditorium Flog Off maps
*Via Michele Mercati 24b, **t** 055 490437; **bus** 4, 14, 28.*
Regular live gigs (the odd big name) Thursday to Saturday in a large student-y venue. In November, it hosts an excellent world music festival, the 'Festival dei Popoli'.

Eskimo C3
*Via dei Canacci 12 (no phone); **bus** A, 12.*
See p.237.

Loonees D4
*Via Porta Rossa 15r, **t** 055 212249; **bus** A, B, 6.*
See p.238.

Palasport Off maps
*Viale Paoli, **t** 055 678841; **bus** 3.*
Near the football stadium in Campo di Marte, this 7,000-capacity sports hall is somewhat lacking in atmosphere but attracts big names such as Eric Clapton, Pat Metheny, Eros Ramozzotti, and Sting.

Saschall Off maps
*Lungarno Aldo Moro 3, **t** 055 650 4112, **w** www.saschall.it.*
Risen from the ashes (not literally) of the old Teatro Tenda, the brand new concert venue with a capacity of 3,000. All kinds of music (including musicals) on the programme. See local press for details.

Tenax Off maps
*Via Pratese 46, out near the airport, **t** 055 308160, **w** www.tenax.org; **bus** 29, 30, and special bus from Piazza Indipendenza.*
The best venue in Florence for live music. Bands range from relative unknowns to heavyweight heavy metal stars or rappers.

Jazz

Cafè La Torre Off maps
*Lungarno Cellini 65r, **t** 055 239 9863; **bus** D, 23.*
Jazz and Latin.

Jazz Club G3
*Via Nuova de' Caccini 3, **t** 055 247 9700; **bus** 6, C.*
A pleasant but smokey atmosphere with live jazz on Friday and Saturday nights, and a free jam session on Tuesdays.

Pinocchio Jazz Off maps
*Viale Giannotti 13 (no phone); **bus** 8, 23, 31, 33.*
Look in *Firenze Spettacolo* for Pinochio's excellent programme of jazz concerts on Saturday nights. The setting is nothing special, but the music (an eclectic mix of trad jazz, Latin, folk, experimental etc.) is good. Doors open 9.15; concerts start at 10.

Sala Vanni B5
*Piazza del Carmine 14, **t** 055 287347; **bus** D.*
Musicus Concentus organize a great jazz series in this concert hall in the Oltrarno from October to May.

Classical Music and Opera

Throughout the year, but especially in the summer, concerts are held in churches, villas, cloisters and piazzas in and around Florence. Look in the local press and on bill boards for details.

Classsical concerts are held in the following venues:

Accademia Bartolomeo Cristofori Off maps
*Via di Camaldoli 7r, **t** 055 221646, **e** abc@dada.it; **bus** D, 6.*
A small concert hall attached to a workshop which restores early keyboard instruments and promotes a series of chamber concerts and recitals featuring keyboard instruments.

Scuola di Musica di Fiesole Off maps
*Villa la Torraccia, San Domenico, Fiesole, **t** 055 597851, **f** 055 599686, **w** www.scuolamusica.fiesole.fi.it; **bus** 7.*
One of Italy's best-known music schools promotes a series of chamber music concerts. The setting – a 16th-century villa and its grounds – is lovely.

Teatro Goldoni B6
*Via Santa Maria 15, **t** 055 210804; **bus** 11, 36, 37.*
A tiny, newly restored theatre with only 400 seats which is occasionally used for chamber opera and concerts.

Teatro del Maggio Musicale Fiorentino E4
*Via del Corso 16, **t** 055 211158, **f** 055 277 9410, **e** tickets@maggiofiorentino.com, **w** www.maggiofiorentino.com; **bus** B, D.*
Symphonic concerts, recitals, opera and ballet are all held at Florence's municipal opera house which attracts major names in conductors, soloists and directors. The Maggio Musicale festival (a mix of all the above) runs from late April to the end of June.

Teatro della Pergola F3–4
*Via della Pergola 12–32, **t** 055 226 4316, **f** 055 610141, **e** info@amicimusica.fi.it, **w** www.amicimusica.fi.it; **bus** C.*
The excellent chamber music series held in the stunning 18th-century Teatro della Pergola is promoted by the Amici della Musica. Internationally known

names usually perform on Saturdays or Sundays.

Teatro Romano, Fiesole Off maps
For Estate Fiesolana, ***t*** *055 597 8308,* ***f*** *055 597044,* ***e*** *efiesole@tin.it;* ***bus*** *7.*
The atmospheric Roman Amphitheatre in Fiesole is the setting for the Estate Fiesolana festival which runs from June through August. Opera, ballet and the odd classical concert make up the programme. The Florence Dance Festival summer edition is also held here.

Teatro Verdi F5
Via Ghibellina 99, ***t*** *055 212320,* ***w*** *www.teatroverdifirenze.it;* ***bus*** *A,14.*
The red and gold Teatro Verdi is home to the excellent Orchestra Regionale Toscana, Tuscany's regional orchestra, who perform there regularly late Nov–May. Light opera and other classical concerts occasionally feature in the mixed-bag programme.

Cinema

For a listing of all current films being shown in Florence (Italian and dubbed in Italian), check the local newspapers.

VO

Cinemas showing English-language films are:

Cinema Astro F4–5
Piazza di San Simeone (Via Isole Stinche), no phone; ***bus*** *A.* ***Open*** *Oct–April.*
Not the latest releases, but this none-too-comfortable cinema shows films in English every night but Monday.

Fulgor Off maps
Via Maso Finiguerra, ***t*** *055 238 1881,* ***w*** *www.cinemafulgor.it;* ***bus*** *1, 17, D.*
Original-language films every Thursday.

Odeon Cinehall D4
Piazza Strozzi 1, ***t*** *055 214068,* ***e*** *cinehall@cinehall.it,* ***w*** *www.cinehall.it;* ***bus*** *A, 22.*
The latest releases are shown in English on Mondays and Tuesdays, sometimes before they are released in the UK.

Ballet and Dance

The ballet (and opera) season at the **Teatro del Maggio** (E4; *see* above) runs roughly from Sept to Dec with other productions appearing in the Maggio festival in the summer. Other venues where you are likely to see such productions are the **Teatro Goldoni** (B6; more dance than opera), **Teatro Verdi** (F4–5; occasionally), **Teatro della Pergola** (F3–4; during the Maggio festival) and at the **Estate Fiesolana** (*see* 'Classical Music and Opera' above for details of venues).

The Teatro del Maggio Musicale's resident company **MaggioDanza** presents half a dozen ballets throughout the year; the standard is very variable although guest *étoiles* can be worth seeing. Guest ballet companies also appear every now and then at the theatre.

The **Florence Dance Cultural Centre** (B5), Borgo Stella 23r, **t** 055 289276, **f** 055 265 4450, **e** *info@florencedance.org*, **w** *www.florencedance.org*, is an innovative dance school and organizer of ballet and dance events. It is responsible for the **Florence Dance Festival** in the summer at the Teatro Romano in Fiesole and a shorter winter festival at the Teatro Goldoni.

Contemporary dance events and ethnic dance groups make frequent appearances on the programme of the **Fabbrica Europa festival** (**w** *www.fabbricaeuropa.net*) which takes place in May/June at the ex-Stazione Leopolda near Porta il Prato.

The **Festival dei Popoli** world music festival at the Auditorium Flog (*see* above) often includes ethnic dance productions.

Theatre

The theatre scene is very active in Florence, but as productions are almost exclusively in Italian, they have limited interest for tourists. However, if you want to have a go, the following theatres are worth looking out for. The theatre season in Florence runs from Oct to May.

Fabbrica Europa
See 'Ballet and Dance' above for details.
This festival always has some theatre (often very avant-garde or roots-based) in its programme.

Teatro delle Limonaia Off maps
Via Gramsci 426, Sesto Fiorentino, ***t*** *055 440852,* ***f*** *055 440852,* ***e*** *info@teatro-limonaia.fi.it,* ***w*** *www.teatro-limonaia.fi.it;* ***bus*** *28.*
A tiny theatre space in the suburbs which puts on fairly alternative productions and fringe events.

Teatro della Pergola F3–4
Via della Pergola 12–32, ***t*** *055 226 4316,* ***e*** *direzione@pergola.firenze.it,* ***w*** *www.pergola.firenze.it;* ***bus*** *C.*
One of Italy's state-run theatres, the Pergola's season runs from Oct to April and is made up of fairly mainstream productions which could include anything from Shakespeare, Brecht, Pirandello, Goldoni, Neil Simon or Oscar Wilde.

Teatro Studio di Scandicci Off maps
Via Donizetti 58, ***t/f*** *055 757348,* ***e*** *teatrostudio@scandiccicultura.org,* ***w*** *www.scandiccicultura.org;* ***bus*** *16.*
Another suburban theatre space which presents exciting new productions. The resident companies are the innovative Compania di Krypton and Kinkaleri; the latter do a lot of physical theatre.

Shopping

Antiques and Art Galleries 244
Auction Houses 244
Books 244
Children 244
Department Stores 244
Fashion and Accessories 244
Food and Wine 246
Jewellery 246
Kitchen and Home 247
Leather 247
Linen 247
Marbled Paper 247
Perfumes and Medieval Cures 247
Shoes 247
Silver, Crystal, Mosaics, Porcelain 248
Street Markets 248

'Made in Italy' has long been a byword for style and quality, especially in fashion and leather, but also in home design, ceramics, kitchenware, jewellery, lace and linens, glassware and crystal, chocolates, hats, straw-work, art books, engravings, hand-made stationery, gold and silverware, a hundred kinds of liqueurs, wine, aperitifs, coffee machines, gastronomic specialities, antique reproductions, as well as the antiques themselves.

Italians don't like **department stores**, but there are a few chains – COIN stores often have good buys in almost the latest fashions. Standa is more like Woolworth's, with a reasonable selection of clothes, houseware, etc., often with a supermarket in the basement. La Rinascente is possibly the most upmarket department store in Italy with men's and women's clothes, household goods, cosmetics etc. All stay open throughout the day.

Note that the attraction of shopping in Italy is strictly limited to luxury items; for less expensive clothes and household items you'll probably do better in Britain or America. Bargains of any kind are rare, and the cheaper goods are often very poor quality.

Italian clothes are lovely, but if you have a large-boned Anglo-American build, you may find it hard to get a good fit, especially on trousers or skirts (Italians are a long-waisted, slim-hipped bunch). Shoes are often narrower than the sizes at home.

Antiques and Art Galleries

Via Maggio, Borgo Ognissanti and the various Lungarni are the places to look for antiques and art galleries.

Antica Maraviglia D5
Via San Jacopo 6r; ***bus*** *D, 37.*
Antique toys and games, objects and porcelain.

Atelier Alice F2–3
Via Faenza 72r; ***bus*** *1, 7, 17.*
Sell Italian carnival masks. You can also learn to make one.

P. Bazzanti e Figli C4
Lungarno Corsini 44; ***bus*** *B.*
Where you can pick up an exact replica of the bronze pig in the Mercato Nuovo.

La Bottega di Marino C5
Via Santo Spirito 8r; ***bus*** *D.*
Restorers and antiques merchants.

Casa dei Tessuti D4
Via de' Pecori 20–24r; ***bus*** *A, 1, 7.*
Keeps Florence's ancient cloth trade alive with lovely linens.

I Mascheroni Atelier E4
Via dei Tavolini 13r; ***bus*** *1, 7, 17.*
Italian carnival masks.

Auction Houses

Serious collectors may want to check Florence's busy auction houses.

Casa d'Aste Pandolfini F4
Borgo degli Albizi 26, ***t*** *055 234 0888;* ***bus*** *A.*

Sotheby's (Associate Office)
Call for an appointment, **t** 055 247 9021.

Books

Bookworms do better in Florence than most Italian cities. Books in English can sometimes cost less than in the UK.

BM Bookshop C4
Borgo Ognissanti 4r; ***bus*** *A, B.*
Books in English and an excellent selection of art books.

Edison D–E4
Piazza della Repubblica 27r; ***bus*** *A.*
Open daily until midnight, Edison is a huge store with a laid-back feel – the nearest thing in Florence to an English or American-style megastore. Good English and travel sections.

Feltrinelli D3–F1
Via Cavour 12–20r, ***bus*** *1, 17.*
The English department is on the first floor and there is also a good selection of art books.

Franco Maria Ricci D4
Via delle Belle Donne 41r; ***bus*** *A.*
A fabulous collection of art books.

The Paperback Exchange G4
Via Fiesolana 31r; ***bus*** *C, 6.*
For the widest selections in English, with many books about Florence.

Seeber D4–5
Via Tornabuoni 70r; ***bus*** *A.*
Books in English, plus books about Florence.

Children

Caponi C4
Borgo Ognissanti 12r; ***bus*** *B.*
Has a fairytale selection of dresses, if you happen to know the kind of little girl who can wear white.

Città del Sole E4
Via Cimatori 21r; ***bus*** *A.*
The best toy shop in Florence.

La Co-operativa dei Ragazzi E2
Via San Gallo 27r; ***bus*** *1, 17, 7.*
Lots of children's books and toys.

Menicucci C6
Via Guicciardini 5; ***bus*** *D.*
Wonderful stuffed toys amongst a large selection.

Department Stores

Deparment stores are open all day.

COIN E4
Via dei Calzaiuoli 56r, ***w*** *www.coin.it;* ***bus*** *A.*

Oviesse D2
Via Nazionale 29; ***bus*** *to station.*
Cheap and cheerful department store near the station.

La Rinascente D–E4
Piazza della Repubblica 1, ***w*** *www.rinascente.it;* ***bus*** *A.*

Standa D3
Via Panzani 31r; ***bus*** *1, 17.*

Fashion and Accessories

With the expansion of Peretola Airport in Florence, and the

important biannual menswear show, Pitti Uomo, Florence is winning back some of its kudos as a fashion centre, after a mass exodus of the big designers to Milan. Many of the big names of the 1960s and '70s, which turned into the international chain stores of the 1980s and '90s, are represented in smart Via de' Tornabuoni, Via della Vigna Nuova and in the streets around the Duomo. Clothes shops generally are to be found in Via Roma and Via Calzaiuoli. For cheaper clothes and shoes go to Borgo San Lorenzo, the streets around the central market, and Il Corso.

Haute Couture

Giorgio Armani C–D4
*Via della Vigna Nuova 51r; **bus** A.*

Emporio Armani D4
*Piazza Strozzi 14–16r; **bus** A.*

Enrico Coveri D4
*Via Tornabuoni 81r; **bus** A.*

Dolce & Gabbana C–D4
*Via della Vigna Nuova 27; **bus** A.*

Gucci D4
Via Tornabuoni 73r.

Luisa E4
*Via Roma 19–21r; **bus** A.*
One-stop designer shopping for men and women, including clothes by Donna Karan, Ralph Lauren, Calvin Klein, Roberto Cavalli, Dolce & Gabbana, Comme des Garçons, Jean-Paul Gaultier...

MaxMara D4
*Via Tornabuoni 89r; **bus** A.*

Prada E5
*Via Vaccheraccia 26r; **bus** A. Also at Via Tornabuoni 67r (D4); **bus** A.*

Valentino C–D4
*Via della Vigna Nuova 47r; **bus** A.*

Versace D4
*Via Tornabuoni 13–15r; **bus** A.*

Classic Women's and Men's Wear

Roberto Biagini E4
*Via Roma 2/4r; **bus** A.*
Traditional men's suits (either made to measure or off the peg) in fine cloths. Also made to measure shoes.

Borsellino Hat E4
*Via dei Cimatori 22r; **bus** A.*
Classic hat makers.

Ferragamo D4
*Via Tornabuoni 14r; **bus** A.*
Best boots in town.

House of Cashmere E4
*Via del Corso 69r; **bus** A.*
Cashmere and shetland sweaters at factory prices; scarves and shawls too.

Madova C5
*Lungarno Guicciardini 1r; **bus** D.*
An incredible selection of gloves made at their own factory.

La Nuova Modisteria D2
*Via Chiara 15r; **bus** A.*
The best for men's women's and children's hats, with a remarkable choice of style and colours.

Oliver E5
*Via Vacchereccia 15r; **bus** A.*
Fashionable casual men's wear.

Principe C–D4
*Via del Sole; **bus** A.*
Principe was recently elbowed out of its premises in Piazza Strozzi and is now squeezed into a smaller space. Classic and expensive 'English-Look' clothes for men, women and children, plus household linens and toiletries.

Roxy D3
*Via Cerretani 33; **bus** 1, 7, 17.*
A huge choice of silk ties and scarves at good prices.

Bargain Fashions

Bargains are to be found in the markets (particularly San Lorenzo and the Tuesday morning Cascine), at secondhand shops and in shops selling the latest fashions – or copies of them – at very reasonable prices in the following streets: Via del Corso (E4), Borgo San Lorenzo (E3), in the streets around the San Lorenzo market, Via Panzani (D3), Via dei Neri (E5). The following are worth a look:

For Women

E-vision D2
*Via Nazionale 154r; **bus** 1, 7, 17.*

The End E4
*Via del Corso 39r (**bus** A) and Via Cerretani 9r (**bus** 1, 7, 17).*

Expensive! E4
*Via Calzaiuoli 78r; **bus** A.*

Maska D4
*Via Strozzi; **bus** A.*
For affordable classic fashion looks.

Andrea Sassi D3
*Via Ceretani 2r; **bus** 1, 7, 17.*

Sonia Sassi D4
*Via dei Pecori 7r; **bus** A.*

For Men

Desii E3
*Borgo San Lorenzo 4–6r; **bus** 1, 7, 17.*

Gerard Loft D4
*Via dei Pecori 34/40r; **bus** A.*

Grigio Perla D4
*Via Strozzi 24r; **bus** A, 22.*

Massimo Ribecchi C–D4
*Via della Vigna Nuova 18/20r; **bus** A.*

Outlet Stores

Alternatively, you could try hunting through the stock at one of several outlet stores in town. It's worth visiting these places regularly as the turnover is fast, but if you are lucky you will find designer labels at knock down prices. Sale times (early January and July/August) turn up some amazing reductions. All the places below sell last season's stock and end of ranges.

Docksteps Store D4
*Via dei Pecori 35r; **bus** 1, 7, 17.*

Grandi Firme E4
*Via Lamberti 16r (**bus** A); also Via del Trebbio 10r (D4; **bus** A).*

Il Guardaroba D2
*Via Nazionale 38 (**bus** 1, 7, 17); also Borgo degli Albizi 85r (F4; **bus** A), and Via Verdi 28r (F4–5; **bus** A, 14).*

Stroll B7–C6
*Via Romana 78r; **bus** D, 11.*

Piazza Pitti 33r C6
Bus D.
A cut above the rest with floaty numbers from Blumarine, the odd piece by Prada or Donna Karan, suits by Alexander McQueen and some excellent Italian knitwear. Men and women.

Out of Town

Gucci
*Via Aretina 63, Leccio, Regello, **t** 055 865 7775.*

Malo
*Via Limite 164, Campi Bisenzio; **bus** 91A.*
Knitwear.

Prada/Miu Miu
*Località SS. Levanella, Montevarchi, **t** 055 919 6528.*

You can take advantage of a private minibus service to the above to and from Florence which costs approx €28 return per person per shop. Call **t** 437 837 4131 for information.

Food and Wine

There are a number of speciality food shops around the Mercato Centrale, or you can try the following:

Allrientar Gastronomia D5
*Borgo SS. Apostoli; **bus** B.*
Pick up items like truffle creams.

La Bolognese B7–C5
*Via de' Serragli 24; **bus** 11, 36, 37.*
For delicious fresh pasta. Try their *ravioli al tartufo* – truffle-flavoured ravioli.

La Bottega del Brunello E3
*Via Ricasoli 81r; **bus** 1, 17.*
Shop divided in two parts – for display and for tasting the wine and specialities on sale.

Casa del Vino D3
*Via dell'Ariento 16r; **bus** 1, 17.*
Wine to taste and to buy plus snacks in the San Lorenzo street market.

Dolce & Dolcezze Off maps
*Piazza Beccaria 8r; **bus** A.*
Worth going out of your way for what are quite simply the best cakes and pastries in Florence. Try the smooth chocolate cake or the fresh raspberry tart.

Dolceforte C3
*Via della Scala 21; **bus** A, 12.*
A fabulous range of chocolates and sweets which include chocolate Davids and Duomos. Try the superb bitter chocolate-dipped orange and lemon peel.

Enoteca dei Giraldi F4
*Via Giraldi; **bus** A, 14.*
Specializes in wines from lesser-known producers. Over 140 labels; you can also eat there.

Enoteca Murgia D3
*Via dei Banchi 57, off Piazza S. Maria Novella; **bus** A.*
Wines and spirits.

Il Fornaio C6
*Via Guicciardini 6r and Via Faenza 39r; **bus** D.*
For a huge choice of breads, foccaccias, pizza by the slice and cakes.

Marchesi de' Frescobaldi C5
*Via di S. Spirito 11; **bus** D.*
One of the largest wine suppliers in Italy; visit their ancient cellars.

Old English Stores D4
*Via Vecchietti 28r; **bus** A.*
For that pot of Marmite or Worcester sauce you've been craving.

Pane & Co E5
*Piazza San Firenze 5r (on corner of Via Condotta); **bus** A.*
Deli with a superb selection of cheeses, meats, pastas, wines and local groceries.

Pitti Gola e Cantina C6
*Piazza Pitti 16; **bus** D.*
A good selction of wines, oils and vinegars, and cookery books (in both English and Italian) to go with them.

La Porta del Tartufo C4
*Borgo Ognissanti 133r; **bus** D.*
Concentrates on different types of truffles or 'truffled' foods ranging from grappa to salmon paste. Also good wines and other typical products.

Il Procacci D4
*Via Tornabuoni 64r; **bus** A.*
This is a high-quality *alimentari* (food shop) selling regional specialities as well as foreign foods.

Suger Blues B7–C5
*Via dei Serragli 57r; **bus** 11, 36, 37.*
One of the few wholefood shops in town. Prices are high.

Vivimarket D3
*Via del Giglio 20–22r; **bus** 1, 17.*
For the best selection of Asian food in town.

Le Volpi e L'Uva D5–6
*Piazza de' Rossi 1 (just south of the Ponte Vecchio); **bus** D.*
Great selection of interesting wines and very helpful staff.

Jewellery

Florence is famous for its jewellery, and the shops on and around the Ponte Vecchio are forced by the nature of their location into wide-open competition. Good prices for Florentine brushed gold (although much of it is now made in Arezzo) and antique jewellery are more common than you may think.

Aprosio e Luthi D6
*Via dello Sprone 1r; **bus** C.*
Fabulous jewellery all made from tiny crystal beads. Also evening bags and belts.

Cibola Off maps
Via XXVII Aprile 47r.
Halfway between a shop and an art gallery – interesting artistic jewellery.

Il Gatto Bianco D5
*Borgo SS. Apostoli 12r; **bus** A.*
Contemporary designs (earrings, rings, necklaces etc.) are crafted on the premises in silver, gold and other metals with pearls and precious stones.

Pepita Studio F4
*Borgo degli Albizi 23r; **bus** A.*
Fun, chunky, young designs in plexiglass, wood and glass. Prices are very reasonable.

Pietro Agnoletti G4
*Via de'Pepi 18, **t** 055 240810.*
Handmade gold jewellery, but you must book for an appointment.

Kitchen and Home

Try also COIN and Rinascente (*see* above under 'Department Stores').

Riccardo Barthe B7–C5
Via dei Serragli 234r; ***bus*** *11, 36, 37.*
A great place to dream of your next kitchen or bath design.

Bartolini E–F3
Via dei Servi 30r; ***bus*** *1, 7, 17.*
A large shop that stocks just about everything.

La Menagère E2–3
Via dei Ginori 4–8r; ***bus*** *1, 7, 17.*
Everything you could possibly want for your kitchen. The stock ranges from Philippe Starck's Alessi designs to Le Creuset and rustic Tuscan terracottaware.

Oltrefrontiera C6
Via Mazzetta 14r; ***bus*** *D.*
Furniture, textiles and unusual objects from Vietnam, the Philippines, Indonesia and other faraway and exotic places.

Le Stanze C4
Borgo Ognissanti 50–52r; ***bus*** *B.*
This shop stocks leading Italian homeware designers such as Cappellini and Porro) plus *objets* from around the world.

Il Tegame F4
Piazza Gaetano Salvemini 7; ***bus*** *A, 14, 23.*
Every surface in this small shop is crammed with ceramics, glass-ware, wooden utensils. Prices are very reasonable.

Leather

Florence is still known for its leather, and you'll see plenty of it in the centre, around Via della Vigna Nuova and Via del Parione, and less expensively at an unusual institution called the Leather School, which occupies part of Santa Croce's cloister (entrance at Piazza Santa Croce 16 or Via S. Giuseppe 5r). Some of the cheapest places for leather jackets are the stalls and shops around San Lorenzo market, but be prepared to bargain and don't always count on the quality.

Il Bisonte C–D4
Via del Parione 31r; ***bus*** *A, B.*
Chunky bags wallets, purses, jackets with signature 'Bison' stamp. Expensive but highest quality.

Fratelli Rossetti D–E4
Piazza Repubblica 43/45; ***bus*** *A.*
One of the largest and best.

Peruzz E–F5
Borgo dei Greci 8–22r; ***bus*** *14, A.*
Huge leather emporium selling shoes, bags, accessories and clothes by designer names.

Linen

Ghezzi E4
Via Calzaiuoli 110r; ***bus*** *A.*
Fashionable towels and bed linens.

Marbled Paper

Florence is one of the few places in the world to make marbled paper, an art brought over from the Orient by Venice in the 12th century. Each sheet is hand-dipped in a bath of colours to create a delicate, lightly coloured, clouded design – no two sheets are alike. The shops listed below (and many others) also carry Florentine paper with its colourful Gothic patterns. Stationery items or just sheets of marbled paper are available at:

La Bottega Artigiana del Libro C4–D5
Lungarno Corsini 40r; ***bus*** *A.*

Giulio Giannini e Figlio C6
Piazza Pitti 36r; ***bus*** *C.*
Originally book binders, now they also produce leather albums and leather desk-top objects as well as handmade paper following a 17th-century technique.

Il Papiro E2–3
*Via Cavour 55r (****bus*** *7, 1, 17); also Piazza del Duomo 24r (E4;* ***bus*** *7, 1, 17), and Lungarno Acciaiuoli 42r (D5;* ***bus*** *B).*
The oldest manufacturer.

Lo Scrittoio D–E2
Via Guelfa 112r; ***bus*** *1, 7, 17.*
Craftsmen work on the premises binding books in either calf or wild boar skin. You can also buy boxes and other accessories in marbled paper.

Il Torchio E6
Via dei Bardi 17, ***t*** *055 234 2862;* ***bus*** *D.*
Sells all types of coloured paper and binds books. The workbench is in the shop so you can see the artisans in action.

Perfumes and Medieval Cures

Farmaceutica di Santa Maria Novella C3
Via della Scala 16n, ***w*** *www.smnovella.it;* ***bus*** *A, 12.*
Housed in a 13th-century frescoed chapel. Sells body lotions, soaps, scents and medicinal remedies, many of them made up to original recipes devised by Dominican monks.

Lorenzo Villoresi E6
Via de' Bardi 14, ***t*** *055 234 1187;* ***bus*** *C, D.*
If you've always wanted to have a perfume designed especially for you, make an appointment; he also has some exotic ready-made perfumes, sold only here in Florence.

Spezieria Erborista Palazzo Vecchio E5
Via Vaccherecia 9r; ***bus*** *A.*
A frescoed, old-fashioned herbalist which sells home-made perfumes and soaps.

Shoes

Shoe shops are to be found along Borgo San Lorenzo (E3; *bus 1, 7, 17*), Via del Corso (E4; *bus A*), Via Roma (E4) and Via Calzaiuoli (E4). For designer shoes, go to Via Tornabuoni (D4; *bus A*). For dreamy creations, ogle Salvatore Ferragamo's window in Via Tornabuoni 2 (*bus A*).

Camper D5
Por San Maria 45r; ***bus*** *A.*
Prices are lower than in the UK for Camper's chunky, hip and practical shoes and boots.

Coccinelle D5
Via Por Santa Maria 49r; ***bus*** *A.*
For contemporary designs in fashion colours at affordable prices.

Divarese E4
Piazza Duomo 55r; ***bus*** *1, 17.*
Huge range of shoes at reasonable prices.

Furla E4
Via Calzaiuoli 47r; ***bus*** *A.*
Contemporary, affordable fasion.

JP Tod's D4
Via Tornabuoni 103r; ***bus*** *A.*
They cost less here than they do in the UK and US.

Roberto Ugolini C6
Via Michelozzi 17r; ***bus*** *D, 11.*
This young shoemaker designs and crafts superb bespoke shoes from about €450 a pair. They will last a lifetime. It will take about 3 months for an order to be made up.

Silver, Crystal, Mosaics, Porcelain

La Botteghina del Ceramista D–E2
Via Guelfa 5r; ***bus*** *1, 7, 17.*
Fabulous handpainted ceramics with multicoloured intricate designs. Anything from an egg-cup to vast platters (which cost up to €44).

Ceramiche Gambone Off maps
Via della Robbia 82; ***bus*** *6.*
Ceramics, crystal, glass and bronze.

Paci Off maps
Viuzzo delle Case Nuove 1; ***bus*** *26.*
A father and son make and restore hard stone mosaic objects. Ronald Reagan shopped here!

A. Poggi E4
Via Calzaiuoli 105r and 116r; ***bus*** *A.*
Has one of the city's widest selections of silver, crystal and porcelain (including Florence's own Richard-Ginori).

Sbigoli Terrecotte F4
Via Sant'Egidio 4r; ***bus*** *A, 14, 23.*
In business for over 150 years.

Street Markets

Florence's lively street markets offer good bargains, fake designer glad rags and even some authentic labels. The huge **San Lorenzo** market (D3) is the largest and most boisterous, where many Florentines buy their clothes; **Sant'Ambrogio** (G–H4) is a bustling food market but has clothes stalls too; the **Mercato Nuovo** or Straw Market (E5) is the most touristic, but not flagrantly so. There's a small market every morning except Sundays where stalls sell food, clothes and shoes in **Piazza Santo Spirito** (C6). Every second Sunday of the month, there's a big craft and flea market and every third Sunday, an organic food market there. There's an extensive clothes and shoes market every Tuesday morning in the **Cascine** (off maps), but perhaps the most fun is the **Mercato delle Pulci** (Flea Market) on Sundays in Piazza dei Ciompi (G4), offering all kinds of desirable junk.

Sports and Green Spaces

Spectator Sports 250
Activities 250
Green Spaces 251

Spectator Sports

Football

'Artemio Franchi' Football Stadium Off maps
*Viale Manfredo Fanti 4, **t** 055 507 2245; **bus** 17.*
Florentines are really into their football or '*calcio*', and the progress of their team, La Fiorentina, is followed avidly. They play regularly at this 45,000 capacity stadium and the season runs from August to May; games usually start at 3pm on Sundays, but times may vary.

Horse-racing

Ippodromo Il Visarno Off maps
*The Cascine, **t** 055 422 6076; **bus** 17C.*
Florence's flat racecourse.

Ippodromo della Mulina Off maps
*The Cascine, **t** 055 411107; **bus** 17C.*
Trotting races.

Medieval Sports

The Florentines play three games of Renaissance football a year (*calcio in costume*), one of which is always played on 24 June.

Motorsport

Autodromo Internazionale del Mugello Off maps
*Via Senni 15, Scarperia, **t** 055 849 9111; **train** to Borgo San Lorenzo or SITA **bus** for Scarperia.*
This race track is set in the rolling green countryside of the Mugello, some 40km north of Florence. It is owned by Ferrari, and the most important event of the year is the Moto Mondiale or World Motorcycle Championships, held in May or June; it also hosts Formula 3000 car racing.

Activities

Golf

Golf Club Ugolino Off maps
*In Gràssina, 7km southeast of the city, on the Chiantigiana (SS222), **t** 055 230 1009, **w** www.golfugolino.it; SITA **bus** to Greve.*
The nearest golf club to Florence: a lovely 18-hole course laid out among olives and cypresses.

Gyms

Body's Off maps
*Via Leonardo Bruni 11, **t** 055 688117, **w** www.bodysgym.com; **bus** 8, 31, 32.*
One of Florence's most popular gyms. It is the only place in town that offers classes in Pilates.

Tropos Off maps
*Via Orcagna 20A, **t** 055 678381, **w** www.troposclub.it; **bus** 14.*
Probably the most desirable health club in town and one of the most expensive. Tropos has a good pool, a well-equipped gym and offers a full range of beauty treatments and massages.

Palestra Ricciardi G2–4
*Borgo Pinti 75, **t** 055 247 8462; **bus** C, 6.*
One of the few gyms in the *centro storico*, Ricciardi offers a full range of exercise machines, weights and classes.

Horse-riding

Horse-riding is increasingly popular, and Agriturist has a number of villa and riding holidays on offer in Tuscany. The National Association of Equestrian Tourism (ANTE) is probably more active here than anywhere in Italy. For any enquiries regarding Agriturism and its services (i.e. places to go riding), it's better to contact the regional headquarters in Florence: Via degli Alfani 67, 50121 Florence, **t** 055 287838, **e** *agritosc@confagricoltura.it*. Although local offices exist, they are not always very efficient. Below are some riding schools (all off maps):

Centro Ippico Cintoia
*Via Cintoia Bassa, Strada in Chianti, **t** 055 854 7973.*
Provides lessons, guided walks and excursions.

Maneggio Marinelle
*Via di Macia 21, Travalle, Calenzano (to the north of Florence); **bus** N28 to Calenzano and arrange to be picked up.*

Rendola Horse Riding Centre
*Loc. Rendola, Montevarchi, **t** 055 970 7045; **train** to Montevarchi.*
In the Chianti hills in a lovely setting. You can stay overnight or ride by the hour. Try one of their special deals: €50 for transport to and from the station, 2 hours' riding and lunch.

Scuola Equitazione Fiorentina
*Via Vicchio e Paterno 12, Bagno a Ripoli; **bus** 33.*
A riding school to the east of the city, but within an easy bus ride.

Rowing

If there's enough water in the Arno, you can try rowing or canoeing; contact the Società Canottieri Comunali, Lungarno Ferrucci 6, **t** 055 681 2151, or the Società Canottieri Firenze, Lungarno dei Medici 2, **t** 055 238 1010 (membership only).

Sailing

The sailing is beautiful among the coves of the Tuscan archipelago and around the Argentario; if you want to learn how, there's a good sailing school in Torre del Lago Puccini, **t** 0584 351211.

Squash

Centro Squash Off maps
*Via Empoli 16, **t** 055 732 3055; **bus** 1.*

Swimming

The one activity most summertime visitors begin to crave after tramping through the sights is a dip in a pool. Some hotel pools allow day membership, or try one of the ones below:

Amici del Nuoto Off maps
*Via del Romito 38, **t** 055 483951.*
Covered and open all the year round.

Bellariva Off maps
*Up the Arno at Lungarno Colombo 2; **bus** 14, 31, 32. **Open** June–Sept 11–5.*
Covered in winter.

Costoli Off maps
*Via Paoli, near Campo di Marte, **t** 055 623 6027; **bus** 3, 10.*
Covered and open year-round.

Piscina le Pavoniere Off maps
*In the Cascine; **bus** 17. **Open** June–Sept 10–6.30.*
The prettiest pool in Florence.

Tennis

Tennis courts are nearly everywhere.

Circolo Tennis Firenze Off maps
*Viale Visarno 1, **t** 055 354326; **bus** 17.*

Tennis Michelangelo G7
*Viale Michelangelo 61, **t** 055 681 1880; **bus** 12, 13.*

Lo Zodiaco Off maps
*Via Achille Gradi, Tavernuzze, **t** 055 202 2847; **bus** 37.*

Green Spaces

Florence is not well off for green space. The only truly green area in the centre of town is the **Boboli Gardens** (C–D7; *see* p.139), but you must pay to get in. It is a marvellous place to wander in, get lost in, dream in and generally cool off but you can't just flop down anywhere for a snooze and/or picnic. There is, however, a big grassy area near the **Porta Romana** (B8) entrance where mothers often take their kids for picnics in the summer.

Forte di Belvedere D7
*Entrance at the top of Costa San Giorgio; **bus** D.*
When the fort which dominates the city is reopened after restoration (but nobody knows when that will be) it will be possible to laze once again in the grounds and enjoy fabulous views of the city and surrounding countryside.

Giardino di Borgo Allegri G4–5
*Borgo Allegri; **bus** A, C.*
A pretty garden near Santa Croce which was once a car park and is now popular with neighbourhood children.

Giardino dell' Orticultura Off maps
*Via Vittorio Emanuele II 4; **bus** 4, 8.*
An impressive horticultural garden dating from 1859 which hosts the colourful annual *Mostra Mercato di Piante e Fiori* flower show in late April. The garden includes a large and unusual greenhouse built in 1879; the only other example of its kind in Europe is in Vienna.

Giardino dei Semplici F2
*Via Michele 3; **bus** 11, 17. **Open** Mon–Fri 9–1.*
Belonging to the University of Florence, this is the botanical garden created for Cosimo I in 1545–46. Still in its original layout, the garden is planted with medicinal and therapeutic herbs, indigenous plants and more exotic flora in the greenhouses. A small, but very pretty, respite from the city.

Parco delle Cascine Off maps
*Viale degli Olmi; **bus** 1, 13.*
Florence's largest park is situated on the north bank of the Arno, west of Porta il Prato. It is perhaps best known to tourists as the setting for the huge Tuesday morning markets, but it is also where Florentine families come to play at weekends. Especially on Sundays, it is full of rollerbladers (you can rent them), joggers, kids on bikes, dogs on walks and strollers. In the summer, you can swim in the pool 'Le Pavoniere' and the park also incorporates a racecourse.

Piazzas

Although hardly 'green', many of Florence's neighbourhood piazzas provide locals with breathing space, a bench, a social life, playspace for their children and dogs, and they are a great way for the visitor to get involved in local life. Many piazzas have a morning market at some point during the week. The following piazzas are worth a look:

Piazza d'Azeglio H3
Bus C, 6.
With a children's playground.

Piazza della Passera C6
Bus D.
A tiny, pretty square between Piazza Pitti and Via Maggio.

Piazza Santa Croce F5
Bus C.
Locals still hang out here, if you can spot them through the tourists.

Piazza Santo Spirito C6
Bus D, 36, 37.

Piazza Tasso Off maps
Bus D.
Actually grassy!

Children and Teenagers' Florence

Even though a declining birthrate and the legalization of abortion may hint otherwise, children are still the royalty of Italy, and are pampered, often obscenely spoiled, probably more fashionably dressed than you are, and never allowed to get dirty. Yet most of them somehow manage to be well-mannered little charmers. If you're bringing your own *bambini* to Italy, they'll receive a warm welcome everywhere.

See also 'Sport and Green Spaces', p.249.

Babysitting

Potential babysitters sometimes post adverts on notice boards at the following:

St James' American Church Off maps
*Via Bernardo Rucellai 9; **bus** 17, 22.*

Paperback Exchange G4
*Via Fiesolana 31r; **bus** C, 6.*

The British Institute C5
*Lungarno Guicciardini 9; **bus** D.*

Or try these agencies. Both deal in babysitting and domestic help:

Help Off maps
*Via Bolognese 4ar, **t** 055 470333.*

Studio B Due Off maps
*Via Lorenzo il Magnifico 94, **t** 055 470608.*

If you can't get a babysitter in, you can always leave your child at the **Canadian Island** kindergarten, Via Gioberti 15, **t** 055 677567; bus 3, 6, 14 (off maps). This playgroup is run in English, but is popular with Italian children too.

Eating Out

Italian restaurants are very child-friendly, but very few actually have a children's menu or official child portions. All you have to do is ask for *pasta al pomodoro* (with tomato sauce), or *pasta al burro* (with butter and parmesan) and even the poshest of chefs will be happy to oblige with a suitable-sized portion. It's really not an issue in Italy and rarely a problem. Very few restaurants supply high chairs, but all will be happy to pile up cushions or put a couple of chairs on top of each other.

There are some Tuscan eating experiences that will appeal more immediately to kids than others, for instance **ice-cream parlours**, **pizzerias**, which sometimes serve kid-sized pizzas (see 'Eating Out', p.223, for both), and ***pasticerrias*** which announce 'Bomboloni Caldi' at around 4pm: piping hot doughnuts dusted with sugar and stuffed with either creamy custard or chocolate come freshly cooked out of the fryer.

Also worth considering:

McDonald's C3
Piazza della Stazione 25/27r; inside the station; Via Cavour 61r.
No surprises here; the usual fare.

Mr Jimmy's American Bakery F6
*Via San Niccolò 47, **t** 055 248 0999; **bus** D.*
For delicious American-style brownies, cheesecakes, muffins etc. A good place to order your child's birthday cake.

Runner Time E6
*Via dei Bardi 58r, **t** 055 214502. **Open** daily 10am–2am.*
A fast-food joint right on the Arno which has a kids' playroom and serves (mediocre) pizzas and hamburgers.

Museums

Florence is not strong on child- or even teenage-friendly museums and monuments. How many children are going to last more than an hour of being dragged around endless Renaissance paintings and boring churches? But with a little research, you can often find a couple of items within a museum or church which stand out as being interesting. Museums such as **La Specola** (C7; *see* p.140) and the **Archeological Museum** (G3, which has lots of mummies; *see* p.122) are good for the gory-minded, while the **Anthropological Museum** in Via Proconsolo (E4; *see* p.92) is full of weird and wonderful curiosities.

The **Museo dei Ragazzi** in Palazzo Vecchio (E5; *see* p.78) organizes activities and special tours for children in Palazzo Vecchio itself, to the Science Museum (E5, where the wonderful working machines are a great attraction; *see* p.87) and to the Stibbert Museum (*see* p.148). Information on **t** 055 276 8224.

Attractions

There is a wonderful old-fashioned **merry-go-round** in Piazza Strozzi (D4; *bus A, 22*), which can provide a good break between sights.

In the summer, the Parterre near Piazza Libertà has a big **inflatables** area where children can bounce till the cows come home. The Parterre also has an **ice rink** for skating during the Christmas/New Year holiday period.

In summer, take them **swimming** to one of the outdoor pools (*see* 'Sport and Green Spaces', p.249).

Anytime you see a notice announcing a '**Lunar Park**', it will be a funfair and is worth a visit. If a **circus** visits town, you're in for a treat; it will either be a sparkling showcase of daredevil skill or a poignant, family-run, modern version of *La Strada*.

Trips out of town (all off maps) include:

Zoo
*Via Pieve a Celle 160, Pistoia, **t** 0573 911219, **w** www.zoodipistoia.it.*
Not exactly the greatest of zoos, but could fill a gap.

Pinocchio Park, Collodi
*Near Pistoia, **t** 0572 429342.*

Parco Preistorico
*Peccioli, near Pontederra, **t** 0587 636030, **w** www.parcsmania.*
A dinosaur park with life-size models of dinosaurs and a playground.

Gay and Lesbian Florence

Organizations

Azione Gay e Lesbica Off maps
Via Manara 12, ***t*** *055 671298,* ***f*** *055 624 1687,* ***w*** *www.azionegayelesbica.it, helpline* ***t*** *055 671320.*
Gay and lesbian community centre which welcomes short-term visitors. Health advice, counselling, political and social meetings, parties, information.

Ireos C5–B6
Via dei Serragli 3, ***t*** *055 216907.*
This gay centre offers a telephone counselling service (Mon–Sat 5–8pm, Wed 9.30–11pm), free AIDS testing, advice on other health issues and group counselling, legal advice and various meetings and social events. They also supply tourist information.

Bookshop

Libreria delle Donne G4
Via Fiesolana 2b, ***t*** *055 240384,* ***w*** *www.women.it/libreriafirenze/fili.htm;* ***bus*** *A, 23.*
Women's and feminist bookshop with some titles in English. They also organize meetings and seminars and have a notice board.

Beaches

There is a strip of beaches frequented by gays in the Versilia between Torre del Lago and Viareggio. The best-known of these is La Lecciona. The beach is lined with bars, restaurants and clubs which are all gay-friendly.

Hotels

The following are gay-friendly:

B&B F4–G2
Borgo Pinti 31, ***t*** *055 248 0056,* ***w*** *www.bnb.it/beb;* ***bus*** *31, A, 14. Singles €47, doubles €83.*
This tiny hotel (there are only four rooms) only accepts women and is non-smoking. Rooms (on the top floor of an old palazzo) are furnished simply but with style and are airy and sunny. The two bathrooms are shared and you help yourself to breakfast.

Morandi alla Crocetta F2
Via Laura 50, ***t*** *055 234 4747,* ***w*** *www.hotelmorandi.it;* ***bus*** *C, 6. Singles €95, doubles €160.*
This small, discreet, family-run *pensione* is housed in a 16th-century ex-convent near Piazza Santissima Annunziata. The 10 rooms are comfortably furnished with antiques; a couple have fresco fragments and two have private terraces.

Dei Mori E4
Via Dante Alighieri 12, ***t*** *055 211438,* ***w*** *www.bnb.it/deimori;* ***bus*** *A. Doubles €115.*
The owners of this cosy B&B situated in the heart of medieval Florence have created a real home-from-home. Breakfast is served in the kitchen, which is also available for guests' use. Some rooms are quite small, but those in the recently acquired flat next door are modern and spacious. The sitting room has TV, a stereo and lots of reading material.

Hotel Porta Rossa D–E4
Via Porta Rossa 19, ***t*** *055 287551;* ***bus*** *A, B. Singles €120, doubles €165.*
One of the oldest hotels in Florence, the popular Hotel Porta Rossa enjoys a wonderfully central position near Via Tornabuoni's chic shops. Rooms vary in standard.

Restaurants

The following are gay-friendly:

Mastro Cigliegia F4
Via M. Palmieri 34r, ***t*** *055 293372;* ***bus*** *A.* ***Open*** *Tues–Sun noon–2.30 and 8–midnight.* ***Inexpensive.***
A lively, cheap eatery (mostly pizzas and pastas).

Momoyama B5
See p.231.

Rose's C–D4
See p.236.

La Vie en Rose G4–5
Borgo Allegri 68r, ***t*** *055 245860;* ***bus*** *A, B.* ***Open*** *Wed–Mon 12–12.* ***Moderate.***
New-wave food and art exhibitions.

Bars

Le Colonnine F5
Via dei Benci 6r, ***t*** *055 234 6417;* ***bus*** *B, C.* ***Open*** *Tues–Sun 8am–1am.*
Caffè by day and popular nightspot later on. Pizzas, pastas, drinks and cigarettes. Mixed.

Il Piccolò Caffè F5
Borgo Santa Croce 23, ***t*** *055 200 1057.* ***Open*** *daily 5pm–1am.*
Frequented by men and women, this popular and friendly little bar organizes art exhibitions and live shows.

Polly Magù Off maps
Via Panicale 27r, ***t*** *055 230 2259;* ***bus*** *A, 1, 17.* ***Open*** *Mon–Sat 8am–1am.*
A gay/straight hangout for coffees, drinks, snacks and light meals. There's music too.

YAG B@r G4–5
Via de' Macci 8r, ***t*** *055 246 9022;* ***bus*** *A, C.* ***Open*** *Mon–Sat 9pm–3am.*
A great late-night dance bar popular with men and women. Internet access and video rooms.

Clubs

Clubs with a gay-friendly night include: **Tenax** (*see* p.238): Saturday nights' 'Nobody's Perfect Party'; and **Auditorium Flog** (*see* p.237): 'Timida Gozilla' one Fri a month. Or try:

Absolut Off maps
Via Mossotti 10, Pisa, ***t*** *050 220 1262.* ***Open*** *daily 8pm–2am.*
You need to be a member of ARCI gay to get into this mixed club.

Crisco F4
Via Sant'Egidio 43r, ***t*** *055 248 0580;* ***bus*** *14, 23, A.* ***Open*** *Mon, Wed, Thurs–Sun 10pm–3am, Fri and Sat 10pm–6am.*
A men-only club/bar with videos, parties and other events.

Tabasco D5
Piazza Santa Cecilia 3r, ***t*** *055 213000;* ***bus*** *A.* ***Open*** *Thurs–Sat 10pm–5am.*
A men-only club and Florence's first gay club.

Festivals

Although festivals in Florence, Siena, Pisa and Lucca are often more show than spirit (though there are several exceptions to the rule), they can add a note of pageantry or culture to your holiday. Some are great costume affairs, with roots dating back to the Middle Ages, and there are quite a few music festivals, antique fairs and, most of all, festivals devoted to food and drink.

Traditional festivals in Florence date back centuries. Easter Sunday's **Scoppio del Carro**, or 'Explosion of the Cart', commemorates Florentine participation in the First Crusade in 1096. The Florentines were led by Pazzino de' Pazzi who, upon returning home, received the special custody of the flame of Holy Saturday, with which the Florentines traditionally relit their family hearths. To make the event more colourful, the Pazzi constructed a decorated wooden ox cart to carry the flame. They lost the job after the Pazzi conspiracy in 1478, and since then the city has taken over the responsibility. In the morning, a firework-filled wooden float is pulled by a long procession of trumpeters, flag throwers, drummers and dignatories dressed in Renaissance costume from Il Prato to the cathedral, where, at 11am, during the singing of the Gloria, it is ignited by a model dove that descends on a wire from the high altar.

On a Sunday in late May, there's the **Festa del Grillo** (cricket festival) in the Cascine; Michelangelo was thinking of its little wooden cricket cages when he mocked Ammanati's gallery on the cathedral dome.

June is the time of the three matches of ***Calcio in Costume*** (historical football in 16th-century costume) in the Piazza Santa Croce, played by 27-man teams from Florence's four quarters, in memory of a defiant football match played in Piazza Santa Croce in 1530, during the siege by Charles V. Flag-throwing and a parade in historical costume are part of the pre-game ceremonies. One match is always played on 24 June, the day of the **festival of San Giovanni**, Florence's patron saint. The best fireworks are reserved for that day too. The **Festa della Rificolona** on 7 September is one of Florence's livelier festivals, with a street party.

Florentines adore cultural events. For further details on concerts, opera and ballet, *see* 'Entertainment', p.240.

January

Epiphany

6 Jan.

Epiphany, or La Befana, is a children's festival in Italy, and a public holiday.

April

Easter

Good Friday.

Way of the Cross candlelight procession, Gràssina, near Florence.

Scoppio del Carro

Easter Sun.

Procession with musicians and flag throwers, Florence.

Settimana dei Beni Culturali

A week of free admission to all state museums, Florence, usually held in early spring. Ask at the tourist office for exact dates.

Flower show

25 April–1 May.

Flower show at the Parterre, Florence.

May

Mille Miglia

Early May Sun.

The 1,000 Miglia vintage car race passes through Florence.

Flower show

Early May Sun.

Flower show, Greve (province of Florence).

Iris festival

All month.

Iris Festival, Florence.

Cantine Aperte

Late May Sun.

Wine estates throughout Tuscany throw open their doors for tastings and tours.

Ascension Day

Cricket Festival, Parco delle Cascine, Florence,with floats, and model crickets sold in little cages.

Maggio Musicale Fiorentino

May and June.

Music and opera festival, Florence.

June

Calcio in Costume

3 weekends.

Renaissance football game, Florence.

San Giovanni festival

24 June.

Celebrations of Florence's patron saint with fireworks, Florence.

La Bruscellata

Last Sun in June.

A week of dancing and old love songs around a flowering tree, San Donato in Poggio (Florence province).

July

Estate Fiesolana

Early July–Aug.

Music, dance and theatre in the Roman amphitheatre in Fiesole.

Pistoia Blues

Mid-July.

Excellent blues festival in Pistoia, province of Florence.

September

Festa della Rificolona

Early Sept.

Procession with lanterns and children, Florence.

Grape festival

End Sept.

Grape festival, Impruneta (near Florence), with food and wine stalls, and a parade of floats.

Artists' Directory

This includes the principal architects, painters and sculptors whose works are found in this book. The works listed are far from exhaustive, bound to exasperate partisans of some artists and do scant justice to the rest, but we have tried to include only the best and most representative works that you'll find.

Agostino di Duccio (Florentine, 1418–81). A precocious and talented sculptor, his best work is in the Malatesta Temple at Rimini – he was exiled from Florence after being accused of theft (Florence: Bargello p.88).

Alberti, Leon Battista (Florentine, b. Genoa, 1404–72). Architect, theorist, and writer, also a sculptor and painter. His greatest contribution was recycling the classical orders and the principles of Vitruvius into Renaissance architecture (Florence: Palazzo Rucellai p.106, façade of S. Maria Novella p.101, SS. Annunziata, p.121).

Allori, Alessandro (1535–1607). Florentine Mannerist painter, prolific follower of Michelangelo and Bronzino (Florence: SS. Annunziata, S. Spirito p.140, Spedale degli Innocenti, p.122).

Ammannati, Bartolommeo (1511–92). Florentine architect and sculptor. Restrained, elegant in building (Florence: S. Trínita bridge p.110, courtyard of Pitti Palace p.136); neurotic, twisted Mannerist sculpture (Florence: Fountain of Neptune p.77, Villa di Castello p.150).

Andrea del Castagno (*c.* 1423–57). Precise, dry Florentine painter, one of the first and greatest slaves of perspective. Died of the plague (Florence: Uffizi p.81, S. Apollonia p.118, SS. Annunziata p.121).

Angelico, Fra (or Beato) (Giovanni da Fiesole, *c.* 1387–1455). Monk first and painter second, but still one of the great visionary artists of the Renaissance (Florence: S. Marco – spectacular *Annunciation* and many more p.116; Fiesole: S. Domenico p.162).

Arnolfo di Cambio (born in Colle di Val d'Elsa, *c.* 1245–1302). Architect and sculptor, pupil of Nicola Pisano and a key figure in his own right. Much of his best sculpture is in Rome, but he changed the face of Florence as main architect to the city's greatest building programme of the 1290s (Florence: cathedral p.66, and Palazzo Vecchio p.78).

Baldovinetti, Alesso (Florentine, 1425–99). A delightful student of Fra Angelico who left few tracks; most famous for fresco work in Florence (SS. Annunziata p.121, Uffizi p.81, S. Niccolò sopr'Arno, S. Miniato p.145).

Bandinelli, Baccio (1488–1559). Florence's comic relief of the late Renaissance; supremely serious, vain, and so awful it hurts – of course he was court sculptor to Cosimo I (Florence: Piazza della Signoria p.75, and SS. Annunziata p.121).

Bartolo di Fredi (Sienese, active *c.* 1353–1410). Student of Ambrogio Lorenzetti, a genuine pre-Raphaelite soul, entirely at home in the Sienese trecento (Siena: Pinacoteca p.181).

Bartolommeo, Fra (*c.*1472–1517) Florentine painter, master of the High Renaissance style (Florence: San Marco p.116, Pitti Palace p.136).

Beccafumi, Domenico (*c.* 1486–1551). Sienese painter; odd mixture of Sienese conservatism and Florentine Mannerism (Siena: Pinacoteca p.181, Palazzo Pubblico p.173, cathedral pavement p.175).

Benedetto da Maiano (Florentine, 1442–97). Sculptor, specialist in narrative reliefs (Florence: S. Croce p.127, Strozzi Palace p.106, Bargello p.88).

Bigarelli, Guido (13th century). Talented travelling sculptor from Como, who excelled in elaborate and sometimes bizarre pulpits (Pisa: Baptistry p.194).

Botticelli, Sandro (Florentine, 1445–1510). Though technically excellent in every respect, and a master of both line and colour, there is more to Botticelli than this. Above every other quattrocento artist, his works reveal the imaginative soul of the Florentine Renaissance, particularly the great series of mythological paintings (Florence: Uffizi p.83). Later, a little deranged and under the spell of Savonarola, he reverted to intense, though conventional religious paintings. Almost forgotten in the philistine 1500s and not rediscovered until the 19th century, many of his best works are probably lost (Florence: Accademia p.119).

Bronzino, Agnolo (1503–72). Virtuoso Florentine Mannerist with a cool, glossy hyper-elegant style, at his best in portraiture; a close friend of Pontormo (Florence: Palazzo Vecchio p.78, Uffizi p.81, S. Lorenzo p.96, SS. Annunziata p.121).

Brunelleschi, Filippo (1377–1446). Florentine architect, credited in his own time with restoring the ancient Roman manner of building – but really deserves more credit for developing a brilliant new approach of his own (Florence: Duomo cupola p.66, Spedale degli Innocenti p.122, S. Spirito p.140, S. Croce's Pazzi Chapel p.130, S. Lorenzo p.96). Also a sculptor (he lost the competition for the Baptistry doors to Ghiberti), and one of the first theorists on perspective.

Buontalenti, Bernardo (1536–1608). Late Florentine Mannerist architect and planner of the new city of Livorno, better known for his Medici villas (Artimino p.152, also the fascinating grotto in Florence's Boboli Gardens p.139, and Belvedere Fort p.145, Uffizi Tribuna p.84).

Cellini, Benvenuto (1500–71). Goldsmith and sculptor. Though a native of Florence, Cellini spent much of his time in Rome. In 1545 he came to work for Cosimo I and to torment Bandinelli (*Perseus*, Loggia dei Lanzi p.76; also works in the Bargello p.88). As famed for his catty *Autobiography* as for his sculpture.

Cimabue (*c.* 1240–1302). Florentine painter credited by Vasari with initiating the 'rebirth of the arts'; one of the first painters to depart from the stylization of the Byzantine style (Florence: mosaics in Baptistry p.70, Crucifix in Santa Croce p.127; Pisa: cathedral mosaic p.193).

Civitali, Matteo (Lucchese, *c.* 1435–1501). Sweet yet imaginative sculptor, apparently self-taught. He would be much better known if all of his works weren't in Lucca (Lucca: cathedral p.206, Guinigi Museum p.208).

Daddi, Bernardo (active 1290–*c.* 1349). Florentine master of delicate altarpieces (Florence: Orsanmichele p.73, S. Maria Novella's Spanish chapel p.104).

Desiderio da Settignano (Florentine, 1428/31–61). Sculptor, follower of Donatello (Florence: S. Croce p.127, Bargello p.88, S. Lorenzo p.96).

Dolci, Carlo (Florentine, 1616–86). Unsurpassed Baroque master of the 'whites of their eyes' school of religious art (Florence: Palazzo Corsini p.111).

Domenico di Bartolo (Sienese, *c.* 1400–46). An interesting painter, out of the Sienese mainstream; the unique naturalism of his art is a Florentine influence (Siena: Pinacoteca p.181).

Domenico Veneziano (Florentine, 1404–61). Painter, teacher of Piero della Francesca; master of perspective with few surviving works (Florence: Uffizi p.81).

Donatello (Florentine, 1386–1466). The greatest Renaissance sculptor appeared as suddenly as a comet at the beginning of Florence's quattrocento. Never equalled in technical ability, expressiveness, or imaginative content, his works influenced Renaissance painters as much as sculptors. A prolific worker, and a quiet fellow who lived with his mum, Donatello was the perfect model of the early Renaissance artist – passionate about art, self-effacing, and a little eccentric (Florence: Bargello p.88 – the greatest works including the original *St George* from Orsanmichele p.73, *David* and *Cupid Atys*, also at San Lorenzo p.96, Palazzo Vecchio p.78, and the Cathedral Museum p.71; Siena: cathedral p.175, baptistry p.181).

Duccio di Buoninsegna (d. 1319). One of the first and greatest Sienese painters, Duccio was to Sienese art what Giotto was to Florence; ignored by Vasari, though his contributions to the new visual language of the Renaissance are comparable to Giotto's (Siena: parts of the great *Maestà* in the Cathedral Museum p.180, also Pinacoteca p.181; Florence: altarpiece in the Uffizi p.81).

Francesco di Giorgio Martini (Sienese, 1439–1502). Architect – mostly of fortresses – sculptor and painter, his works are scattered all over Italy (Siena: Cathedral p.175, Pinacoteca p.181).

Franciabigio (Florentine, 1482–1525). Most temperamental of Andrea del Sarto's pupils but only mildly Mannerist (Florence: Poggio a Caiano p.151, and SS. Annunziata p.121).

Gaddi, Taddeo (*c.* 1300–*c.* 1366). Florentine; most important of the followers of Giotto. He and his son **Agnolo** (d. 1396) contributed some of the finest trecento fresco cycles (notably at S. Croce p.127, and S. Ambrogio p.125, Florence).

Gentile da Fabriano, Francesco di (*c.*1360–1427). Master nonpareil of the International Gothic style, from Fabriano in the Marches. Most of his work is lost (Florence: Uffizi p.81).

Ghiberti, Lorenzo (1378–1455). Goldsmith and sculptor. The first artist to write an autobiography was naturally a Florentine. He would probably be better known had he not spent most of his career working on the doors for the Florence Baptistry, p.70, after winning the famous competition of 1401 (also statues at Orsanmichele p.73, Florence; Siena: Baptistry p.181).

Ghirlandaio, Domenico (Florentine, *c.* 1448–94). The painter of the quattrocento establishment, master of colourful, lively fresco cycles (with the help of a big workshop) in which he painted all the Medici and Florence's banking elite. A great portraitist with a distinctive, dry, restrained style (Florence: Ognissanti p.111, S. Maria Novella p.101, S. Trínita p.109, Spedale degli Innocenti p.122).

Giambologna (1529–1608). A Fleming, born Jean Boulogne; court sculptor to the Medici after 1567 and one of the masters of Mannerist virtuosity – also a man with a taste for the outlandish (Florence: Loggia dei Lanzi p.76, Bargello p.88, Villa della Petraia p.150).

Giotto (*c.* 1266–1337). Shepherd boy of the Mugello, discovered by Cimabue, who became the first great Florentine painter – and recognized as such in his own time. Invented an essential and direct approach to portraying narrative fresco cycles, but is even more important for his revolutionary treatment of space and of the human figure (Florence: S. Croce p.127, cathedral campanile p.69, Horne Museum p.131, S. Maria Novella p.101).

Giovanni da Milano (14th century). An innovative Lombard inspired by Giotto (Florence: S. Croce p.127).

Giovanni di Paolo (d. 1483). One of the best of the quattrocento Sienese painters; like most of them, a colourful, often eccentric reactionary who continued the traditions of the Sienese trecento (Siena: Pinacoteca p.181).

Giovanni di San Giovanni (1592–1633). One of Tuscany's more prolific, but winning Baroque fresco painters (Florence: Pitti Palace p.136, Villa la Petraia p.150).

Gozzoli, Benozzo (Florentine, d. 1497). Learned his trade from Fra Angelico, but few artists could have less in common. The most light-hearted and colourful of quattrocento artists, Gozzoli created enchanting frescoes at the Medici palace (Florence p.99) and Campo Santo (Pisa p.194).

Guido da Siena (13th century). One of the founders of Sienese painting, still heavily Byzantine in style; little is known about his life (Siena: Palazzo Pubblico p.173, Pinacoteca p.181).

Leonardo da Vinci (1452–1519). We could grieve that Florence's 'universal genius' spent so much time on his scientific interests and building fortifications, and that his meagre artistic output was largely unfinished or lost. All that is left in Tuscany is the *Annunciation* (Florence: Uffizi p.81) and also models of all his gadgets at his birthplace, Vinci. As the pinnacle of the Renaissance marriage of science and art, Leonardo requires endless volumes of interpretation. As for his personal life, Vasari records him buying up caged birds in the market-place just to set them free.

Lippi, Filippino (Florentine, 1457–1504). Son and artistic heir of Fra Filippo. Often seems a neurotic Gozzoli, or at least one of the most thoughtful and serious artists of the quattrocento (Florence: S. Maria Novella p.101, S. Maria del Carmine p.141, Badia p.91, Uffizi p.81).

Lippi, Fra Filippo (Florentine, d. 1469). Never should have been a monk in the first place. A painter of exquisite, ethereal Madonnas, one of whom he ran off with (the model, at least, a brown-eyed nun named Lucrezia). The pope forgave them both. Lippi was a key figure in the increasingly complex, detailed painting of the middle 1400s (Florence: Uffizi p.81).

Lorenzetti, Ambrogio (Sienese, d. 1348). He could crank out golden Madonnas as well as any Sienese painter, but Lorenzetti was also a great innovator in subject matter and the treatment of landscapes. Created the first and greatest of secular frescoes, the *Allegories of Good and Bad Government* in Siena's Palazzo Pubblico, p.173, while his last known work, the 1344 *Annunciation* in Siena's Pinacoteca, p.181, is one of the 14th century's most revolutionary treatments of perspective.

Lorenzetti, Pietro (Sienese, d. 1348). Ambrogio's big brother, and also an innovator, standing square between Duccio di Buoninsegna and Giotto; one of the precursors of the Renaissance's new treatment of space. Both Lorenzettis seem to have died in Siena during the Black Death.

Lorenzo di Credi (1439–1537). One of the most important followers of Leonardo da Vinci, always technically perfect if occasionally vacuous (Florence: Uffizi p.81).

Lorenzo Monaco (b. Siena, 1370–1425). A monk at S. Maria degli Angeli in Florence and a brilliant colourist, Lorenzo forms an uncommon connection between the Gothic style of Sienese painting and the new developments in early Renaissance Florence (Florence: Uffizi p.81, S. Trínita p.109).

Martini, Simone (Sienese, d. 1344). Possibly a pupil of Giotto, Martini took the Sienese version of International Gothic to an almost metaphysical perfection, creating luminous, lyrical, and exquisitely drawn altarpieces and frescoes perhaps unsurpassed in the trecento (Siena: Palazzo Pubblico p.173; Pisa: Museo S. Matteo p.197; Florence: Uffizi p.81).

Masaccio (Florentine, 1401–*c.* 1428). Though he died young and left few works behind, this precocious 'shabby Tom' gets credit for inaugurating the Renaissance in painting by translating Donatello and Brunelleschi's perspective onto a flat surface. Also revolutionary in his use of light and shadow, and in expressing emotion in his subjects' faces (Florence: S. Maria del Carmine p.141, S. Maria Novella p.101; Pisa: Museo S. Matteo p.197).

Maso di Banco (Florentine, active 1340s). One of the more colourful and original followers of Giotto (Florence: S. Croce p.127).

Masolino (Florentine, d. 1447). Perhaps 'little Tom' also deserves much of the credit, along with Masaccio, for the new advances in art at the Carmine in Florence, p.141; art historians dispute endlessly how to attribute the frescoes. It's hard to tell, for this brilliant painter left little other work behind to prove his case.

Matteo di Giovanni (Sienese, 1435–95). One Sienese quattrocento painter who could keep up with the Florentines; a contemporary described him as 'Simone Martini come to life again' (Siena: Pinacoteca p.181, Cathedral pavement p.175, S. Agostino p.183).

Memmi, Lippo (Sienese, 1317–47). Brother-in-law and assistant of Simone Martini.

Michelangelo Buonarroti (Florentine, 1475–1564). Born in Caprese (now Caprese Michelangelo) into a Florentine family of the minor nobility come down in the world, Michelangelo's early years and artistic training are obscure; he was apprenticed to Ghirlandaio, but showing a preference for sculpture was sent to the court of Lorenzo de' Medici. Nicknamed Il Divino in his lifetime, he was a complex, difficult character, who seldom got along with mere mortals, popes, or patrons. What he couldn't express by means of the male nude in paint or marble, he did in his beautiful but difficult sonnets. In many ways he was the first modern artist, unsurpassed in technique but also the first genius to go over the top (Florence: Medici tombs and library in San Lorenzo p.97, three works in the Bargello p.88, the *Pietà* in the Museo del Duomo p.71, the *David* in the Accademia p.119, Casa Buonarroti p.126, and his only oil painting, in the Uffizi p.81).

Michelozzo di Bartolomeo (Florentine, 1396–1472). Sculptor who worked with Donatello (as in Florence's Baptistry), he is better known as the classicizing architect favoured by the elder Cosimo de' Medici (Florence: Medici Palace p.98, Chiostro of SS. Annunziata p.121, library of San Marco p.116; Villas at Trebbio and Cafaggiolo).

Mino da Fiesole (Florentine, 1429–84). Sculptor of portrait busts and tombs; like the della Robbias a representative of the Florentine 'sweet style' (Fiesole: cathedral p.160; Florence: Badia p.91, Sant'Ambrogio p.125).

Nanni di Banco (Florentine, 1384–1421). Florentine sculptor at the dawn of the Renaissance (Florence: Orsanmichele p.73).

Orcagna, Andrea (Florence, d. 1368). Sculptor, painter and architect who dominated the middle 1300s in Florence, though greatly disparaged by Vasari, who destroyed much of his work. Many believe he is the 'Master of the Triumph of Death' of Pisa's Camposanto (Florence: Orsanmichele p.73, S. Croce p.127, S. Maria Novella p.101, *Crucifixion* in refectory of S. Spirito p.140, also often given credit for the Loggia dei Lanzi).

Perugino (Pietro Vannucci, Perugia, *c*. 1450–1523). Perhaps the most distinctive of the Umbrian painters; created some works of genius, along with countless idyllic nativity scenes, each with its impeccably sweet Madonna and characteristic blue-green tinted background (Florence: Uffizi p.81, S. Maddalena dei Pazzi p.124, Cenacolo di Foligno p.98).

Piero della Francesca (*c*.1415–92). Painter, born at Sansepolcro, and one of the really unique quattrocento artists. Piero wrote two of the most important theoretical works on perspective, then illustrated them with a lifetime's work reducing painting to the bare essentials: geometry, light and colour. In his best work his reduction creates nothing dry or academic, but dreamlike, almost eerie scenes similar to those of Uccello. And like Uccello or Botticelli, his subjects are often archetypes of immense psychological depth, not to be fully explained now or ever (Florence: Uffizi p.81).

Piero di Cosimo (Florentine, 1462–1521). Painter better known for his personal eccentricities than his art, which in itself is pretty odd. Lived on hard-boiled eggs (Florence: Uffizi p.81; Fiesole: S. Francesco p.160).

Pietro da Cortona (1596–1699). The most charming of Tuscan Baroque painters; his best is in Rome, but there are some florid ceilings in the Pitti Palace (Florence, p.136).

Pinturicchio (Perugia, 1454–1513). This painter got his name for his use of gold and rich colours. Never an innovator, but as an absolute virtuoso in colour, style and grace no one could beat him. Another establishment artist, especially favoured by the popes and, like Perugino, he was slandered most vilely by Vasari (Siena: Piccolomini Library p.179).

Pisano, Andrea (b. Pontedera, *c*. 1290–1348). Artistic heir of Giovanni and Nicola Pisano and teacher of Orcagna; probably a key figure in introducing new artistic ideas to Florence (Baptistry, south doors, p.70). Not related to the other Pisani.

Pisano, Nicola (active *c*. 1258–78). The first great medieval Tuscan sculptor really came from down south in Apulia, which was then enjoying a flowering of classically oriented art under Emperor Frederick II. Created a little Renaissance all his own, when he adapted the figures and composition of ancient reliefs to make his wonderful pulpit reliefs in Siena and Pisa's Baptistry (pp.181 and 194). His son **Giovanni Pisano** (active *c*. 1265–1314) carried on the tradition, notably in the façade sculptures at Siena cathedral, p.175 (also great relief pulpits in Pisa cathedral).

Pollaiuolo, Antonio (Florentine, d. 1498). A sculptor, painter and goldsmith whose fame rests on his brilliant, unmistakable line; he occasionally worked with his less gifted brother Piero (Florence: Uffizi p.81, and Bargello p.88).

Pontormo, Jacopo (Florentine, b. Pontormo, 1494–1556). You haven't seen pink and orange until you've seen the work of this determined Mannerist eccentric. After the initial shock, though, you'll meet an artist of real genius, one whose use of the human body as sole means for communicating ideas is equal to Michelangelo's (Florence: S. Felicità p.139 – his *Deposition* – and Uffizi p.81).

Quercia, Jacopo della (Sienese, 1374–1438). Sculptor who learned his style from Pisano's cathedral pulpit; one of the unsuccessful contestants for the Florence baptistry doors. Maybe Siena's greatest sculptor, though his most celebrated work, that city's Fonte Gaia, is now ruined (Lucca: cathedral tomb of Ilaria del Carretto, p.206; Siena: Baptistry p.181).

Raphael (Raffaello Sanzio, 1483–1520). Born in Urbino in the Marches, Raphael spent time in Città di Castello, Perugia, and Florence before establishing himself in Rome. Only a few of the best works of this High Renaissance master remain in the region; those are in the Pitti Palace and Uffizi, Florence (pp.136 and 81).

Robbia, Luca della (Florentine, 1400–82). Greatest of the famous family of sculptors; he invented the coloured glaze for terracottas that we associate with the della Robbias, but was also a first-rate relief sculptor (the *cantorie* in Florence's cathedral museum p.71). His nephew **Andrea della Robbia** (1435–1525) and Andrea's son **Giovanni** (1469–1529) carried on the blue and white terracotta sweet style in innumerable buildings across Tuscany.

Rosselli, Cosimo (Florentine, 1434–1507). Competent middle-of-the-road Renaissance painter who occasionally excelled (Florence: S. Ambrogio p.125).

Rossellino, Bernardo (1409–64). Florentine architect and sculptor best known as the planner and architect of the new town of Pienza. Also a sculptor (Florence:

S. Croce p.127, S. Miniato p.145). His brother **Antonio Rossellino** (1427–79) was also a talented sculptor (Florence: S. Croce p.127).

Rossi, Vicenzo de' (1525–87). Florentine Mannerist sculptor of chunky male nudes (Florence: Palazzo Vecchio p.78).

Rosso Fiorentino, Giovanni Battista di Jacopo (1494–1540). Florentine Mannerist painter, he makes a fitting complement to Pontormo, both for his tortured soul and for the exaggerations of form and colour he used to create gripping, dramatic effects. Fled Italy after the Sack of Rome and worked for Francis I at Fontainebleau (Florence: Uffizi p.81, and S. Lorenzo p.96).

Salviati, Francesco (Florentine, 1510–63). Friend of Vasari and a similar sort of painter – though much more talented. Odd perspectives and decoration, often bizarre imagery (Florence: Palazzo Vecchio p.78, and Uffizi p.81).

Sangallo, Giuliano da (Florentine, 1443–1516). Architect of humble origins who became the favourite of Lorenzo de' Medici. Often tripped up by an obsession, inherited from Alberti, with making architecture conform to philosophical principles (Poggio a Caiano villa p.151; Florence: S. Maddalena dei Pazzi p.124).

Il Sassetta (Stefano di Giovanni, active *c.* 1390–1450). One of the great Sienese quattrocento painters, though still working in a style the Florentines would have found hopelessly reactionary; an artist who studied Masaccio but preferred the Gothic elegance of Masolino. His masterpiece, the Borgo Sansepolcro polyptych, is dispersed through half the museums of Europe.

Il Sodoma (Giovanni Antonio Bazzi, 1477–1549). Born in Piedmont, but a Sienese by choice, he was probably not the libertine his nickname, and Vasari's biography, suggest. An endearing, serene artist, who usually eschewed Mannerist distortion, he got rich through his work, then blew it all feeding his exotic menagerie and died in the poorhouse (Siena: Pinacoteca p.181, and S. Domenico p.185).

Spinello Aretino (Arezzo, late 14th century–1410). A link between Giotto and the International Gothic style; imaginative and colourful in his compositions (Florence: S. Miniato p.145; Siena: Palazzo Pubblico p.173).

Tacca, Pietro (1580–1640). Born in Carrara, pupil of Giambologna and one of the best early Baroque sculptors (Florence: Piazza SS. Annunziata fountain p.121).

Taddeo di Bartolo (Volterra, 1363–1422). The greatest Sienese painter of the late 1300s – also the least conventional; never a consummate stylist, he often shows a remarkable imagination in composition and treatment of subject matter (Siena: Palazzo Pubblico).

Talenti, Francesco (early 14th century). Chief architect of Florence cathedral and campanile after Arnolfo di Cambio and Giotto; his son **Simone** made the beautiful windows in Orsanmichele, p.73 (and perhaps the Loggia dei Lanzi), in Florence.

Torrigiano, Pietro (1472–1528). Florentine portrait sculptor, famous for his work in Westminster Abbey and for breaking Michelangelo's nose (Siena: cathedral p.175).

Uccello, Paolo (Florentine, 1397–1475). No artist has ever been more obsessed with the possibilities of artificial perspective. Like Piero della Francesca, he used the new technique to create a magic world of his own; contemplation of it made him increasingly eccentric in his later years. Uccello's provocative, visionary subjects (*Noah* fresco in S. Maria Novella p.101, and *Battle of San Romano* in the Uffizi p.81, Florence) put him up with Piero della Francesca and Botticelli as the most intellectually stimulating of quattrocento artists.

Vasari, Giorgio (Arezzo, 1511–74). Florentine sycophant, writer and artist; *see* p.79. Also a fair architect (Florence: Uffizi p.81, Corridoio p.87, and Fish Loggia p.126).

Il Vecchietta (Lorenzo di Pietro, 1412–80). Sienese painter and sculptor, dry and linear, part Sienese Pollaiuolo and part Donatello (Siena: Loggia della Mercanzia p.175, Baptistry p.181).

Verrocchio, Andrea del (1435–88). Florentine sculptor who worked in bronze; spent his life trying to outdo Donatello. Also a painter, a mystic alchemist in his spare time, and interestingly enough the master of both Botticelli and Leonardo (Florence: Uffizi p.81, S. Lorenzo p.96, Orsanmichele p.73, Palazzo Vecchio p.78, and Bargello p.88).

Language

Pronunciation 265
Basic Vocabulary 265
Menu Vocabulary 267

The fathers of modern Italian were Dante, Manzoni and TV. Each did, or has done, their part in creating a national language from an infinity of regional and local dialects. Dante, a Florentine, the first 'immortal' to write in the vernacular, did much to put the Tuscan dialect in the foreground of Italian literature with his *Divina Commedia* (Divine Comedy). Manzoni's revolutionary novel, *I Promessi Sposi* (The Betrothed), heightened national consciousness by using everyday language all could understand in the 19th century. TV in the last decades has performed an even more spectacular linguistic unification; although the majority of Italians still speak a dialect at home, school, work and their TV idols insist on proper Italian.

Perhaps because they are so busy learning their own beautiful language, Italians are not the most adept at learning others. English lessons, however, have been the rage for years, and at most hotels and restaurants in Florence there will be someone who speaks English. The words and phrases below should help you out in most situations. The ideal way to come to Florence is with some Italian under your belt – your visit will be richer, and you're more likely to make Italian friends.

Pronunciation

Italian words are pronounced phonetically. Every vowel and consonant (except 'h') is sounded. Consonants are the same as in English, except 'c' which, when followed by an 'e' or 'i', is pronounced like the English 'ch' (*cinque* thus becomes 'cheen-quay'). Italian 'g' is also soft before 'i' or 'e' as in *gira* ('jee-ra'). The letter 'z' is pronounced like 'ts'.

The consonants 'sc' before the vowels 'i' or 'e' become like the English 'sh' as in *sci*, pronounced 'shee'; 'ch' is pronouced like a 'k' as in Chianti, 'kee-an-tee'; 'gn' as 'ny' in English (*bagno*, pronounced 'ban-yo'); while 'gli' is pronounced like the middle of the word 'million' (Castiglione, for example, is pronounced 'Ca-steely-oh-nay').

Vowel pronunciation is: 'a' as in English father; 'e' when unstressed is like 'a' in 'fate' (*mele*), when stressed it can be the same or like the 'e' in 'pet' (*bello*); 'i' is like the 'i' in 'machine'; 'o', like 'e', has two sounds, 'o' as in 'hope' when unstressed (*tacchino*), and usually 'o' as in 'rock' when stressed (*morte*); 'u' is pronounced like the 'u' in 'June'.

The stress usually (but not always) falls on the penultimate syllable. Accents indicate if it falls elsewhere (as in *città*). Also note that, in the big northern cities, the informal way of addressing someone as you, *tu*, is widely used; the more formal *lei* or *voi* is commonly used in provincial districts, *voi* more in the south.

Basic Vocabulary

yes/no/maybe *sì/no/forse*
I don't know *Non (lo) so*
I don't understand (Italian) *Non capisco (l'italiano)*
Does someone here speak English? *C'è qualcuno qui che parla inglese?*
Speak slowly *Parla lentamente*
Could you assist me? *Potrebbe aiutarmi?*
Help! *Aiuto!*
Please *Per favore*
Thank you (very much) *Grazie (molte/mille)*
You're welcome *Prego*
It doesn't matter *Non importa*
All right *Va bene*
Excuse me *Permesso/Mi scusi*
Be careful! *Attenzione!/Attento!*
Nothing *Niente*
It is urgent! *È urgente!*
How are you? *Come sta?* (formal)/ *Come stai?* (informal)
Well, and you? *Bene, e Lei?/e tu?*
What is your name? *Come si chiama?/Come ti chiami?*
Hello *Salve/Ciao (both informal)*
Good morning *Buongiorno*
Good afternoon/evening *Buonasera*
Good night *Buona notte*
Goodbye *ArrivederLa (formal)/ Arrivederci/Ciao (informal)*
What do you call this in Italian? *Come si chiama questo in italiano?*
What?/Who?/Where? *Che cosa?/ Chi?/Dove?*
When?/Why? *Quando?/Perché?*
How? *Come?*
How much (does it cost)? *Quanto (costa)?*
I am lost *Mi sono perso*
I am hungry/thirsty/sleepy *Ho fame/sete/sonno*
I am sorry *Mi dispiace*
I am tired *Sono stanco*
I feel unwell *Mi sento male*
I am ill *Sono malato*
Leave me alone *Lasciami in pace*
good/bad *buono/cattivo*
well/badly *bene/male*
hot/cold *caldo/freddo*
slow/fast *lento/rapido*
up/down *su/giù*
big/small *grande/piccolo*
here/there *qui/lì*

Travel Directions

One (two) ticket(s) to Naples, please *Un biglietto (due biglietti) per Napoli, per favore*
one way *solo andata*
return *andata e ritorno*
first/second class *prima/ seconda classe*
I want to go to... *Desidero andare a...*
How can I get to...? *Come posso andare a...?*
Do you stop at...? *Si ferma a...?*
Where is...? *Dov'è...?*
How far is it to...? *Quanto è lontano...?*
What is the name of this station? *Come si chiama questa stazione?*
When does the next bus leave? *Quando parte il prossimo autobus?*
From where does it leave? *Da dove parte?*
How much is the fare? *Quant'è il biglietto?*
Have a good trip! *Buon viaggio!*

Public Transport

airport *aeroporto*
bus stop *fermata*
bus/coach *autobus/pullman*
customs *dogana*
platform *binario*
train *treno*
railway station *stazione ferroviaria*
seat (reserved) *posto (prenotato)*
taxi *tassì/taxi*
ticket *biglietto*

Orientation

near/far *vicino/lontano*
left/right *sinistra/destra*
straight ahead *sempre diritto*
forward/backwards *avanti/indietro*
north/south *nord/sud*
east *est/oriente*
west *ovest/occidente*
crossroads *bivio/incrocio*
street/road *strada/via*
square *piazza*
bridge *ponte*

On Wheels

car hire *autonoleggio*
motorbike/scooter/moped *motocicletta/Vespa/motorino*
bicycle *bicicletta*
petrol/diesel *benzina/gasolio*
garage *garage*
This doesn't work *Questo non funziona*
mechanic *meccanico*
map/town plan *carta/pianta*
Where is the road to...? *Dov'è la strada per...?*
breakdown *guasto*
driving licence *patente di guida*
speed *velocità*
danger *pericolo*
parking *parcheggio*
no parking *sosta vietata*
narrow *stretto*
toll *pedaggio*
slow down *rallentare*
one-way *senso unico*

Shopping and Sightseeing

I would like... *Vorrei...*
Where is/are... *Dov'è/Dove sono...*
How much is it? *Quanto costa?*
open/closed *aperto/chiuso*
cheap/expensive *a buon prezzo/caro*
bank *banca*
beach *spiaggia*
bed *letto*
church *chiesa*
entrance/exit *ingresso/uscita*
hospital *ospedale*
money *soldi*
newspaper *giornale*
pharmacy *farmacia*
police station *commissariato*
policeman *poliziotto*
post office *ufficio postale*
sea *mare*
shop *negozio*
room *camera*
tobacco shop *tabaccaio*
WC *toilette/bagno/servizi*
men *Signori/Uomini*
women *Signore/Donne*

Days

Monday *lunedì*
Tuesday *martedì*
Wednesday *mercoledì*
Thursday *giovedì*
Friday *venerdì*
Saturday *sabato*
Sunday *domenica*
Weekdays *feriali*
Holidays *festivi*

Numbers

one *uno/una*
two/three/four *due/tre/quattro*
five/six/seven *cinque/sei/sette*
eight/nine/ten *otto/nove/dieci*
eleven/twelve *undici/dodici*
thirteen/fourteen *tredici/quattordici*
fifteen/sixteen *quindici/sedici*
seventeen/eighteen *diciassette/diciotto*
nineteen *diciannove*
twenty *venti*
twenty-one/twenty-two *ventuno/ventidue*
thirty *trenta*
forty *quaranta*
fifty *cinquanta*
sixty *sessanta*
seventy *settanta*
eighty *ottanta*
ninety *novanta*
hundred *cento*
one hundred and one *centouno*
two hundred *duecento*
one thousand *mille*
two thousand *duemila*
million *un milione*

Time

What time is it? *Che ore sono?*
day/week *giorno/settimana*
month *mese*
morning/afternoon *mattina/pomeriggio*
evening *sera*
yesterday *ieri*
today *oggi*
tomorrow *domani*
soon *fra poco*
later *dopo/più tardi*
It is too early/late *È troppo presto/tardi*

Hotel Vocabulary

I'd like a double room please *Vorrei una camera matrimoniale, per favore*
I'd like a twin room please *Vorrei una camera doppia, per favore*
I'd like a single room please *Vorrei una camera singola, per favore*
...with bath, without bath *...con bagno,senza bagno*
...for two nights *...per due notti*
We are leaving tomorrow morning *Partiamo domani mattina*
May I see the room, please? *Potrei vedere la camera, per cortesia?*
Is there a room with a balcony? *C'è una camera con balcone?*
There isn't (aren't) any hot water/soap... *Manca/Mancano acqua calda/sapone...*
...light/toilet paper/towels *...luce, carta igienica, asciugamani*
May I pay by credit card? *Posso pagare con carta di credito?*
May I see another room please? *Per favore, potrei vedere un'altra camera?*
Fine, I'll take it *Bene, la prendo*
Is breakfast included? *E' compresa la prima colazione?*
What time do you serve breakfast? *A che ora è la colazione?*
How do I get to the town centre? *Come posso raggiungere il centro città?*

Restaurant Vocabulary

Do you have a table for two (three/four)? C'é una tavola per due (tre/quattro)?

Menu Vocabulary

Antipasti (Starters)

antipasto misto mixed starters
bruschetta garlic toast (with olive oil and tomatoes)
carciofi (sott'olio) artichokes (in olive oil)
frutti di mare seafood
funghi (trifolati) mushrooms (with anchovies, garlic, lemon)
gamberi ai fagioli prawns (shrimps) with white beans
mozzarella (in carrozza) soft cow/buffalo cheese (fried with bread in batter)
prosciutto crudo (con melone) Parma ham (with melon)
salsicce sausages

Minestre (Soups) and Pasta

agnolotti meat-stuffed pasta parcels
cappelletti small stuffed pasta parcels, often served in broth
crespelle crêpes
frittata omelette
orecchiette ear-shaped pasta
panzerotto crescent-shaped pastry filled with tomato and tuna or tomato and mozzarella
pasta e fagioli soup with beans, bacon and tomatoes
pastina in brodo tiny pasta in broth
polenta cake or pudding of corn semolina
ravioli flat stuffed pasta parcels
spaghetti all'amatriciana spaghetti with spicy bacon, tomato, onion and chilli sauce
spaghetti alle vongole spaghetti with clam sauce
stracciatella broth with eggs and cheese
tortellini crescent-shaped stuffed pasta parcels

Carne (Meat)

agnello/abbacchio lamb
anatra duck
arrosto misto mixed roast meats
bollito misto meat stew
braciola chop
brasato di manzo braised beef with vegetables
bresaola dried raw meat
bucatini thin pasta tubes
carpaccio thinly sliced raw beef
cervella brains
cervo venison
coniglio rabbit
costoletta/cotoletta chop
guanciale pork cheek
lumache snails
manzo beef
osso buco veal knuckle stewed in its own marrow
pajata veal intestine
pancetta bacon
piccione pigeon
carne alla pizzaiola beef in tomato and oregano sauce
pollo chicken
polpette meatballs
rognoni kidneys
saltimbocca rolled veal, prosciutto and sage, in wine
scaloppine thin slices of veal sautéed in butter
stufato beef and vegetables braised in wine
tacchino turkey
trippa tripe
vitello veal

Pesce (Fish)

acciughe/alici anchovies
anguilla eel
aragosta lobster
baccalà dried salt cod
bonito small tuna
calamari squid
cape sante scallops
cozze mussels
fritto misto mixed fried fish
gamberetti shrimps
gamberi prawns
granchio crab
insalata di mare seafood salad
merluzzo cod
ostriche oysters
pesce spada swordfish
polipi/polpi octopus
sarde sardines
sogliola sole
squadro monkfish
stoccafisso wind-dried cod
tonno tuna
vongole small clams
zuppa di pesce fish soup or stew

Contorni (Vegetables)

aglio garlic
asparagi asparagus
carciofi artichokes
cavolo cabbage
ceci chickpeas
cetriolo cucumber
cicoria green chicory
cipolla onion
fagiolini French (green) beans
fave broad beans
funghi (porcini) mushrooms (cep)
insalata (mista/verde) salad (mixed/green)
lenticchie lentils
melanzane aubergine
patate potatoes
patatine potato chips
peperoncini hot chilli peppers
peperoni sweet peppers
peperonata stewed peppers in tomato and herb sauce
piselli peas
pomodoro(i) tomato(es)
porri leeks
puntarelle stripped curled stalks of *cicoria catalogna*
rucola rocket
spinaci spinach
verdure greens/vegetables
verza Savoy cabbage
zucca pumpkin
zucchine courgettes

Formaggio (Cheese)

bel paese soft white cow's cheese
burrata mozzarella-like cheese with a creamy centre
cacio/caciocavallo pale yellow, sharp cheese
caprino goat's cheese
parmigiano parmesan cheese
pecorino sharp sheep's cheese
provolone sharp, tangy cheese; ***dolce*** is less strong
stracchino soft white cheese

Frutta (Fruit, Nuts)

albicocche apricots
ananas pineapple
arance oranges
banane bananas
ciliegie cherries
cocomero watermelon
fragole strawberries
frutta di stagione fruit in season
lamponi raspberries
limone lemon

macedonia di frutta fruit salad
mandorle almonds
mele apples
more blackberries
nocciole hazelnuts
noci walnuts
pesca peach
pesca noce nectarine
pompelmo grapefruit
prugna/susina prune/plum
uva grapes

Dolci (Desserts)

amaretti macaroons
crostata fruit flan
gelato (produzione propria) ice cream (home-made)
granita (con panna) flavoured ice (with cream), usually lemon or coffee
panettone cake with candied fruit and raisins
semifreddo refrigerated cake
spumone a soft ice cream
tiramisù tiramisù
torta cake, tart
zabaglione creamy dessert of egg yolks and Marsala
zuppa inglese trifle

Bevande (Beverages)

acqua minerale mineral water
gasata/non gasata with/without fizz
aranciata orange soda
birra (alla spina) beer (draught)
caffè coffee
caffè macchiato (freddo/caldo) espresso with a drop of milk (cold/hot)
caffè ristretto extra-short black coffee
cappuccino frothy milky coffee
espresso short black coffee
latte (intero/scremato) milk (whole/skimmed)
latte macchiato milk with a drop of coffee
succo di frutta fruit juice
tè tea
tè freddo sweet iced tea
tisana herbal tea
vino (rosso, bianco, rosato) wine (red, white, *rosé*)

Cooking Terms

aceto (balsamico) vinegar (balsamic)
affumicato smoked
bicchiere glass
burro butter
conto bill
coltello knife
cucchiaio spoon
forchetta fork
forno oven
fritto fried
ghiaccio ice
griglia grill
in bianco plain/without tomato
marmellata jam
menta mint
miele honey
olio (di olivo) olive oil
pane (tostato) bread (toasted)
panini sandwiches (in roll/ciabatta/focaccia etc.)
panna cream
pepe pepper
ripieno stuffed
rosmarino rosemary
sale salt
salvia sage
tavola table
toast toasted sandwich, usually ham and cheese
tovagliolo napkin
tramezzini sandwiches (in sliced bread)
uovo/uova egg/eggs
zucchero sugar

Index

Numbers in **bold** indicate main references. Numbers in *italic* indicate maps.

Accademia 119–20
accommodation *see* where to stay
Agostino di Duccio 40, 259
air travel 42–3, 47–8
Alberti, Leon Battista 38, 259
Albizzi family 24–5
Alexander VI, Pope 27, 28
Allori, Alessandro 259
Amerigo Vespucci airport 47
Ammanati, Bartolommeo 40, 259
  Neptune's Fountain 77
Andrea del Castagno 38, 259
Andrea del Sarto 40
Angelico, Fra 38, 116, 259
Antella Palace 127
Antinori Palace 105
antique shops 244
Antropologia ed Etnologia Museum 92
Archaeology Museum (Artimino) 152
Archaeology Museum (Fiesole) 161
Archaeology Museum (Florence) 122–3
Archaeology Museum (Siena) 183
Argenti Museum 138
Arnolfo di Cambio 37, 72, 259
art and architecture **36–40**
art galleries 244
  see also museums and galleries
Arte della Lana Palace **75**, 155
Arte Moderna Galleria 137–8
Arte della Seta Palace 108
arti 74
Artimino 152
Astrophysical Observatory 145
auction houses 244

babysitting services 253
Badia Fiesolana (Fiesole) 162
Badia Fiorentina **91**, 156
Baldovinetti, Alesso 259
ballet 242
Bandinelli, Baccio 77, 259
Bandini Museum (Fiesole) 161
banks 57–8
Baptistry **70–1**, 155
Bardini Museum 142
Bargello Museum **89–91**, 156
bars 236–7, 255
Bartolini-Salimbeni Palace 109
Bartolo di Fredi 259
Bartolommeo, Fra 259
Basilica Sant'Alessandro (Fiesole) 160
beaches 255
Beccafumi, Domenico 259
Bellosguardo 147
Belvedere Fort 145
Benedetto da Maiano 40, 259
Biblioteca Comunale degli Intronati (Siena) 184
Biblioteca Laurenziana 97
bicycles 51–2
Bigallo 73
Bigarelli, Guido 259
Black Death 24, 170
Blacks 23
Boboli Gardens **139**, 251
Boccaccio, Giovanni 102
Bologna airport 48
Bondi (Fiesole) 162
Bonfire of the Vanities 28, 76
bookshops 244, 255
Borghese Palace 91
Borgo degli Albizi 92
Borgo Allegri gardens 251
Borgo San Frediano 159
Borgo San Jacopo 158
Botanical Museum 118
Botticelli, Sandro 40, 69, 83–4, 259
Bronzino, Agnolo 40, 259
Browning, Elizabeth Barrett 125, 140
Brunelleschi, Filippo 38, 66–7, 71, 103, 122, 259
  death mask 73
  tomb 68
Bruni, Leonardo 128
Buondelmonte dei Buondelmonti 154
Buondelmonti Palace 109
Buontalenti, Bernardo 40, 259
buses 48–9

cafés *see* restaurants and cafés
Caffè di Simo 209
Campaldino, battle of 22
Campanile 69–70
camping 222
Cappelle Medicee 97–8
Capponi Palace 142
Capponi, Piero 27
Careggi Villa 150
Carmignano 149
Carnival 108
carriages 51
Carrozze Museum 138
cars 50–1
  car pound 56
Casa Buonarroti 126
Casa di Dante **91–2**, 156
Casa Fiorentina Antica 108–9
Casa Guidi 140
Casa dei Templari 158
Cascine **147**, 251
Castel di Poggio (Fiesole) 161
Castel di Vincigliata (Fiesole) 161
Castello Villa 150–1
Castruccio Castracani 23, 206
cathedrals
  Fiesole 160
  Florence 66–70
  Lucca 207
  Pisa 193–4
  Siena 166, **175–81**, *176*
  see also churches
Catherine, Saint 185
Cellini, Benvenuto 77, 89, 124, 259
Cenacolo di Foligno 98
Certosa del Galluzzo 149
Charles V 30–1, 170–1
Charles VIII 27
children 244, 253
Chiostro dello Scalzo 118
churches
  Badia Fiesolana (Fiesole) 162
  Badia Fiorentina **91**, 156
  Cappelle Medicee 97–8
  Duomo (Fiesole) 160
  Duomo (Florence) 66–70
  Duomo (Lucca) 207
  Duomo (Pisa) 193–4
  Duomo (Siena) 166, **175–81**, *176*
  Ognissanti 111–12
  opening hours 58
  Oratorio di San Bernardino (Siena) 184
  Orsanmichele **73–5**, 155
  Russian Church 147–8
  San Cristoforo (Lucca) 209
  San Domenico (Fiesole) 162
  San Domenico (Siena) 185–6
  San Firenze 91
  San Francesco monastery (Fiesole) 160–1
  San Francesco (Pisa) 197
  San Francesco (Siena) 184
  San Frediano in Cestello 159
  San Frediano (Lucca) 208–9
  San Gaetano 105–6
  San Giovannino dei Cavalieri 119
  San Jacopo sopr'Arno 158
  San Leonardo in Arcetri 145
  San Leonardo (Artimino) 152

churches cont'd
San Lorenzo 96–7
San Marco 116–17
San Martino Cathedral (Lucca) 206–7
San Martino del Vescovo 91
San Michele (Carmignano) 149
San Michele in Foro (Lucca) 209
San Miniato 145–6
San Nicola (Pisa) 198
San Pancrazio 106
San Salvatore al Monte 146
Sant'Agostino (Siena) 183–4
Sant'Alessandro Basilica (Fiesole) 160
Sant'Ambrogio 125–6
Santa Caterina (Pisa) 196–7
Santa Croce **127–31**, *129*, 156
Santa Felicità 139–40
Santa Lucia dei Magnoli 142
Santa Margherita de'Cerchi 92
Santa Maria degli Angeli 120
Santa Maria del Carmine 141–2
Santa Maria Forisportam (Lucca) 207–8
Santa Maria Maddalena dei Pazzi 124–5
Santa Maria Novella *101*, 101–4
Santa Maria di Provenzano (Siena) 184
Santa Maria dei Servi (Siena) 183
Santa Maria della Spina (Pisa) 198, 200
Santa Trínita 109–10
Santissima Annunziata 121–2
Santo Spirito 140–1
Santo Stefano (Pisa) 196
Santuario e Casa di Santa Caterina (Siena) 184–5
SS. Apostoli 109
Cimabue 37, 259–60
cinemas 242
Civitali, Matteo 40, 260
classical music 241–2
Clement VII, Pope 30
climate 54
clothes shops 244–6
clubs 237–9, 255
coaches 44
Collezione A. della Ragione 124
Comeana 149
Compagnia del Bruco 170
Compi Revolt 24
consulates 55
contrade 171, 173
Corsi Galleria 142
Corsini Galleria 111
Costa San Giorgio 145
Costume Museum 138
Council of Florence 100
Council of Nine 166
Court of Appeals 118
credit cards 57–8
crime 54
Croce del Trebbio 105
crystal 248
customs formalities 47
cycling 51–2

Daddi, Bernardo 260
dancing 242
Dante Alighieri 91–2, 154–7
statue 127, 156
tomb 156
Dante's Stone 73, 155
Davanzati Palace 155
David (Donatello) 90
David (Michelangelo) 77, 119–20
Demidoff 151
department stores 244
Desiderio da Settignano 40, 260
disabled travellers 54–5
Dolci, Carlo 260
Domenico di Bartolo 260
Domenico Veneziano 260
Domus Galilaeana (Pisa) 198
Domus Mazziniana (Pisa) 200
Donatello 38, 89–90, 96, 260
David 90
Judith and Holofernes 77
Mary Magdalene 72
St George 75, 90
St Mark 74–5
driving in Florence 50–1, 56
Duccio di Buoninsegna 38, 260
Duomo (Fiesole) 160
Duomo (Florence) 66–70
Duomo (Pisa) 193–4
Duomo (Siena) 166, **175–81**, *176*

eating out *see* restaurants and cafés
electricity 55
embassies 55
emergencies 56
English Cemetery 125
Enoteca Nazionale (Siena) 186
entertainment and nightlife **236–9**, **241–2**
entry formalities 46–7
Etruscans 20–1
Archaeological Museum (Artimino) 152
art and architecture 36–7
tombs 149, 151
Excavations of Santa Reparata 68

Faesulae 161
fashion shops 244–6
fax facilities 59
Ferdinand I, statue 121
festivals 257
Lucca 204
Palio 173
Pisa 190
Siena 167, 173
Fiesole 159–62, *160*
eating out 233–4
where to stay 219–20
Firenze Com'Era **123–4**, 156
Florence
medieval centre 64–92, *65*
north and east 114–32, *115*
Oltrarno 134–42, *135*, 157–9, *158*
outside the centre *144*, 145–52
west 94–112, *95*
food and drink **224–34**
shopping 246
specialities 224
vegetarians 230
wine 186, 224, 246
see also restaurants and cafés
football 250
Renaissance football match 127
Forte di Belvedere **145**, 251
Fortezza da Basso 147
Fortezza Medicea (Siena) 186
Francesco di Giorgio Martini 260
Franciabigio 260
funfairs 253

G. Marconi airport (Bologna) 48
Gaddi, Agnolo 37, 260
Gaddi, Taddeo 37, 260
Galileo Galilei 198, **199**
Galileo Galilei airport (Pisa) 47–8
galleries *see* museums and galleries
gardens 251
Boboli **139**, 251
Monte Ceceri (Fiesole) 161
Semplici **118**, 251
Villa di Castello 150–1
Gates of Paradise 71
gay and lesbian Florence **255**
gelaterie see restaurants and cafés
Gentile da Fabriano 260
Geology and Palaeontology Museum 118
Ghibellines 21–3
Ghiberti, Lorenzo 38, 71, 260
Ghirlandaio, Domenico 260
Giambologna 40, 77, 260
Mercury 89
Monument to Cosimo 77
il Gioiello 145
Giotto 37, 69–70, 103, 129–30, 260
Giovanni da Milano 37, 260
Giovanni da Paolo 260
Giovanni di San Giovanni 260
Goethe 85
golf 250

Gondi Palace 91
Gozzoli, Benozzo 38, 260
  Procession of the Magi 99
Gualberto, Giovanni 110
Guelphs 21–3
Guido da Siena 38, 260
guilds 74
Guinigi (Lucca) 208
gyms 250

Hawkwood, Sir John 24, 68
health 56
Hermes Trismegistus 177
history **20–34**
homeware shops 247
Horne Museum 131
horse-racing 250
horse-riding 250
hotels *see* where to stay
Huxley, Aldous 85

insurance 56
internet access 56

jazz clubs 241
jewellery shops 246
Jewish Museum 125
John XXIII 70
Judith and Holofernes (Donatello) 77
Julius Caesar 20

kitchen and homeware shops 247

La Petraia 150
La Specola 140
leather goods 247
Lenzi Palace 112
Leo X, Pope 28–30
Leonardo da Vinci 40, 84, 260–1
Leopold II 33
lesbian Florence **255**
libraries
  Biblioteca Comunale degli Intronati (Siena) 184
  Biblioteca Laurenziana 97
  Piccolomini (Siena) 179–80
linen 247
Lippi, Filippino 39, 261
Lippi, Fra Filippo 39, 261
Loggia del Bigallo 73
Loggia dei Lanzi 76–7
Loggia della Mercanzia (Siena) 175
Loggia del Papa (Siena) 183
Loggia del Pesce 126
Loggia dei Rucellai 106
Loggia di San Paolo 105
long stay accommodation 62
Lorenzetti, Ambrogio 38, 261
Lorenzetti, Pietro 38, 261
Lorenzo di Credi 261
Lorenzo Monaco 38, 261
lost property 56
Lucca **202–10**, *202–3*
  Caffè di Simo 209
  churches
    San Cristoforo 209
    San Frediano 208–9
    San Martino Cathedral 206–7
    San Michele in Foro 209
    Santa Maria Forisportam 207–8
  eating out 205
  festivals 204
  getting there 204
  history 202–3, 206
  museums and galleries
    Cattedrale 207
    Guinigi 208
    Pinacoteca Nazionale 210
    Puccini 209–10
  Palazzo Pfanner 209
  Piazza dell'Anfiteatro 208
  Piazza Napoleone 210
  Roman amphitheatre 208
  Torre Guinigi 208
  Torre dell'Ore 209
  tourist information 204
  Via Fillungo 209
  walls 210
  where to stay 204–5
Lunar Park 253

Machiavelli, Niccolò 81
Mannerism 40, 86
marbled paper 247
Marignano, Marquis of 171
Marini, Marino 106
markets 98, 107, 126, 248
Marsuppini, Carlo 128
Martini, Simone 38, 261
Marucelli Palace 119
Mary Magdalene (Donatello) 72
Masaccio 38, 141, 261
Masetti Palace 109
Maso di Banco 37, 261
Masolino 38, 261
Matilda, Countess 20
Matteo di Giovanni 261
Mazzini, Giuseppe 200
media 57
medical emergencies 56
Medici chapels 97–8
Medici family 24–33, *29*
  Alessandro 31
  Anna Maria Ludovica 33
  Cosimo de' 25
  Cosimo I 31–2
  Cosimo II 32
  Cosimo III 33
  Cosimo il Vecchio 25, 98–9, 100
  Ferdinando I 32
  Ferdinando II 32
  Francesco I 32, 80
  Gian Gastone 33
  Giovanni di Bicci 25
  Giovanni (Pope Leo X) 28–30
  Giuliano 28, 69
  Giulio (Pope Clement VII) 30
  Lorenzo, Duke of Urbino 28
  Lorenzo the Magnificent 25–6, 69
  Piero 27
Medici villas 149–52, 161
Medici-Riccardi Palace 98–101
medieval cures 247
medieval sports 127, 250
Memmi, Lippo 261
Mercato Centrale 98
Mercato Nuovo 107
Mercury (Giambologna) 89
Metropolitana (Siena) 180–1
Michelangelo Buonarroti 40, 86, 89, 97–8, 261
  Casa Buonarroti 126
  David 77, 119–20
  Pietà 72
  tomb 128
  Victory 80
Michelozzo di Bartolomeo 261
Mineralogy and Lithology Museum 118
Mino da Fiesole 40, 261
money 57–8
Monte Ceceri (Fiesole) 161
Monteaperti, battle of 22, 166
Montemurlo, battle of 31
Monument to Cosimo (Giambologna) 77
mosaics 248
motorbikes 51–2
motorsports 250
Mozzi Palace 142
museums and galleries
  Antropologia ed Etnologia 92
  Archaeology (Artimino) 152
  Archaeology (Fiesole) 161
  Archaeology (Florence) 122–3
  Archaeology (Siena) 183
  Argenti 138
  Bandini (Fiesole) 161
  Bardini 142
  Bargello **89–91**, 156
  Bigallo 73
  Botanical 118
  Carrozze 138
  Casa Buonarroti 126
  Casa Fiorentina Antica 108–9
  Cattedrale (Lucca) 207
  for children 253
  Civico (Siena) 174–5
  Collezione A. della Ragione 124
  Costume 138

museums and galleries cont'd
Etruscan Archaeological (Artimino) 152
Firenze Com'Era **123–4**, 156
Galleria dell'Accademia 119–20
Galleria d'Arte Moderna 137–8
Galleria Corsi 142
Galleria Corsini 111
Galleria Palatina 136–7
Geology and Palaeontology 118
Guinigi (Lucca) 208
Horne 131
Jewish 125
Marino Marini 106
Metropolitana (Siena) 180–1
Mineralogy and Lithology 118
opening hours 59
Opera del Duomo 71–3
Opera del Duomo (Pisa) 195–6
Opera di Santa Croce 130–1
Palazzo Reale (Pisa) 198
Pinacoteca Nazionale (Lucca) 210
Pinacoteca Nazionale (Siena) 181
Porcelain 138
Porcelain di Doccia 148
Puccini (Lucca) 209–10
San Matteo (Pisa) 197–8
Sant'Apollonia 118–19
Sinopie (Pisa) 195
Spedale 122
Stibbert 148
Storia della Scienza 87–8
Uffizi 81–7
Waxes 140
Zoologico 140
music 241–2

Nanni di Banco 261–2
Neptune's Fountain 77
newspapers 57
nightlife and entertainment **236–9**, **241–2**

Ognissanti 111–12
Oltrarno 134–42, *135*, 157–9, *158*
nightlife 237, 238–9
restaurants and cafés 231–3, *232*
where to stay 218–19
opening hours 58–9
opera 241–2
Opera del Duomo 71–3
Opera del Duomo (Pisa) 195–6
Opera di Santa Croce 130–1
Opificio delle Pietre Dure 120
Oratorio di San Bernardino (Siena) 184
Orcagna, Andrea 37, 262
Tabernacle 75
Orsanmichele **73–5**, 155
Orticultura gardens 251
Ospedale di Bonifazio 119
Ospedale di Santa Maria della Scala (Siena) 181–3

packing 59
Palatina Galleria 136–7
palazzi
dell'Antella 127
Antinori 105
Arte della Lana **75**, 155
Arte della Seta 108
Bartolini-Salimbeni 109
Borghese 91
Buondelmonti 109
Capponi 142
Davanzati 155
Gondi 91
Lenzi 112
Marucelli 119
Masetti 109
Medici-Riccardi 98–101
Mozzi 142
Pandolfini 119
Parte Guelfa 107
Pazzi-Quaratesi 92
Pitti 136–8
Ramirez di Montalvo 92
Ricasoli 111
Rucellai 106
Serristori-Cocchi 127
Signoria 74
Spini-Feroni 109
Strozzi 106–7
Studi 149
Uguccioni 78
Valori 92
Vecchio 78–81
Palio 173
Pandolfini Palace 119
parades 108
parlamento 74
Parte Guelfa Palace 107
passports 46–7
Pazzi conspiracy 26, 69
Pazzi-Quaratesi Palace 92
perfume 247
Perugino 39–40, 262
Petrucci, Pandolfo 170
photography 59
Piazzale Donatello 125
Piazzale Michelangelo 147
piazzas 251
d'Azeglio 125
Ciompi 126
Duomo 66–73
Frescobaldi 158
Goldoni 111
Mozzi 142
Peruzzi 132
Repubblica 107
San Firenze 91
San Lorenzo 96–7
San Marco 116–20
San Pier Maggiore 92
Santa Croce 127
Santa Maria Novella 105
Santa Trínita 109
Santissima Annunziata 121–6
Santo Spirito 140–2
Signoria 75–8
Piccolomini, Aeneas Silvius 170, **179**
Piccolomini Library (Siena) 179–80
Piero di Cosimo 262
Piero della Francesca 38, 262
Pietà (Michelangelo) 72
Pietro da Cortona 40, 262
Pinacoteca Nazionale (Lucca) 210
Pinacoteca Nazionale (Siena) 181
Pinturicchio 40, 262
Pisa **188–200**, *188–9*
airport 47–8
Baptistry 194
Campo del Miracoli 192–4
Campo Santo 194–5
churches
Duomo 193–4
San Francesco 197
San Nicola 198
Santa Caterina 196–7
Santa Maria della Spina 198, 200
Santo Stefano 196
Domus Galilaeana 198
Domus Mazziniana 200
eating out 191
festivals 190
getting there 190
history 188, 192
Hunger Tower 196
Leaning Tower 192–3
museums and galleries
Opera del Duomo 195–6
Palazzo Reale 198
San Matteo 197–8
Sinopie 195
Palazzo della Carovana 196
Piazza dei Cavalieri 196
Roman Ships 198
shopping 190
tourist information 190
Via Santa Maria 196
where to stay 190–1
Pisano, Andrea 37, 262
Pisano, Giovanni 37, 262
Pisano, Nicola 37, 262
Pitti Palace 136–8
Poggio a Caiano 151–2
Poggio Imperiale 152
police 54
Pollaiuolo, Antonio 38, 262
Pollaiuolo, Piero 38
Ponte alla Carraia 111

Ponte alle Grazie 142
Ponte all'Indiano 147
Ponte a Mensola 148
Ponte Santa Trínita 110–11
Ponte Vecchio 88, 157–8
Pontormo, Jacopo 40, 262
porcelain 248
  museums 138, 148
Porta della Mandorla 66
Porta San Frediano 159
Porta San Giorgio 145
Porta Santa Maria 154
post offices 59–60
practical A–Z **54–62**
priori 74
Procession of the Magi (Gozzoli) 99
processions 108
public holidays 58
Puccini (Lucca) 209–10

Quercia, Jacopo della 40, 172, 262

radio 57
railways 43–4, 49–50, 105
Ramirez di Montalvo Palace 92
Raphael 262
Renaissance 38–40
Renaissance football match 127
Il Reppiedi (Fiesole) 162
restaurants and cafés **224–34**, *226–7*, *232*
  for children 253
  Fiesole 233–4
  gay and lesbian 255
  Lucca 205
  medieval centre 225
  north and east Florence 229–31
  Oltrarno 231–3, *232*
  Pisa 191
  Siena 168–9
  specialities 224
  vegetarians 230
  west Florence 225–9
  see also food and drink
Ricasoli Palace 111
Robbia, Andrea della 262
Robbia, Giovanni della 262
Robbia, Luca della 40, 262
rock concerts 241
Roman Ships (Pisa) 198
Romans 20–1
  art and architecture 36–7
rooms to let 221
Rosai, Ottone 40
Rosselli, Cosimo 262
Rossellino, Antonio 40
Rossellino, Bernardo 40, 262
Rossi, Vincenzo de' 262
Rosso Fiorentino 40, 262–3
Rotunda di Santa Maria degli Angeli 120
rowing 250
Rucellai, Giovanni 106
Rucellai Palace 106
Russian Church 147–8

sailing 250
St George (Donatello) 75, 90
St Mark (Donatello) 74–5
Salviati, Francesco 69, 263
San Cristoforo (Lucca) 209
San Domenico (Fiesole) 162
San Domenico (Siena) 185–6
San Firenze 91
San Francesco monastery (Fiesole) 160–1
San Francesco (Pisa) 197
San Francesco (Siena) 184
San Frediano in Cestello 159
San Frediano (Lucca) 208–9
San Gaetano 105–6
San Giovannino dei Cavalieri 119
San Jacopo sopr'Arno 158
San Leonardo in Arcetri 145
San Leonardo (Artimino) 152
San Lorenzo 96–7
San Marco 116–17
San Martino Cathedral (Lucca) 206–7
San Martino del Vescovo 91
San Matteo (Pisa) 197–8
San Michele (Carmignano) 149
San Michele in Foro (Lucca) 209
San Miniato 145–6
San Nicola (Pisa) 198
San Pancrazio 106
San Salvatore al Monte 146
Sangallo, Giuliano da 263
Sant'Agostino (Siena) 183–4
Sant'Alessandro Basilica (Fiesole) 160
Sant'Ambrogio 125–6
Sant'Apollonia 118–19
SS. Apostoli 109
Santa Caterina (Pisa) 196–7
Santa Croce **127–31**, *129*, 156
Santa Felicità 139–40
Santa Lucia dei Magnoli 142
Santa Margherita de'Cerchi 92
Santa Maria degli Angeli 120
Santa Maria del Carmine 141–2
Santa Maria del Fiore 66–70
Santa Maria Forisportam (Lucca) 207–8
Santa Maria Maddalena dei Pazzi 124–5
Santa Maria Novella *101*, 101–4
Santa Maria Nuova 123
Santa Maria di Provenzano (Siena) 184
Santa Maria dei Servi (Siena) 183
Santa Maria della Spina (Pisa) 198, 200
Santa Reparata 68
Santa Trínita 109–10
Santissima Annunziata 121–2
Santo Spirito 140–1
Santo Stefano (Pisa) 196
Santuario e Casa di Santa Caterina (Siena) 184–5
Il Sassetta 263
Sassetti, Francesco 110
Sasso di Dante 73, 155
Savonarola, Girolamo 27–8, 76
Second World War 34
Semplici gardens **118**, 251
Serristori-Cocchi Palace 127
Settignano 148–9
shoe shops 247–8
shopping **244–8**
  markets 98, 107, 126, 248
  opening hours 58
  Pisa 190
  Siena 167
  weights and measures 55
Siena **164–86**, *165*
  Baptistry 181
  Biblioteca Comunale degli Intronati 184
  Campo 172
  Cappella della Piazza 174
  churches
    Duomo 166, **175–81**, *176*
    Oratorio di San Bernardino 184
    San Domenico 185–6
    San Francesco 184
    Sant'Agostino 183–4
    Santa Maria di Provenzano 184
    Santa Maria dei Servi 183
    Santuario e Casa di Santa Caterina 184–5
  contrade 171, 173
  Croce del Travaglio 175
  eating out 168–9
  Enoteca Nazionale 186
  festivals 167
  Fonte Gaia 172–3
  Fortezza Medicea 186
  getting there 167
  history 164–72
  Loggia della Mercanzia 175
  Loggia del Papa 183
  museums and galleries
    Archeologico 183
    Civico 174–5
    Metropolitana 180–1
    Pinacoteca Nazionale 181
  Ospedale di Santa Maria della Scala 181–3
  Palazzo Piccolomini 183

Siena cont'd
Palazzo Pubblico 170, **173–5**
Palio 173
Piazza del Duomo 175–81
Piccolomini Library 179–80
shopping 167
Terzo di Camollia 171
Terzo di Città 171
Terzo di San Martino 171
Torre del Mangia 173
tourist information 167
where to stay 167–8
Signoria Palace 74
silver 248
Sinopie (Pisa) 195
smoking 60
Soderini, Piero 28
Il Sodoma 40, 263
specialist tour operators 44–6, 54–5
Spedale degli Innocenti 122
Spedale Museum 122
Spinello Aretino 263
Spini-Feroni Palace 109
sports **250–1**
squash 250
Stazione Centrale 105
Stibbert Museum 148
Storia della Scienza Museum 87–8
street markets *see* markets
Strozzi, Filippo 106–7
Strozzi Palace 106–7
Strozzi, Piero 171
student discounts 43
students 60
Studi Palace 149
swimming 250–1
synagogue 125

Tacca, Pietro 40, 263
Taddeo di Bartolo 263
Talenti, Francesco 263
Talenti, Simone 263
i Tatti 148, 161
taxis 51
Teatro della Pergola 124
telephones 60–1
television 57
temperature chart 54
tennis 251
theatres 242
time 61
tipping 61
toilets 61
Tomba dei Boschetti 149
Tomba di Montefortini 149
Torre della Castagna 156
Torre del Gallo 145
Torre dei Marsili 158
Torre dei Rossi Cerchi 158
Torrigiano, Pietro 263
Torrino di Santa Rosa 159
tour operators 44–6, 54–5
tourist offices 61–2
trains 43–4, 49–50, 105
travel **42–52**
air travel 42–3, 47–8
bicycles 51–2
buses 48–9
carriages 51
cars 50–1
coaches 44
disabled travellers 54–5
entry formalities 46–7
insurance 56
lost property 56
motorbikes 51–2
packing 59
specialist tour operators 44–6, 54–5
student discounts 43
taxis 51
trains 43–4, 49–50
women travellers 62
traveller's cheques 57
Tribunale di Mercanzia 78
True Cross 131

Uccello, Paolo 38, 263
Uffizi 81–7
Uguccioni Palace 78
university 117–18

Valori Palace 92
Vasari, Giorgio 32, 40, **79**, 263
corridor 157–8
Il Vecchietta 40, 263
vegetarians 230
Venus de'Medici 85
Verrocchio, Andrea del 39, 263
Vespucci, Amerigo 111
Via de'Bardi 142
Via Bentaccordi 132
Via de'Calzaiuoli 73–5
Via Dante Alighieri 156
Via Por Santa Maria 154–5
Via San Gallo 119
Via di Santo Spirito 158–9
Via de'Tornabuoni 105–7
Via Torta 132
Victory (Michelangelo) 80
villa hotels 220–1
villa rentals 222
villas
Artimino 152
Bellosguardo 147
Bondi (Fiesole) 162
Careggi 150
di Castello 150–1
Demidoff 151
i Tatti 148, 161
il Gioiello 145
Il Reppiedi (Fiesole) 162
La Petraia 150
Medici (Belcanto) 161
Poggio a Caiano 151–2
Poggio Imperiale 152
visas 46–7
Visconti, Giangaleazzo 170

walks
Dante's Florence 154–7, *155*
Fiesole 159–62, *160*
Oltrarno 157–9, *158*
Waxes Museum 140
weights and measures 55
where to stay **212–22**, *214–15*
camping 222
Fiesole 219–20
gay and lesbian accommodation 255
long stay accommodation 62
Lucca 204–5
medieval Florence 212–13
north and east Florence 217–18
Oltrarno 218–19
Pisa 190–1
rooms to let 221
Siena 167–8
villa hotels 220–1
villa rentals 222
west Florence 213–17
youth hostels 221–2
Whites 23
wine 186, 224, 246
women travellers 62
working in Italy 62

youth hostels 221–2

zoo 253
Zoological Museum 140

Florence Street Maps

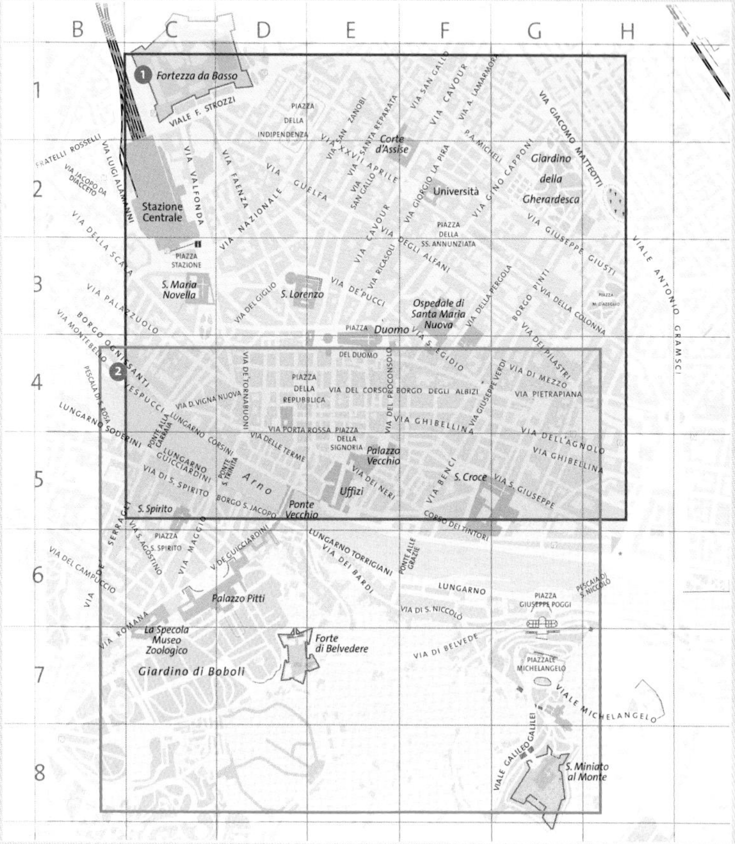

B C D E F G H

1 2 3 4 5 6 7 8

Fortezza da Basso
Viale F. Strozzi
Piazza della Indipendenza
Via San Zanobi
Via Santa Reparata
Via San Gallo
Via Cavour
Via A. Lamarmora
Corte d'Assise
P.A. Micheli
Via Giacomo Matteotti
Giardino della Gherardesca
Via Gino Capponi
Università
Via Giorgio La Pira
Via XXVII Aprile
Via Guelfa
Via Nazionale
Via Faenza
Via Valfonda
Via Luigi Alamanni
Fratelli Rosselli
Via Jacopo da Diacceto
Stazione Centrale
Piazza Stazione
Via della Scala
S. Maria Novella
Via Palazzuolo
Borgo Ognissanti
Via Montebello
S. Lorenzo
Via del Giglio
Via de' Pucci
Via Ricasoli
Via degli Alfani
Piazza della SS. Annunziata
Ospedale di Santa Maria Nuova
Via della Pergola
Borgo Pinti
Via della Colonna
Via Giuseppe Giusti
Viale Antonio Gramsci
Piazza del Duomo
Duomo
Via S. Egidio
Via dei Pilastri
Via di Mezzo
Via Pietrapiana
Via de' Tornabuoni
Piazza della Repubblica
Via del Corso
Borgo degli Albizi
Via del Proconsolo
Via Giuseppe Verdi
Via Ghibellina
Via dell'Agnolo
Via D. Vigna Nuova
Vespucci
Lungarno Soderini
Pescaia di S. Rosa
Ponte alla Carraia
Lungarno Corsini
Via Porta Rossa
Piazza della Signoria
Palazzo Vecchio
Via delle Terme
Lungarno Guicciardini
Ponte S. Trinita
Via di S. Spirito
Arno
Via dei Neri
Uffizi
Via Benci
S. Croce
Via S. Giuseppe
S. Spirito
Borgo S. Jacopo
Ponte Vecchio
Corso dei Tintori
Serragli
Piazza S. Spirito
Via S. Agostino
Via Maggio
V. de' Guicciardini
Lungarno Torrigiani
Via dei Bardi
Ponte alle Grazie
Via del Campuccio
Palazzo Pitti
Lungarno
Piazza Giuseppe Poggi
Pescaia di S. Niccolò
Via di S. Niccolò
Via Romana
La Specola Museo Zoologico
Forte di Belvedere
Via di Belvedere
Piazzale Michelangelo
Giardino di Boboli
Viale Michelangelo
Viale Galileo Galilei
S. Miniato al Monte

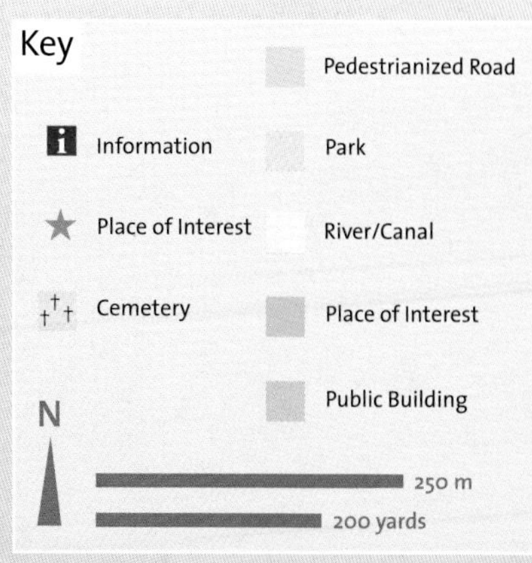

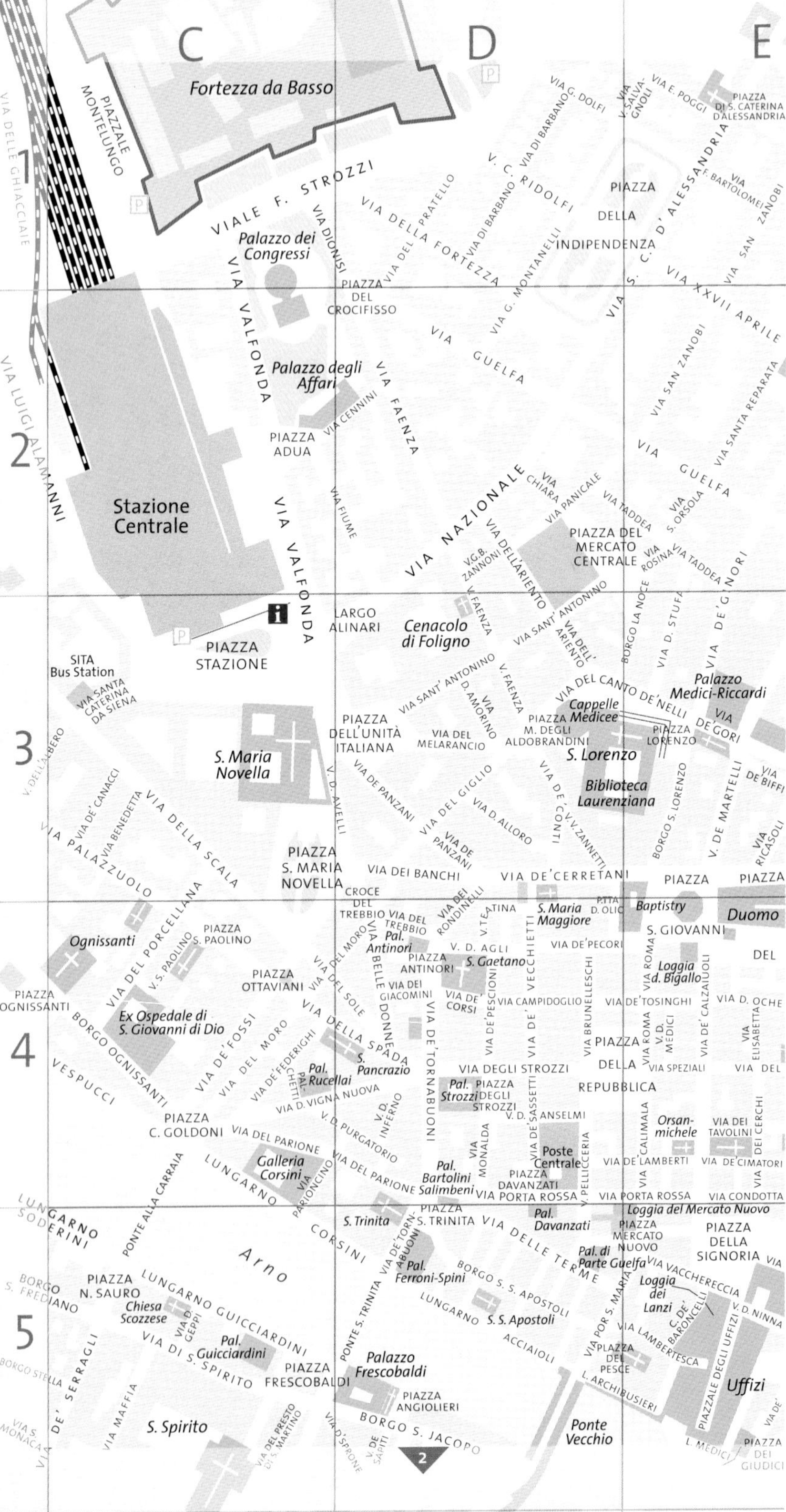
C
D
E
1
2
3
4
5
Fortezza da Basso
Piazzale Montelungo
Viale F. Strozzi
Palazzo dei Congressi
Via Valfonda
Piazza del Crocifisso
Palazzo degli Affari
Piazza Adua
Stazione Centrale
Via Nazionale
Via Faenza
Via Guelfa
Piazza della Indipendenza
Via XXVII Aprile
Piazza del Mercato Centrale
Largo Alinari
Cenacolo di Foligno
Piazza Stazione
SITA Bus Station
Piazza dell'Unità Italiana
S. Maria Novella
Piazza S. Maria Novella
Cappelle Medicee
Piazza M. degli Aldobrandini
S. Lorenzo
Biblioteca Laurenziana
Palazzo Medici-Riccardi
Piazza S. Lorenzo
Via de' Cerretani
Via dei Banchi
Via della Scala
Via Palazzuolo
Ognissanti
Piazza Ognissanti
Ex Ospedale di S. Giovanni di Dio
Borgo Ognissanti
Piazza Ottaviani
Pal. Antinori
Piazza Antinori
S. Gaetano
S. Maria Maggiore
Baptistry
Duomo
Piazza S. Giovanni
Loggia d. Bigallo
Via de' Tornabuoni
Pal. Rucellai
S. Pancrazio
Via degli Strozzi
Pal. Strozzi
Piazza degli Strozzi
Piazza della Repubblica
Piazza C. Goldoni
Galleria Corsini
Pal. Bartolini Salimbeni
Poste Centrale
Orsanmichele
Piazza Davanzati
Via Porta Rossa
Pal. Davanzati
Loggia del Mercato Nuovo
Piazza Mercato Nuovo
Piazza della Signoria
S. Trinita
Piazza S. Trinita
Via delle Terme
Pal. Ferroni-Spini
Pal. di Parte Guelfa
Loggia dei Lanzi
Arno
Lungarno Corsini
Lungarno Soderini
Ponte alla Carraia
Piazza N. Sauro
Chiesa Scozzese
Lungarno Guicciardini
Pal. Guicciardini
Via di S. Spirito
Piazza Frescobaldi
Palazzo Frescobaldi
Piazza Angiolieri
Borgo S. Jacopo
Ponte S. Trinita
Lungarno Acciaioli
S. S. Apostoli
Borgo S. S. Apostoli
Ponte Vecchio
Uffizi
Piazzale degli Uffizi
Piazza dei Giudici
S. Spirito
Via Maffia
Via de' Serragli
Borgo S. Frediano
2

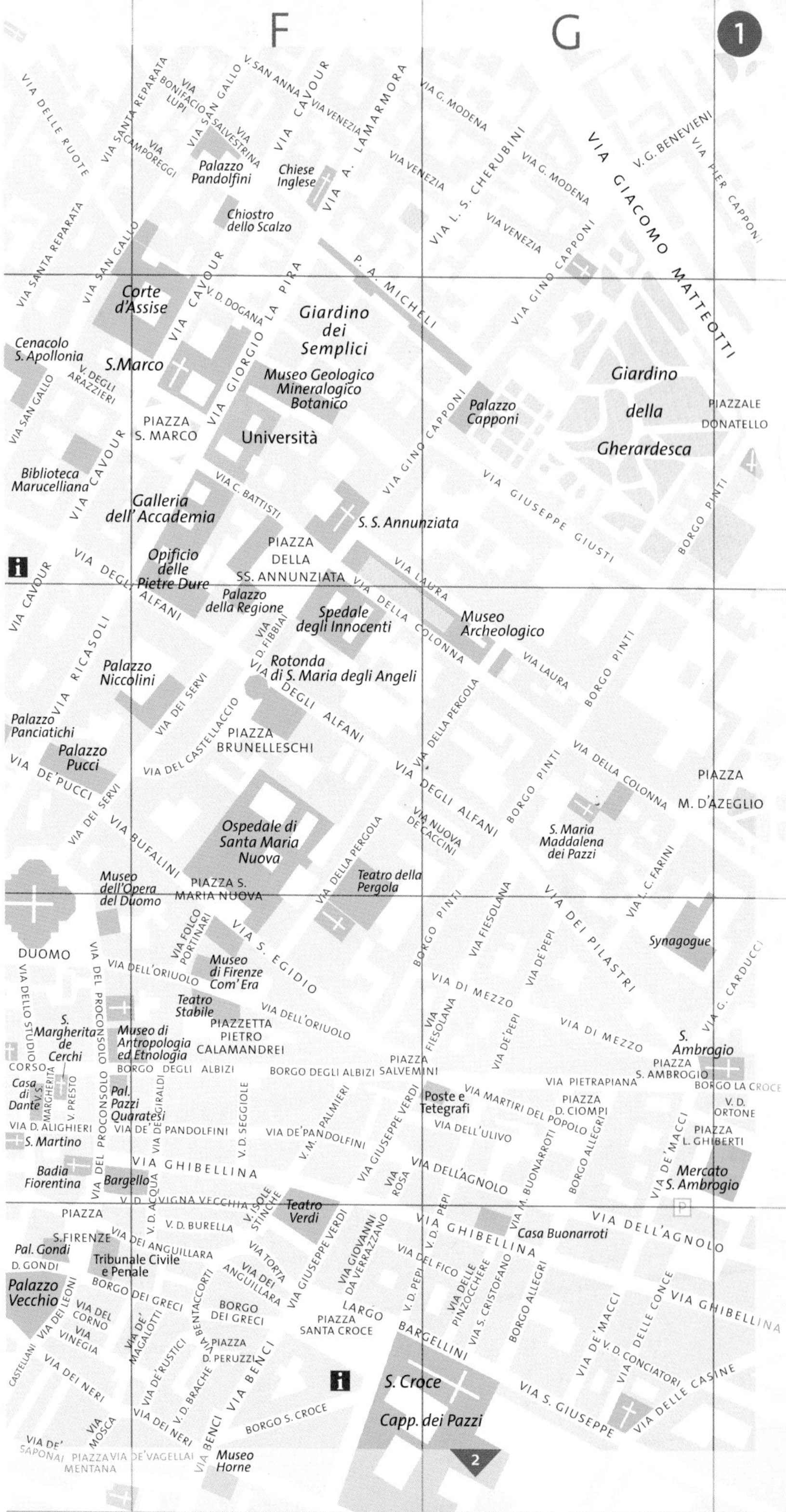

F
G
1
Palazzo Pandolfini
Chiese Inglese
Chiostro dello Scalzo
Corte d'Assise
Giardino dei Semplici
Cenacolo S. Apollonia
S.Marco
Museo Geologico Mineralogico Botanico
Giardino della Gherardesca
Palazzo Capponi
PIAZZA S. MARCO
Università
PIAZZALE DONATELLO
Biblioteca Marucelliana
Galleria dell' Accademia
S. S. Annunziata
PIAZZA DELLA SS. ANNUNZIATA
Opificio delle Pietre Dure
Palazzo della Regione
Spedale degli Innocenti
Museo Archeologico
Palazzo Niccolini
Rotonda di S. Maria degli Angeli
Palazzo Panciatichi
Palazzo Pucci
PIAZZA BRUNELLESCHI
PIAZZA M. D'AZEGLIO
Ospedale di Santa Maria Nuova
S. Maria Maddalena dei Pazzi
Museo dell'Opera del Duomo
PIAZZA S. MARIA NUOVA
Teatro della Pergola
DUOMO
Synagogue
Museo di Firenze Com' Era
Teatro Stabile
S. Margherita de Cerchi
Museo di Antropologia ed Etnologia
PIAZZETTA PIETRO CALAMANDREI
PIAZZA SALVEMINI
S. Ambrogio
PIAZZA S. AMBROGIO
Casa di Dante
Pal. Pazzi Quaratesi
Poste e Tetegrafi
PIAZZA D. CIOMPI
PIAZZA L. GHIBERTI
S. Martino
Badia Fiorentina
Bargello
Mercato S. Ambrogio
Teatro Verdi
PIAZZA S.FIRENZE
Pal. Gondi
Tribunale Civile e Penale
Casa Buonarroti
Palazzo Vecchio
BORGO DEI GRECI
LARGO PIAZZA SANTA CROCE
PIAZZA D. PERUZZI
S. Croce
Capp. dei Pazzi
Museo Horne
PIAZZA MENTANA
2
VIA DELLE RUOTE
VIA SANTA REPARATA
VIA BONIFACIO LUPI
VIA SAN GALLO
V. SAN ANNA
VIA CAVOUR
VIA VENEZIA
VIA A. LAMARMORA
VIA G. MODENA
VIA L. S. CHERUBINI
VIA GIACOMO MATTEOTTI
V. G. BENEVIENI
VIA PIER CAPPONI
VIA SALVESTRINA
VIA SCAMPOREGGI
P. A. MICHELI
VIA GINO CAPPONI
V. D. DOGANA
VIA LA PIRA
VIA GIORGIO LA PIRA
V. DEGLI ARAZZIERI
VIA C. BATTISTI
VIA GIUSEPPE GIUSTI
BORGO PINTI
VIA LAURA
VIA DEGLI ALFANI
VIA DELLA COLONNA
VIA D. FIBBIAI
VIA RICASOLI
VIA DEI SERVI
VIA DEL CASTELLACCIO
VIA DELLA PERGOLA
VIA DE' PUCCI
VIA NUOVA DE' CACCINI
VIA BUFALINI
VIA L. C. FARINI
VIA DEI PILASTRI
VIA FOLCO PORTINARI
VIA S. EGIDIO
VIA FIESOLANA
VIA DE' PEPI
VIA G. CARDUCCI
VIA DELLO STUDIO
VIA DEL PROCONSOLO
VIA DELL'ORIUOLO
VIA DI MEZZO
CORSO
V. S. MARGHERITA
V. PRESTO
BORGO DEGLI ALBIZI
VIA PIETRAPIANA
BORGO LA CROCE
V. D. ORTONE
VIA DE' GIRALDI
V. D. SEGGIOLE
V. M. PALMIERI
VIA GIUSEPPE VERDI
VIA MARTIRI DEL POPOLO
VIA D. ALIGHIERI
VIA DE' PANDOLFINI
VIA DELL'ULIVO
VIA M. BUONARROTI
BORGO ALLEGRI
VIA DE' MACCI
VIA GHIBELLINA
VIA ROSA
VIA DELL'AGNOLO
V. D. ACQUA
V. D. VIGNA VECCHIA
V. ISOLE STINCHE
V. D. BURELLA
VIA DEI ANGUILLARA
VIA TORTA
VIA GIOVANNI DA VERRAZZANO
V. D. PEPI
VIA DEL FICO
VIA DELLE PINZOCCHERE
VIA S. CRISTOFANO
VIA DELLE CONCE
D. GONDI
BORGO DEI GRECI
VIA BENTACCORDI
VIA DEL CORNO
VIA DEI LEONI
VIA VINEGIA
VIA DE' MAGALOTTI
VIA DE' RUSTICI
V. D. BRACHE
VIA BENCI
BARGELLINI
V. D. CONCIATORI
VIA DELLE CASINE
VIA S. GIUSEPPE
CASTELLANI
VIA DEI NERI
VIA MOSCA
BORGO S. CROCE
VIA DE' SAPONAI
VIA DE' VAGELLAI

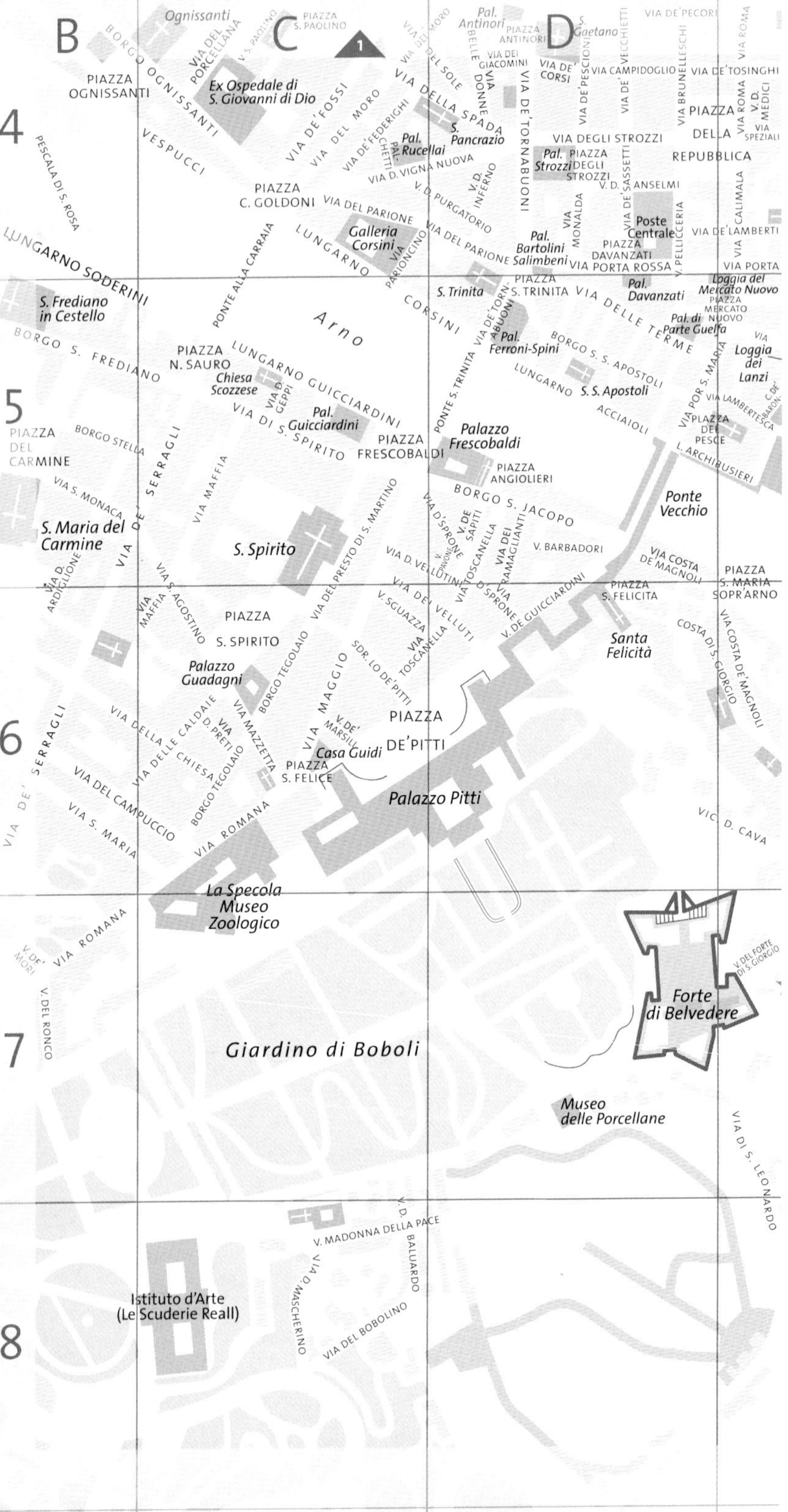

B
C
D
4
5
6
7
8
Ognissanti
PIAZZA OGNISSANTI
BORGO OGNISSANTI
VIA DEL PORCELLANA
Ex Ospedale di S. Giovanni di Dio
VESPUCCI
PESCAIA DI S. ROSA
VIA DE' FOSSI
VIA DEL MORO
VIA DEL SOLE
VIA DELLA SPADA
VIA DE' FEDERIGHI
Pal. Rucellai
S. Pancrazio
VIA D. VIGNA NUOVA
PIAZZA C. GOLDONI
VIA DEL PARIONE
V. D. PURGATORIO
V. D. INFERNO
Galleria Corsini
LUNGARNO SODERINI
S. Frediano in Cestello
BORGO S. FREDIANO
PONTE ALLA CARRAIA
Arno
CORSINI
PIAZZA N. SAURO
LUNGARNO GUICCIARDINI
Chiesa Scozzese
Pal. Guicciardini
VIA DI S. SPIRITO
PIAZZA FRESCOBALDI
Palazzo Frescobaldi
PIAZZA ANGIOLIERI
BORGO S. JACOPO
Pal. Antinori
PIAZZA ANTINORI
S. Gaetano
VIA DE' TORNABUONI
VIA DEGLI STROZZI
Pal. Strozzi
PIAZZA DEGLI STROZZI
V. D. ANSELMI
PIAZZA DELLA REPUBBLICA
Poste Centrale
Pal. Bartolini Salimbeni
PIAZZA DAVANZATI
VIA PORTA ROSSA
S. Trinita
PIAZZA S. TRINITA
VIA DELLE TERME
Pal. Davanzati
Loggia del Mercato Nuovo
Pal. di Parte Guelfa
Pal. Ferroni-Spini
BORGO S.S. APOSTOLI
S. S. Apostoli
LUNGARNO ACCIAIOLI
Loggia dei Lanzi
PIAZZA DEL PESCE
PONTE S. TRINITA
Ponte Vecchio
PIAZZA DEL CARMINE
BORGO STELLA
VIA S. MONACA
S. Maria del Carmine
VIA DE' SERRAGLI
VIA MAFFIA
S. Spirito
VIA DEL PRESTO DI S. MARTINO
V. BARBADORI
VIA COSTA DE MAGNOLI
PIAZZA S. MARIA SOPR'ARNO
PIAZZA S. FELICITA
Santa Felicità
PIAZZA S. SPIRITO
VIA S. AGOSTINO
Palazzo Guadagni
BORGO TEGOLAIO
VIA MAGGIO
PIAZZA DE' PITTI
Casa Guidi
PIAZZA S. FELICE
Palazzo Pitti
VIA ROMANA
VIA DEL CAMPUCCIO
VIA S. MARIA
La Specola Museo Zoologico
Forte di Belvedere
Giardino di Boboli
Museo delle Porcellane
VIA DI S. LEONARDO
V. MADONNA DELLA PACE
V. D. BALUARDO
VIA D. MASCHERINO
VIA DEL BOBOLINO
Istituto d'Arte (Le Scuderie Reall)
V. DEL RONCO
VIC. D. CAVA

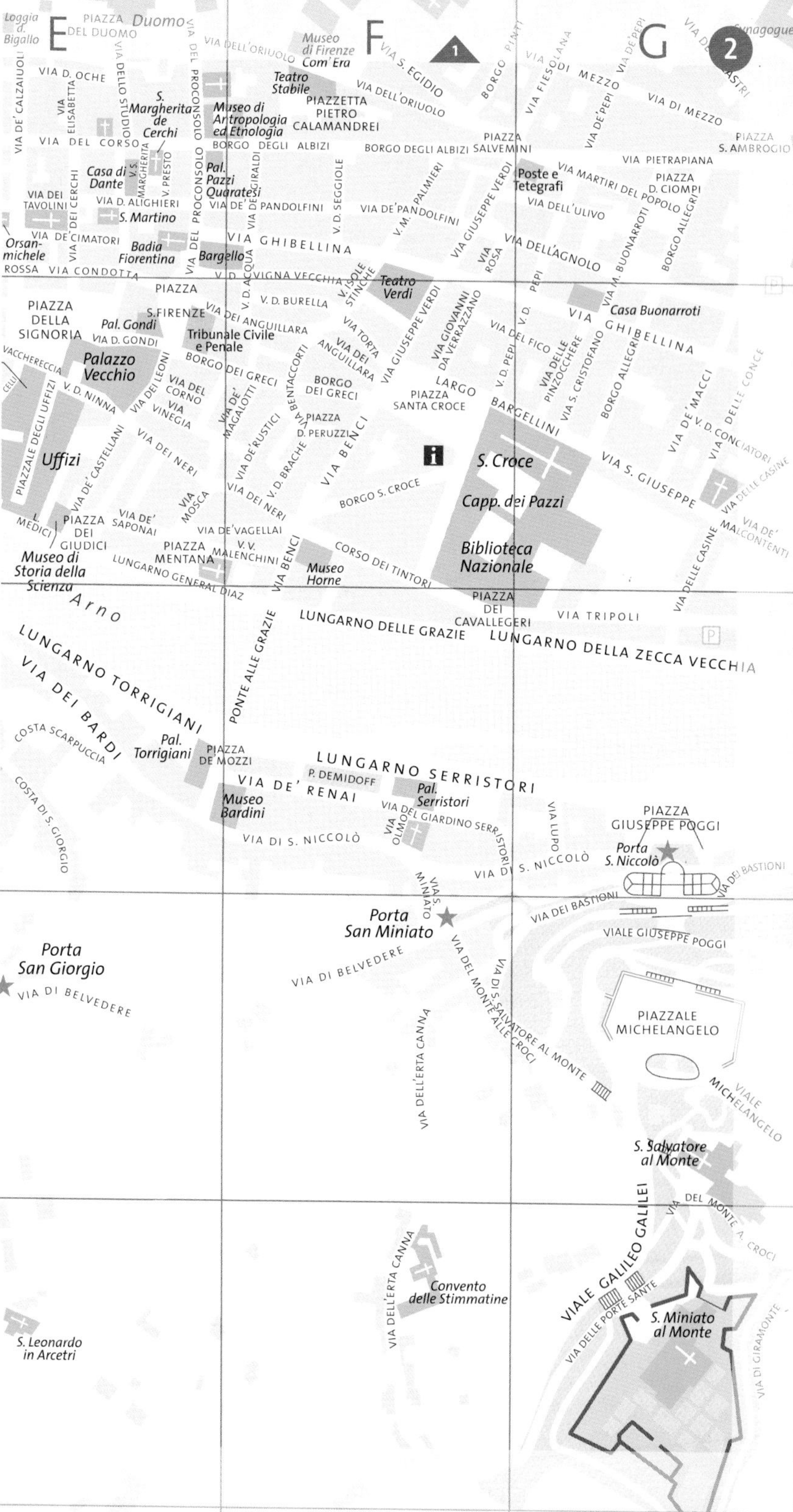

E
F
G
1
2
Loggia d. Bigallo
PIAZZA DEL DUOMO
Duomo
Synagogue
Museo di Firenze Com'Era
Teatro Stabile
PIAZZETTA PIETRO CALAMANDREI
S. Margherita de Cerchi
Museo di Antropologia ed Etnologia
Casa di Dante
Pal. Pazzi Quaratesi
S. Martino
Orsanmichele
Badia Fiorentina
Bargello
Poste e Tetegrafi
PIAZZA SALVEMINI
PIAZZA S. AMBROGIO
PIAZZA D. CIOMPI
Teatro Verdi
Casa Buonarroti
PIAZZA DELLA SIGNORIA
PIAZZA S.FIRENZE
Pal. Gondi
Tribunale Civile e Penale
Palazzo Vecchio
Uffizi
PIAZZA SANTA CROCE
S. Croce
Capp. dei Pazzi
Biblioteca Nazionale
PIAZZA DEI GIUDICI
Museo di Storia della Scienza
PIAZZA MENTANA
Museo Horne
PIAZZA DEI CAVALLEGERI
Arno
LUNGARNO DELLE GRAZIE
LUNGARNO DELLA ZECCA VECCHIA
LUNGARNO TORRIGIANI
VIA DEI BARDI
PONTE ALLE GRAZIE
Pal. Torrigiani
PIAZZA DE' MOZZI
LUNGARNO SERRISTORI
Museo Bardini
P. DEMIDOFF
Pal. Serristori
VIA DE' RENAI
VIA DI S. NICCOLÒ
PIAZZA GIUSEPPE POGGI
Porta S. Niccolò
Porta San Miniato
Porta San Giorgio
VIA DI BELVEDERE
VIALE GIUSEPPE POGGI
PIAZZALE MICHELANGELO
VIALE MICHELANGELO
S. Salvatore al Monte
VIALE GALILEO GALILEI
Convento delle Stimmatine
S. Miniato al Monte
S. Leonardo in Arcetri
VIA GHIBELLINA
VIA DEI NERI
CORSO DEI TINTORI
LUNGARNO GENERAL DIAZ
VIA DELL'ERTA CANNA
VIA DEL MONTE ALLE CROCI
VIA DI S. SALVATORE AL MONTE
VIA DELLE PORTE SANTE
VIA DI GIRAMONTE

Attractions Finder

Badia Fiorentina **E4**
Baptistry **E4**
Bargello **E4**
Borgo degli Albizi **F4**
Cappelle Medicee **D3**
Casa Buonarroti **G5**
Casa di Dante **E4**
Casa Guidi **C6**
Cenacolo di Foligno **D3**
Chiostro dello Scalzo **F1**
Croce del Trebbio **D4**
Duomo **E4**
English Cemetery **H2**
Forte di Belvedere **D7**
Fortezza da Basso **C1**
Galleria Corsini **C4**
Galleria dell'Accademia **F2**
Giardino di Boboli **C/D7**
La Specola **C6/7**
Loggia dei Lanzi **E5**
Loggia del Bigallo **E4**
Mercato Nuovo **E5**
Mercato S. Ambrogio **H4**
Museo Archeologico **G3**
Museo Bardini/Galleria Corsi **F6**
Museo dell'Opera del Duomo **E4**
Museo della Casa Fiorentina Antica/Palazzo Davanzati **D5**
Museo di Firenze Com'Era **F4**
Museo di Storia della Scienza **E5**
Museo Horne **F5**
Museo Nazionale di Antropologia ed Etnologia **E4**
Ognissanti **C4**
Opificio delle Pietre Dure **F2**
Orsanmichele **E4**
Palazzo Medici-Riccardi **E3**
Palazzo Pitti **C/D6**
Palazzo Rucellai **C4**
Palazzo Strozzi **D4**
Palazzo Vecchio **E5**
Piazza d'Azeglio **H3**
Piazza dei Ciompi **G4**
Piazza della Repubblica **D/E4**
Piazza della Signoria **E5**
Piazza Goldoni **C4**
Piazza San Firenze **E4**
Piazza Santa Maria Novella **C3**
Piazza Santa Trínita **D5**
Piazza Santissima Annunziata **F2**
Piazza Santo Spirito **C6**
Piazzale Donatello **H2**
Ponte Santa Trínita **D5**
Ponte Vecchio **E5**
Rotonda di Santa Maria degli Angeli **F3**
San Frediano in Cestello **B5**
San Leonardo in Arcetri **E8**
San Lorenzo **D3**
San Marco **F2**
San Miniato al Monte **G8**
San Pancrazio/Museo Marino Marini **D4**
San Salvatore al Monte **G7**
Sant'Ambrogio **H4**
Sant'Apollonia **E2**
Santa Croce **G5**
Santa Felicità **D6**
Santa Margherita de' Cerchi **E4**
Santa Maria del Carmine **B5**
Santa Maria Maddalena dei Pazzi **G3**
Santa Maria Novella **C3**
Santa Maria Nuova **F3**
Santa Trínita **D5**
Santissima Annunziata **F2**
Santo Spirito **C5**
Spedale degli Innocenti **F3**
Stazione Centrale **C2**
Synagogue **G4**
Teatro della Pergola **F3/4**
Teatro Verdi **F5**
Uffizi **E5**
Università and its Museums **F2**
Via de' Calzaiuoli **E4**
Via de' Tornabuoni **D4/5**
Via San Gallo **E2**

ROME
Dana Facaros & Michael Pauls
CADOGANguides
PARIS
Dana Facaros & Michael Pauls
CADOGANguides
BRUSSELS
Antony Mason
CADOGANguides